Alpheus Crosby

A lexicon to Xenophon's Anabasis

Alpheus Crosby

A lexicon to Xenophon's Anabasis

ISBN/EAN: 9783337223434

Printed in Europe, USA, Canada, Australia, Japan

Cover: Foto ©Paul-Georg Meister /pixelio.de

More available books at **www.hansebooks.com**

A

LEXICON TO XENOPHON'S ANABASIS,

Adapted to all the common Editions.

FOR THE USE BOTH OF BEGINNERS AND OF MORE
ADVANCED STUDENTS.

BY

ALPHEUS CROSBY,
PROFESSOR EMERITUS OF THE GREEK LANGUAGE AND LITERATURE IN
DARTMOUTH COLLEGE.

TOGETHER WITH

INTRODUCTION TO ANABASIS, NOTES ON THE SEVEN BOOKS, GEOGRAPHICAL NOTES, RECORDS OF MARCHES,
ETC., ETC.

THE NOTES, ETC., EDITED FROM PROFESSOR CROSBY'S MSS.
By J. A. SPENCER, S. T. D.,
PROFESSOR OF GREEK IN THE COLLEGE OF THE CITY OF NEW YORK.

NEW YORK AND CHICAGO:
POTTER, AINSWORTH, AND COMPANY.
1875.

simplicity of manners, integrity, and patriotism, till his death in the winter of 361-0, at the age of 80. He was lame, and insignificant in general appearance. He was sent into Asia Minor, B. C. 396, to prosecute the war against the Persians; but was recalled from the plans and promise of great accomplishment, in 394, to sustain Sparta against the Thebans, Athenians, &c., over whom he gained the battle of Coronēa. Xenophon served under him in Asia, and returned with him to Greece. v. 3. 6.

Ἀγίας, ου, *Agias*, a Cyrean general from Arcadia, slain through the treachery of Tissaphernes. He prob. commanded troops left by Xenias or Pasion. ii. 5. 31; 6. 30.

ἄγκος, εος, τό, a bend *or* hollow, *valley, glen, dell*, iv. 1. 7. Cf. Lat. uncus, angulus.

†ἄγκυρα, ας, ancŏra, *an* ANCHOR, iii. 5. 10.

ἀ-γνοέω, ήσω, ήγνόηκα, (γνο- in γιγνώσκω) *not to know or recognize, to be ignorant or in doubt*, CP., iv. 5. 7: vi. 5. 12: vii. 3. 38.

†ἀγνωμοσύνη, ης, *want of sense*; pl. *misunderstandings*, ii. 5. 6.

ἀ-γνώμων, ον, g. ονος, (γνώμη) *devoid of sense, thoughtless, inconsiderate, ignorant*, vii. 6. 23, 38.

ἀγορά, ᾶς, (ἀγείρω) *an assembly; place of assembly* (Lat. forum), *marketplace* (the same open place in a city being commonly used for both purposes); *market, provisions or supplies* for sale; i. 2. 10; 3. 14: v. 7. 3: vi. 6. 3: παρέχειν ἀγοράν *to afford or provide a market, offer provisions for sale*, ii. 3. 26 s: οἱ ἐκ τῆς ἀγορᾶς ἔφευγον *those in the market fled from it, or the market-men fled*, 704 a, i. 2. 18: ἀγορὰ πλήθουσα, *the time of full market*, the middle of the forenoon, and from that time till noon, i. 8. 1. See Κεραμῶν.

†ἀγοράζω, άσω, ἠγόρακα, *to buy, purchase*: *M. to buy for one's self*: A.: i. 3. 14; 5. 10: vii. 3. 5.

†ἀγορᾱ-νόμος, ου, ὁ, (νέμω) *a superintendent or inspector of the market, market-director, market-master;* having the general care and direction in respect to order, fairness of dealing, the quality of the provisions, and often their price; v. 7. 2, 23 s.

†ἀγορεύω, εύσω, ἠγόρευκα, (comm. f. ἐρῶ, pf. εἴρηκα, 2 a. εἶπον) *to address an assembly, harangue, speak, introduce* a subject, A. εἰς, v. 6. 27.

†ἀγρεύω, εύσω, (ἄγρα field-roaming, hunting) *to hunt, take in the chase*, A., v. 3. 8.

†ἄγριος, α, ον, *living in the field, wild,* i. 2. 7; 5. 2. Cf. agrestis.

ἀγρός, οῦ, ὁ, (cog. ager, Germ. *acker, our acre*) *field, land, country* as opp. to city, v. 3. 9: vi. 2. 8.

ἀγρ-υπνέω, ήσω, (ἄγρ-υπνος sleephunting? *sleepless) to lie awake, watch,* πρό, vii. 6. 36.

ἄγω,* ἄξω, ἦχα, 2 a. ἤγαγον, ago, *to put in motion, to lead a person, army, animal*, &c.; *conduct, direct, bring, carry, convey; lead on, advance;* A. εἰς, ἐπί, &c.; i. 3. 5; 6. 10; 9. 27: iv. 3. 5; 8. 12: vi. 3. 18: ἡσυχίαν *or* εἰρήνην ἄγειν *to lead a quiet or peaceful life,* iii. 1. 14: φέρειν καὶ ἄγειν ferre et agere, *to carry and lead off, to plunder, spoil, despoil, harry, by carrying off things and leading off cattle,* A. (of booty taken or persons robbed), v. 5. 13: ii. 6. 5: ἄγε (δή), ἄγετε (δή), *come (now)!* ii. 2. 10: v. 4. 9: ἄγων *bringing, with,* 674 b, v. 4. 11: *M. to bring* one's own things, A., i. 10. 17.

†ἀγώγιμος, ον, *portable;* τὰ ἀγώγιμα, the things to be carried, *freight,* v.1.16.

†ἀγών, ῶνος, ὁ, *a bringing together, gathering, assembly*, especially *to witness a game or contest;* hence *a game or games, contest, strife, encounter, struggle,* i. 2. 10; 7. 4. Der. AGONY.

†ἀγωνίζομαι, ἴσομαι ιοῦμαι, ἠγώνισμαι, *to contend, strive, struggle, fight,* AE., πρός, περί, ii. 5. 10 : iii. 1. 43 : iv. 8. 27. Der. AGONIZE.

†ἀγωνο-θέτης, ου, (τίθημι) *an institutor, director, or judge of a contest, umpire*, iii. 1. 21.

ἀ-δειπνος, ον, (δεῖπνον q. v.) *supperless*, i. 10. 19: iv. 5. 21.

ἀ-δελφός, οῦ, (ἀ- cop., δελφύς matrix) *a brother,* i. 3, 8 : viii. 9. 22. 25, 38.

ἀ-δεώς adv., (δέος *fear*) *without fear, fearlessly, securely*, i. 9. 13 : vi. 6. 1.

ἀ-δηλος, ον, *uncertain, doubtful, unknown,* D., v. 1. 10: vi. 1. 21.

ἀ-διάβατος, ον, *impassable, unfordable,* ii. 1. 11 : iii. 1. 2.

†ἀδικέω, ήσω, ἠδίκηκα, *to be unjust,*

ἀδικία 3 αἱ

act unjustly, do wrong, be in the wrong; to treat unjustly, wrong, injure, harm; A. AE., P.; i. 3. 10; 4. 9; 6. 7 s: vii. 7. 3: pr. as pf. *to be guilty of doing wrong, to have wronged,* 612, i. 5. 11: v. 7. 26, 29 : μηδὲν ἀ. *to do no wrong, be guilty of no crime,* i. 9. 13.

†ἀδικία, ας, *injustice, wrong-doing,* ii. 6. 18.

ἄ-δικος, ον, s., (δίκη) *unjust, guilty, criminal, wicked, unprincipled,* περί, i. 6. 8; 9. 13: ii. 6. 20 : τὸ ἄδικον *injustice,* i. 9. 16.

‡ἀδίκως, s.? *unjustly, wrongfully,* v. 7. 29 : vii. 1. 16 (or adj.).

ἀ-δόλως adv., (δόλος *guile, fraud) without guile* or *treachery, faithfully,* ii. 2. 8 ; 3. 26 ; iii. 2. 24.

Ἀδραμύτ[τ]ιον, see Ἀτραμύττιον.

ἀ-δύνατος, ον, *impossible, impracticable ; unable, powerless, inefficient;* ii. 4. 6 : iv. 1. 25 : v. 6. 10 : vii. 7. 24.

ᾄδω,* ᾄσομαι, *to sing,* A., iv. 3. 27 ; 7. 16 : vi. 1. 6.

ἀεί, less Att. αἰεί, *always, continually ; at any time* (esp. between the art. and a pt., or after a rel. w. ἄν), *on each occasion, successively;* i. 9. 19 : iii. 2. 31, 38 : iv. 7. 23 : v. 4. 15.

ἀετός, less Att. αἰετός, οῦ, ὁ, *an eagle.* This bird was regarded by the Greeks as sacred to Zeus, and as sent by him to give omens of the future. It gave to the Assyrians and Persians, as to some modern nations, a symbol of royalty or power. i. 10. 12: vi. 1. 23.

ἄ-θεος, ον, s., (θεός) *godless, impious,* ii. 5. 39. Der. ATHEIST.

[Ἀθηνᾶ, ᾶς, *Athēna, Pallas,* or *Minerva;* in Greek mythology the daughter of Zeus, sprung from his head, the goddess of wisdom and warlike prowess, and the especial patroness of Athens.]

‡Ἀθῆναι, ῶν, αἱ, *Athens,* the capital of Attica, and the city in which Greek, indeed ancient civilization culminated (799), "the eye of Greece." According to tradition, it was founded by Cecrops, named for the goddess Athēna (who bestowed upon it the gift of the olive), and greatly enlarged by Theseus, who united the people of Attica as its citizens. At its zenith, it is supposed to have contained, with its harbor the Piræus, about 200,000 inhabitants, or about two fifths of the whole population of Attica. From the Persian wars, in which it acquired such glory at Marathon and Salamis, and was burned by Xerxes, to the Peloponnesian war, in which it was conquered by Sparta, it was the leading state of Greece. In politics, it was the head of the democratic, as Sparta of the aristocratic interest. The latter war had closed, with the prostration of Athens and the exaltation of Sparta, B. C. 404, about three years before the expedition of Cyrus. Preserved from destruction through the desolations of so many centuries, it became, A. D. 1834, the capital of the new kingdom of Greece. iii. 1. 5.

‡Ἀθηναία, ας, poet. for Ἀθηνᾶ, chosen as a password, from the kinship which Seuthes claimed to the Athenians, vii. 3. 39 ?

‡Ἀθηναῖος, ου, ὁ, *an Athenian :* e. g. Xenophon, Lycius, Polycrates, &c. No Athenian is mentioned in the Anabasis dishonorably. i. 8. 15 : iii. 3. 20.

‡Ἀθήνησι or -ῃσι, old d. pl. as adv., *at Athens,* 380 c, iv. 8. 4 : vii. 7. 57.

ἆθλον, ου, (ἆθλος *contest*) *prize* of a contest, i. 2. 10. Der. ATHLETE.

†ἀθροίζω, οἴσω, ἤθροικα, *to assemble, collect, muster, levy,* esp. troops, A.: M., *to assemble, muster,* intrans.: i. 1. 2, 6 s ; 2. 1 ; 10. 5 : ii. 1. 1.

ἀ-θρόος, α, ον, (ἀ- cop., θρόος *noise*) *rustling together, close* or *thick together, in a body, collected, assembled,* esp. of persons, i. 10. 13 : iv. 6. 13 : vii. 3. 9.

†ἀθῡμέω, ήσω, *to be discouraged, disheartened, dispirited,* or *dejected ; to despond, want courage* or *heart ;* D., πρός, ἕνεκα, ὅτι : iii. 2. 18 ; 4. 20 : v. 4. 19 : vi. 2. 14 : vii. 1. 9.

‡ἀθῡμητέον (ἐστὶν ἡμῖν) *we must be disheartened* [there is to be discouragement to us], 682, iii. 2. 23.

†ἀθῡμία, ας, *discouragement, despondency, dejection, faintheartedness,* iii. 2. 8 ; 3. 11.

ἄ-θῡμος, ον, c., (θυμός), *without spirit* or *courage, dispirited, discouraged, dejected, desponding, fainthearted, spiritless, disinclined,* πρός, i. 4. 9 : iii. 1. 36.

‡ἀθύμως *despondingly, dejectedly, dispiritedly, without heart:* ἀθύμως ἔχειν *to be disheartened* or *dejected :* iii. 1. 3, 40 : vi. 4. 26.

αἰ, αἴ, αἷς, see ὁ, ὅς, i. 1. 6 : v. 4. 33.

αἰγι-αλός, οῦ, ὁ, (ἀΐσσω to rush, ἅλς sea) that over which the sea rushes, sea-shore, beach, vi. 4. 1, 4, 7.

†Αἰγύπτιος, α, ον, Egyptian, ii. 1. 6: Αἰγύπτιος subst., an Egyptian, i. 4. 2; 8. 9. The Egyptians mentioned in i. 8. 9 may have entered the Persian service before the revolt stated below, or have been otherwise unaffected by it; or they may have been so called as descendants of the Egyptians settled in Asia by Cyrus the Elder. See Cyr. 7. 1. 45.

Αἴγυπτος, ου, ἡ, Egypt, the northeastern country of Africa, on both sides of the Nile, so famed for its fertility in the basin of this river, its early and peculiar civilization, its varied history, and its wonderful remains so defying the hand of time. It was conquered by Cambyses, the son of the great Cyrus, B. C. 525, and made a Persian province. Its inhabitants, always impatient of the yoke (the more on account of the religious antagonism of the two nations), had succeeded under Amyrtæus in asserting their independence, B. C. 414. The Persians were chagrined at the loss of so important a province, and eager for its reconquest, ii. 1. 14; 5. 13. This was at length effected in the reign of Artaxerxes III., B. C. 346. Not long after, B. C. 332, Egypt submitted to the arms of Alexander; and after his death became the kingdom of one of his generals, Ptolemy. In the year 30 B. C., it became a Roman province.

αἰδέομαι, ἐσομαι, ᾔδεσμαι, α. ᾐδέσθην, to respect, reverence, revere, regard, A., iii. 2. 4 s.

‡αἰδήμων, ον, g. ονος, s. ονέστατος, respectful, modest, i. 9. 5.

‡αἰδοῖον, ου, private part, groin, iv. 3. 12.

‡αἰδώς,* όος, ἡ, respect, reverence, G., ii. 6. 19.

αἰεί, αἰετός, v. l. for ἀεί, ἀετός.

Αἰήτης, ου, Æetes, a king of the Phasians, regarded as a successor, in both sovereignty and name, to the father of Medēa and keeper of the golden fleece which it was the object of the Argonautic expedition to recover, v. 6. 37.

†αἰθρία, ας, (αἰθήρ ether) open air, clear sky, iv. 4. 14 ?

αἴθω (in pr. & ipf.), ch. poet., to set on fire, kindle, burn, A., iv. 7. 20 : M. to be on fire, blaze, burn, intrans., vi. 3. 19.

αἰκίζω, oftener αἰκίζομαι, ἴσομαι ιοῦμαι, ᾔκισμαι, (αἰκία insult, abuse) to abuse, maltreat, insult, outrage, torture, mangle, A. AE., ii. 6. 29 : iii. 1. 18 ; 4. 5.

αἷμα, ατος, τό, blood, v. 8. 15.

Αἰνείας or Αἰνέας, ου, ὁ, Æneas, a lochage from Stymphalus, iv. 7. 13.

Αἰνιάν, ᾶνος, ὁ, an Ænianian. The Æniānes were a tribe of southwestern Thessaly, occupying the upper valley of the river Sperchīus (now the Hellāda). i. 2. 6 : vi. 1. 7.

αἴξ, αἰγός, ἡ ὁ, (ἀΐσσω to leap) a goat [leaper], iv. 5. 25; 6. 17. Der. ÆGIS.

Αἰολίς, ίδος, ἡ, Æolis, a region in the northwest part of Asia Minor, colonized by Æolians. Its cities (twelve especially) were united in a tribal bond, and had a common temple and rites at Cyme ; but attained no great power or distinction. v. 6. 24.

†αἱρετέος, α, ον, to be taken, that must be taken, iv. 7. 3.

†αἱρετός, ή, όν, chosen, selected : οἱ αἱρετοί, the persons chosen, deputies, delegates. i. 3. 21.

αἱρέω,* ήσω, ᾕρηκα, 2 a. εἷλον, a. p. ᾑρέθην, to take, seize, catch, capture, A., i. 4. 8 : iv. 2. 13 : M. to take for one's self, choose, elect, prefer, adopt, A., 2 A., I., ἀντί, i. 3. 5, 14 ; 7. 3 s: ii. 6. 6 : iv. 8. 25 : v. 7. 28 : P. to be taken or chosen, 588, iii. 1. 46 : v. 4. 26. See ἁλίσκομαι. Der. HERESY, HERETIC.

αἴρω,* ἀρῶ, ἦρκα, a. ἦρα, to lift up, raise, A., i. 5. 3 : v. 6. 33.

αἰσθάνομαι,* θήσομαι, ᾔσθημαι, 2 a. ᾐσθόμην, to perceive, notice, observe, learn, become aware of, hear, G., A. P., CP., i. 1. 8 ; 2. 21 ; 9. 21, 31 : ii. 6. 25 : v. 7. 19 : vi. 1. 31. Der. ÆSTHETIC.

†αἴσθησις, εως, ἡ, perception, means of or chance for discovery, iv. 6. 13.

αἴσθομαι r. for αἰσθάνομαι ; v. l. αἴσθεσθαι, ii. 5. 4.

αἴσιος, ον, (αἶσα fate, luck) lucky, auspicious, ominous for good, vi. 5. 2.

Αἰσχίνης, ου, Æschines, of Acarnania, a commander of targeteers, iv. 3. 22 ; 8. 18.

[αἶσχος, εος, τό, disgrace, shame.]

‡αἰσχρός, ά, όν, c. αἰσχίων, s. αἰσχι-

αἰσχρῶς 5 ἀκούω

στος,* *disgraceful, shameful, base, infamous,* πρός, i. 9. 3 : ii. 5. 20 : v. 7. 12 : vii. 6. 21.

†αἰσχρῶς *disgracefully, with dishonor,* iii. 1. 43 : vii. 1. 29.

†αἰσχύνη, ης, *shame, disgrace, dishonor:* ὥστε πᾶσιν αἰσχύνην εἶναι so *that all were ashamed,* ii. 3. 11 : αἰ. ἀλλήλων *a sense of shame before each other,* iii. 1. 10.

†αἰσχύνω, ὑνῶ, ᾔσχυγκα l., *to shame, disgrace:* M. *to be* or *feel ashamed,* I., P., ὅτι, i. 3. 10 : vi. 5. 4 : vii. 6. 21 : *to be ashamed before, reverence, stand in awe of,* A. I., CP., i. 7. 4 : ii. 3. 22 (a. p. as m. ᾐσχύνθην); 5. 39 ; 6. 19.

αἰτέω, ήσω, ᾔτηκα l., *to ask* for a thing, *demand,* A., 2 A., παρά, i. 1. 10 ; 3. 14, 16 : ii. 1. 10 : M. (more subjective, earnest, or humble) *to ask as a favor to* one's self, *entreat, beseech, beg ; to obtain by entreaty ;* A. I., παρά, ii. 3. 18 s : v. 1. 11 : vi. 6. 31.

†αἰτία, ας, [ground of demand] *cause; blame, reproach, censure, charge,* vi. 6. 15 s : αἰτίαν (αἰτίας) ἔχειν *to incur censure (reproaches), be blamed,* ὑπό, vii. 1. 8 ; 6. 11, 15.

†αἰτιάομαι, άσομαι, ᾐτίαμαι, dep.mid., *to blame, accuse, complain of, charge, reprove,* A. I., ὅτι, i. 2. 20 : iii. 1. 7 ; 3. 11 s : v. 5. 19 : vi. 2. 9.

†αἴτιος, a, ον, *causative, causing, productive;* hence, *chargeable with, responsible, guilty, to blame :* ὁ αἴ. *the author,* τὸ αἴ. *the cause :* G. (444 f), I. (A.); i. 4. 15 : ii. 5. 22 : iv. 1. 17 : vi. 6. 8 : vii. 7. 48.

αἰχμ-άλωτος, ον, (αἰχμή *point of a spear,* ἁλίσκομαι) *taken in war, captured :* οἱ αἰ. *the prisoners of war, captives :* τὰ αἰ. *the things taken in war, prizes of war,* including both prisoners and booty : iii. 3. 19 : iv. 1. 12 s ; 8. 27 : v. 3. 4.

[ἀκ- *point,* a root appearing in ἀκμή, ἄκων *dart,* ἄκρος, αἰχμή, ὀξύς, perh. ἀκούω *to point the ear ;* Lat. acus, acuo, acies ; Sans. açan *dart ;* &c.]

Ἀκαρνάν, ᾶνος, ὁ, *an Acarnanian.* Acarnania was the most western province of Greece Proper, lying between Ætolia, the Ionian Sea, and the Ambracian Gulf (now the Gulf of Arta); and was occupied by colonists of different tribes, none of which attained much eminence or refinement. iv. 8. 18.

ἄ-καυστος, ον, (καίω) *unburnt,* iii. 5. 13.

ἀ-κέραιος, ον, (κεράννῡμι) *unmixed, undisturbed ;* of troops,*fresh,* vi. 5. 9.

ἀ-κήρυκτος, ον, (κηρύσσω) *without intercourse by heralds, without truce, implacable,* iii. 3. 5.

ἀκῑνάκης, ου, (fr. Pers.) a *straight poniard, dagger,* or *short-sword,* used by the Persians, and commonly attached to the girdle on the right side, i. 2. 27; 8. 29.

ἀ-κίνδυνος, ον, *without danger, safe, secure,* vi. 5. 29.

†ἀκινδύνως *without danger, safely, securely,* ii. 6. 6.

ἄ-κληρος, ον, (κλῆρος *lot, portion, estate*) *without estate, portionless, poor, in poverty,* iii. 2. 26 ?

†ἀκμάζω, άσω, *to be at the acme of life,* in one's fullest maturity and strength, I., iii. 1. 25.

ἀκμή, ῆς, (ἀκ-) *point, tip,* ACME : ἀκμήν adv., in puncto temporis, *on the point, in the act, just, even now,* iv. 3. 26.

ἀ-κόλαστος, ον, (κολάζω) *unchastised,* ii. 6. 9.

†ἀκολουθέω, ήσω, ἠκολούθηκα, *to accompany, follow,* D. or σύν, vii. 5. 3.

ἀ-κόλουθος, ον, (ἀ- cop., κέλευθος *road, way*) *going the same way, accompanying, following, consistent,* ii. 4. 19. Der. AN-ACOLUTHON.

†ἀκοντίζω, ἴσω ιῶ, *to throw, hurl,* or *fling* a dart or javelin ; *to shoot, hit,* or *pierce* with a javelin, A.; i. 8. 27 ; 10. 7 : iii. 3. 7 : vii. 4. 18.

ἀκόντιον, ου, (ἀκ-; dim. of ἄκων *javelin,* 371 f) *a javelin* or *dart,* for throwing, smaller and lighter than the δόρυ, iv. 2. 28.

†ἀκόντισις, εως, ἡ, *use of the dart, throwing the javelin,* i. 9. 5.

†ἀκοντιστής, οῦ, *javelin-thrower, javelin-man, darter,* iii. 3. 7 : iv. 3. 28.

ἀκούω,* ἀκούσομαι, ἀκήκοα, a.ἤκουσα, (ἀκ-?) *to hear, hear of, listen to, learn* by hearing ; *to hear to, heed, obey ;* G., A., P., I. (w. subj. A.), CP., παρά, περί, — the gen. properly expressing the cause or source of the hearing or learning, whether person or thing (sometimes even the noise itself), while that which is heard or learned is comm. in the acc. or in a complementary clause ; i. 2. 5, 21 ; 3. 20 s ;

ἄκρα 6 ἀλλά

8. 16 : ii. 5. 15 s, 26 ; iii. 5. 16: iv. 7. 24 : εὖ ἀκούειν bene audire, *to be spoken well of*, ὑπό, 575 a, vii. 7. 23 : pr. as pf., ἀκούομεν *we hear = we have heard, are informed*, 612, v. 1. 13 ; 5. 8. Der. ACOUSTIC.

ἄκρα, ας, (fem. of ἄκρος) arx, a *fortified summit, stronghold* or *fortress* on a height, *citadel*, v. 2. 17 s.

ἄ-κρᾱτος, ον, (κεράννῡμι) *unmixed, pure, strong.* The use of wine without mixture was accounted barbaric by the ancient Greeks, who usually tempered it with a much larger portion of water. iv. 5. 27 : v. 4. 29.

ἄ-κριτος, ον, (κρίνω) *unjudged, untried, without trial*, v. 7. 28 s.

†ἀκρο-βολίζομαι, ίσομαι, (βάλλω) *to throw from a height* or *a distance, fight with missiles, skirmish*, D., iii. 4. 18, 33 : v. 2. 10.

‡ἀκροβόλισις, εως, ἡ, *a skirmish, skirmishing*, iii. 4. 16, 18.

†ἀκρό-πολις, εως, ἡ, (πόλις) the [topmost city] *citadel, acropolis*, i. 2. 1, 8 s.

ἄκρος, α, ον, s., (ἀκ-) at the point, tip, or top ; *highest, topmost, extreme :* τὸ ἄκρον the highest point, *height, top, summit, eminence, peak ;* often τὰ ἄκρα the *heights, summits, hills ;* i. 2. 21 : iii. 4. 49 s : τὸ ἀκρότατον the *loftiest summit*, v. 4. 15. Der. ACRO-STIC.

‡ἀκρ-ωνυχία, ας, (ὄνυξ *claw, nail*) *nail-tip ;* hence, *extreme edge, sharp ridge* or *spur* of a mountain, iii. 4. 37 s.

ἀκτή, ῆς, (ἄγνῡμι *to break*) where the sea breaks, *promontory, headland, shore*, vi. 2. 1.

ἀ-κῡρος, ον, (κῦρος *authority*) *without authority* or *force, null, void*, vi. 1. 28.

ἄκων, ουσα, ἄκον, g. οντος, ούσης, (ἀ-, ἑκών) *un-willing, reluctant*, vii. 7. 14 : w. pt., *involuntarily, unintentionally*, iv. 8. 25 : ἄκοντος Κύρου [C. being unwilling] *against the will of C.,* or *without his consent*, i. 3. 17.

ἀλαλάζω, ἄξομαι, a. ἠλάλαξα, ch. poet., (ἀλαλά *war-cry*) *to raise the war-cry, shout* for battle, D., iv. 2. 7 : v. 2. 14 ? vi. 5. 26.

ἀλεεινός, ή, όν, (ἀλέα *warmth*) *warm,* iv. 4. 11 ?

ἀλέξω,* ἀλεξήσω Ep., f. m. ἀλεξήσομαι or ἀλέξομαι, a. m. ἠλεξάμην or ἠλεξησάμην, (akin to ἀλκή *prowess*) *to ward* or *keep off : M. to keep off* from one's self, *defend one's self, repel, require*, A., i. 3. 6 ; 9. 11 : iii. 4. 33.

ἀλέτης, ου, (ἀλέω *to grind*) *a grinder :* as adj., 506 f, ὄνος ἀλέτης a [grinder] *mill-stone*, i. 5. 5.

ἄλευρον, ου, (ἀλέω *to grind*) *flour,* esp. *wheat-flour*, comm. pl., i. 5. 6.

†ἀλήθεια, ας, *truth ; reality ; sincerity, uprightness ;* ii. 6. 25 ; vi. 2. 10.

†ἀληθεύω, εύσω, *to tell* or *speak the truth ; to speak, state, report, predict,* or *promise truly*, A.; i. 7. 18 : iv. 4. 15.

ἀ-ληθής, ές, (λανθάνω or λήθω) unconcealed, *true, real, sincere :* τὸ ἀληθές [the true] *truth*, 507 a : ii. 5. 24 ; 6. 22 : v. 5. 24.

‡ἀληθινός, ή, όν, *truthful, trusty, genuine*, i. 9. 17.

‡ἀληθῶς *truly, in truth*, iv. 7. 7 ?

ἀλιευτικός, ή, όν, (ἀλιεύω *to fish,* fr. ἅλς *sea*) *for fishing :* ἁ. πλοῖον *fishing-boat*, vii. 1. 20.

ἁλίζω, a. p. ἡλίσθην, (ἁλής *crowded*) *to collect* or *assemble* (trans.): *M. to collect* or *assemble* (intrans.), *rendezvous :* ii. 4. 3 : vi. 3. 3.

ἀ-λιθος, ον, (λίθος) *free from stones, not stony,* vi. 4. 5.

ἅλις adv., in crowds, heaps, or abundance ; *abundantly, sufficiently, enough :* subst., G., v. 7. 12.

Ἁλισάρνη, ης, *Halisarne,* a small town in southwestern Mysia, not far from Pergamum, belonging to the principality of the descendants of the Spartan Damarātus, vii. 8. 17 ?

ἁλίσκομαι,* ἁλώσομαι, ἑάλωκα & ἥλωκα, 2 a. ἑάλων & ἥλων, (as pass. of αἱρέω) *to be taken, captured,* or *caught,* P. ; *to be taken prisoner ;* i. 4. 7 ; 5. 2 : iii. 4. 8, 17 ; 5. 14 : vii. 1. 36.

ἄλκιμος, ον, s., (ἀλκή *prowess, courage*) *brave, valiant, warlike,* iv. 3. 4.

ἀλλ᾽ ἤ* exceptive conj., (fr. ἀλλα or ἄλλο ἤ, cf. ἀλλά) *other than, except,* iv. 6. 11 : vii. 7. 53.

ἀλλά,* sometimes adv., but comm. adversative conj., (ἄλλα neut. pl. of ἄλλος, w. accent changed) *otherwise, on the other hand, on the contrary, but, yet, still, however, nay, but only ;* often after a negation ; and often in transitions, to introduce questions, commands, exhortations, &c.; i. 1. 4 ; 4. 18 ; 6. 3 : ii. 5. 18 s, 22 : iv. 7. 7 : ἁ. (καί) *but also, but even,* iii. 2. 19 ; 5. 16 : v. 6. 10 : ἁ. (μᾶλλον) *but rather,*

ἀλλαχοῦ 7 ἅμα

iii. 1. 35 : vii. 8. 16 : ἄ. ὁμῶς *but yet, yet nevertheless*, i. 8. 13 : ἄ. οὐδέ *nay* (or *yet*) *not even, nor yet*, i. 3. 3 ? 4. 8. A speaker, from reference to something before expressed or mutually understood, often commences with ἀλλά, which may then be frequently translated adverbially (*well, well indeed, indeed, for my part*, &c.) or omitted in translation (sometimes, w. μέν, seeming almost as if used prospectively, cf. ἄλλος, 567), i. 8. 17 : ii. 1. 4, 10, 20 : iii. 1. 45. See δέ, γάρ, μήν.

ἀλλαχοῦ (ἄλλος, 380e) *v. l.* for ἄλλῃ, ii. 6. 4 : so ἀλλαχῇ or -ῇ, vii. 3. 47.

ἄλλῃ (dat. of ἄλλος, as adv., 380c) *in another place, direction, way*, or *manner; elsewhere, otherwise;* i. 9. 14? ii. 6. 4? iv. 2. 4, 10 : ἄ. καὶ ἄ. *here and there*, v. 2. 29 ? See ἄλλος c.

ἀλλήλων * g. pl., οις, αις, &c., reciprocal pron., (ἄλλος) *one another, each other,* i. 2. 27. Der. PAR-ALLEL.

ἀλλοθεν (ἄλλος) *from another place* or *point*, i. 10. 13. See ἄλλος c.

ἄλλομαι,* ἁλοῦμαι, a. ἡλάμην & ἡλόμην, *to leap, jump*, iv. 2. 17: vi. 1. 5.

ἄλλος,* η, ο, alius, *other, another, else, remaining, rest, besides; one*, pl. *some:* (a) other than has been mentioned, i. 1. 7; 4. 14; 8. 9 : ἄ. στράτευμα *another army*, τὸ ἄ. στράτευμα *the* [remaining] *rest of the army*, 523 f, i. 1. 9 ; 2. 25 : τὰ ἄλλα or τἄλλα [as to the rest] *in other respects*, i. 7. 4 : τί καὶ ἄλλο ὕλης *also* [any thing else] *any other kind of shrub*, i. 5. 1: τῇ ἄλλῃ, sc. ἡμέρᾳ, *the next day*, ii. 1. 3 : οὐδὲ ἄλλο οὐδὲν δένδρον *nor, besides, a single tree,* 567 e, i. 5. 5 : — (b) other than is to be mentioned, i. 3. 3 : ii. 1. 7 : οὐδὲν ἄλλο ἤ *nothing else than*, iii. 2. 18 : ἄλλο τι [sc. ἐστιν] ἤ; [is there aught else than this ?] *is it not certain that ?* 567 g, iv. 7. 5 : οἱ ἄλλοι Κρῆτες *the rest, the Cretans*, 567 e, v. 2. 31: (b, a) ἄλλος ἄλλον εἷλκε *one drew up another* (alius alium), v. 2. 15 : — (c, repeated or joined with a der., 567 d) *different from each other*, as ἄλλοι ἄλλως alii aliter, [different persons in different ways] *some in one way and others in another*, i. 6. 11 : ἄλλοι ἄλλοθεν some from one point and others from another, *in various directions*, i. 10. 13: ἄλλος (ἄλλοι) ἄλλῃ *one* (some) *one way and another* (others) *another, in different directions*, iv. 8. 19 : ἄλλος ἄλλα λέγει *one says one thing, another another*, ii. 1. 15.

‡ἄλλοτε *at another time, at other times*, iv. 1. 17: ἄ. καὶ ἄ. *at one time and at another, now and then, from time to time*, ii. 4. 26 : v. 2. 29 ?

‡ἀλλότριος, α, ον, aliēnus, *belonging to another* or *others, another's, foreign*, iii. 2. 28 ; 5. 5 : vii. 2. 33.

‡ἄλλως *in another* or *any other manner* or *way, otherwise, differently ; on any other condition ;* [otherwise than should be] *at random ;* i. 6. 11 (see ἄλλος c): iii. 2. 39 : v. 1. 7 : vi. 6. 10 (pleon.): ἄ. πως ἤ *in any other way than*, iii. 1. 20, 26: ἄ. ἔχειν *to be otherwise*, iii. 2. 37: ἄ. τε καί *both otherwise and in particular, especially*, v. 6. 9. Cf. Lat. aliter.

ἀ-λόγιστος, ον, (λογίζομαι) *inconsiderate, unreasoning*, ii. 5. 21.

ἄλσος, εος, τό, (ἀλδαίνω *to make grow*) *a grove*, esp. *a sacred grove*, v. 3. 11 s.

Ἅλυς, υος, ὁ, the *Halys*, the largest river of Asia Minor. It flows into the Euxine, and formerly separated the Lydian and Persian kingdoms (and afterwards Paphlagonia and Pontus). Crœsus crossed this river, trusting to a deceptive oracle, and fought near it a great battle with Cyrus. v. 6. 9. ‖ The *Kizil-Irmak*, i. e. Red River.

ἄλφιτον, ου, comm. in pl., *groats*, esp. *barley-groats, barley-meal*, i. 5. 6.

ἀλωπεκῆ, -ῆς, or -ίς, ίδος, ἡ, (ἀλώπηξ *fox*) *a fox-skin, fox-skin cap*, vii. 4. 4.

ἁλῶ, ἁλώσομαι, see ἁλίσκομαι, i. 4. 7.

‡ἁλώσιμος, ον, *easy to take, liable to be taken, easily captured*, v. 2. 3.

ἅμα *at the same time; at the same time with, together with, with,* D.; i. 2. 9 : ii. 4. 9 : ἅμα (τῇ) ἡμέρᾳ *at the same time with the day, at daybreak, at the dawn of day*, ἅμα ἡλίῳ ἀνίσχοντι or ἀνατέλλοντι (δύνοντι or δυομένῳ) *at sun-rise* (-set), i. 7. 2: ii. 1. 2s; 2. 13. It is often joined with the earlier of two words or clauses, when acc. to the Eng. idiom, it would rather be joined with the later ; or with both, instead of one only ; vii. 6. 20 : iii. 4. 19 : so with a pt., rather than the verb, ἅμα ταῦτ' εἰπὼν ἀνέστη [having said this, he at the same time rose] *as soon as he had said this, he rose*, 662, iii. 1. 47:

Ἀμαζών 8 **Ἀμφίδημος**

ἐμάχοντο ἅμα πορευόμενοι, *fought* [at the same time] *while marching*, vi. 3. 5.

Ἀ-μαζών, όνος, ή, (μαζός *breast*) an *Amazon* (so called as *wanting a breast*, the right breast having been removed for the better use of arms). The Amazons were fabled as a nation of female warriors, dwelling about the Thermōdon in the north part of Asia Minor, and having as their capital Themiscȳra (now Thermeh?). iv. 4. 16.

ἅμαξα, ης, (ἅμα, ἄγω) a *wagon*, esp. for freight (cf. ἅρμα); *wagon-load*; i. 5. 7 s; 7. 20: iv. 7. 10.

†ἁμαξιαῖος, α, ον, *large enough to load a wagon*, *each a wagon-load*, iv. 2. 3.

†ἁμαξ-ιτός, όν, (ἰτός, verbal of εἷμι) *passable by wagons*: ὁδὸς ἁ. *a wagon-way, carriage-road*, i. 2. 21.

ἁμαρτάνω,* ἁμαρτήσομαι, ἡμάρτηκα, 2 a. ἥμαρτον, *to fail of hitting, miss*, G.; *to fail* or *err* in conduct, *do wrong, sin against one*, AE. περί; i. 5. 12: iii. 2. 20; 4. 15: μικρὰ ἁμαρτηθέντα *small things done wrong, small errors* or *mistakes*, v. 8. 20.

ἀ-μαχεί adv., (μάχομαι) *without fighting, resistance*, or *a battle*, i. 7. 9: iv. 6. 12: vi. 5. 15 (v. l. ἀμαχί).

†ἀ-μαχητί = ἀμαχεί, iv. 2. 15 (v. l. ἀμαχητεί).

Ἀμβρακιώτης or **Ἀμπρακιώτης**, ου, an *Ambraciot* or *Ambracian*. Ambracia (now Arta), the most celebrated city in Epīrus, was a colony of Corinth, about seven miles north of the Ambracian Gulf. Siding with Sparta in the Peloponnesian war, it suffered greatly. It was chosen by Pyrrhus for his capital, and won much fame by its brave and resolute defence against the siege of the Romans, B. C. 189. The entrance of the gulf was the scene of the decisive victory of Augustus over Antony, B. C. 31. i. 7. 18: v. 6. 16.

ἀμείνων,* ον, as c. of ἀγαθός, *better, superior, braver*: for emphasis, ἀμείνων καὶ κρείττων *better and more efficient*, nearly = *far better*: ἄμεινον as adv., c. of εὖ, *in a better way, better*: i. 7. 3: ii. 1. 20: iii. 1. 21, 23.

†ἀμέλεια, as, *neglect, carelessness in guarding*, G., iv. 6. 3.

†ἀμελέω, ήσω, ἠμέληκα, *to be careless* or *negligent of, neglect, slight*, G., i. 3. 11: v. 1. 15: vii. 2. 7.

ἀ-μελής, ές, (μέλει) *careless, heedless, negligent.*]

†ἀμελῶς *carelessly, heedlessly, without caution, incautiously*, v. 1. 6.

ἄ-μετρος, ον, (μέτρον) *measureless, immense*, im-mensus, iii. 2. 16.

Ἀμεινσικλείδης, see Ναυσικλείδης.

ἀ-μήχανος, ον, (μηχανή) *without means, resources*, or *expedients;* of persons, *destitute of means or resources, resourceless, helpless;* of things, *impracticable, impossible, insurmountable, inextricable;* i. 2. 21: ii. 3. 18; 5. 21.

ἁμιλλάομαι, ἥσομαι, ἡμίλλημαι, (ἅμιλλα *strife, competition*) *to compete, contend;* w. ἐπί or πρός, *to race for* or *towards, vie for the attainment of, struggle to reach*, iii. 4. 44, 46.

ἄμπελος, ου, ή, (ἀμφὶ ἑλίσσω *to twine round*) *a vine*, i. 2. 22: vi. 4. 6.

Ἀμπρακιώτης, see Ἀμβρακιώτης.

ἀμυγδάλινος, η, ον, (ἀμυγδάλη *almond*) *of almonds, made from almonds*, iv. 4. 13.

ἀ-μύζω, see μύζω, iv. 5. 27 ?

ἀμύνω, ἀμυνῶ, 1 a. ἤμυνα, (cf. mūnio) *to ward* or *keep off: M. to* [keep off from one's self] *defend one's self, act in self-defence*, one means of which is retaliation; hence *to avenge one's self upon, requite, punish*, A.; ii. 3. 23: iii. 1. 14, 29: v. 4. 25.

ἀμφί prep.,* (akin to ἄμφω and Lat. ambo, amb-) *on both sides of*, hence *on different sides of, about, around:* (a) w. Acc. of place, i. 2. 3: of person (the person himself often included, 527 a), οἱ ἀμφὶ Τισσαφέρνην [those about T.] *T. and those with him*, iii. 5. 1: of object of concern or relation, τὰ ἁ. τάξεις [the things about] *matters relating to tactics*, ii. 1. 7; ἁ. εἷναι or ἔχειν *to be busy about* or *occupied with*, iii. 5. 14: v. 2. 26: of time or number, *about*, i. 8. 1; ἁ. τὰ εἴκοσιν *about* [the] *twenty*, 531 d, iv. 7. 22: — (b) w. GEN., poet. or r.: of object sought or cause, *about*, iv. 5. 17. In compos. as above. Cf. περί.

ἀμφι-γνοέω,* ἥσω, ipf. ἠμφιγνόουν or ἠμφεγνόουν, (γνο- in γιγνώσκω) to think on both sides, *to be puzzled, in doubt*, or *at a loss, to wonder*, CP., ii. 5. 33.

Ἀμφί-δημος, ου, *Amphidēmus*, an Athenian, father of Amphicrates.

Ἀμφι-κράτης, εος, Amphicrates, a lochage from Athens, iv. 2. 13, 17.

ἀμφι-λέγω,* λέξω, λέλεχα l., to speak on both sides, to dispute or quarrel about, A., i. 5. 11.

Ἀμφιπολίτης, ου, (Ἀμφί-πολις) an Amphipolite, i. 10. 7. Amphipolis was a city of western Thrace mostly surrounded by the Strymon near its mouth (whence its name), a greatly prized colony of the Athenians, for the loss of which in the Peloponnesian war the historian Thucydides was banished. ǁ Neokhorio.

ἀμφορεύς, έως, ὁ, (shortened from ἀμφι-φορεύς, a vessel carried on both sides, i. e. with two handles; φέρω) amphora, a two-handled vessel (commonly of clay and with a small neck), jar, v. 4. 28.

†ἀμφότερος, α, ον, both (taken or viewed together); from its signification rarely in the sing.: of two individuals, pl. or dual: ἀμφότεροι both or the two persons or parties. With the article, it is placed acc. to the order of statement, as τὼ παῖδε ἀμφοτέρω both the children, ἀμφότερα τὰ ὦτα both ears, 523 b. i. 1. 1; 4. 4; 5. 14, 17: ii. 4. 10: iii. 1. 31: iv. 7. 14.

‡ἀμφοτέρωθεν from or on both sides, at both ends, G., i. 10. 9: iii. 4. 29; 5. 10.

ἄμφω,* ουν, both, ch. substantively, and of two persons, ii. 6. 30: iv. 2. 21.

ἄν* adv., a contingent particle which has no corresponding word in Eng. (though it may sometimes be expressed by perhaps, or, if joined with a rel. pron. or adv., by -ever or -soever); but verbs with which it is connected are commonly translated by the potential mode. It is post-positive, and is thus distinguished from ἄν if. i. 1. 10. See 618 s.

ἄν * conj., (contr. fr. ἐάν q. v.) if, i. 3. 20; 7. 4; 8. 12: ii. 1. 8?

ἀν-, see ἀ- and ἀνά.

ἀνά,* by apostr. ἀν᾿, prep., up, opp. to κατά: w. Acc. of place, up through, along, upon, iii. 5. 16: of standard, ἀνὰ κράτος [up to one's strength] at full speed, i. 8. 1; 10. 15: of number (distributively), ἀνὰ ἑκατόν by the hundred, each a hundred, iii. 4. 21: v. 4. 12: ἀνὰ πέντε παρασάγγας τῆς ἡμέρας at the rate of 5 parasangs a day, iv. 6. 4. In compos., up, up again, again, back.

ἀνα-βαίνω,* βήσομαι, βέβηκα, 2 a. ἔβην, to go up, march up, climb up, ascend, mount, as a height, horse, ship, &c.; to go on board a vessel, embark; often, to go up from the coast of Asia into the interior; ἐπί, &c.; i. 1. 2; 2. 22; 8. 3; vi. 1. 14.

ἀνα-βάλλω,* βαλῶ, βέβληκα, 2 a. ἔβαλον, to throw up; to lift or put upon a horse, A. ἐπί: iv. 4. 4: v. 2. 5.

ἀνά-βασις, εως, ἡ, (ἀνα-βαίνω) ascent, upward-march, expedition into the interior, i. 4. 9: iv. 1. 1, 10.

ἀνα-βιβάζω, βιβάσω βιβῶ, (βιβάζω to make go) to lead up, i. 10. 14.

ἀνα-βοάω, ἤσομαι, βεβόηκα, to raise a cry, call or shout aloud, v. 4. 31.

ἀνα-βολή, ῆς, (ἀνα-βάλλω) earth thrown up, rampart, v. 2. 5.

ἀν-αγγέλλω,* ελῶ, ἤγγελκα, a. ἤγγειλα, to bring back word, re-port, A. D., i. 3. 19, 21.

ἀνα-γιγνώσκω,* γνώσομαι, ἔγνωκα, 2 a. ἔγνων, [to know again, as persons or characters before seen] to recognize, read, i. 6. 4: iii. 1. 5: v. 8. 6.

†ἀναγκάζω, άσω, ἠνάγκακα, to compel, force, oblige, require, constrain, A. I., ii. 1. 6: iii. 3. 12; 4. 19, 49.

†ἀναγκαῖος, α, ον, or ος, ον, necessary, indispensable, inevitable: ἀναγκαῖόν τι some necessity: οἱ ἀναγκαῖοι [those connected by necessary ties] necessarii, kinsmen, relatives : i. 5. 9 : ii. 4. 1.

ἀνάγκη, ης, necessity, constraint, necessary cause: ἀνάγκη (ἐστίν) there is a necessity, it is necessary, indispensable, or unavoidable, it must be, I. (A.) : i. 3. 5 : ii. 4. 26 : iv. 5. 15.

ἀνα-γνούς, see ἀνα-γιγνώσκω, i. 6. 4.

ἀν-άγω,* ἄξω, ἦχα, 2 a. ἤγαγον, to lead up, bring or carry up, A., ii. 3. 21; 6. 1: to bring upon the high sea; M. to put out to sea, weigh anchor, set sail, v. 7. 17: vi. 1. 33 s. Cf. κατ-άγω.

ἀνα-ζεύγνυμι,* ζεύξω, ἔζευξα l., to yoke up, harness up, break up the camp, prepare to start, ii. 4. 37: iv. 6. 1.

ἀνα-θαρρέω, ήσω, τεθάρρηκα, to become confident again, regain confidence or courage, vi. 4. 12.

ἀνα-θεῖναι, -θείς, see ἀνα-τίθημι.

‡ἀνά-θημα, ατος, τό, a sacred gift or votive offering set up in a temple, as a statue, tripod, &c., G., v. 3. 5.

ἀνα-θορυβέω, ήσω, τεθορύβηκα, (θόρυβος) to raise a shout or clamor, cry ἀναθρέψας 10 ἀναρχία

out, shout, cheer, applaud, ὥς: v. 1.3: vi. 1. 30.
ἀνα-θρέψας, see ἀνα-τρέφω, iv. 5. 35.
ἀν-αιρέω,* ήσω, ἤρηκα, 2 a. εἷλον, *to take up;* sp. to take up a question for reply, hence, through an oracle or omen, *to respond, answer, signify, direct, point out,* A. D., I., iii. 1. 6 s: vii. 6. 44 : *M. to take* or *pick up* for one's self, *undertake;* sp. *to take up* or *carry off* one's dead for burial (to which the Greeks attached great importance, believing that the souls of the unburied dead were long debarred from repose; so *A.* rarely, vi. 4. 9); A., iv. 1. 19 ; v. 7. 21, 27.
ἀνα-καίω & Att. κάω,* καύσω, κέκαυκα, *to light up* a fire, *kindle,* A., iii. 1. 3.
ἀνα-καλέω,* καλέσω καλῶ, κέκληκα, *to call* [with raised voice] *aloud,* A., vi. 6. 7 : *M. to call back* to one's self, *summon, sound a retreat,* iv. 4. 22.
ἀνά-κειον or ἀνα-κεῖον, ου, (κεῖμαι) *an upper floor,* v. 4. 29?
ἀνα-κοινόω, ώσω, pf. m. κεκοίνωμαι, *to bring up* from concealment in the breast and *communicate* to another; *to consult,* as a god : *M. to consult* or *confer with,* as with a friend, *to communicate:* D. A., περί : iii. 1. 5 : v. 6. 36 : vi. 1. 22.
ἀνα-κομίζω, ίσω ιῶ, κεκόμικα, *to bring up : M. to lay up* for one's self, *store,* A., iv. 7. 1, 17.
ἀνα-κράζω r., κράξω 1., κέκραγα, 2 a. ἔκραγον, *to raise a cry, cry out, cry aloud, exclaim, shout,* AE., ὡς or ὅτι, iv. 4. 20 : v. 8. 10, 12 : vii. 3. 33.
ἀν-αλαλάζω, ἀξομαι, *to raise the battle-shout, to shout the war-cry,* iv. 3. 19.
ἀνα-λαμβάνω,* λήψομαι, εἴληφα, 2 a. ἔλαβον, *to take up, take with one* or *away, rescue,* A., i. 10. 6 : iv. 7. 24.
ἀνα-λάμπω,* ψω, λέλαμπα, *to blaze up, burst into flames,* v. 2. 24.
ἀνα-λέγω,* λέξω, *to gather up, recount, relate, repeat,* A., ii. 1. 17 ?
ἀν-ᾱλίσκω,* -ᾱλώσω, -ήλωκα, a. -ήλωσα, (ἁλίσκω *to take, A.* as trans. not in use) to take up, *use up, expend, spend, consume,* A., iv. 7. 5, 7, 10.
ἀν-άλωτος, ον, (ἁλίσκομαι) *not to be taken, impregnable,* v. 2. 20.
ἀνα-μένω,* μενῶ, μεμένηκα, *to remain, stay ; wait for,* A.I., iii. 1. 14.

ἀνα-μίγνῡμι,* μίξω, μέμιχα 1., pf. p. μέμιγμαι, *to mix up, mingle,* ἐν, iv. 8. 8.
ἀνα-μιμνήσκω,* μνήσω, a. *p.* ἐμνήσθην, *to remind of, make mention of,* 2 A., iii. 2. 11 : *P.* and *M. to be reminded of, call to mind, remember,* reminiscor, A.P., CP., vi. 1. 23 ; 5. 23.
ἄν-ανδρος, ον, (ἀνήρ) *un-manly, weak, cowardly,* ii. 6. 25.
Ἀναξίβιος, ου, *Anaxibius,* a Spartan admiral, false, corrupt, and cruel. He was afterwards sent out to oppose the Athenians on the Hellespont, and having been surprised by the Athenian general Iphicrates, died fighting like a Spartan, B. C. 388. v.i. 4: vii. 1. 2 s.
ἀναξυρίδες, ίδων, αἱ (fr. Pers.), *trowsers,* such as the Persians wore, i. 5. 8.
ἀνα-παύω, παύσω, πέπαυκα, *to refresh : M. to refresh* or *rest one's self, take one's rest, go to rest* (as for the night), *repose, rest, take breath ; to desist,* G.; i. 10. 16 : ii. 2. 4 : v. 6. 31?
ἀνα-πείθω,* πείσω, πέπεικα, *to bring over* to another opinion, *gain over, persuade, induce,* A. I., i. 4. 11.
ἀνα-πετάννυμι or -ύω,* πετάσω πετῶ, (πετάννῡμι *to spread out) to throw wide open again,* A., vii. 1. 17.
ἀνα-πηδάω, ήσομαι, πεπήδηκα, (πηδάω *to leap) to leap* or *spring up, spring upon* or *mount* a horse, iii. 4. 27 ? vii. 2. 20.
ἀνα-πνέω,* πνεύσομαι, πέπνευκα, a. ἔπνευσα, *to breathe again, take* or *recover breath,* iv. 1. 22.
ἀνα-πράττω,* πράξω, πέπρᾱχα, *to* [make up] *exact,* A. D. παρά, vii. 6. 40.
ἀνα-πτύσσω,* ύξω, (πτύσσω *to fold) to fold back, swing back, wheel round,* A., i. 10. 9. [v. 2. 24 s ?
ἀν-άπτω,* ἄψω, *to light up, kindle,* ἀνα-πυνθάνομαι,* πεύσομαι, πέπυσμαι, 2 a. ἀν-επυθόμην, *to inquire again* or *closely, learn by close inquiry,* A. P., περί, v. 5. 25 ? 7. 1.
ἀν-αρίθμητος, ον, (ἀριθμέω *to number,* fr. ἀριθμός) *in-numerable, countless,* iii. 2. 13.
ἀν-άριστος, ον, (ἄριστον) *without breakfast,* i. 10. 19 : iv. 2. 4 : vi. 5. 21.
ἀν-αρπάζω,* άσω or ἄσομαι, ἥρπακα, *to snatch up, seize, carry-off,* A., i. 3. 14 ? vii. 1. 15.
ἀν-αρχία, ας, (ἀρχή) *want of government,* ANARCHY, iii. 2. 29.

ἀνα-σκευάζω, άσω, to pack up, remove, A., vi. 2. 8.
ἀνα-στάς, -στῆναι, see ἀν-ίστημι.
ἀνα-σταυρόω, ώσω, (σταυρός) to fix or exhibit on a stake or polc, A., iii. 1. 17.
ἀνα-στέλλω,* ελῶ, ἔσταλκα, to send or drive back, keep back or in check, A., v. 4. 23. [μι.
ἀνα-στήσας,-στήσομαι, see ἀν-ίστη-
ἀνα-στρέφω,* ἐψω, ἔστροφα 1., 2 a. p. as m. ἐστράφην, to turn back, retreat, retire, turn or wheel round : M. to move round, carry one's self ; face about, rally: i. 4.5 ; 10. 8, 12 : ii. 5.14.
ἀνα-σχέσθαι, -σχωμαι, see ἀν-έχω.
ἀνα-ταράττω,* άξω, τετάραχα 1., to stir up, confuse : pf. p. pt. [having been put] in disorder, i. 7. 20.
ἀνα-τείνω,* τενῶ, τέτακα, a. ἔτεινα, to stretch or lift up, hold up, raise, elevate, A. : ἀνα-τεταμένος, elevated, acc. to some with expanded wings: i. 10. 12 : iii. 2. 9 : vii. 4. 9 ?
ἀνα-τέλλω,* τελῶ, τέταλκα, (τέλλω to raise, rise) to rise up, ii .3. 1.
ἀνα-τίθημι,* θήσω, τέθεικα, a. ἔθηκα (θῶ, &c.), to put up ; put, place, or lay upon : sp. to set up as a sacred gift, consecrate, deposit : A. ἐπί, εἰς : ii. 2. 4 : iii. 1. 30 : v. 3. 5 s.
ἀνα-τρέφω,* θρέψω, τέτροφα, to [feed up] fatten, iv. 5. 35.
ἀνα-φεύγω,* φεύξομαι, πέφευγα, 2 a. ἔφυγον, to flee or escape up, ἐπί, vi. 4.24.
ἀνα-φρονέω, ήσω, πεφρόνηκα, to become rational again, come to one's senses, iv. 8. 21.
ἀνα-χάζω,* (χάζω drive back, ch. poet.) M. to draw back, retire, retreat, iv. 7. 10: so Α. iv. 1. 16.
ἀνα-χωρέω, ήσω, κεχώρηκα, to go back, retreat, retire, withdraw, return, iii. 3. 13 : iv. 3. 6 : vi. 4. 10.
ἀνα-χωρίζω, ίσω ιῶ, to separate again, draw off, A., v. 2. 10.
ἄνδρες, -ός, &c., see ἀνήρ, i. 1. 6.
‡ἀνδρ-αγαθία, as, (ἀγαθός) virtus, manly excellence, esp. valor, v. 2. 11.
‡ἀνδρά-ποδον, ου, (πούς) [a man's footstool, as the captive often fell at the feet of the conqueror, and the foot of the latter was sometimes placed on his neck] a slave, esp. one made in war, a captive, i. 2. 27 : ii. 4. 27.
‡ἀνδρεῖος, a, ον, manly, brave, valiant, vi. 5. 24.

‡ἀνδρειότης, ητος, ἡ, virtus, manliness, bravery, valor, vi. 5. 14.
‡ἀνδρίζω, ίσω, to make one a man : M. to make one's self a man, to act the man, act manfully, display one's valor, iv. 3. 34 : v. 8. 15.
ἀν-έβην, see ἀνα-βαίνω, i. 1. 2.
ἀν-εγείρω,* ἐγερῶ, ἐγήγερκα 1., a. p. ἠγέρθην, to wake up another, rouse: P. to be aroused, to awake, iii. 1. 12 s.
ἀν-εῖλον, see ἀν-αιρέω, iii. 1. 6.
ἀν-εῖναι, see ἀν-ίημι, vii. 6. 30 ?
ἀν-ειπεῖν, 2 a. inf. (see εἰπεῖν), to [speak up] proclaim, announce, I. (A.), ὅτι, ii. 2. 20 : v. 2. 18.
ἀν-εκ-πίμπλημι,* πλήσω, πέπληκα, to fill out again, fill up, A., iii. 4. 22 ?
ἀν-ελέσθαι, see ἀν-αιρέω, iv. 1. 19.
ἄνεμος, ου, ὁ, (akin to Lat. animus, anima) wind, iv. 5. 3 s.
ἀν-επιλήπτως, (ἐπι-λαμβάνω) in a way not to be taken hold of, blamelessly, without blame or censure, vii. 6. 37.
ἀν-ερεθίζω, ίσω ιῶ, ἠρέθικα, (ἐρέθω irrīto, to provoke) to stir up, excite, inflame, instigate, A., vi. 6. 9.
ἀν-ερωτάω,* ἐρωτήσω & ἐρήσομαι, ἠρώτηκα, to ask [up] directly and as one who has a right to know, demand, question, inquire of, A. CP., ii. 3. 4 : iv. 5. 34.
ἀν-έστην, see ἀν-ίστημι, iii. 2. 1.
ἀν-εστράφην, see ἀνα-στρέφω.
ἄνευ adv. as prep., without, G., i. 3. 11, 13 : ii. 6. 6, 18.
ἀν-ευρίσκω,* εὑρήσω, εὕρηκα or ηὕρηκα, to find again, discover, find, A., vii. 4. 14.
ἀν-έχω and ἀν-ίσχω,* ἔξω and σχήσω, ἔσχηκα, 2 a. ἔσχον, to hold or lift up ; of the sun, to [lift itself up] rise, ii. 1. 3 : M. (ipf. w. double aug. ἠνειχόμην, 2 a. ἀν-εσχόμην, oftener ἠνεσχόμην, 282 b) to hold up under, sustain, endure, bear, tolerate, hold firm against, restrain or control one's self, A., G. (661 b), P., i. 7. 4 ; 8. 11, 26 : ii. 2. 1.
ἀνεψιός, οῦ, ὁ, a cousin, kinsman (in Byzantine law, NEPHEW), vii.8.9.
ἀν-ήγαγον, -ηγμένος, see ἀν-άγω.
ἀν-ηγέρθην, see ἀν-εγείρω, iii. 1. 12.
ἀν-ήκεστος, ον, (ἀκέομαι to heal) incurable, irremediable, irreparable, ii. 5. 5 : vii. I. 18.
ἀν-ήκω, ήξω, to [come up to] reach, extend, εἰς, vi. 4. 3, 5.
ἀνήρ,* ἀνδρός, vir, a man in dis-

tinction from a woman or child (as ἄνθρωπος is a *man* in distinction from a higher or a lower being, as from a god or a beast); hence a *man* emphatically, as a *husband*, a *warrior* or *soldier* (though hostile, or even cowardly, vi. 6. 24), a *brave man*, a *man of full age*, a *man to be honored*. A more specific name with adjective force is often joined with it (esp. in address, where ἄνδρες is the term of respect in addressing a company of men), and it need not then be always translated. i. 1. 6, 11; 2. 20; 3. 3; 7. 4: iv. 5. 24.

ἀν-ηρώτων, see ἀν-ερωτάω, ii. 3. 4.
ἀν-ήχθην, see ἀν-άγω, ii. 6. 1.
ἀνθ', by apostr. for ἀντί, i. 3. 4.
ἀνθέμιον, ου, (ἄνθος *flower*) a *flower, figure of a flower, pattern of flowers*, v. 4. 32.
ἀνθ-ίστημι,* στήσω, ἕστηκα, *to set against*: *M.* *to stand against, withstand, resist*, vii. 3. 11.
†ἀνθρώπινος, η, ον, *human*, ii. 5. 8.
ἄνθρωπος, ου, ὁ ἡ, homo, *a man* (one of the race, see ἀνήρ), *human being, person, fellow*; pl. *men, persons, people, mankind*; i. 3. 15; 5. 9; 6. 6. In the expression of respect, ἀνήρ is the rather used; of contempt, ἄνθρωπος, i. 7. 4: iii. 1. 27, 30; and in speaking of one's self, it is more modest to use ἄνθρωπος, vi. 1. 26. Yet, without special expression, ἄνθρωπος is often used as a more general and unemphatic term, where ἀνήρ might have been used, as in speaking of soldiers, i. 8. 9; with a more specific name, vi. 4. 23; &c. Der. PHILANTHROPY. See ὤψ.
ἀνιάω, άσω, ἠνίακα l., (ἀνία *grief, distress*) *to annoy, trouble*, A.: *M. to be grieved, troubled*, or *distressed*: i. 2. 11: iii. 3. 19: iv. 8. 26.
ἀν-ίημι,* ἥσω, εἷκα, a. ἧκα (ὦ, &c.) *to* [let one get up] *let go* or *escape*, A. P., vii. 6. 30?
ἀν-ιμάω, (ἱμάς *leathern strap* used in drawing) *to draw up*, A., iv. 2. 8.
ἀν-ίστημι,* στήσω, ἕστηκα, 1 a. ἕστησα, 2 a. ἕστην, *to raise, rouse*, or *start up* another, A.: *M.*, w. pf. and 2 a. act., *to raise one's self up, stand up, get up, rise* (sp. for speaking): i. 3. 13; 5. 3; 6. 10: iv. 5. 8, 19, 21.
ἀν-ίσχω, see ἀν-έχω, ii. 1. 3: v. 7. 6.
ἄν-οδος, ου, ἡ, (ἀνά, ὁδός), = ἀνά-

βασις, *the way up, upward march, ascent*, ii. 1. 1.
ἄν-οδος, ον, (ἀ-, ὁδός) *pathless, inaccessible*, or *difficult of access*, iv. 8. 10.
ἀ-νόητος, ον, .(νοέω) *senseless, demented, foolish*, ii. 1. 13.
ἀν-οίγω,* ἀν-οίξω, ἀν-έῳχα, ipf. ἀν-έῳγον, (οἴγω *to open*) *to* [open up or again] *open*, A., v. 5. 20: vii. 1. 16.
ἀνομία, ας, (ἄ-νομος) *lawlessness*, v. 7. 33 s.
ἀν-ομοίως, (ἀν-όμοιος *un-like*) *differently*: a. ἔχειν *to be differently situated* or *esteemed*, vii. 7. 49.
ἄ-νομος, ον, (νόμος) *lawless*, vi. 6. 13.
ἀντ' or ἀνθ', by apostr. for ἀντί.
ἀντ-αγοράζω, άσω, ἠγόρακα, *to buy* or *purchase in return*, A., i. 5. 5.
ἀντ-ακούω,* ἀκούσομαι, ἀκήκοα, *to hear in return, listen in turn*, ii. 5. 16.
Ἄντανδρος, ου, ἡ, *Antandros*, an old town of Troas, south of Mt. Ida and on the north shore of the Adramyttian Gulf, where Virgil makes Æneas build his fleet (Æn. 3. 6). It was later colonized by Æolians, and was sometimes under Greek, and sometimes under Persian power. vii. 8. 7. ‖ Avjilar.
ἀντ-εμ-πίπλημι,* πλήσω, πέπληκα, *to fill in return*, A. G., iv. 5. 28.
ἀντ-επιμελέομαι,* ἥσομαι, ἐπιμεμέλημαι, *to take heed* or *care in return*, ὅπως, iii. 1. 16.
ἀντ-ευ-ποιέω,* ήσω, πεποίηκα, *to do well* or *a service in return*, v. 5. 21; also written, through tmesis, ἀντ' εὖ ποιέω, 699 i.
ἀντί* prep., *over against, against* (*behind*, iv. 7. 6); *instead of, in place of, in preference to, in return for*; G.: in compos., *against, instead, in turn* or *return*: i. 1. 4; 3. 4. 21; 7. 3 s.
ἀντι-δίδωμι,* δώσω, δέδωκα, a. ἔδωκα (δῶ, &c.), *to give instead* or *in return*, A., iii. 3. 19.
ἀντι-θέω,* θεύσομαι, *to run against*, ἐπί, iv. 8. 17?
ἀντι-καθ-ίστημι,* στήσω, ἕστηκα, a. p. ἐστάθην, *to appoint instead*, A., iii. 1. 38.
ἀντι-λέγω,* λέξω, *to speak* or *say against* or *in opposition, gainsay, oppose, object*, D. I. (A.), ὡς, ii. 3. 25; 5. 29.
Ἀντι-λέων, οντος, *Antileon*, a Cyrean from Thurii, a flourishing Athenian colony in Italy, on the Tarentine Gulf. Among its colonists were the historian Herodotus and the orator Lysias. v. i. 2.

ἀντίος, α, ον, (ἀντί) set against; opposite, fronting, over against; ἐκ τοῦ ἀντίου [sc. μέρους] from the opposite part, in front; w. ἰέναι, &c., as adv., against: opposed, contrary, different (other than, ἤ): D.: i. 8. 17, 23 s? 10. 10: iv. 3. 26: vi. 6. 34.

ἀντι-παρα-θέω,* θεύσομαι, to run [along against] sidewise to meet or oppose, ἐπί, iv. 8. 17?

ἀντι-παρα-σκευάζομαι, άσομαι, ἐσκεύασμαι, to prepare in turn, make preparation against, i. 2.5.

ἀντι-παρα-τάττομαι, τάξομαι, τέταγμαι, to [array one's self] draw up or form against, A. or κατά, iv. 8. 9.

ἀντι-πάρ-ειμι,* ipf. ᾔειν, to march [along over against] abreast, iv. 3. 17.

ἀντι-πάσχω,* πείσομαι, πέπονθα, to suffer in turn or return, ii. 5. 17.

ἀντι-πέρᾱς or ἀντι-πέρᾱν, over against, on the other side of, G., i. 1. 9: iv. 8. 3: see κατ-αντιπέρας.

ἀντι-ποιέω, ήσω, πεποίηκα, to do or act in return, retaliate, A., iii. 3.7,12: M. to [make for or claim in opposition to another] contest, dispute, contend, or strive with one about or for; to vie in, seek distinction for; D. G., περί: ii. 1. 11; 3. 23: iv. 7. 12: v. 2. 11.

ἀντι-πορεύομαι, εύσομαι, &c., to march against, iv. 8. 17?

ἀντί-πορος, ον, ch. poet., opposite to, over against, D., iv. 2. 18.

ἀντι-στασιάζω, άσω, to form a party against, to contest or contend with, D., iv. 1. 27.

ἀντι-στασιώτης, ου, (στασιώτης partisan) one of an opposite party, opponent, adversary, antagonist, i. 1. 10.

ἀντι-στοιχέω, ήσω, (στοῖχος row) to stand in opposite rows, front each other, D., v. 4. 12.

ἀντι-στρατοπεδεύομαι, εύσομαι, ἐστρατοπέδευμαι, to encamp or take the field against, vii. 7. 33.

ἀντι-τάττω,* τάξω, τέταχα, to array against, draw up or marshal against, oppose to, A. D.: M. to array one's self against, D.: pf. p. as pret. to [have been marshalled] stand in array or be drawn up against: i. 10. 3: ii. 5. 19: iii. 2. 14: iv. 8. 5.

ἀντι-τῑμάω, ήσω, τετίμηκα, to honor in return, A. ἀντί, v. 5. 14.

ἀντι-τοξεύω, εύσω, to shoot in return, shoot back, iii. 3. 15: v. 2. 32.

ἀντι-φυλάττω,* άξω, πεφύλαχα, to guard in turn; M. to be on one's guard in turn, ii. 5. 3.

ἄντρον, ου, antrum, cave, cavern, grot, ANTRE, i. 2. 8. [3. 11.
†ἀντρώδης, ες, (εἶδος) cavernous, iv.
†ἀνυστός, όν, practicable, possible, i. 8. 11.

ἀνύω & Att. ἀνύτω,* ύσω, ἤνυκα, to accomplish, effect; M., for one's own advantage, A., vii. 7. 24.

ἄνω, c. ἀνωτέρω, s. -τάτω, adv., (ἀνά) up, upwards, high up, above, in the ascent; into the air; up the country, from the sea-coast into the interior, in the interior: ὁ ἄνω the upward, upper, inland: τὸ ἄνω [sc. μέρος] the part or division above: οἱ ἄνω those above: τὰ ἄνω the [places above] high ground, heights: G.: i. 2. 1; 4. 17: iii. 1. 8; 4. 17: iv. 3. 3, 23, 25; 6. 26; 8. 28.

†ἀνώ-γαιον, ου, or ἀνώγεων, ω, (γαῖα = γῇ) an upper floor, v. 4. 29?

†ἄνωθεν, from above, from the interior, iv. 7. 12: v. 2. 23: vii. 7. 2.

ἀξία, ας, (fem. of ἄξιος) value, desert, due, vi. 6. 33. [i. 5. 12.
ἀξίνη, ης, (ἄγνυμι to break?) an axe,
ἄξιος, α, ον, c., s., (ἄγω to bring or weigh) [bringing or weighing so much] worth, worthy, deserving, worth one's while, befitting, becoming, adequate, G. D., I.: πολλοῦ ἄ. worth much, valuable, of great value: i. 3. 12; 4. 7; 7. 3; 9. 1, 29: ii. 1. 14; 3. 25: vii. 3. 27.

†ἀξιο-στράτηγος, ον, c., worthy to be a general or to command, iii. 1. 24.

†ἀξιόω, ώσω, ἠξίωκα, to deem worthy, A. G., I.; to deem fit, proper, or reasonable, to approve, A.; hence to claim, demand, ask, request, or desire, as fit, proper, or reasonable, A., I. (A.); i. 1. 8; 7. 8; 9. 15? iii. 2. 7: v. 5. 12.

†ἀξίωμα, ατος, τό, dignity, vi. 1. 28. Der. AXIOM.

ἄξω, f. of ἄγω, ii. 3. 6.
ἄξων, ονος, ὁ, (ἄγω) axis, Germ. Achse, an AXLE, i. 8. 10.

ἄ-οπλος, ον, (ὅπλον) without armor, unarmed, ii. 3. 3.

ἀπ', ἀφ', by apostr. for ἀπό, i. 7. 18.
ἀπ-αγγέλλω, ελῶ, ἤγγελκα, to bring or carry word, a message, or tidings from a person or place; comm. to bring or carry back word, a message, or tidings, to re-port, announce; A. D., CP., παρά, περί, &c.; i. 4. 12s; 10. 14s.

ἀπ-αγορεύω 14 ἀπῄειν

ἀπ-αγορεύω, εύσω, ἠγόρευκα, (comm. f. ἐρῶ, pf. εἴρηκα, 2 a. εἶπον) to [speak off from a thing, bid farewell to it] *renounce, resign, give up; to give out, become exhausted* or *fatigued, tire, ὑπό*: also, *to* [bid one away from a thing] *forbid*: ἀπ-είρηκα, as pret., *I* [have become fatigued] *am fatigued, tired,* or *weary*, P.: i. 5. 3 : ii. 2. 16 : v. 1. 2 ; 8. 3. See ἀπεῖπον.

ἀπ-άγω,* ἄξω, ἦχα, 2 a. ἤγαγον, *to lead, conduct, bring,* or *curry away;* comm. *to lead*, &c., *back: M. to carry off* one's own : A. διά, εἰς, &c. : i. 3. 14; 10. 6 : ii. 3. 29 : v. 2. 8 s : vi. 6. 1.

‡ἀπ-αγωγή, ῆς, a *leading away, removal*, vii. 6. 5.

ἀ-παθής, ές, (πάθος) *free from suffering,* G., vii. 7. 33.

ἀ-παίδευτος, ον, (παιδεύω) *uneducated, ignorant, stupid,* ii. 6. 26.

ἀπ-αίρω,* ἀρῶ, ἦρκα, a. ἦρα, to lift from its resting-place, as a vessel, &c.; hence *to set sail, depart,* vii. 6. 33 ?

ἀπ-αιτέω, ήσω, *to ask* from, *demand*, esp. one's due, as the payment of a debt ; *to ask back;* 2 A.; i. 2. 11: ii. 5. 38 : iv. 2. 18 : vii. 6. 2, 17.

ἀπ-αλλάττω,* ἄξω, ἤλλαχα, 2 a. p. ἠλλάγην (ἀλλάττω *to change,* fr. ἄλλος) *to* [change from or off] *put away, get rid of, escape,* A. : *M.* and *P. to be rid* or *quit of, to be freed from,* G.; *to depart from, leave, withdraw, ἀπό, ἐκ* : i. 10. 8 : iii. 2. 28 : iv. 3. 2 : v. 6. 32.

ἀπαλός, ή, όν, c., (ἄπτω) *soft* to the touch, *tender*, i. 5. 2 : v. 4. 32.

ἀπ-αμείβομαι, ψομαι, a. p. ἠμείφθην, ch. poet., esp. Ep., (ἀμείβω *to interchange*) *to* [give back in exchange] *reply*, ii. 5. 15.

ἀπ-αντάω, ήσω, ἤντηκα, (ἀντάω *to meet*, fr. ἀντί) *to go* or *come* from the other side in order *to meet* or *to oppose, to meet* as a friend or foe, *encounter, go against*, D., ii. 3. 17 : iv. 6. 5.

ἅπαξ *once* (after ἐπεί, ἐάν, ὡς, as in Lat. ut semel), i. 9. 10 : ii. 2. 12.

ἀ-παρα-σκεύαστος or ἀ-παρά-σκευ-ος, ον, c., s., (σκευάζω, σκεῦος) *unprepared*, i. 1. 6 ; 5. 9 : ii. 3. 21.

ἅ-πᾱς, ᾱσα, αν, (πᾶς strengthened by α- cop.) *all together, all, the whole* or *entire*: πεδίον ἅπαν, *all a plain*, *a level region throughout* : i. 4. 4, 15 ; 5. 1 ; 6. 10 : iv. 4. 1.

ἀπ-αυθημερίζω, ίσω ιῶ, (αὐθημερόν)

to come back or *return on the same day,* ἐπί, v. 2. 1.

ἀπ-εγνωκέναι, see ἀπο-γιγνώσκω.
ἀπ-εδόμην, -έδωκα, see ἀπο-δίδωμι.
ἀπ-έδρᾱν, 2 a. of ἀπο-διδράσκω.
ἀπ-έθανον, 2 a. of ἀπο-θνῄσκω, i. 8. 27.

ἀπειθέω, ήσω, (ἀ-πειθής *disobedient*, fr. πείθομαι) *to be disobedient, disobey*, ii. 6. 4 : iii. 2. 31.

†ἀπειλέω, ήσω, *to threaten*, D. A., CP., v. 5. 22 ; 6. 34.

ἀπειλή, ῆς, a *threat*, vii. 7. 24.

ἄπ-ειμι,* ἔσομαι, (εἰμί) absum, *to be away* or *absent, to absent one's self,* D., i. 5. 37 : vi. 6. 20.

ἄπ-ειμι * (often as f. of ἀπ-έρχομαι), ipf. ᾔειν or ᾖα, (εἶμι) *to go from* or *away, depart, withdraw, retire, retreat, desert ; to go back, return ;* AE. *ἀπό, ἐκ, ἐπί, εἰς,* &c., i. 3. 11 ; 9. 29 : ii. 2. 4, 10 s ; 3. 7, 29.

ἀπ-εῖπον, 2 a. associated with ἀπα-γορεύω q. v., *to renounce, resign,* A.; *to forbid,* D. I. ; vii. 1. 41 ; 2. 12.

ἀπ-είρηκα, pf. associated with ἀπα-γορεύω q. v., ii. 2. 16.

ἀ-πείρος, ον, c., (πείρα) *in-experienced, un-skilled, un-acquainted with,* G., ii. 2. 5 : iii. 2. 16 : v. 1. 8 ; 6. 29.

ἀπ-εῖχον, see ἀπ-έχω, iii. 1. 2.
ἀπ-έκτονα, see ἀπο-κτείνω, ii. 1. 8.
ἀπ-ελαύνω,* ἐλάσω ἐλῶ, ἐλήλακα, a. ἤλασα, *to drive off* or *away, dislodge,* A. ἀπό : *to* [drive a horse or army] *ride* or *march off, away,* or *back, to retreat,* εἰς, &c. : i. 4. 5 ; 8. 17 : iii. 4. 40.

ἀπ-ελθών, see ἀπ-έρχομαι, i. 4. 7.
ἀπ-ερύκω,* ὐξω Ep., a. ἤρυξα, ch. poet., *to keep off*, A., v. 8. 25.

ἀπ-έρχομαι,* ἐλεύσομαι, ἐλήλυθα, 2 a. ἦλθον, *to come* or *go from* or *away, depart, withdraw, retire, retreat, desert ; to go back, return ;* παρά, ἐπί, εἰς, πρός, &c.; i. 1. 4 ; 3. 17 ; 9. 29.

ἀπ-εχθάνομαι,* -εχθήσομαι, -ἤχθη-μαι, 2 a. -ηχθόμην, (ἔχθος) *to incur one's hate* in return, *displease, offend,* D., ii. 6. 19 : v. 8. 25 : vii. 6. 34.

ἀπ-έχω,* ἔξω, ἔσχηκα, 2 a. ἔσχον, *to* [have one's self away from] *be off from* or *distant,* G. A. of extent, ἀπό : *M. to hold* or *exclude one's self from, refrain* or *abstain from, refrain from injuring, spare, decline,* G. : i. 3. 20 : ii. 4. 10 ; 6. 10 : iii. 1. 22 : iv. 3. 5 : vi. 1. 31.

ἀπ-ήγαγον, 2 a. of ἀπ-άγω, i. 10. 6.
ἀπ-ῄειν, see ἀπ-ειμι (εἶμι), i. 9. 29.

ἀπ-ήλασα,-ήλαυνον, see ἀπ-ελαύνω.
ἀπ-ῆλθον, 2 a. of ἀπ-έρχομαι, i. 9. 29.
ἀπ-ηλλάγην, see ἀπ-αλλάττω, i. 10. 8.
ἀπ-ῆρα, a. of ἀπ-αίρω, vii. 6. 33?
ἀπ-ιέναι, -ιθι, -ιμεν, -ἴοιμι, &c., see ἄπ-ειμι (εἶμι), i. 3. 11.
†ἀπιστέω, ήσω, ήπίστηκα, to distrust, mistrust, suspect; to disobey; D.; ii. 5. 6, 15 s; 6. 19 : vi. 6. 13.
†ἀπιστία, as, want of faith; distrust, mistrust; faithlessness, perfidy, treachery, πρός; ii. 5. 4, 21 : iii. 2. 4, 8.
ἄ-πιστος, ον, void of faith ; void of credit, distrusted, D., ii. 4. 7: vii. 7. 23 s.
ἀπ-ιτέον ἐστίν (ἀπ-ειμι) it is necessary to depart, 682 ; v. 3. 1.
ἀπ-ίω, -ιών, &c., see ἄπ-ειμι (εἶμι).
ἄ-πλετος or ἄ-πλᾶτος, ον, (πελάω to approach) [un-approachable] immense, vast, prodigious, iv. 4. 11.
ἀ-πλόος,* όη, όον, contr. οὖς, ῆ, οὖν, simplex, simple, sincere ; τὸ ἁπλοῦν simplicity, sincerity, 507 a ; ii. 6. 22 : v. 8. 18.
ἀπό,* by apostr. ἀπ' or ἀφ', prep., ab, from ; w. GEN. of PLACE, from, away from, i. 1. 2 ; 2. 5 (so of persons or things from which a separation takes place, i. 8. 3, 28): of TIME, from (either before or after), i. 7. 18: ii. 6. 5 ; ἀφ' οὗ [from the time when, 557 a] since, iii. 2. 14 : of SOURCE (origin, cause, means, &c.), from, by means of, by, with, through, upon, i. 1. 9 ; 5. 10 : ii. 5. 7. In compos., from, away, off, back (hence where something is due); sometimes strengthening, and sometimes reversing the idea of the simple.
ἀπο-βαίνω,* βήσομαι, βέβηκα, 2 a. ἔβην, to [step off from a vessel] disembark, εἰς, ἐπί : to [come off] be fulfilled or prove true: v. 7. 9 : vii. 8. 22.
ἀπο-βάλλω,* βαλῶ, βέβληκα, 2 a. ἔβαλον, to throw away, lose, A., iv. 6. 10 : vi. 1. 21 : vii. 6. 31.
ἀπο-βιβάζω, βιβάσω βιβῶ, (βιβάζω to make go, causative of βαίνω) to disembark or land another, A., i. 4. 5.
ἀπο-βλέπω, ἔψομαι, βέβλεφα 1., to look off to, as one does to a quarter from which help is expected ; hence to look expectantly or intently upon, gaze at, watch, εἰς, i. 8. 14 : vii. 2. 33.
ἀπο-γιγνώσκω,* γνώσομαι, ἔγνωκα, 2 a. ἔγνων, to decide away from something, i. e. to abandon or relinquish the idea of it, to renounce or give up

the thought or intention of, G., i. 7. 19.
ἀπο-δέδρᾱκα, see ἀπο-διδράσκω, i. 4. 8.
ἀπο-δείκνῡμι,* δείξω, δέδειχα, a. p. ἐδείχθην, to point off or out, show, direct, declare, publish, A. D., I., CP.; to de-signate, appoint, 2 A.; i. 1. 2 : ii. 3. 14: iii. 2. 36: v. 8. 7 : M. to express or show one's opinion or feeling, A. I. (A.), CP., v. 2. 9 ; 5. 3 ; 6. 37.
ἀπο-δέρω,* δερῶ, 2 a. p. ἐδάρην (δέρω to skin) to take off the skin, to skin, flay, A., iii. 5. 9.
ἀπο-δέχομαι, δέξομαι, δέδεγμαι, to receive from one, accept, vi. 1. 24.
ἀπο-δημέω, ήσω, (ἀπό-δημος away from one's people) to leave home, vii. 8. 4.
ἀπο-διδράσκω,* δράσομαι, δέδρᾱκα, 2 a. ἔδρᾱν, to run off or away, flee, desert, withdraw, escape, esp. by stealth, secretly, or unobserved (cf. φεύγω, ἀποφεύγω); to escape by concealment, slip away, hide one's self ; A., εἰς, ἐκ, &c.; i. 4. 8 : ii. 2. 13 ; 5. 7 : vi. 4. 8.
ἀπο-δίδωμι,* δώσω, δέδωκα, a. ἔδωκα (δῶ, &c.), to give back, restore or return, give or deliver up ; hence esp. to give or pay what has been borrowed or is due, A. D., i. 2. 11 s ; 4. 15: iv. 2. 19, 23 : M. to [give up for one's own profit] sell, Λ., vii. 2. 3, 6 ; 8. 6.
ἀπο-δοκέω,* δόξω, to seem away from one's interest ; only as impers., ἀποδοκεῖ, it does not seem good or expedient, it is decided not to, D. I., ii. 3. 9.
ἀπο-δοῦναι, see ἀπο-δίδωμι, i. 7. 5.
ἀπο-δραίην, -δρᾶναι, -δράς, see ἀποδιδράσκω, ii. 2. 13 ; 5. 7.
ἀπο-δραμοῦμαι, f. of ἀπο-τρέχω.
ἀπο-δύω,* δύσω, δέδῡκα, 2 a. as m. ἔδυν, to take off from or strip another, despoil, A.; M. to strip one's self, take off one's own clothes; iv. 3. 17 : v. 8. 23.
ἀπο-δώσω, f. of ἀπο-δίδωμι, i. 4. 15.
ἀπο-θανεῖν, -θανών, see ἀπο-θνήσκω.
ἀπο-θαρρέω, ήσω, to be confident, v. 2. 22?
ἄποθεν or ἄπωθεν, (ἀπό) from a distance, i. 8. 14?
ἀπο-θνήσκω,* θανοῦμαι, τέθνηκα, 2 a. ἔθανον, to die off, die, fall in battle ; as p. of ἀποκτείνω, to be killed, slain, or put to death, ὑπό : i. 6. 11 ; 8. 27: ii. 6. 29 s : iii. 2. 39.
ἀπο-θύω (ὕ),* θύσω, τέθῠκα, to sacrifice in payment of a vow, pay a sacrifice, A. D., iii. 2. 12 : iv. 8. 25.

ἀποικία   16   ἀποπήγνυμι

†ἀποικία, as, *a colony*, iv. 8. 22.
ἄπ-οικος, ον, transplanted from home, *colonized*: subst. ἡ ἄποικος [sc. πόλις] *colony*; οἱ ἄποικοι *colonists*; v. 3. 2; 5. 10: vi. 1. 15; 2. 1.
ἀπο-καίω & Att. ἀπο-κάω,* καύσω, κέκαυκα, *to burn off*; also of intense cold (ne frigus adūrat, Virg. G. 1. 92), *to blast, freeze off*, A., iv. 5. 3: vii. 4. 3.
ἀπο-καλέω,* καλέσω καλῶ, κέκληκα, *to call aside* or *apart*, A., vii. 3. 35.
ἀπο-κάμνω,* καμοῦμαι, κέκμηκα, 2 a. ἔκαμον, *to fall off from work through fatigue, become fatigued, grow tired* or *weary*, iv. 7. 2.
ἀπό-κειμαι,* κείσομαι, *to be laid away* or *laid up, to be reserved, stored,* or *kept in store*, D., ii. 3. 15: vii. 7. 46?
ἀπο-κλείω,* κλείσω, κέκλεικα, *to shut off* or *out, intercept, exclude*, A. G.; *to shut*, A.; iv. 3. 20s: vi. 6. 13: vii. 6. 24.
ἀπο-κλίνω,* κλῖνῶ, κέκλῐκα 1., *to turn aside*, ii. 2. 16.
ἀπο-κόπτω,* κόψω, κέκοφα, 2 a. *p.* ἐκόπην, *to cut off, strike off, beat off*, A., iii. 4. 39: iv. 2. 10, 17: vii. 4. 15.
ἀπο-κρίνομαι,* κρῐνοῦμαι, κέκρῐμαι, a. ἐκρῑνάμην (later ἀπ-εκρῐθην), *to* [decide back] *reply, answer*, D. AE., CP., πρός, i. 3. 20; 4. 14; 6. 7s: ii. 1. 15, 22s.
ἀπο-κρύπτω,* κρύψω, κέκρυφα, *to hide away, conceal, cover*, A.: *M. to conceal one's own, hoard*: i. 9. 19? iv. 4. 11.
ἀπο-κτείνω,* κτενῶ, 2 pf. ἔκτονα, a. ἔκτεινα, (*P.* supplied by ἀποθνήσκω) *to kill off, kill, slay, put to death*, A., i. 1. 3, 7; 2. 20: ii. 1. 8.
ἀπο-κτίννῡμι,* = ἀποκτείνω, vi. 3. 5.
ἀπο-κωλύω (ῡ), σω, κεκώλῠκα, *to hinder* or *prevent from*, A. G., I., iii. 3. 3? vi. 4. 24.
ἀπο-λαμβάνω,* λήψομαι, εἴληφα, 2 a. ἔλαβον, a. *p.* ἐλήφθην, *to take* or *receive back, re-take, recover; to receive* what is due; *to take* or *cut off, intercept, arrest*; A.; i. 2. 27; 4. 8: ii. 4. 17: vii. 7. 21, 33, 55?
ἀπο-λείπω,* λείψω, 2 pf. λέλοιπα, 2 a. ἔλιπον, *to leave behind, forsake, desert, quit, fail; to leave* [out] *a space;* A.: *P.* and *M. to be left behind, fall behind, fail to observe*, G.: i. 4. 8: ii. 6. 12: iv. 3. 22: v. 4. 20: vi. 3. 26; 5. 11.
ἀπό-λεκτος, ον, (λέγω) *picked out, select, choice*, ii. 3. 15.
ἀπο-ληφθῶ, -λήψομαι, see ἀπο-λαμβάνω, i. 4. 8: ii. 4. 17.

ἀπ-όλλῡμι,* ὀλέσω ὀλῶ, ὀλώλεκα, (ὄλλῡμι *to destroy*) *to destroy* [off or utterly], *slay*, A.; *to lose, be deprived of*, A. ὑπό: *M.* (f. ὀλοῦμαι, 2 a. ὠλόμην) *to perish, die*, ὑπό: 2 pf. as *m.* ἀπ-όλωλα perii, *I have perished, I am lost* or *undone*: i. 2. 25; 5. 5: ii. 5. 17, 39, 41: iii. 1. 2; 4. 11: vi. 6. 23.
'Ἀπόλλων,* ωνος, ωνι, ωνα and ω, Ἀπολλον, *Apollo*, son of Jupiter and Latōna, and twin-brother of Diāna, one of the chief divinities of the Greeks, and regarded as the patron of divination, music, poetry, archery, &c. His oracles were numerous, and that at Delphi in Phocis was the most famous of all the Greek oracles. "Apollo had more influence upon the Greeks than any other god. It may safely be asserted that the Greeks would never have become what they were, without the worship of Apollo: in him the brightest side of the Grecian mind is reflected." *Dr. Schmitz.* i. 2. 8.
‡Ἀπολλωνία, as, *Apollonia*, a small town of Mysia near Lydia, vii. 8. 15.
‡Ἀπολλωνίδης, ου, *Apollonides*, a mean-spirited lochage, a Lydian by birth, but serving as a Greek in the division of Proxenus, iii. 1. 26.
ἀπο-λογέομαι, ήσομαι, -λελόγημαι, (λόγος) *to plead off from a charge, speak* or *say in defence*, APOLOGIZE, περί, ὅτι, v. 6. 3.
ἀπο-λύω,* λύσω, λέλῠκα, *to loose from, acquit*, A. G., vi. 6. 15.
ἀπ-ολώλεκα, see ἀπ-όλλῡμι, ii. 5. 39.
ἀπο-μάχομαι,* χέσομαι χοῦμαι, μεμάχημαι, *to fight off, resist, refuse*, vi. 2. 6.
ἀπό-μαχος, ον, (μάχη) Fr. hors de combat, *kept from fighting, disabled, non-combatant, out of the ranks*, iii. 4. 32: iv. 1. 13.
ἀπο-νοστέω, ήσω, (νόστος *a return*) *to return* [back] *home*, iii. 5. 16.
ἀπο-πέμπω,* πέμψω, πέπομφα, *to send off, away,* or *back; to send* what is due, *re-mit;* A. D., εἰς, ἐπί, &c.: *M. to send away* or *back* from one's self, *dismiss*, A.: i. 1. 3, 5, 8; 2. 1. 20.
ἀπο-πέτομαι,* πετήσομαι, comm. πτήσομαι, 2 a. a. ἔπτην or ἔπτᾶν, *to fly off* or *away*, i. 5. 3?
ἀπο-πήγνῡμι,* πήξω, πέπηχα 1., *to form curds* from a liquid: *M. to curdle, become congealed, freeze*, v. 8. 15.

ἀπο-πηδάω, ήσομαι, πεπήδηκα, (πηδάω to leap) to leap or spring off, away, or back, iii. 4. 27?

ἀπο-πλέω,* πλεύσομαι or πλευσοῦμαι, πέπλευκα, a. ἔπλευσα, to sail off, away, or back, to sail for home, ἐκ, &c., i. 3. 14 ; 4. 7 : vi. 6. 9 : vii. 1. 38.

‡ἀπό-πλοος, contr. ους, ου, ὁ, a voyage back or home, v. 6. 20.

ἀπο-πορεύομαι, εὔσομαι, πεπόρευμαι, to go away, depart, vii. 6. 33.

†ἀπορέω, ήσω, ἠπόρηκα, to be without resource or means ; to be at a loss what to do, to be perplexed, puzzled, or in doubt, D. (M. in like sense, CP., I.); to be destitute or in want, to want, lack, G.; i. 3. 8 ; 7. 3 : vi. 1. 22 ? vii. 3. 29.

†ἀπορία, ας, lack of resource or means ; perplexity, embarrassment, distress ; difficulty, I.; want, lack, G.; i. 3. 13 : ii. 5. 9 : iii. 1. 2, 11 s.

ἄ-πορος, ον, without way, resource, or means ; impracticable, impossible, difficult ; of places, impassable ; of persons, without resource, devoid of means, I.; subst. ἄπορον something impassable, an insuperable obstacle, pl. obstacles, difficulties, straits : ii. 4. 4 ; 5. 21 : iii. 2. 22 ; 3. 4 : v. 6. 20.

ἀπό-ρ-ρητος, ον, (ῥε- to speak) [away from speaking] not to be spoken, forbidden to be told, secret, i. 6. 5 : vii. 6. 43. See ποιέω.

ἀπο-ρ-ρώξ, ῶγος, ὁ ἡ, ch. poet., (ἀπο-ρ-ρήγνυμι to break off) broken off, ab-rupt, steep, vi. 4. 3.

ἀπο-σήπω,* ψω, 2 pf. as m. σέσηπα, (σήπω to rot) to rot off (trans.): M. to rot off (intrans.), be mortified ; τοὺς δακτύλους ἀποσεσηπότες [mortified as to] having lost their toes, ὑπό, iv. 5. 12.

ἀπο-σκάπτω,* άψω, ἔσκαφα, (σκάπτω to dig) to trench off, dig a trench to intercept, AE., ii. 4. 4.

ἀπο-σκεδάννυμι,* σκεδάσω σκεδῶ, to scatter abroad (trans.): P. and M. to be scattered or dispersed, scatter or disperse (intrans.), stray or straggle : οἱ ἀποσκεδαννύμενοι the stragglers : iv. 4. 9, 15 : vii. 6. 29.

ἀπο-σκηνέω, ήσω, or -σκηνόω, ώσω, to encamp at a distance from, iii. 4. 35.

ἀπο-σπάω,* άσω, ἔσπακα, a. p. ἐσπάσθην, to draw off, separate, A. ἀπό : also intrans. to separate one's self from, outstrip (or M.), 577 c : P. to be separated or removed from, G.,

ἀπό : i. 5. 3 ? 8. 13 : ii. 2. 12 : vii. 2. 11 ; 3. 41.

ἀπο-σταίην, -στάς, see ἀφ-ίστημι.

ἀπο-σταυρόω, ώσω, to stake or palisade off, A., vi. 5. 1.

ἀπο-στέλλω,* στελῶ, ἔσταλκα, to send away or back, A., ii. 1. 5.

ἀπο-στερέω,* ήσω, ἐστέρηκα, to deprive, rob, de-fraud, 2 A., vi. 6. 23.

ἀπο-στῆναι, see ἀφ-ίστημι, i. 1. 7.

ἀπο-στρατοπεδεύομαι, εύσομαι, ἐστρατοπέδευμαι, to encamp at a distance, G., iii. 4. 34 : vii. 7. 1.

ἀπο-στρέφω,* ψω, ἔστροφα 1., to turn back, recall, A. ἐξ, ii. 6. 3.

‡ἀπο-στροφή, ῆς, a [turning aside or back] retreat, refuge, resort (place as well as act), ii. 4. 22 : vii. 6. 34.

ἀπο-συλάω, ήσω, (συλάω to strip) to strip off, despoil, rob, 2 A., i. 4. 8.

ἀπο-σχεῖν, -σχω, see ἀπ-έχω, ii. 2. 12.

ἀπο-σώζω,* σώσω, σέσωκα, to lead or bring back in safety, to restore safe, A. εἰς, ii. 3. 18.

ἀπο-ταφρεύω, εύσω, (τάφρος) to trench off, complete a trench, vi. 5. 1.

ἀπο-τείνω,* τενῶ, τέτακα, pf. p. τέταμαι, to stretch off, ex-tend, εἰς, i. 8. 10.

ἀπο-τειχίζω, ίσω ιῶ, τετείχικα, to wall off, build a wall to intercept, ii. 4. 4.

ἀπο-τέμνω,* τεμῶ, τέτμηκα, 2 a. ἔτεμον, a. p. ἐτμήθην, to cut off, intercept, A. : ἀποτμηθέντες τὰς κεφαλὰς beheaded, 481 : i. 10. 1 : ii. 6. 1 : iii. 1. 17 ; 4. 29.

ἀπο-τίθημι,* θήσω, τέθεικα, a. ἔθηκα (θῶ, &c.), to put away, lay up, store, A., ii. 3. 15.

ἀπο-τίνω,* τίσω, τέτικα, (τίνω to pay) to pay back, or what is due, A. D. : M. to get pay from, take vengeance, requite, punish, A. : iii. 2. 6 : vii. 6. 16.

ἀπο-τμηθείς, see ἀπο-τέμνω, ii. 6. 1.

‡ἀπότομος, ον, cut sharp off, precipitous, iv. 1. 2 ; 7. 2 ?

ἀπο-τρέπω,* ψω, τέτροφα, 2 a. m. ἐτραπόμην, to turn off or back, trans. : M. to turn off, aside, or back, intrans., iii. 5. 1 : vii. 3. 7 ; 6. 11.

ἀπο-τρέχω,* δραμοῦμαι, δεδράμηκα, 2 a. ἔδραμον, to run off or back, retreat, return, v. 2. 6 : vii. 6. 5.

ἀπο-φαίνω,* φανῶ, πέφαγκα, a. ἔφηνα, to show off or forth : M. to show one's self or one's own ; appear ; express, A. ; i. 6. 9 : v. 7. 12.

ἀπο-†εύγω,* φεύξομαι, πέφευγα,

2 a. ἔφυγον, *to flee away, escape*, esp. through speed (cf. ἀπο-διδράσκω), ἐκ, εἰς, i. 4. 8: ii. 5. 7: iii. 4. 9: iv. 2. 27.

ἀπόφραξις, εως, ἡ, (ἀπο-φράττω *to fence off, obstruct*) *obstruction, blockade*, G., iv. 2. 25 s.

ἀπο-χωρέω, ήσω or ήσομαι, κεχώρηκα, *to go back, retreat, return*, i. 2. 9.

ἀπο-ψηφίζομαι, ίσομαι ιοῦμαι, ἐψήφισμαι, *to vote* [off from] *otherwise or against*, i. 4. 15.

ἀ-πρόθῡμος, ον, *not inclined, disinclined, un-willing*, vi. 2. 7.

ἀ-προσδόκητος, ον, (προσ-δοκάω) *unexpected, sudden; ἐξ ἀπροσδοκήτου ex improviso, of a sudden, suddenly, unexpectedly, by surprise*, iv. 1. 10.

ἀ-προφασίστως adv., (προφασίζομαι) *without making excuses, promptly, without hesitation*, ii. 6. 10.

ἅπτω,* ἅψω, *to fasten, kindle; M. to fasten one's self to, touch, engage in*, G., i. 5. 10: v. 6. 28.

ἀπ-ωλόμην, see ἀπ-όλλῡμι, i. 5. 5.

ἀπ-ών, see ἀπ-ειμι (εἰμί), ii. 5. 37.

[ἀρ-, *to fit, suit, please, unite.*]

↓ἄρα* postpos. adv., a particle expressing inference or relation, and often throwing force upon the preceding word. It is variously translated: *accordingly, therefore, then, now, indeed, in truth; it seems; perhaps* (as w. εἰ or ἐάν); i. 7. 18: ii. 2. 3; 4. 6: iv. 6. 15?

↓ἆρα * interrog.adv.,(a stronger form of ἄρα) *indeed? surely?* often not expressed in Eng., except by the mode of utterance. ̓Ἀρ᾽ οὐ expects an affirmative, and ἆρα μή a negative answer. iii. 1. 18: vi. 5. 18: vii. 6. 5.

Ἀραβία, ας, (Ἄραψ *Arab*) *Arabia*, the great southwestern peninsula of Asia, so extensively desert, and mostly occupied in ancient as in modern times by nomadic and predatory tribes. Its limits on the north were not fixed, and Xenophon so extends them as to include a desert region beyond the Euphrates. i. 5. 1: vii. 8. 25.

Ἀράξης, ου, *the Araxes*, prob. the same with the Χαβώρας, now Khabûr (the Chebar, the scene of the prophet Ezekiel's sublime visions, Ezek. 1. 1), the largest affluent of the Euphrates above its junction with the Tigris, i. 4. 19.

ἀράτω, see αἴρω, v. 6. 33.

Ἀρβάκας, or Ἀρβάκης, ου, *Arbacas* or *-ces*, satrap of Media, and commander of a fourth part of the army of Artaxerxes, i. 7. 12: vii. 8. 25.

Ἀργεῖος, ου, ὁ, (Ἄργος) *an Argive.* Argos was the chief city of Argolis, the most eastern province of Peloponnesus; and according to tradition was the oldest city in Greece. Its early importance was such that its name is applied by Homer, not only to the surrounding district, of which Mycēnæ was the Homeric capital, but even to the whole Peloponnese; and sometimes the name Ἀργεῖοι, to the Greeks in general. Other cities afterwards so eclipsed and depressed it, that it played no great part either in Greek politics or civilization. In the Persian wars, it was inactive; in domestic wars, as the Peloponnesian, it was generally inclined to side with the enemies of Sparta. It worshipped Hēra (Juno) as its especial patroness. iv. 2. 13, 17.

ἀργός, όν, (contr. fr. ἀ-εργός, fr. ἔργον) *without work, at ease, idle*, iii. 2. 25.

†ἀργύρεος, α, ον, contr. ἀργυροῦς, ᾶ, οῦν (772 c), *of silver*, iv. 7. 27.

†ἀργύριον, ου, dim., *silver* in small pieces for money, *silver-money, money,* i. 4. 13: ii. 6. 16: iii. 2. 21.

†ἀργυρό-πους, ὁ ἡ, g. -ποδος, *silverfooted*, iv. 4. 21.

[ἄργυρος, ου, ὁ, (ἀργός shining, *white*) *silver.*]

Ἀργώ, όος, ἡ, *the Argo*, the vessel, small in size but great in mythic fame, in which Jason with his band of fifty heroes sailed from Iolcos in Thessaly to Æa in Colchis, in quest of the golden fleece, about a generation before the Trojan war, vi. 2. 1.

ἄρδην adv., (αἴρω) [all taken up] *altogether, wholly, quite*, vii. 1. 12?

ἄρδω (in Att. only pr. and ipf.) *to water, irrigate*, A., ii. 3. 13.

ἀρέσκω,* ἀρέσω, (ἀρ-) *to please, satisfy, suit*, D., ii. 4. 2.

↓ἀρετή, ῆς, *goodness, excellence, virtue, magnanimity; good service, περί*; esp. goodness in war (virtus), *manhood, valor, prowess, courage*; i. 4. 8 s: ii. 1. 12 s: iv. 7. 12.

ἀρήγω, ήξω, ch. poet., (akin to ἀρκέω) *to give aid* or *succor*, esp. in war, i. 10.5.

‡'Ἀρηξίων, ωνος, *Arexion*, a soothsayer in the Cyrean army, from Parrhasia in Arcadia, vi. 4. 13 ; 5. 2, 8.

Ἀριαῖος, ου, *Ariæus*, chief commander under Cyrus of the barbarian troops, but treacherous to the Greeks after the battle of Cunaxa. He is mentioned as in command at Sardis, B. C. 395. i. 8. 5 ; 9. 31: ii. 4. 1 s.

ἀριθμός, οῦ, ὁ, *number; numbering, enumeration ; summary, total, whole extent*, τῆς ὁδοῦ: i. 2. 9 ; 7. 10 : ii. 2. 6. Der. ARITHMETIC. From ἀρ-?

Ἀριστ-αρχος, ου, *Aristarchus*, Spartan harmost at Byzantium, corrupt and cruel, vii. 2. 5 s, 12 s. — 2. See Ἀριστέας.

ἀριστάω, ήσω, ἠρίστηκα, (ἄριστον q. v.) *to breakfast, take the first or morning meal*, iii. 3. 6 : iv. 3. 10.

Ἀριστέας, ου, *Aristeas*, of Chios, a brave and useful commander of light-armed troops, iv. 1. 28 (v. l. Ἀρίσταρχος) ; 6. 20.

ἀριστερός, ά, όν, (fr. ἄριστος by euphemism? cf. εὐώνυμος) *left* in distinction fr. *right* : ἡ ἀριστερὰ χείρ *the left hand, the left* (the art. and χείρ oftener omitted): ii. 3. 11 ; 4. 28 : iv. 8. 2.

Ἀρίστ-ιππος, ου, *Aristippus*, of Larissa in Thessaly, one of the noble family of the Aleuadæ. Obtaining money from Cyrus, he enlisted troops to withstand an opposing party, and from these sent a force under his favorite Menon to the service of Cyrus. i. 1. 10 ; 2. 1 : ii. 6. 28.

ἄριστον, ου, τό, (cf. ἦρι *early*) the first of the two usual and regular Greek meals, the *morning* or *forenoon meal, breakfast ;* not usually taken very early, and sometimes corresponding to our early *dinner*, or the English *lunch* (Lat. prandium) ; i. 10. 19.

‡ἀριστο-ποιέω, ήσω, *to prepare breakfast : M. to prepare* one's own *breakfast, get breakfast*, iii. 3. 1, cf. 6.

ἄριστος, η, ον, s. to ἀγαθός, (ἀρ-) *most fitting, best, most useful* or *advantageous* (often coupled with κάλλιστος, ii. 1. 9, 17); *best* or *first in rank, noblest, most eminent ; best in war, bravest*: ἄριστα adv. (s. to εὖ), *in the best way, best, most successfully* or *advantageously* : i. 3. 12; 5. 7; 6. 1, 4 ; 9. 5 : iii. 1. 6. Der. ARISTO-CRAT.

‡Ἀρίστων, ωνος, *Ariston*, an Athenian sent by the Cyreans on an embassy to Sinōpe, v. 6. 14.

‡Ἀριστ-ώνυμος, ου, *Aristonymus*, a lochage from Methydrium in Arcadia, one of the bravest and most adventurous of the Cyreans, iv. 1. 27.

†Ἀρκαδικός, ή, όν, *Arcadian :* τὸ Ἀρκαδικόν [sc. στράτευμα or πλῆθος] *the Arcadian force*, iv. 8. 18.

Ἀρκάς, άδος, ὁ, *an Arcadian*. Arcadia was the mountainous central province of the Peloponnese, inhabited by a brave and energetic but not wealthy people, many of whom, like the modern Swiss, sold their services abroad for more liberal rewards than could be obtained at home. Their pastoral habits led to the especial worship of Pan and culture of music. Arcadia was the Greek province most largely represented in the army of Cyrus ; and its modern inhabitants are said to be the bravest people in the Morea. i. 2. 1: vi. 2. 10.

ἀρκέω, έσω, *to be sufficient* or *enough ; to suffice, content, satisfy :* ἀρκῶν as adj., *sufficient, enough :* D., *πρός :* ii. 6. 20 ; v. 6. 1 ; 8. 13 : vi. 4. 6.

ἄρκτος, ου, ἡ, comm. epicene, *a bear; the Northern Bear* (Ursa Major), *the north ;* i. 7. 6 ; 9. 6. Der. ARCTIC.

ἅρμα, ατος, τό, (ἀρ-) *a yoked vehicle, a chariot*, esp. for war, with two wheels, and open behind. Its use in battle (except as scythe-armed among barbarian nations) belonged rather to the Homeric than to later times. i. 2. 16 ; 7. 10 s, 20 ; 8. 3, 10. Cf. ἄμαξα &

‡ἁρμ-άμαξα, ης, a covered *carriage*, esp. for women and children, i. 2. 16.

†Ἀρμενία, ας, *Armenia*, an elevated region of Western Asia, containing the head-waters of the Euphrātes, Tigris, and several other rivers. Here the garden of Eden seems to be most naturally located ; here the ark of Noah is comm. supposed to have rested ; and this region prefers strong claims to be regarded as an especial cradle of Caucasian civilization. The Cyreans found its winter climate severe ; and its heights occupied by hardy and brave, but rude tribes. iii. 5. 17.

Ἀρμένιος, α, ον, *Armenian :* οἱ Ἀ. *the Armenians :* iv. 3. 4, 20 ; 5. 33.

Ἀρμήνη, ης, *Harmēne*, a village and harbor about five miles west of

Sinōpe and belonging to it: *v. l. Ἀρμήνη*: vi. 1. 15, 17. ‖ Ak-Liman, i. e. *White Haven.*

ἁρμοστής, οῦ, (ἁρμόζω *to regulate*) *a regulator, director, governor* of a dependent state, *harmost;* a title esp. given to the officers who were sent by Sparta during her supremacy to regulate and control the affairs of subject states, and whose arbitrary and corrupt conduct brought so much odium upon the Spartan rule; v. 5. 19 s.

ἄρνειος, α, ον, (ἀρνός *lamb's*) *of a lamb, lamb's*, iv. 5. 31.

†**ἁρπαγή**, ῆς, *seizure, robbery, rapine, pillage, plunder*; καθ' ἁρπαγήν [with reference to] *for plunder*: iii. 5. 2.

ἁρπάζω,* άσω, oftener ἅσομαι, ἥρπακα, pf. *p.* ἥρπασμαι, rapio, *to snatch up, seize, carry away, capture; to plunder, pillage, rob*: οἱ ἁρπάζοντες *the pillagers*: A.: i. 2. 25, 27; 10. 3 s.

Ἅρπασος, ου, ὁ, *the Harpasus*, prob. the same river with the Acampsis (now Choruk-Su), flowing into the southeastern Euxine, iv. 7. 18.

[**Ἀρτα-**, *great* or *honored*, a common prefix in Persian names.]

Ἀρτα-γέρσης, ου, *Artagerses*, commander of the body-guard of Artaxerxes, i. 7. 11; 8. 24.

Ἀρτα-κάμας, α, *Artacamas*, satrap of Phrygia, vii. 8. 25.

Ἀρτά-οζος, ου, *Artaozus*, a follower of Cyrus, who made his submission to the king, ii. 4. 16; 5. 35.

Ἀρτα-ξέρξης, ου, (translated by Herodotus μέγας ἀρήϊος *great warrior*, 6. 98, see Ξέρξης) *Artaxerxes* II., surnamed Mnemon from his great memory, eldest son of Darius Nothus, and his successor upon the Persian throne, reigning B. C. 405 – 359. Before his accession, his name was Arsaces. Of natural mildness and easy temper, he was a weak king, yielding undue power to his mother, the unprincipled and cruel Parysatis, and leaving the government too much to slaves and eunuchs. His subjects were rebellious; his arms had little success; and his last years were embittered and shortened by the quarrels and crimes of his sons. i. 1. 1, 3 s.

Ἀρτα-πάτης or **-ας**, ου or α, *Artapates* or *-as*, the personal attendant in whom Cyrus most confided, i. 6. 11.

ἀρτάω, ήσω, ἤρτηκα 1., *to fasten, hang*, or *suspend* one thing to another, A., iii. 5. 10.

Ἄρτεμις, ιδος, ιδι, ιν or ιδα, ι, *Artemis* or *Diāna*, twin-sister of Apollo, the goddess of virginity and of the chase. She was greatly worshipped by the Greeks, and with especial honor at Ephesus and in Arcadia. i. 6. 7.

ἄρτι adv., (ἀρ-) *exactly, just, just now*, iv. 6. 1: vii. 4. 7.

Ἀρτίμας, α, *Artimas*, satrap of Lydia, vii. 8. 25.

†**ἀρτο-κόπος**, ου, ὁ ἡ, (κόπτω) α [bread-beater] *baker*, iv. 4. 21: v. l. ἀρτο-ποιός, οὗ, (ποιέω) *a bread-maker.*

ἄρτος, ου, ὁ, *a loaf of bread*, esp. of wheat, bread, i. 9. 26: ii. 4. 28.

Ἀρτούχας, ου or α, *Artūchas*, a commander of forces for the king, prob. a ruler of the Mardonii or Mardi, iv. 3. 4.

Ἀρύστας, ου or α, *Arystas*, an Arcadian, a great eater, vii. 3. 23 s: v. l. Ἄριστος, Ἄρυστος.

†**Ἀρχ-αγόρας**, ου or α, *Archagoras*, a lochage, an exile from Argos, iv. 2. 13.

†**ἀρχαῖος**, α, ον, [in the beginning] *old, ancient*: Κῦρος ὁ ἀ. C. *the Elder*: τὸ ἀρχαῖον, as adv., *of old, formerly*: i. 1. 6; 9. 1: iii. 1. 4: iv. 5. 14.

†**ἀρχή**, ῆς, *beginning; rule, command, dominion, sovereignty*, G.; *government, realm, empire, principality, satrapy, province*: ἀρχήν, as adv., *in the first place, at all* (followed by a negative): i. 1. 2 s: ii. 1. 11: vi. 3. 1: vii. 7. 25, 28.

†**ἀρχ-ηγός**, οῦ, ὁ, (ἄγω) *a leader, commander, officer*, iii. 1. 26?

†**ἀρχικός**, ή, όν, *fitted to command, qualified for command*, ii. 6. 8, 20.

ἄρχω, ἄρξω, ἦρχα r., *to be foremost, take the lead;* in time, *to begin* or *commence*, esp. for others to follow, G., I.; in rank or office, *to lead, command, rule, govern, reign*, G.; ἄρχων subst., *a leader, commander, officer, ruler, governor, prince, chief*: P. *to be ruled, governed*, or *commanded*, hence *to submit to authority, to obey* or *serve*, ὑπό· οἱ ἀρχόμενοι *those under command, the common soldiers*, "*the men*"; πρὸς ἄλλους ἀρχομένους ἀπιέναι *to go as soldiers to other officers* (ii. 6. 12; v. l. ἄρχοντας, ἀρξομένους, &c.): *M. to begin* or *commence* for one's self, I., G.; w. ἀπό, *to begin* [from] *at* or *with* (ἀπὸ θεῶν *with the gods*, i. e. by consulting them,

ἄρωμα 21 ἀτάρ

vi. 3. 18): i. 1. 2, 8 ; 3. 1, 15; 4. 10, 15: ii. 1. 3 ; 6. 14 s, 19 : vi. 4. 1. Der. ARCH-, -ARCH, -ARCHY, in compounds.
ἄρωμα, ατος, τό, *an* AROMATIC, *spice*, i. 5. 1.
†**ἀσέβεια,** as, *impiety, ungodliness,* iii. 2. 4.
ἀ-σεβής, ές, (σέβομαι *to revere*) *irreverent, impious, ungodly*, πρός, ii. 5. 20 : v. 7. 32.
†**ἀσθενέω,** ήσω, *to be sick, feeble*, or *infirm*, i. 1. 1 : iv. 5. 19, 21.
ἀ-σθενής, ές, (σθένος *strength*) *weak, feeble*, i. 5. 9.
Ἀσία, as, *Asia*, a name sometimes applied by the Greeks to Asia Minor (Anatolia) or the nearer part of it, and sometimes to all they knew of the grand division now bearing this name. The latter was sometimes divided into ἡ κάτω Ἀσία *Lower Asia*, the part west of the Halys, and ἡ ἄνω Ἀσία *Upper Asia*, the part east of this river. v. 3. 6 : vii. 1. 1 s ; 2. 2.
Ἀσιδάτης, ου, *Asidates*, a Persian of rank and wealth, vii. 8. 9, 12, 21.
Ἀσιναῖος, ου, ὁ, (Ἀσίνη, a small town on the Laconian gulf, nearly south of Sparta) *an Asinæan*, v. 3. 4 : vi. 4. 11. || Passava ?
ἀ-σινῶς adv., s. ἀσινέστατα, (ἀ-σινής *harmless*, fr. σίνομαι) *without doing harm, without injury* or *depredation, harmlessly*, ii. 3. 27: iii. 3. 3.
ἄ-σιτος, ον, (σῖτος) *without* or *in want of food, fasting*, ii. 2. 16 : iv. 5. 11.
ἀσκέω, ήσω, ήσκηκα, *to practise, cultivate, observe, maintain*, ii. 6. 25.
ἀσκός, οῦ, ὁ, *a skin*, esp. of a goat, *a leathern bag*, iii. 5. 9 s : vi. 4. 23.
ἄσμενος, η, ον, (ἥδω) *well-pleased, glad ;* always with a verb, and like an adv. in force, *gladly, willingly, cheerfully*, ii. 1. 16 : iii. 4. 24.
ἀσπάζομαι, ἀσομαι, (σπάω) *to* [draw to one's self] *embrace ; to salute, greet, welcome, take leave of ;* A.; vi. 3. 24.
Ἀσπένδιος, ου, ὁ, (Ἄσπενδος) *an Aspendian.* Aspendus was a city of Pamphylia on the Eurymedon (now Capri-Su), about six miles from the sea, an Argive colony. Here Thrasybūlus, the deliverer of Athens from the tyranny of the Thirty, lost his life, B. C. 389. i. 2. 12. || Balkésu.
ἀσπίς, ίδος, ἡ, *a shield ;* here sp. applied to the large oval shield of the Greek hoplites, comm. made of several thicknesses of stout leather strengthened by a metallic front and rim, and convex outwardly (so that it could even be used as a vessel to receive blood, ii. 2. 9): as a collective noun, *heavy-armed infantry ;* ἀσπὶς μυρία 10,000 [shield] *shield-men* or *hoplites* (cf. "10,000 horse," i. e. horsemen): παρ' ἀσπίδας [by the shields] *by* or *to the left*, since the shield was carried on the left arm (while, in a posture of waiting in readiness for action, it was also supported in part by the bent knee, i. 5. 13): i. 2. 16 ; 7. 10 ; 8. 9, 18 : iv. 3. 26.
†**Ἀσσυρία,** as, *Assyria* (the kingdom of Asshur, Gen. 10. 11), a name applied, with varying extent, to the famous country of which Nineveh was the capital ; in a narrower sense confined to the region between Media and the Tigris, but in a wider sense extending over Mesopotamia to the Euphrates. It was the seat of one of the greatest of the early empires, which was overthrown by the Medes and Babylonians about 625 B. C. vii. 8. 25.
Ἀσσύριος, α, ον, *Assyrian*, pertaining to Assyria, vii. 8. 15.
ἀ-σταφίς, ίδος, ἡ, = σταφίς (ἀ- euphon.) *a dried grape, raisin*, iv. 4. 9 ?
ἀστράπτω, ἄψω 1., (akin to ἀστήρ *star*) *to gleam, flash, glisten*, i. 8. 8.
†**ἀσφάλεια,** as, *safety, security*, v. 7. 10 : vii. 6. 30.
ἀ-σφαλής, ές, c. έστερος, s. έστατος, (σφάλλω) *not liable to fall, firm, safe, secure :* ἐν ἀσφαλεῖ *in a safe place* or *position, in safety :* i. 8. 22: iii. 2. 19.
ἄσφαλτος, ου, ἡ, ASPHALT, *bitumen,* much used of old for mortar, ii. 4. 12.
ἀσφαλῶς, c. έστερον, s. έστατα, (ἀσφαλής) *safely, securely*, i. 3. 11, 19.
ἀσχολία, as, (ἀ-σχολος *without leisure, busy*, fr. σχολή) *occupation, engagement*, vii. 5. 16.
†**ἀτακτέω,** ήσω, *to be disorderly* or *out of order*, v. 8. 21.
ἄ-τακτος, ον, (τάττω) *disarranged, out of order, in disorder* or *confusion, disorderly*, i. 8. 2 : iii. 4. 19 : v. 4. 21.
ἀ-ταξία, as, (τάττω) *want of order* or *discipline, disorder, leaving the ranks*, iii. 1. 38 ; 2. 29 : v. 8. 13.
ἀτάρ conj., *but, yet*, as in a question expre sing objection, τί ; iv. 6. 14.

Ἀταρνεύς, έως, ὁ, *Atarneus*, a city in southwest Mysia, on the Ægean, over against Lesbos, vii. 8. 8. || Dikeli-Koi.

ἀτασθαλία, as, (ἄτη *infatuation*) *recklessness, wantonness*, iv. 4. 14?

ἄ-ταφος, ον, *un-buried*, vi. 5. 6.

ἄτε * (neut. pl. of the relative ὅστε, used as an adv. of manner) *just as, as;* W. P., expressing cause and = *inasmuch as* w. verb; iv. 2. 13; 8. 27.

ἀτέλεια, as, (ἀ-τελής *exempt from tax*, fr. τέλος) immunitas, *exemption, immunity;* ἄλλην τινὰ ἀ. *some exemption from other service*, iii. 3. 18.

†**ἀτιμάζω**, άσω, ἠτίμακα, *to dishonor, disgrace, hold in dishonor*, A., i. 1. 4.

ἄ-τιμος, ον, c., (τιμή) *without honor, dis-honored, in dis-honor, ἐν,* vii. 7. 24, 46, 50.

ἀτμίζω, ίσω, (ἀτμός *vapor*) *to exhale* or *send up vapor, to steam*, iv. 5. 15.

Ἀτραμύττιον, ον, *Adramyttium*, a city in Mysia, at the head of the gulf bearing its name, and called by Strabo an Athenian colony: v. l. Ἀδραμύτιον, Ἀτραμύτειον, &c.: vii. 8. 8. || Adramiti or Edremit.

ἀ-τριβής, ές, (τριβή) *without wear, un-worn, untrodden*, non tritus, iv. 2. 8; vii. 3. 42.

Ἀττικός, ή, όν, (ἀκτή) *Attic, Athenian*, i. 5. 6.

αὖ post-pos. adv., *again, back*, in respect either to time, or to the order or relations of the discourse (often w. δέ; δ' αὖ); *further, moreover, on the other hand, in turn;* i. 1. 7, 9 s; 6. 7; 10. 5, 11: ii. 6. 7, 18.

αὐαίνω, αὐανῶ, ch. poet. & Ion., (αὔω *to dry*) *to dry*, trans.: M. (ipf. αὐαινόμην & ηὐαινόμην, 278 d) *to dry up, wither*, intrans., ii. 3. 16?

αὐθ-αίρετος, ον, (αὑτός) *self-chosen, sc'f-elected, self-appointed*, v. 7. 29.

αὐθ-ημερόν or **αὐθήμερον** adv., (αὐτός, ἡμέρα) *on the same day*, iv. 4. 22 s.

αὖθις adv., (αὖ) *again, back; moreover, besides; at another time, afterwards, hereafter;* i. 10. 10 : ii. 4. 5.

αὐλέω, ήσω, (αὐλός) *to play* on a flute or other wind instrument: *M. to have the flute played for one's self*, 581, πρός : vi. 1. 11 : vii. 3. 32.

αὐλίζομαι, ίσομαι, ηὐλισάμαι l., a. ηὐλισάμην in Thuc., but ηὐλίσθην in Xen., (αὐλή *court*) *to lodge* or *be lodged,*

encamp, quarter, be quartered, take quarters, bivouac, ii. 2. 17 : iv. 3. 1 s.

αὐλός, οῦ, ὁ, (ἄω *to blow*) *a flute*, differing from that common with us, in having a mouthpiece and a fuller tone; *a pipe, oboe, clarinet;* vi. 1. 5.

†**αὐλών**, ῶνος, ὁ, *a water-pipe, canal*, ii. 3. 10.

αὔριον adv., *to-morrow :* ἡ αὔριον [sc. ἡμέρα] *the morrow, the next day :* ii. 2. 1? iv. 6. 8 : vi. 4. 15.

αὐστηρότης, ητος, ἡ, (αὐστηρός *harsh*, AUSTERE, fr. αὔω *to dry*) *harshness, roughness, strength*, of wine, v. 4. 29.

αὐτῇ, **αὐταῖ**, see οὗτος, i. 1. 7.

†**αὐτίκα** at the very time, *at once, immediately, forthwith, directly, speedily, presently,* i. 8. 2 : iii. 2. 32 s ; 5. 11.

†**αὐτόθεν** from the very spot, *from this* or *that place, hence, thence*, iv. 2. 6 : v. 1. 10.

†**αὐτόθι** ibidem, in the very place, *here, there*, i. 4. 6 : iv. 5. 15 ; 8. 20.

†**αὐτο-κέλευστος**, ον, (κελεύω) *self-bidden, self-prompted, of one's own impulse*, iii. 4. 5.

†**αὐτο-κράτωρ**, ορος, ὁ ἡ, (κρατέω) *ruling by one's self, sole, absolute* (cf. AUTOCRAT), vi. 1. 21.

†**αὐτό-ματος**, η, ον, or ος, ον, (μάομαι *to seek*) *self-moved,* or *prompted : ἀπὸ* or *ἐκ τοῦ αὐτομάτου of one's own motion* or *accord, of one's self, spontaneously, by chance :* i. 2. 17 ; 3. 13 : iv. 3. 8 : vi. 4. 18. Der. AUTOMATON.

†**αὐτο-μολέω**, ήσω, ηὐτομόληκα, *to desert :* οἱ αὐτομολοῦντες, *the deserters :* παρά, πρός, &c.: i. 7. 13 : ii. 1. 6 ; 2. 7.

†**αὐτό-μολος**, ον, (μολ- *to go*) [going off of one's self] *a deserter*, i. 7. 2.

†**αὐτό-νομος**, ον, *self-ruling, independent*, vii. 8. 25. Der. AUTONOMY.

αὐτός,* ή, ὁ, (αὖ, old definitive τός) *very, same :* (a) preceded by the art., ὁ αὐτός idem, *the same*, D.: τὰ αὐτὰ ταῦτα *these same things, the same course :* ἐκ τοῦ αὐτοῦ, ἐν τῷ αὐτῷ, εἰς ταυτό, *from (in, into) the same place :* i. 1. 7 ; 8. 14 : ii. 6. 22. (b) Not preceded by the art., it is either the common pron. of the 3d pers. (*him, her, it, them*, but only in the oblique cases, and not beginning a clause); or is used as an adjective or appositive, with an emphatic or reflexive force, as in Lat. ipse, and in Eng. the compounds of *self (myself, himself,*

&c.), the adjectives *very, own,* &c. (sometimes expressed by *alone, apart, simply, quite, close, directly,* as χωρεῖ αὐτός he goes [himself only] *alone,* iv. 7.11; ἐπ' αὐτὸν τὸν ποταμόν *to the very river, quite t*e *the river,* iv. 3. 11): i. 1. 2 s; 3. 7 s ; 9. 21: αὐταῖς ταῖς τριήρεσι [with the triremes themselves] *triremes and all,* 467 c, i. 3. 17 ? ἡμέτερος αὐτῶν *our own,* 498, vii. 1. 29. Distinguish carefully the adv. αὐτοῦ, the forms of οὗτος (αὕτη, αὗται), and those of the contr. reflexive αὑτοῦ. Der. AUTO- in compounds.

‡**αὐτόσε** to the very place, *thither,* iv. 7. 2.

‡**αὐτοῦ** adv., in the very place, *in this* or *that place, here, there,* often followed by a prepositional phrase defining the place, i. 3. 11 : iv. 3. 28.

‡**αὐτοῦ** contr. fr. ἑ-αυτοῦ q. v., i. 3. 2.

‡**αὕτως** or **αὔτως**, see ὡσαύτως, v. 6.9.

αὐχήν, ένος, ὁ, *the neck ; neck* of land, *isthmus,* vi. 4. 3.

ἀφ' by apostr. for ἀπό, before the rough breathing, iii. 2. 14.

ἀφ-αιρέω,* αἱρήσω, ᾕρηκα, 2 a. εἶλον, a. p. ᾑρέθην, *to take from* or *away, detach,* A.: oftener *M. to take* to one's self *from* another, *take away; to rescue* from another ; *to deprive* or *rob* another *of;* 2 A., A. G., 485 d : *P. to be taken away* or *rescued ; to be deprived of,* A.: i. 3. 4 : iv. 4. 12 : vi. 5. 11 ; 6. 23, 26 s : vii. 2. 22.

ἀ-φανής, ές, (φαίνω) not appearing, *unseen, unobserved; out of sight, gone; secret, private, doubtful, little known;* i. 4. 7: ii. 6. 28 : iv. 2. 4.

‡**ἀφανίζω**, ἴσω ιῶ, ἠφάνικα, *to make invisible, hide from view, annihilate,* A., iii. 2. 11; 4. 8.

ἀφ-εῖκα,-**εῖμαι**,-**εῖναι**,-**εἰς**, see ἀφ-ίημι.
ἀφ-ειλόμην, -ελών, see ἀφ-αιρέω.
ἀφ-έξεσθαι, see ἀπ-έχω, ii. 6. 10.
ἀφ-έστηκα, -εστήκειν or -ειστήκειν, -εστήξω, see ἀφ-ίστημι, i. 1. 6 : ii. 4. 5.

ἀφ-ηγέομαι, ἡγήσομαι, ἥγημαι, *to lead off* in conversation, *relate, tell,* D. CP., vii. 2. 26.

ἀφ-ήσω, -ήκα, see ἀφ-ίημι, v. 4. 7.
†**ἀφθονία**, as, *abundance,* i. 9. 15.

ἄ-φθονος, ον, c., (φθόνος) *without grudging, bounteous ; of land, fertile ; abundant, copious, plentiful ;* iii. 1. 19 : v. 6. 25 : ἐν ἀφθόνοις *amid abundant supplies, in abundance,* iii. 2. 25 ; ἐν πᾶσιν ἀφθόνοις *in* [all things abundant] *great abundance,* iv. 5. 29 : ἐν ἀφθονωτέροις [sc. πλοίοις] *in vessels more abundantly provided,* or *in a more abundant supply* or *greater number of them,* v. 1. 10.

ἀφ-ίημι,* ἥσω, εἷκα, a. ἧκα (ὦ, &c.), pf. p. εἶμαι, *to send off, away,* or *back; to dismiss, let go, allow to depart, suffer to escape ; to let loose, set free, release, give up ; to let flow,* as water ; *to let sink* or *drop,* as anchors ; i. 3. 19 : ii. 2. 20 ; 3. 13, 25 : iii. 5. 10.

ἀφ-ικνέομαι,* ἴξομαι, ἷγμαι, 2 a. ἱκόμην, (ἵκω), *to arrive, reach, come to,* or *return to,* from another place, D. εἰς, πρός, &c., i. 1.5 ; 2.4,12 ; 5.4 : iii.1.43.

ἀφ-ιππεύω, εύσω, (ἵππος) *to ride away* or *back,* i. 5. 12.

ἀφ-ίστημι,* στήσω, ἕστηκα, 2 a. ἔστην, f. pf. ἑστήξω, *to withdraw* (trans.), *alienate from,* A. ἀπό, vi. 6. 34 : *M.,* w. act. complete tenses and 2 a., *to stand off* or *aloof, forsake, desert, revolt from, go over* to another, *withdraw* or *retire* (intrans.), G., πρός els: i. 1. 6 s: ii. 6. 27. Der. APOSTATE.

ἀφ-οδος, ου, ἡ, (ὀδός) a [way back or off] *retreat, departure,* iv. 2. 11.

ἀφροντιστέω, ήσω, (ἀ-φρόντιστος *heedless,* fr. φροντίζω) *to be heedless of* or *indifferent to, neglect, make light of,* G., v. 4. 20 : *v. l.* ἀμελέω.

†**ἀφροσύνη**, ης, *folly, infatuation, want of consideration,* v. 1. 14.

ἄ-φρων, ον, g. ονος, (φρήν *mind*) *without understanding, senseless, foolish, infatuated, delirious,* iv. 8. 20.

†**ἀφυλακτέω**,ήσω,*to be off* one's *guard,* vii. 8. 20.

ἀ-φύλακτος, ον, (φυλάσσω) *unguarded,* ii. 6. 24 : v. 7. 14.

‡**ἀφυλάκτως**, *unguardedly,* v. 1. 6.

Ἀχαιός, οῦ, *an Achœan,* a man of Achaia, the hilly province on the north of the Peloponnese, along the Corinthian Gulf. In the early history of Greece, the Achæans were so dominant a race that the name most frequently applied by Homer to the Greeks in general is Ἀχαιοί. On the conquest of their old seats in the

ἀχάριστος 24 βαρβαρικός

Peloponnese by the Dorians, many of the Achæans retired to the northern shore, expelling from it, it is said, Ionian settlers, and giving to it their own name. Here they formed a confederacy of twelve cities, none of which attained any great power or distinction. For a long time, the Achæans took little part in the general affairs of Greece, remaining for the most part neutral in the great contests, whether foreign or internal. In a later period of its history, the Achæan League became eminent. The Arcadians and Achæans constituted more than half of the Greek army of Cyrus. i. 1. 11.

ἀ-χάριστος, ον, (χαρίζομαι) without grace or thanks: of things, *unpleasing, disagreeable; unrewarded*: of persons, *ungrateful*, εἰς : λέγεις οὐκ ἀχάριστα *you speak* [things not without grace] *quite rhetorically* or *entertainingly*: i. 9. 18 : ii. 1. 13 ? vii. 6. 23.

‡ἀχαρίστως adv., *without thanks, gratitude*, or *reward; ungratefully;* ii. 3. 18 : vii. 7. 23.

ἄ-χαρις, ι, g. ιτος, or ἀ-χάριτος, ον, (χάρις) = ἀχάριστος, ii. 1. 13 ?

Ἀχερουσιάς, άδος, ἡ, (Ἀχέρων, a fabled river in Hades) as an adj., *Acherusian*. Ἀ. Χερρόνησος *the Acherusian Peninsula*, a promontory near the Bithynian Heraclēa, with a very deep mephitic hole, fabled as the place of Hercules' descent to Hades, vi. 2. 2. ǁ Baba-Burun.

ἄχθομαι,* ἀχθέσομαι, ἤχθημαι 1., a. *p.* ἠχθέσθην, *to be* [burdened] *vexed, displeased, offended, provoked, troubled, distressed, nettled*, or *chagrined*, D., G. P., AE., τοῦτο (483 b), ὅτι, ἐπί, i. 1. 8: iii. 2. 20: vii. 5. 5 s ; 6. 10 ; 7. 21.

ἀ-χρεῖος, ον, (χρεία *use*) *use-less, unfit for use, unserviceable*, iv. 6. 26.

ἀ-χρηστος, ον, (χράομαι) *use-less, inappropriate*, ii. 1. 13 ? iii. 4. 26.

ἄχρι (and, before a vowel, less Att. ἄχρις) adv., *as far as, even to*, εἰς : conj., *till, until*, ἄν w. subj.: ii. 3. 2 : v. 5. 4. Akin to ἄκρος : cf. μέχρι.

ἀψίνθιον, ου, *wormwood*, i. 5. 1.

B.

Βαβυλών, ῶνος, ἡ, *Babylon*, one of the greatest and most magnificent cities of the ancient world, and the seat of successive empires. It was situated on both sides of the lower Euphrates, in a rich alluvial plain. According to Herodotus, it was square, with a circuit of more than 50 miles ; and was surrounded by a wall more than 300 feet high and 80 broad, with 100 brazen gates, and with a deep moat without. It was taken by Cyrus through a diversion of the river, B. C. 538 ; and opened its gates to Alexander, after the battle of Arbēla, B.C. 331. It is now for the most part in utter ruin, the more from the perishable nature of its chief material, brick, and from the removal of this for the construction of other cities. i. 4. 11, 13: ii. 2. 6 : v. 5. 4. ǁ Hillah.

‡Βαβυλώνιος, α, ον, *Babylonian* : ἡ Βαβυλωνία [sc. χώρα] *Babylonia*, the alluvial region around Babylon and west of the Tigris, comm. regarded as extending from the Wall of Media, which separated it from Mesopotamia, to the Persian Gulf. Watered by the overflowing of the Euphrātes and Tigris, and by canals drawn from them, it had great fertility. i. 7. 1: ii. 2. 13.

βάδην adv., (βαίνω) *step ly step, in regular step : β. ταχύ in rapid step :* iv. 6. 25 ; 8. 28 : vi. 5. 25.

‡βαδίζω, ἴσομαι ἰοῦμαι, βεβάδικα, *to walk, march, set foot, go*, v. 1. 2.

†βάθος, εος, τό, *depth*, i. 7. 14.

βαθύς, εῖα, ύ, *deep*, i. 7. 14 s: v. 2. 3.

βαίνω,* βήσομαι, βέβηκα, 2 a. ἔβην, *to step, go :* pf. pret., *I* [have planted foot] *stand, stand firm*, iii. 2. 19.

‡βακτηρία, ας, baculum, *a staff, cane*, ii. 3. 11 : iv. 7. 26.

βάλανος, ου, ἡ, glans, *an acorn* or like fruit, *nut, date*, i. 5. 10 : ii. 3. 15.

βάλλω,* βαλῶ, βέβληκα, 2 a. ἔβαλον, *to throw, cast, hurl ; to throw at, hit* with a missile, *pelt* (esp. w. stones), *stone*, A. D. of the missile: οἱ ἐκ χειρὸς βάλλοντες [those throwing from the hand] *the javelin-men* or *darters :* i. 3. 1: iii. 3. 15 : iv. 6. 12: v. 4. 23.

βάπτω,* βάψω, *to dip*, A., ii. 2. 9. Der. BAPTISM.

†βαρβαρικός, ή, όν, BARBARIC, *barbarian, foreign ;* here esp. *Persian :* τὸ βαρβαρικόν [sc. στράτευμα] *the barbarian force* or *army :* i. 2. 1 ; 5. 6 s : iv. 5. 33 ; 8. 7.

βαρβαρικῶς 25 βοεικός

‡βαρβαρικῶς in the barbarian tongue, in Persian, i. 8. 1.

βάρβαρος, ον, s., BARBAROUS, barbarian, rude: βάρβαρος subst., a barbarian, foreigner. The Greeks so termed all other nations. i. 1. 5 : ii. 5. 32 : v. 4. 34 ; 5. 16.

βαρέως (βαρύς heavy) heavily, with heavy heart: β. φέρειν graviter ferre, to take ill, be smitten with grief: ii. 1. 4, 9.

Βασίας, ου, Basias, an Arcadian in the army of Cyrus, iv. 1. 18. — 2. A soothsayer from Elis, vii. 8. 10 ?

†βασιλεία, ας, kingdom, royal power, regal authority, sovereignty, i. 1. 3.

†βασίλειος, ον, royal, regal, kingly: βασίλειον [sc. δῶμα], oftener pl., [royal building or buildings] a royal residence, a palace of a king or satrap : i. 2. 7 s, 20 ; 10. 12 : iii. 4. 24.

βασιλεύς, έως, a king, esp. applied (often w. μέγας, and comm. without the art.) to the Persian king: i. 1. 5 s ; 2. 8, 12 s : iii. 1. 12. Der. BASILISK.

‡βασιλεύω, εύσω, to be king, to reign, G.: ὡς βασιλεύσοντι [as about to reign] as the future king : i. 1. 4 ; 4. 18.

‡βασιλικός, ή, όν, s., relating to or fit for a king, kingly, royal, the king's, i. 9. 1 : ii. 2. 12, 16. Der. BASILICA.

βάσιμος, ον, (βαίνω) passable (for a horse), iii. 4. 49.

βατός, ή, όν, (βαίνω) passable, D., iv. 6. 17.

βέβαιος, α, ον, (βαίνω) standing firm, firm, constant, i. 9. 30.

‡βεβαιόω, ώσω, to make firm, confirm, make good, fulfil, complete, A. D., vii. 6. 17.

βεβηκώς, see βαίνω, iii. 2. 19.

Βέλεσυς, υος, Belesys, satrap of Syria, i. 4. 10 : v. l. Βέλεσις, ιος.

βέλος, εος, τό, (βάλλω) a missile, iii. 3. 16 : iv. 3. 6 ; 8. 11.

βελτίων,* ον, βέλτιστος, η, ον, (βελτ-, akin to βέλος ?) better, best, as c. and s. to ἀγαθός q. v.; braver, nobler, more expedient or advantageous, &c.; i. 1. 6 : ii. 2. 1 ; 5. 41 : iii. 3. 5.

βῆμα, ατος, τό, (βαίνω) a step, pace, iv. 7. 10.

βία, ας, vis, force, violence : βίᾳ w. G., in spite of or despite : i. 4. 4 : iii. 4. 12 : vi. 6. 25 : vii. 8. 17.

‡βιάζομαι, άσομαι, βεβίασμαι, to use force, force one's way; to force or com-

pel, A. I.; to force back, A.; i. 3. 1 s ; 4. 5 : vii. 8. 11.

‡βίαιος, α, ον, violent : βιαιόν τι [sc. πρᾶγμα] any violent act or violence : v. 5. 20 : vi. 6. 15.

‡βιαίως, forcibly, violently, with great force, i. 8. 27.

[βιβάζω, βιβάσω βιβῶ, (causative of βαίνω) to make go.]

βίβλος, ου, ἡ, the inner bark of the papȳrus ; hence, paper made from this ; a book : β. γεγραμμέναι (?) manuscripts, vii. 5. 14. Der. BIBLE.

Βιθῡνός, ή, όν, Bithynian : Βιθῡνός subst., a Bithynian. The Bithȳni, driven by more powerful tribes, crossed from Thrace into Asia, and gave their name to a region south of the Euxine and east of the Propontis (also called Asiatic Thrace). vi. 2. 17 ; 5. 30.

βῖκος or βίκος, ου, ὁ, a large earthen vessel, esp. for wine ; a jar, flagon ; i. 9. 25.

βίος, ου, ὁ, (cf. Lat. vivo) vita, life; a living, livelihood, subsistence ; i. 1. 1: v. 5. 1: vi. 4. 8. Der. BIO-GRAPHY.

‡βιοτεύω, εύσω, to live, pass one's life, ἐν, iii. 2. 25.

Βισάνθη, ης, Bisanthe, a pleasant town in Thrace, on the Propontis, founded by the Samians, vii. 2. 38 ; 5. 8. ‖ Rodosto.

Βίων or Βίτων, ωνος, Bion or Biton, a Spartan envoy who brought money to the Cyreans, vii. 8. 6.

βλάβη, ης, ἡ, or βλάβος, εος, τό, (βλάπτω) harm, injury, detriment, ii. 6. 6 : vii. 7. 28.

βλᾰκεύω, εύσω, (βλάξ lazy) to be lazy, loiter, shirk, yield to sloth, ii. 3. 11: v. 8. 15.

βλάπτω,* ἄψω, βέβλαφα, to harm, hurt, injure, 2 A., ii. 5. 17: iii. 3. 11. iv. 1. 20. See ὁράω.

βλέπω, ἔψομαι, βέβλεφα 1., to look : of scythes, to be directed or point towards; πρός, εἰς : i. 8. 10 : iii. 1. 36 : iv. 1. 20. See ὁράω.

βλώσκω,* μολοῦμαι, μέμβλωκα, 2 a. ἔμολον, ch. poet., to go, come, arrive, vii. 1. 33.

βοάω,* ἤσομαι, βεβόηκα 1., (βοή) boo, to cry or call out or aloud, shout, D. I., ὅτι, i. 8. 1, 12, 19.: iv. 7. 23 s.

βοεικός, ή, όν, (βοῦς) relating to oxen, of oxen ; ζεῦγος β. a yoke of oxen, an ox-team, vii. 5. 2, 4 : v. l. βοϊκός.

LEX. AN. 2

βοή 26 **γάμος**

βοή, ῆς, *a loud cry, shout, shouting, outcry*, iv. 7. 23.

‡**βοήθεια**, ας, *help, assistance, succor, rescue; auxiliary troops;* ii. 3. 19: iii. 5. 4.

‡**βοηθέω**, ήσω, βεβοήθηκα, (βοη-θός *assisting*, running to a cry for help, βοή, θέω) *to run to the rescue, hasten to help, bring aid, go or come to the assistance of another; to succor, help, assist, give assistance:* D., ἐπί, ὑπέρ: i. 9. 6 : ii. 4. 25 : iii. 4. 13 ; 5. 6.

βόθρος, ου, ὁ, (cf. βαθύς & Lat. puteus) *a pit,* iv. 5. 6 : v. 8. 9.

Βοΐσκος, ου, *Boïscus*, a Thessalian boxer, lazy and lawless, v. 8. 23.

†**Βοιωτία**, ας, *Bœōtia*, iii. 1. 31.

†**βοιωτιάζω**, άσω, *to resemble a Bœotian,* iii. 1. 26.

Βοιωτός, οῦ, & **Βοιώτιος**, ου, ὁ, *a Bœotian.* Bœotia, lying northwest of Attica, was a very fertile province, whose inhabitants were in general regarded by their neighbors as wanting in spirit, vivacity, intellect, and refinement. It had, however, a short period of glory under Epaminondas and Pelopidas. Its chief city was Thebes; and in Greek politics, except Platææ, it was oftener opposed to Athens. i. 1. 11: v. 3. 6 ; 6. 19.

βορέας,* ου, contr. **βορρᾶς**, ᾶ, *boreas, the north-wind,* iv. 5. 3 : v. 7. 7.

βόσκημα, ατος, τό, (βόσκω *to feed*) *a fed or pastured animal;* pl. *cattle,* iii. 5. 2.

†**βουλεύω**, εύσω, βεβούλευκα, *to plan, devise, counsel,* A. D., ii. 5. 16 : *M. to take counsel* with one's self, *deliberate, consider; to consult together; to meditate, consult, concert, plan, devise, propose, purpose, resolve;* A., I., CP., περί, πρός, &c.; i. 1. 4, 7 ; 3. 11, 19 s ; 10. 5 : ii. 3. 20 s: iii. 2. 8 ?

βουλή, ῆς, (βούλομαι) *will, plan, counsel, consideration,* vi. 5. 13.

βουλιμιάω, άσω, (βου-λιμία *bulimy, intense hunger, faintness from hunger,* βοῦς, λιμός) *to have or suffer from the bulimy, to be faint with hunger,* iv. 5. 7 s.

βούλομαι* (2 sing. βούλει, iii. 4. 41 s), λήσομαι, βεβούλημαι, volo, *to will, be willing, wish, desire, choose, prefer, consent;* ὁ βουλόμενος *he or any one that wishes, whoever pleases:* I. (A.), often supplied from the context :

i. 1. 1,11; 3. 4 s, 9 : ii. 4. 4; 5. 5; 6. 6. See ἐθέλω.

†**βου-πόρος**, ον, (πείρω *to pierce*) *ox-piercing;* β. ὀβελίσκος *an ox-spit,* vii. 8. 14.

βοῦς,* βοός, ὁ ἡ, bos, *an ox, cow;* pl. *oxen, kine,* neat *cattle:* ἡ, *an ox-hide:* in compos., sometimes augmentative : ii. 1. 6 : iv. 5. 32 ; 7. 22.

†**βραδέως** *slowly,* i. 8. 11.

βραδύς, εῖα, ύ, s. ὕτατος, *slow,* vii. 3. 37.

βραχύς, εῖα, ύ, c. ὕτερος, *short:* βραχύ *or* ἐπὶ βραχύ [sc. χωρίον, or διάστημα *distance*] *a short distance:* βραχύτερα *a shorter distance:* i. 5. 3 : iii. 3. 7, 17. Cog. brevis, *brief.*

βρέχω,* βρέξω l., a. p. ἐβρέχθην, *to wet,* A., i. 4. 17 : iii. 2. 22 : iv. 5. 2.

βροντή, ῆς, *thunder,* iii. 1. 11.

βρωτός, ή, όν, (βιβρώσκω *to eat*) *eatable,* iv. 5. 5.

†**Βυζάντιον**, ου, *Byzantium,* a city founded by the Megarians, B. C. 657, in an admirable situation upon the Propontis at the entrance of the Thracian Bosphorus. The Athenians and Spartans contended repeatedly and earnestly for its control. The Cyreans found it, as so many Greek cities at this time, under the rule of a Spartan harmost. The Roman Emperor Constantine made it his capital, A. D. 330, and gave to it a new name from his own. vi. 4. 2 : vii. 1. 3. ∥ Constantinople *or* Stambûl.

Βυζάντιος, α, ον, (Βύζας, αντος, *Byzas,* the reputed founder of Byzantium) *Byzantine:* οἱ Βυζάντιοι *the Byzantines,* vii. 1. 19, 39.

βωμός, οῦ, ὁ, (βαίνω) *a raised place,* esp. for sacrifice ; *an altar,* whether of rude stones or earth, or of elaborate workmanship. Altars were common places of refuge. i. 6. 7 : iv. 8. 28.

Γ.

γαλήνη, ης, (akin to γελάω ?) *a* [*smile upon the sea* ?] *calm,* v. 7. 8. Der. GALENA.

†**γαμέω**,* γαμῶ, γεγάμηκα, *to marry* (of the man): *M. to marry or be married* (of the woman), iv. 5. 24.

γάμος, ου, ὁ, *marriage, wedlock:* ἐπὶ γάμῳ [on terms of marriage] *in*

marriage, as his wife, ii. 4. 8. Der. POLY-GAMY.

Γάνος, ου, ἡ, Ganus, a small town of Thrace, on the west shore of the Propontis, vii. 5. 8. ‖ Ganos.

γάρ* post-pos. conj., (γε ἄρα at least in accordance with this) a particle commonly marking the accordance between a fact, statement, &c., and its ground or reason, explanation or specification, confirmation, &c. It is commonly translated for; but sometimes since, as, or because (as a causal conj.), that or namely (in specification), indeed or certainly (in explanation or confirmation), then, now, &c.; i. 2. 2; 7. 4 : ii. 3. 1; 5. 11 : iii. 1. 24. It often occurs in elliptic construction (as in questions, replies, &c., i. 6. 8 ; 7. 9 : ii. 5. 40); and may frequently be either explained as a conj. by supplying an ellipsis, or as an adv. without doing so : ἀλλὰ γάρ at enim, but (enough, no more, not so, no, &c.,) for, or but indeed, yet indeed, iii. 2. 25 s, 32 : καὶ γάρ etenim, and (this the rather, &c.,) because, or for indeed, and indeed, for even, i. 1. 6, 8 : ii. 2. 15 : καὶ γὰρ οὖν and (this is apparent, for) therefore, and consequently, accordingly, i. 9. 8, 12, 17 : ii. 6. 13.

γαστήρ,* τέρος, sync. τρός, ἡ, the belly, abdomen, paunch, stomach, ii. 5. 33 : iv. 5. 36. Der. GASTRIC.

γαυλικός or **γαυλιτικός**, ή, όν, (γαῦλος a round-built freighting vessel) pertaining to a γαῦλος : γ. χρήματα cargoes of freighting vessels, v. 8. 1.

Γαυλίτης, ου, Gaulites, an exile from Samos, faithful to Cyrus, i. 7. 5.

γέ,* a post-pos. and encl. adv. giving emphasis or force, more frequently to the preceding word, or to a word or clause which this introduces, and often with an associate idea of restriction or limitation ; quidem, at least, indeed, even, surely, certainly ; but often expressed in Eng. simply by emphasis; i. 3. 9, 21; 6. 5 : ii. 5. 19 : γὲ δή [surely now] indeed, iv. 6. 3 : γὲ μέντοι, γὲ μήν, certainly at least, and or but certainly, moreover, i. 9. 14, 16, 20 : ii. 3. 9.

γεγένημαι, **γέγονα**, see γίγνομαι, i. 6. 8.

γείτων, ονος, ὁ ἡ, (γῆ) a neighbor, D. or G., ii. 3. 18 : iii. 2. 4.

γελάω, ἄσομαι, a. ἐγέλασα, to laugh, smile, ἐπί, ii. 1. 13 : v. 4. 34.

‡**γελοῖος** or **γέλοιος**, α, ον, laughable, ridiculous, v. 6. 25 : vi. 1. 30.

‡**γέλως**, ωτος, ὁ, laughter, i. 2. 18.

‡**γελωτο-ποιός**, οῦ, ὁ, (ποιέω), a laughter-maker, jester, buffoon, vii. 3. 33.

γέμω, only in pr. and ipf., to be full of or stored with, G., iv. 6. 27.

γενεά, ᾶς, (γεν- in γίγνομαι) birth : ἀπὸ γενεᾶς from birth, of age, ii. 6. 30. Der. GENEA-LOGY.

γενειάω, άσω, (γένειον chin) to have a beard or be bearded, ii. 6. 28.

γενέσθαι, γενοίμην, γενήσομαι, &c., see γίγνομαι, i. 6. 8 ; 9. 1 : iii. 1. 13.

†**γεννιότης**, ητος, ἡ, (γενναῖος of good birth) nobleness, generosity, vii. 7. 41.

γένος, εος, τό, (γεν- in γίγνομαι) genus, birth, descent, race, i. 6. 1.

γεραιός, ά, όν, c. αἴτερος, (γερ- in γέρων) old, v. 7. 17.

γερόντιον, ου, τό, (dim. fr. γέρων) a feeble old man, vi. 3. 22.

γέῤῥον, ου, an oblong shield of wicker-work, comm. covered with oxhide, and sometimes strengthened with metallic plates, much used by the Asiatics ; a wicker-shield, ii. 1. 6.

‡**γεῤῥο-φόρος**, ου, ὁ, (φέρω) a wicker-shield-bearer, a soldier with a wicker-shield, i. 8. 9.

γέρων, οντος, ὁ, (cf. γῆρας) an old man, iv. 3. 11 : vii. 4. 24.

γεύω, γεύσω, to make one taste : M. gusto, to taste, G., i. 9. 26 : iii. 1. 3.

γέφυρα, ας, a bridge, whether firm or floating, i. 2. 5 ; 7. 15 : vi. 5. 22.

†**γεώδης**, ες, (εἶδος) earthy, vi. 4. 5.

γῆ, γῆς, (contr. fr. γέα) earth, land, country, ground, i. 1. 7 ; 5. 1 ; 8. 10 : iii. 2. 19. Der. GE-OLOGY, GEORGE.

‡**γήϊνος**, ον, made of earth, earthen, vii. 8. 14.

‡**γή-λοφος**, ου, ὁ, (λόφος) an elevation of earth, hill, eminence, height, i. 5. 8 ; 10. 12 : iii. 4. 24 s.

γῆρας, αος, τό, (cf. γέρων) old age, advanced age, iii. 1. 43.

γίγνομαι,* Ion. or later **γίνομαι**, γενήσομαι, γεγένημαι & 2 pf. γέγονα, 2 a. ἐγενόμην, (cf. gigno) to come to be (more briefly translated be or come), become, get (intrans.); to take place, happen, occur, result (ἂν εὖ γένηται if it come out well, if the result be favorable, i. 7. 7); to come to be in a place,

γιγνώσκω 28 Γυμνιάς

arrive, come, get, extend, (ἐν ἑαυτῷ ἐγένετο *came to* [be within] *himself,* i. 5. 17); *to be ascertained, shown,* or *proved to be, to prove* or *show one's self to be;* D., διά, ἐκ, ἐν, ἐπί, κατά, &c. It is variously translated according to the subject or other words with which it is connected, and sometimes by a pass. verb (as if supplying the pass. of ποιέω, &c.): of children, *to be born* or *descended,* G., ἀπό· of rain or snow, *to fall;* of a cry, shout, laughter, tumult, war, &c., *to arise;* of the day, *to dawn;* of a road, *to pass* or *lead;* of income, *to accrue* (τὰ γιγνόμενα *the proceeds,* vii. 6. 41); of numbers, *to amount to;* of acts, *to be performed,* ὑπό· of meetings, *to be held;* of oaths or pledges, *to be taken, given,* or *exchanged;* of sacrifices, *to* [result as they should] *take effect, be favorable* or *auspicious,* I.; &c.; i. 1. 1, 8; 6. 5, 8; 8. 8, 23 s: ii. 2. 3, 10: — w. dat. of possessor (459), δρόμος ἐγένετο τοῖς στρατιώταις [to the soldiers there came to be a running] *the soldiers began to run,* i. 2. 17; ἐγένετο καὶ Ἕλληνι καὶ βαρβάρῳ πορεύεσθαι [it came to be, became possible to, &c.] *both Greek and barbarian could go,* i. 9. 13; τὴν ἡμέραν αὐτοῖς ἐγένετο *occupied them through the day,* iv. 1. 10; &c. The aor. and complete tenses of γίγνομαι sometimes seem to supply these tenses for εἰμί.

γιγνώσκω,* Ion. or later γινώσκω, γνώσομαι, ἔγνωκα, 2 a. ἔγνων, a. p. ἐγνώσθην, gnosco, *to* KNOW, *recognize, understand, perceive, discern, judge, decide, think* (pf. *have recognized the fact, reflect,* iii. 1. 43): A. P., I. (A), CI'., 2 A., περί: i. 3. 2, 12s; 7. 4: ii. 5. 8, 35: iii. 1. 27, 45. See ὁράω.

Γλοῦς,* οὗ, οὗ, οὖν, οὗ, *Glus,* an Egyptian, son of the admiral Tamos. He was a favorite officer of Cyrus; and was afterwards taken into favor by Artaxerxes. He was probably appointed to the command of the Persian fleet; but slain, after a victory over the Cyprians, as he was meditating revolt, B.C. 383. i. 4. 16: ii. 4. 24.

Γνήσ-ιππος, ου, *Gnesippus,* an Athenian lochage, vii. 3. 28.

γνοίην, γνούς, γνῶναι, γνώσομαι, &c., see γιγνώσκω, i. 7. 4; 9. 20.

†γνώμη, ης, *understanding, judgment, conviction, sentiment, thought,* *opinion, design, plan, expectation; mind, disposition, inclination, preference, favor, consent:* τὴν γνώμην ἔχειν *to have one's mind made up* or *fixed, to be assured, inclined, disposed,* or *attached,* D., πρός, ὡς w. P. absolute: γνώμῃ *on principle:* i. 3. 6, 13; 6. 9s; 7. 8; 8. 10: ii. 5. 29; 6. 9: vi. 6. 12. Der. GNOMIC.

Γογγύλος, ου, *Gongylus,* the name of a father and son sprung from Gongylus, an Eretrian who was banished for aiding the treason of Pausanias, but rewarded by Xerxes with four cities in western Asia Minor, vii. 8. 8, 17.

γοητεύω, see κατα-γοητεύω, v. 7. 9?

γονεύς, έως, ὁ, (γεν· in γίγνομαι) *father:* pl. *parents,* iii. 1. 3: v. 8. 18.

γόνυ,* γόνατος, τό, genu, *the* KNEE; *a joint* or *knot* in a plant; i. 5. 13: iii. 2. 22: iv. 5. 36.

Γοργίας, ου, *Gorgias,* a celebrated sophist and rhetorician from Leontini in Sicily, who taught at Athens and elsewhere in Greece, for large price, dazzling his hearers by the ingenuity of his reasoning and the glitter of his declamation. He is introduced by Plato into a dialogue bearing his name. ii. 6. 16.

Γοργίων, ωνος, *Gorgion,* a son of Gongylus and Hellas, vii. 8. 8.

γοῦν adv., (γὲ οὖν) *at least* then, *at any rate, at all events, certainly, assuredly,* iii. 2. 17: v. 8. 23: vii. 1. 30.

γρᾴδιον, cont. γρᾴδιον, ου, τό, (dim. fr. γραῦς *old woman*) a feeble *old woman,* iii. 3. 22.

†γράμμα, ατος, τό, litera, *a letter;* pl. *letters, an inscription,* v. 3. 13. Der. GRAMMAR.

γράφω,* γράψω, γέγραφα, pf. p. γέγραμμαι, *to* GRAVE, *write, paint,* A., CP., i. 6. 3: vii. 8. 1. Der. GRAPHIC.

γυμνάζω, άσω, γεγύμνακα, (γυμνός) *to* [train naked] *train, exercise,* A., i. 2. 7. Der. GYMNASTIC.

γυμνής, ῆτος, ὁ, or γυμνήτης, ου, (γυμνός) as adj., [naked] *light-armed;* comm. subst., *a light-armed soldier;* a term applied to all foot-soldiers except the hoplites, and with special propriety to archers and slingers (to slingers only, v. 2. 12): i. 2. 3: iii. 4. 26: iv. 1. 6, 28.

Γυμνιάς, άδος, ἡ, *Gymnias,* a large city of the Scythini in Armenia, iv.

γυμνικός　20　δασύς

7. 19. v. l. Γυμνίας or -νάς. ‖ Gumish Kaneh? — acc. to some, Erzrum, &c.

†γυμνικός, ή, όν, gymnastic, iv. 8. 25.

γυμνός, ή, όν, naked: less strictly, lightly clad, in one's under-garment only; exposed without defensive armor, πρός: i. 10. 3: iv. 3. 6, 12.

γυνή,* γυναικός, voc. γύναι, a woman, wife, i. 2. 12. Der. MISO-GYNIST.

Γωβρύας, ου or α, Gobryas, commander of a fourth part of the army of Artaxerxes, i. 7. 12.

Δ.

δ' by apostr. for δέ, i. 1. 4 s.

δάκνω,* δήξομαι, δέδηχα l., a. p. ἐδήχθην, to bite, A., iii. 2. 18, 35.

δακρύω, ύσω, δεδάκρῡκα l., (δάκρυ a tear) to shed tears, weep, i. 3. 2.

†δακτύλιος, ου, ὁ, a finger-ring. Rings were greatly worn by the Greeks for use as seals, and also as ornaments or amulets. They were most worn on the fourth finger of the left hand, and were often embellished with stones cut with exquisite art. iv. 7. 27.

δάκτυλος, ου, ὁ, (cf. δείκνυμι and δέχομαι) digitus, finger, toe (τῶν ποδῶν), iv. 5. 12: v. 8. 15. Der. DACTYL.

Δᾶμ-άρᾱτος, ου, Damarātus, a king of Sparta, deposed through the intrigues of his colleague Cleomenes, B. C. 491, but kindly received by king Darius Hystaspis. He attended Xerxes in his invasion of Greece, and gave him wise counsel in vain. His service was however rewarded by the gift of a small principality in southwestern Mysia. ii. 1. 3. V. l. Δημάρατος.

Δάνα, ης, ἡ, or Δάνα, ων, τά, Dana or Tyana, an important city in southern Cappadocia, at the northern foot of Mt. Taurus, on the way to the Cilician Pass. It was the native place of Apollonius, the Pythagorean thaumaturgist. i. 2. 20: v. l. Θόανα. ‖ Kiz-Hissar (Girls' Castle), or Kilissa-Hissar.

δαπανάω, ήσω, δεδαπάνηκα, (δαπάνη expense, akin to δάπτω) to expend, spend; to live upon, consume (τὰ ἑαυτῶν δαπανῶντες at their own expense, v. 5. 20); A. εἰς, ἀμφί: i. 1. 8; 3. 3.

δά-πεδον, ου, (διά, πέδον ground) ch. poet., the ground, iv. 5. 6.

[δάπτω, δάψω, poet., to devour.]

Δαράδαξ, ακος, ὁ, see Δάρδας, i. 4. 10?

Δαρδανεύς, έως, ὁ, (Δάρδανος) a Dardanian. Dardanus was an Æolic town of Troas, on the southern part of the Hellespont. Its name remains in the modern Dardanelles. iii. 1. 47.

Δάρδας, ᾱτος, or Δάρδης, ητος, ὁ, the Dardas or -es, supposed (with some dissent) to have been a short canal from the Euphrates to the princely residence of Belesys, where was afterwards the city Barbalissus (field of Belesys; now Bâlis) i. 4. 10: v. l. Δαράδαξ.

†δᾱρεικός, οῦ, ὁ, [sc. στατήρ coin] a daric, a Persian gold coin stamped with the figure of a crowned archer, = about $5.00 by weight, but in exchange with Attic silver coins, reckoned at 20 drachmæ = about §4.00 (3000 darics = 10 talents, i. 7. 18). It was struck of great purity by Darius Hystaspis, and either named from him or from the Pers. darâ, king; cf. the Eng. sovereign. i. 1. 9; 3. 21.

Δαρεῖος, ου, Darīus II., king of Persia, natural son of Artaxerxes I. (Longimanus), and hence surnamed Nothus. This prince, whose previous name was Ochus, ascended the throne, B. C. 424, through the murder of his half-brother Sogdiānus, who had himself become king in a similar way. He aided the Spartans in their war with Athens; and his weak reign was disturbed by various revolts, of which the most important and successful was that of Egypt. He was greatly under the influence of his ambitious and imperious wife Parysatis; but, in opposition to her wishes, appointed as his successor his eldest son Arsaces, rather than the younger Cyrus. He died, B. C. 405, leaving, according to Ctesias, four children of thirteen born of Parysatis. Δαρεῖος, like Ξέρξης and Ἀρταξέρξης, seems to have been rather a title of dignity than a simple name, and to have signified controller or lord (ἑρξης Hdt. 6. 98; Pers. darâ king).

†δάσμευσις, εως, ἡ, division, distribution, vii. 1. 37.

δασμός, οῦ, ὁ, (δαίομαι to divide) a portion paid to a ruler, a tax, impost, tribute, revenue, i. 1. 8: iv. 5. 24.

δασύς, εῖα, ύ, thick or dense with trees, shrubs, hair, &c.; bushy, shag-

Δαφναγόρας 30 Δελφοί

gy, hairy, with the hair on: τὸ δασύ the thicket: ii. 4. 14 : iv. 7. 6 s, 22.

Δαφν-αγόρας, ου, Daphnagoras, a guide sent by Hellas, vii. 8. 9.

δαψιλής, ές, (δάπτω) abundant, in abundance, plentiful, ample, iv. 2. 22.

δέ* distinctive conj. and adv., postpos., but, and; yet, however; on the other hand, on the contrary; also, further, moreover; sometimes translated while, for, or, then (as after a conditional clause, v. 6. 20), now, indeed, even, or omitted in translation; i. 1. 1 s : iv. 5. 4 : v. 7. 6 : vi. 6. 16 : καί .. δέ and [not only so, but] also, and indeed, and even, i. 1. 2 ; 5. 9 ; 8. 2 : οὐδὲ .. δέ nor yet further, nor indeed, nor even, i. 8. 20. Δέ (to which μέν corresponds) is the common particle of contradistinction, intermediate in its force between the copulative καί and, and the adversative ἀλλά but. Καί adds without implying distinction; while δέ implies some distinction, and ἀλλά not only distinction, but even opposition. See μέν, ὁ.

[-δε* an inseparable encl. particle, denoting direction towards, affixed in demonstratives, and also as a prep. to accusatives to form adverbs of place.]

δέδια & δέδοικα, see δείδω : i. 3. 10.

δέδογμαι, see δοκέω, iii. 2. 39.

δέδομαι, see δίδωμι, i. 4. 9.

δεηθῆναι, δεήσας, &c., see δέω, i.2.14.

δεῖ impers., see δέω, i. 3. 5.

δείδω* Ep., δείσομαι Ep. & vii. 3. 26 ? pret. δέδοικα & 2 pf. δέδια, a. ἔδεισα, to fear, be afraid, A., μή, i. 3. 10 ; 7. 7; 10. 9 : iii. 2. 5, 25.

δείκνυμι & -ύω,* δείξω, δέδειχα, indico, to point out, show, indicate, make signs, A. D., CP., iv. 5. 33 ; 7. 27.

δείλη, ης, afternoon, both early (πρῶτα) and late (ὀψία); evening : δείλης or τῆς δείλης in the afternoon, at evening : ἀμφὶ δείλην about the coming of afternoon, early in the afternoon: i. 8. 8 : ii. 2. 14 : iii. 3. 11.

δειλός, ή, όν, (δείδω) timid, cowardly, i. 4. 7 ? iii. 2. 35 : vi. 6. 24.

δεινός, ή, όν, (δείδω) dreadful, frightful, fearful, terrible, perilous; outrageous, intolerable, insufferable, grievous, severe; strange, wondrous; very powerful, able, skilful, clever, or adroit; I. (φαγεῖν δεινός a terrible fellow to eat, vii. 3. 23): δεινόν subst.,

peril, danger, obstacle : i. 9. 19 : ii. 3. 13, 22 ; 5. 15 ; 6. 7 : iv. 6. 16.

↓δεινῶς terribly : εἶχον δεινῶς they were [in a terrible condition] suffering severely, vi. 4. 23.

†δειπνέω, ήσω, δεδείπνηκα, to take the second or afternoon meal, to dine or sup, ii. 2. 4 : iii. 5. 18 : iv. 6. 17, 22.

δεῖπνον, ου, (akin to δάπτω and Lat. daps, though it has been fancifully referred to δεῖ πονεῖν, as the meal that must be worked for) cœna, the second of the two usual or regular Greek meals, the afternoon or evening meal, supper, often corresponding to our later dinner; the meal for which most preparation was made, and to which guests were especially invited ; ii. 4. 15 : iv. 2. 4 : vii. 3. 15 s.

↓δειπνο-ποιέω, ήσω, to prepare supper for another; but M., for one's self, vi. 3. 14 ; 4. 26.

δεῖσαι, -σας, &c., see δείδω, iii. 2. 5.

δεῖσθαι, δεῖται, &c., see δέω, i. 1. 10.

δέκα indecl., ten, i. 2. 10, 14. Der. DECADE.

↓δεκα-πέντε indecl., fifteen, vii. 8. 26.

‡δεκατεύω, εύσω, to take a tenth of, tithe, A., v. 3. 9.

↓δέκατος, η, ον, tenth : ἡ δεκάτη [sc. μοῖρα part] the tenth part, tithe: v. 3. 4.

Δέλτα, τό, indecl., the Delta, a part of Thrace between the Euxine and Propontis, so named from its shape, vii. 1. 33 ; 5. 1.

δελφίς, ῖνος, ὁ, a dolphin, v. 4. 28.

Δελφοί, ῶν, οἱ, Delphi, a small city of Phocis, famed for the natural sublimity and beauty of its situation overhung by the cliffs of Mt. Parnassus, and for its temple and oracle of Apollo, the most celebrated in the world. It was the seat of the Pythian games, and one of the two places for the meeting of the Amphictyonic council ; and was accounted by the Greeks the central point of the earth. It abounded in consecrated gifts and works of the choicest and richest art ; and here several states, as the Athenians, Corinthians, &c., had sacred treasuries, esp. for the keeping of such gifts as should not stand in the open air. Its oracle was finally silenced by the emperor Theodosius in his general prohibition of Pagan worship, A.D. 390. v. 3. 5 ; vi. 1. 22. ‖ Kastri.

δένδρον,* ου, (dat. pl. δένδροις or δένδρεσι, iv. 7. 9; 8. 2), *a tree*, i. 2. 22.

δέξασθαι, -ομαι, &c., see δέχομαι.

†**δεξιόομαι, ώσομαι,** *to give the right hand to another, welcome, greet, congratulate,* vii. 4. 19.

δεξιός, ά, όν, (akin to δέχομαι and δείκνυμι, from the use of the right hand in taking and pointing) *dexter, right* in distinction fr. *left, on the right* (the auspicious side in Greek augury, as the left in Roman): ἡ δεξιά [sc. χείρ] *the right hand,* often used, as now, in greeting, and also in solemn asseveration ; hence, a *pledge* or *solemn assurance,* esp. of friendship or peace ; ἐν δεξιᾷ, *on the right* (*hand*), G.: τὸ δεξιόν [sc. κέρας, μέρος, &c.] *the right* (*wing*) of an army (a position of special honor), *the right side* or *part* (so τὰ δεξιά), *the right; ἐπὶ δεξιά to* or *on the right:* i. 2. 15 ; 5. 1 ; 6. 6 ; 8. 4 s, 13 : ii. 4. 1: iv. 3. 17: vi. 1. 23 ; 4. 1.

Δέξ-ιππος, ου, *Dexippus,* a Laconian, prob. a lochage in the division of Clearchus, faithless and slanderous, v. 1. 15 : vi. 1. 32 ; 6. 5.

Δερκυλ[λ]ίδας, ου, *Dercyl[l]idas,* a Spartan general of great ability (surnamed Sisyphus from his varied resources), under whom as the successor of Thibron, the Cyreans, after their return, served against the Persians. He had previously commanded for the Spartans in the region of the Hellespont (sent out B. C. 411). Plutarch informs us, that his generalship did not secure him from insult at Sparta for being unmarried. v. 6. 24.

δέρμα, ατος, τό, (δέρω *to flay*) the *skin* stripped off, *hide,* i. 2. 8 : iv. 8. 26.

‡**δερμάτινος,** η, ον, *of skin, leathern;* δερματίνη [sc. ἀσπίς or πέλτη] *a buckler* of leather or skin, iv. 7. 26?

Δέρνης, ου or εος, *Dernes,* satrap of Arabia, vii. 8. 25.

†**δεσμεύω,** εύσω, *to chain* or *tie up,* A., v. 8. 24?

δεσμός, οῦ, ὁ, (δέω *to bind*) a *band, strap, yoke-strap,* iii. 5. 10.

δεσπότης, ου, (cf. Lat. *potis*) *a master, lord,* ii. 3. 15. Der. DESPOT.

δεῦρο adv., *hither, here,* i. 3. 19.

δεύτερος, α, ον, (c. form fr. δύο, 376 c) *second :* δεύτερον or τὸ δεύτερον, as adv., *the second time:* i. 8. 16 : ii. 2. 4: iii. 4. 28. Der. DEUTERO-NOMY.

δέχομαι,* δέξομαι, δέδεγμαι, *to receive, accept, take* what is offered ; *to receive* hospitably, *admit, welcome* (οἰκίᾳ δέχεσθαι *to receive* [with] *into one's house,* vii. 2. 6); *to receive* an enemy, *to meet* or *await* his charge or attack (εἰς χεῖρας δέχεσθαι *to receive* an enemy *hand to hand, to meet* him *in close combat,* iv. 3. 31); A. εἰς, ἐπί : i. 8. 17; 10. 6, 11 : iv. 5. 32 : v. 5. 2 s, 19 s.

δέω,* δήσω, δέδεκα, pf. *p.* δέδεμαι, *to bind, tie, fasten,* A., iii. 4. 35 ; 5. 10 : iv. 3. 8 ; 6. 2. Der. DIA-DEM.

δέω,* δεήσω, δεδέηκα, a. *p.* as *m.* ἐδεήθην, *to need, want, lack,* G. I.; as αὐτοῦ ὀλίγου δεήσαντος καταλευσθῆναι *when he had wanted little* [to be] *of being stoned to death,* had narrowly escaped or come near this, i. 5. 14 ; πολλοῦ δεῖν *to lack much of, be far from,* vii. 6. 18 :—*M. to need* for one's self, *stand in need of, want, require, desire ; to beg, entreat, beseech, ask, request ;* G. I. (A.), A. of neut. pron.; i. 1. 10 ; 2. 14 ; 3. 4 ; 4. 14s: ὑπὸ τοῦ δεῖσθαι *by want* or *poverty,* ii. 6. 13.— Impers. **δεῖ** (δέῃ, δέοι, δεῖν, δέον, f. δεήσει, a. ἐδέησε) *there is need* of, G.; *there is need* that, *it is necessary, due,* or *proper, it behooves* (often translated personally by *must* or *ought, am obliged,* &c.), I. (A., r. D.), iii. 4. 35) : οὐδὲν (τὶ, τί, ὅ τι) δεῖ, *there is no* (*some, any,* &c.) *need* (adv. acc. or of spec., *used as to nothing,* &c., ii. 4. 7 : iii. 4. 23) : τὸ δέον *the thing needed* or *proper :* εἰς τὸ δέον *satisfactorily :* ὡς δεήσον *as it would be necessary* (pt. abs., v. 2. 12) : i. 3. 5 s, 8 : iii. 2. 28, 33, 36.

δή* post-pos. adv., (δέ) *indeed, truly, surely, forsooth, even, accordingly, of course, just, so, then, now, pray.* It is also translated by other strengthening words, or sometimes by emphasis only. i. 1. 4 ; 2. 3 s ; 9. 28 s.

δῆλος, η, ον, *evident, manifest, plain, clear :* δῆλον (ἐστίν) *it is evident :* by personal constr. for impers., δῆλος ἦν ἀνιώμενος *it was manifest that he was grieved,* or *he was manifestly grieved* (so often w. a pt., 573, i. 2. 11 ; 5. 9 : cf. v. 2. 26): δῆλον ὅτι parenthetically, also written δηλονότι as an adv., [it is evident that] *evidently :* i. 3. 9 : ii. 3. 1, 6 : iii. 2. 26, 34.

‡**δηλόω,** ώσω, δεδήλωκα, *to manifest, show, make evident ; to set forth, relate,*

δημαγωγέω 32 διαζεύγνυμι

declare; A., CP. D., πρός: i. 9. 28: ii. 1.1; 2. 18 (ἐδήλωσε τοῦτο *this showed itself, became evident*, 577 c; or *he showed this*); 5. 26: vii. 7. 35.

δημ-αγωγέω, ήσω, (δημ-αγωγός a DEMAGOGUE, δῆμος, ἄγω) *to play the demagogue* or *curry favor* with, *win by popular arts*, A., vii. 6. 4.

Δημ-άρᾱτος, ου, *Demarātus*, *v. l.* for Δαμάρατος, ii. 1. 3: vii. 8. 17.

Δημο-κράτης, εος, *Democrates*, a Temenite, a trusty scout, iv. 4. 15.

Δημοσ-άδης, *v. l.* for Μηδοσάδης. [**δῆμος**, ου, ὁ, *the people, the commons*. Der. DEMO-CRACY.]

‡**δημόσιος**, α, ον, belonging to the people, being *public property :* τὰ δημόσια *the public money :* iv. 6. 16.

δηόω, ώσω, δεδήωκα 1., (δήϊος *hostile*) *to ravage, lay waste*, A., v. 5. 7.

δή-που adv., *doubtless, surely, certainly, of course*, iii. 1. 42; 2. 15.

δῆσαι, -σας, -σω, see δέω, *to bind*.

δηχθείς, see δάκνω, iii. 2. 18.

διά,* by apostr. δι', prep. w. G. and A., (akin to δύο and Lat. dis-) *through :* more literally, w. GEN. (of place, time, means, manner, &c.), i. 2. 5: ii. 5. 21 s: iv. 6. 22: διὰ ταχέων through quick measures, *rapidly*, i. 5. 9 : αὐτοῖς διὰ φιλίας ἰέναι to go to them through the way of friendship, *to seek their friendship*, διὰ παντὸς πολέμου αὐτοῖς ἰέναι *to wage utter war with them*, iii. 2. 8: διὰ τέλους through the completion, *throughout*, vi. 6. 11: — w. ACC., causal, *through the influence, agency,* or *aid of; on account of, by reason of, for the sake of, for, through;* i. 2. 8 ; 7. 5 s: vii. 7.7, 49 s. In compos., *through* (of place, time, completion, &c.); *apart, asunder, about, abroad*, denoting division or distribution, cf. Lat. dis-.

Δία, Διΐ, Διός, see Ζεύς, i. 7. 9.

δια-βαίνω,* βήσομαι, βέβηκα, 2 a. ἔβην, *to go* or *pass through, over,* or *across, to cross*, A., διά : *to step apart, stride, straddle:* i. 2. 6; 4. 14 s: iv. 3. 8.

δια-βάλλω,* βαλῶ, βέβληκα, 2 a. ἔβαλον, to pierce with words like darts, *to calumniate, traduce, slander, accuse* or *state falsely* or *maliciously, insinuate*, A., AE., πρός, ὡς, i. 1. 3 : vii. 5. 8.

†**διάβασις**, εως, ἡ, *the act, means,* or *place* of *crossing; a crossing, passage; ford, bridge, ferry; temporary bridge;* i. 5. 12 : ii. 3. 10.

†**διαβατέος**, α, ον, *that must be crossed, to be crossed*, ii. 4. 6: vi. 5. 12 s.

†**διαβατός, ή, όν**, *that may be crossed, passable, fordable*, i. 4. 18 : ii. 5. 9.

δια-βέβηκα, -βάς, -βῆναι, -βῶ, &c., see δια-βαίνω, i. 2. 6 ; 4. 14, 16, 18.

‡**δια-βιβάζω**, βιβάσω βιβῶ, (βιβάζω *to make go*, causative of βαίνω) *to carry* or *bring across* or *over, take* or *lead across, transport*, A., iii. 5. 2, 8.

διαβολή, ῆς, (δια-βάλλω) *calumny, slander, false accusation*, ii. 5. 5.

δι-αγγέλλω, ελῶ, ἤγγελκα, to carry word through, *report, announce, communicate*, A. D., εἰς : *M. to pass the word* [through] *one to another:* i. 6. 2 : ii. 3. 7 : iii. 4. 36 : vii. 1. 14.

δια-γελάω, άσομαι, *to make sport of* among others, *expose to ridicule, laugh at, jeer at, mock*, A., ii. 6. 26.

δια-γίγνομαι,* γενήσομαι, γεγένημαι & 2 pf. γέγονα, 2 a. ἐγενόμην, *to come* or *get through, subsist, continue, pass time*, A. P., ἐν, i. 5. 6; 10.19 : ii. 6. 5.

δι-αγκυλόομαι, ώσομαι, ἠγκύλωμαι, (ἀγκύλη *a loop*, the leathern thong of a javelin, fr. ἄγκος) *to insert one's finger in the thong* of a javelin, in immediate preparation for hurling it : διηγκυλωμένοι *with their fingers in the thongs*. The ἀγκύλη (Lat. amentum) was prob. fastened to the javelin at or near the centre of gravity, and was so used in throwing as to give greater force or (through rotation) steadiness to the motion. iv. 3. 28 : v. 2. 12 : *v. l.* δι-αγκυλίζομαι, ἰσομαι, ἤχα, ἠγκύλισμαι.

δι-άγω,* ἄξω, ἦχα, 2 a. ἤγαγον, *to lead* or *carry through* or *across, bring over, transport*, A.; *to pass* time, A.; without an acc. expressed, *to pass the time, live, continue, be constantly*, P.; i. 2. 11 : ii. 4. 28 : iii. 1. 43 ; 5. 10.

δι-αγωνίζομαι, ἴσομαι ιοῦμαι, ἠγώνισμαι, *to contend throughout* or *constantly*, πρός, iv. 7. 12.

δια-δέχομαι, δέξομαι, δέδεγμαι, to receive one from another through a line, *to relieve one another, succeed*, i. 5. 2.

δια-δίδωμι,* δώσω, δέδωκα, a. ἔδωκα (δῶ, δοίην, &c.), *to dis-tribute*, A. D. Ι., i. 9. 22; 10. 18 : v. 8. 7: vii. 7. 56.

διάδοχος, ου, ὁ, (δια-δέχομαι) *a successor*, D., vii. 2. 5.

δια-ζεύγνυμι,* ζεύξω, ἔζευχα 1., pf. *p.* ἔζευγμαι, *to un-yoke, disunite, separate*, A. ἀπό, iv. 2. 10.

δια-θεάομαι, άσομαι, τεθέαμαι, to look through, observe, consider, CP. G. of theme, iii. 1. 19.

δι-αιθριάζω, άσω, (αίθρία) dis-serenasco, to be clearing up or away [the clouds dispersing, hence διά], iv. 4. 10 : v. l. συν-αιθριάζω.

δι-αιρέω,* ήσω, ήρηκα, 2 a. εΐλον, to take apart, and thus destroy or remove, A., ii. 4. 22 : v. 2. 21.

διά-κειμαι,* κείσομαι,to be arranged, dis-posed, or affected, ch. of the state of the mind, D., πρός, ii. 5. 27; 6. 12 : iii. 1. 3 : vii. 3. 17 (impers.; yet by some, of the gift, to be disposed of).

δια-κελεύομαι, εύσομαι, to exhort or encourage through an undertaking, &c., to cheer on, D., iii. 4. 45 : iv. 7. 26.

δια-κινδυνεύω, εύσω, to expose one's self throughout, meet all dangers, incur all risks, hazard a battle, i. 8. 6.

δια-κλάω, κλάσω l., (κλάω to break) to break in pieces, A., vii. 3. 22.

διᾱκονέω, ήσω, δεδιᾱκόνηκα, (διά-κονος a waiter, one who goes through the dust, κόνις · or akin to διώκω) to wait upon, serve, iv. 5. 33.

δια-κόπτω,* κόψω, κέκοφα, 2 a. p. έκόπην, to cut through or in pieces, break through, A., i. 8. 10 : iv. 8. 11.

διᾱκόσιοι, αι, α, (δίς, έκατόν) two hundred, i. 2. 9.

δια-κρίνω,* κρῐνῶ, κέκρῐκα, to judge between, decide, vi. 1. 22.

δια-λαγχάνω,* λήξομαι, είληχα, 2 a. έλαχον, to divide, assign, or take by lot, to allot, A., iv. 5. 23.

δια-λαμβάνω,* λήψομαι, είληφα, 2 a. έλαβον, to take apart, separate, divide; to take severally, each his share ; A.; iv. 1. 23 : v. 3. 4.

δια-λέγομαι,* λέξομαι, είλεγμαι, έλέχθην, to share the talk, converse, confer, or treat with, D., πρός, AE., περί, i. 7. 9 : iv. 2. 18 s. Der. DIALOGUE.

δια-λείπω,* λείψω, λέλοιπα, 2 a. έλιπον, to leave an interval, to be or stand apart or at intervals, be distant, A. άπό : τό διαλεΐπον the interval : i. 7. 15 ; 8. 10 : iv. 7. 6 ; 8. 12 s.

δι-αμαρτάνω,* άμαρτήσομαι, ήμάρτηκα, 2 a. ήμαρτον, to stray apart from, fail to find, miss, G., vii. 4. 17.

δια-μάχομαι,* χέσομαι χοῦμαι, μεμάχημαι, to fight [through] hard, contend or resist earnestly or obstinately, D., I., περί, v. 8. 23 ; 6. 25 ? vii. 4. 10.

δια-μένω,* μενῶ, μεμένηκα, to remain through, still remain, vii. 1. 6 : v. 4. 22?

δια-μετρέω, ήσω, to distribute by measure, measure out, A. D., vii. 1. 40 s.

δι-αμπερές (for δι-ανα-περές fr. πείρω to pierce) ch. Ep., quite through, adv., or as prep. w. A., iv. 1. 18 : vii. 8. 14.

δια-νέμω,* νεμῶ, νενέμηκα, a. ένειμα, to distribute, apportion, A. D., vii. 5. 2.

δια-νοέομαι, ήσομαι, νενόημαι, a. ένοήθην, to dis-pose one's thoughts, purpose, purpose, design, intend, I., AE., ii. 4. 17 : v. 7. 15 : vi. 1. 19 : vii. 7. 48 s.

‡διάνοια, as, a design, intent, purpose, project, v. 6. 31.

δια-παντός adv., or διὰ παντός, through everything, throughout, vii. 8. 11.

δια-πέμπω,* πέμψω, πέπομφα, to send about or round, A., i. 9. 27.

δια-περάω, άσω, πεπέρᾱκα, to pass through, cross, A., iv. 3. 21 ?

δια-πλέω,* πλεύσομαι, πέπλευκα, to sail across, είς, vii. 2. 9 ; 3. 3.; 8. 1.

δια-πολεμέω, ήσω, πεπολέμηκα, to carry the war through, fight it out, D., iii. 3. 3.

δια-πορεύω, εύσω, pf. m. πεπόρευμαι, to carry or convey across or over, A.: M. to carry one's self over, to cross, to march or pass through or over, A.: i. 2. 11 ; 5. 18 : iii. 3. 3 : vi. 5. 19.

δι-απορέω, ήσω, ήπόρηκα, A. and M. to be at a loss or in doubt between two courses, vi. 1. 22.

δια-πράττω,* πράξω, πέπρᾱχα, pf. m. and p. πέπραγμαι, to work through, work out, effect, accomplish, obtain, gain ; διαπράξαι όπως εισέλθοι to obtain for him [how he might enter] the privilege of entering : M. much as A., to work out for one's self, effect one's desire, accomplish one's aim, obtain one's request, gain one's point ; to negotiate, stipulate, make an agreement, arrange or settle affairs : A. D., I. (Λ.), CP., παρά, πρός, περί : ii. 3. 20, 25 : iii. 5. 5 : v. 7. 29 : vii. 1. 38 ; 2. 7.

δι-αρπάζω,* άσομαι, ήρπακα, pf. p. ήρπασμαι, di-ripio, to snatch apart, plunder, sack, seize, carry off, A., i. 2. 19, 26 ; 10. 2, 18 : ii. 2. 16 ; 4. 27.

δια-ῥ-ρέω = v. l. διά . ῥέω, v. 3. 8.

δια-ῥ-ρίπτω or ῥιπτέω,* ῥίψω, ἔῥρῑφα, to throw about, scatter, A., v. 8. 6.

†διάρριψις, εως, ἡ, a throwing about, scattering, v. 8. 7.
δια-σημαίνω, ανῶ, a. ἐσήμηνα or ᾶνα, to signify or indicate a decision between two courses, CP., ii. 1. 23.
δια-σκηνέω (intrans.), ήσω, & δια-σκηνόω (trans.?), ώσω, to encamp apart, separate for quarters, κατά, εἰς, iv. 4. 8, 10; 5. 29.
†δια-σκηνητέον ἐστίν, it is necessary to encamp apart, εἰς, iv. 4. 14.
δια-σπάω,* σπάσω, ἔσπᾶκα, pf. p. ἔσπασμαι, a. p. ἐσπάσθην, to draw apart, separate, scatter, disperse, A., i. 5. 9 : iii. 4. 20 : iv. 8. 10, 17.
δια-σπείρω,* σπερῶ, ἔσπαρκα 1., pf. p. ἔσπαρμαι, 2 a. p. ἐσπάρην, to scatter, disperse, spread, trans.: M., intrans.: i. 8. 25 : ii. 4. 3 : vi. 3. 19 ; 5. 28.
δια-στάς, -στῆναι, see δι-ίστημι.
δια-σφενδονάω, ήσω, to sling or throw in all directions, iv. 2. 3.
διά-σχω, -σχοιμι, see δι-έχω.
δια-σώζω, σώσω, σέσωκα, a. p. ἐσώθην, to preserve through danger, save, keep or bring safe: P. & M. to be saved or brought safe, save one's self or one's own, arrive safely: A. D., εἰς, πρός: v. 4. 5; 5. 13; 6.18 : vi. 6. 5.
δια-τάττω,* τάξω, τέταχα, a. p. ἐτάχθην, to arrange, draw up, or distribute, in order of battle, A., i. 7. 1.
δια-τείνω,* τενῶ, τέτακα, a. ἔτεινα, to stretch out: M. to strain or exert one's self; πᾶν πρὸς ὑμᾶς δ. to use every effort with you, vii. 6. 36.
δια-τελέω,* ἔσω ῶ, τετέλεκα, to finish through or entirely, complete, A.: w. A. understood (476. 2) to finish the way, complete the distance ; to fill up the time, to continue, be continually or constantly, P.: i. 5. 7 : iii. 4. 17 : iv. 3. 2 ; 5. 11.
δια-τήκω,* τήξω, 2 pf. τέτηκα, to melt through, trans.: M. and 2 pf., intrans., iv. 5. 6.
δια-τίθημι,* θήσω, τέθεικα, a. ἔθηκα (θῶ, &c.), dis-pono, to dis-pose in mind ; to dispose of, handle, treat or serve ; A., i. 1. 5 : iv. 7. 4 : M. to dispose of for one's own profit, sell, A.: vi. 6. 37: vii. 4. 2.
δια-τρέφω,* θρέψω, τέτροφα, 2 a. p. ἐτράφην, to feed through, nourish, sustain, A., iv. 7. 17.
†δια-τρῑβή, ῆς, delay, vi. 1. 1.
δια-τρίβω, τρίψω, τέτρῑφα, to rub through, wear away, waste, pass or spend time, A.; w. A. understood, to spend the time, delay, tarry ; i. 5. 9 : ii. 3. 9: iv. 6. 9: vii. 2. 3.
δια-φαίνω,* φανῶ, πέφαγκα, to show through : M. to appear or shine through, v. 2. 29 : 2 a. p. impers. διεφάνη [it] the light shone through, vii. 8. 14.
†διαφανῶς (διαφανής transparent) transparently, clearly, manifestly, vi. 1. 24.
†διαφερόντως surpassingly, pre-eminently, peculiarly, i. 9. 14.
δια-φέρω,* οἴσω,ἐνήνοχα, a.ἤνεγκα or -ον, dif-fero, to DIF-FER from, surpass, excel, G. AE., ἤ · impers. w. I., διέφερεν ἀλέξασθαι it was different or easier to repel ; or by pers. constr., διέφερον ἀλέξασθαι they were [different] better able, or found it easier to repel, 573 ; or ii. 3. 15 : iii. 1. 37 ; 4. 33 : οἱ ποταμοὶ διοίσουσιν [v. l. διήσουσιν] the rivers will [carry us across] permit us to cross (acc. to some, will differ in size), iii. 2. 23: M. to differ with, quarrel, be at variance, ἀμφί, πρός, iv. 5. 17.
δια-φεύγω,* φεύξομαι, πέφευγα, 2 a. ἔφυγον, to flee through, get away, escape, A. ἐξ, v. 2. 3: vi. 3. 4: vii. 3. 43.
δια-φθείρω,* φθερῶ, ἔφθαρκα, 2 a. p.˙ ἐφθάρην, to spoil utterly, ruin, destroy; to corrupt, seduce, bribe ; A.: P. to be destroyed or ruined, go to ruin, waste away, &c.: iii. 3. 5 : iv. 1. 11 ; 5. 12.
διάφορος, ον, s., (δια-φέρω) at variance : neut. subst., variance, disagreement, cause of difference or dissension, iv. 6. 3 : vii. 6. 15.
δια-φυή, ῆς, (φυή growth, fr. φύω) growth between, a partition or division, v. 4. 29.
δια-φυλάττω, άξω, πεφύλαχα, to guard throughout : M. to take care or exercise precaution throughout, AE. ώς, vii. 6. 22 ?
δια-χάζω,* (χάζω to drive back, ch. Ep.) to draw apart, separate, intrans., iv. 8. 18 ?
δια-χειμάζω, άσω, (χεῖμα winter, fr. χέω to pour) to go through or pass the winter, to winter, vii. 6. 31.
δια-χειρίζω, ίσω ιῶ, κεχείρικα, (χείρ) to pass through one's hands, administer, manage, A., i. 9. 17.
δια-χωρέω, ήσω, κεχώρηκα, to go or work through : impers. κάτω διεχώρει αὐτοῖς they had a diarrhœa, iv. 8. 20.

†διδάσκαλος, ου, ὁ, a teacher, ii. 6. 12.
διδάσκω,* ἄξω, δεδίδαχα, to teach, instruct, inform, A. CP., I.: P. to be taught, learn: i. 7. 4: ii. 5. 6: iii. 3. 4; 4. 32: vi. 5. 18. Der. DIDACTIC.
δίδημι,* ch. Ep., a prolonged form of δέω to bind, q. v.; v. 8. 24.
δίδωμι,* δώσω, δέδωκα, a. ἔδωκα (δῶ, &c.), pf. p. δέδομαι, a. p., ἐδόθην, Lat. do, to give, grant, bestow, A. D., i. 1. 6, 8 s; 2. 12, 27: δοθῆναι αὐτῷ σώζειν that it should be granted to him to save, the privilege of saving, 663 b, ii. 3. 25; cf. vii. 3. 13. Der. DOSE.
δι-έβαινον, -έβην, see δια-βαίνω.
δι-εγενόμην, see δια-γίγνομαι, ii. 6. 5.
δι-είργω,* εἴρξω, to intercept (sc. αὐτούς), intervene, iii. 1. 2.
δι-εῖχον, see δι-έχω, i. 8. 17.
δι-ελαύνω,* ἐλάσω ἐλῶ, ἐλήλακα, a. ἤλασα, to ride, drive, or charge, through, i. 5. 12; 10. 7: ii. 3. 19.
δι-ελθεῖν, -ελήλυθα, see δι-έρχομαι.
δι-ελών, see δι-αιρέω, ii. 4. 22.
δι-εξ-έρχομαι,* ἐλεύσομαι, ἐλήλυθα, 2 a. ἦλθον, to come out through, εἰς, vi. 6. 38?
δι-έρχομαι,* ἐλεύσομαι, ἐλήλυθα, 2 a. ἦλθον, to go or come through, pass or march through, cross, A., διά: of a rumor, to go abroad, spread: i. 4. 7: ii. 4. 12: iv. 1. 3, 5; 5. 22: v. 4. 14.
δι-ερωτάω, to appeal to, v. l. for ἐρωτάω, iv. 1. 26.
δι-εσπάρθαι, see δια-σπείρω, ii. 4. 3.
δι-έχω,* ἕξω, ἔσχηκα, ipf. εἶχον, 2 a. ἔσχον, [to have one's self apart] to be apart, distant, or separated, to diverge, G., ἀπό: τὸ διέχον, the intervening space, interval: i. 8. 17: iii. 4. 22.
δι-ηγέομαι, ἡσομαι, ἥγημαι, to lead through a story, to relate or state in detail, narrate, A., iv. 3. 8: vii. 4. 8.
δι-ήλασα, see δι-ελαύνω, i. 10. 6.
δι-ῆλθον, see δι-έρχομαι, i. 4. 7.
δι-ίημι,* ἥσω, εἶκα, a. ἧκα (ὦ, &c.), to send through, permit to go through, let pass, A. διά, iii. 2. 23? iv. 1. 8.
δι-ίστημι,* στήσω, ἔστηκα, 2 a. ἔστην, to station apart: M., w. pf. and 2 a. act., to stand apart, be stationed at intervals, open the ranks, i. 5. 2; 8. 20.
δίκαιος, α, ον, c., s., (δίκη) just, right, righteous, upright, proper, reasonable, I., i. 3. 5: iii. 1. 37: τὸ δίκαιον justice, right, pl. rights: ἐκ τοῦ δικαίου [out of] according to justice, in a just

way, i. 9. 19: δίκαια ποιεῖν to do what is right, i. 3. 5; τὰ δίκαια λαμβάνειν to take justice, vii. 7. 17: οὓς ἐδόκουν δικαιοτάτους εἶναι whom they deemed to be the most proper to invite, or the best entitled to an invitation, = v. l. οὓς ἐδόκει δικαιότατον εἶναι whom it seemed to be the most proper to invite, 573, vi. 1. 3.
↓δικαιοσύνη, ης, justice (as a quality), uprightness, righteousness, i. 9. 16.
↓δικαιότης, ητος, ἡ, = δικαιοσύνη, ii. 6. 26.
↓δικαίως justly, with reason, reasonably, properly, deservedly, ii. 3. 19.
†δικαστής, οῦ, (δικάζω to judge) a judge, v. 7. 34.
δίκη, ης, justice or right; just retribution either (1) to him who has suffered, or (2) to him who has done wrong (ἡ ἐσχάτη δίκη the severest retribution or punishment, v. 6. 15); also (3) sing. or pl., a process of justice, judicial proceedings, trial; G. Thus, (1, 3) δίκην διδόναι poenas dare, to give retribution or satisfaction, make amends, pay the penalty, suffer punishment; to render a judicial account of one's conduct; D.; ii. 6. 21: v. 7. 29; 8. 1: δίκην λαμβάνειν poenas sumere, to take satisfaction, obtain amends or justice, inflict punishment, v. 8. 17: δίκην ἔχειν to have satisfaction, vii. 4. 24: — (2, 3) δίκην ἐπιτιθέναι to inflict retribution, punishment, or just desert, p. i. 3. 10, 20: iii. 2. 8: τῆς δίκης τυχεῖν to receive one's desert, vi. 6. 25: ἔχειν τὴν δίκην to have one's desert or due, receive the punishment due, ii. 5. 38, 41: ὑπέχειν δίκην to undergo retribution, make amends, submit to an investigation, trial, or punishment, render account, D., v. 8. 1, 18: vi. 6. 15: εἰς δίκας καταστῆσαι to present for trial, bring to trial, v. 7. 34.
δι-μοιρία, ας, (δίς, μοῖρα portion) a double portion, twice as much, vii. 2. 36.
δινέω, ήσω, ch. poet., (δίνη a whirl) to whirl, trans.: M., intrans., vi. 1. 9.
διό adv. = δι' ὅ, on account of which, wherefore, i. 2. 21: v. 5. 10: vii. 6. 39.
δί-οδος, ου, ἡ, a way or journey through, passage, v. 4. 9.
δι-οίσω, see δια-φέρω, iii. 2. 23?
δι-οράω,* ὄψομαι, ἑώρακα or ἑδράκα, to see through, perceive, discover, A., v. 2. 30.

δι-ορύττω, * ύξω, ὀρώρυχα, to dig through, A., vii. 8. 13 s.

διότι* conj., (δι' ὅ τι) on account of this that, because, ii. 2. 14.

†δί-πηχυς, υ, g. εος, (πῆχυς) two cubits long, iv. 2. 28.

†δι-πλάσιος, α, ον, (πλάττω to form) two-fold, double, twice as much or many: διπλάσιον double the distance, twice as far, G.: iii. 3. 16 : iv. 1. 13.

†δι-πλεθρος, ον, (πλέθρον) two hundred feet long or wide, iv. 3. 1.

†δι-πλόος, όη, όον, contr. δι-πλοῦς, ῆ, οῦν, (-πλοος, akin to πλέκω) duplex, two-fold, double, vii. 6. 7. Der. DIPLOMA.

[δίς adv., also in compos. δι-, (δύο) twice, doubly.]

‡δισ-χίλιοι, αι, α, two thousand, i. 1. 10 ; 2. 9.

διφθέρα, ας, (δέφω to tan) a tanned or prepared skin, a leathern bag or pouch, i. 5. 10 : v. 2. 12. Der. DIPHTHERIA.

‡διφθέρινος, η, ον, made of skins, leathern, ii. 4. 28.

δί-φρος, ου, ὁ, (δίς, φέρω) a seat, originally for two, as in the old chariot for the warrior and the driver, i. 8. 10 : vii. 3. 29.

δίχα adv., (δίς) in two, asunder: δίχα ποιεῖν to divide, vi. 4. 11.

‡διχάζω, άσω, to divide or separate, intrans., iv. 8. 18 ?

διψάω (contr. -ῶ, -ῇς, -ῇ),* ήσω, δεδίψηκα, (δίψα thirst) to thirst, be thirsty, iv. 5. 27.

†διωκτέος, α, ον, to be pursued: διωκτέον ἐστίν it is necessary to pursue, chase must be given, iii. 3. 8.

διώκω,* ώξω, oftener ώξομαι, δεδίωχα, (δίω to run away, flee) to make flee or run, pursue, chase, give chase, drive or follow as an enemy, A. εἰς, &c., i. 4. 7 s; 5. 2 s; 8. 21 : as intrans., to hasten or gallop off, vii. 2. 20.

‡δίωξις, εως, ἡ, act of pursuing, pursuit, iii. 4. 5.

†διῶρυξ, υχος, ἡ, (δι-ορύττω) a canal, trench, i. 7. 15 : ii. 4. 13, 17.

†δόγμα, ατος, τό, a decree, ordinance, DOGMA, iii. 3. 5 : vi. 4. 11 ; 6. 8, 27.

δοθῆναι, δοίην, see δίδωμι, ii. 3. 25.

δοκέω,* δόξω, δεδόκηκα poet., (1) of the action of the mind itself, to think, suppose, imagine, expect, I. (A.), i. 7. 1 ; 8. 2 : δεδογμένος thought best, approved, determined, resolved on, voted, iii. 2. 39 : τούτους τί [sc. παθεῖν] δοκεῖτε; what do you think [these suffered] was the case with these? v. 7. 26: — (2) of the action of an object upon the mind, to seem, appear, Lat. videor ; to seem good, best, expedient, right, proper; to be approved, determined, resolved on, adopted, or voted; both personally and impersonally, and with the former construction for the latter (the two combined, iii. 1. 11 ?), 573 ; D. I. (A.; the inf. often supplied fr. the context); i. 2. 1; 3. 11 s, 18, 20; 4. 7, 15 : δόξαν ταῦτα [sc. ποιεῖν fr. the context, or see 502] it having been voted to pursue this course, or this resolved on, 675 a, iv. 1. 13. With the uses 1 and 2, compare I think and methinks = me-seems = it seems to me. Δοκέω is much used for greater modesty or courtesy of expression, i. 3. 12 ; 7. 4 (αἰσχύνεσθαί μοι δοκῶ, me-thinks I am ashamed): iii. 1. 38 ; cf. 70 m, 654.

δοκιμάζω, άσω, (δόκιμος accepted on proof, fr. δέχομαι) to approve on examination, iii. 3. 20.

δόλιος, α, ον, (δόλος) deceitful, treacherous, perfidious, i. 4. 7 ?

δόλιχος, ου, ὁ, the long race, protracted to several miles, by an extension of the course, or a repetition of it, iv. 8. 27.

δόλος, ου, ὁ, dolus, a wile, fraud, deceit, treachery, v. 6. 29.

Δόλοψ, οπος, ὁ, a Dolopian. The Dolopes were a rude but hardy tribe, living on both sides of the southern range of Mt. Pindus. i. 2. 6.

†δόξα, ης, opinion, expectation; reputation, credit, glory, εἰς : ii. 1. 18 : vi. 1. 21 ; 5. 14. Der. ORTHO-DOXY.

‡δοξάζω, άσω, to commend, extol, A., vi. 1. 32 ?

δόξαι, δόξω, see δοκέω, i. 3. 20 ; 4. 15.

δοράτιον, ου, τό, (dim. of δόρυ) a short spear, of special use in carrying booty or baggage, yet also used as a weapon, vi. 4. 23.

δορκάς, άδος, ἡ, (δέρκομαι, pf. δέδορκα, to look keenly) a small, swift, and beautiful antelope, so named from the lustre of its eye, a gazelle, i. 5. 2 : v. 3. 10. Hence prop. name DORCAS.

δορπηστός, οῦ, or δόρπηστος, ου, ὁ, (δόρπον supper) supper-time, i. 10. 17 : v. l. δόρπιστος.

δόρυ,* δόρατος, τό, (cf. δρῦς oak) a beam or large stick, the shaft of a spear; hence comm. *a spear, lance, pike*, Lat. hasta. The common spear of the Greek hoplite consisted of a long wooden shaft, with a sharp steel point (αἰχμή), and upon the reverse end an iron spike (σαυρωτήρ) for thrusting the spear into the ground in time of rest. Ἐπὶ δόρυ [spear-ward] *to the right*, since the spear was carried in the right hand; cf. παρ' ἀσπίδας. i. 8. 18: iii. 5. 7: iv. 3. 29; 7. 16.

‡δορυ-φόρος, ου, ὁ, (φέρω) *a spear-bearer, spear-man*, a forager carrying a spear, v. 2. 4: cf. δοράτιον.

†δουλεία, as, *slavery, servitude, bondage, subjection*, vii. 7. 32.

†δουλεύω, εύσω, δεδούλευκα, *to be a slave*, iv. 8. 4.

δοῦλος, ου, ὁ, (δέω to bind) *a slave, bondman, bond-servant*; under an absolute government, *a subject*; i. 9. 15, 29: ii. 5. 32, 38: iii. 1. 17.

δοῦναι, δούς, see δίδωμι, i. 2. 12.

†δουπέω,* ήσω, δέδουπα, ch. Ep., *to make a din, to clash*, D. of instrument, πρός, i. 8. 18. Onomatopoetic.

δοῦπος, ου, ὁ, ch. poet., *a loud noise, din, uproar, hubbub*, ii. 2. 19.

Δρακόντιος, ου, *Dracontius*, a Spartan exile, iv. 8. 25: vi. 6. 30.

δράμοιμι, δραμοῦμαι, see τρέχω.

†δρεπανη-φόρος, ον, (φέρω) *scythe-bearing, scythe-armed*, i. 7. 10s; 8. 10.

δρέπανον, ου, τό, or poet. δρεπάνη, ης, (δρέπω to pluck) *a scythe, sickle*, i. 8. 10.

Δρίλαι, ῶν, the *Drilæ*, a warlike people dwelling near Trebizond, v. 2. 1s.

δρόμος, ου, ὁ, (τρέχω, pf. δέδρομα) the act or place of running; *a run, running, race; race-course*: δρόμῳ *upon the run, as in a race, at full speed, rapidly*: δρόμος ἐγένετο τοῖς στρατιώταις the soldiers began to run, 459: i. 2. 17; 8. 18s: iv. 8. 25s.

δύναμαι,* δυνήσομαι, δεδύνημαι, ipf. ἐδυνάμην or ἠδυνάμην, a. p. ἐδυνήθην, ἠδυνήθην, or r. ἐδυνάσθην, *to be able (can), have power*, I. (often understood); hence elliptically, *to be strong or powerful; to be equal or equivalent to, to mean*, A.; i. 1. 4; 5. 6; 7. 5: ii. 2. 12s: iv. 5. 11s: οἱ μέγιστον (or μέγιστα) δυνάμενοι [sc. ποιεῖν] *the most powerful*, ii. 6. 21: οὐκ ἐδυνάμην ζῆν *I could not (consent to) live*, vii. 2. 33.

It is often used or to be supplied with a rel. and superl., 553 c: ὡς μάλιστα ἐδύνατο ἐπικρυπτόμενος [concealing it as he best could] *as secretly as possible*, i. 1. 6; ᾗ ἐδύνατο τάχιστα [as he could most rapidly] *as rapidly as he could*, i. 2. 4; ὡς ἄν δύνηται πλείστους *as many as he could*, i. 6. 3.

‡δύναμις, εως, ἡ, *ability, power, might, strength, force; military force, forces, troops, army* (so pl. i. 5. 9): κατὰ or εἰς δύναμιν *according to* or *to the extent of one's ability*: i. 1. 6; 6. 7: ii. 3. 23: iii. 2. 9. Der. DYNAMIC.

‡δυνάστης, ου, *a chief* or *powerful man, lord, nobleman*, i. 2. 20. Der. DYNASTY.

‡δυνατός, ή, όν, c., s., actively, *able, competent, powerful, strong*, I.; passively, *possible, practicable, feasible*, D. I.; i. 3. 17; 9. 24: ii. 6. 8, 19: iv. 1. 12, 24: ἐκ τῶν δυνατῶν *from [the possibles] the means in their power*, iv. 2. 23. It is often used or to be supplied with a rel. and superl., 553 c: ᾗ δυνατὸν μάλιστα [so as is possible, most implicitly] *as implicitly as possible*, i. 3. 15; ὅτι ἀπαρασκευαστότατον [according to what is possible, most unprepared] *as unprepared as possible*, ὅτι πλείστους *as many as possible*, i. 1. 6; ὡς τάχιστα πορεύεσθαι *to proceed as speedily as possible*, i. 3. 14.

δύω,* δύσω, *to make enter, put on*: hence δύνω & δύομαι, δύσομαι, δέδυκα, 2 a. ἔδυν, of the sun, *to enter* the western sea, *to set*, i. 10. 15: ii. 2. 3.

δύο,* δυοῖν, or, w. plur. nouns, indecl., *duo, TWO*, i. 1. 1: iii. 2. 37: vi. 4. 12: vii. 5. 9; 6. 1. Der. DUAL.

[δυσ-* inseparable particle, *ill, mis-, un-*, DYS-, *with difficulty*.]

δυσ-βατος, ον, *difficult of access*, v. 2. 2: iv. 1. 25?

δυσ-διάβατος, ον, *difficult to pass*, vi. 5. 19?

δυσμή, ῆς, (δύνω) usu. in pl., *setting of the sun; ἡλίου δυσμαί sun-set*; vi. 4. 26; 5. 32: vii. 3. 34.

δυσ-πάριτος, ον, (πάρ-ειμι to pass) *hard* or *difficult to pass*, iv. 1. 25: v. l. δυσπόριστος (for δυσπρόσιτος *difficult of access?*) or δύσβατος.

δυσ-πόρευτος, ον, (πορεύω) *difficult of passage* or *to pass*, D., i. 5. 7.

†δυσπορία, as, *difficulty of crossing, difficult passage*, G., iv. 3. 7.

δύσ-πορος, ον, difficult of passage, hard to cross, ii. 5. 9: v. 1. 13: vi. 5. 12.

δύσ-χρηστος, ον, (χράομαι) hard to use or manage, of little use, unserviceable, iii. 4. 19.

δυσ-χωρία, ας, (χῶρος) the ruggedness or difficulty of the country, difficult ground, iii. 5. 16.

δῶ, δώσω, see δίδωμι, i. 7. 7.

δώ-δεκα indecl., (δύο, δέκα) twelve, i. 2. 10; 7. 15.

†δωρέομαι, ήσομαι, δεδώρημαι, to make or give a present, to present, give, A. D., vii. 3. 18, 26 s; 5. 3.

†δωρο-δοκέω, ήσω, (δέχομαι) to receive a gift, take a bribe, vii. 6. 17.

δῶρον, ου, (δίδωμι) a gift, present, reward, i. 2. 27; 9. 14, 22 : ii. 1. 10.

E.

ἐᾷ, ἐᾶν, &c., see ἐάω, iii. 3. 3.
ἑάλωκα, ἑάλων, see ἁλίσκομαι, iii. 4. 8.
ἐάν,* (εἰ, ἄν) contr. ἤν or "ἄν, conj. followed by the subj., if perhaps, if haply, if, in case that : ἐὰν μὴ if not, unless, except : ἐάν τε . . ἐάν τε [both if . . and if] whether . . or : i. 3. 14, 18 s; 4. 12 : vii. 1. 31; 3. 37.

‡ἐάν-περ, if indeed, if only, iv. 6. 17?
ἐαρίζω, ίσω ιῶ, (ἔαρ ver, spring) to pass or spend the spring, iii. 5. 15.

ἑ-αυτοῦ,* ἦς, contr. αὐτοῦ, ἧς, refl. pron., (ἕ him, αὐτός) sui, of himself, herself, itself, ch. used when the reflex reference is emphatic or direct. In the gen., it often supplies the place of a possessive pron. (suus): οἱ ἑαυτοῦ his own men, τὰ ἑαυτῶν their own affairs, interests, or possessions. i. 1. 5; 2. 7, 15: iii. 1. 16. V. l. for ἐμαυτοῦ or σαυτοῦ, 539 d, vi. 6. 15: vii. 5. 5 : often for αὐτοῦ, or the common form.

ἐάω,* ἐάσω, εἴᾱκα, ipf. εἴων, to permit, allow, suffer, let, A. I.: to let be, let alone, leave, dismiss, have nothing to do with, A. D.: οὐκ ἐᾶν to forbid, prohibit, protest, 686 i : i. 4. 7, 9; 9. 18 : vii. 3. 2; 4. 10 s, 20, 24.

†ἑβδομήκοντα indecl., seventy, iv. 7. 8.
ἕβδομος, η, ον, (ἑπτά) seventh, vi. 2. 12.

'Εβροζέλμις or 'Εβολζέμιος, ου, v. l. for 'Αβροζέλμης, vii. 6. 43.

ἐγ-, the form which ἐν takes in compos. before a palatal, 150.

ἐγ-γίγνομαι,* γενήσομαι, γεγένημαι & 2 pf. γέγονα, to take place, be produced, or arise in, D., v. 8. 3.

‡ἔγ-γονος, ου, ὁ, a descendant, iii.2.14?

ἐγγυάω,* ἤσω, ἠγγύηκα, (ἐγ-γύη a pledye in hand, fr. γυῖον limb, hand) to put in hand, pledge : M. to pledge one's self, engage, promise, I. (A)., vii. 4. 13.

†ἐγγύθεν adv., from nigh at hand, iv. 2. 27.

ἐγγύς* adv., c. & s. ἐγγύτερον, τατα, or τέρω, τάτω, near, nigh, close at hand, G.; nearly, closely : superl. w. art. the nearest, last : i. 8. 8; 10. 10 : ii. 2. 11, 16 s; 4. 1: iv. 2. 28.

ἐγείρω,* ἐγερῶ, ἐγήγερκα 1., to wake another : 2 pf. pret. ἐγρήγορα to be or keep awake, keep watch, iv. 6. 22.

ἐγενόμην, ἐγιγνόμην, see γίγνομαι.

ἐγ-καλέω,* καλέσω καλῶ, κέκληκα, to call upon as responsible, make a demand upon, charge, blame, throw the blame upon, find fault with, D. CP.; to call upon one for, demand, A.; vii. 5. 7; 7. 33, 44, 47.

ἐγ-καλύπτω, ύψω, κεκάλυφα 1., (καλύπτω to wrap, cover) to wrap up in a covering, A., iv. 5. 19.

ἔγ-κειμαι,* κείσομαι, to lie in or therein, iv. 5. 26.

ἐγ-κέλευστος, ον, (κελεύω) urged on, instructed, incited, bidden, i. 3. 13.

ἐγ-κέφαλος, ου, ὁ, (κεφαλή) the brain; the brain, crown, or cabbage of the palm, a large cabbage-like bud at the top of the stalk, ii. 3. 16.

ἐγ-κρατής, ές, (κράτος) in power over, in possession of, master of, G., i. 7. 7: v. 4. 15.

ἔγνωκα, ἔγνων, ἐγνώσθην, see γιγνώσκω, i. 3. 2 : ii. 4. 22 : iii. 1. 43.

ἐγρήγορα, -ειν, see ἐγείρω, iv. 6. 22.

ἐγ-χαλῑνόω, ώσω, pf. p. κεχαλίνωμαι, to put a bit in the mouth of, to bridle, A., vii. 2. 21; 7. 6.

ἐγ-χειρέω, ήσω, ἐγ-κεχείρηκα, (χείρ) to take in hand, undertake, make an attempt, v. 1. 8.

ἐγ-χειρίδιον, ου, τό, (χείρ) a handknife, dagger, iv. 3. 12.

ἐγ-χειρίζω, ίσω ιῶ, κεχείρικα, (χείρ) to put in the hands of another, commit, entrust, A. D., iii. 2. 8.

ἐγ-χέω,* f. χέω or χεῶ, κέχυκα, (χέω to pour) to pour in wine for a libation, D., iv. 3. 13.

ἐγώ,* ἐμοῦ or μοῦ, pl. ἡμεῖς, (the

ἔγωγε　39　εἰμί

forms beginning w. ἐ- having comm. some emphasis, and those w. μ- being enclitic) ego, mei, nos, *I*, *we*, i. 3. 3, 5 s: πρός με for πρὸς ἐμέ, 788 e, iii. 2. 2: ἡμᾶς = ἐμέ, i. 7. 7: ἐγῷμαι by crasis for ἐγὼ οἶμαι, *I think*, iii. 1. 35? Der. EGOTISM.

‡ἔγω-γε,* ἐμοῦ γε, ἔμοιγε, ἔμεγε or ἐμέ γε, equidem, *I at least, I for my part, I certainly*, i. 4. 8 : vii. 1. 30.

ἔδει, ἐδεῖτο, see δέω, i.5.14: iv.1.13.

ἔδεισα, ἐδεδοίκειν, see δείδω, i. 10. 9.

ἐδήδοκα, see ἐσθίω, iv. 8. 20.

ἐδόκουν, ἔδοξα, see δοκέω, i. 3. 20.

ἔδραμον, see τρέχω, iv. 3. 33.

ἔδωκα, ἔδοσαν, see δίδωμι, i. 2. 27.

ἔζων, ἔζη, see ζάω, i. 5. 5 : v. 8. 10.

†ἐθελοντής, οῦ, ὁ, *a volunteer;* as adj. *voluntary, willing, of one's own accord*, i. 6. 9 : iv. 1. 26 s.

†ἐθελοντί adv., *willingly*, iii. 3. 18 ?

†ἐθελούσιος, α, ον, *voluntary, of one's own accord*, iv. 6. 19: vi. 5. 14.

ἐθέλω,* ἐθελήσω, ἠθέληκα, by a shorter but less frequent form θέλω, θελήσω, *to be willing, consent, wish, desire, will, choose, please, prefer*, I., τί : οὐκ ἐθέλω, *I am not willing, I will not, I refuse:* ἐθέλων w. adverbial force, *willingly:* i. 2. 26 ; 3. 6, 8 ; 9. 13 s : iv. 4. 5 : vi. 2. 6. Ἐθέλω and βούλομαι are nearly synonymous and may be often interchanged; yet, in strict distinction, ἐθέλω expresses the *wish* or *will* more as a *feeling*, and βούλομαι more as a *rational purpose* or *preference*. Simple *inclination, acquiescence*, or *desire* is rather expressed by ἐθέλω, and *plan* or *determination* by βούλομαι : εἰ ὑμεῖς ἐθέλετε ἐξορμᾶν, ἕπεσθαι βούλομαι *if you are willing to take the lead, I am resolved to follow*, iii. 1. 25 : cf. v. 6. 20 ; 7. 27 s.

ἐθέμην, ἔθηκα, see τίθημι, i. 5. 14.

ἔθνος, εος, τό, *a nation, tribe: κατὰ ἔθνη* or *ἔθνος, according to their nations* or *tribes, by nations* or *tribes:* i. 8. 9: iv. 5. 28: v. 5. 5. Der. ETHNO-LOGY.

εἰ * conj. (becoming ἐάν before the subj., 619 a), si, *if, supposing, provided, in case that*, i. 2. 2 : εἰ μή nisi, *if not, unless, except*, i. 4. 18 : iv. 2. 4 : εἰ δὲ μή *but if not, otherwise*, used even after negative sentences, ii. 2. 2 : iv. 3. 6 : εἴ τις *if any*, sometimes, as a more moderate form of expression, supplying the place of ὅστις *whoever*,

whatever, 639, i. 5. 1 ; 6. 1 ; καὶ εἴ τις νόσῳ *and a few perhaps by sickness*, v. 3. 3 : καὶ εἰ, εἰ καὶ *even if, although, though*, iii. 2. 22, 24 : vi. 6. 27 : — εἰ as compleni., *if, whether, whether not*, i. 3. 5 ; 10. 5 : iii. 2. 22 ; so elliptically, *to see* or *try if, to ascertain whether*, iv. 1. 8 : v. 4. 3.

εἴα, εἴασα, see ἐάω, i. 4. 7 ; 9. 13, 18.

εἶδον, εἰδῶ, εἰδέναι, εἰδώς, &c., see ὁράω. Cf. video, Sans. vid, *to wit*.

‡εἶδος, εος, τό, *appearance, form, beauty*, ii. 3. 16.

εἴην, εἴησαν or εἶεν, see εἰμί, i. 1. 5.

εἰκάζω,* ἄσω, εἴκακα l., pf. *p.* εἴκασμαι or ᾔκασμαι, *to make like, liken*, A.; *to think likely, conjecture, suppose, estimate*, I. (A.), i. 6. 1, 11 ; 10. 16 : pf. *p.* to have been made like, *to resemble*, D., v. 3. 12 ; 4. 12 : — 2 pf. pret. ἔοικεν, 2 plup. ἐῴκειν, *to be like, resemble, seem like*, D. ; *to seem ;* ii. 1. 13 ; 2. 18.

‡εἰκός, ότος, (neut. pt. of εἴκα = ἔοικα) *likely, probable, reasonable, proper, natural*, w. frequent ellipsis of ἐστί or ἦν, I. (A.) : τὸ εἰκός *the likelihood, probability*, &c. : ii. 2. 19 ; 3. 6 : iii. 1. 21.

εἴκοσι(ν) indecl., *twenty*, i. 2. 5, 8.

εἰκότως adv., (εἰκός) *reasonably, naturally, with good reason*, ii. 2. 3.

εἴληφα, -ειν, see λαμβάνω, iv. 5. 35.

εἴληχα, -ειν, see λαγχάνω, iv. 5. 24.

εἵλκον, see ἕλκω, iv. 2. 28 : v. 2. 15.

εἱλόμην, εἷλον, see αἱρέω, i. 3. 5 ; 9. 9.

εἰμί,* ἔσομαι (3 sing. ἔσται), ipf. ἦν, sum, *to be, exist*, the chief substantive verb, variously translated acc. to the context, i. 1. 4 : w. GEN., *to be of* or *one's, belong to; be the property* or *part of*, &c., 437 a, 440, 443, i. 1. 6 : ii. 1. 4, 9 : ὄντα τὸ εὖρος πλέθρου *being* [of] *a plethron in width*, i. 4. 9 : w. DAT., *to be to* or *for* (where *have* is frequent in translation, 459), i. 2. 7 ; 3. 21 : w. a PART., often a stronger form of expression for the simple verb, 679, ii. 2. 13 ; 3. 10 : τὰ ὄντα the things being, *facts, effects, possessions*, iv. 4. 15 : vii. 8. 22 : τῷ ὄντι *in reality* or *fact, really*, v. 4. 20. — Its IMPERS. use (which may usu. be also explained personally, 571 f, h) is extensive : ἔστι *there is* or *it is, it is possible, the part of*, &c., I. (A.), i. 5. 2 s ; ii. 1. 9 : often w. a neut. adj. sing. or pl., as δῆλον ii. 3. 6, ἄβατα iii. 4. 49 : w. a relative,

εἰμι 40 εἰσφέρω

often forming a complex indefinite, 559 a, as ἔστι δ' ὅστις but there is who = but some one, i. 8. 20, ἦν οὕς = some, i. 5. 7, ἔσθ' ὅτε there is when = sometimes, ii. 6. 9; and negatively, οὐκ ἦν ὅπου there was [not where] no place where, iv. 5. 31 (cf. ii. 3. 23), οὐκ ἔστιν ὅπως [there is not how] it cannot be that, ii. 4. 3 (cf. the personal use τοῦτ' ἔστιν ὅπως; is this possible, how? is it possible that? v. 7. 7): τὸ κατὰ τοῦτον εἶναι so far as regards him, τὸ νῦν εἶναι for the present, 665 b, i. 6. 9: iii. 2. 37. — For the accent of the pres. ind., see 787 c, 788 a, b, d, f.

εἶμι,* ipf. ἤειν or ᾖα, to go, come; the pres. regularly used in the ind., and sometimes in other modes, as fut. (εἶμι I am going = I shall go, cf. ἔρχομαι): imv. ἴθι age, come! AE., D. διά, εἶς, ἐπί, &c.: i. 2. 11; 3. 1, 6; 4. 8: iv. 6. 12: vii. 2. 26. For M. ἴεμαι, see ἵημι.

εἶπα, εἶπον, see φημί, i. 3. 7: ii. 1. 21.

εἴ-περ if indeed, if in fact or really, i. 7. 9: ii. 4. 7: iv. 6. 16.

εἰπόμην, see ἔπομαι, iii. 4. 18.

εἴργω or **εἴργω**,* ῥξω, to bar, debar, shut in or out, hem in, exclude, keep off, prevent, A. ἀπό, ἐκ: M. to shut one's self out, get one's self excluded: iii. 1. 12; 3. 16: vi. 3. 8; 6. 16.

εἴρηκα, εἴρημαι, see φημί, i. 2. 5.

εἰρήνη, ης, (εἴρω to join, or to talk) peace, ii. 6. 2, 6: iii. 1. 37.

εἰς,* sometimes **ἐς**, (ἐν-s, 688 d) prep., w. ACC. of place, into, more briefly to or in; at, on, or upon; [to go into] for; sometimes for ἐν by const. præg. 704 a; i. 1. 2 s; 2. 2 s, 24: so of state or action, ii. 6. 17: iii. 1. 43: — of a collection of persons or things, among, to, into the land of, against, i. 1. 11; 6. 7: ii. 2. 20: v. 6. 27 s: — of time, [in passing into] on or upon, in, at, i. 7. 1: ii. 1. 17: iii. 1. 3: — of number or measure, up to, even to, to the number, extent, or depth of, i. 1. 10: ii. 3. 23: vi 4. 16; εἰς ἀφθονίαν [to] in abundance, abundantly, vii. 1. 33; εἰς δύο two by two, ii. 4. 26; εἰς ὀκτώ eight deep, vii. 1. 23: — of aim, end, result, object of reference, &c., for, in respect to, concerning, i. 1. 9; 3. 3; 9. 5, 16, 23: ii. 6. 30. In compos., into, in, &c.

εἶς,* μία, ἕν, g. ἑνός, μιᾶς, one, a single one, an individual; used more strictly as a numeral than one in Eng.;

i. 2. 6; 9. 22: καθ' ἕνα one by one, singly, iv. 7. 8: εἷς τις any single one, εἷς ἕκαστος each individual, each singly, ii. 1. 19: vi. 6. 12, 20.

εἰσ-άγω,* ἄξω, ἦχα, 2 a. ἤγαγον, a. ὄπου there was [not where] no place p. ἤχθην, to lead or bring into or in, A. εἰς, πρός, i. 6. 11? vi. 1. 12.

εἰσ-ακοντίζω, ἴσω ιῶ, to throw or hurl darts in, vii. 4. 15.

εἰσ-βαίνω,* βήσομαι, βέβηκα, 2 a. ἔβην, to go into a vessel, embark, εἰς, v. 7. 15?

εἰσ-βάλλω,* βαλῶ, βέβληκα, 2 a. ἔβαλον, to throw one's self into, effect an entrance or make an irruption into, enter; of streams, to empty into; εἰς; i. 2. 21; 7. 15: v. 4. 10.

εἰσ-βιβάζω, βιβάσω βιβῶ, to put into or on board a vessel, A., v. 3. 1.

εἰσ-βολή, ῆς, (εἰσ-βάλλω) irruption, entrance, pass, i. 2. 21: v. 6. 7.

εἰσ-δύομαι,* δύσομαι, to enter or sink into, εἰς, iv. 5. 14.

εἰσ-έδραμον, -δραμών, see εἰσ-τρέχω.

εἴσ-ειμι,* ipf. ᾔειν, (εἶμι q. v.) to go or come into or in, enter, εἰς, παρά: to enter one's mind, occupy one's thoughts, A. CP.: i. 7. 8: vi. 1. 17: vii. 2. 14.

εἰσ-ελαύνω,* ἐλάσω ἐλῶ, ἐλήλακα, a. ἤλασα, to ride into, enter, εἰς, i. 2. 26.

εἰσ-ελθεῖν, see εἰσ-έρχομαι, i. 2. 21.

εἰσ-έρχομαι,* ἐλεύσομαι, ἐλήλυθα, 2 a. ἦλθον, to come or go into or in, to penetrate into, enter, εἰς, ἐπί, i. 2. 21: iv. 8. 13: vii. 1. 27.

εἰσ-ήειν, -ήεσαν or -ῇσαν, see εἴσ-ειμι, i. 7. 8.

εἰσ-ήλασα, see εἰσ-ελαύνω, i. 2. 26.

εἰσ-ηνέχθην, see εἰσ-φέρω, i. 6. 11?

εἰσ-ήχθην, see εἰσ-άγω, i. 6. 11?

εἴσ-οδος, ου, ἡ, a way in, entrance, εἰς, iv. 2. 3: vi. 5. 1.

εἴσομαι, see ὁράω, i. 4. 15.

εἰσ-πηδάω, ήσομαι, πεπήδηκα, a. ἐπήδησα, (πηδάω to leap) to leap into, εἰς, i. 5. 8.

εἰσ-πίπτω,* πεσοῦμαι, πέπτωκα, 2 a. ἔπεσον, to fall into or upon, burst or rush into, εἰς, i. 10. 1: vii. 1. 17, 19.

εἰσ-πλέω,* πλεύσομαι, πέπλευκα, to sail into, εἰς, vi. 4. 1.

εἰσ-πορεύομαι, εὔσομαι, πεπόρευμαι, to march into, εἰς, iv. 7. 27?

εἰστήκειν or **ἑστήκειν**, see ἵστημι.

εἰσ-τρέχω,* δραμοῦμαι, δεδράμηκα, 2 a. ἔδραμον, to run into or in, v. 2. 16.

εἰσ-φέρω,* οἴσω, ἐνήνοχα, a. ἤνεγκα

or -ον, a. p. ἠνέχθην, to bring or carry into or in, A. D., εἰς, i. 6. 11? vii. 3. 21.
εἰσ-φορέω, ήσω, πεφόρηκα, to bring into, A. εἰς, iv. 6. 1.
εἴσω, sometimes ἔσω, adv., (εἰς or ἐς) within, inside of, G., i. 2. 21 ; 4. 5.
εἰσ-ωθέω,* ώσω, to push into or in, trans.: M. intrans., v. 2. 18 ?
εἶτα adv., (εἰ τά if those things are, cf. ἔπειτα) then, in that case, thereupon, after that, next, i. 2. 16, 25.
εἴ-τε .. εἴ-τε si-ve .. si-ve, both if .. and if, whether .. or, ii. 1. 14 : iii. 1. 40 ; 2. 7. See εἰ.
εἶχον, εἰχόμην, see ἔχω, i. 1. 6.
εἴωθα,* I [have accustomed myself] am wont or accustomed, I.; intrans. 2 pf. pret. of ἐθίζω, ἴσω ἰῶ, εἴθικα, to accustom: 2 plup. εἰώθειν, vii. 8. 4.
εἴων, εἶας, εἶα, see ἐάω, i. 4. 9.
ἐκ, the form which the prep. ἐξ takes before a consonant, 165, i. 1. 6.
†ἑκασταχόσε in each direction, iii. 5. 17.
ἕκαστος, η, ον, (see ἑκάτερος) quisque, each of more than two, every, each or every one ; pl. several, respective, each body, all, or translated as sing. or like an adv. (severally). Its sing. is often joined, esp. through apposition, with a plural. i. 1. 6; 2. 15 ; 7. 15 ; 8. 9 : ii. 2. 17 : v. 5. 5.
‡ἑκάστοτε at each time, uniformly, always, ii. 4. 10.
ἑκάτερος, α, ον, (a compar. in form w. ἕκαστος as sup., perhaps derived fr. εἷς, 376 c, d) uterque, each of two; pl. both, each party, or translated as sing. : καθ' ἑκάτερα on each side, G.: i. 8. 27: iii. 2. 36 : v. 5. 25; 6. 7: vi. 1. 9.
‡ἑκατέρωθεν from or on each or both sides, i. 8. 13, 22 : vi. 4. 3 ; 5. 25.
‡ἑκατέρωσε to each side of two, in both directions, i. 8. 14 ?
ἑκατόν indecl., a hundred, i. 2. 25.
Ἑκατ-ώνυμος, ov, Hecatonymus, an envoy to the Cyreans from Sinôpe, v. 5. 7 ; 6. 3.
ἐκ-βαίνω,* βήσομαι, βέβηκα, 2 a. ἔβην, to go out, forth, or aside, from a road, valley, river, vessel, &c.; to sally forth; to disembark; εἰς, &c.; iv. 2. 1, 10, 25 s ; 3. 3, 23 : v. 4. 11.
ἐκ-βάλλω,* βαλῶ, βέβληκα, 2 a. ἔβαλον, a. p. ἐβλήθην, to throw or cast out or away (out of one's hands, quiver, &c.); to drive out, banish, expel; ἐξ,

εἰς : i. 1. 7 ; 2. 1 : ii. 1. 6 : vii. 1. 16 ; 5. 6. Cf. ἐκ-πίπτω = passive.
ἔκ-βασις, εως, ἡ, (ἐκ-βαίνω) egress, outlet, passage, pass, iv. 1. 20 ; 2. 1s.
Ἐκβάτανα, ων, τά, Ecbatana (also written Agbatana, and Achmetha, Ezra 6. 2) the capital of Media, favorably situated for coolness and good air, and containing the strongly fortified and magnificent summer residence of the Persian king, ii. 4. 25 : iii. 5. 15. || Hamadan.
ἐκ-βληθείην, see ἐκ-βάλλω, vii. 5. 6.
ἐκ-βοηθέω, ήσω, βοήθηκα, to rush or come forth to the rescue, ἐξ, vii. 8. 15.
ἔκ-γονος, ον, (γίγνομαι) born from : οἱ ἔκγονοι the descendants: τὰ ἔκγονα the young of animals : iii. 2. 14 ? iv. 5. 25 ?
ἐκ-δεδράμηκα, ἐκ-δραμών, see ἐκ-τρέχω, v. 2. 17 ; 4. 16.
ἐκ-δέρω,* δερῶ, a. ἔδειρα, (δέρω to skin) to take out of one's skin, to flay, A., i. 2. 8 : v. l. ἐκδείρειν.
ἐκ-δίδωμι,* δώσω, δέδωκα, pf. p. δέδομαι, to give forth or up, A.: to give forth in marriage, settle with a husband, A. παρά : iv. 1. 24 : vi. 6. 10.
ἐκ-δύνω,* δύσομαι, δέδυκα, 2 a. ἐδῦν, to get out of one's clothes, to strip one's self, iv. 3. 12.
ἐκεῖ adv., there, in that place, yonder, i. 3. 20 ; 10. 8 : iv. 1. 24.
‡ἐκεῖθεν thence, from that place or region, v. 6. 24.
‡ἐκεῖνος,* η, ο, that, that one ; often as a strong pers. pron., he, she, it ; i. 1.4 ; 3.9 ; 7.18 : iii.1.35. See ἐπ-έκεινα.
‡ἐκεῖσε thither, to that place, there (= thither), vi. 1. 33 ; 6. 36.
ἐκήρυξε, -ύχθη, see κηρύττω, ii. 2. 21.
ἐκ-θλίβω,* ίψω, τέθλιφα 1., (θλίβω to squeeze) to press or crowd out, A., iii. 4. 19 s.
ἐκ-καθαίρω, *αρῶ, pf. p. κεκάθαρμαι, to cleanse from defilement, burnish ; or
ἐκ-καλύπτω, ύψω, pf. p. κεκάλυμμαι (καλύπτω to cover, veil) to un-cover, to take the shield out of the leather case (σάγμα) in which it was commonly carried on the march to preserve its brightness ; i. 2. 16.
ἐκκλησία, ας, (ἐκ-καλέω to call forth) a convocation, assembly, i. 3. 2 ; 4. 12.
‡ἐκκλησιάζω,* άσω, to call an assembly, v. 6. 37. Der. ECCLESIASTIC.

ἐκ-κλίνω,* κλῖνῶ, κέκλικα 1., (κλίνω clino, to bend) to bend out of line, turn to flight, give way, i. 8. 19. Cf. IN-CLINE.

ἐκ-κομίζω, ἴσω ιῶ, κεκόμικα, to bring or carry out, to lead out (of the Pontus, vi. 6. 36) : M. to carry out or off for one's self : A.: i. 5. 8 : v. 2. 19.

ἐκ-κόπτω,* κόψω, κέκοφα, to cut trees out of a wood, cut down, fell; to lay waste or destroy by cutting down trees; A.; i. 4. 10 : ii. 3. 10.

ἐκ-κυβιστάω, ήσω, to throw a somerset, a feat often performed among the Greeks over swords pointing upwards, vi. 1. 9. See κυβιστάω.

ἐκ-κυμαίνω, ανῶ, (κῦμα wave) to [wave out of line] bend out or swell forth like a wave, i. 8. 18.

ἐκ-λέγω,* λέξω, εἴλοχα, (λέγω lego, to LAY, gather) to lay or gather out, to pick or single out, select ; so M., more subjectively ; A.; ii. 3. 11 : iii. 3. 19 : v. 6. 20. Der. ECLECTIC.

ἐκ-λείπω,* λείψω, λέλοιπα, 2 a. ἔλιπον, to leave (going out of), quit, abandon, desert, forsake, A. εἰς: of snow, to disappear: i. 2. 24 : iii. 4. 8 : iv. 1. 8 ; 3. 24 ; 5. 15. Der. ECLIPSE.

ἐκ-μηρύομαι, ύσομαι, (μηρύομαι to wind) to wind out ; of an army, to defile, vi. 5. 22.

ἐκ-πέμπω,* πέμψω, πέπομφα, to send out, conduct forth : M. to send forth of one's own company : A.: iii. 2. 24 : v. 2. 21.

ἐκ-πέπληγμαι, see ἐκ-πλήττω.

ἐκ-πεπτωκώς, see ἐκ-πίπτω, i. 1. 7.

ἐκ-περαίνω, ανῶ, to finish out, fully accomplish, A. D., v. 1. 13.

ἐκ-πεσών, see ἐκπίπτω, v. 2. 31.

ἐκ-πηδάω, ήσομαι, πεπήδηκα, to leap or spring out or forth, vii. 4. 16.

ἐκ-πίμπλημι,* πλήσω, πέπληκα, to fill out or up, A., iii. 4. 22 ?

ἐκ-πίνω,* πίομαι, πέπωκα, 2 a. ἔπιον, to drink [out] up, A., i. 9. 25.

ἐκ-πίπτω,* πεσοῦμαι, πέπτωκα, 2 a. ἔπεσον, to fall or be thrown out : out of one's home, to be driven out, banished, or exiled ; οἱ ἐκπεπτωκότες the exiles : of trees, out of their places, to fall down : out of the sea, to be thrown ashore or wrecked : to throw one's self out, rush or hurry out, tumble out : ἔξ: i.1.7: ii.3.10: v.2.17s: vii.5.12s.

ἐκ-πλαγείς, see ἐκ-πλήττω, i. 8. 20.

ἐκ-πλέω,* πλεύσομαι, πέπλευκα, to sail out, forth, or away, e. g. out of the Pontus, ἐξ, ii. 6. 2 : vii. 1. 1, 39.

ἐκ-πλέως, ων, (πλέως* full) filled out, entirely full, complete, iii. 4. 22.

ἐκ-πλήττω,* πλήξω, πέπληγα, pf. p. πέπληγμαι, 2 a. p. ἐπλήγην, but ἐξεπλάγην, to strike out of one's selfpossession ; to strike with surprise, astonishment, alarm, or terror ; to surprise, amaze, astonish, confound, confuse, alarm, terrify; A.; i. 5. 13; 8.20.

ἐκ-ποδών adv., (ποῦς) out of the way of the feet, out of the way : ἑ. ποιεῖσθαι to put out of the way : i. 6. 9 : ii. 5. 29.

ἐκ-πορεύομαι, εύσομαι, πεπόρευμαι, to march or go out or forth, v. 1. 8.

ἐκ-πορίζω, ίσω ιῶ, πεπόρικα, to bring out, provide, procure, A. D., v. 6. 19 ?

ἔκ-πωμα, ατος, τό, (πίνω) drinkingcup, beaker, iv. 3. 25 ; 4. 21 : vii. 3. 18.

ἐκ-ταθείς, see ἐκ-τείνω, v. 1. 2.

ἐκταῖος, α, ον, (ἕκτος) on the sixth day, vi. 6. 38.

ἐκ-τάττω,* τάξω, τέταχα, to draw out or up in battle-order, trans.: M., intrans. or refl., v. 4. 12 ? vii. 1. 24.

ἐκ-τείνω,* τενῶ, τέτακα, a. ἔτεινα, a. p. ἐτάθην, to stretch out, ex-tend, A., v. 1. 2 ; 8. 14.

ἐκ-τοξεύω, εύσω, to shoot forth arrows (out of a tower), vii. 8. 14.

ἕκτος, η, ον, (ἕξ) sixth, vi. 2. 12.

ἐκ-τρέπω,* ἕψω, τέτροφα, 2 a. m. ἐτραπόμην, to turn out or aside, trans.; M., intrans., iv. 5. 15.

ἐκ-τρέφω,* θρέψω, τέτροφα, 2 a. p. ἐτράφην, to bring up (out of childhood), vii. 2. 32.

ἐκ-τρέχω,* δραμοῦμαι, δεδράμηκα, 2 a. ἔδραμον, to run out or forth, to sally forth, v. 2. 17 ; 4. 16.

ἐκτώμην, see κτάομαι, i. 9. 19.

ἐκ-φαίνω,* φανῶ, πέφαγκα, a. ἔφηνα, to show forth, A.: πόλεμον ἐκφαίνειν to make hostile demonstrations, iii. 1. 16.

ἐκ-φέρω,* οἴσω, ἐνήνοχα, a. ἤνεγκα or -ον, to bring or carry out or forth ; to report :. ἑ. πόλεμον to make open war : A. εἰς, πρός : i. 9. 11 : iii. 2. 29.

ἐκ-φεύγω,* φεύξομαι, πέφευγα, 2 a. ἔφυγον, to flee out of danger, escape, A., G. or I., πρός, i. 3. 2 ; 10. 3.

ἑκών, οὖσα, όν, g. όντος, ούσης, willing ; w. force of adv., willingly, voluntarily, of free will or one's own accord, i. 1. 9 ; 9. 9 : ii. 4. 4 : iii. 2. 6.

ἔλαβον, see λαμβάνω, i. 2. 26.
†ἐλαία & Att. ἐλάα, ας, olīva, an OLIVE; the olive-tree, fabled as the gift of Athena, and sacred to her: vi. 4. 6: vii. 1. 37.
ἔλαιον, ου, oleum, OIL, esp. olive-oil, iv. 4. 13: v. 4. 28: vi. 6. 1.
ἐλάττων,* ον, ἐλάχιστος, η, ον, c. & s. of ἐλαχύς Ep., usu. referred to μικρός small, little, or ὀλίγος little, few: τούλάχιστον (= τὸ ἐλ.) at least: ii. 4. 13: iii. 2. 28: v. 7. 8: vi. 2. 4s: vii. 1. 27.
ἐλαύνω,* ἐλάσω ἐλῶ, ἐλήλακα, a. ἤλασα, to drive, ride, A.; intrans., or w. ἵππον, ἅρμα, στράτευμα, &c., understood, to ride, drive, advance, march, charge, AE. διά, &c.: i. 2. 23; 5. 7, 13, 15; 8. 1, 10, 24: iv. 7. 24. Der. ELASTIC.
†ἐλάφειος, ον, of a deer: κρέα ἐλάφεια deer's meat, venison, i. 5. 2.
ἔλαφος, ου, ὁ ἡ, (in Att. ἡ as a generic term), a deer, stag, v. 3. 10.
‡ἐλαφρός, ά, όν, [deer-like] light in motion or weight, nimble, agile, iii. 3. 6: iv. 2. 27.
‡ἐλαφρῶς lightly, nimbly, with agility, vi. 1. 12: vii. 3. 33.
ἐλάχιστος, η, ον, see ἐλάττων, iii. 2. 28.
ἐλέγχω,* ἐγξω, pf. p. ἐλήλεγμαι, a. p. ἠλέγχθην, to examine, question, or inquire, closely; to convict, prove; A. CP., P.; ii. 5. 27? iii. 5. 14 (A. by attr., 474 b): iv. 1. 23.
ἐλεινός, ή, όν, (ἔλεος pity) piteous, iv. 4. 11?
ἐλεῖν, ἐλέσθαι, &c., see αἱρέω.
ἐλελίζω, ίξω, (ἐλελεῦ a war-cry) to raise the war-cry, to shout in battle, i. 8. 18: v. 2. 14?
ἔλεξα, ἐλέχθην, see λέγω, i. 4. 13.
†ἐλευθερία, ας, freedom, liberty, independence, i. 7. 3: iii. 2. 13: vii. 7. 32.
ἐλεύθερος, α, ον, (ἐλευθ-? see ἔρχομαι) going and coming at pleasure, free, independent, ii. 5. 32: iv. 3. 4.
ἐλήφθην, see λαμβάνω, i. 7. 13.
ἐλθεῖν, -οιμι, -ω, -ών, see ἔρχομαι.
Ἐλισάρνη, ης, v. l. for Ἀλισάρνη, vii. 8. 17.
ἕλκω,* ἕλξω, ipf. εἷλκον, to draw, drag, pull, A., iv. 2. 28; 5. 32: v. 2. 15.
†Ἑλλάς, άδος, ἡ, Hellas, Greece; originally, it is said, the name of a town or district in southern Thessaly, settled by Hellen. The name was afterwards so extended as to include all Greece except the Peloponnesus; and yet further, so as to include not only this, but even all the Greek colonies, wherever situated. i. 2. 9; 4. 7. — 2. Hellas, wife of Gongylus, friendly to Xenophon, vii. 8. 8.
Ἕλλην, ηνος, ὁ, Hellen, a Greek; originally, it is said, the name of a son of Deucalion, and the father of Æolus and Dorus, and grandfather of Achæus and Ion. Passing to his posterity, it became the general name of all the Greeks (Hellēnes), while their great divisions were named from his children and grandchildren. As an adj., Greek. i. 1. 2; 2. 14, 18; 10. 7.
‡ἑλληνίζω, ίσω, to speak Greek; vii. 3. 25. Der. HELLENIST.
‡Ἑλληνικός, ή, όν, Hellenic, Grecian, Greek: τὸ Ἑλληνικόν [sc. στράτευμα] the Greek army or force: i. 1. 6; 8. 14s.
‡Ἑλληνικῶς adv., in the Greek language, in Greek, i. 8. 1.
‡Ἑλληνίς, ίδος, (fem. adj. = Ἑλληνική, 235) Grecian, Greek, iv. 8. 22.
‡Ἑλληνιστί adv., (spoken) in Greek, vii. 6. 8.
†Ἑλλησποντιακός, ή, όν, Hellespontic or Hellespontian, i. 1. 9: v. l. -ικός, -ιος.
Ἑλλήσ-ποντος, ου, ὁ, [the sea of Helle, who was here drowned, according to fable, in endeavoring to escape through the air to Colchis, with her brother Phrixus, on the back of a golden-fleeced ram] the Hellespont, a strait about 40 miles long and from 1 to 4 miles wide, connecting the Propontis and Ægean, and separating Europe and Asia. It was bridged by Xerxes, and was the scene, in the Peloponnesian war, of the great naval battles of Cynossēma and Ægospotami. The name was also applied to the region lying about this strait. i. 1. 9. ‖ The Dardanelles, or Strait of Gallipoli.
ἔλοιμι, -οίμην, -όμενος, see αἱρέω.
†ἐλπίζω, ίσω ἰῶ, ἤλπικα 1., to hope, expect, I. (A.), iv. 6. 18: vi. 5. 17.
ἐλπίς, ίδος, ἡ, (ἔλπω to give hope) hope, expectation: ἐλπίδας λέγων speaking or expressing hopes: τῶν μυρίων ἐλπίδων μία one [of the 10,000 expectations] chance in ten thousand: G., I. (A.): i. 2. 11: ii. 1. 19; 5. 12: iii. 2. 8.
ἐλῶν, see ἐλαύνω, i. 8. 10.
ἐμ-, the form which the prep. ἐν takes in compos. before a labial, 150.
ἔμαθον, see μανθάνω, v. 2. 25.

ἐμαυτοῦ 44 ἐν

ἐμ-αυτοῦ,* ἧς, refl. pron., (ἐμέ, αὐτός) of myself: ἡ ἐμαυτοῦ ἀρχή my own province: i. 3. 10: ii. 3. 29; 5. 10.

ἐμ-βαίνω,* βήσομαι, βέβηκα, 2 a. ἔβην, to step or go into; to go on board, embark; εἰς, i. 3. 17; 4. 7: ii. 3. 11.

ἐμ-βάλλω,* βαλῶ, βέβληκα, 2 a. ἔβαλον, to throw or thrust in or upon, insert; to inflict blows; to [thrust in] give fodder to horses; A. D.; i. 5. 11; 9. 27: reflexively, to throw one's self into or upon, fall upon, attack, charge; to strike into, invade, enter; ἐμβάλλειν εἰς αὐτούς to [enter among them] invade their country; of a river, to empty into; εἰς· i. 2. 8; 8. 24: iii. 5. 16 s.

ἐμ-βάς, -βάντες, see ἐμ-βαίνω, i. 4. 7.

ἐμ-βιβάζω, βιβάσω βιβῶ, to put into or on board a vessel, make one embark, A. εἰς, v. 3. 1; 7. 8.

ἐμ-βολή, ῆς, (ἐμ-βάλλω) an irruption, invasion, inroad, entrance, iv. 1. 4.

ἐμ-βρόντητος, ον, (βροντάω to thunder, fr. βροντή) thunder-struck; hence, stupefied, insane, panic-struck: iii. 4. 12.

ἔμεινα, see μένω, i. 2. 6, 10, 14.

ἐμέω,* ἐμέσω ἐμῶ, ἐμήμεκα, vomo, to VOMIT, iv. 8. 20. Der. EMETIC.

ἐμ-μένω,* μενῶ, μεμένηκα, to remain or abide in, ἐν, iv. 7. 17.

†ἐμός, ή, όν, my, mine, i. 6. 6.

ἐμοῦ, ἐμοί, ἐμέ (by apostr. ἐμ'), oblique cases of ἐγώ, i. 3. 3, 6; 5. 16.

ἔμ-παλιν adv., on the return, backwards, back, back again: so τοὔμπαλιν (by crasis for τὸ ἔμπαλιν) & εἰς τοὔμπαλιν [to that which is on the return], i. 4. 15: iii. 5. 13: v. 7. 6.

ἐμ-πεδόω, ώσω, (πέδον the ground) to fix in the ground, make firm; hence, to hold fast or sacred, sacredly observe, A., iii. 2. 10.

ἔμ-πειρος, ον, s., (πεῖρα) in acquaintance with, acquainted with, experienced in, familiar with, G., iv. 5. 8: v. 6. 1, 6: vii. 3. 39. Der. EMPIRIC.

‡ἐμ-πείρως adv., in acquaintance with, G.; ἐμπείρως ἔχειν to be acquainted with, ii. 6. 1.

ἐμ-πέπτωκα, -πεσών, see ἐμ-πίπτω.

ἐμ-πίνω,* πίομαι, πέπωκα, to drink in, take a drink, vi. 1. 11?

ἐμ-πίπλημι or -πίμπλημι,* πλήσω, πέπληκα, a. ἐν-επλήσθην, to fill into, fill up, cover with; to satisfy, content; A. G., P.; i. 7. 8; 10. 12: vii. 7. 46.

ἐμ-πίπρημι or -πίμπρημι,* πρήσω, πέπρηκα, a. ἐν-έπρησα, (πίμπρημι to burn) to put fire in, set fire to, set on fire, A., iv. 4. 14: v. 2. 3: vii. 4. 15.

ἐμ-πίπτω,* πεσοῦμαι, πέπτωκα, 2 a. ἔπεσον, to fall into, upon, or among; to throw one's self into; to attack; to [fall into one's mind] occur to; D., εἰς: ii. 2. 19; 3. 18: iii. 1. 13: iv. 8. 11?

ἐμ-πλεως, ων, (πλέως* full) filled in with, full of, abounding in, G., i. 2. 22?

†ἐμ-ποδίζω, ίσω ιῶ, im-pedio, to IMPEDE, hinder, be in the way of, A., iv. 3. 29.

†ἐμ-πόδιος, ον, in the way, presenting an obstacle, D., vii. 8. 3 s.

ἐμ-ποδών adv., (ἐν ποδῶν ὁδῷ) in the way of the feet: ἐμποδών εἶναι to be in the way, hinder, prevent, D. I. (w. τό or τοῦ), iii. 1. 13: iv. 8. 14: v. 7. 10.

ἐμ-ποιέω, ήσω, πεποίηκα, to create or produce in, inspire in, impress upon, D. A., CP., ii. 6. 8, 19; vi. 5. 17.

ἐμ-πολάω, ήσω, ἠμπόληκα, (akin to πωλέω) to obtain or realize from a sale, A., vii. 5. 4?

†ἐμ-πόριον, ου, a place of trade, EMPORIUM, mart, i. 4. 6.

ἔμ-πορος, ου, ὁ, a person on a journey for trade, a merchant, v. 6. 19.

ἔμ-προσθεν adv., in front, before (in place or time), G., i. 8. 23: vii. 7. 36: ὁ ἔ. the foregoing, preceding, or past, ii. 1. 1: οἱ ἔ. those in front, iv. 3. 14: τὰ ἔ. the fore parts or places in front, v. 4. 32: vi. 3. 14.

ἐμ-πωλέω, ήσω, to sell, obtain by sale, A., vii. 5. 4?

ἐμ-φαγεῖν 2 aor. (ἐν-έφαγον, ἐμ-φάγω, οιμι, &c.; see ἐσθίω, the pr. ἐν-εσθίω not being in use), to take in food, eat a little or hastily, A., iv. 2. 1; 5. 8.

ἐμ-φανής, ές, (φαίνω) shining in, manifest: ἐν τῷ ἐμφανεῖ in public, publicly, openly, ii. 5. 25.

‡ἐμ-φανῶς openly, v. 4. 33.

ἐν* prep., Lat. in w. abl., IN: w. DAT. of place or persons, in, within, on, upon, at, among, i. 1. 6 s; 5. 1; 6. 1: iv. 7. 9; ἐν Βαβυλῶνι [in the region of B.] at or near B., v. 5. 4: — of time, in, at, on, during, within; ἐν τούτῳ [sc. χρόνῳ] in or during this time, meanwhile; ἐν ᾧ during which time, or [in the time when, 557 a] while, whilst; i. 2. 20; 5. 15s; 7. 18; 10. 10: — of state, manner, means, instru-

ment, &c., *in, under, with,* i. 3. 21; 7. 20; 9. 1: iv. 3. 7 s. In compos. (ἐμ- before a labial, and ἐγ- bef. a palatal, 150), *in, into* (698 d ʳ), *among, upon, at.*
ἔν, ἑνός, ἑνί, see εἶς, i. 9. 12: vii. 5. 4.
ἐν-αγκυλάω, ήσω, (ἀγκύλη, see διαγ- κυλόομαι) *to* [put in a] *fit with a thong,* iv. 2. 28.
†**ἐναντιόομαι,** ώσομαι, ἠναντιώμαι, *to oppose, withstand,* D. περί or G., vii. 6. 5.
ἐν-αντίος, α, ον, *on the opposite side, opposite, opposed to, contrary, hostile to; in an opposite direction; over against, against, in front of, before, in one's face;* often w. an adv. force: οἱ ἐνάντιοι *the enemy:* ἐκ τοῦ ἐναντίου [from] *on the opposite side:* τἀναντία (= τὰ ἐναντία) *in the opposite direction,* &c.: τούτου ἐναντίον *in this man's presence:* D., G., ᾗ: i. 8. 23 ? iii. 2. 10: iv. 3. 28, 32; 7. 5: v. 8. 24: vii. 6. 23.
ἐν-άπτω, ἄψω, *to set on fire, set fire to, kindle,* A., v. 2. 24 s ?
ἔνατος, later **ἔννατος,** η, ον, (ἐννέα q. v.) *ninth,* iv. 5. 24.
ἐν-αυλίζομαι, ίσομαι, ηύλισμαι l., a. p. ηὐλίσθην, *to en-camp, lodge for the night,* vii. 7. 8.
ἔνδεια, ας, (ἐν-δέω) *need, want, poverty, lack of provisions,* i. 10. 18.
ἐν-δείκνυμι,* δείξω, δέδειχα, in-dico, *to in-dicate, express;* M. *to show* or *express* one's own feelings, A., vi. 1. 19.
ἐν-δέκατος, η, ον, (ἕν-δεκα *eleven) eleventh,* i. 7. 18.
ἐν-δέω,* δεήσω, δεδέηκα, *to lack in* anything: impers. ἐν-δεῖ *there is lack* or *need* of, G. D.; ἑώρα πλείονος ἐνδέον *he saw there* [being] *was need of more explicitness:* M. *to lack* for one's own support, G.: vi. 1. 31: vii. 1. 41; 3. 3 ?
ἔν-δηλος, ον, *among evident things, evident, manifest, plain;* used like δῆλος w. a participle; ii. 4. 2; 6. 18.
ἔν-δημος, ον, *within a nation, at home;* τὰ ἔνδημα *the home revenues,* vii. 1. 27. Der. ENDEMIC.
ἐν-δίφριος, ον, (δίφρος) *sitting on the same seat,* or *at table,* with another (the Thracians sitting at their meals): ἐνδίφριος subst., *a table-companion:* vii. 2. 33, 38.
†**ἔνδοθεν** adv., *from within,* v. 2. 22.
ἔνδον adv., (ἐν) *within,* ii. 5. 32.
ἔν-δοξος, ον, (δόξα) *in repute, honorable, glorious, betokening honor,* vi. 1. 23.

ἐν-δύνω & **ἐν-δύομαι,*** δύσομαι, δέ- δυκα, 2 a. ἔδῦν, (cf. in-duo) *to put on* one's self, A.: plup. *had put on, wore:* i. 8. 3 : v. 4. 13.
ἐν-ε-: for augmented forms thus beginning, look under ἐγ- before a palatal, and under ἐμ- before a labial.
ἐν-έβαλον, sec ἐμ-βάλλω, i. 5. 11.
ἐν-έδρα, as, (ἕδρα *a seat) a seat within* (in a hidden place), *ambush, ambuscade,* Lat. in-sidiæ, iv. 7. 22.
↓**ἐνεδρεύω,** εύσω, a. ἐν-ήδρευσα, *to form* or *place an ambush, lie in wait,* i. 6. 2.
ἔν-ειμι,* ἔσομαι, (εἰμί) *to be in* or *on,* ἐν: *to be* [in a place] *there:* i. 5. 1 s; 6. 3: ii. 4. 21 s, 27. See ἔνι.
ἕνεκα,* sometimes **ἕνεκεν** (esp. before a vowel), adv., *for the sake of, on account of, for the purpose of, for,* G.; comm. following, but sometimes preceding or dividing its complement: τούτου ἕνεκα *on this account:* i. 4. 5, 8: ii. 3. 13, 20 ; 5. 14: v. 1. 12; 8. 13.
ἐν-εκείμην, see ἔγ-κειμαι, iv. 5. 26.
ἐνενήκοντα indecl., (ἐννέα) *ninety,* i. 5. 5 ; 7. 12.
ἐνεός (v. l. ἐννεός), ά, όν, *deaf and dumb,* v. 5. 33.
ἐν-επλήσθην, see ἐμ-πίπλημι.
ἐν-έπρησα, see ἐμ-πίπρημι, iv. 4. 14.
ἐν-ετός, ή, όν, (ἵημι) *sent in, incited, prompted,* ὑπό, vii. 6. 41 ?
ἐν-εχείρισα, see ἐγ-χειρίζω, iii. 2. 8.
ἐν-έχυρον, ου, (ἐχυρός) *a pledge in* hand, *security,* vii. 6. 23.
ἐν-έχω or **ἐν-ίσχω,*** ἕξω or σχήσω, ἔσχηκα, *to hold fast in, catch* or *entangle in,* A. D., vii. 4. 17.
ἐν-ῆν, see ἔν-ειμι, i. 5. 1 : ii. 4. 27.
ἔνθα adv. demonst., rel., and complem., (ἐν) of place, *there, here, where;* sometimes of time (esp. w. δή), *thereupon, then, when:* i. 5. 8 ; 8. 1 s, 4: iv. 1. 2 ; 5. 22, 29 : v. 1. 1.
↓**ἐνθά-δε** (-δε adding demonstr. force, cf. 252 a) *there, here:* (-δε signifying *to,* 688 e) *thither, hither:* ii. 1. 4 ; 3. 21: iii. 3. 2 : v. 1. 10.
↓**ἔνθα-περ** *in the very place where, just where, where,* iv. 8. 25 : vi. 4. 9.
ἐν-θείην, -θέμενος, &c., see ἐν-τίθημι.
ἔνθεν adv., (ἐν, cf. ἔνθα) *thence, hence, whence* (sc. ἐκεῖσε ii. 3. 6 ; sc. ταύτας iii. 5. 13): ἔνθεν μὲν .. ἔνθεν δέ hinc .. illinc, *hence .. thence,* [from] *on this side .. and on that:* ἔνθεν καὶ ἔν- θεν *on each side,* G.: i. 10. 1 : ii. 4. 22.

ἐνθένδε 46 ἐνωμοτία

✝ἐνθέν-δε (-δε adding demonst. force) from this very spot, from this place, hence (for ἀφ᾽ ὑμῶν, vii. 7. 17): v. 6. 10.

ἐν-θυμέομαι, ἥσομαι, ἐν-τεθύμημαι, a. p. ἐν-εθυμήθην, (θῦμός) to have or bear in mind, reflect, consider, ponder, A. CP., ii. 4. 5 : iii. 1. 20, 43 ; 2. 18.

✝ἐν-θύμημα, ατος, τό, a thought, consideration, conception, device, plan, iii. 5. 12 : vi. 1. 21. Der. ENTHYMEME.

ἐν-θωρακίζω, ἴσω, pf. p. τεθωράκισμαι, to put in a cuirass or corselet, to clothe in mail, fully arm, A., vii. 4. 16.

ἐνί a prolonged poet. form for ἐν in; also used, even in prose, with the accent drawn back (ἔνι), for ἔν-εστι or ἔν-εισι, fr. ἔν-ειμι, 699 e, 785, v. 3. 11.

ἐνί, ἑνός, see εἷς, i. 9. 12 : iii. 2. 19.

ἐνι-αυτός, οῦ, ὁ, (ἐνί, αὐτός, or fr. ἔνος annus, year) a period returning into itself, a cycle, year ; ii. 6. 29 : iii. 2. 12 : vii. 8. 26. See κατά.

ἐν-ιδών, see ἐν-οράω, vii. 7. 45.

ἔνι-οι, αι, α, (ἔνι οἵ there are who, 559 a) some, i. 5. 8 ; 7. 5 : ii. 4. 1.

ἐνί-οτε (ἔνι ὅτε there is when, 559 a), sometimes, at times, i. 5. 2 : ii. 6. 9.

ἐν-ίσχω, see ἐν-έχω, vii. 4. 17 ?

ἐννέα indecl., nine, i. 4. 19. In its derivatives, ἐννα-, for ἐνα-, is a less classic form. Der. ENNEA-GON.

ἐν-νοέω, ἥσω, νενόηκα, A. & M. (w. a. p.) to have or bear in mind, consider, reflect, ponder, think, devise ; to take thought, be anxious or apprehensive, apprehend ; A. CP., μή: ii. 2. 10 ; 4. 5, 19 : iii. 1. 2 s, 41 ; 5. 3 : iv. 2. 13.

✝ἔννοια, ας, a thought, reflection, consideration, iii. 1. 13.

Ἐν-οδίας, ου, Enodias, a lochage, vii. 4. 18 ?

ἐν-οικέω, ἥσω, ᾤκηκα, to dwell in, in-habit : οἱ ἐνοικοῦντες the inhabitants : i. 2. 24 ; 3. 4 ; 5. 5 : v. 6. 25.

ἐν-όντων, see ἔν-ειμι, ii. 4. 22.

ἐν-όπλιος, ον, (ὅπλον) in arms, martial, adapted to movements in armor, vi. 1. 11.

ἐν-οράω,* ὄψομαι, ἑώρακα or ἐόρακα, 2 a. εἶδον, to see or discern in a person or thing, A. D., i. 3. 15 : vii. 7. 45.

ἔνος, η, ον, last year's, v. 4. 27 ?

ἐν-οχλέω, ἥσω, ἠνώχληκα, (ὄχλος) to crowd upon, disturb, annoy, interfere with, D., ii. 5. 13 : iii. 4. 21.

ἐν-τάττω,* τάξω, τέταχα, to post among other troops ; to enrol ; iii. 3. 18 ?

ἐνταῦθα adv., (by metath. for Ion. ἐνθ-αῦτα, fr. ἔνθα & αὐτός) in this or that very place, here, there ; sometimes hither, thither : of time, hereupon, upon this, thereupon, then : i. 2. 1, 6 s ; 3. 21 ; 10. 1, 4, 12 s, 16 s : v. 5. 4.

ἐν-τείλασθαι, see ἐν-τέλλομαι.

ἐν-τείνω,* τενῶ, τέτακα, in-tendo, to stretch out upon, inflict upon, A. D. ; πληγὰς ἐνέτεινον came to blows, ii. 4.11.

ἐν-τελής, ές, (τέλος) at its end, complete, full, i. 4. 13.

ἐν-τέλλομαι,* τελοῦμαι, τέταλμαι, a. ἐτειλάμην, (τέλλω to raise) to put upon, enjoin upon, charge, command, D. I., v. 1. 13.

ἔντερον, ου, (ἐντός) an intestine ; pl. intestines, ENTRAILS, bowels, ii. 5. 33.

ἐντεῦθεν (fr. ἔνθεν, after the analogy of ἐνταῦθα fr. ἔνθα) from this or that very place or time, hence, thence ; after this, afterwards, hereupon, thereupon ; sometimes from or in consequence of this, therefore ; i. 2. 7, 10 : iii. 1. 31 : iv. 4. 10 : vii. 1. 25.

ἐν-τίθημι,* θήσω, τέθεικα, a. ἔθηκα (θῶ, θείην, &c.) to put in, inspire in, A. D., vii. 4. 1 : M. to put on board for one's self, A., i. 4. 7 : v. 7. 15.

ἐν-τιμος, ον, c., s., (τιμή) held in honor, honored, respected, v. 6. 32 : vi. 3. 18.

✝ἐν-τίμως in honor, ii. 1. 7.

ἐν-τόνως (ἔντονος strained, strenuous, fr. ἐν-τείνω) strenuously, vii. 5. 7.

ἐντός adv., (ἐν) within, of place or time, G. : ἐντὸς αὑτῶν within their line : i. 10. 3 : ii. 1. 11 : vii. 5. 9 ; 8. 16.

ἐν-τυγχάνω,* τεύξομαι, τετύχηκα, 2 a. ἔτυχον, to happen or light upon, fall in or meet with, find, D., i. 2. 27 ; 8. 1, 10 : ii. 3. 10.

Ἐννάλιος, ου, (Ἐνύω Bellōna, goddess of war) Enyalius (the warlike), another name for Mars (Ἄρης), the god of war ; a sonorous word specially used in the battle-cry ; i.8.18 : v.2.14.

ἐν-ύπνιον, ου, (ὕπνος) a thing seen in sleep, a dream, vii. 8. 1 : v. l. τὰ ἐνοίκια the interior ; Toup conjectured τὰ ἐνώπια the inner walls.

✝ἐνωμοτ-άρχης or ἐνωμότ-αρχος, ου, (ἄρχω) a leader of an ἐνωμοτία, enomotarch, iii. 4. 21 : iv. 3. 26.

ἐν-ωμοτία, ας, (ἐν-ώμοτος sworn in, fr. ὄμνυμι) a band of sworn soldiers,

ἐξ 47 ἐξεπλάγην

an enomŏty; comm. of about 25 men, the fourth part of a λόχος ; iii. 4. 22.

ἐξ,* before a cons. ἐκ, prep., *out of:* w. GEN. of place, *out of, forth from, from;* ἐκ τῶν Ταόχων *from the land of the Taochi;* ἐξ ἀριστερᾶς [from] *on the left;* i. 2. 1, 3, 7, 18 : iv. 7. 17; 8. 2: — of time, *from, after, upon,* often denoting not mere succession of time, but also consequence ; ἐκ τούτου *from this time, upon* or *after this, hereupon, in consequence of this;* ἐκ παίδων *from boyhood;* i. 2. 17 ; ii. 5. 27 ; 6. 4 : iv. 6. 14, 21 : ἐξ οὗ or ὅτου *from* [what time] *the time when, since,* 557 a, v. 7. 34 : vii. 8. 4 :— of source, cause, agent, means, manner, &c., *from, of, in consequence of, on account of, by, by means of, with, according to,* &c., i. 1. 6 ; 9. 16, 19, 28 : iii. 1. 11 s, 43 : ἐκ τούτων from this state of affairs, *in these circumstances,* i. 3. 11. In compos., *out, forth, off, from;* sometimes implying completeness (cf. *utterly*).

ἕξ indecl., sex, SIX, i. 1. 10: ii. 4. 27.

ἐξ-αγγέλλω, ελῶ, ἤγγελκα, a. ἤγγειλα, *to bring out word, report, repeat, state,* A. D., CP., i. 6. 5 ; 7. 8 : ii. 4. 24.

ἐξ-άγω,* ἄξω, ἦχα, 2 a. ἤγαγον, a. p. ἤχθην, *to lead out* or *forth; to induce;* A. I., ἐπί, πρός, &c.; i. 6. 10 ; 8. 21.

†**ἐξ-αίρετος,** ον, *picked out, select, choice,* vii. 8. 23 : cf. Lat. *eximius* fr. *ex-imo*.

ἐξ-αιρέω,* ήσω, ᾕρηκα, 2 a. εἷλον, a. p. ᾑρέθην, *to take out, remove, set apart,* A. G., D.: M. *to take out for one's own benefit, select, choose,* A., ἐκ : ii. 1. 9 ; 3. 16 ; 5. 4, 20 : v. 3. 4.

ἐξ-αιτέω, ήσω, ᾔτηκα 1., *to demand:* M. *to beg off* as a favor to one's self, *to rescue by entreaty :* A.: i. 1. 3 : vi. 6. 11 (v. *l.* ζητέω).

ἐξ-αίφνης, softer but less Att. form ἐξαπίνης, (αἴφνης *suddenly,* fr. ἀ- & φαίνω) *of a sudden, suddenly, unexpectedly,* 380 b, iii. 3. 7 : v. 6. 19 s.

ἑξακισ-χίλιοι, αι, α, (ἑξάκις *six times,* fr. ἕξ) *six thousand,* i. 7. 11 : ii. 2. 6.

ἐξ-ακοντίζω, ίσω ιῶ, *to shoot forth* with darts, D. of instrument, v. 4. 25.

ἑξακόσιοι, αι, α, (ἕξ, ἑκατόν) *six hundred,* i. 8. 6, 24.

ἐξ-αλαπάζω, άξω, poet., (ἀλαπάζω *to plunder) to sack, desolate,* A., vi. 1. 29.

ἐξ-άλλομαι,* ἁλοῦμαι, a. ἡλάμην & ἡλόμην, *to spring aside,* vii. 3. 33.

ἐξ-αμαρτάνω,* τήσομαι, ἡμάρτηκα, *to err from the right, do wrong, offend, sin,* AE. περί : τοιαῦτα ἐξαμαρτάνοντες [sinning such sins] *so sinning* or *offending, guilty of such misconduct,* v. 7. 33.

ἐξ-αν-ίστημι,* στήσω, ἕστηκα, 2 a. ἕστην, *to raise up out of* one's seat, &c., A.: M., w. pf. & 2 a. a., *to stand, rise,* or *start up,* iv. 5. 18 : vi. 1. 10 ?

†**ἐξ-απατάω,** ήσω, ἠπάτηκα, (f. m. as p., 576 a, vii. 3. 3) *to deceive* utterly or grossly, *mislead, cheat, impose upon,* A. AE. ὡς, ὥστε, ii. 6. 22 : v. 7. 6 s, 9.

ἐξ-απάτη, ης, (ἀπάτη *deceit*) gross *deceit, imposition,* vii. 1. 25.

ἐξ-ά-πηχυς, υ, g. εος, *six cubits long,* v. 4. 12 : v. *l.* ἑξ-πηχυς.

ἐξαπίνης, see ἐξαίφνης, iii. 3. 7 ; 5. 2.

ἐξ-αρκέω, έσω, *to suffice fully,* vii. 7. 54 ?

ἐξ-άρχω, ἄρξω, ἦρχα, *to lead off; lead off in, take the lead in,* G.; v. 4. 14 : vi. 6. 15.

ἐξ-αυαίνω, ανῶ, *to dry up,* trans.: M. *to dry up, wither away* or *entirely,* intrans., ii. 3. 16 ?

ἐξ-αυλίζομαι, ίσομαι, ηὔλισμαι 1., *to leave* or *change one's quarters,* εἰς, vii. 8. 21.

ἐξ-ε- : for augmented forms thus beginning, look under ἐκ-.

ἐξ-έβαλον, -εβλήθην, see ἐκ-βάλλω.

ἔξ-ειμι,* ἔσομαι, (εἰμί) *to be out of* confinement or restraint, *to be free* or *permitted;* only used impers., ἔξεστι, ἐξείη, ἐξῆν, &c., *it is permitted* or *allowed, it is in one's power, one may,* D. I.; pt. abs. ἐξόν, *it being permitted, when it is* or *was permitted* or *in one's power, when he may* or *might;* ii. 3. 26 ; 5. 18, 22 s; 6. 6, 12, 28 : iii. 1. 22.

ἔξ-ειμι,* ipf. ᾔειν, (εἶμι q. v.) *to go* or *come out* or *forth, march out* or *forth,* iii. 5. 13 : v. 1. 8, 17 : vi. 6. 1 s.

ἐξ-ελαύνω,* ελάσω ελῶ, ἐλήλακα, *to drive out, expel,* A. ἐξ : intrans. or w. A. understood (see ἐλαύνω), *to drive* or *ride forth, advance, proceed, march,* διά, &c. : i. 2. 5 s ; 4. 4 : vii. 7. 7.

ἐξ-ελέγχω,* έγξω, *to prove fully, convict,* A. P., ii. 5. 27 ?

ἐξ-ελήλυθα, -ελθεῖν, see ἐξ-έρχομαι.

ἐξ-έλιπον, see ἐκ-λείπω, i. 2. 24.

ἐξ-ελοίμι, -ελοίμην, see ἐξ-αιρέω.

ἐξ-ενέγκειν, see ἐκ-φέρω, iii. 2. 29.

ἐξενίσθαι, see ξενίζω, vii. 3. 8 ?

ἐξ-επλάγην, see ἐκ-πλήττω, ii. 2. 18.

ἐξ-έπλει, see ἐκ-πλέω, ii. 6. 2.
ἐξ-έρπω, ἔρψω, (ἕρπω serpo, to creep) to creep out or forth, vii. 1. 8.
ἐξ-έρχομαι,* ἐλεύσομαι, ἐλήλυθα, 2 a. ἦλθον, to come or go out or forth, depart, escape, ἐξ : of time, to expire, elapse : i. 3. 17 : iii. 1. 12 : vii. 5. 4.
ἔξ-εστι, -έσται, see ἔξ-ειμι (εἰμί).
ἐξ-ετάζω, άσω, ἐξ-ήτακα, (ἐτεός true) to search out the truth of, examine, inspect : M. to present one's self for inspection, pass review, v. 4. 12 ?
‡ἐξ-έτασις, εως, ἡ, inspection or review of troops, i. 2. 9, 14 ; 7, 1 s.
ἐξ-ετράφην, see ἐκ-τρέφω, vii. 2. 32.
ἐξ-ευ-πορίζω, ίσω ιῶ, πεπόρικα, to provide well or fully, v. 6. 19 ?
ἐξ-έφηνα, see ἐκ-φαίνω, iii. 1. 16.
ἐξ-έφυγον, see ἐκ-φεύγω, i. 3. 2.
ἐξ-ηγέομαι, ἡσομαι, ἥγημαι, to lead forth : to bring out to another, communicate, impart ; ἀγαθόν τι ἑ. to render some service, esp. by information or guidance : A. D., εἰς : iv. 5. 28 : vi. 6. 34. Der. EXEGESIS.
ἐξ-ἤειν, -ἤεσαν or ἦσαν, see ἔξ-ειμι.
ἐξήκοντα indecl., (ἕξ) sexaginta, sixty, ii. 2. 6 : iv. 8. 27.
ἐξ-ἥκω, ἥξω, ἧκα 1., to come or have come out ; of time, to have run out, expired, or passed by, pr. as pf., 612, vi. 3. 26.
ἐξ-ἦλθον, see ἐξ-έρχομαι, i. 6. 5.
ἐξ-ἦν, see ἔξ-ειμι (εἰμί), vi. 6. 2.
ἐξ-ἤνεγκα, -ον, see ἐκ-φέρω, v. 6. 29.
ἐξ-ἤχθην, see ἐξ-άγω, i. 8. 21.
ἐξ-ιέναι, -ιών, see ἔξ-ειμι (εἶμι), v. 1. 8.
ἐξ-ικνέομαι,* ἵξομαι, ἷγμαι, to come out to ; to fly or send far enough to hit, to reach, of both missiles and senders, G. ; to amount to, suffice, εἰς : i. 8. 19 : iii. 3. 7, 15, 17 : vii. 7. 54.
ἐξ-ίστημι,* στήσω, ἕστηκα, to place out of : M. to stand out of, withdraw from, ἐξ, i. 5. 14.
ἔξ-οδος, ου, ἡ, a way out, outlet ; egress, departure, excursion, expedition ; v. 2. 9: vii. 4. 17. Der. EXODUS.
ἔξομεν, ἕξομαι, see ἔχω, i. 3. 11.
ἐξ-όν, see ἔξ-ειμι (εἰμί), ii. 5. 22 ; 6. 6.
ἐξ-οπλίζω, ίσω ιῶ, ὥπλικα 1., to arm fully or completely : M. so to arm or accoutre one's self : ἐξωπλισμένος in full armor : i. 8. 3: ii. 1. 2 : iii. 1. 28.
‡ἐξ-οπλισία, as, the arming, military equipment or array, i. 7. 10.
ἐξ-ορμάω, ἡσω, ὥρμηκα, to urge forth,

incite, animate, Α. ἐπί : A. & M. intrans., to start or set out or forth, go forth, ἐπί : iii. 1. 24 s : v. 2. 4 ; 7. 17.
ἐξ-ουσία, ἀς, (ἔξ-ειμι fr. εἰμί) permission, license, authority : ἐξουσίαν ποιεῖν to give license, D., v. 8. 22.
ἔξ-πηχυς, υ, g. εος, = v. l. ἐξ-ά-πηχυς.
ἔξω adv., (ἐξ) out, out of, without, outside, on the outer side of, abroad ; beyond, beyond the reach of ; besides : τὸ ἔξω the outer : G.; i. 4. 4 s ; 8. 13 : ii. 2. 4 ; 6. 3, 12 : iii. 4. 15 : vii. 3. 10.
‡ἔξωθεν from without, outside of, iii. 4. 21: v. 7. 21.
ἔοικα, see εἰκάζω, ii. 1. 13.
ἑόρακα or ἑώρακα, see ὁράω, ii. 1. 6.
ἑορτή, ἦς, (ὄρνυμι to stir, excite ?) a festival, feast, v. 3. 9 s.
ἐπ- or ἐφ-, by apostr. for ἐπί, i. 2. 2.
ἐπ-αγγέλλω, ελῶ, ἤγγελκα, to announce to : M. to announce or declare one's self, to promise, offer, consent, propose one's self, D. I., ii. 1. 4: iv. 7. 20 : vii. 1. 33.
ἐπ-άγω,* ἄξω, ἦχα, to bring or propose against, A. D. περί, vii. 7. 57.
ἔπαθον, see πάσχω, i. 3. 4 ; 9. 6.
†ἐπ-αινέω,* ἔσω & ἔσομαι, ᾕνεκα, (αἰνέω to speak) to speak for or in favor of, applaud, approve, commend, praise ; to thank, acknowledge gratefully (even in civilly declining) ; A. ἐπί : i. 3. 7 ; 4. 16 : ii. 6. 20 : iii. 1. 45 : vii. 7. 52.
ἔπ-αινος, ου, ὁ, (αἶνος speech) praise, commendation, applause, v. 7. 33.
ἐπ-αίρω,* ἀρῶ, ἦρκα, a. ἦρα, to raise to, stir up, excite, induce, influence, A. I., vi. 1. 21 : vii. 7. 25.
ἐπ-αίτιος, ον, charged against, D. : ἐπαίτιόν τι [something charged against] a ground of accusation, iii. 1. 5 ?
ἐπ-ακολουθέω, ἡσω, to follow upon or after, pursue, D., iii. 2. 35: iv. 1. 1.
ἐπ-ακούω,* οὔσομαι, ἀκήκοα, a. ἥκουσα, to listen to, overhear, A., vii. 1. 14.
ἐπάν or ἐπήν, (ἐπεὶ ἄν, 619 b) rel. adv. or conj. w. subj., when-ever, when, after, as soon as : ἐπὰν τάχιστα as soon as, 553 b : i. 4. 13 : ii. 4. 3 ? iv. 6. 9.
ἐπ-ανα-τείνω,* τενῶ, τέτακα, a. ἔτεινα, to stretch up for another to strike, to present upstretched, A., vii. 4. 9 ?
ἐπ-ανα-χωρέω, ἡσω, κεχώρηκα, to go back to, retreat, return, εἰς, iii. 3. 10.
ἐπ-αν-έρχομαι,* ἐλεύσομαι, ἐλήλυθα, 2 a. ἦλθον, to go up or back to, return, εἰς, vi. 5. 32 : vii. 3. 4 s.

ἐπ-άνω, on the upper side, *above:* τὰ ἐπάνω *the preceding narrative,* vi. 3. 1.
ἐπ-απειλέω, ἤσω, *to threaten besides, add threats,* vi. 2. 7.
ἐπ-εγ-γελάω, άσομαι, *to laugh at in one's face, to insult,* D., ii. 4. 27.
ἐπ-εγείρω,* ἐρῶ, ἐγήγερκα l., a. ἤγειρα, *to rouse to, awaken, wake up,* trans., iv. 3. 10.
ἐπ-εθέμην, ἐπ-έθεσαν, see ἐπι-τίθημι.
ἐπεί rel. adv. or conj. (upon this that, ἐπί): of time, *after, when, now that, since; whenever, as often as;* ἐπεὶ τάχιστα *as soon as,* 553 b: causal, *since, inasmuch as, for; ἐπεί γε certainly* or *of course since:* i.1.1; 3.1 s, 5s, 9; 5. 2; 8. 20: iii. 1. 31: vi. 3. 21.
‡ἐπειδάν (ἐπει-δὴ ἄν) rel. adv. or conj. w. subj., *whenever now* or *indeed, when indeed, when, after, as soon as:* ἐπειδὰν τάχιστα *as soon as:* i. 4. 8: ii. 2. 4; 3. 29: iii. 1. 9.
‡ἐπει-δή rel. adv. or conj.: of time, *when now* or *indeed, after, as soon as;* causal, *since now* or *indeed;* ἐπειδή γε *certainly since, inasmuch as:* i. 1. 3? 2. 17; 7.16; 9.24: iii.5.18: vii.7.18.
ἐπ-εῖδον, see ἐφ-οράω, vii. 6. 31.
ἔπ-ειμι,* ἔσομαι, (εἰμί) *to be upon* or *over,* ἐπί, i. 2. 5; 7. 15: iv. 4. 2.
ἔπ-ειμι,* ipf. ἤειν, (εἶμι q. v.) *to go* or *come upon* or *against, advance against, attack,* D.; *to advance, proceed, come up* or *forward:* of time, *to follow, succeed;* ἡ ἐπίουσα ἕως (ἡμέρα, νύξ) *the coming, following,* or *next morning,* &c.: i. 2. 17; 7. 1 s, 4; iv. 3. 23, 27; 7. 23: v. 7. 12.
ἐπεί-περ conj., *since indeed, inasmuch as,* ii. 2. 10: 5. 38, 41: iv. 1. 8.
ἔπεισα, ἐπείσθην, see πείθω, i.2.26.
ἔπ-εισι(ν), see ἔπ-ειμι (εἰμί), i. 7. 15: see ἔπ-ειμι (εἶμι), v. 7. 12.
ἔπειτα adv. (ἐπεί τά *when* or *since those things* are, cf. εἶτα ; or fr. ἐπί and εἶτα), *thereupon, thereafter, then, afterwards, next; then also, moreover, further:* ὁ ἔπειτα χρόνος *the coming time:* i. 3. 10; 9. 5, 14: ii. 1. 17; 4. 13; 5. 20.
ἐπ-έκεινα adv. (also written ἐπ' ἐκεῖνα) *upon yonder side, beyond:* ἐκ τοῦ ἐ. *from the region beyond,* v. 4. 3.
ἐπ-εκ-θέω,* θεύσομαι, *to run out against, sally out upon,* v. 2. 22.
ἐπ-έλιπον, see ἐπι-λείπω, i. 5. 6.
ἐπ-έξ-ειμι,* ipf. ήειν, *to go out against,* vi. 5. 4?

ἐπ-εξ-έρχομαι,* ἐλεύσομαι, ἐλήλυθα, *to come* or *sally out against,* v. 2. 7.
ἐπ-εξόδιος, ον, (ἔξ-οδος) *relating to an expedition:* ἐπεξόδια [sc. ἱερά] *sacrifices respecting an excursion,* vi. 5. 2: *v. l. ἐπ' ἐξόδῳ* (-οδείᾳ or -οδίᾳ), ὑπεξόδια.
ἐπεπάμην, see πάομαι, i. 9. 19.
ἐπ-έπεσον, see ἐπι-πίπτω, iv. 1. 10.
ἐπεπράγμην, see πράττω, vii. 6. 32.
ἐπεπράκειν, see πιπράσκω, vii. 2. 6.
ἐπ-έρχομαι,* ἐλεύσομαι, ἐλήλυθα, 2 a. ἦλθον, *to go to* or *upon, traverse,* A., vii. 8. 25.
ἐπ-ερωτάω,* ἐρωτήσω & ἐρήσομαι, ἠρώτηκα, 2 a. ἠρόμην, *to put a question to, inquire of, question, ask; to question further, again to ask;* A. CP.; iii. 1. 6: v. 8. 5: vii. 3. 12 ; 4. 10.
ἔπεσον, see πίπτω, vi. 1. 5 ; 4. 9.
ἐπ-έστην, -έστησα, -εστάθην, see ἐφ-ίστημι, i. 5. 7: iii. 4. 21; 3. 20.
ἐπ-έσχον, see ἐπ-έχω, iii. 4. 36.
ἐπ-ετετάγμην, see ἐπι-τάττω, ii.3.6.
ἐπ-εύχομαι, εὔξομαι, εὖγμαι or ηὖγμαι, *to imprecate upon one's self, appeal to the gods,* v. 6. 3.
ἐπ-εφάνην, see ἐπι-φαίνω, ii. 4. 24.
ἐπεφεύγειν, see φεύγω, v. 4. 18.
ἐπ-έχω,* ἕξω or σχήσω, ἔσχηκα, 2 a. ἔσχον, *to hold upon, hold back from, delay, refrain from,* G., iii. 4. 36. Der. EPOCH.
ἐπ-ῄειν, -ῄεσαν or -ῇσαν, see ἔπ-ειμι (εἶμι), i. 2. 17; 5. 15; 10. 10.
ἐπ-ήκοος, ον, (ἀκούω) *listening to; favorable for hearing:* εἰς ἐπήκοον [sc. χωρίον] *into a hearing place, within hearing distance* (so ἐν ἐπηκόῳ), ii. 5. 38: iii. 3. 1: vii. 6. 8.
ἐπ-ῆκτο, see ἐπ-άγω, vii. 7. 57.
ἐπήν, see ἐπάν, ii. 4. 3.
ἐπ-ῆν, see ἔπ-ειμι (εἰμί), i. 2. 5.
ἐπ-ῄνεσαν, see ἐπ-αινέω, i. 3. 7.
ἐπ-ῆρα, see ἐπ-αίρω, vi. 1. 21.
ἐπ-ηρόμην, see ἐπ-ερωτάω, iii. 1. 6.
ἐπί* prep., by apost. ἐπ' or ἐφ', *on, upon,* or *against* (as in cases of *resting, leaning, pressing,* &c., *on* or *against*): (a) w. GEN. of place, *on* or *upon* (the relation often closer than that indicated by the dat.), *in, on board of; on the bank* or *borders of* a *river* or *country; upon* a place as an object of aim, *for, towards;* i. 4. 3 ; 7. 20 : ii. 1. 3: iv. 3. 6, 28:—of military or other support, and hence of association in place or time, *by, with,* ——

ἔπίασιν 50 ἐπικύπτω

deep, at, in, in or at the time of; ἐπὶ τεττάρων upon four ranks as the support of the line, four deep, i. 2. 15; ἐφ' ἑνὸς one by one, v. 2. 6; ἐφ' ἑαυτῶν by themselves, ii. 4. 10; ἐπὶ φάλαγγος in line of battle, iv. 6. 6; ἐφ' ἡμῶν in our time, i. 9. 12: — (b) w. DAT. of place, on, upon, at, near, by, i. 2. 8; 4. 1. 4 s: — of purpose, end, object, condition, terms, occasion, or cause, for, on account of, in respect to, on, at, in, i. 3. 1; 6. 10: ii. 4. 5: iii. 1. 27, 45; ἐφ' ᾧ on condition that, ἐφ' ᾧτε in order that, I., 557 a, iv. 2. 19: vi. 6. 22:— of persons or things on which one depends or exerts authority, in the power of (Lat. penes), dependent upon, subject to; over, in charge or command of; i. 1. 4; 4.2:—denoting succession, upon, after, in addition to, in reply to, ii. 2. 4; 5. 41: iii. 2. 4: — (c) w. ACC. of place or person, on or upon (implying motion), to, at, against; ἐπὶ τὸν Μαίανδρον [upon the bank of] to the Mæander (so often, where water is spoken of); i. 1. 3; 2. 4 s, 17, 22: — of extent in space, time, &c., to the extent of, to, over, through, till, i. 7. 15: vi. 6. 36; ἐπὶ πολύ (πάμπολυ, βραχύ, πλέον, ὅσον, &c.) to or over a great or wide extent or distance, &c., i. 8. 8; ἐπὶ πᾶν ἔλθοι would go to all lengths, resort to every expedient, iii. 1. 18; ἐπὶ πολλοὺς τεταγμένοι arranged to the depth of many ranks, drawn up many deep (where gen. more comm.), iv. 8. 11: — of the object to be reached, obtained, or affected, to, for, after, to obtain, i. 2. 2; 6. 10: iv. 3. 11: v. 1. 8: — (d) in compos., on, upon, to, for, at, against, over, after, besides; often rather strengthening the sense of the simple, than adding a new idea.

ἐπ-ίασιν, see ἔπ-ειμι (εἶμι), i. 7. 4.

ἐπι-βάλλω,* βαλῶ, βέβληκα, to throw or put on, A., iii. 5. 10: M. pf. to have [put] one's arrow on the string (pt. with one's arrow on the string), ἐπί, iv. 3. 28: v. 2. 12.

ἐπι-βοηθέω, ήσω, βεβοήθηκα, to come to the aid of, give support to, D., vi. 5. 9.

†ἐπι-βουλεύω, εύσω, βεβούλευκα, to plan or plot against, plot, conspire or intrigue against, form designs against or to get, D., I., i. 1. 3: ii. 6. 23 s: v. 6. 29.

ἐπι-βουλή, ῆς, a design against, plot, D., πρός, i. 1. 8: ii. 5. 1, 38: v. 6. 29.

ἐπι-γίγνομαι,* γενήσομαι, γεγένημαι & 2 pf. γέγονα, 2 a. ἐγενόμην, to come or fall upon, attack, D., iii. 4. 25: vi. 4. 26.

ἐπι-γράφω, άψω, γέγραφα, to write upon, inscribe, v. 3. 5. Der. EPIGRAM.

ἐπι-δείκνυμι & δεικνύω,* δείξω, δέδειχα, to point out, show, display, or exhibit to others: M. to show, display, or exhibit one's self or in one's self: A.D., CP.: i. 2. 14; 3. 13, 16; 9. 7, 10, 16: iv. 6. 15 s: v. 4. 34.

ἐπ-ιδεῖν, -ιδών, see ἐφ-οράω, iii. 1. 13.

ἐπι-διώκω, ώξω, oftener ὤξομαι, δεδίωχα, to follow upon the steps of, pursue, give chase, i. 10. 11: iv. 1. 16.

ἐπι-δραμεῖν, see ἐπι-τρέχω, iv. 3. 31.

ἐπιεζόμην, see πιέζω, iii. 4. 48.

ἐπι-θαλάττιος, ον, (θάλαττα) lying upon the sea, on the sea-coast, maritime, v. 5. 23.

ἐπι-θεῖναι, -θῶ, -θέσθαι, -θῶμαι, -θοίμην, -θήσω, &c., see ἐπι-τίθημι.

‡ἐπί-θεσις, εως, ἡ, an attack, assault, iv. 4. 22: vii. 4. 23.

ἐπι-θυμέω, ήσω, -τεθύμηκα, (θυμός) to set one's heart upon, to desire, long for, wish, covet, G., I., i. 9. 12, 21.

‡ἐπι-θυμία, as, desire, ii. 6. 16.

ἐπι-καίριος, ον, (καιρός) opportūnus, proper for the occasion, appropriate, suitable, important, chief, vii. 1. 6.

ἐπι-κάμπτω,* κάμψω, (κάμπτω to bend) to wheel [against] forward, bend one's line of battle, i. 8. 23.

ἐπι-κατα ῥ-ρίπτω or -ριπτέω,* ρίψω, ἔρρῑφα, to throw down upon, A., iv. 7. 13.

ἐπί-κειμαι,* κείσομαι, (cf. in-sto) to press upon, attack, assault, D., iv. 1. 16; 3. 7, 30: v. 2. 5, 26.

ἐπι-κίνδυνος, ον, c., dangerous, perilous, D.: ἐπικίνδυνόν ἐστιν there is danger: i. 3. 19: ii. 5. 20: vii. 7. 54.

ἐπι-κουρέω, ήσω, (ἐπί-κουρος an auxiliary, κοῦρος young man) to assist, defend, protect against; to relieve, avert; D. A., v. 8. 21, 25.

‡ἐπι-κούρημα, ατος, τό, a protection, defence, relief, G., iv. 5. 13.

ἐπι-κράτεια, as, (ἐπι-κρατής in power over, κράτος) power over, control, command, mastery, vi. 4. 4: vii. 6. 42.

ἐπι-κρύπτω,* ύψω, κέκρυφα, to throw a veil over, conceal : M. to conceal one's self or one's own doings, hence pt. secretly, 674 b, d, i. 1. 6.

ἐπι-κύπτω, κύψω, κέκυφα, to bend or stoop to or over, iv. 5. 32?

ἐπικυρόω 51 ἐπίσταμαι

ἐπι-κῠρόω, ώσω, (κῦρος authority) to add authority, confirm, vote, iii. 2. 32.
ἐπι-κωλύω v.l. = ἀπο-κωλύω, iii. 3.3.
ἐπι-λαμβάνω,* λήψομαι, εἴληφα, 2 a. ἔλαβον, to reach or extend to, take in, A.: M. to seize upon, lay hold of, G.: iv. 7. 12 s: vi. 5. 5 s. Der. EPI-LEPSY.
ἐπι-λανθάνομαι,*λήσομαι,λέλησμαι, 2 a. ἐλαθόμην, to let a thing lie hid for or escape one's self, to forget, G., iii. 2. 25.
ἐπι-λέγω, λέξω, to say in addition, say besides or also, A., i. 9. 26. Der. EPI-LOGUE.
ἐπι-λείπω,* λείψω, λέλοιπα, 2 a. ἔλιπον, to leave behind; of things, to fail, give out, be wanting; A.; i.5.6; 8.18?
ἐπί-λεκτος, ον, (λέγω to pick, choose) picked for service, select, chosen, iii. 4. 43: vii. 4. 11.
ἐπι-μαρτύρομαι, ὑροῦμαι l., a. ἐμαρτῡράμην, (μάρτυς) to call to witness, appeal to, A., iv. 8. 7.
ἐπί-μαχος, ον, s., (μάχομαι) that may be fought against, open to attack, assailable, v. 4. 14.
†ἐπι-μέλεια, as, care bestowed upon, attention, diligence, thoughtfulness, i. 9. 24, 27.
†ἐπι-μελής, ές, c. ἐστερος, caring for, careful, attentive, vigilant, iii. 2. 30.
ἐπι-μέλομαι or -μέλεομαι,* μελήσομαι, μεμέλημαι, a. p. ἐμελήθην, to care for, to take care or charge of, attend to, give attention to, take thought, observe or watch carefully, G. CP., i. 1. 5 ; 8. 21 : iii. 1. 38 ; 2. 37 : iv. 3. 30.
ἐπι-μένω,* μενῶ, μεμένηκα, a. ἔμεινα, to wait for, wait, tarry; to remain over or in charge of, abide by, ἐπί : v. 5. 2 : vii. 2. 1.
ἐπι-μίγνῡμι,* μίξω, μέμιχα l., (μίγνῡμι misceo, to mix) A. or M. to mingle or associate with, have intercourse or dealings with, πρός, iii. 5. 16.
ἐπίμπλην, see πίμπλημι, i. 5. 10.
ἐπι-νοέω, ήσω, νενόηκα, (νόος) to think upon or of, have in mind, intend, purpose, propose, A., ι., ii. 2. 11 ; 5. 4.
†ἐπιορκέω, ήσω, ἐπιώρκηκα, to perjure or forswear one's self, commit perjury; swear falsely by, A.: τὸ ἐπιορκεῖν perjury: ii. 4. 7; 5. 38, 41; 6. 22: iii. 1. 22.
†ἐπιορκία, as, perjury, false swearing, πρός, ii. 5. 21: iii. 2. 4, 8.
ἐπί-ορκος, ον, (ὅρκος) against an oath, perjured, swearing falsely, addicted to perjury, ii. 6. 25.
ἐπι-πάρ-ειμι,* ἔσομαι, (εἰμί) to be present in addition, to be also at hand, iii. 4. 23 ?
ἐπι-πάρ-ειμι,* ipf. ἤειν, (εἶμι) to come up or march by the side or abreast (in addition to or in support of others, also or higher up), iii. 4. 23? 30.
ἐπι-πίπτω,* πεσοῦμαι, πέπτωκα, 2 a. ἔπεσον, of snow, to fall upon ; of men, to fall upon, make a descent upon, attack, D.; i. 8. 2 : iv. 1.10; 4.11; 5.17.
ἐπιπολύ as adv., better written ἐπὶ πολύ, i. 8. 8 : see ἐπί.
ἐπί-πονος, ον, c., for toil, toilsome, laborious ; portending toil ; i. 3. 19 : vi. 1. 23.
ἐπι-ῥ-ρίπτω or ῥιπτέω,* ῥίψω, ἔρρῑφα, to throw upon others, throw down, A., v. 2. 23.
ἐπί-ῥ-ρυτος, ον, (ῥέω) flowed upon, well-watered, i. 2. 22.
ἐπι-σάττω, a. ἔσαξα, (σάττω to pack) to put a pack on, to saddle, A., iii. 4.35.
Ἐπι-σθένης, εος, Episthenes, from Amphipolis in Thrace, a commander of targeteers, discreet and trustworthy, i. 10. 7 : iv. 6. 1. — 2. An Olynthian lochage, noted for his love of handsome boys, vii. 4. 7 s.
ἐπι-σῑτίζομαι, ίσομαι ιοῦμαι, σεσίτισμαι, (σῖτος) to add to one's stock of provisions, to collect, obtain, or lay in provisions ; to provision one's self, procure food, forage; i. 4. 19 ; 5. 4.
↓ἐπι-σῑτισμός, οῦ, ὁ, obtaining provisions, provisioning; a supply of provisions ; i. 5. 9 : vii. 1. 9.
ἐπι-σκέπτομαι, comm. σκοπέω,* σκέψομαι, ἔσκεμμαι, to in-spect, review, A.; to ascertain by inspection, CP.; ii. 3. 2 : iii. 3. 18.
ἐπι-σκευάζω, άσω, to repair, keep in repair, v. 3. 13.
ἐπι-σκοπέω, see ἐπι-σκέπτομαι, ii. 3. 2.
ἐπι-σπάω,* σπάσω, ἔσπακα, to draw to or upon; M. to draw upon one's self, drag along or after, A., iv. 7. 14.
ἐπι-σποίμην, see ἐφ-έπομαι, iv. 1. 6.
ἐπ-ίσταμαι,* ἐπι-στήσομαι, ipf. ἠπιστάμην, (ἐπί, ἵσταμαι, 167 a) to stand upon a subject as mastering it, while in Eng. we say "to under-stand it," as able to carry it in the mind ; to understand, know, know about, be aware, be acquainted with, be assured,

ἐπιστάs 52 Ἐπύαξα

A. P., CP.; *to know how*, I.; i. 3. 12, 15; 4. 8, 15 : iii. 2. 23 : vi. 6. 17. See ὁράω.
ἐπι-στάς, -στᾶσαν, see ἐφ-ίστημι.
†ἐπί-στασις, εως, ἡ, *a stopping, halt*, ii. 4. 26.
†ἐπι-στατέω, ήσω, (ἐπι-στάτης one who stands over, in command or charge, ἵστημι) *to act as commander, command, take the charge*, ii. 3. 11.
ἐπι-στέλλω,* στελῶ, ἔσταλκα, a. ἔστειλα, *to send to*, D. A., CP.; *to command, enjoin, charge*, D. I.; v. 3. 6: vii. 2. 6; 6. 44.
ἐπιστήμων, ον, g. ονος, (ἐπ-ίσταμαι) *acquainted* or *conversant with, skilled* or *versed in*, G., ii. 1. 7.
ἐπι-στήσας, &c., see ἐφ-ίστημι.
ἐπιστολή, ῆς, (ἐπι-στέλλω) *an* EPISTLE, *letter*, i. 6. 3 : iii. 1. 5.
†ἐπι-στρατεία, ας, *an expedition against*, ii. 4. 1.
ἐπι-στρατεύω, εὐσω, ἐστράτευκα, *to march* or *make an expedition against, make war upon*, ii. 3. 19.
ἐπι-σφάττω,* άξω, *to slay upon : M. to slay one's self upon :* A. D. : i. 8. 29.
ἐπι-τάττω,* τάξω, τέταχα, *to lay upon, command, enjoin, commit*, D. I. : *M. to station behind* one's own line, A. D. : ii. 3. 6 : vi. 5. 9 : vii. 6. 14.
ἐπι-τελέω, έσω ῶ, τετέλεκα, *to bring to an end, complete, accomplish, consummate*, A., iv. 3. 13.
ἐπιτήδειος, α, ον, s., (ἐπιτηδές *to the purpose*) *suited to a purpose, suitable, appropriate, proper, fitting, fit, suited to one's needs*, I., i. 3. 18: ii. 3. 11 ; 5. 18 : τὰ ἐπιτήδεια (art. sometimes om.) *the things suited to the support of life, the necessaries of life, provisions, supplies*, i. 3. 11: iv. 4. 17 : οἱ ἐπιτήδειοι *the suitable* or *proper persons;* sometimes *the persons suited to one*, i. e. *his friends;* vii. 7. 13, 57.
ἐπι-τίθημι,* θήσω, τέθεικα, a. ἔθηκα (θῶ, &c.) *to put* or *place upon, inflict*, A. D., i. 3. 10, 20 : vi. 4. 9 : *M.* to put one's self upon, *fall* or *press upon, attack, assail*, D., ii. 4. 3. Der. EPITHET.
ἐπιτοπολύ as adv., better written ἐπὶ τὸ πολύ, iii. 1. 42 : see πολύς.
ἐπι-τρέπω,* τρέψω, τέτροφα, *to turn* or *give over to, commit, entrust, confide* (ἐπιτρεπόμεναι *committed* or *committing themselves* to his charge, i. 9. 8), A. D. I.; *to permit, suffer, allow, direct*, D. (or A.) I.; *to refer* or *leave it to*, D. CP.;

i. 2. 19 : iii. 2. 31 ; 5. 12: vi. 1. 31; 5. 11 ? vii. 7. 3, 8, 18.
ἐπι-τρέχω,* δραμοῦμαι, δεδράμηκα, 2 a. ἔδραμον, *to run upon* a foe, *to make a quick attack* or *rapid onset*, iv. 3. 31.
ἐπι-τυγχάνω,* τεύξομαι, τετύχηκα, 2 a. ἔτυχον, *to happen* or *light upon, fall in* or *meet with, find*, D., i. 9. 25.
ἐπι-φαίνω,* φανῶ, πέφαγκα, 2 a. p. as m. ἐφάνην, *to show to : M. to show one's self to, appear, make one's appearance, come in view, be in sight*, D., ii. 4. 24 : iii. 4. 13, 39 s ; 5. 2.
ἐπι-φέρω,* οἴσω, ἐνήνοχα, *to bring upon : M. to bear one's self onward, rush upon*, i. 9. 6 : v. 8. 20.
ἐπι-φθέγγομαι, ἔγξομαι, ἔφθεγμαι, *to sound* [onward] *the charge*, iv. 2. 7 ?
ἐπι-φορέω, ήσω, πεφόρηκα l., *to carry* or *bring upon*, A., iii. 5. 10.
ἐπί-χαρις, ι, g. ιτος, *agreeable, pleasing, gracious, winning*, in one's manner, ii. 6. 12.
ἐπι-χειρέω, ήσω, ἐπι-κεχείρηκα, (χείρ) *to lay hand to, undertake, attempt, try, endeavor*, I., i. 9. 29 : ii. 5. 10 ; 6. 26.
ἐπι-χέω,* χέω or χεῶ, κέχυκα l., (χέω *to pour*) *to pour upon* or *in, add* by pouring, A., iv. 5. 27.
ἐπι-χωρέω, ήσω, κεχώρηκα, *to move upon* or *against, to advance*, i. 2. 17.
ἐπι-ψηφίζω, ίσω ιῶ, ἐψήφικα, *to put to vote, put the question, call the vote*, A. : *M. to vote for, vote*, A. : v. 1. 14 ; 6. 35 : vi. 1. 25 : vii. 3. 14 ; 6. 14 ?
ἐπ-ιών, -έναι, see ἔπειμι (εἶμι), i. 7. 2.
ἔπλευσα, see πλέω, i. 9. 17.
ἐπλήγην, see πλήττω, v. 8. 2, 12.
ἐπ-οικοδομέω, ήσω, pf. p. ᾠκοδόμημαι, *to build upon*, A. ἐπί, iii. 4. 11.
ἕπομαι,* ἕψομαι, ipf. εἱπόμην, 2 a. ἐσπόμην, sequor, *to follow* as a friend or as an enemy ; *to pursue; to attend, accompany ;* D., σύν, ἐπί : i. 3. 6, 17 s; 4. 13 s ; 8. 19 : ii. 3. 17 ; 6. 13.
ἐπ-όμνυμι,* ὀμοῦμαι, ὀμώμοκα, a. ὤμοσα, *to swear to* a statement, *add an oath*, vii. 5. 5 ; 8. 2.
ἐπράχθην, see πράττω, ii. 1. 1.
ἑπτά indecl., *septem*, SEVEN, i. 2. 5 s ; 6. 4. Der. HEPT-ARCHY.
†ἑπτα-καί-δεκα indecl., also written ἑπτὰ καὶ δέκα, *seventeen*, ii. 2. 11.
†ἑπτακόσιοι, αι, α, (ἑκατόν) *seven hundred*, i. 2. 3 ? 4. 3.
Ἐπύαξα, ης, *Epyaxa*, queen of the Cilicians, friendly to Cyrus, i. 2. 12.

ἐπυθόμην 53 ἔσχατος

ἐπυθόμην, see πυνθάνομαι, i. 5. 15.
ἐράω & M. poet. ἔραμαι,* a. p. as m.
ἠράσθην, to love, desire ardently, long
for, G., iii. 1. 29 : iv. 6. 3. Cf. φιλέω.
†ἐργάζομαι,* ἄσομαι, εἴργασμαι, to
work, labor, perform, do, 2 A.; to work
upon land, &c., till; ii. 4. 22 : v. 6. 11.
ἔργον, ου, (Ϝεργ-) WORK, deed, act,
action ; operation, execution ; fact,
event, result : τὰ εἰς τὸν πόλεμον ἔργα,
military or warlike exercises : i. 9. 5,
10, 18 : iii. 2. 32; 3. 12; 5. 12. Der.
ENERGY.
ἐρεῖ, ἐρεῖν, &c., see φημί, i. 3. 5.
ἐρέσθαι, see ἐρωτάω, ii. 3. 20.
Ἐρετριεύς, έως, ὁ, an Eretrian.
Eretria, an Ionian city on the southwest shore of Euboea (now Negropont),
was, next to Chalcis, the chief city in
the island. It was destroyed by the
Persians, B. C. 490, but rebuilt on a
new site (now Kastri). vii. 8. 8.
†ἐρημία, as, solitude, loneliness, isolation, privacy, ii. 5. 9 : v. 4. 34. Der.
EREMITE, HERMIT.
ἔρημος, ον, or ος, η, ον, c., devoid of men,
deserted, desert, desolate, uninhabited,
unoccupied ; without inhabitants, occupants, drivers, defenders, persons
near or around, &c.; destitute or void
of, deprived of, G.: σταθμὸς ἔρημος a
desert march, i. e. through a region
without inhabitants : i. 3. 6 ? 5. 1. 4 s :
ii. 1. 6 : iii. 4. 40 : iv. 6. 11, 13.
‡ἐρημόω, ώσω, to make lonely or desolate, deprive of company, A. G., i. 3. 6?
ἐρίζω, ίσω 1., ἤρικα 1., (ἔρις strife) to
contend or vie with, D., i. 2. 8 : iv. 7. 12.
ἐρίφειος, ον, (ἔριφος kid) of a kid,
kids', iv. 5. 31.
ἑρμηνεύς, έως, ὁ, (Ἑρμῆς Mercury,
the god of speech) an interpreter, i. 2.
17 : iv. 5. 10, 34.
‡ἑρμηνεύω, εύσω, to interpret, v. 4. 4.
Der. HERMENEUTIC.
ἐροῦντα, -τες, &c., see φημί, ii. 5. 2.
ἐρρωμένος, η, ον, c. ἐρρωμενέστερος,
(pf. pt. of ῥώννυμι to strengthen) strengthened, strong, resolute ; neut. subst.,
energy, resolution ; πρός : ii. 6. 11: iii.
1. 42.
‡ἐρρωμένως energetically, resolutely,
vi. 3. 6.
ἐρύκω ch. poet. & Ion., ὕξω Ep., a.
ἤρυξα, to keep or ward off, A. ἀπό, iii.
1. 25 : akiu to
ἔρυμα, ατος, τό, (ἐρύομαι to defend)

a defence, protection ; fortification, fortress, rampart ; i. 7. 16 : iv. 5. 9 s.
Ἐρύ-μαχος, see Εὐρύ-μαχος, v. 6. 21.
ἐρυμνός, ή, όν, (ἐρύομαι to defend)
fortified, defensible, strong for defence :
τὰ ἐρυμνά the strongholds : i. 2. 8 : iii.
2. 23 : v. 5. 2.
ἔρχομαι,* ἐλεύσομαι, ἐλήλυθα, 2 a.
ἦλθον, to come, go, AE., D. εἰς, ἐπί, παρά,
πρός, &c., i. 1. 10 s; 3. 20 ; 7. 4 : iii.
1. 6, 18. For the pres. except in the
ind., the ipf., and the fut., the Att.
comm. used other verbs, esp. εἶμι.
ἐρῶ, εἴρηκα, see φημί, i. 4. 8 : ii. 5. 12.
ἐρῶντες, see ἐράω, iii. 1. 29.
‡ἔρως, ωτος, ὁ, love, ardent desire or
wish, I. as A. or G., ii. 5. 22. Der.
EROTIC.
ἐρωτάω,* ἐρωτήσω & ἐρήσομαι, ἠρώτηκα, a. ἠρώτησα or 2 a. m. ἠρόμην, to
inquire, ask, question, interrogate (directly or through another, v. 4. 2), 2 A.,
CP., i. 3. 18, 20 ; 7. 9 : iv. 4. 5, 17.
ἐς = the more comm. εἰς, 688 d.
ἔσθ' by apostr. for ἐστί, fr. εἰμί.
ἐσθής, ῆτος, ἡ, (ἕννυμι to clothe) vestis, clothing, raiment, apparel, iii. 1.
19 : iv. 3. 25.
ἐσθίω,* f. ἔδομαι, ἐδήδοκα, 2 a. ἔφαγον, to eat, feed upon, A., G. partitive,
i. 5. 6 : ii. 3. 16 : iv. 8. 20. Cf. ἔdo.
ἔσομαι, ἐσοίμην, see εἰμί, i. 4. 11.
ἐσπείσαμην, see σπένδω, iv. 4. 6.
†Ἑσπερῖται, ων, οἱ, the Hesperitæ,
or the inhabitants of western Armenia,
subject to Tiribazus, iv. 4. 4 : vii. 8. 25.
ἕσπερος, α, ον, of evening : subst.
ἑσπέρα, ας, [sc. ὥρα] vespera, the evening ; [sc. χώρα] the west, cf. Germ.
Abend : iii. 1. 3 ; 5. 15 : iv. 4. 4 ; 7. 27.
Der. VESPER.
ἔσται, ἐστέ, ἐστί(ν), ἔστω, see εἰμί.
ἐσταλμένος, see στέλλω, iii. 2. 7.
ἔσταμεν, -τε, -σαν, -ναι, see ἵστημι.
ἔσ-τε,* by apostr. ἔστ', adv., as far
as, as long as, even, ἐπί, iv. 5. 6 : conj.,
unto this that, until, till ; while,
whilst, as long as ; i. 9. 11 : ii. 3. 9 ;
5. 30 : iii. 1. 19 ; 3. 5.
ἕστηκα, -κειν, ἑστώς, ἔστην, see
ἵστημι, i. 3. 2 ; 5. 8 ; 8. 5.
ἐστιγμένος, see στίζω, v. 4. 32.
ἐστραμμένος, see στρέφω, iv. 7. 15.
ἔσχατος,* η, ον, (sup. fr. ἐξ) extremus, last, farthest, frontier ; uttermost, utmost, extreme, severest, worst :
i. 2. 10, 19 : ii. 5. 24 : iii. 1. 18.

ἐσχάτως 54 εὐθύς

✝ἐσχάτως *to the last degree, extremely,* ii. 6. 1.

ἔσχον, see ἔχω, i. 8. 4.

ἔσω adv., *within,* see εἴσω. Der. ESOTERIC.

✝ἔσωθεν adv., *from within, on the inner side; within, inside:* τὸ ἔσωθεν *the inner,* i. 4. 4.

ἔσωσα, see σώζω, i. 10. 3.

✝ἑταίρα, as, a *female companion, concubine, mistress, courtesan,* iv. 3. 19.

ἑταῖρος, ου, ὁ, (akin to ἔτης *clansman*) a *companion, comrade, associate,* iv. 7. 11 ; 8. 27 ? vii. 3. 30.

ἔταξα, ἐτάχθην, see τάττω, i. 2. 15.

Ἐτεό-νῑκος, ου, *Eteonicus,* a Spartan officer, prob. the same that had been harmost in Thasos, and afterwards held this office in Ægīna, vii. 1. 12.

ἕτερος,* α, ον, (a compar. form, cf. Lat. alter, Germ. ander, Eng. either, other) alter, *the* OTHER *of two, one of two, the next,* in this sense comm. taking the art., and used in the plur. with reference to two classes, parties, or sets ; *other than, different from, differently situated from,* G.; *other, much like* ἄλλος, but with a sense of *difference ; besides :* εἰς τὴν ἑτέραν ἐκ τῆς ἑτέρας πόλεως *to one city from the next :* i. 2. 20; 4. 2 : iv. 1. 23 : v. 4. 31: vi. 1. 5 ; 4. 8. See θάτερα & μηδέτερος.

ἐτετίμημην, see τιμάω, i. 8. 29.

ἐτετρώμην, see τιτρώσκω, ii. 2. 14.

ἔτι adv., YET, *still, further, still further; furthermore, moreover; henceforth, hereafter, afterwards, any more* or *longer* (w. neg. *no more, no longer*), *in future;* w. compar., intensive, *still, even ;* i. 1. 4; 3. 9 ; 6. 8 ; 7. 18 ; 9. 10 ; 10. 10 : iii. 1. 23 ; 2. 2.

ἕτοιμος, η, ον, or ος, ον, (prob. akin to ἔτυμος & ἐτεός *real, &* εἰμί) *ready, prepared ; ready to one's hand;* D., I.; i. 6. 3 : iv. 6. 17 : vi. 1. 2 : vii. 8. 11.

✝ἑτοίμως *readily, promptly, at once,* ii. 5. 2 : v. 7. 4.

ἔτος, εος, τό, *a year :* τριάκοντα ἔτη γεγονότες, or ἔτων τριάκοντα, 30 *years old :* ii. 3. 12 ; 6. 20. Der. ETESIAN.

ἐτραπόμην, see τρέπω, ii. 6. 5.

ἐτράφην, see τρέφω, iii. 2. 13.

ἔτρωσα, ἐτρώθην, see τιτρώσκω.

ἔτυχον, see τυγχάνω, i. 5. 8.

εὖ adv., (fr. neut. of Ep. ἐΰς *good,* but compared as if neut. of ἀγαθός) *well, fortunately, happily, prosperously, successfully, rightly ; kindly, beneficially; easily;* sometimes, in compos., *very;* i. 3. 4; 7. 5. Der. EU-LOGY.

✝εὐ-δαιμονία, as, *prosperity, happiness,* ii. 5. 13.

✝εὐ-δαιμονίζω, ίσω ιῶ, *to call* or *esteem happy, congratulate,* A. G. or ὑπέρ, i. 7. 3.

✝εὐ-δαιμόνως, c. νέστερον, s. νέστατα, *happily,* iii. 1. 43.

εὐ-δαίμων, ον, g. ονος, c. ονέστερος, s. ονέστατος, (δαίμων *dæmon, fortune*) of *good fortune, fortunate, happy ; prosperous, flourishing, opulent, wealthy, rich ;* i. 2. 6 s ; 5. 7; 9. 15 : iii. 5. 17.

εὔ-δηλος, ον, *very clear, quite evident,* iii. 1. 2 : v. 6. 13.

εὐ-δία, as, (Ζεύς, Διός) when Zeus is kind, *fine weather,*· *a calm ;* hence, *quiet, security ;* v. 8. 19.

εὔ-δοξος, ον, (δόξα) of *good fame, portending glory,* vi. 1. 23 ?

εὐ-ειδής, ές, c. ἔστερος, s. ἔστατος, (εἶδος) of *good appearance, fine-looking, well-formed, handsome,* ii. 3. 3.

εὔ-ελπις, ι, g. ιδος, of *good hope, hopeful, confident,* ii. 1. 18.

εὐ-επί-θετος, ον, (ἐπι-τίθημι) *easy of attack,* D.: εὐεπίθετον ἦν (impers.) τοῖς πολεμίοις *it was easy for the enemy to make an attack,* iii. 4. 20.

✝εὐεργεσία, as, *well-doing, good service, beneficence ; a benefit, kindness, favor ;* ii. 5. 22 ; 6. 27.

✝εὐεργετέω, ήσω, εὐεργέτηκα or εὐηργέτηκα, *to do a favor, confer benefits,* ii. 6. 17.

εὐ-εργέτης, ου, (ἔργον) a *well-doer, benefactor,* ii. 5. 10 : vii. 7. 23 (as adj.).

εὔ-ζωνος, ον,. s., (ζώνη) *well-girt* as for exercise, *prepared for active movement, lightly equipped ;* hence, *active, agile, nimble :* iii. 3. 6 : iv. 2. 7 ; 3. 20.

✝εὐήθεια, as, *simplicity, folly, stupidity,* i. 3. 16.

εὐ-ήθης, ες, (ἦθος *disposition*) well-dispositioned, *guileless ; simple, foolish, stupid ;* i. 3. 16. ·

εὐθέως adv., (εὐθύς) *straightway, immediately,* iv. 7. 7 ?

✝εὐθυμέω, ήσω, *to make cheerful : M. to be in good spirits, enjoy one's self,* iv. 5. 30.

εὔ-θυμος, ον, c., *in good spirits, cheerful,* iii. 1. 41.

εὐθύς, εῖα, ύ, *straight, direct :* hence adv. εὐθύς *straightway, directly, forthwith, immediately ; at the outset ;*

εὐθύωρον 55 εὔτολμος

sometimes joined with a part. instead of the leading verb, 662 : εὐθὺς παῖδες ὄντες immediately [being] while children, from their very childhood (= εὐθὺς ἐκ παίδων iv. 6. 14): εὐθὺς ἐπειδὴ ἀνηγέρθη immediately [when he awoke] on his awaking, or as soon as he awoke : i. 5. 8, 13, 15 ; 9. 4 : iii. 1. 13 ; 5. 12.

‡ εὐθύ-ωρον adv., (ὥρα ?) straight forward, right onward, ii. 2. 16.

εὔ-κλεια, as, (κλέος) good fame, glory, honor, vii. 6. 32 s.

‡ Εὐκλείδης, ου, Euclides, a soothsayer from Phlius in Peloponnesus, and a friend of Xenophon. Acc. to most mss., the same man or another of the same name was associated with Bi[t]on in his agency. vii. 8. 1, 3, 6 ?

εὐκλεῶς (εὐ-κλεής glorious, fr. κλέος) gloriously, with glory, vi. 3. 17.

εὐ-μενής, ές, c. ἕστερος, (μένος temper) well-disposed, kind, gentle, favorable, 2 D., iv. 6. 12.

εὐ-μετα-χείριστος, ον, (μετα-χειρίζω to handle, fr. χείρ) easily handled, easy to manage or impose upon, ii. 6. 20.

† εὔνοια, as, good-will towards, G.; affection, fidelity ; i. 8. 29 : iv. 7. 20.

† εὐνοϊκῶς with good-will, affectionately : εὖ. ἔχειν to be attached, D., i. 1. 5.

εὔ-νοος, ον, contr. εὔνους, ουν, c. οὐστερος, well-minded, well-disposed, friendly, affectionate, attached, D., i. 9. 20, 30 : ii. 4. 16: vii. 7. 30.

εὐξάμην, see εὔχομαι, iii. 2. 9.

εὔ-ξενος, Ion. εὔ-ξεινος, (ξένος) hospitable : Πόντος Εὔξεινος the Euxine or Black Sea, a sea whose early navigation was attended with so many dangers that it was called Πόντος Ἄξεινος, the inhospitable sea. The establishment of Greek, chiefly Milesian, colonies upon its shores removing some of these dangers, its name was changed on this account, or for better omen (cf. εὐώνυμος), to Πόντος Εὔξεινος, the hospitable sea. The Greeks carried on an extensive commerce with the Euxine, exchanging their manufactures, wine, oil, works of art, &c., for corn, honey, wax, timber, salt-fish, slaves, &c. iv. 8. 22 : v. 1. 1.

† Εὐ-οδεύς, έως, either a proper name, Euodeus ; or a patrial, a Euodian, from the name of some place in Elis if the Hieronymus before mentioned is here meant; vii. 4. 18 : v. l. Ἐυοδίας.

εὔ-οδος, ον, s., easy of travel or access, practicable, accessible, D.: impers. εὔοδόν ἐστιν the access is easy : iv. 2. 9; 8. 10, 12.

εὔ-οπλος, ον, s., (ὅπλον) well-armed, ii. 3. 3.

εὐ-πετῶς adv., (εὐ-πετής falling well, of dice, &c., fr. πίπτω) without trouble, easily, with ease, ii. 5. 23.

† εὐ-πορία, as, case of passage, transit, or provision ; abundance, plenty of means, sufficiency ; v. 1. 6 ? vii. 6. 37.

εὔ-πορος, ον, easily passable, easy of passage or to pass, easy, ii. 5. 9 : iii. 5. 17.

εὔ-πρακτος, ον, c., (πράττω) easy to effect, practicable, ii. 3. 20.

εὐ-πρεπής, ές, (πρέπω) well-looking, comely, handsome, iv. 1. 14.

εὐ-πρόσ-οδος, ον, s., easy of access, accessible, v. 4. 30.

† εὕρημα, ατος, τό, something found, an unexpected good fortune, a godsend, windfall : εὕρημα ἐποιησάμην I esteemed it a piece of good fortune : ii. 3. 18: vii. 3. 13.

εὑρίσκω,* εὑρήσω, εὕρηκα or ηὕρηκα, 2 a. εὗρον or ηὗρον, to find, discover, invent, devise, A. P.: M. to find for one's self, obtain, A. παρά : i. 2. 25 : ii. 1. 8 ; 3. 21 : iv. 1. 14: vi. 1. 29.

† εὖρος, εος, τό, width, breadth ; often in nom. with ἐστί understood, or to be supplied w. ἐστί· or in acc. of specif., both w. and without the art.; i. 2. 5, 8, 23 ; 4. 1, 4, 10 s ; 7. 14s.

† Εὐρύ-λοχος, ου, Eurylochus, a lochage from Lusi in Arcadia, eminent for valor and enterprise, iv. 2. 21 ; 7. 11.

† Εὐρύ-μαχος or Ἐρύ-μαχος, ου, E[u]rymachus, a Dardanian, a messenger for Timasion, v. 6. 21.

εὐρύς, εῖα, ύ, wide, broad, spacious, iv. 5. 25 : v. 2. 5.

‡ Εὐρ-ώπη, ης, Europe, a name in Hom. (Apoll. 251) for the main land north of the Peloponnesus, but in Hdt. and henceforth for the northwest division of the Old World, vii. 1. 27 ; 6. 32.

εὔ-τακτος, ον, c., (τάττω) well-ordered, well-disciplined, well-behaved, orderly, ii. 6. 14 : iii. 2. 30.

‡ εὐ-τάκτως in an orderly manner, in good order, vi. 6. 35.

εὐ-ταξία, as, (τάττω) good order, discipline, i. 5. 8 : iii. 1. 38.

εὔ-τολμος, ον, (τόλμα courage) of

good courage, courageous, spirited, brave, i. 7. 4.

εὐ-τυχέω, ήσω, εὐτύχηκα or ηὐτύχηκα, (τύχη) to be fortunate or successful, to succeed, AE., i. 4. 17 : vi. 3. 6.

†εὐ-τύχημα, ατος, τό, a success: εὐτυχεῖν εὐτύχημα to gain or obtain a success, vi. 3. 6.

Εὐφράτης, ου, the Euphrātes, a noted river of western Asia, linked with the very dawn of history, and with some of its greatest empires and most signal events. It rises by two great branches in the mountains of Armenia ; and, after an estimated course of 1780 miles, enters the Persian Gulf, having formed with the Tigris a large alluvial tract, which is still rapidly increasing. The Cyreans forded the main river at Thapsacus, and the eastern branch not far from its source in Armenia. i. 3. 20 ; 4. 11: iv. 5. 2. ‖ FRAT ; below the junction of the Tigris, Shat-el-A'rab; the northern branch, Kará-Su (Black Water); the eastern and greater branch, Murád-Su (Water of Desire).

†εὐχή, ῆς, prayer, wish, i. 9. 11.

εὔχομαι, εὔξομαι, εὖγμαι or ηὖγμαι, to pray, vow, make or offer one's prayers or vows ; to express a wish, to wish ; I. (A.) D., A.: εὔχοντο αὐτὸν εὐτυχῆσαι wished him success : i. 4. 7, 17; 9. 11 : iii. 2. 9, 12 : iv. 3. 13 ; 8. 16, 25.

εὐ-ώδης, ες, (ὄζω, pf. ὄδωδα, to smell) sweet-smelling, fragrant, odoriferous, i. 5. 1 : iv. 4. 9 : v. 4. 29.

εὐ-ώνυμος, ον, (ὄνομα) of good name or omen, left : τὸ εὐώνυμον (κέρας) the left (wing) of an army. In the Greek system of augury (here unlike the Roman), indications from the left were deemed inauspicious. Hence, to avert any ill omen from mentioning this unlucky quarter, the Greeks applied to it, by euphemism, the term εὐώνυμος, just as they named the Furies Εὐμενίδες, the gracious goddesses ; cf. ἀριστερός, Εὔξεινος. i. 2. 15 ; 8. 4 s, 9, 13, 23.

εὐ-ωχέω, ήσω, (ἔχω) to entertain or feed another well or generously : M. to feed one's self or fare generously, to feast : iv. 5. 30 : v. 3. 11. [1. 4.

†εὐ-ωχία, as, feast, entertainment, vi.

ἐφ' by apost. for ἐπί, i. 2. 16.

ἔφαγον, see ἐσθίω, ii. 3. 16.

ἐφάνην, see φαίνω, i. 10. 19.

ἔφασαν, see φημί, i. 4. 12.

ἐφ-εδρος, ον, (ἕδρα seat) sitting by : subst. ἔφεδρος, ου, ὁ, an athlete sitting by when two were contending, ready to contest the prize with the conqueror ; hence, successor in the contest, avenger, ii. 5. 10: v. l. ἔφορος.

ἐφ-έπομαι,* ἕψομαι, ipf. εἱπόμην, 2 a. ἑσπόμην, to follow upon or after, accompany ; to pursue as a foe, press upon ; D.; ii. 2. 12 : iv. 1. 6 s ; 6. 25.

†Ἐφέσιος, a, ον, Ephesian, v. 3. 4, 6.

Ἔφεσος, ου, ἡ, Ephesus, a famed city of Ionia in Asia Minor, at the mouth of the Caÿster. It was specially devoted to the worship of Diāna (Ἄρτεμις), which attracted to it hosts of worshippers, and gave to it a kind of sacred character that brought it favor and saved it from many of the evils of war. Its great temple of the goddess was burned, for the sake of notoriety, by Herostratus, on the night in which Alexander the Great was born ; but by the contributions of the Ionian and other cities it rose with more than its former splendor, and was then the largest of all the Greek temples, and accounted one of the wonders of the world. Ephesus was afterwards the seat of one of the most influential of the Christian churches, where Paul, Timothy, and John labored. It was a common landing-place for passengers on the way to Sardis, like the Cyrean Greeks ; and Xenophon here begins his computation of the length of the march to Cunaxa. i. 4. 2 : ii. 2. 6. ‖ Ayasaluk.

ἐφ-εστήκεσαν, ἐφ-ειστήκεσαν, or ἐφ-έστασαν, see ἐφ-ίστημι, i. 4. 4.

ἔφην, ἔφησθα, ἔφη, see φημί, i. 6. 7.

ἐφθός, ή, όν, (ἕψω) boiled, cooked, v. 4. 32.

ἐφ-ίημι,* ἥσω, εἷκα, a. ἧκα (ὦ, &c.), to send to : M. to yield one's self to, permit, D. I., vi. 6. 31 ?

ἐφ-ίστημι,* στήσω, ἔστηκα, 1 a. ἔστησα, 2 a. ἔστην, a. p. ἐστάθην, to bring to a stand, A.: hence, to stop or halt an army; to check a horse [sc. τὸν ἵππον, i. 8. 15]; to place, set, or appoint over, A. D.; ii. 4. 25 : v. 1. 15 s :—M. (w. pf., plp., & 2 a. act.) to stand upon, by, or over, ἐπί · hence, to stop or halt, intrans.; to command, D.; i. 4. 4 ; 5. 7 : ii. 4. 26 : iv. 7. 9 : vi. 5. 11.

ἐφ-όδιον, ου, (ὁδός) viaticum, *provision for the way* or *journey*, *travelling-money*, vii. 3. 20 ; 8. 2.

ἔφ-οδος, ου, ἡ, *a way to* or *upon, access, approach*, ἐπί, ii.2.18 : iii.4.41.

ἐφ-οράω,* ὄψομαι, ἑώρᾱκα or ἑόρᾱκα, 2 a. εἶδον, *to look upon, view, behold, witness; to keep in view* or *charge, watch over, guard;* A.; iii. 1. 13 : vi. 3. 14 : vii. 1. 30 ; 6. 31.

ἐφ-ορμέω, ήσω, *to lie moored against, to blockade*, vii. 6. 25.

ἔφ-ορος, ου, ὁ, (ἐφ-οράω) *an overseer, guardian; an Ephor*, a popular magistrate in some of the Doric states. The Spartan Ephori, five in number, were elected annually from the whole body of citizens as their especial representatives, and as general overseers of the state.. During their brief term of office, they were endowed with great powers, administrative, judicial, and censorial, even above those of the kings. ii. 6. 2 s : 5. 10 ?

ἔφυγον, see φεύγω, i. 2. 18 ; 9. 31.

ἐχθές = χθές *yesterday*, vi. 4. 18 ?

[**ἔχθος**, εος, τό, *hate, hatred*.]

†**ἔχθρα**, ας, inimicitia, *enmity, hostility, animosity*, ii. 4. 11.

‡**ἐχθρός**,* ά, όν, c. ἐχθίων & s. ἔχθιστος as fr. root ἐχθ-, inimīcus, *inimical, hostile:* subst. **ἐχθρός,οῦ**, *an enemy* or *foe*, esp. *a private* or *personal enemy*, one cherishing feelings of personal hatred or enmity ; while πολέμιος (hostis) denotes rather a *public enemy*, one who is at war with another: οἱ ἔχθιστοι *the bitterest foes, worst enemies:* i. 3. 12, 20 : iii. 2. 3, 5.

†**ἐχυρός**, ά, όν, *fit for holding, strong, fortified, secure*, ii. 5. 7 : cf. ὀχυρός.

ἔχω & **ἴσχω**,* εἴξω & σχήσω, ἔσχηκα, ipf. εἶχον & ἴσχον, 2 a. ἔσχον (σχῶ, σχοίην, σχές, &c.) *to have* or *hold (have* belonging rather to ἔχω, ἕξω, and *hold* to ἴσχω, σχήσω ; but the translation often varying according to the grammatical object, while this object w. ἔχω often forms a periphrasis for a corresponding verb), A.; hence, *to possess, occupy, contain, obtain, retain; to wear* or *carry; to feel ; to detain, withstand, restrain, keep from*, A. G.; *to have the ability* or *power* [sc. δύναμιν], *be able* (*can*), i. : ἔχων *having*, often where we use *with:* i. 1. 2, 8 ; 2. 6, 15 s ; 4. 7 ; 5. 8 : iii. 5. 11 : εἰρή-

νην ἔχειν *to live in peace*, ἔνδηλον ἔ. *to make evident*, ἡσυχίαν ἔ. *to remain quiet, keep still*, ii. 6. 6, 18 : iv. 5. 13. Ἔχω is sometimes used w. a part., as a stronger form of expression than the simple verb, 679 b, i. 3. 14 : iv. 7. 1. Ἔχω refl. or intrans., *to have one's self*, hence *to be* (w. an adv. comm. = εἰμί w. an adj., 577 d), *be affected* or *related, be situated, stand, lie, fare;* ὥσπερ εἶχεν *just as he* [had himself] *was;* οὕτως ἔχει impers., *so it is, thus the matter stands;* κακῶς or καλῶς ἔχειν *to be* or *go ill* or *well;* ἐντίμως ἔ. *to be held in honor;* i. 1. 5 ; 3. 9 ; 5. 16 : iii. 1. 3, 31, 40 : iv. 1. 19 ; 5. 22. — *P. to be occupied, held* as prisoners, &c.; (ἐν) ἀνάγκῃ ἔχεσθαι *to be bound by necessity;* ii. 5. 21: iv. 6. 22. — *M.* ἔχομαι *to have* or *lay hold of, hold fast to, cling to, struggle for ; hence, to follow closely, come* or *be next to, adjoin;* G.; i. 8. 4, 9 : vi. 3. 17 : vii. 6. 41. — See ἴσχω.

ἑψητός, ή, όν, (ἔψω) *boiled, obtained by boiling*, ii. 3. 14.

ἔψομαι, see ἕπομαι, i. 3. 6.

ἕψω,* ἑψήσω, *to boil, cook*, ii. 1. 6.

ἕωθεν adv., (ἕως) *from dawn, at daybreak, early in the morning*, iv. 4. 8.

ἑώκειν, see εἰκάζω, iv. 8. 20.

ἑῶν, ἑῶσι, see ἐάω, v. 8. 22.

ἑώρων, ἑώρᾱκα, see ὁράω, i. 9. 14.

ἕως,* ἕω, ἕῳ, ἕω (199. 3), ἡ, *dawn, daybreak, early morning; the east;* i. 7. 1 : ii. 4. 24 : iii. 5. 15 : iv. 3. 9.

ἕως adv. or conj., (ὅς) *as long as, while, whilst, until*, i. 3. 11 ; 4. 8 : ii. 1. 2 : ἕως οὗ *until the time when*, 557 a, iv. 8. 8 ?

Z.

Ζάβατος or **Ζαπάτας**, ου, ὁ, *the Zabatus* or *Zapatas*, a large affluent entering the Tigris a little below the site of Nineveh. Its oriental name Zaba was sometimes translated by the Greeks into Λύκος, *wolf*. ii. 5. 1 : iii. 3. 6. || The Great Zab.

ζάω * (ζάεις ζῇς, inf. ζῆν, &c., 120 g), ζήσω, ἔζηκα, ipf. ἔζων, *to live :* ζῶν *living, alive :* A. of extent, P. of means, ἀπό: i. 5. 5 ; 6. 2 ; 9. 11 : iii. 2. 25, 39 : vi. 1. 1.

ζειά, ᾶς, comm. pl., Lat. *far, spelt*, *a kind of grain*, v. 4. 27.

ζειρά, ᾶς, a long *overcoat* or *wrapper*, worn by the Thracians, vii. 4. 4.

†ζευγηλατέω, ήσω, to *drive a team*, vi. 1. 8.

†ζευγ-ηλάτης, ου, (ἐλαύνω) the *driver of a team, a teamster*, vi. 1. 8.

ζεύγνῡμι,* ζεύξω, ἔζευχα 1., pf. p. ἔζευγμαι, to *yoke, join, connect, fasten; to span, form by the union of;* A. D. of means, παρά, πρός : i. 2. 5 : ii. 4. 13, 24 : iii. 5. 10 : vi. 1. 8. Cf. jungo.

‡ζεῦγος, εος, τό, jugum, a *yoke, span,* or *team*, of oxen, horses, &c., iii. 2. 27.

Ζεύς,* Διός, Διΐ, Δία, Ζεῦ, *Zeus* or *Jupiter* (cf. Ζεῦ πάτερ), son of Kronos (Saturn) and Rhea, king of gods and men, ruling especially over the heavens and solid earth, i. 7. 9. His name appears in the Anabasis with the surnames σωτήρ, as protector from danger, i. 8. 16 ; βασιλεύς, as king, and patron of kings, iii. 1. 12 ; ξένιος, as the god of hospitality and maintainer of its rights, iii. 2. 4 ; μειλίχιος, as gracious to those who propitiate him by offerings, vii. 8. 4. Xenophon was directed by the Delphic oracle to Ζεὺς Βασιλεύς for special guidance and protection in his Asiatic journey ; and was advised by Euclides to propitiate Ζεὺς Μειλίχιος, as a deity offended by neglect.

ζῇ, ζῆν, see ζάω, i. 9. 11 : ii. 1. 1.

Ζήλ-αρχος, ου, *Zelarchus*, a director of the market, who was believed by the Cyreans to have wronged them, v. 7. 24, 29.

ζηλωτός, ή, όν, (ζηλόω to envy, fr. ζῆλος ZEAL, emulation) *enviable, to be envied;* of a person, *an object of envy*, D. ; i. 7. 4.

ζημιόω, ώσω, ἐζημίωκα, (ζημία loss, penalty) to *punish*, A. D. of penalty, vi. 4. 11.

ζητέω, ήσω, ἐζήτηκα, to *seek, inquire* or *ask for*, A., I., ii. 3. 2 : v. 4. 33.

ζυμίτης, ου, (ζύμη leaven, ζέω to bubble up) adj., *leavened*, vii. 3. 21 : v. l. ζυμής, ῆτος, or ζυμήτης, ου.

ζωγρέω, ήσω, (ζωός, ἀγρέω to catch) to *take alive, to take captive* or *prisoner*, A., iv. 7. 22.

ζῶν, ζῶντες, ζώην, see ζάω, ii. 6. 29.

ζώνη, ης, (ζώννῡμι to gird) a *girdle, belt*, ZONE. The girdle was important to the ancients for confining their loose dresses, and raising them when too long for convenience (as in work); and also for sustaining weapons, pouches, &c. It was sometimes highly ornamented and costly ; so that the Persian queens had the income of villages appropriated for their girdles (εἰς ζώνην *for girdle-money*, cf. "pin-money"). i. 4. 9 ; 6. 10.

ζωός, ή, όν, (ζάω) *alive, living*, iii. 4. 5. Der. ZODIAC, ZOO-LOGY.

H.

ἤ * alternative conj., *aut, vel, or:* ἤ . . ἤ *either . . or: πότερον . . ἤ, πότερα . . ἤ,* or sometimes *εἰ . . ἤ, utrum . . an, whether . . or:* i. 3. 5 ; 4. 13, 16 (= otherwise) ; 10. 5 : ii. 4. 3 ; 5. 17 : — comparative conj. (after comparatives, and some other words of distinction, as ἄλλος, ἄλλως, ἀντίος, διαφέρω, πρόσθεν), *quam, than*, i. 1. 4 s : ii. 2. 13 : iii. 1. 20 ; 4. 33. See ἀλλ' ἤ.

ἤ * adv., *indeed, truly, surely, certainly, assuredly;* sometimes introducing a direct question ; i. 6. 8 : v. 8. 6 : vii. 4. 9 ; 6. 4.

ἤ, see ὁ. — ᾗ, ᾗς, ᾗ (often as adv., *where, which way*), ἥν, see ὅς. — ᾗ, see εἰμί, i. 3. 20.

ἡβάσκω, in pr. & ipf., (inceptive of ἡβάω to *be of age*, fr. ἥβη *youthful prime*) to *become of age, come to manhood*, iv. 6. 1 : vii. 4. 7.

ἤγαγον, see ἄγω, iv. 6. 21.

ἡγάσθην, see ἄγαμαι, i. 1. 9.

ἤγγειλα, ἤγγελλον, see ἀγγέλλω.

ἠγγυάμην, see ἐγγυάω, vii. 4. 13.

†ἡγεμονία, ας, *leadership, lead, foremost place, precedence*, G., iv. 7. 8.

†ἡγεμόσυνος, ον, *relating to guidance:* ἡγεμόσυνα [sc. ἱερά] *thank-offerings for safe guidance* or *conduct*, iv. 8. 25.

†ἡγεμών, όνος, ὁ, a *leader; a guide, conductor*, whether human or divine (as Hercules for the Greeks, vi. 5. 24s); a *leader* in war, *commander, chief;* a *superior* or *sovereign*, applied to a controlling state ; G. ; i. 3. 14, 16 s ; 6. 2 ; 7. 12 : vi. 1. 27 ; 2. 15.

ἡγέομαι, ἥσομαι, ἥγημαι, (ἄγω) to *lead, go before ; to guide, conduct ; to take the lead* or *advance, lead the way, be in the advance* or *van ; to lead* in war, *command ;* G., D., AE., εἰς, ἐπί,

&c.: mentally, to lead to a conclusion (cf. Lat. duco), *think, consider, deem, suppose, believe,* I. (A.): ὁ ἡγούμενος *the leader:* τὸ ἡγούμενον *the leading division* of an army, *the van, advance,* or *front:* i. 2. 4; 4. 2; 7. 1; 9. 31: ii. 1. 11; 2. 4, 8; 4. 5, 26: v. 4. 10, 20.

‡**Ἡγήσ-ανδρος,** ου, *Hegesander,* one of the 10 commanders chosen by the Arcadians and Achæans, vi. 3. 5.

ἥδειν, ἥδεσαν, see ὁράω, i. 8. 21.

ἡδέως adv., c. ἥδιον, s. ἥδιστα, (ἡδύς) *agreeably, pleasantly, at ease; with pleasure, gladly, cheerfully, cordially:* c. *more cheerfully, rather:* ἥδιστ' ἂν ἀκούσαιμι *I should most gladly hear,* or *be most glad to hear,* i. 2. 2; 4. 9; 9. 19: ii. 5. 15: vi. 5. 17: vii. 7. 46.

ἤ-δη adv., (ἡ δή *surely now*) comm. referring to the present with the recent past, or in strong distinction from the past; but sometimes to the present with the immediate future, in distinction from a more distant future: jam, *already, by this time, just now, now, recently, at length; presently, forthwith:* τὸ ἤδη κολάζειν *the immediate chastisement:* i. 2. 1; 3. 1, 11; 8. 1: ii. 2. 1: vi. 1. 17: vii. 1. 4; 7. 24.

ἡδονή, ῆς, *pleasure, delight, enjoyment; an object of pleasure, gratification; delicious flavor;* ii. 3. 16; 6. 6: iv. 4. 14. From ἥδω.

ἡδυνάμην, -ήθην, see δύναμαι.

†**ἡδύ-οινος,** ον, *producing sweet wine,* vi. 4. 6.

ἡδύς, εῖα, ύ, c. ἡδίων, s. ἥδιστος,(ἥδω) *sweet, delicious, pleasing, pleasant, agreeable,* i. 5. 3; 9. 25: vi. 5. 24.

ἥδω, ἥσω 1., *to please:* P. & M. (f. ἡσθήσομαι, a. ἥσθην) *to be pleased, delighted,* or *gratified; to delight in, be fond of;* D., P.; i. 2. 18; 4. 16: ii. 6. 28.

ἥειν, ἥεσαν, or ἦσαν, see εἶμι.

ἤθελον, ἠθέλησα, see ἐθέλω, i. 8. 13.

ἧκα, see ἵημι, iv. 5. 18.

ἥκιστα, see ἥττων, i. 9. 19.

ἥκω, ἥξω, ἧκα 1., *to come; to come back, return;* often as pf., *to have come* or *arrived* (cf. *I am come*), *be here,* 612; i. 2. 1, 6; 5. 12, 15; 6. 3: ii. 1. 9, 15. Cf. οἴχομαι.

ἥλασα, ἤλαυνον, see ἐλαύνω, i. 2. 23.

ἤλεγχον, see ἐλέγχω, iii. 5. 14.

Ἠλεῖος, ου, ὁ, (Ἦλις) *an Elean.* Elis was the most western province of Peloponnesus, containing a city of the same name, and also Olympia, famed for the temple and great games in honor of Jupiter. It was hence regarded as a sacred territory; and was thus mainly protected, even in its unwalled towns, from invasion and ravage. Permitted and disposed to take little part in the quarrels of Greece, it enjoyed a long period of quiet and prosperity. It was natural and wise in Xenophon to choose it for residence, on his withdrawal from military and civil life. ii. 2. 20: iii. 1. 34.

ἤλεκτρον, ου, (ἔλη *brightness*) *amber; electrum,* an alloy of about four parts gold to one of silver; ii. 3. 15. Der. ELECTRICITY.

ἦλθον, see ἔρχομαι, i. 2. 18.

†**ἠλί-βατος,** ον, poet., (βαίνω) *inaccessible, precipitous,* i. 4. 4.

[**ἤλιθα** Ep. adv., (ἄλη *wandering*) *in vain.*]

‡**ἠλίθιος,** α, ον, *foolish, silly, senseless, stupid, stolid:* τὸ ἠλίθιον *folly, stupidity:* ii. 5. 21; 6. 22: v. 7. 10.

ἡλικία, ας, (ἡλίκος *how old*) *time of life, age,* i. 9. 6: iii. 1. 14, 25.

‡**ἡλικιώτης,** ου, (v. l. ἧλιξ, ικος) *an equal in age, comrade,* i. 9. 5.

ἥλιος, ου, ὁ, (akin to ἔλη *brightness*) *sol, the sun,* an object of religious worship among the Greeks, and still more among the Persians, i. 10. 15: iv. 5. 35. See ἅμα. Der. HELIO-TROPE.

ἥλπιζον, see ἐλπίζω, vii. 6. 34.

ἥλωκα, ἥλων, see ἁλίσκομαι, iv. 2. 13.

[**ἦμαι,** ἧσο, ἧσθαι, &c., pret., *to sit.*]

ἡμεῖς *we,* pl. of ἐγώ, i. 3. 9 s, 18.

ἠμελημένως, (fr. pf. p. pt. of ἀμελέω) *carelessly, incautiously,* i. 7. 19.

ἦμεν, ἦτε, ἦσαν, see εἰμί, vii. 6. 9.

ἡμέρα, ας, (as if from ἥμερος, sc. ὥρα, *the mild time*) *the day* (w. the art. often om., 533 d), *a day,* i. 2. 6; 7. 2, 14, 18: ii. 1. 2 s; 6. 7. See ἅμα, μετά. Der. EPH-EMERAL.

ἥμερος, ον, *mild, tame; cultivated* or *garden* (trees), v. 3. 12.

ἡμέτερος, α, ον, (ἡμεῖς) *our:* ἡ ἡμετέρα, sc. χώρα, *our territory:* τὰ ἡμέτερα *our affairs,* sometimes by periphr. for ἡμεῖς: i. 3. 9: iii. 5. 5 s: iv. 8. 6.

ἡμι- in compos., *semi-, half-,* HEMI-.

ἡμί-βρωτος, ον, *half-eaten,* i. 9. 26.

ἡμι-δαρεικόν, ου, (δαρεικός) *a half-daric,* i. 3. 21.

ἡμι-δεής, ές, (δέω to want) wanting half, half-emptied, half-full, i. 9. 25.
ἡμι-οβόλιον, ου, (ὀβολός) a half-obol, i. 5. 6?
ἡμι-όλιος, α, ον, (ὅλος) half as much again: neut. subst., the whole and a half, a half more, G., i. 3. 21.
†ἡμιονικός, ή, όν, of mules, vii. 5. 2.
ἡμί-ονος, ου, ὁ ἡ, a half-ass, a mule, v. 8. 5.
ἡμί-πλεθρον, ου, a half-plethrum, about 50 feet, iv. 7. 6.
ἥμισυς, εια, υ, (ἥμι-) semis, half: τὸ ἥμισυ [sc. μέρος] the half [part]: ἡμίσεα ἄρτων half-loaves of bread: i. 8. 22; 9. 26: iv. 2. 9; 3. 15.
ἡμι-ωβόλιον = ἡμι-οβόλιον, i. 5. 6?
ἥμουν, see ἐμέω, iv. 8. 20.
ἡμφεγνόουν, see ἀμφι-γνοέω, ii. 5. 33?
ἤν, contr. fr. ἐάν, if, i. 1. 4; 4. 15.
ἤν, ἦσθα, ἦν, see εἰμί, iii. 1. 27.
ἤν, ἤν-περ, see ὅς, ὅσ-περ, ii. 2. 10.
ἠνειχόμην, ἠνεσχόμην, see ἀν-έχω.
ἠνέχθη, see φέρω, iv. 7. 12.
ἡνίκα rel. adv., (ὅς) when, ch. w. ind., and more specific than ὅτε, 53;; i. 8. 1, 8, 17: iii. 5. 18 (G., see ὥρα)?
ἡνί-οχος, ου, ὁ, (ἡνία rein, ἔχω) a rein-holder, driver of a chariot, i. 8. 20.
ἤν-περ, contr. fr. ἐάν-περ, if indeed, if only, ii. 4. 17? iii. 2. 21: iv. 6. 17?
ἤξειν, ἥξοιμι, see ἥκω, i. 7. 1; 6. 3.
ἥ περ just as, just where, see ὅσ-περ.
ἠπιστάμην, see ἐπ-ίσταμαι, v. 1. 10.
†Ἡράκλεια, ας, Heraclēa (city of Hercules), a prosperous commercial city on the Bithynian coast of the Euxine, a Megarian colony, v. 6. 10: vi. 2. 1; 4. 2. ‖ Herakli, or Eregli.
†Ἡρακλείδης, ου, Heraclides, from Maronēa in Thrace, an unprincipled and trickish agent of Seuthes, vii. 3. 16.
†Ἡρακλεώτης, ου, (a man of Ἡράκλεια) a Heracleot or Heraclean, v. 6. 19: vi. 2. 3, 17 s.
†Ἡρακλεῶτις, ιδος, ἡ, (sc. γῆ) Heracleōtis, the territory belonging to Heraclēa, vi. 2. 19.
Ἡρα-κλῆς,* έους, εῖ, ἐα, εις, Heracles or Hercules, son of Jupiter and Alcmēne, the most celebrated of all the heroes of antiquity. The greatest of the twelve labors which he performed at the bidding of Eurystheus, was his descent into Hades and bringing thence the monster Cerberus, whom he showed to his taskmaster and then restored. Tradition connected this descent with various localities, most commonly with a cave near Cape Taenarum in Laconia. His exploits in removing the dangers of travel from wild beasts and robbers, led to his especial worship as a conductor in perilous journeys (ἡγεμών). iv. 8. 25: vi. 2. 2; 5. 24 s.
ἡράσθην, see ἔραμαι, iv. 6. 3.
ἡρέθην, ᾕρημην, see αἱρέω, iii. 1. 47 s.
ἡρμήνευον, see ἑρμηνεύω, v. 4. 4.
ἡρξάμην, ἠρχόμην, see ἄρχω.
ἡρόμην, ἠρώτων, ἠρώτησα, see ἐρωτάω, i. 3. 20; 6. 7 s; 7. 9.
ἧς, ἧσ-περ, see ὅς, ὅσ-περ, iii. 2. 21.
ἧσαν, ἦσθα, ἤστην, see εἰμί, i. 1. 6.
ἧσαν or ᾖεσαν, see εἶμι, iv. 4. 14.
ᾐσθημαι, ᾐσθόμην, see αἰσθάνομαι.
ᾔσθην, see ἥδομαι, i. 2. 18.
ᾔσθιον, see ἐσθίω, ii. 1. 6.
†ἡσυχάζω, άσω, to keep quiet or still, keep one's place, v. 4. 16.
†ἡσυχῇ or ἡσυχῆ, quietly, stilly, noiselessly, i. 8. 11.
†ἡσυχία, ας, ease, quiet, rest, tranquillity: καθ' ἡσυχίαν at one's ease, in quiet, quietly, peaceably, without molestation: ii. 3. 8. See ἄγω & ἔχω.
ἥσυχος, ον, (ἥμαι?) still, quiet, without clamor, vi. 5. 11? [5. 11?
‡ἡσύχως quietly, without clamor, vi.
ᾔτε, ᾔτε, see εἰμί, εἶμι, ii. 5. 39.
ᾔτησα, ᾐτούμην, see αἰτέω, ii. 4. 2.
ἧτρον, ου, (ἦτορ heart) the abdomen, esp. below the navel: μέχρι τοῦ ἥτρου as far as the groin, iv. 7. 15.
†ἡττάομαι, ἡττήσομαι, oftener p. ἡττηθήσομαι, ἥττημαι, a. ἡττήθην, to be inferior, surpassed, or worsted, G. P.; to be conquered, defeated, or vanquished, as pass. of νικάω and sometimes, like this, w. the pres. as pf., 612; i. 2. 9: ii. 3. 23; 4. 6, 19; 6. 17: iii. 2. 39.
ἥττων, ἥκιστος, c. & s. (as fr. Ep. adv. ἧκα slightly, aspirated) referred to μικρός or κακός, less, least, or worse, worst: c. weaker, inferior, v. 6. 13, 32: neut. as adv., c. ἧττον less, the less, less likely or ably, ii. 4. 2: vi. 1. 18: vii. 5. 9; s. (otherwise rare) ἥκιστα least, the least, least of all, i. 9. 19.
ηὐξάμην, ηὐχόμην, ηὕρισκον, ηὗρον, ηὐτύχησα, see εὔχομαι, εὑρίσκω, εὐτυχέω, i. 4. 7? 9. 29? iv. 8. 25? vi. 3. 6?
ἠχθέσθην, ἠχθόμην, see ἄχθομαι.
ἤχθην, see ἄγω, vi. 3. 10.

Θ.

θ' for τί, by apostr. before au aspirated vowel, i. 3. 9.

θάλαττα (-σσα), ης (ἅλς sal, salt?) the sea, a general name for the great connected body of salt- or sea-water (often without the art. 533 d): θάλαττα μεγάλη a great or heavy sea, i. e. a great or violent rush of the sea (cf. magnum mare, Lucr. 2. 553): i. 1. 7 ; 2. 22 ; 4. 1, 4: iv. 7. 24: v. 8. 20. Cf. πόντος.

θάλπος, εος, τό, warmth, heat; pl. calōres, attacks of heat, heat, iii. 1. 23.

θαμινά adv. = θαμά (ἅμα) often, frequently, iv. 1. 16.

θάνατος, ου, ὁ, (θνήσκω) death; kind of death, mode of execution: ἐπὶ θανάτῳ for death, in token of death, as a sign of execution : i. 6. 10: ii. 6. 29 : iii. 1. 43. Der. EU-THANASY.

‡θανατόω, ώσω, to condemn to death, A., ii. 6. 4.

θάπτω,* θάψω, 2 a. p. ἐτάφην, to bury, inter, A., iv. 1. 19 : v. 7. 20.

†θαρραλέος, a, ον, c., courageous, bold, daring, confident, πρός, iii. 2. 16.

‡θαρραλέως courageously, boldly, fearlessly, confidently, with confidence, πρός: τὸ ἔχειν θ. to have one's self confidently, a feeling of confidence, fearlessness: i. 9. 19 : ii. 6. 14 : vii. 3. 29 ; 6. 29.

†θαρρέω, ήσω, τεθάρρηκα, to be courageous or of good courage ; to be bold, fearless, or confident ; to take heart; to have no fear of, A.: pt. as adv., confidently, with confidence, without fear, 674 d : i. 3. 8 : iii. 2. 20 ; 4. 3.

θάρρος, εος, τό, courage, confidence, vi. 5. 17.   [7. 2.

‡θαρρύνω, ὔνῶ, to encourage, cheer, i.

θαρσ- v. l. for θαρρ- in θάρρος, &c.

Θαρύπας, ου, Tharypas, a favorite of Menon, ii. 6. 28.

θάτερον or θάτερον, &c., by crasis for τὸ ἕτερον, &c., 125 b ; pl. ἐκ τοῦ [sc. χωρίου] ἐπὶ θάτερα [sc. μέρη], from [the region upon] the other or farther side, v. 4. 10.

θάττων, ον, c. of ταχύς, i. 2. 17.

θαῦμα, ατος, τό, (θάομαι to gaze upon) wonder or a subject of wonder, a marvel, vi. 3. 23.

‡θαυμάζω, ἄσομαι, less Att. άσω, τεθαύμακα, a. ἐθαύμασα, to wonder, marvel, admire, be surprised or astonished, CP., A., G., 472 e, i. 2. 18 ; 3. 2 s ; 8. 16 ; 10. 16 : vi. 2. 4.

‡θαυμάσιος, a, ον, s., wonderful, marvellous, admirable, G.? ii. 3. 15: iii. 1. 27.

‡θαυμαστός, ή, όν, s., to be wondered at, wonderful, wondrous, strange, surprising, D., i. 9. 24 ? ii. 5. 15 : iv. 2. 15.

†Θαψακηνός, οῦ, ὁ, a Thapsacene, a man of Thapsacus, i. 4. 18.

Θάψακος, ου, ἡ, Thapsacus (Tiphsah, i. e. passage or ford, 1 Kings 4. 24), a city near a much-frequented ford of the Euphrates, though the Thapsacenes flattered Cyrus by saying that the river had never before been fordable at that point. Alexander here crossed by two bridges, doubtless of boats ; but Lucullus forded the stream with his army, and Ainsworth states that the depth of the water was reduced to 20 inches in the autumn of 1841. i. 4. 11. ‖ Ruins near the Ford of the Anese-Beduins.

θέα, as, (akin to θάομαι to gaze upon) a sight, spectacle, iv. 8. 27.

θεά, ᾶς, (θεός) a goddess, vi. 6. 17 (elsewhere ἡ θεός, 174 b, v. 3. 6 s, 13).

‡Θεα-γένης, εος, see Θεο-γένης.

†θέαμα, ατος, τό, a sight, spectacle, iv. 7. 13.

θεάομαι, άσομαι, τεθέαμαι, (θέα) to look on, gaze at, behold, observe, witness, watch, perceive, see, with surprise, wonder, or admiration often implied, A. P., CP., i. 5. 8 : v. 7. 26 : vi. 5. 16. Cf. ὁράω. Der. THEATRE.

θεῖν to run, see θέω, i. 8. 18.

θεῖος, a, ον, (θεός) divine, by divine interposition, supernatural, miraculous, i. 4. 18.

θέλω to wish, will, see ἐθέλω.

θέμενος, θέντες, &c., see τίθημι.

†Θεο-γένης, εος, Theogenes, a lochage from Locris, vii. 4. 18 : v. l. Θεα-γένης.

†Θεό-πομπος, ου, Theopompus, an Athenian, only mentioned by some mss., ii. 1. 12. Other mss. have here ξενοφῶν, and two have ξενοφῶν in the text, and θεόπεμπος in the margin. We cannot suppose that there was a general named Theopompus, and it is extremely improbable that a person of inferior rank, so quiet and insignificant as to be nowhere else mentioned, should have interfered in an interview of the generals with the

θεός   62   Θήβη

king's heralds. But Xenophon, who was with the army simply as the intimate friend of Proxenus, and by the special invitation of Cyrus, held no position of inferiority. With entire propriety, he might be invited by Proxenus to attend him in the interview as a friend ; and might take part in the conversation to support him, if a fit occasion should arise. Compare i. 8. 15 : ii. 5. 37. Hence, also, Diodorus might naturally ascribe to Proxenus himself (xiv. 25) the words spoken by one who was present as his companion. How then could the change of name have arisen in some of the best mss.? Perhaps as follows : in view of the subsequent preservation of the army through Xenophon, an enthusiastic reader may have written in the margin, by the side of his name, θεῖπομπος, *the heaven-sent* (= θεό-πεμπτος, while in the marginal θεόπεμπτος the two forms seem blended) ; and, through a common mistake, a subsequent copyist may have understood as a correction what was simply meant as a comment, and have substituted it in the text.

θεός, οῦ, ὁ ἡ, deus, *a god, deity, divinity*, (ἡ θεός goddess, iii. 2. 12 : v. 3. 6 s): σὺν τοῖς θεοῖς *with the help of the gods*, or *by their will* or *favor :* πρὸς θεῶν *before* or *by the gods*. The art. is often omitted w. θεοί, 533 c. The Anabasis abounds in appeal or reference to "the gods," as a general expression for the Divine and Supreme Power (so ὁ θεός *the Deity*, vi. 3. 18); but makes comparatively little mention of any particular god, showing how far polytheism had lost its hold upon the Greek mind. i. 4. 8 ; 6. 6 : ii. 3. 22 s : iii. 1. 5 s, 23 s. Der. THEISM, ATHEIST.

‡θεο-σέβεια, as, (σέβω *to revere) piety, religion*, ii. 6. 26.

†θεραπεύω, εύσω, τεθεράπευκα, *to take care of, provide for, cherish, court*, A., i. 9. 20 : ii. 6. 27. Der. THERAPEUTIC.

θεράπων, οντος, ὁ, (θέρω *to warm) an attendant, waiter, servant*, i. 8. 28 ?

θερίζω, ίσω ιῶ, (θέρος *summer*, fr. θέρω *to warm) to spend* or *pass the summer*, iii. 5. 15.

θερμασία, as, (θερμός *warm*, fr. θέρω *to warm) warmth*, v. 8. 15.

Θερμώδων, οντος, ὁ, *the Thermōdon*,

a river of Asia Minor, flowing into the Euxine. Its banks were the fabled abode of the Amazons. v. 6. 9 : vi. 2. 1. ∥ Thermeh-Chai.

θέσθαι, θέσθε, see τίθημι, i. 6. 4.

†Θετταλία (older Θεσσαλία), as, *Thessaly*, a large, fertile, and populous, but rude province in the northeast of Greece. It consists mostly of the rich basin of the Penēus, surrounded by mountains, among which are the famed Olympus and Ossa (with the beauties of Tempe between), and Pelion. Its institutions were mostly oligarchic, a few noble families domineering. Its rank was highest in the early history of Greece, when it contained the original Hellas, and sent Jason to the Argonautic adventure, and Achilles to Troy. i. 1. 10.

Θετταλός (older Θεσσαλός), ου, ὁ, a man of Thessaly, *a Thessalian*, i. 1. 10.

θέω,* θεύσομαι, ipf. ἔθεον, (other tenses supplied by τρέχω) *to run*, δρόμῳ, εἰς, ἐπί, πρός, &c., i. 8. 18 : ii. 2. 14 : iv. 3. 21, 29.

θεωρέω, ήσω, τεθεώρηκα, (θεωρός *spectator*, fr. θεάομαι) *to view, behold, observe, witness ; to inspect* or *review* an army; *to attend* games or rites *as a sacred deputy ;* A.; i. 2. 10, 16 : ii. 4. 25 s : v. 3. 7. Der. THEOREM, THEORY.

Θηβαῖος, ου, ὁ, a man of Thebes, *a Theban*, ii. 1. 10. Thebes (Θῆβαι) was the chief city of Bœotia, said to have been founded by the Phœnician Cadmus and walled to the music of Amphion. It was wonderfully rich in legendary story, e. g. as the birthplace of Bacchus and Hercules, and the scene of the tragic fortunes of Œdipus and Niobe. In the historical age, it commonly held the rank of the third city in Greece ; but, for a short period after the battle of Leuctra, of the first.

Θήβη, ης, *Thebe*, a town of western Mysia (also assigned to Lydia, as early occupied by the Lydians), under Mt. Placus. According to Homer, Andromache was the daughter of its king ; and the capture of the beautiful Chryseïs, in connection with its sack by Achilles, gave occasion to the action of the Iliad. Perishing itself, it left its name to a fertile plain in the vicinity of Adramyttium. vii. 8. 7.

θήρ 63 θυμός

[θήρ, θηρός, ὁ, fera, *a wild beast;* cf. Germ. *thier*, Eng. *deer.*]

‡θήρα, ας, *a hunt* or *chase* of wild beasts, v. 3. 8, 10.

‡θηράω, άσω, τεθήρᾱκα, *to hunt, chase*, or *pursue* wild beasts; *to prey upon;* A.; i. 5. 2: iv. 5. 24: v. 1. 9.

‡θηρεύω, εύσω, τεθήρευκα, *to hunt* or *chase* wild beasts; *to catch* or *take*, as a hunter his prey; A.; i. 2. 7, 13.

‡θηρίον, ου, dim. of θήρ, but comm. used in prose for it, 371 f; *a wild beast* or *animal*, i. 2. 7; 5. 2; 9. 6.

θησαυρός, οῦ, ὁ, (τίθημι) thesaurus, *a store* laid up, TREASURE; *treasury;* v. 3. 5; 4. 27.

Θήχης, ου, *Theches,* a mountain from which the Cyreans obtained their first and transporting view of the Euxine, iv. 7. 21. ‖ Acc. to Strecker, *Kolat-Dagh;* to others, *Tekieh-Dagh,* &c.

Θίβρων, ωνος, *Thibron,* a Spartan general who was sent in the winter of 400 – 399 B. C., to protect the Ionian cities from the Persians, and who took the returned Cyreans into his service. From want of efficiency and good discipline, he was superseded, in about a year, by Dercyllidas. In a later command against the Persians, B. C. 391, his carelessness cost him his life. vii. 6. 1; 8. 24: *v. l.* Θίμβρων.

θνήσκω* (oftener ἀπο-θνήσκω, exc. in the complete tenses), θανοῦμαι, τέθνηκα, 2 a. ἔθανον, 2 pf. pl. τέθναμεν, &c., inf. τεθνάναι, pt. τεθνεώς, *to die, fall in battle;* as pass. of κτείνω, *to be slain:* pf. pret., *to* [have died] *be dead,* pt. *dead; τεθνάναι ἐπηγγέλλετο* he offered or consented to be a dead man, i. e. *to die* or *be put to death immediately:* i. 6. 11 : ii. 1. 3 : iv. 1. 19; 7. 20.

‡θνητός, ή, όν, *mortal, liable* or *exposed to death,* iii. 1. 23.

Θόανα *v. l.* for Δάνα, i. 2. 20.

θόρυβος, ου, ὁ, (akin to θρέομαι *to cry,* and Lat. turba) *noise, outcry, uproar, tumult, alarm, murmur,* i. 8. 16 : ii. 2. 19 : iii. 4. 35 s : iv. 2. 20.

Θούριος, ου, ὁ, *a Thurian,* a man of Thurii, a flourishing city founded by an Athenian colony, B. C. 443, near the ruins of Sybaris on the Tarentine Gulf in southern Italy. Among the colonists were the historian Herodotus and the orator Lysias. v. 1. 2. ‖ Ruins near Terra-Nuova.

Θράκη, ης, (Θρᾷξ) *Thrace,* a rude country in southeastern Europe, north of the Ægean and Propontis. If this region was occupied early by more civilized tribes, to which Orpheus, Musæus, Thamyris, &c., belonged, they prob. moved southward into Greece. v. 1. 15. ‖ Rumelia. — 2. A neighboring district in Asia, across the Bosphorus, so called as occupied by Thracian tribes; oftener called Bithynia, from the chief of these tribes; vi. 4. 1.

‡Θράκιον, ου, *Thracium,* or *the Thracian Area,* in Byzantium, probably near the Thracian Gate, vii. 1. 24.

‡Θράκιος, α, ον, *Thracian,* vii. 1. 13.

Θρανίψαι *v. l.* for Τρανίψαι.

Θρᾷξ, Θρᾳκός, ὁ, *a Thracian,* a man of Thrace (in Europe or Asia); as adj., *Thraeian.* The Thracians were not wanting in activity, energy, or courage; but, though claiming relationship to their Greek neighbors, they partook but scantily of the Greek culture. Among their too prevalent characteristics were ferocity, cruelty, intemperance, and faithlessness. i. 1. 9; 2. 9 : vi. 4. 2 : vii. 1. 5 ; 3. 26.

†θρασέως adv., *boldly,* iv. 3. 30.

θρασύς, εῖα, ύ, c. ύτερος, (having the same stem w. θράσος = θάρσος or θάρρος) *bold, daring, spirited,* v. 4. 18 ; 8. 19.

θρέψομαι, see τρέφω, vi. 5. 20.

θρόνος, ου, ὁ, *a seat,* esp. the elevated seat of a ruler, *a* THRONE, ii. 1. 4.

θυγάτηρ,* (τέρος) τρός, τρί, τέρα, θύγατερ, ἡ, Germ. *toehter, a* DAUGHTER, ii. 4. 8 : iv. 5. 24.

θύλακος, ου, ὁ, *a sack, bag,* vi. 4. 23.

θῦμα, ατος, τό, (θύω) *a victim, sacrifice,* v. 4. 20 : vii. 8. 19.

Θύμβριον, ου, *Thymbrium,* a city of Phrygia, now represented acc. to some by Akshehr (i. e. *white city*), and acc. to others by Ishakli ; while the copious fountain Olu-Bunár (i. e. *great fountain*), between these towns, has been regarded by some as the famed spring of Midas. i. 2. 13.

†θῦμο-ειδής, ές, or θυμώδης, ες, c.ἐστερος, (εἶδος) *spirited, mettlesome,* iv. 5. 36.

†θυμόομαι, ώσομαι, τεθύμωμαι, *to be angry, provoked, incensed,* or *enraged,* D., ii. 5. 13.

θυμός, οῦ, ὁ, (θύω *to rush*) the rush of feeling, *spirit, anger, passion, resentment,* vii. 1. 25.

Θυνοί, ῶν, οἱ, *the Thyni*, a Thracian tribe near Byzantium, especially formidable in the night. A part of this tribe crossed, like the Bithyni, into Asia. vii. 2. 22, 32; 4. 14.

θύρα, ας, (cf. Lat. foris, Germ. *thür*) *a* DOOR, often in the plur., even when a single entrance is spoken of: pl. *door* or *doors, gates, quarters, residence, court* (cf. *sublime porte*): ἐπὶ ταῖς θύραις *at the very door* or *gates*, sometimes used as a strong expression for nearness: i. 2. 11; 9. 3: ii. 4. 4; 5. 31.

‡**θύρετρον, ου**, *a door, gate*, v. 2. 17.

†**θυσία, ας**, *a sacrifice, offering to a god*, iv. 8. 25 s: v. 3. 9: vi. 4. 15.

θύω (ῠ), θύσω, τέθυκα, *to sacrifice, offer to a god*, D. A., AE.: τὰ Λύκαια ἔθυσε *offered the Lycœan sacrifices, celebrated the Lycœan rites* or *festival*: i. 2. 10: iii. 2. 9, 12: *M. to sacrifice for learning the will of the gods* or *future events, to take* or *consult the auspices*, AE., D. (of the god, or of the person for whom), CP., I., ἐπί, περί, ὑπέρ, ii. 2. 3: v. 6. 22, 27 s: vii. 8. 4 s.

†**θωρακίζω, ίσω, to arm with a cuirass;** τεθωρακισμένος *equipped with a corselet, clad in armor: M. to put on one's own cuirass* or *armor, arm one's self:* ii. 2. 14; 5. 35: iii. 4. 35.

θώραξ, ακος, ὁ, *a cuirass, corselet, breastplate*. The Greek cuirass comm. consisted of two metallic plates, adapted to the shape of the body, one for the front, and the other for the back. These were ch. united by shoulder-pieces, the belt, and hinges or buckles at the sides. The cavalry cuirass was esp. heavy. Some nations wore corselets of thick, firm layers of flaxen cloth or felting. i. 8. 3, 26: iii. 4. 48: iv. 7. 15. Der. THORAX.

Θώραξ, ακος, an officer from Bœotia, who often contended with Xenophon, v. 6. 19, 25, 35.

I.

Ἰάομαι, ἀσομαι, ἴαμαι 1., *to heal, cure, dress* a wound, i. 8. 26.

Ἰασόνιος, α, ον, ('Ἰάσων *Jason*) *Jasonian:* Ἰασονία ἀκτή *the Jasonian Shore*, a promontory not far from Cotyōra, where Jason was supposed to have landed in the Argonautic Expedition, vi. 2. 1. ‖ Yasun-Burun, or Cape Bona.

ἰατρός, οῦ, ὁ, (ἰάομαι) *a healer, surgeon, physician*, i. 8. 26: iii. 4. 30.

ἰδεῖν, ἴδοιμι, ἴδω, ἰδών, see ὁράω, i. 2. 18; 9. 13: ii. 1. 9. Der. IDEA.

Ἴδη, ης, *Ida*, a mountain-range in Mysia, south of Troy. Here, in the old myths, Paris awarded the prize to Venus, and the gods sat to watch the strife about Troy. Its highest point, Gargaron (now Kaz-Dagh), is about 4650 feet high. vii. 8. 7.

ἴδιος, α, ον, *one's own, private, personal:* εἰς τὸ ἴδιον *for one's private* or *personal use* or *benefit, for one's self:* ἰδίᾳ, as adv., *privately, in private, personally, by one's self, on one's own account:* i. 3. 3: v. 6. 27. Der. IDIOM.

‡**ἰδιότης, ητος, ἡ**, *peculiarity*, ii. 3. 16.

‡**ἰδιώτης, ου**, *a private* or *common person* or *soldier, a private*, i. 3. 11: vi. 1. 31: vii. 7. 28. Der. IDIOT.

‡**ἰδιωτικός, ή, όν,** *relating to a private person*, or *denoting a private station*, vi. 1. 23.

ἱδρόω,* ώσω, ἵδρωκα l., (ἴδος *sweat*) *sudo, to sweat, perspire*, i. 8. 1.

ἴδω, ἰδών, see ὁράω, i. 2. 18.

ἵεμαι or **ἴεμαι,** see ἵημι, i. 5. 8.

ἰέναι, ἴθι, ἴοιμι, ἴω, ἰών, see εἶμι.

†**ἱερεῖον, ου**, *a victim for sacrifice, an animal* such as were used for sacrifice or food (since the two uses were so intimately united); pl. *cattle;*. iv. 4. 9: vi. 1. 4, 22; 5. 1 s.

†**Ἱερὸν ὄρος, τό**, *the Sacred Mountain* (Mons Sacer), a mountain west of the Propontis, on the direct route from Byzantium to the Chersonese, vii. 1. 14; 3. 3. ‖ Tekir-Dagh.

ἱερός, ά, όν, *sacred, consecrated, holy, hallowed,* G. 437 b: τὸ ἱερόν [sc. δῶμα] *the temple:* τὰ ἱερά *the sacred rites, sacrifices, auspices;* from their esp. use in divination, *the entrails*[sacred parts] of the victim: τὰ ἱερὰ γίγνεται *the sacrifices take effect, are auspicious:* i. 8. 15; ii. 1. 9; 2. 3: iv. 3. 9; 5. 35: v. 3. 9 s, 11, 13. Der. HIERO-GLYPHIC.

‡**Ἱερ-ώνυμος, ου**, *Hieronymus*, an Elean, the oldest lochage in the division of Proxenus, and influential for good, iii. 1. 34: vi. 4. 10.

ἵημι,* ἤσω, εἶκα, a. ἧκα (εἷμεν, ὤ, εἵην, &c.) *to send, throw, hurl, shoot, let fly,* A., D. of missile, κατά, εἰς, i. 5:

ἵητε   65   ἵστημι

12 : iv. 5. 18. *M. ἵεμαι (v. l. ἵεμαι,* referred to εἷμι, 45 p) to send one's self, *hasten, hurry on, rush, spring,* ἐπί, &c., i. 5. 8 ; 8. 26 : iv. 2. 7 s, 20.

ἵητε, ἵθι, see εἷμι, vii. 2. 26 ; 3. 4.

ἱκανός, ή, όν, c., (ἵκω) reaching the desired end, *sufficient, enough; adequate, required; able, capable, competent, qualified, adapted :* ἱκανόν [sc. χωρίον] *a sufficient distance:* I., D., ὅς, ὡς, ὥστε : i. 1. 5; 2. 1 ; 3. 6; 7. 7: ii. 3. 4 : v. 2. 30 ; 6. 12, 30 : vi. 4. 3.

‡ἱκανῶς *sufficiently, adequately,* iv. 2. 31.

†ἱκετεύω, εύσω, *to supplicate, entreat, beseech,* Α. Ι., vii. 4. 7, 10, 22.

ἱκέτης, ου, (ἵκω) one who comes for aid, *a suppliant,* vii. 2. 33.

Ἰκόνιον, ου, *Iconium,* an old city of Phrygia, near Lycaonia, in which it was afterwards included. Paul visited the city more than once, and made many converts. In the eleventh century, it became the capital of a powerful Seljuk sovereignty, which gave it a prominent place in the history of the Crusades. It is still an important city, and the capital of a pashalic. i. 2. 19. ‖ Konieh.

["ἵκω * poet., *to come, arrive, reach,* akin to ἥκω, 114 d.]

ἵλεως, ων, Att. contr. fr. ἵλᾶος, ον, *propitious, gracious, kind,* vi. 6. 32.

ἴλη, ης, *a troop,* esp. of horse, often set at 64 men, i. 2. 16: fr. εἴλω *to coil.*

ἱμάς, άντος, ὁ, a leathern *strap* or *thong,* iv. 5. 14.

ἱμάτιον, ου, (ἕννυμι *to clothe) a garment, vestment,* esp. an outer garment; pl. *clothes, clothing;* iv. 3. 11 s.

ἵνα * final conj., *in order that, so that, that,* comm. w. subj. or opt., i. 3. 4, 15 ; 4. 18 ; 10. 18.

ἴοιμι, ἰόντος, ἰόντων, &c., see εἷμι.

†ἵππ-αρχος, ου, ὁ, (ἄρχω) *a hipparch, commander of cavalry, master of horse,* iii. 3. 20.

†ἱππασία, ας, *riding about, movements* on horse, ii. 5. 33.

†ἱππεία, ας, *cavalry,* v. 6. 8.

†ἱππεύς, έως, ὁ, *horseman, knight;* pl. *cavalry, horse* (collectively). The Greek horseman was comm. armed much like the hoplite ; exc. that he usually carried no shield, and hence wore a stouter cuirass. Metallic armor was also provided for the head, breast, and sides of the horse. From the mountainous character of their country, however, and their habits of city life, the Greeks used cavalry very much less than the eastern nations. i. 2. 4 ; 5. 2, 13 ; 6. 2 s; 8. 7.

†ἱππικός, ή, όν, *of* or *for cavalry :* subst. ἱππικόν [sc. στράτευμα or πλῆθος] *cavalry* [force]: i. 3. 12 ; 9. 31.

†ἱππό-δρομος, ου, ὁ, *a race-course* for horses, *hippodrome,* i. 8. 20.

ἵππος, ου, ὁ ἡ, *a horse, mare :* ἀπὸ ἵππου [from a horse] *on horseback:* οἱ ἵπποι sometimes = οἱ ἱππεῖς *the horse, cavalry :* i. 2. 7 ; 8. 3, 18 : vii. 3. 39. Der. HIPPO-POTAMUS *(river-horse).*

Ἶρις, ιος or ιδος, ὁ, *the Iris,* a considerable river in the northeast part of Asia Minor, flowing into the Euxine, v. 6. 9 : vi. 2. 1. ‖ The Yeshil-Irmak, i. e. *Green River.*

ἴσθι, ἴσμεν, ἴστε, ἴσᾶσι, see ὁράω.

ἰσθμός, οῦ, ὁ, (εἷμι) the place to go on, *an* ISTHMUS: as a prop. name, the *Isthmus of Corinth,* the neck of land (about five miles across, where narrowest) connecting the Peloponnese w. the mainland of Greece, and separating the Corinthian and Saronic Gulfs. Repeated attempts were made and abandoned, to connect these gulfs by a canal. The famed Isthmian Games were here celebrated in honor of Neptune. ii. 6. 3.

†ἰσό-πλευρος, ον, (πλευρά) *equal-sided, equi-lateral,* iii. 4. 19.

ἴσος, η, ον, *equal,* D.: ἐν ἴσῳ *on an even line, with equal step:* ἐξ ἴσου from *equal ground, on an equality* or *par :* εἰς τὸ ἴσον *upon equal ground, to a level:* ἴσον κρατεῖν *to bear equal sway* or *have equal power:* i. 8. 11: ii. 5. 7 : iii. 4. 47 : iv. 6. 18 : v. 4. 32. Hence ISO- in many compounds.

‡ἰσο-χειλής, ές, (χεῖλος *lip, brim) level with* or *up to the brim,* iv. 5. 26.

Ἰσσοί, ῶν, οἱ, and Ἰσσός, οῦ, ἡ, *Issus* or *Issi,* an important city in the eastern part of Cilicia, at the head of a gulf bearing its name (now the Gulf of Scanderoon). Near it, B. C. 333, Alexander won a great victory over Darius III. i. 2. 24; 4. 1. ‖ Ruins near the northeast extremity of the gulf.

ἴστε, see ὁράω, i. 5. 16 ; 7. 3.

ἵστημι,* στήσω, ἔστηκα (2 pf. ἕσταμεν, &c., ἑστάναι, ἑστώς), plp. ἑστήκειν

LEX. AN.   E

ἱστίον 66 καθίζω

or εἱστήκειν, 1 a. ἔστησα, 2 a. ἔστην, to set up, STATION; to make stand or halt, to stop (trans.); A.; i. 2. 17; 10. 14: — M., w. act. 2 a. and complete tenses (used preteritively), sto, to STAND, intrans.; to stand one's ground, make a stand; but 1 a. m. to set up for one's self, erect, A.; i. 3. 2; 5. 2, 13; 10. 1, 11: iv. 6. 27; 7. 9.

ἱστίον, ου, (dim. of ἱστός web) a sail, i. 5. 3.

† ἰσχυρός, ά, όν, s., strong, mighty, powerful; vehement, severe; i. 5. 9: ii. 5. 22: iv. 5. 20; 7. 1: v. 8. 14.

† ἰσχυρῶς, c. ὅτερον, strongly, forcibly, vigorously; energetically, strenuously, resolutely; vehemently, severely; exceedingly, very; i. 2. 21; 5. 11: iii. 2. 19.

ἰσχύς, ύος, ή, (ἴς vis, strength) strength, might, force; a force of soldiers, a strong force; i. 8. 22: iii. 1. 42.

ἴσχω (strengthened form of ἔχω q. v.) to hold, arrest, check, A., vi. 5. 13: impers. ἴσχετο it was held or held itself, the matter stuck, the negotiation was suspended, vi. 3. 9.

ἴσως adv., (ἴσος) with equal chances, perhaps, probably; sometimes, from Greek courtesy, where we might rather say doubtless; ii. 2. 12: iii. 1. 37.

Ἰταβέλιος, ου, Itabelius, a Persian commander, who went to the aid of Asidates, vii. 8. 15: v. l. Ἰταμένης, &c.

ἰτέον (fr. εἶμι) ἐστίν it is necessary, proper, or best to go, one must or should go, 682, iii. 1. 7: vi. 5. 30.

ἴτυς, υος, ή, a rim, as of a shield; a shield-rim; iv. 7. 12.

ἴτωσαν, see εἶμι, i. 4. 8?

ἰχθύς, ύος, ὁ, a fish, i. 4. 9. Der. ICHTHYO-LOGY. The Syrian gods Dagon and Derceto (who had also other names) were worshipped in a form human above, but fish-like below.

ἴχνος, εος, τό, and dim. in form

ἴχνιον, ου, a track, trace, footstep, i. 6. 1; 7. 17: vii. 3. 42.

Ἰωνία, as, (Ἴωνες Ionians) Ionia, the central part of the western coast of Asia Minor, so named from its early colonization by the Ionians, whose descent was traced from Ion, grandson of Deucalion. It was the favorite seat (with the adjacent islands) of early Greek letters and art, the home of Epic and Elegiac poetry, of Ionic architecture, &c.; but unfortunately, from

its position, could not maintain its independence against the Lydians and afterwards the Persians. Assistance given to the Ionians was a pretext with the Persians for invading Greece. i. 4. 13: ii. 1. 3.

† Ἰωνικός, ή, όν, Ionian, pertaining to Ionia, i. 1. 6.

K.

κἀ- often in crasis for καὶ ἀ- or καὶ ἐ-.

κἀγαθός, κἀγώ = καὶ ἀγαθός, καὶ ἐγώ.

καθ' by apostr. for κατά, before an aspirated vowel, i. 10. 4.

καθά rel. adv., (καθ' ἅ) according as, as, vii. 8. 4?

καθαίρω, ἀρῶ, κεκάθαρκα, a. ἐκάθηρα or ἐκάθαρα, (καθαρός pure) to cleanse, purge; to purify in a religious sense; A.; v. 7. 35.

καθάπερ rel. adv., (καθ' ἅπερ) just according as, just as, even as, v. 4. 28.

καθαρμός, οῦ, ὁ, (καθαίρω) purification, v. 7. 35.

καθ-έζομαι,* f. καθ-εδοῦμαι, ipf. ἐκαθεζόμην, (ἕζομαι to sit, poet.) to seat one's self, sit down; to halt, rest; i. 5. 9: iii. 1. 33: v. 8. 14.

καθ-ειστήκειν, see καθ-ίστημι.

καθ-έλκω,* ἕλξω, ipf. εἷλκον, to draw or haul down, as vessels into the sea, to launch, A., vii. 1. 19.

καθ-έντας, see καθ-ίημι, vi. 5. 25.

καθ-εύδω,* εὑδήσω, ipf. ἐκάθευδον or καθηῦδον, (εὕδω to sleep) to lie down and sleep, to sleep, repose, i. 3. 11.

καθ-ηγέομαι, ἡσομαι, ἥγημαι, to lead down: ταῦτα καθηγεῖσθαι to conduct this enterprise, vii. 8. 9.

καθ-ηδυ-παθέω, ἥσω, (ἡδύς, πάσχω) to revel down, to spend, waste, or squander, in luxury or pleasure, A., i. 3. 3.

καθ-ήκω, ἥξω, ἧκα 1., to come down to, to reach or extend down, εἰς, ἐπί, ἀπό: to appertain to, belong as a duty, D. I.: i. 4. 4; 9. 7: iii. 4. 24: iv. 3. 11.

κάθ-ημαι* pf. m. pret., f. pf. καθήσομαι 1., plp. ἐκαθήμην or καθήμην, (ἧμαι to sit) to sit down, be seated, be in session, be encamped or stationed, i. 3. 12; 7. 20: iv. 2. 5 s: vi. 2. 5.

καθῆραι or -ᾶραι, see καθαίρω.

καθ-ίζω,* καθίσω ἰῶ, κεκάθικα 1., a. ἐκάθισα and καθῖσα, (ἵζω to seat, poet.)

καθίημι   67   κακῶς

to make sit down, *seat, set, place*, A. εἰς, ii. 1. 4 : iii. 5. 17.

καθ-ίημι,* ἥσω, εἶκα, a. ἧκα (ὧ, εἶς, &c.), *to let down*, as a spear for action, *to lower, couch*, A. εἰς, vi. 5. 25, 27.

καθ-ίστημι,* στήσω, ἕστηκα, 1 a. ἕστησα, 2 a. ἔστην, *to fix or set down, settle, arrange, station, place, establish, restore, bring, render*, A.; *to constitute or appoint*, 2 A., εἰς, ἐπί: i. 4. 13; 10. 10: iii. 2. 1, 5: — *M*., w. act. 2 a. and complete tenses (used pret.), *to station, set, place, fix,* or *establish one's self, to take one's place* or *station; to be established, set, settled,* or *placed; to result* or *eventuate;* εἰς, ἐπί (to set one's self to, *undertake*, vi. 1. 22): but 1 a. *m. to station, set*, or *appoint* for one's self, A.: i. 1. 3; 3. 8; 8. 3 s, 6 : iv. 5. 19, 21.

καθ-οράω,* ὄψομαι, ἑώρακα or ἑόρᾱκα, 2 a. εἶδον (ἴδω, &c.), *to look down upon, view, inspect, descry, discern, perceive, see*, A., i. 8. 26 ; 10. 14.

καί * conj. & adv., (akin to Lat. que) *and;* often with a strengthened idea, which we express in Eng. by adding an adverb, *and also, and even, and indeed, and especially, and the rather, and therefore; also, even* (sometimes translated by other adverbs of like force, *further, moreover, really, indeed, yet, still, only*, &c.); i. 1. 1 s ; 3. 6, 13, 15 ; 6. 10: iv. 5. 15: vi. 2. 10 : καὶ δή (καί) *and now* (even), in supposition, v. 7. 9 : καὶ εἰ (or ἐάν, &c.), εἰ καί *even if, although* (and so καί w. a part., like καίπερ q. v.), iii. 2. 10, 22, 24 : τέ . . καί, καί . . καί, *both . . and*, i. 3. 3 ; 8. 27 ; see ἄλλως. Καί is often used where in Eng. no connective, or one more specific would be preferred (as *for, when, but, as*, &c.), 702 c, 705, ii. 2. 10 ; 3. 18: iv. 6. 2 : v. 4. 21. In annexing several particulars, the Eng. more frequently uses the copulative w. the last only; but the Greek w. all or none, i. 2. 22: iii. 1. 3. The special relation of καί to the word following (and not to the word preceding, as in the case of so many particles) will not fail to be observed. For καὶ γάρ, καὶ γὰρ οὖν, see γάρ. Cf. δέ.

Κάϊκος (ῑ), ου, ὁ, *the Caïcus*, a river in the southwest part of Mysia, flowing near Pergamum and through a fertile plain, vii. 8. 8, 18 ? || The Bakir-Chai.

Καιναί, ῶν, αἱ, *Coenae*, a large city on the west bank of the Tigris (perhaps the Canneh of Ezek. 27. 23), ii. 4. 28. || Kaleh Sherghât, so interesting in its remains, and believed by some to have been, for a long period, the capital of the Assyrian Empire.

καί-περ adv., *even indeed*, used w. a part. (as also καὶ even) to express concession, where the Eng. familiarly uses *though* or *although* with a verb, 674 f : καίπερ εἰδότες *even* [indeed knowing] *though they knew*, i. 6. 10. Cf. ii. 3. 25 : iii. 1. 29 : iv. 3. 33 : v. 5. 17 s.

καιρός, οῦ, ὁ, *occasion, opportunity, season, juncture, crisis, a fitting, proper, special*, or *particular time*, I.: καιρός ἐστιν *it is the proper time, there is occasion;* hence, *there is need, it is necessary* or *proper: ἐν καιρῷ in season, opportunely, according to the occasion, to the purpose:* προσωτέρω τοῦ καιροῦ *farther than there was occasion, farther than was necessary* or *expedient:* i.7.9: iii. 1. 36, 39, 44 : iv. 3. 34 ; 6. 15.

καί-τοι conj., *and indeed, and certainly, and yet, however; though, although;* i. 4. 8 : v. 7. 10 : vii. 7. 39.

καίω & Att. κάω,* καύσω, κέκαυκα, *to burn* (trans.), *set on fire, consume* by fire ; *to kindle, maintain*, or *keep up a fire, keep a fire burning;* of a surgeon, *to cauterize;* A.: *M.* or *P., to burn*, intrans.: i. 6. 1 s : iii. 5. 3, 5 s: iv. 5. 5 s: v. 8. 18. Der. CAUSTIC.

κἀκεῖνος = καὶ ἐκεῖνος, ii. 6. 8 ?

†κακό-νοια, ας, *ill-will*, πρός, vii. 7. 45.

†κακό-νοος, ον, contr. κακό-νους, ουν, *evil-minded, ill-disposed, ill-affected, inimical*, D., ii. 5. 16, 27.

†κακο-ποιέω, ήσω, *to do evil to, treat ill, maltreat*, A., ii. 5. 4 ?

κακός, ή, όν, c. κακίων, s. κάκιστος, *bad, evil, ill, wicked, vile, base, worthless*, D., περί : bad in war, *cowardly:* subst. κακόν, οῦ, *an evil, harm, injury, mischief:* i. 3. 18 ; 4. 8 ; 9. 15 : ii. 5. 5, 16, 39. Der. CACO-PHONY.

‡κακουργέω, ήσω, *to work evil to, to injure, harm, harass, annoy*, A., vi. 1. 1.

‡κακοῦργος, ον, (ἔργον) *working evil, criminal:* masc. subst., *an evil-doer, malefactor:* i. 9. 13.

‡κακόω, ώσω, pf. *p.* κεκάκωμαι, *to injure*, A., iv. 5. 35.

‡κακῶς adv., c. κάκιον, s. κάκιστα, *badly, ill; injuriously; wretchedly,*

κάκωσις 68 καρπόω

miserably, uncomfortably; i. 4. 8 ; 5. 16 ; 9. 10 : iii. 1. 43 : iv. 4. 14. See ἔχω, πάσχω, ποιέω, πράττω.

‡κάκωσις, εως, ἡ, *ill-treatment, abuse,* G., iv. 6. 3.

†καλάμη, ης, *straw,* v. 4. 27.

κάλαμος, ου, ὁ, calamus, *a reed;* collectively, for plants of this kind ; i. 5. 1 : iv. 5. 26. Der. CALAMITY.

καλέω,* καλέσω καλῶ, κέκληκα, a. ἐκάλεσα, a. p. ἐκλήθην, calo, *to* CALL, *summon, invite,* A. ἐπί : *to call, name,* 2 A.: τὸ Μηδίας καλούμενον τεῖχος *the so-called wall of Media :* sometimes *M., to call to* or *for one's self,* A.: i. 2. 2, 8: ii. 4. 12 : iii. 3.1: vii. 3. 15; 6. 38.

καλινδέομαι in pr. & ipf., (akin to κυλίω) *to roll,* intrans., v. 2. 31 ?

†καλλ-ιερέω, ήσω, κεκαλλιέρηκα, (ἱερόν) *A.* & *M. to sacrifice favorably* or *with good omens, to obtain good auspices* in sacrifice, v. 4. 22 : vii. 1. 40 ; 8. 5.

†Καλλί-μαχος, ου, *Callimachus,* a brave and ambitious lochage from Parrhasia in Arcadia, iv. 1. 27; 7. 8.

†καλλίων, κάλλιστος, see καλός.

†κάλλος, εος, τό, *beauty,* ii. 3. 15. Der. CALLI-STHENICS.

‡καλλ-ωπισμός, οῦ, ὁ, (ὤψ *face*) fine appearance, *ornament, adornment,* i. 9. 23.

καλός,* ἡ, όν, c. καλλίων, s. κάλλιστος, *beautiful* (of both physical and moral beauty, and also with reference to use or promise), *beauteous, handsome, fine, fair ; honorable, noble ; favorable, propitious, auspicious; excellent, good;* I.: τὸ καλόν *honorable conduct, honor:* εἰς καλόν *for good, opportunely :* i. 2. 22 ; 8. 15 : ii. 6. 18 s, 28 : iv. 7. 3 ; 8. 26. Ἀγαθός refers more to the essential quality of an object, and καλός more to the impression which it produces upon the eye or mind. See ἄριστος.

Κάλπη, ης, *Calpe,* a place with a good harbor, on the Bithynian coast of the Euxine, where Xenophon evidently longed to found a city, vi. 2. 13 ; 3. 24 ; 4. 1. ∥Kirpeh.

Καλχηδονία, Καλχηδών, = Χαλκηδονία, Χαλκηδών, 167 b, vi. 6. 38 ?

καλῶς adv., c. κάλλιον, s. κάλλιστα, (καλός) *beautifully, handsomely, finely, honorably, properly ; favorably, prosperously, successfully, advantageously, well :* καλῶς ἔχειν or εἶναι *to be, go,* or *result well, be right, proper, safe, in good condition, properly arranged,* &c.: i. 2. 2 ; 8. 13 ; 9. 17 s, 23 : iii. 1. 6 s, 16, 43. See ἔχω, πράττω.

κάμνω, καμοῦμαι, κέκμηκα, 2 a. ἔκαμον, *to labor, toil ; to be weary, fatigued, exhausted, disabled, sick :* οἱ κάμνοντες *the sick* or *disabled:* P.: iii. 4. 47 : iv. 5. 17 s : v. 5. 20.

κἀμοί, κἄν, κἄν, κἀντεῦθεν, κἄπειτα, by crasis for καὶ ἐμοί, καὶ ἄν, καὶ ἐν, καὶ ἐντεῦθεν, καὶ ἔπειτα, i. 3. 20 : ii. 3. 9.

κάνδυς, υος, ὁ, an outer garment with large sleeves, worn by the Medes and Persians; *an overcoat, robe;* i. 5. 8.

καπηλεῖον, ου, (κάπηλος caupo, *huckster*) *a huckster's shop, an inn,* i. 2. 24.

καπίθη, ης, *a capithe,* a Persian measure = 2 χοίνικες, i. 5. 6.

καπνός, οῦ, ὁ, *smoke,* ii. 2. 15, 18.

Καππαδοκία, ας, *Cappadocia,* a mountainous region in the eastern part of Asia Minor, north of the Taurus, chiefly pastoral, and noted for its fine horses. Its men were reputed as of little worth. i. 2. 20 ; 9.7: vii. 8. 25.

κάπρος, ου, ὁ, aper, *a wild boar,* ii. 2. 9.

καρβατίνη, ης, *a carbatine* or *brogue,* a rude protection for the foot, resembling a low moccasin, and said to have been named from its Carian origin, iv. 5. 14 (777. 2).

καρδία, ας, cor, *the heart,* ii. 5. 23. Der. CARDIAC.

†Καρδούχειος or Καρδούχιος, α, ον, *Carduchian* (Koordish), iv. 1. 2 s.

Καρδοῦχος, ου, ὁ, *a Carduchian.* The *Carduchi* were a race of fierce, independent, and predatory mountaineers, living east of the Tigris, from whom the modern Koords have derived their name, lineage, and character. iii. 5. 15 : iv. 1. 8 s. ∥ *A Koord,* in Armenian *Kordu,* plur. *Kordukh* (to the plur. ending of which, the -χοι in Καρδοῦχοι seems analogous).

Κάρκασος, ου, ὁ, *Carcasus,* a small and otherwise unknown stream, vii. 8. 18 : v. l. Κάϊκος.

†καρπαία, ας, *the Carpœan* or [Crop] *Farm Dance,* a mimic dance of the Thessalians, vi. 1. 7.

καρπός, οῦ, ὁ, *the produce, fruits,* or *crops* of the earth, ii. 5. 19.

‡καρπόω, ώσω, *to bear fruit : M. to gather the fruits of, reap,* A., iii. 2. 23.

Κάρσος or **Κέρσος**, ου, ὁ, *the Carsus* or *Cersus*, *a small stream separating Cilicia from Syria.* i. 4. 4. ǁ *The Merkez.*

κάρυον, ου, *a nut;* in the Anab., *the chestnut,* which afterwards became so common an article of food in southern Europe, v. 4. 29, 32. [i. 5. 10.

κάρφη, ης, (κάρφω Ep., *to dry) hay,*

Καστωλός, οῦ, ἡ, *Castōlus*, a town of Lydia, which gave its name to one of the great muster-fields of the Persian army. Kiepert places this field at the junction of the Hermus and Cogamus, a few miles northeast of Sardis. i. 1. 2; 9. 7.

κατά* prep., by apostr. **κατ'** or **καθ'**, *down*, opp. to ἀνά: w. GEN. of place, *down from, down,* i. 5. 8: iv. 2. 17; κατὰ γῆς [down from] *under the earth,* vii. 1. 30 : — w. ACC. of place or person, *down along, along, along side of;* also translated *by, over, over against, against, opposite, upon, in, at, about, near, to, throughout,* &c.; i. 5. 10; 8. 12, 26; 10. 9: iv. 6. 23 s : vii. 2. 1, 28; κ. γῆν (θάλατταν) *by land* (*sea*), i. 1. 7 ; κ. τὴν γέφυραν *along* or *over the bridge,* vi. 5. 22 ; κ. ταῦτα *along this shore,* vii. 5. 13 : — denoting conformity, connection, purpose, manner, *according to, in respect to, as to, for, in, by,* &c., ii. 2. 8 ; 3. 8 : iii. 5. 2 ; κ. χώραν [according to place] *in the proper places* or *order,* i. 5. 17 : vi. 4. 11 ; τὸ κ. τοῦτον εἶναι *so far as regards him* or *he is concerned,* 665 b, i. 6. 9 ; κ. ταυτά *according to the same method, in the same way,* v. 4. 22 ; καθ' αὑτόν *by himself,* vi. 2. 13 : forming adv. phrases w. abstract nouns, see ἡσυχία, κράτος : — distributively, *by, among, each* or *every,* &c., w. sing. or plur., i. 2. 16 ; κ. ἔθνη or ἔθνος, *by nations,* or *nation by nation,* i. 8. 9 : v. 5. 5 ; καθ' ἕνα *one by one,* iv. 7. 8 ; κ. τετρακισχιλίους *4000 at a time,* iii. 5. 8 ; κ. ἐνιαυτόν *each year, yearly, annually,* iii. 2. 12 ; κ. τοὺς χώρους *in the different places, through the region,* vii. 2. 3. — In compos., *down, downwards, along, against;* often strengthening the idea, or implying completeness (*downright*), or rendering the verb transitive.

κ ιτα-βαίνω,* βήσομαι, βέβηκα, 2 a. ἔβην, *to go* or *come down, descend,* as from the interior to the sea-coast, from a hill, horse, carriage, into the arena, &c.; *to dismount; to enter the lists;* εἰς, πρός, ἀπό: i. 2. 22s : ii. 2. 14 ; 5. 22 : iv. 2. 20 ; 8. 27.

↓**κατά-βασις**, εως, ἡ, *the way* or *passage down, descent,* εἰς, ἐκ : *return to the sea-coast;* iii. 4. 37 : v. 2. 6 ; 5. 4.

κατα-βλακεύω, εύσω, *to treat negligently* or *slothfully,* A., vii. 6. 22.

κατ-αγάγοιμι, see κατ-άγω, i. 2. 2.

κατ-αγγέλλω, ελῶ, ἤγγελκα, *to inform against, expose, denounce,* A., ii. 5. 38.

κατά-γειος or -**γαιος**, ον, (γῆ) *underground, subterranean,* iv. 5. 25.

κατα-γελάω,* ἄσομαι, a. ἐγέλασα, *to laugh* [against] *at, jeer at, deride, ridicule,* G.; *to mock, exult, triumph;* i. 9. 13 : ii. 4. 4 ; 6. 23, 30.

κατ-άγνυμι,* ἄξω, 2 pf. pret. intrans. ἔαγα, a. ἔαξα, (ἄγνυμι *to break*) *to break* in pieces, *crush,* A., iv. 2. 20.

κατα-γοητεύω or γοητεύω, εύσω, (γόης *a wizard*) *to bewitch, spell-bind,* A., v. 7. 9.

κατ-άγω,* ἄξω, ἦχα, 2 a. ἤγαγον, *to lead* or *bring down* or *back, restore, to bring* [down from the high sea] *ashore* or *into port,* A.: sc. πλοῖα, &c., *to put in, come ashore : M. to return, arrive,* ἐπί: i. 1. 7 ; 2. 2 : iii. 4. 36 : v. 1. 11s : vi. 6. 3.

κατα-δαπανάω, ἤσω, δεδαπάνηκα, *to expend to the bottom, wholly consume,* trans., ii. 2. 11.

κατα-δειλιάω, άσω, (δειλός) *to cower down, shrink from through fear,* A., vii. 6. 22.

κατα-δικάζω, άσω, δεδίκακα l., (δικάζω *to judge,* δίκη) *to give sentence against, condemn, pass judgment,* G. I., ὅτι, v. 8. 21 : vi. 6. 15.

κατα-διώκω,* ώξω or ώξομαι, δεδίωχα, *to chase* or *drive down* or *off,* A., iv. 2. 5.

κατα-δοξάζω, άσω, *to judge* to any one's discredit, I. (A.), vii. 7. 30.

κατα-δραμεῖν, -ών, see κατα-τρέχω.

κατα-δύω,* δύσω, δέδυκα, 1 a. ἔδυσα, 2 a. ἔδυν, *to sink* down, *drown,* A., i. 3. 17 ; M., w. pf. & 2 a. act., *to sink* or *drown,* intrans., κατά, μέχρι, iii. 5. 11 : iv. 5. 36 : vii. 7. 11.

κατα-θεάομαι, άσομαι, τεθέαμαι, *to look down upon, view* or *survey, take a view* or *survey,* A., i. 8. 14 : vi. 5. 30.

κατα-θέμενος, see κατα-τίθημι.
κατα-θέω,* θεύσομαι, to run down, εἰς, ἐπί, vi. 3. 10 ? vii. 3. 44.
κατα-θύω (ῠ),* θύσω, τέθῠκα, to lay down as an offering, to sacrifice, offer, A. D., iii. 2. 12 : iv. 5. 35 : v. 3. 13.
κατ-αισχύνω, ῠνῶ, to shame down, disgrace, dishonor, put to shame, prove unworthy of, A., iii. 1. 30 ; 2. 14.
κατα-καίνω,* κανῶ, 2 pf. r. κέκονα or κέκανα, 2 a. ἔκανον, (καίνω = κτείνω) to cut down, kill, slay, put to death, A., i. 6. 2; 9. 6: iii. 2. 39: vii. 6. 36.
κατα-καίω & Att. -κάω,* καύσω, κέκαυκα, to burn down or, from a different form of conception, burn up ; to consume, burn, destroy or lay waste by fire ; A.; i. 4. 10, 18 : iii. 3. 1 ; 5. 13.
κατά-κειμαι,* κείσομαι, to lie down, lie on the ground, lie inactive, lie, recline, rest, repose, ἐν, iii. 1. 13 s.
κατα-κεκόψεσθαι, see κατα-κόπτω.
κατα-κηρύττω, ύξω, κεκήρῡχα, to enjoin by proclamation, A., ii. 2. 20.
κατα-κλείω, κλείσω, κέκλεικα, pf. p. κέκλειμαι or -εισμαι, a. p. ἐκλείσθην, to shut down or, from a different form of conception, to shut up, enclose, confine, A., εἰς, εἴσω, iii. 3. 7 ; 4. 26.
κατ-ακοντίζω, ίσω ιῶ, to shoot down or to death, vii. 4. 6.
κατα-κόπτω,* κόψω, κέκοφα, f. pf. κεκόψομαι, 2 a. p. ἐκόπην, to cut down, off, or to pieces, to slay, A., i. 2. 25; 5. 16.
κατα-κτάομαι, κτήσομαι, κέκτημαι, to win over, acquire, gain, A., vii. 3. 31 ?
κατα-κτείνω,* κτενῶ, 2 pf. ἔκτονα, 1 a. ἔκτεινα, 2 a. ch. poet. ἔκτανον, A., to cut down, kill, slay, i. 9. 6 ? ii. 5. 10 : iv. 8. 25 : v. 7. 27.
κατα-κωλύω (ῠ), ύσω, κεκώλυκα, to hinder downright, detain, keep, stop, A., v. 2. 16 : vi. 6. 8.
κατα-λαμβάνω,* λήψομαι, εἴληφα, 2 a. ἔλαβον, pf. p. εἴλημμαι, a. p. ἐλήφθην, to take down, seize upon, seize, occupy, take possession of, take by surprise, overtake, catch, A.; to light upon, find, A. P.; i. 3. 14; 8. 20; 10. 16, 18: ii. 2. 12 : iii. 1. 8 ; 3. 8 s: iv. 5. 7, 24, 30.
κατα-λέγω,* λέξω, to reckon or charge against one, account, A. ὅτι, ii. 6. 27.
κατα-λείπω,* λείψω, 2 pf. λέλοιπα, 2 a. ἔλιπον, p. ἐλείφθην, to leave down in its place, leave behind, leave, abandon, desert, A.: M. to remain behind : i. 2. 18; 8. 25 : iii. 1. 2; 2. 17; 5. 5 : v. 6. 12.
κατα-λεύω, λεύσω, a. p. ἐλεύσθην, (λεύω to stone) to stone [down] to death, A., i. 5. 14 : v. 7. 2, 19, 30.
κατα-λήψομαι, -ληφθῶ, see κατα-λαμβάνω, i. 10. 16 : iv. 7. 4.
κατα-λιπεῖν, -λιπών, see κατα-λείπω.
κατ-αλλάττω,* ἄξω, ἤλλαχα, 2 a. p. ἠλλάγην, (ἀλλάττω to change, ἄλλος) to change to a settled or calm state, as from enmity to friendship, to reconcile : P. to be or become reconciled, i. 6. 1.
κατα-λογίζομαι, ίσομαι ιοῦμαι, λελόγισμαι, to set down to one's account, compute, reckon, consider, A., v. 6. 16.
κατα-λύω,* λύσω, λέλῠκα, to loose from under, unyoke ; hence, to halt, rest ; to dissolve, terminate, A. ; to cease from action or contest, make peace, πρός : i. 1. 10; 8. 1; 10. 19 : vi. 2. 12.
κατα-μανθάνω,* μαθήσομαι, μεμάθηκα, 2 a. ἔμαθον, to learn thoroughly, observe well, understand, perceive, find, A. CP., P., i. 9. 3 : ii. 3. 11 : v. 8. 14.
κατ-αμελέω, ήσω, ἠμέληκα, to be quite negligent, v. 8. 1.
κατα-μένω,* μενῶ, μεμένηκα, a. ἔμεινα, to remain upon the spot, remain, stay behind, settle down, v. 6. 17, 19, 27 : vi. 6. 2, 28.
κατα-μερίζω, ίσω ιῶ, to divide into portions, distribute, A. D., vii. 5. 4.
κατα-μηνύω, ύσω, μεμήνῠκα, to inform against, expose, make known, A., ii. 2. 20 ?
κατα-μίγνῡμι or -ύω,* μίξω, (μίγνῡμι misceo, to mix) to mingle down : M. intrans. κατεμιγνύοντο εἰς τὰς πόλεις they [mingled down into the cities] settled in the cities, mingling with the inhabitants, vii. 2. 3.
κατα-νοέω, ήσω, νενόηκα, to observe, watch, or consider carefully, discern, reflect upon, A., i. 2. 4 : vii. 7. 43, 45.
κατ-αντι-πέρᾱς or -ᾱν (also written κατ' ἀντιπέρας or -αν) [along the region over against] over against, opposite, G., i. 1. 9 : iv. 8. 3.
κατα-πέμπω,* πέμψω, πέπομφα, to send down, as fr. the interior to the sea-coast, A., i. 9. 7.
κατα-πεσεῖν, -ών, see κατα-πίπτω.
κατα-πετρόω, ώσω, to stone [down] to death, A., i. 3. 2.
κατα-πηδάω, ήσομαι, πεπήδηκα, a.

ἐπήδησα, (πηδάω to leap) to leap or spring down, ἀπό, i. 8. 3, 28.

κατα-πίπτω,* πεσοῦμαι, πέπτωκα, 2 a. ἔπεσον, to fall down or to the ground, fall off from a horse, iii. 2. 19.

κατα-πολεμέω, ήσω, πεπολέμηκα, to war down, conquer in war, A., vii.1.27.

κατα-πράττω,* πράξω, πέπραχα, to accomplish, achieve, gain: M. to accomplish, &c., for one's self: A. D.: i. 2. 2: vii. 7. 17, 27, 46.

κατ-αράομαι,* ἄσομαι, ἤραμαι, (ἀράομαι to pray) to pray against, invoke curses upon, execrate, curse, D., v. 6. 4: vii. 7. 48.

κατα-σβέννυμι,* σβέσω, ἔσβηκα, (σβέννυμι to quench) to extinguish or put out entirely, A., vi. 3. 21, 25.

κατα-σκεδάννυμι,* σκεδάσω σκεδῶ, A. or M. to sprinkle or throw down, as the wine remaining in one's cup, A. G.? vii. 3. 32?

κατα-σκέπτομαι,* σκέψομαι, ἔσκεμμαι, to look down upon, inspect, examine, A., i. 5. 12.

κατα-σκευάζω, άσω, pf. p. ἐσκεύασμαι, to prepare fully or well, furnish, equip, improve, A. εἰς: M. to make arrangements: i.9.19: iii.2.24; 3.19.

κατα-σκηνέω, ήσω, or -σκηνόω, ώσω, to camp down, encamp, ἐν, εἰς, ii. 2. 16: iii. 4. 32 s: vii. 4. 11.

κατα-σκοπή, ῆς, (κατα-σκέπτομαι) inspection, espionage, vii. 4. 13.

κατα-σπάω,* άσω, ἔσπακα, a. p. ἐσπάσθην, to drag or pull down, A., i. 9. 6.

†κατά-στασις, εως, ἡ, condition, constitution, v. 7. 26.

κατα-στήσομαι, -σω, -σας, see καθίστημι, i. 3. 8 ; 4. 13 : iii. 2. 1.

κατα-στρατοπεδεύω, εύσω, to fix down in camp : M. to encamp, iii. 4. 18 : iv. 5. 1 : vi. 3. 20.

κατα-στρέφω,* ἐψω, ἔστροφα 1., to bend down, overturn: M. to subjugate to one's self, subdue, conquer, A., i. 9. 14 : vii. 5. 14 ; 7. 27.

κατα-σφάττω,* άξω, 2 a. p. ἐσφάγην, to put to death, A., iv. 1. 23.

κατα-σχεῖν, see κατ-έχω, iv. 8. 12.

κατα-σχίζω, ίσω, to split or hew down, cut or burst through, A., vii. 1. 16.

κατα-τείνω,* τενῶ, τέτακα, to stretch tight, strain, urge, insist, ii. 5. 30.

κατα-τέμνω,* τεμῶ, τέτμηκα, to cut down or in pieces; cut or dig ditches; A.; ii. 4. 13 : iv. 7. 26.

κατα-τίθημι,* θήσω, τέθεικα, 2 a. m. ἐθέμην, to put down: M. to put down or deposit one's own or for one's self, to lay or treasure up, reserve, secure, A. D., εἰς, ἐν, παρά, i. 3. 3 : ii. 5. 8 : v. 2. 15 : vii. 6. 34.

κατα-τιτρώσκω,* τρώσω, to wound severely, A., iii. 4. 26 ? iv. 1. 10.

κατα-τρέχω,* δραμοῦμαι, δεδράμηκα, 2 a. ἔδραμον, to run down, v. 4. 23.

κατ-αυλίζομαι, ίσομαι, ηὔλισμαι 1., a. p. ηὐλίσθην, to camp down, encamp, ἐν, vii. 5. 15.

κατα-φαγεῖν, see κατ-εσθίω, iv.8.14.

κατα-φανής, ές, (φαίνω) clearly seen, in plain view, conspicuous, visible, in sight, i. 8. 8 : ii. 3. 3 ; 4. 14.

κατα-φεύγω,* φεύξομαι, πέφευγα, 2 a. ἔφυγον, to flee for refuge, take refuge, escape, εἰς, i.5.13: iii. 4. 11.

κατα-φρονέω, ήσω, πεφρόνηκα, to think [down] inferior, despise, regard with contempt, iii. 4. 2 : v. 7. 12 ?

κατα-χωρίζω, ίσω ιῶ, to [set down] station or arrange separately, assign distinct places to, place, A., vi. 5. 10.

κατ-έαξα, see κατ-άγνυμι, iv. 2. 20.

κατ-έβην, see κατα-βαίνω. [1. 22.

κατ-εγγυάω v. l. = παρ-εγγυάω, vii.

κατ-εθέμην, see κατα-τίθημι, i. 3. 3.

κατ-εῖδον, see καθ-οράω, iv. 6. 6.

κατ-είληφα, -είλημμαι,' -ελήφθην, see κατα-λαμβάνω, i. 8. 20 : iv. 1. 20 s.

κάτ-ειμι,* ipf. ἥειν, (εἶμι) to go or come down, descend, v. 7. 13.

κατ-εῖχον, see κατ-έχω, iv. 2. 6.

κατ-εργάζομαι,* άσομαι, εἴργασμαι, a. εἰργασάμην, to work out, accomplish, achieve, gain, A., i. 9. 20 : vi. 2. 10.

κατ-έρχομαι,* ἐλεύσομαι, ἐλήλυθα, 2 a. ἦλθον, to go or come down or back, return, vii. 2. 2.

κατ-εσθίω,* ἔδομαι, ἐδήδοκα, 2 a. ἔφαγον, to eat down or, from a different form of conception, eat up, devour, iv. 8. 14.

κατ-έστην, -έστησα, see καθ-ίστημι.

κατ-ετετμήμην, see κατα-τέμνω.

κατ-έτρωσα, see κατα-τιτρώσκω.

κατ-έχω,* ἔξω or σχήσω, ἔσχηκα, ipf. εἶχον, 2 a. ἔσχον, to hold down or fast, retain, restrain, A. ; to forbid, compel, A. I.; to occupy, hold, possess, A. ; to [have one's self or one's vessel] come from the high sea to the shore, *to arrive* by sea, *land;* ii. 6. 13 : iii. 1. 20: iv. 2. 5 s: vi. 1. 33 : vii. 7. 28 s.

κατ-ηγορέω, ήσω, κατ-ηγόρηκα, (ἀγορεύω) *to speak against, accuse, charge, denounce,* G. CP., πρός, v.7.4 : vii.7.44.

↓ κατ-ηγορία, as, *an accusation, charge,* v. 8. 1.

κατ-ηρεμίζω, ἰσω ιῶ, or κατ-ηρεμέω, ήσω, (ἠρέμα *quietly*) *to quiet* down, *calm, tranquillize,* A., vii. 1. 22, 24.

κατ-ιδεῖν, -ἰδοιμι, -ιδών, see καθ-οράω, i.10.14: iv. 3. 11 ; 4. 9.

κατ-ιών, see κάτ-ειμι, v. 7. 13.

κατ-οικέω, ήσω, ᾤκηκα, *to dwell* as a settled resident, *reside,* ἐν, v. 3. 7.

κατ-οικίζω, ἰσω ιῶ, *to found* or *build* a city, A., v. 6. 15 : vi. 4. 7.

κατ-ορύττω, ύξω, ὀρώρυχα, a. *p.* ὠρύχθην, *to sink by digging, bury,* A., iv. 5. 29 : v. 8. 9, 11.

κάτω adv., (κατά) *down, downwards, in the descent; below, beneath :* τὸ κάτω [sc. μέρος] *the lower part:* iv. 2. 28 ; 5. 25 ; 8. 20, 28.

καῦμα, ατος, τό, (καίω) *burning heat, heat,* i. 7. 6.

καύσιμος, ον, (καίω) *combustible,* vi. 3. 15, 19.

Καΰστρου Πεδίον, Caÿstri Campus, *the Plain of Caÿster,* a town of Phrygia, at the crossing of two great thoroughfares, (not on the Caÿster which flowed by Ephesus, and was noted for its swans), i. 2. 11. ‖ Near *Bulavadin.*

κάω an Att. form for καίω, q. v.

κέγχρος, ου, ὁ, milium (akin to μελίνη q. v.), a kind of *millet,* a plant which bears abundantly a small grain valued in some countries for food ; or the grain itself ; i. 2. 22.

κέκραγα, see κράζω, vii. 8. 15.

κεῖμαι,* κείσομαι, ipf. ἐκείμην, (cf. Lat. cubo) *to lie ; to lie dead,* or as if dead ; *to rest; to be laid, placed,* or *situated,* sometimes used as a pass. of τίθημι: ἐν, ἐπί, &c.: i. 8. 27 : ii. 4. 12: iii. 1. 21 ; 4. 10 : iv. 8. 21.

κέκτημαι, see κτάομαι, i. 7. 3.

Κελαιναί, ῶν, αἱ, Celœnæ, a city of Phrygia, having a strong citadel and two palaces, i. 2. 7 s. ‖ Dinair.

κελεύω, εὐσω, κεκέλευκα, (κέλλω *to impel,* cf. Lat. cello, celer) *to bid* (to tell a person to do a thing, whether in the way of command, counsel, request, or permission) ; *to command, order, direct, urge, advise, exhort,* *request, invite ;* A. I., AE.; i. 1. 11 ; 3. 8, 16 ; 5. 8 ; 6. 2 s : ii. 5. 2 : vi. 6.14.

κενός, ή, όν, *empty, void, vacant, unoccupied, without,* G.; *groundless, idle ;* i. 8. 20 : ii. 2. 21 : iii. 4. 20.

↓ κενο-τάφιον, ου, (τάφος) an empty tomb, CENOTAPH, vi. 4. 9. The superstition of the Greeks respecting the essential importance of burial rites, inclined them especially to pay this tribute to the unrecovered dead.

κεντέω, ήσω, *to prick, goad, torture,* A., iii. 1. 29. Der. CENTRE.

Κεντρίτης, ου, *Centrites,* a branch of the Tigris, separating Armenia from the land of the Carduchi, iv. 3. 1. ‖ Buhtán-Chai.

†κεράμιον, ου, an earthen *jar;* as a measure for liquids, the *ceramium* = about 6 gallons, estimated by Hussey at 5 gall. 7.577 pts. ; vi. 1. 15 ; 2. 3.

κεράμιος, α, ον, (κέραμος clay) *made of clay, earthen,* iii. 4. 7 : *v. l.* κεραμεοῦς (ᾶ, οῦν), κεράμειος, κεράμινος.

Κεραμῶν 'Αγορά, Forum Ceramorum, *Market of the Ceramians,* a town of Phrygia near the confines of Mysia, i. 2. 10. ‖ Near *Ushak.* See p. 152.

κεράννυμι,* κεράσω l., κεκέρακα l., a. ἐκέρασα, a. *p.* ἐκράθην or ἐκεράσθην, *to mix, mingle,* esp. wine w. water, A. D., i. 2. 13 : v. 4. 29.

κέρας,* κέρατος κέρως, τό, *a horn* of an animal ; hence, as originally made from this, *a horn* for blowing or to drink from, *a cornet, a drinking-cup* or *beaker; a* sharp mountain *peak* (cf. the Swiss *Schreck-horn,* &c.); *the* [horn] *wing* of an army ; a body of troops marching in column, *a column* of soldiers (κατὰ κέρας *in column,* iv. 6. 6); i. 7. 1 : ii. 2. 4 : v. 6. 7 : vi. 5. 5 : vii. 3. 24. Der. RHINO-CEROS. Cf. cornu.

†Κερασούντιος, ου, ὁ, *a Cerasuntian,* v. 5. 10 ; 7. 17 ; a man of

Κερασοῦς, οῦντος, ἡ, (*abounding in cherries,* fr. κερασός cerasus, CHERRY-TREE, 375 f, 207 c) *Cerasus,* a city of Pontus, on the Euxine, a Sinopean colony. The cherry was sent to Italy from this region by Lucullus, about 70 B. C. v. 3. 2. ‖ Kerasun-Dereh.

κεράτινος, η, ον, (κέρας) *made of horn, horn,* vi. 1. 4.

Κέρβερος, ου, ὁ, *Cerberus,* the huge, fierce, many-headed watch-dog of Hades, vi. 2. 2.

†κερδαίνω,* ανῶ, κεκέρδηκα, to gain, A., ii. 6. 21.

†κερδαλέος, α, ον, c. ώτερος, gainful, profitable, lucrative, i. 9. 17.

κέρδος, εος, τό, gain, profit, wages, pay, i. 9. 17 : vi. 2. 10.

Κέρσος, v. l. = Κάρσος, i. 4. 4.

Κερτωνός (ή) or -όν, οὗ, Certōnus or -um, a town in southwest Mysia, vii. 8. 8 : v. l. Κερτώνιον, Κερτώνιον, Κυτώνιον. ‖ Aiwaly.

†κεφαλ-αλγής, ές, (ἄλγος pain) apt to cause headache, ii. 3. 15 s.

κεφαλή, ῆς, caput, the head, i. 8. 6 ; 10. 1. Der. CEPHALIC.

κεχ- in redupl. for χεχ-, 159 a.

†κηδεμών, όνος, ὁ, a guardian, protector, intercessor, iii. 1. 17.

κήδομαι* to care or provide for, G., vii. 5. 5.

κηρίον, ου, (κηρός beeswax, cf. Lat. cēra) a honeycomb, iv. 8. 20.

†κηρύκειον or κηρύκιον, ου, caduceus, a herald's wand or staff, v. 7. 30.

†κῆρυξ or κήρυξ, ῦκος, ὁ, a herald, whose office and person were sacred, ii. 1. 7 ; 2. 20.

κηρύττω, ύξω, κεκήρυχα, to proclaim, as a herald, or by a herald, D. I. (A.), AE., CP., ii. 2. 21 : iii. 4. 36 (ἐκήρυξε, sc. ὁ κῆρυξ, proclamation was made, 571 b) : iv. 1. 13 : vii. 1. 7, 36.

Κηφισό-δωρος, ου, ὁ, Cephisodōrus, a lochage from Athens, iv. 2. 13, 17 ; son of

Κηφισο-φῶν, ῶντος, ὁ, Cephisophon, an Athenian, iv. 2. 13.

κιβώτιον, ου, (dim. of κιβωτός a wooden box) a chest, vii. 5. 14.

†Κιλικία, ας, Cilicia, the southeast province of Asia Minor, occupying a narrow, but well-watered and fertile space between Mt. Taurus and the Mediterranean. Cicero was proconsul of Cilicia, B. C. 51 ; and here Pompey subdued the pirates, B. C. 67. i. 2. 20 s. Its name remains in the present Ichili.

Κίλιξ, ικος, ὁ, a Cilician, i. 2. 12 : 4. 4. — Feminine

↓Κίλισσα, ης, a Cilician woman (or queen), i. 2. 12, 14.

†κινδυνεύω, εύσω, κεκινδύνευκα, to be in peril, incur or encounter danger, AE.; to be in danger of, to be likely, I.; κινδυνεύει as impers., there is danger: i. 1. 4 : iv. 1. 11 : v. 6. 19 : vii. 6. 36.

κίνδυνος, ου, ὁ, danger, peril, risk:

LEX. AN. 4

κίνδυνός (ἐστιν) there is danger, I. (A.), μή : τοῦτο κίνδυνος this is a danger, there is danger of this : i.7.5 : ii.5.17: iv. 1. 6 : v. 1. 6 : vii. 7. 31.

κινέω, ήσω, κεκίνηκα, to move, stir, remove, keep in motion, trans.; but M., w. aor. p., intrans.; ἀπό, ἐκ : iii. 4. 28 : iv. 5. 13 : v. 8. 15 : vi. 3. 8.

κιττός, οῦ, ὁ, the ivy, v. 4. 12.

Κλε-αγόρας, ου, Cleagoras, a painter who embellished the Lyceum at Athens with pictures of dreams, prob. from the old myths ; or, as some think, an author who wrote a book entitled "Dreams in the Lyceum"; vii. 8. 1 : yet see ἐνύπνιον.

Κλε-αίνετος, ου, Cleænetus, a lochage, v. 1. 17.

Κλέ-ανδρος, ου, Cleander, a Spartan harmost at Byzantium, for a time prejudiced against Xenophon, but afterwards his friend ; first disappointing the Cyreans, and then favoring them ; vi. 2. 13 ; 6. 1 : vii. 1. 8 ; 2. 6.

Κλε-άνωρ, ορος, Cleānor, of Orchomenus in Arcadia, one of the oldest and most trusted of the Greek generals ; prob. first commanding troops left by Xenias or Pasion, afterwards elected to succeed Agias ; ii. 1. 10.

Κλε-άρετος, ου, (ἀρετή) Clearetus, a lochage, quite unworthy of his name, v. 7. 14, 16 : v. l. Κλεάρατος.

Κλέ-αρχος, ου, Clearchus, a Spartan commander during the latter part of the Peloponnesian War, brave, skilful, and much trusted in battle, but tyrannical as harmost of Byzantium. After the peace, his passion for war led him to disobey the Spartan government, and he was sentenced to death. Escaping, he fled to Cyrus, was taken into his confidence, raised troops for his expedition, and was the general most honored and trusted by him. He loved war for its own sake, and this ruling passion threw its malign influence over his whole character. i. 1. 9 ; 2. 9 : ii. 3. 11 ; 6. 1. Κλέαρχοι Clearchuses [men like C.], iii. 2. 31.

†κλεῖθρον, ου, a bar or bolt, vii. 1. 17. Older Att. κλῆθρον.

κλείω, είσω, κέκλεικα, to shut, close, A., v. 5. 19 : ἐκέκλειντο were kept closed, 599 c, vi. 2. 8. Older Att. κλῄω.

[κλέος, τό, fame, glory, an element in many proper names.]

κλέπτω,* έψω, κέκλοφα, *to steal ; to seize, occupy,* or *keep, by stealth* or *secretly ; to steal by with, smuggle by;* A., G. partitive; iv. 1. 14 : 6. 15 s.

Κλε-ώνυμος, ου, *Cleonymus,* a Spartan spoken well of, iv. 1. 18.

†κλῖμαξ, ακος, ἡ, *a ladder,* iv. 5. 25. Hence CLIMAX.

†κλίνη, ης, *a couch, bed,* iv. 4. 21. [κλίνω,* κλῖνῶ, κέκλῖκα 1., clīno, *to bend, in-*CLINE, *lean.*]

κλοπή, ῆς, (κλέπτω) *theft, stealing,* iv. 6. 14.

‡κλωπεύω or κλοπεύω, εύσω, *to seize* or *intercept stealthily* or *by stealth,* A., vi. 1. 1.

κλώψ, κλωπός, ὁ, (κλέπτω) *a thief, plunderer, marauder,* iv. 6. 17.

κνέφας, αος, Att. ους (224 b), *darkness, dark, dusk,* iv. 5. 9.

κνημίς, ίδος, ἡ, (κνήμη *the leg* between the knee and ankle) *a greave* or *leggin,* a defence for the lower leg, comm. metallic among the Greeks. The use of such greaves indicated completeness of armor, and hence, in Homer, the frequent use of ἐϋκνήμῑδες, *well-greaved,* as an epithet for the Greeks. i. 2. 16.

κόγχη, ης, concha, *a muscle* or *cockle,* a kind of shell-fish, v. 3. 8. Der. CONCH.

‡κογχυλιάτης, ου, adj., *shelly, containing* petrified *shells,* iii. 4. 10.

κοῖλος, η, ον, *hollow,* cut by deep valleys, v. 4. 31. Cf. cœlum.

κοιμάω, ήσω, (akin to κεῖμαι) *to put to sleep : M.,* w. aor. p., *to go to sleep* or *rest, to sleep, repose,* ii. 1. 1.

κοινός, ή, όν, (ξύν, cf. Lat. con-) commūnis, *common, joint, owned* or *shared in common, public,* D.: τὸ κοινόν *the common stock, the public* or *general council* or *authority* (so, w. art. om., ἀπὸ κοινοῦ): κοινῇ as adv., *in common, jointly, σύν, μετά* : iii. 1. 43, 45 ; 3. 2 : iv. 7. 27: v. 1. 12 ; 7. 17 s.

↓ κοινόω, ώσω, *to make common : M. to communicate, consult,* D., v. 6. 27 : vi. 2. 15.

‡κοινωνέω, ήσω, κεκοινώνηκα, *to share in, have the common benefit of,* G., vii. 6. 28.

↓κοινωνός, οῦ, ὁ, *a sharer, partaker, partner,* G., vii. 2. 38.

Κοιρατάδης or -ας, ου, *Cœratades* or -*as,* a Theban, who commanded Bœotian troops under Clearchus, when the latter was harmost at Byzantium,

B. c. 408. Taken prisoner by the Athenians, but afterwards escaping, he made himself ridiculous by wandering about Greece in search of military command. vii. 1. 33, 40.

Κοῖτοι, ων, or Κοῖται, ῶν, οἱ, *the Cœti* or -*æ,* perhaps another name for the Τάοχοι, vii. 8. 25.

κολάζω, άσω, *A. & M. to chastise, punish,* A., ii. 5. 13 ; 6. 9 : v. 8. 18.

↓κόλασις, εως, ἡ, *chastisement, punishment,* vii. 7. 24. Cf. κόλος *clipped.*

Κολοσσαί, ῶν, αἱ, *Colossæ,* a city in southwest Phrygia, on the Lycus, a branch of the Mæander. It was the seat of one of the early Christian churches, to which Paul wrote an epistle. i. 2. 6. ‖ Ruins near Khonós.

†Κολχίς, ίδος, ἡ, *Colchis,* a land southeast of the Euxine, watered by the Phasis and other rivers, whose golden sands, it has been thought, suggested the fable of the golden fleece, iv. 8. 23. As fem. adj., *Colchian,* v. 3. 2.

Κόλχος, ου, ὁ, *a Colchian.* The Colchi were thought by Hdt., from their complexion, language, practice of circumcision, linen manufactures, &c., to be of Egyptian descent, perhaps a colony remaining behind from the army of Sesostris. The Cyreans seem to have met with only a border and weaker tribe of this people. iv. 8. 8 s, 24 : v. 2. 1.

κολωνός, οῦ, ὁ, collis, *a hill, mound, cairn,* iv. 7. 25.

Κομανία, ας, *Comania,* a castle or town in southwest Mysia, not far from Pergamum, vii. 8. 15.

†κομιδή, ῆς, *conveyance, transport,* v. 1. 11.

κομίζω, ίσω ιῶ, κεκόμικα, (κομέω *to tend*) *to take care of; to convey, bring, carry : M. to convey, bring, take,* or *remove* one's own : A. ἐπί, &c. : iii. 2. 26 : iv. 5. 22 ; 6. 3 : v. 4. 1 ; 5. 20.

†κονιᾱτός, ή, όν, (κονία *plaster*) *plastered, cemented,* iv. 2. 22.

†κονι-ορτός, οῦ, ὁ, (ὀρνῡμι *to stir up*) *a cloud* or *body of dust,* i. 8. 8.

[κόνις, ιος, Att. εως, ἡ, *dust.*]

κόπος, ου, ὁ, (κόπτω) *fatigue, weariness,* v. 8. 3.

κόπρος, ου, ἡ, *dung, ordure,* i. 6. 1.

κόπτω,* κόψω, κέκοφα, *to strike, smite, cut, cut down, slaughter ; to beat* or κόρη 75 Κρής

knock upon a door or gate for admission; A.; ii. 1. 6 : iv. 8. 2 : vii. 1. 16.

κόρη, ης, (κόρος *boy, lad*) *a girl, maiden, damsel,* iv. 5. 9.

Κορσωτή, ῆς, *Corsōte,* a large city on the north side of the Euphrates, which the Cyreans found deserted (perhaps only temporarily, on account of the approach of the army). The Mascas, which flowed around it, is supposed to have been a canal that still exists and makes with the Euphrates the island Werdi, on which are extensive ruins. i. 5. 4.

Κορύλας, ου or α, *Corylas,* a prince of Paphlagonia, who aspired at independence, and disobeyed the summons of Artaxerxes to join him with his army, of which the cavalry was especially excellent. v. 5. 12 ; 6. 11.

κορυφή, ῆς, (κόρυς *helmet*) *the top of* the head, of a mountain, &c.; *highest point, summit, peak* ; iii. 4. 41.

Κορώνεια, ας, *Coronēa,* an ancient city in the western part of Bœotia. On the plain before it, the Bœotians won their independence by defeating the Athenians, B. C. 447; and here the Spartans under Agesilāus gained the victory in a hard-fought battle with the Bœotians, Athenians, and their allies, B. C. 394. v. 3. 6 ? ‖ Ruins near Camari.

†κοσμέω, ήσω, κεκόσμηκα, *to regulate, arrange, order, marshal ; to decorate, adorn ;* A.; i. 9. 23 : iii. 2. 36. Der. COSMETIC.

†κόσμιος, α, ον, *orderly, well-disciplined,* vi. 6. 32.

κόσμος, ου, ὁ, (κομέω *to tend ?*) *order, equipment, ornament, decoration, garniture,* D., i. 9. 23 ? iii. 2. 7. Der. COSMICAL, MICRO-COSM.

Κοτύωρα, ων, τά, *Cotyōra,* a city on the southern shore of the Euxine, a Sinopean colony. Here the long and severe foot-march of the Cyreans was relieved by sailing. v. 5. 3. ‖ Ordu.

↓Κοτυωρίτης, ου, *a Cotyorite* or *Cotyorian,* v. 5. 6 s, 19.

κοῦφος, η, ον, *light* (not heavy) : χόρτος κοῦφος [light] *dry grass, hay,* i. 5. 10 : vi. 1. 12.

↓κούφως *lightly, nimbly,* vi. 1. 5.

κράζω * r., άξω l., 2 pf. pret. κέκραγα, *to cry* or *call aloud, make outcry,* vii. 8. 15.

κράνος, εος, τό, (κάρα *head*) *a helmet* or *casque ;* among the Greeks, comm. of metal, with movable pieces for fuller protection, lined, and fastened under the chin ; among some nations, of leather ; i. 2. 16 ; 8. 6 : v. 4. 13.

κρατέω, ήσω, κεκράτηκα, (κράτος) *to have power over, to rule, control, be superior, be sovereign over ; to master, conquer, worst, vanquish, overcome ; to hold* or *maintain* a military post ; G., A.; i. 7. 8 : ii. 5. 7 : v. 6. 7, 9.

κρᾱτήρ, ῆρος, ὁ, (κεράννῡμι) a mixing-vessel, esp. for mixing wine and water ; *a large bowl,* iv. 5. 26, 32.

κράτιστος, κράτιστα, see κρείττων.

κράτος, εος, τό, *strength, might, power, force :* κατὰ κράτος [according to force] *with might and main, with vigor, by force of arms,* i. 8. 19 : vii. 7. 7. Der. AUTO-CRAT. See ἀνά.

κραυγή, ῆς, (κράζω) *a loud cry, outcry, shout, shouting, noise, clamor,* i. 2. 17 ; 5. 12 ; 8. 11 : iii. 4. 45.

κρέας, κρέαος, contr. κρέως, τό, *caro, flesh :* pl. κρέα *pieces of flesh, flesh, meat,* esp. *cooked,* i. 5. 2 s : iv. 5. 31.

κρείττων,* ον, κράτιστος, η, ον, c. & s. of the Ep. κρατύς *strong,* but comm. referred to ἀγαθός, D., I.: *c. better, superior ; stronger, more powerful ; more efficient, useful, serviceable,* or *valuable ;* i. 2. 26 ; 7. 3 : iii. 1. 4 : s. *best, ablest, noblest, highest in rank ; most powerful, distinguished, eminent, useful,* or *valuable ;* i. 5. 8 : 9. 2, 20 s : iii. 4. 41 : — adv. κράτιστα (as s. to εὖ, c. κρεῖττον) *best ; most stoutly, bravely, successfully,* or *advantageously ; to the best advantage ;* iii. 2. 6, 27.

κρέμαμαι,* ἥσομαι, *to hang* (intrans.), *be hung up,* ἐπί, ὑπέρ, iii. 2. 19 : iv. 1. 2.

↓κρεμάννῡμι,* κρεμάσω κρεμῶ, a. p. ἐκρεμάσθην, *to hang up, suspend,* A., i. 2. 8 : vii. 4. 17.

κρήνη, ης, (κάρα, κάρηνον, *head ?*) *a fountain, spring* of water, i. 2. 13.

κρηπίς, ίδος, ἡ, crēpīdo, *a foundation, base,* iii. 4. 7, 10.

Κρής, Κρητός, ὁ, *a Cretan,* a man of Κρήτη (*Crete,* now Candia), the large island south of the Ægean, prominent in the early history of Greek civilization ; where, according to fable, Zeus was born, where Minos reigned and gave laws, which Homer styles ἑκατόμπολις *hundred-citied,* and credits with 80 vessels sent to the siege of Troy. Its soldiers had a high reputation as light-armed troops, and 200 Cretan bowmen rendered good service to the Cyreans. i.2.9: iv.2.28; 8.27. Der. CRETACEOUS.

κριθή, ῆς, ch. pl., *barley*, i. 2. 22.
‡κρίθινος, η, ον, *of barley*: οἶνος κ. [barley wine] *beer*: iv. 5. 26, 31.

κρίνω,* κρῐνῶ, κέκρῐκα, a. ἔκρῖνα, a. p. ἐκρίθην, *to distinguish, select; to judge, decide, be of opinion; to try* a person accused; A. I.; i. 5. 11; 9. 5, 20, 28, 30: vi. 6. 16, 25. Der. CRITIC.

κρῐός, οῦ, ὁ, (κέρας?) *a ram*, ii. 2. 9.

κρίσις, εως, ἡ, (κρίνω) *trial, judgment*, i. 6. 5: vi. 6. 20. Der. CRISIS.

κρόμμυον or κρόμυον, ου, *an onion*, vii. 1. 37.

†κροτέω, ἥσω, *to strike together*, A., vi. 1. 10?

†κρότος, ου, ὁ, *clapping, applause*, vi. 1. 13.

κρούω, ούσω, κέκρουκα, *to strike, clash, strike together*, A., iv. 5. 18: vi. 1. 10 (v. l. κροτέω).

κρύπτω,* ὑψω, κέκρυφα, *to hide, conceal*, 2 A., i. 4. 12; 9. 19: vi. 1. 18. Der. CRYPT.

κρωβύλος or κρώβυλος, ου, ὁ, *a tuft* of hair or leathern thongs, v. 4. 13.

κτάομαι,* κτήσομαι, κέκτημαι, *to acquire, procure, get, gain, win: πολεμίους κ. to gain as enemies, to make enemies*: pf. pret. *to* [have acquired] *possess, enjoy*: A.: i. 7. 3; 9. 19: ii. 6. 17s, 26: v. 5. 17.

κτείνω, κτενῶ, 2 pf. ἔκτονα, (usu. ἀπο-κτείνω) *to kill, slay*, A., ii. 5. 32.

†κτῆμα, ατος, τό, *a possession*, vii.7.41.

†κτῆνος, εος, τό, *a domestic animal*, as property once consisted chiefly of these (cf. *cattle*, orig. the same with *chattel*); pl. *cattle*; iii. 1. 19: v. 2. 3.

‡Κτησίας, ου, *Ctesias*, a celebrated physician and historian from Cnidus in Caria, who passed a number of years at the Persian court as the king's physician, and carefully availed himself of this peculiar opportunity of obtaining historic information. He was surgeon to Artaxerxes at the battle of Cunaxa. i. 8. 26s.

κυβερνήτης, ου, (κυβερνάω guberno, *to steer*) *a steersman, helmsman, pilot*, v. 8. 20.

[κυβιστάω, ήσω, (κύβος CUBE, *die*, or κύβη *head*) *to throw one's self down head foremost*, or as dice are thrown; while ἐκ-κυβιστάω is strictly *to recover* from this position.]

Κύδνος, ου, ὁ, *the Cydnus*, a river of Cilicia, rising in Mt. Taurus, and flowing through the capital Tarsus to the Mediterranean. It was noted for the coldness of its water, which nearly cost Alexander his life. The luxurious state in which Cleopatra sailed up the Cydnus to meet and conquer Antony is depicted in Plutarch and Shakspeare. i. 2. 23. ‖ Mesarlyk-Chai.

†κυζικηνός, οῦ, ὁ, (sc. στατήρ), *a Cyzicene* [stater], a widely current gold coin from the famed mint of Cyzicus, = 28 Att. drachmæ, or about $5½, v. 6. 23: vi. 2. 4: vii. 2. 36.

Κύζικος, ου, ἡ, *Cyzicus*, an old and important commercial city beautifully situated on an island, afterwards a peninsula, in the Propontis. It was colonized by the Milesians. vii. 2. 5. ‖ Bal-Kiz (Παλαία Κύζικος).

κύκλος, ου, ὁ, *circulus, a circle, ring, round, enclosure; a circle, group*, or *knot* of men; *a circular form* or disposition of troops, presenting shields on every side: κύκλῳ *in a circle* or *circuit, all around, around, round about* (strengthened by πάντη, as it is sometimes used where the circle is not complete, iii. 1. 2), περί: ἡ κύκλῳ χώρα *the surrounding country*: i.5.4: iii.1.12; 4. 7: v. 7. 2: vii. 8. 18. Der. CYCLE.

‡κυκλόω, ώσω, κεκύκλωκα, *to surround, encircle, hem in*, A.: *M. to stand* or *gather around, περί* : i.8.13 : iv.2.15: vi. 4. 20.

‡κύκλωσις, εως, ἡ, *a surrounding, enclosing*, i. 8. 23.

κυλίνδω or κυλινδέω, ήσω l., (also κυλίω r. or l.) *to roll, roll down* or *off*, trans.; but *M*., intrans.; iv. 2. 3s, 20; 7. 6; 8. 28? Der. CYLINDER.

Κυνίσκος, ου, *a Spartan general*, who carried on war from the Chersonese against the Thracians, vii. 1. 13.

κυπαρίττινος, η, ον, (κυπάρισσος or -ριττος, cupressus, CYPRESS), *made of cypress*, v. 3. 12.

κύπτω, κύψω, κέκυφα, (akin to Lat. cubo) *to stoop down, bend forward*, iv. 5. 32?

Κύρειος or Κυρεῖος, α, ον, (Κῦρος)

Cyrēan, of Cyrus, belonging to Cyrus, i. 10. 1 : iii. 2. 17 (subst.) : vii. 2. 7.

κύριος, α, ον, (κῦρος *authority*) *invested with authority, possessed of power,* I., v. 7. 27.

Κῦρος, ου, (Pers. Khur, *sun*) *Cyrus* the Great, or the Elder, son of Cambȳses, a Persian noble, and Mandāne, daughter of Astyages, king of the Medes. He founded the Persian monarchy by dethroning his tyrannical grandfather, B. C. 558 ; and enlarged it by conquering Crœsus, king of Lydia, B. C. 554, and taking Babylon, B. C. 538. He was slain in battle with the Scythians, B. C. 529. Such, in general, is the account of Hdt., from which those of Ctesias and Xenophon vary. i. 9. 1.—2. *Cyrus* the Younger, second son of Darius II. and Parysatis, born soon after his father's accession to the throne, while his elder brother Arsaces was born before this accession. As, therefore, the first-born of Darius *the king,* he was the heir to the throne, according to the peculiar principle of succession which gave the crown to Xerxes. Both the ambitious Cyrus and his fond mother seem to have hoped that this precedent would be regarded by Darius. Cyrus was so precocious in the qualities of command, that he was appointed by his father, when a mere youth of seventeen, B. C. 407, satrap of Lydia, Phrygia, and Cappadocia, and instructed to assist Sparta in her war against Athens. This he did so zealously and liberally, that the Spartans afterwards felt under obligation to render him aid in return. Desirous of making his government a model for order and security, and perhaps more jealous for his authority than an older ruler would have been, he was not only lavish in rewarding faithful service, but also rigorous in punishing the disobedient and criminal, — we should say, perhaps, too rigorous, but it was the Persian habit to be severe in punishment. The better to secure his dignity, he imprudently required in those who approached him an etiquette which had been regarded as due only to royalty ; and when two of his cousins, sons of a sister of his father, refused to observe it, he enforced the rule by putting them to death. On complaint of their parents, and apprehending the approach of death, Darius sent for the young prince, B. C. 405. Cyrus went to his father, taking with him, as if a friend, Tissaphernes, the wily and treacherous satrap of Caria, — in truth perhaps because he did not wish to leave him behind. Darius died soon after, and disappointed Cyrus by leaving the sceptre, "which had glittered before his young imaginings," to his elder brother. Hereupon Tissaphernes, who doubtless hoped thus to add the rich province of Cyrus to his own, and who was capable of any deceit and calumny, brought against him the monstrous charge of designing the assassination of the new king during the very rites of coronation. Unfortunately this crime, which was so remote from the open and manly, even if excessive, ambition of Cyrus, had precedents in Persian history ; and Artaxerxes, either believing the charge or willing to make it a pretext, arrested his brother to put him to death. The young prince was only saved from speedy execution by the full power of his mother's prayers and tears, and was sent back to his distant satrapy, burning with the sense of injustice, disgrace, and danger. There was no real reconciliation between the two brothers ; and Cyrus had reason to feel that his danger was only deferred, not past, especially with such a neighbor as Tissaphernes in the king's confidence, and that he must either at length fall a sacrifice to the jealousy of Artaxerxes or reign in his stead. He was thus stimulated, with the encouragement of his mother's favor, to attempt the ill-fated expedition of which Xenophon wrote the history, — an expedition which certainly cannot be justified on Christian or even Socratic principles, but which was almost in the regular line of oriental history. i. 1. 1 s ; 9. 1.

Κυτώνιον, ου, *Cytonium,* see Κερτωνός, vii. 8. 8 ?

κύων, κυνός, ὁ ἡ, canis, *dog, bitch,* iii. 2. 35 : v. 7. 26 ; 8. 24 : vi. 2. 2. Der. CYNIC.

κωλύω (ῠ), ύσω, κεκώλυκα, *to hinder, prevent, forbid, oppose:* τὸ κωλῦον *the*

κωμάρχης 78 λαφυροπώλης

hindrance, obstacle: A. G., I.: i. 2. 21s; 3. 16; 6. 2: iv. 5. 20. Cf. κόλος *clipped.*
†κωμ-άρχης, ου, (ἄρχω) *the ruler or head-man of a village, village-chief,* iv. 5. 10, 24; 6. 1 s.
κώμη, ης, *a village,* comm. unfortified, i. 4. 9 : iv. 4. 7. Der. COMEDY.
‡κωμήτης, ου, *a villager,* iv. 5. 24.
κώπη, ης, (cf. Lat. capio) *the handle of an oar,* &c.; *an oar,* vi. 4. 2.

Λ.

λαβεῖν, -οιμι, -ών, see λαμβάνω.
λαγχάνω,* λήξομαι, εἴληχα, 2 a. ἔλαχον, *to draw* or *obtain by lot, to obtain* perchance or by fate, A., iii. 1. 11 : iv. 5. 24.
λαγώς, ώ, ῴ, ών or ώ, ὁ, lepus, *a hare,* iv. 5. 24 : v. *l.* λαγῶς, ῶ.
λαθεῖν, -ών, see λανθάνω, i. 3. 17.
‡λάθρα or λάθρᾳ clam, *secretly, without the knowledge of,* G., i. 3. 8.
†Λακεδαιμόνιος, ου, ὁ, *a Lacedæmonian, a Spartan,* the most common term for the citizens of Sparta, i.1.9 : ii. 6. 2: iii. 2. 37. See Σπαρτιάτης.
Λακεδαίμων, ονος, ἡ, *Lacedæmon, Sparta,* v. 3. 11. See Σπάρτη.
λάκκος, ου, ὁ, (cf. Lat. lacus) *an underground cistern* or *cellar,* such as are now frequent in Kurdistan and Armenia, iv. 2. 22.
λακτίζω, ίσω ιῶ, (λάξ *with the foot*) *to kick,* A., iii. 2. 18.
Λάκων, ωνος, ὁ, *a Laconian,* an inhabitant of Laconia ; a term wider in extent than Λακεδαιμόνιος, but not unfrequently used in its place ; ii. 1. 3, 5 ; 5. 31 (cf. i. 4. 3 ; 1. 9) : v. 1. 15. See Σπάρτη, Σπαρτιάτης.
‡Λακωνικός, ἡ, όν, *Laconian:* ὁ Λακωνικός *the Laconian:* iv. 1. 18 ; 7. 16: vii. 2. 29 ; 3. 8.
λαμβάνω,* λήψομαι, εἴληφα, 2 a. ἔλαβον, a. *p.* ἐλήφθην, *to take; to take* captive or by force, as prisoners, prey, plunder, a military post, &c., *to seize, catch, capture; to take* by gift, bargain, or loan, *to receive, obtain, procure; to take* as instruments, arms, supplies, pledges, companions, military force, &c., *to obtain, procure, enlist* (λαβών *having taken* = *with,* i. 2. 3); *to overtake, come upon, catch, find, detect;* A. G., G. partitive, ἀπό, ἐκ, εἰς, παρά,

&c.; i. 1. 2, 6, 9 ; 2. 1 s ; 5. 2 s, 7, 10 ; 6. 6 s, 10 ; 7. 13 ; 10. 18. See δίκη, δίκαιος, πεῖρα. Der. DI-LEMMA.
†λαμπρός, ά, όν, c., *brilliant, illustrious, glorious,* vii. 7. 41.
‡λαμπρότης, ητος, ἡ, *brilliancy, splendor,* i. 2. 18.
λάμπω,* ψω, λέλαμπα, *to make shine, light up: M. to shine, blaze, be in a blaze:* iii. 1. 11 s. Der. LAMP.
†Λαμψακηνός, οῦ, ὁ, *a Lampsacene,* vii. 8. 3 ; a man of
Λάμψακος, ου, ἡ, *Lampsacus,* a city of Mysia on the Hellespont, an Ionian colony. On account of its good wine, Artaxerxes I. assigned it to Themistocles as a means of his support. It was the reputed birthplace of Priāpus, and the especial seat of his worship. vii. 8. 1. || Lamsaki.
λανθάνω &, ch. poet., λήθω,* λήσομαι, λέληθα, 2 a. ἔλαθον, *to escape the notice* or *knowledge* or *elude the observation of* any one, *lie hid* or *be concealed* from him, *be unobserved* by him, *elude,* A. W. a pt., it is oftener translated by an adv., adverbial phrase, or adj., and the pt. by a finite verb, 677 f; as, τρεφόμενον ἐλάνθανεν *was* [concealed in being maintained] *secretly maintained,* i. 1. 9 s ; λαθεῖν αὐτὸν ἀπελθών *to* [elude him departing] *depart without his knowledge,* i. 3. 17 ; ἔλαθον ἐγγὺς προσελθόντες *they drew near unobserved,* iv. 2. 7 ; ἐλάνθανον αὐτοὺς γενόμενοι [were not observed by themselves in having come] *came unconsciously to themselves, unawares,* or *unexpectedly,* vi. 3. 22. See, also, iv. 6. 11 : v. 2. 29 : vi. 3. 14: vii. 3. 38, 43. Der. LETHE. Cf. lateo.
Λάρισσα, ης, *Larissa,* (anciently Calah, while some have traced the name to Resen, Gen. x. 11s) a part of the extensive ruins of "great Nineveh," and abounding in the most interesting remains, which lay buried more than 2000 years to be recently brought to light and surprise the world, iii. 4. 7. || Nimrúd. See Μέσπιλα.
λάσιος, α, ον, (akin to δασύς) *bushy:* τὰ λάσια *the thickets:* v. 2. 29 : vi. 4. 26.
λάφυρον, ου, (λαμβάνω) ch. pl., *spolia, the spoils* of war, *booty,* vi. 6. 38 ?
‡λαφυρο-πωλέω, ήσω, *to sell booty,* vi. 6. 38 ? [*salesman* of booty, vii. 7. 56.
‡λαφυρο-πώλης, ου, *a booty-seller,*

λαχεῖν, λαχών, see λαγχάνω.
‡λάχος, εος, τό, ch. poet., *a portion*, esp. by lot, *share, part, division*, v. 3. 9: vi. 3. 2?

λέγω,* λέξω, λέλεχα 1., (classic εἴρηκα), a. p. ἐλέχθην, *to say, speak, tell, express, relate, report, state; to speak of, mention, name, account; to bid, propose, advise:* A. D., CP., I. (A.), περί, πρός, εἰς, ἐν: i. 2. 12, 21; 3. 8, 13, 15, 19; 4. 11: ii. 5. 25. In the pass., the personal construction w. the inf., for the impers., is the more common, 573, i. 2. 8: ii. 2. 6: cf. i. 8. 6: iv. 1. 3. Der. LEXICON, DIA-LECT.

λεία, as, *booty, plunder, spoils,* v. 1. 8, 17: vii. 4. 2.

λειμών, ῶνος, ὁ, (λείβω *to pour*) a moist place, *meadow*, v. 3. 11.

λεῖος, α, ον, lēvis, *smooth, gently sloping, of easy ascent,* iv. 4. 1.

λείπω,* ψω, λέλοιπα, 2 a. ἔλιπον, a. p. ἐλείφθην, f. pf. λελείψομαι, linquo, *to* LEAVE, *quit, forsake, abandon, desert; to leave behind, spare;* A.; i. 2. 21: vii. 4. 1: — *P. to be left;* hence, *to remain, survive; to be left behind, fall behind, be inferior,* G. 405 b: λελείψεται *will* [have been left] *remain:* ii. 4. 5: iii. 1. 2: vii. 7. 31. Der. EL-LIPSIS.

* λεκτέος, α, ον, (λέγω) *to be* or *that must be said* or *spoken,* v. 6. 5.

λελείψομαι, λελοιπώς, see λείπω.
λέξω, λέξον, λεξάτω, see λέγω, i. 3. 13.

Λεοντῖνος, ου, ὁ, *a Leontine, a man of Leontini* (Λεοντῖνοι, now Lentini), a city of eastern Sicily, a Chalcidian colony, situated in a region of extraordinary fertility, and early prosperous, but overshadowed by its powerful Doric neighbor, Syracuse, ii. 6. 16.

†λευκο-θώραξ, ᾱκος, ὁ ἡ, *with a white corselet,* doubtless of linen, i. 8. 9. See θώραξ.

λευκός, ή, όν, (akin to λεύσσω *to see,* LOOK, and Lat. luceo) *bright, white,* i. 8. 8: v. 4. 32 s.

λεχθείς, λεχθῆναι, see λέγω, iii. 1. 1.
λήγω, ξω, (λέγω *to* LAY) *to allay;* comm. intrans., *to abate, cease, end, close, come to an end,* iii. 1. 9: iv. 5. 4.

λήζομαι, ίσομαι, or Att. λήσομαι, λήσομαι, λέλησμαι, (λεία) *to plunder, ravage, pillage, rob; to seize as booty* or *spoil, take as prey* or *by force;* A., ἐκ: iv. 8. 23: v. 1. 9: vi. 1. 1: vii. 3. 31.

λῆρος, ου, ὁ, *nonsense, trumpery, a trifle,* vii. 7. 41.

†ληστεία, ας, *robbery, plunder, pillage,* vii. 7. 9.

ληστής, οῦ, (λήζομαι) *a robber, plunderer, pillager,* vi. 1. 8; 6. 28.

λήσω, see λανθάνω, vii. 3. 43.
ληφθῆναι, λήψομαι, see λαμβάνω.
λίαν adv., *very, exceedingly,* vi. 1. 28.
†λίθινος, η, ον, *of stone,* iii. 4. 7, 9.

λίθος, ου, ὁ, *a stone,* often such as are used for an attack: *stone,* the material: i. 5. 12: iii. 3. 17; 4. 10; 5. 10: iv. 7. 4 s. Der. LITHO-GRAPH.

λιμήν, ένος, ὁ, (akin to λείβω *to pour?*) *a harbor, haven, port,* vi. 2. 13.

λιμός, οῦ, ὁ, (λείπω) *failure of food, hunger, famine,* i. 5. 5: ii. 2. 11; 5. 19.

λίνεος, α, ον, contr. λινοῦς, ῆ, οῦν, (λίνον *flax*) *flaxen,* LINEN, iv. 7. 15.

†λογίζομαι, ίσομαι ιοῦμαι, λελόγισμαι, *to consider, calculate, expect,* A., I., ii. 2. 13: iii. 1. 20.

λόγος, ου, ὁ, (λέγω) *a word; speech, discourse; conversation, discussion; a statement, narrative, report, rumor; an argument, plea:* pl. *words, conference, discussion,* πρός: εἰς λόγους ἔρχεσθαι *to enter into a conference* or *come to an interview* with, D.: i. 4. 7; 6. 5: ii. 1. 1; 5. 4, 16, 27; 6. 4: v. 8. 18: vi. 1. 18. Der. LOGIC, -LOGY, -LOGUE.

λόγχη, ης, (cf. Lat. lancea) *the point* or *spike of a spear, the spear-head,* early made by the Greeks of bronze, but afterwards of iron; comm. fr. 6 in. to a foot in length: hence often, by synecdoche, *a spear* or LANCE (esp., in the Anab., of those used by the barbarians): i. 8. 8: ii. 2. 9: iv. 7. 16; 8. 7.

λοιδορέω, ήσω, λελοιδόρηκα, (λοίδορος *a railer*) *to rail at, revile, abuse, reproach, reprove,* A., iii. 4. 49.

λοιπός, ή, όν, (λείπω) re-liquus, *left behind, remaining, the rest* or *remainder of,* D., iv. 2. 13 s: λοιπόν (ἐστιν) *it* [is left] *remains,* iii. 2. 29: τὴν λοιπὴν [sc. ὁδόν] *the rest of the way,* iii. 4. 46: τὸ λοιπόν *the rest,* G. partitive, iii. 4. 6: τοῦ λοιποῦ [sc. χρόνου], oftener τὸ λοιπόν, *in* or *during the rest* of the time, *in future, afterwards, henceforth, thenceforth,* 482 e, ii. 2. 5: iii. 2. 8: v. 7. 34.

Λοκρός, οῦ, ὁ, *a Locrian,* a man of Locris, a central region of Greece in three separate parts (two north of Bœotia and Phocis, and the third, the

Λουσιάτης 80 λύπη

larger but ruder portion, west of Phocis). The eastern Locrians are credited with 40 ships sent to the Trojan War under the lesser Ajax. vii. 4. 18.

Λουσιάτης or -ώτης, ου, & **Λουσιεύς**, έως, ὁ, *a Lusian*, a man of Lusi (Λουσοί), a town in the north of Arcadia, having a celebrated temple of Artemis (Diana), which was revered through the Peloponnese as an inviolable asylum, iv. 2. 21; 7. 11s: vii. 6. 40. ‖ Sudheuá.

λόφος, ου, ὁ, (λέπω *to rub off, peel*) *the neck* of a horse or ox, as rubbed by the yoke; hence, in general, *an elevation* or *crest; an eminence* or *ridge* of land, *a hill, height,* = γή-λοφος: i. 10. 13 s (cf. 12): iii. 4. 39 (cf. 37).

†**λοχαγέω**, ήσω, *to be a lochage* or *captain*, vi. 1. 30.

†**λοχᾱγία**, ας, the command of a λόχος, *a captaincy*, i. 4. 15: iii. 1. 30.

†**λοχ-ᾱγός**, οῦ, ὁ, (ἄγω) the leader of a λόχος, *a lochage, centurion, captain*, who comm. received twice the pay of a private. The word has the Dor. form, as a term of war, in which the Doric race so excelled, 386 c. i. 7. 2: vi. 3. 6 (where the term is applied to the commander of a tenth of the Arcadian and Achæan force, also termed στρατηγός): vii. 2. 36.

†**λοχίτης**, ου, *a soldier* belonging to a λόχος, *a member of a company*, vi. 6. 7, 17.

λόχος, ου, ὁ, (λέγω *to collect*) *a company* or *division* of soldiers, not fixed in number, but usu. of about 100 men. For the subdivision of the common λόχος, see iii. 4. 21 s. i. 2. 25: iv. 8. 15: vi. 3. 2, 4 s; 5. 9 s.

†**Λυδία**, ας, *Lydia*, a fertile province of Asia Minor, west of Phrygia, once a powerful kingdom. It was early distinguished for its industry, wealth, and progress in the arts; and exerted much influence in the development of Greek civilization. It reached its acme under Crœsus, whose defeat by Cyrus made it a part of the Persian Empire. Its people, before warlike, were then forbidden the use of arms, and naturally became both effeminate themselves and the teachers of effeminacy to their conquerors. i. 2. 5; 9. 7: vii. 8. 7 ? 25.

†**Λύδιος**, α, ον, *Lydian*, i. 5. 6.

Λῡδός, οῦ, ὁ, *a Lydian*, a man of Lydia, iii. 1. 31.

Λύκαιος or **Λυκαῖος**, α, ον, *Lycæan*, pertaining to Mt. Lycæus, a lofty height in southwestern Arcadia, presenting a view of a large part of the Peloponnese, and sacred to Zeus (hence surnamed Lycæan) and Pan: τὰ Λύκαια [sc. ἱερά], *the Lycæan Rites* or *Festival*, in honor of Lycæan Jove, celebrated by the Arcadians with sacrifices and games, i. 2. 10. ‖ Diofórti, 4659 feet high.

†**Λυκαονία**, ας, an elevated region of Asia Minor, north of Cilicia, occupied by a rude, warlike, independent, and predatory race. It was an early scene of the missionary labors of the apostle Paul, who here found Timothy. i. 2. 19: vii. 8. 25.

Λυκάων, ονος, ὁ, *a Lycaonian*, iii. 2. 23.

Λύκειον, ου, *the* LYCEUM, the chief of the Athenian gymnasia, situated without the eastern wall, adorned with fine trees, covered walks, and other embellishments, and consecrated to Lycéan Apollo. Here Aristotle taught while walking, from which his philosophy was named Peripatetic (περιπατέω *to walk around*). vii. 8. 1.

Λύκιος, ου, *Lycius*, a Syracusan, sent by Clearchus for observation, i. 10. 14. — 2. An Athenian, appointed commander of cavalry, and so rendering good service, iii. 3. 20: iv. 3. 22.

λύκος, ου, ὁ, lupus, *a wolf*, the largest beast of prey in Greece, ii. 2. 9 (prob. sacrificed on this occasion as sacred to Ahriman, the Persian god of evil). Der. LYCO-PODIUM.

‡**Λύκος**, ου, ὁ, *the Lycus* or *Wolf-River*, a name given to several streams, seemingly from their destructive character. A small river so named entered the Euxine near Heraclēa, vi. 2. 3. ‖ Kilij-Su, i. e. *Sword Water*.

Λύκων, ωνος, *Lycon*, a factious Achæan, v. 6. 27: vi. 2. 4, 9.

λυμαίνομαι, λυμανοῦμαι, λελύμασμαι, (λύμη *outrage*) *to ruin, spoil, frustrate*, A. D., i. 3. 16.

†**λῡπέω**, ήσω, λελύπηκα, *to pain, grieve, trouble, distress, annoy, molest*, A., i. 3. 8: ii. 3. 23; 5. 14: iii. 1. 11.

λύπη, ης, *pain, grief, sorrow, distress*, iii. 1. 3.

λυπηρός 81 μανθάνω

‡λῦπηρός, ά, όν, c., *painful, grievous, distressing, troublesome, annoying*, D., ii. 5. 13 : vii. 7. 28.

λύσι-τελέω, ήσω, (λύω *to pay*, τέλος *expense*) *to pay expenses, to be profitable, advantageous,* or *expedient*, D. I., iii. 4. 36 ? [zy, v. 7. 26.

λύσσα or λύττα, ης, *madness, frenzy*.

λύω,* λ*ύ*σω, λέλυκα, solvo, *to* LOOSE, *let loose, release, set free ; to undo, break, break down, destroy, remove, violate* (a treaty or oath); A.; ii. 4. 17, 19 s : iii. 1. 21 ; 4. 35 : = *v. l.* λυσιτελέω, iii. 4. 36 : λελυμένος *unbound, free from bonds*, iv. 6. 2 : — *M. to ransom, redeem*, A., vii. 8. 6. Der. ANA-LYSIS.

λωτο-φάγος, ου, ὁ, (λωτός the *lotus,* φαγεῖν *to eat*) a *lotus-eater*. The Cyrenean lotus (now *jujube*) was a small sweet date-like fruit, so delicious that, according to the old fable (Hom. Od. ι. 94), all who ate of it forgot their homes, and wished only to remain and feed upon it; while in Arab poetry it is the fruit of paradise. The Lotophagi of Homer, upon whose shore Ulysses landed, have been located by most geographers upon the coast of Tripoli and Tunis in North Africa. iii. 2. 25.

λωφάω, ήσω, λελώφηκα, (λόφος, as if *to withdraw the neck from the yoke ?*) *to rest, cease*, iv. 7. 6.

λῴων,* contr. fr. c. λωίων referred to ἀγαθός, *more desirable, better*, D. I., iii. 1. 7: for emphasis, λῷον καὶ ἄμεινον *more desirable and advantageous, preferable and better*, vi. 2. 15 : vii. 6. 44.

M.

μά* *by*, an adv. of swearing, comm. negative, unless preceded by ναί, A., i. 4. 8 : v. 8. 6, 21.

μάγαδις, ιος, dat. (ιι) ῑ, 218. 2, ἡ, (a foreign word) *the magadis*, a kind of harp with 20 strings arranged in octaves ; or, acc. to some, a kind of flute ; vii. 2. 32.

Μάγνης, ητος, ὁ, a *Magnesian*, a man of Magnesia, a narrow mountainous region occupying the east coast of Thessaly, vi. 1. 7. Cf. MAGNET.

μαθεῖν, -ω, -οιμι, &c., see μανθάνω.

Μαίανδρος, ου, ὁ, *the Mæander*, the largest river entering the Ægean from

Asia, so remarkable for its winding course through its rich alluvial plain, that it has given a name to the winding of rivers. Its deposit has greatly extended and changed the coast at its mouth. i. 2. 5, 7 s. ǁ Mendere-Chai.

μαίνομαι,* μανοῦμαι ι., 2 pf. μέμηνα, 2 a. p. ἐμάνην, *to be mad, insane*, or *frenzied*, ii. 5. 10, 12. Der. MANIAC.

Μαισάδης, ου, *Mæsades*, a Thracian prince, father of Seuthes, vii. 2. 32.

μακαρίζω, ίσω ιῶ, (μακάρ *happy*) *to count* or *esteem happy* or *fortunate*, A., iii. 1. 19.

‡μακαριστός, ή, όν, *esteemed happy, envied* or *enviable, being an object of envy*, D., i. 9. 6.

Μακίστιος (or Μακέστιος), ου, ὁ, a *Macistian*, a man of Macistus (Μάκιστος), an old town of Triphylia in Elis, vii. 4. 16. ǁ Heights of Khaiaffa.

μακρός, ά, όν, c., s., (μῆκος *length*, cf. μέγας magnus) *long*, of both space and time : μακράν [sc. ὁδόν] a *long way, a great distance, far* (so c. & s.): μακρότερον adv., *farther: μακρόν ἦν it was a long distance*, or *too far* : i. 5. 7 : ii. 2. 11 s : iii. 4. 16 s, 42.

Μάκρων, ωνος, ὁ, a *Macronian*. The Macrōnes were a warlike tribe dwelling not far from Trebizond. iv. 7. 27 ; 8. 5 : v. 5. 17.

μάλα, by apostr. μάλ', c. μᾶλλον, s. μάλιστα, adv. (much used with adjectives and adverbs to express degree, 510), *very, very much, greatly, exceedingly ; very well, certainly* ; iii. 4. 15 ; 5. 3 ; οὐ μάλα *not at all, by no means*, ii. 6. 15 ; by exceptional arrangement, αὐτίκα μάλα *very speedily, instantly, at once*, iii. 5. 11, εὖ μάλα *very easily*, vi. 1. 1 :—c. *more, rather, more certainly,* (sometimes joined w. another compar. for clearness or emphasis, iv. 6. 11) ἤ or G. (as c.), i. 1. 4 s, 8 ; 9. 5, 24 :—s. *most, most of all, in the highest degree, best, especially ; most* or *very nearly, about* (w. numbers); i. 1. 6 ; 9. 22, 29 : vi. 4. 3 : vii. 2. 22.

μαλακίζομαι, f. p. ισθήσομαι l., (μαλακός *soft*) *to be self-indulgent, yield to sloth*, v. 8. 14.

μανείς, -έντες, see μαίνομαι, ii. 5. 10.

μανθάνω,* μαθήσομαι, μεμάθηκα, 2 a. ἔμαθον, *to learn, ascertain*, A., I., G. CP., παρά, i. 9. 4 : ii. 5. 37 : iii. 2. 25 : iv. 8. 5 : v. 2. 25. Der. MATHEMATICS.

LEX. AN. 4* F

† μαντεία, as, *prophecy, oracle,* iii. 1. 7. [μαντεύομαι,εύσομαι,(μάντις) *to prophesy, declare by oracle.*]

† μαντευτός, ή, όν, *declared or pointed out by an oracle,* D. ἐκ, vi. 1. 22.

Μαντινεύς, έως, ὁ, *a Mantinean,* a man of Mantinēa (Μαντίνεια), an ancient and, before the building of Megalopolis, the largest city of Arcadia, situated in the eastern part. It was noted for the excellence of its political institutions, and for five important battles fought near it. In one of these, B. C. 362, the Theban Epaminondas conquered the Spartans and Athenians at the expense of his own life, and the two sons of Xenophon fought; the elder, Gryllus, falling after signal feats of valor, among which some reckoned the slaying of the Theban general. vi. 1. 11. ‖ Paleópoli.

μάντις, εως, ὁ ἡ, (μαίνομαι) one who speaks in a state of divine frenzy, *a prophet, seer; a diviner, soothsayer, augur;* i. 7. 18. Der. NECRO-MANCY.

Μαρδόνιοι or Μάρδοι, ων, *the Mardonii* or *Mardi,* or *-ians,* a warlike people, prob. dwelling near the southern boundary of Armenia, iv. 3. 4: *v.l.* Μυγδόνιοι.

Μαριανδῡνοί, ῶν, *the Mariandȳni* or *-ians,* a people of Bithynia, dwelling around Heraclēa, and at length subjected by this city, vi. 2. 1 : *v. l.* Μαριανδηνοί, Μαρυανδηνοί.

μάρσιπος or μάρσιππος, ου, ὁ, *marsupium, a bag, pouch,* iv. 3. 11. Der. MARSUPIAL.

Μαρσύας, ου, *Marsyas,* fabled as a Phrygian satyr or peasant who invented the flute, and was most cruelly punished for his presumption in contending with Apollo, i. 2. 8. — 2. *The Marsyas,* a small river of Phrygia, flowing into the Mæander, and fabled to have risen from the tears shed by the shepherds and rural divinities of Phrygia for the cruel fate of their favorite musician, i. 2. 8.

† μαρτυρέω, ήσω, μεμαρτύρηκα, *to bear witness for* or *in favor of, testify in behalf of,* D., iii. 3. 12 : vii. 6. 39.

† μαρτύριον, ου, *testimony, witness, proof,* iii. 2. 13.

μάρτυς, g. μάρτυρος, d. pl. μάρτυσι, ὁ ἡ, *a witness,* vii. 7. 39. Der. MARTYR.

Μαρωνείτης, ου, *a Maronite,* a man of Maronēa (Μαρώνεια), a town of the Cicones in Thrace on the Ægean, afterwards colonized from Chios. It was noted for its excellent wine, which even Homer mentions (Od. *ι.* 196 s), and for the too free use of it by its inhabitants. vii. 3. 16. ‖ Marogna.

μασθός, οῦ, ὁ, *v. l.* for μαστός, i. 4. 17.

Μάσκας,* α, or Μασκᾶς, ᾶ, *the Mascas,* a stream in Mesopotamia, prob. a short canal flowing from and re-entering the Euphrātes, i. 5. 4.

μαστεύω, εύσω, ch. poet. , (μάομαι *to seek) to seek, search out, eagerly desire,* A., I., iii. 1. 43 : v. 6. 25 : vii. 3. 11.

† μαστῑγόω, ώσω, *to whip, lash, scourge,* iv. 6. 15.

μάστῑξ, ῑγος, ἡ, *a whip, lash, scourge,* iii. 4. 25.

μαστός, οῦ, ὁ, (μάσσω *to squeeze) one of the breasts;* hence, *a round hill, knoll, hillock;* i. 4. 17 ? iv. 2. 6, 14 s.

μάταιος, α, ον, (μάτην *in vain) useless, vain, idle, without avail,* vii. 6. 17; 7. 24.

† μάχαιρα, as, *a sword,* esp. a short or curved sword in distinction from ξίφος, the longer, straight sword (though the distinction is not always made, vii. 4. 16); *a sabre; a dagger, large knife;* i. 8. 7 : iv. 6. 26 : vii. 2. 30.

† μαχαίριον, ου, dim., *a dagger, dirk, knife,* iv. 7. 16.

† μάχη, ης, *a battle, fight, encounter, combat:* ἀπὸ τῆς μάχης *from the* (place of the) *battle, from the battle-ground:* i. 2. 9 : ii. 2. 6. Der. LOGO-MACHY.

† μάχιμος, η, ον, *fit for fighting, warlike,* vii. 8. 13.

μάχομαι, μαχέσομαι μαχοῦμαι, μεμάχημαι, a. ἐμαχεσάμην, *to fight, give battle; withstand, contend;* D., περί, πρό, σύν : i. 5. 9 ; 7. 9, 17 s : ii. 1. 12; 5. 19.

μέ (μ') me, μοί, μοῦ, see ἐγώ, i. 3. 3.

Μεγάβυζος, ου, *Megabyzus,* a general name borne by the keeper of the temple of Diāna at Ephesus, according to custom a eunuch, v. 3. 6 s.

μεγάλη, -ου, &c., see μέγας, i. 2. 6.

‡ μεγαλ-ηγορέω, ήσω, (ἀγορεύω) to talk big, *speak boastfully, boast, vaunt,* vi. 3. 18.

‡ μεγαλο-πρεπής, ές, (πρέπω) befitting the great, *magnificent,* i. 4. 17?

‡ μεγαλο-πρεπῶς, c. ἔστερον, s. ἔστατα, *magnificently, on a magnificent scale, with great liberality,* i. 4. 17?

†**μεγάλως** adv., *greatly, grossly*, iii. 2. 22.

Μεγαρεύς, έως, ό, (Μέγαρα, capital of Megaris) *a Megarian*. Megara was early included in Attica; but was conquered by the Dorians, and for a time was subject to Corinth. After it won its independence, its advantages for commerce gave it great prosperity, so that it established several flourishing colonies (Byzantium, &c.), and even vied with Athens in naval power. As an ally of Sparta, it suffered greatly in the Peloponnesian War. Though not distinguished for letters, it claimed the invention of comedy, and gave its name to a school of philosophy founded by Euclides, a disciple of Socrates. i. 2. 3 : vi. 2. 1.

μέγας,* μεγάλη, μέγα, g. μεγάλου, -ης, c. μείζων, s. μέγιστος, *magnus, great, large, stately; mighty, powerful; of great moment* or *obligation, important;* of a sound, *loud;* i. 2. 4, 7s; 4.9s: ii.5.14: iii.2.25: iv.7.23. The neut., sing. and pl., is much used as the acc. of effect or adv. acc., or as an appositive to the sentence or to a part of it : τὰ μεγάλα εὖ ποιεῖν [to do well the great acts] *to confer great favors*, i. 9. 24 : μέγα ὀνῆσαι or ὠφελῆσαι, βλάψαι μεγάλα, *to benefit* or *injure greatly*, iii. 1. 38 ; 3. 14 : τὸ μέγιστον *as the chief reason, chiefly*, i. 3. 10.

Μεγαφέρνης, ου, a Persian of high rank, put to death by Cyrus, i. 2. 20.

μέγεθος, εος, τό, (μέγας) *greatness, magnitude, size;* of a river, *width:* ii. 3. 15 : iv. 1. 2.

μέδιμνος, ου, ό, *the medimnus*, the common Attic corn-measure, = very nearly a bushel and a half, vi. 1. 15.

μεθ' by apostr. for μετά, before an aspirated vowel, ii. 2. 7.

μεθ-ίημι,* ήσω, εἷκα, *to let go with* or *after, let go, give up, resign*, A., vii. 4. 10.

μεθ-ίστημι,* στήσω, ἔστηκα, 1 a. ἔστησα, 2 a. ἔστην, *to place differently, remove: M.,* w. 2 a. and complete tenses act., *to change one's own place, to withdraw;* but 1 a. *m. to place apart* from one's self, *set aside*, A.; ii. 3. 8, 21.

Μεθυδριεύς, έως, ό, *a Methydrian*, a man of Methydrium (Μεθ-ύδριον), a city of central Arcadia, so called from its situation between two streams. Its inhabitants were removed to people Megalopolis. iv. 1. 27 ; 7. 12. || Ruins near Pyrgo.

μεθύω,* ύσω l., *to be drunk* or *intoxicated*, iv. 8. 20 : v. 8. 4.

μείζων, ον, *greater*, see μέγας, i. 2. 4.

μειλίχιος, α, ον, (μειλίσσω *to soothe*) *mild, gracious*, vii. 8. 4 : see Ζεύς.

μεῖναι, μείνας, &c., see μένω, i. 5. 13.

μειράκιον, ου, τό, (in form dim. of μεῖραξ, ὁ ἡ, *a youth*) *a youth, stripling, boy*, in his teens, ii. 6. 16, 28.

†**μείωμα**, ατος, τό, (μειόω *to lessen*) *a deficiency*, v. 8. 1.

μείων, ον, c. referred to μικρός or ὀλίγος, *less*, in respect to size, power, number, &c.; *smaller, weaker, fewer;* i. 9. 10: iv. 5. 36 : μεῖον ἔχειν *to have* [less success] *the worst, be worsted*, i. 10. 8 : τοῦτο μεῖον ἔχειν *to have this as a disadvantage* or *a disadvantage in this*, iii. 2. 17. The neut. μεῖον is sometimes used as an indecl. subst. or adj.; and also (as an adv.) with ἤ omitted, though the gen. does not follow ; 507 e, f, 511 c, v. 6. 9: vi. 4. 3, 24.

Μελανδῖται, ῶν, *the Melanditæ*, a people of Thrace, vii. 2. 32: *v. l.* Μελανδέπται.

†**μελανία**, as, *blackness, duskiness*, i. 8. 8.

μέλας,* αινα, άν, g. άνος, αίνης, *black, dark*, iv.5.13,15. Der. MELAN-CHOLY.

μελετάω, ήσω, μεμελέτηκα, (μέλω) *to give attention to, practise*, I., iii. 4. 17: iv. 6. 14.

†**μελετηρός**, ά, όν, s., *diligent* or *assiduous in practising*, G., i. 9. 5.

μελίνη, ης, sing. and pl., panicum, *panic*, a kind of *millet*, cf. κέγχρος· ἐπὶ τὰς μελίνας *upon the panic (fields)*: i. 2. 22 ; 5. 10: ii. 4. 13 : vi. 4. 6.

†**Μελινο-φάγοι**, ων, (φαγεῖν) *the* [panic-eaters] *Melinophagi*, a Thracian people near Salmydessus on the Euxine, perhaps Strabo's Ἀστοί, vii. 5. 12.

μέλλω,* μελλήσω, a. ἐμέλλησα or ἠμέλλησα, *to be about to* or *going to, be on the point of, intend ;* also translated by *will, would, shall, should, must, am to, were to*, &c., cf. 598 a ; *to be only about to, to delay:* τὸ μέλλον *the future:* I.: i.8.1 ; 9. 28: ii.6.10: iii. 1. 2, 8, 46 s ; 5. 17: vi. 1. 21.

μέλω, μελήσω, μεμέλητκα, *to concern, be a care to*, D.: comm. impers., as ἐμοὶ μέλει *it concerns* or *is a care to me, it* *is my care, I take care, I look* or *see to it,* ὅπως: i. 4. 16; 8. 13: vi. 4. 20: τῇ θεῷ μελήσει *the goddess will see to it,* by euphemism for *the goddess will punish his neglect,* v. 3. 13.

μέμνημαι, -ήσομαι, see μιμνήσκω.

μέμφομαι, ψομαι, *to blame, reproach, find fault with,* A. εἰς, ii. 6. 30.

μέν post-pos. adv. or secondary conj. (66 f), *on the one hand, indeed, in the first place, first,* but often omitted in translation. It is usu. a prospective particle of distinction, marking the words with which it is connected as distinguished fr. others which follow, and with which a retrospective particle, (comm. δέ, but sometimes ἀλλά, μέντοι, εἶτα, ἔπειτα, καί, &c.) is regularly joined. i. 1. 1 s; 3. 2, 10: ii. 1. 13: iii. 1. 19 s. The regular sequence is sometimes neglected, esp. after intervening clauses, i. 10. 16: iii. 2. 8. In some combinations of particles, μέν has a force like that of the confirmative μήν, *indeed, truly:* μὲν δή *now indeed, indeed, truly, so then, then, accordingly,* i. 2. 3: iii. 1. 10: οὐ μὲν δή *nor* [now] *yet indeed, yet surely not,* i. 9. 13: ii. 2. 3: ἐγὼ μὲν οὖν *I* [indeed] *for my part then,* ii. 4. 7 (μέν emphasizing ἐγώ, cf. i. 9. 1): ἀλλά .. μέν (or μέντοι) *but* or *well certainly,* vii. 6. 11, 39. The words upon which μέν throws its emphasis regularly precede it, either wholly or in part. If, as has been supposed, μέν and δέ (of which μήν and δή are longer forms) are derived from the first and second numerals (cf. μία, δύο), then their original force would seem to have been, *for one thing . . for another thing;* hence, *on the one hand . . on the other hand, in the first place . . in the second place, first . . secondly, indeed . . but* or *and,* &c. See δέ, ὁ.

†μέν-τοι *indeed truly, assuredly, really, indeed, withal, to be sure; yet, still, however, but;* i. 3. 10: ii. 3. 9 s, 22 s: καί .. μέντοι *and indeed, and certainly, and moreover, and yet,* i. 9. 6, 29: iv. 6. 16. See μέν.

μένω, μενῶ, μεμένηκα, a. ἔμεινα, maneo, *to* REMAIN, *wait, stay, tarry, continue; to wait for,* A.; i. 2. 6, 9 s; 3. 11: ii. 3. 24: iv. 4. 19 s.

Μένων, ωνος, *Menon,* a general from Pharsālus in Thessaly, whose character Xenophon depicts in dark colors. He was a favorite of Aristippus, who placed him, while yet a young man, in command of a mercenary force levied with money furnished by Cyrus. From this he brought 1500 men to the Cyrean army. When the other generals who had been seized through the treachery of Tissaphernes were put to death, Menon was spared, prob. because he claimed the merit of having aided that treachery, and through the intercession of his intimate Ariaeus; but he afterwards perished by lingering torture, prob. from having fallen into the hands of the vengeful Parysatis, who thus punished him for his supposed treason. A dialogue of Plato bears his name. i. 2. 6: ii. 6. 28 s.

†μερίζω, ίσω ιῶ, *to divide, distribute,* A., v. 1. 9 ?

μέρος, εος, τό, (μείρομαι *to share*) *a share, part, portion, division, quota, detachment; specimen:* ἐν τῷ μέρει, κατὰ (τὸ) μέρος *in* or *according to one's share, part, place,* or *turn:* i. 5. 8; 6. 2: iii. 4. 23: v. 1. 9: vi. 4. 23: vii. 6. 36.

†μεσ-ημβρία, ας, (ἡμέρα, 146 b) *midday, noon;* the place of the sun at noon, *the south;* i. 7. 6: iii. 5. 15.

†μεσό-γαια or -γεια, ας, (γῆ) *the inland, interior,* vi. 2. 19; 3. 10; 4. 5.

μέσος, η, ον, (akin to μετά) medius, MIDDLE, of space or time; *central; the middle* or *midst of* (in this use as an adj., not immediately preceded by the article, 508 a, 523 b); i. 2. 7, 17; 8. 13: iv. 8. 8 *(among* or *with):* subst. μέσον, ον, *the middle, midst,* or *centre; the interval* or *space between;* G.; i. 2. 15; 4. 4; μέσον ἡμέρας *midday, noon,* i. 8. 8; μέσον τὸ ἑαυτοῦ *his own centre,* i. 8. 13? (cf. i. 8. 22, 23); διὰ μέσου, ἐν (τῷ) μέσῳ, εἰς τὸ μέσον, *through, in,* or *into the midst* or *the interval between,* sometimes = *between,* i. 4. 4; 5. 14; 7. 6: ii. 2. 3; ἐκ τοῦ μέσου *out of* [the space between] *the way,* i. 5. 14. Der. MESENTERY.

†μεσόω, ώσω, *to form* or *be in the middle:* μεσοῦσα ἡ ἡμέρα *midday,* vi. 5. 7.

Μέσπιλα, ης or ων, ἡ or τά, (referred by some to the oriental "mashpil," *desolate,* and perhaps the origin of the name Mosul) *Mespila,* the ruins of Nineveh in its stricter sense. These lie upon the east bank of the Tigris, opposite Mosul; and include the great mounds of Koyunjik, containing the remains of the magnificent palaces of Sennacherib and his grandson, and Nebbi Yunas, sacred in Mohammedan tradition as the burial-place of the prophet Jonas. The name Nineveh, in its wider sense, seems to have applied to a vast aggregation of palaces and towns (some specially walled and having also other names, cf. modern London) situated north of the junction of the Tigris and Upper Zab, and together constituting the splendid capital of the mighty Assyrian Empire. It is represented as "an exceeding great city of three days' journey" (Jonah 3. 3.), having according to Diodōrus (2. 3) a circuit of 480 stadia (the longer sides 150 stadia, and the shorter 90). Mespila was in the northwest part of its wide-spread ruins, and Larissa (now Nimrúd, where the wonderful remains of the palaces of Esarhaddon and others have been disinterred, ch. through the efforts of Layard) in the southwest. The distance between them is set by Xen. at 6 parasangs, and is now estimated to be about 18 miles. The other two corners of the immense quadrangle (which, like the enclosure of Babylon, was doubtless occupied in part by pleasure grounds and land for culture) have been recognized at Khorsabád, where was the beautiful palace of Sargon, and at Keremles, giving an extent not greatly differing from the statement of Diodorus. Nineveh lost its glory in its capture and the overthrow of the Assyrian Empire by the Medes and Babylonians, B.C. 625; but it is represented by Xen. as not wholly destroyed till the Medes were overpowered by the Persians (B.C. 558). iii. 4. 10.

μεστός, ή, όν, *full of, abounding in; filled, stored,* or *laden with;* G.; i. 4. 19; 10. 18 : ii. 5. 9.

μετά* prep., by apostr. μετ' or μεθ', a-MID, *among* (akin to μέσος medius, and Germ. *mit*): (a) w. GEN., ch. of persons, *among;* hence, *with; in the army* or *under the command of;* i. 2. 20, 24; 7. 10 : ii. 2. 7: μεθ' ὑμῶν εἶναι *to be associated with you, adhere to you,* i. 3. 5? μετὰ ἀδικίας *with, by means of,* or *through injustice,* ii. 6. 18 : — (b) w. ACC., *after* (orig., in order to be among or with), in respect to PLACE, RANK, or oftenest TIME ; *next after, next to;* i. 3. 16 ; 7. 2 ; 8. 4: vii. 7. 22 : μετὰ ταῦτα or τοῦτο *after this, hereupon, thereupon,* i. 4. 9: iv. 6. 4: μεθ' ἡμέραν after the coming of day, hence *by day,* iv. 6. 12 : — (c) in compos., *among, after,* often denoting *distribution* or *interchange* among, and hence, in general, *change.*

μετα-βάλλω,* βαλῶ, βέβληκα, to throw to a different position : *M. to throw* or *turn* one's shield *behind,* as in retreat, A., vi. 5. 16.

μετα-γιγνώσκω,* γνώσομαι, ἔγνωκα, 2 a. ἔγνων, *to think differently, change one's mind,* ii. 6. 3.

μετα-δίδωμι,* δώσω, δέδωκα, a. ἔδωκα (δῶ, δοίην, &c.), *to distribute, impart to, share with,* D. A., G., iii. 3. 1 : iv. 5. 5 s : vii. 8. 11.

μετα-μέλει, μελήσει, *it repents* one, or he *repents,* D. P., i. 6. 7 : vii. 1. 34.

μεταξύ adv., (μετά) *in the midst, in the mean while, between,* G.: μεταξὺ γίγνεσθαι *to intervene, elapse:* i. 7. 15 : iii. 1. 27 ; 4. 37 : v. 2. 17.

†μετά-πεμπτος, ον, *sent for, having been sent for,* i. 4. 3.

μετα-πέμπω,* πέμψω, πέπομφα, *to send* one *after* or *for* another : *M. to send for* to come to one's self, *summon,* A. ἀπό, πρός, εἰς, i. 1. 2 ; 2. 26 ; 3. 8 ; 4. 5, 11 : vii. 1. 3.

μετα-στάς, -στησάμενος, see μεθίστημι, ii. 3. 8, 21.

μετα-στρέφω,* ἔψω, ἔστροφα l., *to turn about* or *round,* trans.; but *M.* intrans., vi. 1. 8.

μετά-σχοιμι, &c., see μετ-έχω.

μετα-χωρέω, ήσω, κεχώρηκα, *to remove* to another place, *change one's encampment,* vii. 2. 18.

μέτ-ειμι,* ἔσομαι, *to be with* or *shared among :* οὐδενὸς ἡμῖν μέτεστι there is to us a share of none, *we share in none.* D. G. partitive, 421 a, iii. 1. 20.

μετ-έχω,* ἕξω, ἔσχηκα, ipf. εἶχον, 2 a. ἔσχον, *to have a share of, partake of, share* with another, *participate in,* G., v. 3. 9 : vi. 2. 14 : vii. 6. 28.

μετ-έωρος, ον, (αἴρω) *uplifted, raised from the ground,* i. 5. 8 (raising them from the ground). Der. METEOR.

μετρέω 86 μήν

†μετρέω, ήσω, metior, *to* MEASURE, iv. 5. 6. Der. GEO-METRY.

†μετρίως adv., *in due measure, moderately, temperately, in a conciliatory way*, ii. 3. 20.

μέτρον, ου, *a measure*, iii. 2. 21. Der. METRE, DIA-METER; Lat. metrum.

μέχρι * &, before a vowel, less Att. μέχρις, (akin to μακρός) adv. of place or time with a prep. or another adv., but oftener w. G. as a prep., *as far as, even to, up* or *down to, until*: μέχρι οὗ *to the region where* or *time when, until*, 557 a: i. 7. 6, 15 : iv. 1. 1 : v. 1. 1 ; 4. 16 ; 5. 4 : — temporal conj., *until, till*, i. 4. 13 : ii. 3. 7, 24 ; 6. 5 ?

μή * (a) the subjective neg. adv., used in expressing negation as desired, feared, or assumed, and esp. w. the subj., imv., and inf., *not*, 686 (cf. οὐ); but often redundant w. the inf. after words implying some negation (so even the strengthened μὴ οὐ), 713 d; i. 1. 10 ; 3. 2 s : iii. 1. 13, 24 : ὅπου μή *where not, except where*, i. 5. 9 : μὴ πορίσας [not] *without having supplied*, ii. 3. 5 : μὴ οὐ for μή with inf. after negative clauses, expressions of shame, &c., 713 f, ii. 3. 11 : — (b) the neg. final conj., ch. w. subj. and opt., 624s, *that not, lest, that* (after words of fearing, 625 a), i. 3. 17 ; 8. 13 : iii. 4. 1. — (c) It has similar uses in compos.; where it is often repeated without doubling the negation, 713, i. 3. 14 : vii. 1. 6. See εἰ, ἐάν, οὐ.

†μηδ-αμῇ or -αμῇ adv., (ἀμῇ *anywhere*) *nowhere*, vii. 6. 29 (713 d).

†μηδ-αμῶς adv., (ἀμῶς *in any way*) *in no way*, vii. 7. 23.

μη-δέ, by apostr. μηδ', conj., *and not, but not, nor, neither* (cf. μήτε), ii. 4. 1 ; 5. 29 : iii. 2. 17 : — emphatic adv., ne . . quidem, *not even, neither*, i. 3. 14 : iii. 2. 21 : vii. 6. 18 s, 23. For its compounds μηδείς, &c., the stronger forms μηδὲ εἷς, &c., are also found.

‡μηδ-είς, μηδε-μία, μηδ-έν, *not even one, no one, no, none* : μηδέν subst., *nothing*; as adv., as *to nothing, not at all, by no means* : i. 3. 15 ; 9. 7 s.

‡μηδέ-ποτε not even at any time, never, iii. 2. 3 : iv. 5. 13.

‡μηδ-έτερος, α, ον, *neither* of two, vii. 4. 10.

Μηδία or Μήδεια, as, (Μῆδος) *Media* (or *Medea*), the country of the

Medes, which Xen. extends to the river Tigris, making the region especially called Assyria a part of it. In a more limited sense, Media lay northeast of the valley of the Tigris, extending from the Araxes to Persis, with great variety of climate, soil, and products (now the northwest part of Persia). Τὸ Μηδίας τεῖχος *the Median wall*, a wall built at the head of the Babylonian plain, to prevent the incursions of the Medes (as "the Picts' Wall" in England means the wall against the Picts). i. 7. 15 : ii. 4. 12, 27. — 2. The wife of the last Median king (acc. to the common account, Astyages), iii. 4. 11. — In the first sense, Μηδία is to be preferred, and perhaps Μήδεια in the second.

Μήδοκος, ου, *Medocus*, a king of the Odrysae, reigning at a distance from the Propontis, the most powerful and, we might judge, the best of the Thracian princes of his time. He was claimed by Alcibiades as a friend. vii. 2. 32 ; 3. 16 ; 7. 11.

Μῆδος, ου, ὁ, *a Mede*, iii. 2. 25 ; 4. 7. The Medes were early a brave people, esp. skilled in the use of the bow and horse, and holding the kindred Persians subject. But after the conquest of Assyria, they became more luxurious, and the sovereignty passed to the Persians, B. C. 558.

Μηδοσάδης, ου, *Medosades*, chief minister of the Thracian prince Seuthes, vii. 1. 5 ; *v. l.* Δημοσάδης, &c.

μήθ' for μήτε, before an aspirated vowel, iii. 2. 23.

μη-κ-έτι, 165 c, *not henceforth* or *in future, not again, no longer, no more*, i. 2. 27 ; 4. 16 ; 6. 9.

μῆκος, εος, τό, (akin to μακρός) *length*, i. 5. 9 (pl.): ii. 4. 12 : v. 4. 32.

μήν confirmative adv. post-pos. (μέν) vero, *indeed, in truth, surely, certainly; yet, however;* comm. attached to other particles : ἀλλὰ μήν (. . γε) *but surely* (at least), *and certainly, yet further*, i. 9. 18 : iii. 2. 16 : ἢ μήν (. . γε) *indeed certainly* (at least), *most certainly, positively, assuredly*, in swearing or strong asseveration, ii. 3. 26 s : vi. 1. 31 : καὶ μήν *and indeed, and yet*, i. 7. 5 : iii. 1. 17 : οὐ μήν (. . γε) *not indeed* (at least), *yet* (*certainly*) *not*, i. 10. 3, 13. See γέ.

μήν, μηνός, ό, mensis, a MONTH: τοῦ μηνός (433 f) or κατὰ μῆνα, by the month, a month, monthly. The Attic months were lunar, beginning with the new moon, and consisting alternately of 29 and 30 days. i. 1. 10 ; 3. 21 ; 9. 17. Der. MENISCUS.

†μηνο-ειδής, ές, (εἶδος) crescent-shaped, in the form of a crescent, v. 2. 13 ?

μηνύω, ύσω, μεμήνυκα, to disclose, make known, expose, A., ii. 2. 20.

μή-ποτε n-unquam, n-cver, i. 1. 4.

μή-πω non-dum, not yet, iii. 2. 24.

μηρός, οῦ, ό, the thigh, vii. 4. 4.

μή-τε* conj., by apostr. μήτ' or μήθ', ne-que, and not, nor: μήτε .. μήτε neither .. nor: μήτε .. τε neque .. et, both not .. and, not only not .. but also. Μήτε is comm. doubled in whole or in part as above, and is thus distinguished fr. the conj. μηδέ. i. 3. 14: ii. 2. 8: iii. 1. 30 : iv. 4. 6.

μήτηρ,* μητρός, ή, mater, a MOTHER, i. 1. 3 s: ii. 4. 27. Der. MATERNAL.

†μητρό-πολις, εως, ή, mother-city, chief city, METROPOLIS, v. 2. 3 ; 4. 15.

†μηχανάομαι, ήσομαι, μεμηχάνημαι, machinor, to contrive, devise, scheme, seek or try by artifice, AE., I., ἐκ, ii. 6. 27: iv. 7. 10. Der. MACHINATION.

μηχανή, ῆς, (μῆχος an expedient) machina, a contrivance, device, means, iv. 5. 16. Der. MACHINE, MECHANISM.

μία, see εἷς, ii. 1. 19.

[μίγνυμι & μίσγω, μίξω, μέμιχα l., misceo, to MIX, MINGLE.]

Μίδας, ου, Midas, a king of Phrygia, who had been a pupil of Orpheus, but became proverbial for his folly. Having caught the satyr Silēnus by the sure trap of a fountain mingled with wine, he treated him with such kindness that he was permitted by Bacchus to fix his own reward. He chose the power of changing all he touched to gold, a fatal gift, from which he was relieved by bathing in the Pactolus, whose sands were thenceforth golden. Appointed judge between Apollo and Pan, he awarded the prize for musical skill to the latter; and the indignant god of the lyre punished him for his bad taste by changing his ears to those of an ass. i. 2. 13.

Μιθριδάτης, ου, Mithridātes, a partisan of Cyrus, but one who, after C.'s death, dealt treacherously with the Greeks; according to vii. 8. 25, satrap of Lycaonia and Cappadocia. The name seems to mean a gift of or to Mithrā (the Sun-God, — da, to give), and hence to have been common among his worshippers. ii. 5. 35: iii. 3. 1 ; 4. 2: v. l. Μιθραδάτης.

μικρός,* ά, όν, c. μείων or ἐλάττων, s. ἐλάχιστος, q. v., little, small ; weak, insignificant ; short (of time or distance), brief; ii. 4. 13 : iii. 2. 10 : μικρόν a little, a short distance, a short space only, (hence narrowly, i. 3. 2), ii. 1. 6 : iii. 1. 11 : κατὰ μικρόν or μικρά according to small measure, in or into small parts or portions, v. 6. 32 : vii. 3. 22 : μικρὰ ἁμαρτηθέντα small things done wrong, small mistakes, trifling errors, v. 8. 20. Der. MICRO-SCOPE.

†Μιλήσιος, α, ον, Milesian, belonging to Milētus : subst. Μιλήσιος a Milesian man, Μιλησία a Milesian woman, i. 1. 11 ; 9. 9 : 10. 3.

Μίλητος, ου, ή, Milētus, an Ionian city with four harbors, situated on the northwestern coast of Caria, near the mouth of the Mæander. It was remarkable for the extent of its commerce, the number of its colonies, and the arts, wealth, and luxury of its inhabitants. It suffered greatly from its capture by the Persians, B. C. 494, after which it never regained its former importance. It is prominent in the early history of Greek philosophy as the birthplace of Thales, Anaximander, and Anaximenes. It was also the birthplace of the early historians Cadmus and Hecatæus, of Aspasia, &c. i. 1. 6 s ; 4. 2. ‖ Ruins buried by the deposits of the Mæander.

Μιλτοκύθης, ου, Miltocythes, a Cyrean officer from Thrace, who deserted to the king, ii. 2. 7.

μιμέομαι, ήσομαι, μεμίμημαι, (μῖμος a MIMIC) imitor, to imitate, mimic, act as in a play, iii. 1. 36 : vi. 1. 9.

μιμνήσκω,* μνήσω, a. p. as m. ἐμνήσθην, to remind : M. to remind one's self, call to mind, make mention of, mention, suggest ; pf. pret. μέμνημαι, f. pf. μεμνήσομαι, memini, I have been reminded, re-MEMBER, mention ; G., I., CP.; i. 7. 5 : iii. 2. 39 : v. 8. 25 s.

μισέω, ήσω, μεμίσηκα, (μῖσος hatred) to hate, be angry or displeased with, A., vi. 2. 14. Der. MIS-ANTHROPE.

†μισθο-δοσία, ας, (δίδωμι) *the payment of wages*, ii. 5. 22.

†μισθο-δοτέω, ήσω, *to pay wages, give pay*, D., vii. 1. 13.

†μισθο-δότης, ου, (δίδωμι) *a paymaster, employer*, D., i. 3. 9.

μισθός, οῦ, ὁ, *wages, pay, hire, reward, recompense*, G.: μισθὸν τῆς ἀσφαλείας *pay for the security* or *preservation*: i.1.10 : ii.2.20 : iii.5.8: v.6.31.

‡μισθο-φορά, ᾶς, or μισθο-φορία, ας, (φέρω) *the receipt of pay, service for pay, employment for wages, wages*, v. 6. 23, 35 s : vi. 1. 16 ; 4. 8.

‡μισθο-φόρος, ον, (φέρω) *receiving pay,serving for hire,mercenary*: subst. μισθοφόροι *hired soldiers, mercenaries*: i. 4. 3 : iv. 3. 4 : vii. 8. 15.

‡μισθόω, ώσω, μεμίσθωκα, *to let for hire*, A.: *M. to hire*, A.: *P. to be hired*, 588, ἐπί: i. 3. 1 : vi. 4. 13 : vii. 7. 34.

μνᾶ,* ᾶς, *a* MINA = 100 drachmæ, or ₁⁄₆₀ of a talent ; as a weight, at Athens, = about 15.2 oz.; as a sum of money, = about $20 ; i. 4. 13 : v. 8. 1.

μνήμη, ης, (μιμνήσκω) *remembrance, memory*, vi. 5. 24. [μνήμων *mindful*.]

‡μνημονεύω, εύσω, ἐμνημόνευκα, *to call to mind, recall, recount, reflect* or *dwell upon*, G., iv. 3. 2.

‡μνημονικός, ή, όν, s., *having a good memory*, vii. 6. 38. Der. MNEMONICS.

μνησθῶ, see μιμνήσκω, vi. 4. 11.

‡μνησι-κακέω, ήσω, (κακός) *to remember an injury, cherish resentment* or *bear ill-will* towards a person for anything, D. G., ii. 4. 1.

μόλις & earlier μόγις,(μῶλος & μόγος, *toil*, cf. Lat. mōles) *with toil* or *difficulty, hardly, scarcely*, iii. 4. 48.

†μολυβδίς or μολιβδίς, ίδος, ἡ, *a leaden ball* or *bullet*, iii. 3. 17.

μόλυβδος or μόλιβδος, ου, ὁ, plumbum, *lead*, iii. 4. 17.

μόλω, see βλώσκω, vii. 1. 33.

μον-αρχία, ας, (μόνος, ἄρχω) *sole command*, MONARCHY, vi. 1. 31.

μοναχῇ or -χῇ adv., (μόνος) *by one way only, singly, only* : ᾗπερ μοναχῇ *by which way only*, iv. 4. 18.

μονή, ῆς, ἡ, (μένω) mansio, *a stay, staying, remaining*, v. 1. 5 ; 6. 22, 27.

†μονο-ειδής, ές, (εἶδος) *uni-form, regular*, v. 2. 13?

†μονό-ξυλος, ον, (ξύλον) *made of a single log, hollowed from a single trunk*, v. 4. 11.

μόνος, η, ον, (μένω?) *remaining* or *left alone, alone, only, sole* : μόνον adv., *only, solely, alone*: i.4.15 : ii.5.14,20. Der. MONO-, MON-, MONK, MONAD.

μόσσυν or μόσυν, ῦνος, d. pl. μοσσύνοις, 225 f, ὁ, (a foreign word) *a wooden tower*, v. 4. 26.

‡Μοσ[σ]ύνοικοι, ων, οἱ, (οἰκέω) *the* ['l'ower-dwellers] *Mos*[*s*]*ynœci*, a rude, piratical people on the southern coast of the Euxine, with singular customs, v. 4. 2, 15, 27, 30.

μόσχειος, ον, (μόσχος *calf*) *of a calf* : κρέα μόσχεια *veal*, iv. 5. 31.

μοχθέω, ήσω, (μόχθος, akin to μόγος, *toil*) *to toil, labor, undergo toil* or *hardship*, AE., περί, vi. 6. 31.

μοχλός, οῦ, ὁ, *a bar, bolt, for fastening gates,* &c., vii. 1. 12, 15.

Μυγδόνιοι *v. l.* for Μαρδόνιοι, iv. 3. 4.

μύζω* or ἀ-μύζω, (356 p ; μύω *to close* the mouth) *to suck*, iv. 5. 27.

Μυρίανδος or Μυρί-ανδρος, ου, ἡ, *Myriandus* or *-drus*, a commercial town, built by the Phœnicians on the Gulf of Issus. i. 4. 6. ǁ Between Iscanderun and Arsús.

†μυριάς, άδος, ἡ, *a* MYRIAD, *the number of* 10,000, i. 4. 5 ; 7. 10 s.

μύριος, α, ον, 10,000, the greatest number expressed in Greek by one word (comm. pl., exc. w. a collective noun, i. 7. 10); sometimes less definitely for a very large number; i.1.9 ; 2. 9: ii. 1. 19 : iii. 2. 31.

μύρον, ου, (μύρω *to flow?*) *a fragrant oil* or *unguent, precious ointment*, iv. 4. 13.

†Μυσία, ας, *Mysia*, a province in the northwest of Asia Minor, south of the Propontis. The name was applied in a narrower sense to the southern inland part of this province. vii. 8. 8.

†Μυσός, a, ον, *Mysian*, i. 2. 10.

Μυσός, οῦ, ὁ, *a Mysian*. The Mȳsi were a rude people in Mysia, supposed to have emigrated from Thrace, who maintained a species of independence in their mountain fastnesses, and were troublesome to their neighbors by their predatory habits. From their low repute, Μυσῶν ἔσχατος became proverbial as a term of reproach. i. 6. 7 ; 9. 14. — 2. *Mysus*, the proper name of a Mysian, who was both useful and entertaining to his comrades, v. 2. 29; vi. 1. 9.

μυχός, οῦ, ὁ, (μύω to close) a recess, nook, iv. 1. 7.

μῶρος, α, ον, later **μωρός**, ά, όν, s., morus, foolish, silly, stupid, iii. 2. 22.

‡**μώρως** or **μωρῶς** foolishly, stupidly, vii. 6. 21.

N.

ναί * confirmative adv., næ, certainly : ναί & ναὶ μά W. A., certainly by, yes by, by, v. 8. 6 : vi. 6. 34 : vii. 6. 21.

νᾱός, * οῦ, contr. **νεώς**, νεώ, ὁ, (ναίω to dwell) the dwelling of a god (cf. ædes), a temple, v. 3. 8 s, 12 s.

νάπη, ης, ἡ, & **νάπος**, εος, τό, (νάω to flow?) a woody vale, dell, glen, hollow, ravine, iv. 5. 15, 18 : vi. 5. 12 s.

†**ναυ-αρχέω**, ήσω, to be admiral, command the fleet, v. 1. 4 : vii. 2. 7.

†**ναύ-αρχος**, ου, ὁ, (ἄρχω) a naval commander, admiral, esp. a Spartan high-admiral, i. 4. 2 : vi. 1. 16 : vii. 2. 5.

†**ναύ-κληρος**, ου, ὁ, (κλῆρος allotment) a ship-owner, ship-master, vii. 2. 12.

†**ναῦλος**, ου, ὁ, or **ναῦλον**, ου, naulum, passage-money, fare, v. 1. 12.

†**ναυ-πηγήσιμος**, ον, (πήγνυμι) fit for ship-building, vi. 4. 4.

ναῦς, * νεώς, νηΐ, ναῦν, ἡ, (akin to νέω to swim) navis, a ship, esp. a warvessel, with banks of rowers, i. 4. 2 s : v. 4. 10 : vii. 5. 12. Der. NAUTILUS, NAVY. Cf. πλοῖον, τριήρης.

‡**Ναυσι-κλείδης**, ου, Nausiclides, a Spartan envoy who brought money to the army, vii. 8. 6 : v. l. Ἀμευσικλείδης, ἅμα Εὐκλείδης.

‡**ναυσί-πορος**, ον, traversed by ships, navigable, ii. 2. 3.

‡**ναυτικός**, ή, όν, NAVAL, NAUTICAL, i. 3. 12.

νεανίσκος, ου, ὁ, (dim. in form, νέος) a young man, sometimes applied even up to the age of 40, ii. 1. 13 : iv. 3. 10.

νεῖμαι, see νέμω, vi. 6. 33.

νεκρός, οῦ, ὁ, a dead body, corpse : οἱ νεκροὶ the dead : ἄνευ πολλῶν νεκρῶν without the loss of many lives : iv. 2. 18, 23 : v. 2. 9. Der. NECRO-MANCY.

νέμω, * νεμῶ, νενέμηκα, a. ἔνειμα, to divide, distribute, portion out, award, assign, regulate ; to carve ; to assign or occupy for pasture : A. D. : νέμεται αἶξι it is pastured with goats : M. of animals, to be at pasture, to graze : ii. 2. 15 : iv. 6. 17 : vi. 6. 33 : vii. 3. 21.

†**νεό-δαρτος**, ον, (δέρω to skin) newly skinned or stripped : iv. 5. 14.

νέος, α, ον, c., s., novus, NEW, fresh, young, i. 1. 1 : iv. 1. 27 ; 2. 16 : v. 4. 27. See τεῖχος. Der. NEO-PHYTE.

νεῦμα, ατος, τό, (νεύω to nod) a nod, v. 8. 20 (where we should rather say wink).

†**νευρά**, ᾶς, a string, esp. of a bow, bowstring, iv. 2. 28 : v. 2. 12.

νεῦρον, ου, nervus, a string, cord, sinew, NERVE, iii. 4. 17.

νεφέλη, ης, (νέφος nubes, cloud) nebula, a cloud, mist, i. 8. 8 : iii. 4. 8. Der. NEBULAR.

νέω, * νευσοῦμαι or νεύσομαι, νένευκα, no, nato, to swim, iv. 3. 12 ? v. 7. 25.

νέω, * νήσω, to pile up, heap together, A., v. 4. 27.

νεω-κόρος, ου, ὁ, (νεώς, κορέω to sweep) a temple-sweeper, sexton, sacristan, keeper of a temple, v. 3. 6.

Νέων, ωνος, Neon, from Asine in Laconia, lieutenant and successor to Chirisophus, an ambitious and contentious man, v. 3. 4 ; 6. 36 : vi. 4. 11.

†**νεώριον**, ου, (ὥρα care) a place for the care of ships, dock-yard, dock, vii. 1. 27.

νεώς, νεών, see ναῦς, i. 4. 3.

νεώς, * ώ, see νᾱός, v. 3. 8.

νεωστί adv., (νέος) newly, recently, lately, iv. 1. 12.

νή * affirmative adv. of swearing, truly by, yes by, by, A. (oftenest Δία), i. 7. 9 : v. 7. 22.

νηΐ, νῆες, see ναῦς, i. 4. 2.

νῆσος, ου, ἡ, (νέω to swim, as if floating land?) insula, an island, isle, ii. 4. 22. Der. POLY-NESIA.

†**Νίκ-ανδρος**, ου, Nicander, a Laconian, who slew the faithless and intriguing Dexippus, v. 1. 15.

†**Νίκ-αρχος**, ου, Nicarchus, an Arcadian, who was severely wounded, ii. 5. 33. — 2. An Arcadian lochage, who deserted (doubtless a different person from the preceding, who could not have recovered so quickly), iii. 3. 5.

†**νῑκάω**, ήσω, νενίκηκα, to conquer, prevail over, overcome, defeat, surpass, excel, outdo ; to be victor or victorious over, hence in pres., to have conquered, 612 : τὰ πάντα ν. to have [conquered the whole] gained a complete victory : ἐκ τῆς νικώσης [sc. γνώμης or ψήφου] according to the [prevailing vote] vote

νίκη 90 Ξενοφῶν

of the majority: A., AE.: i.2.8; 9.11; 10.4: ii. 1. 1, 4, 8 s: vi. 1. 18; 5. 23. Der. NICO-LAS.

νίκη, ης, *victory,* i. 5. 8; 8. 16.

†Νικό-μαχος, ου, *Nicomachus,* an Œtæan, a commander of light-armed troops, iv. 6. 20.

νοέω, ήσω, νενόηκα, (νόος) *to perceive, observe; to think, devise;* A.; iii.4.44: v. 6. 28. Der. NOETIC.

νόθος, η, ον, *illegitimate, natural, bastard,* ii. 4. 25.

νομή, ῆς, (νέμω) *pasture-ground, pasturage; a herd* (at pasture): iii. 5. 2: v. 3. 9.

†νομίζω, ίσω ιῶ, νενόμικα, to observe or regard as a custom (*P. to be observed as a custom, to be customary,* iv. 2. 23): hence, in general, *to regard, esteem, consider, believe, suppose, think, be assured,* 2 A., I. (A.), P., i. 1. 8; 2. 27; 3. 6, 10; 4. 9, 16: vi. 6. 24.

†νόμιμος, η, ον, *customary, according to law, appointed by law,* D. I., iv.6.15.

νόμος, ου, ὁ, (νέμω) *an assignment* or *regulation, custom, rule, law; a law for song, tune, strain;* i. 2. 15: iv. 6. 14: v. 4. 17, 33. Der. ECO-NOMY.

νόος,* ου, contr. νοῦς, νοῦ, ὁ, *mind, intellect,* NOUS (sportive): ἔχειν ἐν νῷ *to have in mind, to purpose, intend:* i. 5. 9: ii. 4. 2: iii. 3. 2. See προσέχω.

†νοσέω, ήσω, νενόσηκα, *to be sick* or *diseased, to be in a disordered state,* vii. 2. 32.

νόσος, ου, ἡ, *sickness, disease,* v. 3. 3: vii. 2. 32. Der. NOSO-LOGY.

νότος, ου, ὁ, notus, auster, *the south wind,* v. 7. 7.

νου-μηνία, ας, contr. fr. νεο-μηνία, (νέος, μήν) *the new moon, beginning of the month,* v. 6. 23, 31.

νοῦς, νοῦ, νῷ, see νόος, i. 5. 9.

†νυκτερεύω, εύσω, *to pass the night, to bivouac,* iv. 4. 11; 5. 11: vi. 4. 27.

νυκτός, -ί, -α, &c., see νύξ, i. 7. 1.

†νυκτο-φύλαξ, ακος, ὁ, *a night-guard* or *sentinel, watchman,* vii.2.18; 3.34.

†νύκτωρ adv., noctu, *in* or *during the night, by night,* iii.4.35: iv. 4. 9; 6.12.

νῦν, (νέον, neut. of νέος?) nunc, Germ. NUN, NOW, *at present,* often including the near past or future: ὁ νῦν χρόνος (βασιλεύς) *the present time (king):* τὸ νῦν εἶναι *for the present,* 665 b: i. 4. 14; 7.5: iii. 1. 40, 46; 2. 12, 36 s; 4. 46: vi. 6. 13. — Softened it becomes

↓νύν encl., *now, then,* of inference, or sequence in discourse, vii. 2. 26?

↓νῦν-ί (Att. emphatic -ι, 252 d) *just now, even now, now certainly,* v. 6. 32: vii. 3. 3.

νύξ, νυκτός, ἡ, nox, Germ. *Nacht,* NIGHT: (τῆς) νυκτός *in the night, by night,* ii. 2. 1; 6. 7: (τὴν) νύκτα *through* or *during the night,* 482 e, iv. 2. 1: vi. 1. 14: διὰ νυκτός *throughout the night,* iv. 6. 22: μέσαι νύκτες the middle hours of the night, *midnight,* i. 7. 1: iii. 1. 33.

νῶτον, ου, *the back,* v. 4. 32.

Ξ.

Ξανθι-κλῆς, έους, *Xanthicles,* an Achæan chosen general to succeed Socrates, iii. 1. 47: v. 8. 1: vii. 2. 1.

†ξενία, ας, *a bond of hospitality:* ἐπὶ ξενίᾳ *on terms of hospitality* or *as guests:* vi. 1. 3? 6. 35: vii. 6. 3?

†Ξενίας, ου, *Xenias,* from Parrhasia in Arcadia, the general (in the service of Cyrus) of whom mention is earliest made, i. 1. 2; 2. 1; 4. 7: v. l. Ξεννίας.

†ξενίζω, ίσω ιῶ, *to receive* or *entertain as a guest,* A., v. 5. 25: vii. 3. 8; 6. 3.

†ξενικός, ή, όν, *of* or *relating to foreigners:* ξενικόν [sc. στράτευμα or πλῆθος] *a foreign force,* i. 2. 1: ii. 5. 22.

†ξένιος, α, ον, *of* or *pertaining to hospitality:* Ζεὺς ξένιος Zeus the god of hospitality or protector of guests: τὰ ξένια *the gifts* or *rites of hospitality, hospitable* or *friendly gifts* or *presents:* ἐπὶ ξένια *to a friendly entertainment, as guests:* iii. 2. 4: iv. 8. 23 s: vii. 6.3?

†ξενόομαι, ώσομαι, *to become a guest,* D., παρά, vii. 8. 6, 8.

ξένος, ου, ὁ, hospes, a person related by the ties of hospitality, *a guest-friend, a guest* or *host,* G. or D.: *a foreigner, foreign soldier, mercenary* (ξένοι *foreign* or *hired troops,* &c.): i. 1. 10 s; 3. 3: ii. 4. 15: iii. 1. 4.

↓Ξενο-φῶν, ῶντος, (contr. fr. Ξενοφάων *giving light to guest-friends,* φάω *to give light*) *Xenophon,* son of Gryllus, an Athenian of the tribe Ægeis, the demus Erchēa, and the order of Knights. There is strong evidence that he was not born till about 430 B. C., though some prefer an earlier date. He became early a pupil of

Socrates through the invitation of the sage, who was won by the attractive appearance of the youth; and also received instruction in oratory from Isocrates. He joined the Cyrean expedition, which was then professedly against the Pisidians, not as one of the army, but simply as the friend of Proxenus, and by the special request of Cyrus. After the treacherous seizure of the generals, he roused the Greeks from their dejection; and having been chosen successor to Proxenus, was the leading spirit of the famous retreat, though the nominal precedence belonged to Chirisophus as a Spartan, and an older man and general. When the Cyreans enlisted under the standard of Thibron, Xenophon appears to have returned to Athens; but not long after to have rejoined his old comrades in aiding the Spartans against the Persians. As a friend of Sparta and enemy of Persia, Xenophon was sentenced to exile from Athens, probably about the time when Athens took a position friendly to Persia and hostile to Sparta, B. C. 395.

On the recall of the Spartan king Agesilāus, the next year, to defend his native city, Xenophon returned with him; and thus was present at the battle of Coronēa, though it is not probable that he took part in it. He now withdrew from military and political life, making no attempt to obtain revenge for his banishment, but settling for a quiet, rural, literary, and, through his charge of a temple, sacred life, under Lacedæmonian protection, at Scillus in Triphylian Elis. At the same time, his vicinity to Olympia gave him signal advantages for renewing or forming acquaintance with persons from the whole Greek world. He was followed from Asia Minor by a wife, Philesia (perhaps a second wife, the first having died before the Cyrean expedition), and two sons, Gryllus and Diodōrus. The latter received a military training at Sparta, and when Sparta and Athens were united against Thebes, so that there could be no conflict between regard for his native and for his patron city, were sent by Xenophon to serve in the Athenian army. In the battle of Mantinēa, B. C. 362, Gryllus fell fighting most bravely, and according to some having slain the Theban commander Epaminondas. Xenophon resided at Scillus more than 20 years; but was forced to leave this delightful retreat, when the Eleans took possession of it, after the battle of Leuctra (B. C. 371). He retired to Lepreum and afterwards to Corinth, which seems from this time to have been his chief residence, and where he is stated to have died, well advanced in age (probably a few years after 357 B. C.). As his sentence of banishment was repealed, upon the motion, it is said, of its very proposer, Eubūlus, he may have spent a part of his old age in his native Athens.

Besides his longer works, the Anabasis, Cyropædīa, Hellenica, and Memoirs of Socrates, he wrote several shorter essays, or sketches. The Anabasis appears to have been based upon a journal kept by him during the Expedition, and to have been mainly completed for his own use and that of his friends soon after his return; but not to have received its last touches till after his establishment at Scillus. Its publication seems, however, to have been preceded by an abstract of it, or a work based upon it, put forth, doubtless with Xenophon's consent, by Themistogenes, a Syracusan. The character of Xenophon was marked by energy, courage, sagacity, a keen sense of honor, attachment to friends, uprightness, and piety. i. 8. 15 : ii. 5. 37 : iii. 1. 4 s, 47.

Ξέρξης, ου, (Pers. kshérshé, *king;* Hdt. translates by ἀρήϊος *warrior*, 6. 98) *Xerxes* I., king of Persia B. C. 486 – 465, the son of Darīus I. and Atossa, a daughter of Cyrus. Darius had older sons born before his accession to the throne; but, through the influence of Atossa, appointed Xerxes his successor, as the first-born of Darius *the king*. The reign of Xerxes was most noted for his invasion of Greece in pursuance of his father's plans, with a countless host, for his bridging the Hellespont and cutting off Mt. Athos, for the checks at Thermopylæ and Artemisium, and the signal defeats of Salamis, Platæœ, and Mycale. The disasters, follies, and vices of his reign terminated in his assassination by two of his chief officers, the crown descending to his son Artaxerxes I. i. 2. 9 : iii. 2. 13. See Δαρεῖος.

†ξεστός, ή, όν, smoothed, polished, wrought, iii. 4. 10.

[ξέω or ξύω to scrape, shave, polish.]
†ξηραίνω, ανῶ, to dry, A., ii. 3. 15.
ξηρός, ά, όν, dry, SERE, iv. 5. 33.
ξίφος, εος, τό, (ξέω?) a sword, esp. a large, straight, pointed, and double-edged sword. This was comm. carried by the Greeks in a sheath on the left side, by a belt from the right shoulder. ii. 2. 9. Cf. μάχαιρα.

ξόανον, ου, (ξέω) an image or statue, esp. one carved of wood, v. 3. 12.

ξυγ- older for συγ-, see ξύν.
ξυήλη, ης, (ξύω, see ξέω) a curved Spartan dagger, iv. 7. 16 : 8. 25.
†ξυλίζομαι, ίσομαι., to gather or collect wood, ii. 4. 11.
†ξύλινος, η, ον, of wood, wooden, i. 8. 9.
ξύλον, ου, (ξύω, see ξέω) a stick or log of wood, pole, i. 10. 12: comm. pl., wood, fuel, trees, i. 5. 12 : ii. 1. 6 ; 2. 16 : iv. 5. 5 : vi. 4. 4 s. Der. XYLO-GRAPHY.

ξύν * (in compos. also ξυ-, ξυγ-, ξυλ-, ξυμ-, ξυρ-, ξυσ-) an older form for σύν cum, with, ii. 3. 19 ; 5. 2. For all words in which it is found, see σύν and its compounds. Some editors now exclude it from the Anab., even in passages where it appears in the best mss.

O.

ὅ which, ὅ τι whatever, see ὅς, ὅστις, i. 3. 17, 19. — ὁ- prefixed to an indefinite or interrogative beginning with π, makes an indefinite relative.

ὁ, ἡ, τό,* the definite or prepositive article, the (often not translated, 520 a); also as a demonstrative or personal pron. (after καί, taking the orthotone forms ὅς, ἥ, οἵ, αἵ, 518 f), that, this, he, she, it ; 249 s, 518 s : i. 1. 1 s; 8. 16 s : ὁ μέν . . ὁ δέ this (on the one hand, indeed) . . (on the other hand, but, and) that, the one . . the other, one . . another, &c., οἱ μέν . . οἱ δέ these . . those, some . . others, the one party . . the other party, &c., i. 1. 7; 10. 4 : iii. 4. 16 : vii. 2. 2 (so w. τὶς, 530 b, iv. 3. 33):

cf. i. 9. 6 : ὁ μέν . . οἱ δέ he (indeed) . . and the rest, ii. 2. 5 ; cf. 3. 10, 23 s : ὁ (ἡ, οἱ, αἱ) δέ but or and he (she, they), comm. w. a change of subject, 518 c, i. 1. 3 s, 9 ; 2. 2, 16 s : iv. 5. 10 : τὰ μέν . . τὰ δέ, [as to some things . . as to others] partly . . partly, now . . now, iv. 1. 14 : τῇ μέν [sc. χώρᾳ or ὁδῷ] . . τῇ δέ in this place . . in that place, here . . there, in one view or respect . . in another view or respect, iii. 1. 12 ? iv. 8. 10. The art. is sometimes doubled, and sometimes omitted where it would be regularly used, 523 a, j, 533 s, i. 4. 4. It is often used w. an ellipsis of its subject (which also explains its pronominal use), 527 s : οἱ παρά (σύν, ἐξ, μετά, &c.), the men or those from (with, &c.), οἱ ἐκείνου his men, i. 1. 5 ; 2. 15, 18 : οἱ τότε [the then men] those then living, οἱ ἔνδον (ἔξω) those within (without), 526, ii. 5. 11, 32 : τὰ πρὸς Κύρου the [affairs] relation of Cyrus, τὰ παρὰ βασιλέως the messages or communications from the king, τὰ περὶ Προξένου the fate of Proxenus, i. 3. 9 : ii. 3. 4 ; 5. 37 : εἰς τὸ πρόσθεν [to the region before] forward, i. 10. 5 : τὸ ἐπὶ τούτῳ [as to that depending upon him] so far as depended upon him, vi. 6. 23. It is thus used in forming many adverbial phrases, 529 : τὸ πρῶτον at first, τὸ πρόσθεν before, i. 10. 10. A noun, or a relative and verb, are often used in translating an art. and part., 678 a : οἱ φεύγοντες (ἐκπεπτωκότες) the exiles, ὁ ἡγησόμενος who will guide, i. 1. 7 : ii. 4. 5 : τὸν βουλόμενον [him that] any one that wished, i. 3. 9. It often implies a possessive, genitive, or distributive pronoun, 530 e, 522 b : πρὸς τὸν ἀδελφόν to [the] his brother, τῷ στρατιώτῃ to each soldier, i. 1. 3 ; 3. 21 ; cf. 8. 3.

[ὀβελός] & dim. ὀβελίσκος, ου, ὁ, (βέλος) a spit, vii. 8. 14. Der. OBELISK.
†ὀβολός, οῦ, ὁ, (supposed to have been so named from its shape or stamp) obolus, an obol, = ⅙ drachma, or about 3½ cents, i. 5. 6.
†ὀγδοήκοντα indecl., octoginta, eighty, iv. 8. 15.
ὄγδοος, η, ον, (ὀκτώ) octāvus, eighth, iv. 6. 1.

ὅ-δε, ἥ-δε, τό-δε,* demonstr. pron., (ὁ, -δε) hic, hic-ce, this, this one, the following ; more deictic than οὗτος, ὁδεύω 93 οἴομαι

and often referring to that which follows, as οὗτος to that which precedes, while both are nearer in reference than ἐκεῖνος: τῇδε [sc. χώρᾳ or ὁδῷ] in this place or way, *here, thus:* i. 1. 9; 5. 15s; 9.29: ii.3.19; 5.41: vii.2.13.
†ὁδεύω, εὔσω, *to pursue one's way, travel, journey,* vii. 8. 8?
†ὁδοι-πορέω,* ήσω, ὁδοι-πεπόρηκα or ὡδοι-πόρηκα, (πόρος) *to journey, travel,* esp. *to proceed by land,* v. 1. 14?
†ὁδο-ποιέω,* ήσω, ὡδο-ποίηκα or -πεποίηκα, ipf. ὡδο-ποίουν, *to make, prepare,* or *repair a road,* D., AE., iii. 2. 24: iv. 8. 8: v. 1. 13s; 3. 1.
ὁδός, οῦ, ἡ, via, iter, *a way, path, road, highway, route; a way, method, means; length of the way, distance; a journey, march, expedition;* i. 2. 13; 4. 11 : ii. 6. 22 : iv. 3. 16 : often understood w. an adj. or art., iii. 5. 15 : iv. 2. 9. Der. METH-OD, METH-ODIST.
'Οδρύσης, ου, *an Odrysian*. The Odrysæ were a numerous and powerful people of Thrace, whose special seat was about the Hebrus, but who long bore sway from the Ægean to the Euxine. Their earlier known kings reigned as follows : 1. Teres, about 500 B. C.; 2. his son Sitalcas, who invaded Macedonia with an army of 150,000; and 3., was succeeded, B. C. 424, by his nephew, Seuthes I., whose yearly revenue reached 400 talents, besides a larger amount in presents; 4. Medocus (already reigning, B. C. 405) and Mæsades, prob. sons of Seuthes. With this division of the sovereignty was connected a decline of the power of the Odrysæ. Mæsades was soon driven from his kingdom, and died, leaving to his son, Seuthes II. (the prince whom the Cyreans assisted), only an empty title. vii. 2. 32; 7. 11. As adj., *Odrysian,* vii. 7. 2. — 2. Acc. to some, *Odryses,* from whom the Odrysæ took their name, father of Teres, vii. 5. 1.
'Οδυσσεύς, έως, *Ulysses,* king of Ithaca, one of the most famous of the besiegers of Troy, especially renowned for prudence, skill, firmness, eloquence, and cunning, and for his ten years' wanderings in returning home, v. 1. 2.
ὅθεν adv., (ὅς) unde, from which or what place, *whence, from which* or *whence, from what source* or *quarter,*

i. 2. 8 ; 3. 17 (sc. ἐκεῖσε): ii. 3. 14, 16; 5. 26.
↓ὅθεν-περ from which very place, *whence indeed, whence,* ii. 1. 3.
οἱ *the,* see ὁ. — οἵ *who,* see ὅς. — οἷ *they,* see ὁ, vii. 6. 4. — οἵ enclit., *to him,* see οὗ, i. 1. 8. — οἵ adv., (ὅς) quo, *whither,* i. 6. 10?
οἶδα (οἶδ') novi, οἶσθα, see ὁράω.
οἴει 2 sing. of οἴομαι, i. 7. 9.
†οἴκα-δε (-δε, 225 i) *to one's home, for home, home-ward, home :* ἡ οἴκαδε ὁδός *the way home:* i.2.2; 7.4: iii.2.24s.
†οἰκεῖος, α, ον, s., familiāris, belonging to the house or family, *domestic, akin, familiar, intimate:* οἱ οἰκεῖοι *the members of a family, household, kindred, friends, relatives:* D., G.: ii.6.28 : iii. 2. 26, 39 ; 3. 4.
†οἰκείως *in a familiar* or *friendly way, familiarly, kindly,* vii. 5. 16.
†οἰκέτης, ου, *a member of a family; a domestic, servant;* ii. 3. 15 : iv. 5. 35.
†οἰκέω, ήσω, ᾤκηκα, *to inhabit, occupy, dwell* or *live (in),* A., ὑπέρ, ἀνά, ἐν, ἐπί, παρά, &c., i. 1. 9 ; 2. 6 ; 4. 6, 11 : iii. 2. 23 ; 5. 16 : v. 1. 13.
†οἴκημα, ατος, τό, *a dwelling,* vii. 4. 15.
†οἴκησις, εως, ἡ, *a residence,* vii. 2. 38.
†οἰκία, ας, *a house, dwelling,* ii. 2. 16.
†οἰκίζω, ίσω ιῶ, ᾤκικα l., *to build a house* or *city ; to colonize* or *people a place ; to settle* or *establish in a residence ;* A.; v. 3. 7; 6. 17: vi.4.14; 6.3.
†οἰκο-δομέω, ήσω, ᾠκοδόμηκα, (δέμω *to build) to build, construct, erect,* a house, wall, tower, &c., A., i. 2. 9.
†οἴκοθεν adv., *from home,* iii. 1. 4.
†οἴκοι adv., *at home, in one's own country :* οἱ οἴκοι *those at home, one's family* or *countrymen:* τὰ οἴκοι *things at home :* i. 1. 10 ; 2. 1 ; 7. 4 : v. 6. 20.
†οἰκο-νόμος, ου, ὁ, (νέμω) *a steward, manager,* ECONOMIST, i. 9. 19.
οἶκος, ου, ὁ,. (akin to Lat. vicus, Eng. *-wick, -wich,* 139) *a house, home,* ii. 4. 8.
οἰκτείρω,* ερῶ, (οἶκτος pity, fr. οἴ oh!) *to pity, commiserate,* A., i. 4. 7 : iii.1.19.
οἶμαι methinks, see οἴομαι, i. 3. 6.
οἶνος, ου, ὁ, vinum, WINE, 141, i. 2. 13 ; 5. 10 : iv. 4. 9 ; 5. 26.
↓οἰνο-χόος, ου, ὁ, (χέω *to pour*) *a wine-pourer, cup-bearer,* iv. 4. 21.
οἴομαι * (nude 1 sing. οἶμαι, ipf. ᾤμην, more comm., esp. when the verb

is parenthetic ; 2 s. οίει), οίήσομαι, ᾤημαι, a. p. ᾠήθην, to think, suppose, believe, expect; sometimes used not from doubt, but for modesty or irony; I. (A.); i. 3. 6 ; 7. 4, 9, 14 : iii. 1. 15, 17, 29 (parenthetic, methinks), 35.

οίος,* a, ον,rel. pron.of quality,sometimes complem., (ὅς) qualis, of which or what kind,sort,or nature; such as,what kind of, what (in quality), how great; = ὅτι τοιοῦτος that such, 558: i. 3. 13; 7. 4: ii. 3. 15 ; 6. 8 : [such as to] suitable, proper, I., 556 c, ii. 3. 13 : οἷον χαλεπώτατον such as is most difficult, of the most difficult kind, 556 a, iv. 8. 2 : οἷον adv., as, as for instance, as if, iv. 1. 14 : vii. 3. 32 : οἷός τε [such as to] competent, able, possible, (w. ἐστί often understood) I., i. 3. 17 : ii. 4. 6, 24 : v. 4. 9 ; ὡς οἷόν τε μάλιστα πεφυλαγμένως [so as is possible, most guardedly] as guardedly as possible, ii. 4. 24.

↓οῖος-περ, ἅπερ, ονπερ, also written separately, = οἷος strengthened, just such as, such indeed as, just such a one as, just as, &c.; i. 3. 18 ; 8. 18.

οὔ-περ, see ὅσ-περ, iii. 2. 10.

οἷς,* οἰός, ἡ ὁ, ovis, a sheep, iv. 5. 25.

οἶσθα, see ὁράω, ii. 3. 21.

†ὀϊστός, contr. οἰστός, οῦ, ὁ, an arrow, ii. 1. 6.

οἴσω, f. of φέρω, ii. 1. 17.

Οἰταῖος, ον, an Œtæan, a man from the region of Mt. Œta (now Katavóthra, 7071 feet high), in the south of Thessaly, iv. 6. 20.

οἵ-τινες, see ὅστις, i. 3. 18.

οἴχομαι,* οἰχήσομαι, ᾠχημαι? pf. α. οἴχωκα or ᾤχωκα, to go, depart ; hence, to disappear, perish : pres. as pf., I have gone or departed, I am gone or absent, opposed to ἥκω I am come, 612; and ipf. as both plp. and aor.: i. 4. 8 ; 10. 16 : iv. 5. 24, 35 : ὁπόθεν οἴχοιτο [whencesoever, he was gone] where he was missing, iii. 1. 32. The part. of a verb of motion is often used with οἴχομαι as a stronger form of expression for the simple verb, 679 d ; as ᾤχετο ἀπελαύνων he [departed riding off] rode off, ᾤχετο πλέων he sailed away, ii. 4. 24 ; 6. 3 : cf. iii. 3. 5.

οἰωνός, οῦ, ὁ, (οἶος alone) a bird that flies alone, as an eagle, vulture, &c., esp. observed for auguries; hence, an augury,omen, présage,token, G., iii.2.9.

ὀκέλλω,* a. ὤκειλα, (κέλλω to impel) of a vessel, to run aground, strike, vii. 5. 12.

ὀκλάζω, άσω, (κλάω to break, bend) to bend the knee, sink on bended knee, kneel or crouch down, vi. 1. 10.

†ὀκνέω, ήσω, to hesitate, be reluctant or apprehensive, fear, I., μή, i. 3. 17 : ii. 3. 9 ; 4. 22.

†ὀκνηρῶς adv., (ὀκνηρός reluctant) reluctantly, vii. 1. 7.

ὄκνος, ου, ὁ, reluctance, hesitation, backwardness, iv. 4. 11.

†ὀκτακισ-χίλιοι, αι, α, eight thousand, v. 3. 3 ; 5. 4.

†ὀκτακόσιοι, αι, α, (ἑκατόν) octingenti, eight hundred, i. 2. 9.

ὀκτώ indecl., octo, Germ. acht, EIGHT, i. 2. 6 ; 8. 27. Der. OCTAVE.

↓ὀκτω-καί-δεκα (or ὀκτώ καί δέκα) indecl., octō-decim, eighteen, iii. 4. 5.

ὄλεθρος, ου, ὁ, (ὄλλυμι to destroy) destruction, loss, i. 2. 26.

ὀλίγος, η, ον, c. ἐλάσσων & μείων, s. ὀλίγιστος, small, little ; of time or distance, short; pl. few, a few: ὀλίγον adv., little, a little : ἐπ' ὀλίγων few deep, κατ' ὀλίγους [by few] in small parties : see ἐπί, κατά, παρά : i. 5. 2 ? 14 : iii. 3. 9 : iv. 8. 11 : v. 8. 12 (ὀλίγας, sc. πληγάς, too few blows) : vii. 2. 20 ; 6. 29. Der. OLIG-ARCHY.

ὀλισθάνω,* ὀλισθήσω I., ὤλισθηκα I., 2 a. ὤλισθον, to slip, slide, iii. 5. 11.

↓ὀλισθηρός, ά, όν, slippery, iv. 3. 6.

ὁλκάς, άδος, ἡ, (ἕλκω) a vessel which is towed ; hence, a ship of burden, merchantman, i. 4. 6. Der. HULK.

†ὁλοί-τροχος, ου, ὁ, (τροχός wheel, fr. τρέχω) a stone making an entire wheel, a round stone, iv. 2. 3.

†ὁλο-καυτέω, ήσω, (καίω) to burn whole, offer a HOLOCAUST, A., vii. 8. 4s.

ὅλος, η, ον, tōtus, WHOLE, entire, all, i. 2. 17 : ii. 3. 16 : iii. 3. 11 : iv. 8. 11. Der. CATH-OLIC.

Ὀλυμπία, ας, Olympia, a consecrated spot on the north bank of the river Alphēus, near Pisa in Elis, noted for its temple of Jupiter Olympius, and the quadrennial celebration (about midsummer) of the great Olympic games, on which the Greek system of chronology was based. v. 3. 7, 11. || The vale of Andilalo.

Ὀλύνθιος, ου, an Olynthian, a man of Olynthus (Ὄλυνθος), a flourishing ὁμαλής 95 ὀπηνίκα

and powerful city on the northern coast of the Ægean, at the head of the Toronaic Gulf, a Chalcidian colony. Some of the most familiar orations of Demosthenes were delivered for the preservation of this city from the machinations of Philip of Macedon, but in vain. It was destroyed B. C. 347. i. 2. 6. ‖ Aio Mamás.

ὁμαλής, ές, & ὁμαλός, ή, όν, (ὁμός) even, level, smooth; sometimes w. χώριον ground, or ὁδός way, understood; i. 5. 1: iv. 6. 12. Der. AN-OMALOUS.

‡ὁμαλῶς evenly, in an even line, uniformly, i. 8. 14.

ὅμ-ηρος, ου, ὁ, (ὁμοῦ, ἀρ-) one who joins together, a surety, hostage, i. fut. as gen., iii. 2. 24: vii. 4. 12s, 24.

ὁμιλέω, ήσω, ὡμίληκα, (ὅμιλος a crowd, assembly) to associate or be intimate with, D., iii. 2. 25. Der. HOMILY.

ὁμίχλη, ης, a mist, fog, iv. 2. 7.

ὄμμα, ατος, τό, (ὀπ-, see ὁράω) a look, eye, vii. 7. 46.

ὄμνυμι * & ὀμνύω, ὀμοῦμαι, ὀμώμοκα, a. ὤμοσα, to swear, take an oath; to swear by, 472 f; A. D., I. (A.), AE., ἐπί: ii. 2. 8s: iii. 2. 4: vi. 1. 31; 6. 17.

†ὅμοιος, α, ον, like, alike, similar, the same kind of; in like condition or on an equality with; D. G. (iv.1.17?): at Sparta, οἱ ὅμοιοι the peers, those who had the full rights of citizenship, iv. 6. 14 : ἐν τῷ ὁμοίῳ in a like position, on equal ground, iv. 6. 18 : ὅμοιοι ἦσαν θαυμάζειν or θαυμάζοντες (or -ουσιν) they seemed to be wondering, 657 j, iii. 5. 13: ὁμοίοις καί 705 c, v. 4. 21 : ὅμοια ἅπερ [things like to those which] the same kind of things which, or just as, v. 4. 34. Der. HOMŒO-PATHY.

†ὁμοίως in like or the same manner, alike, i. 3. 12 : vi. 5. 31 (ὁ. ὥσπερ): vii. 6. 10.

†ὁμο-λογέω, ήσω, ὡμολόγηκα, (λέγω) to speak in agreement with another, to agree, agree upon, acknowledge, confess; to consent, promise; A., I. (A.); i. 6. 7 s ; 9. 1, 14 : ii. 6. 7 : vii. 4. 13.

‡ὁμο-λογουμένως adv., (fr. pt. of preceding) confessedly : ὁ. ἐκ πάντων [confessedly by all] by the acknowledgment, admission, or consent of all, ii. 6. 1.

†ὁμο-μήτριος, α, ον, (μήτηρ) born of the same mother, iii. 1. 17.

†ὁμο-πάτριος, α, ον, (πατήρ) by the same father, iii. 1. 17.

[ὁμός, ή, όν, Ep., one and the same. Der. HOMO- in compounds.]

ὀμόσαι, -σας, see ὄμνυμι, ii. 3. 27.

ὁμόσε (ὁμός) to the same place with the enemy, or to meet them; to the charge, to close quarters; iii. 4. 4 : v. 4. 26.

ὁμο-τράπεζος, ον, (ὁμός, τράπεζα) sitting at the same table : masc. subst., a table-companion, partaker at the same table; among the Persians, a courtier who was specially honored by admission to the prince's table: D. : i. 8. 25 : iii. 2. 4. So συν-τράπεζος, i. 9. 31.

ὁμοῦ adv., (ὁμός) in the same place; together, in union or combination; at the meeting of arms, in collision; at the same time; i. 10. 8 : iv. 2. 22 ; 6. 24 (D. or G. 450, 445 c): v. 2. 14: vii.1.28.

ὀμφαλός, οῦ, ὁ, umbilicus, the navel, iv. 5. 2.

ὅμως adv., (ὁμός) at the same time, however, nevertheless, notwithstanding, yet, still; often w. a conj., as δέ, ἀλλά, &c.; i. 3. 21 ; 8. 13, 23 : ii. 2. 17 ; 4. 23.

ὅν, see εἰμί. — ὅν whom, see ὅς.

ὄναρ,* τό, ὄνειρος, ὁ, or ὄνειρον, τό, g. ὀνείρου or ὀνείρατος, pl. ὀνείρατα or ὄνειρα, a dream, night-vision, iii. 1. 11 s : iv. 3. 8, 13. Der. ONEIRO-MANCY.

ὀνίνημι,* ὀνήσω, a. ὤνησα, a. p, ὠνήθην, to benefit, do one a service, 2 A., iii. 1. 38 ? v. 5. 2 ; 6. 20.

ὄνομα, ατος, τό, (γνο- in γιγνώσκω) Lat. nōmen (fr. nosco), what one is known by; a NAME; re-NOWN, reputation; i. 2. 23 ; 4. 11 ; 5. 4 : ii. 6. 17. Der. AN-ONYMOUS. [vii. 4. 15.

‡ὀνομαστί adv., by name, vi. 5. 24 :

ὄνος, ου, ὁ ἡ, asinus, an ass : ὄνος ἄγριος onager, the wild ass : ὁ. ἀλέτης a grinding-jack, a mill-stone, esp. the upper one : i. 5. 2, 5 : ii. 1. 6 ; 2. 20.

ὄντος, -ι, -α, -ες, &c., see εἰμί, i. 1. 11. Der. ONTO-LOGY.

†ὄξος, εος, τό, Fr. vin-aigre, sour wine, vinegar, ii. 3. 14.

ὀξύς, εῖα, ύ, sharp, acid, sour, v. 4. 29. Der. OXY-GEN.

ὅ-περ, see ὅσ-περ, iii. 2. 29.

ὅ-πη or ὅ-πῃ adv., wherever, where; by or in whatever or what way, how, as ; in whatever or what direction, whither (soever); i.3.6; 4.8: ii.1.19: iv. 2. 12, 24 : vi. 1. 21.

ὀ-πηνίκα adv., (πηνίκα; at what point of time?), at whatever point of time, G., iii. 5. 18 ?

ὄπισθεν 96 ὁράω

ὄπισθεν adv., (akin to ἕπομαι) *from behind, behind, in the rear*: ἐκ τοῦ ὄπισθεν *from behind*, εἰς τοὔπισθεν *backwards*: οἱ ὄπισθεν *those behind* or *in the rear*, *the rear*: τὰ ὄπισθεν *the rear*: c.: i. 7. 9; 10. 6, 9: iii. 3. 10; 4. 40: iv. 1. 6; 2. 25 s.

‡ ὀπισθο-φυλακέω, ήσω, *to form the rear-guard; to guard, cover, bring up*, or *command the rear*; ii. 3. 10.

‡ ὀπισθο-φυλακία, ας, *the charge of the rear*, iv. 6. 19.

‡ ὀπισθο-φύλαξ, ακος, ὁ ἡ, *guarding the rear, of the rear-guard*: οἱ ὀπισθοφύλακες subst., *the rear-guard*: iii. 3. 7: iv. 1. 6, 17; 3. 27; 5. 16; 7. 8.

ὀπίσω adv., (akin to ἕπομαι) *behind*, vi. 1. 8.

†ὁπλίζω, ἴσω ιῶ, ὥπλικα 1., *to arm, equip*, A.: *M. to arm one's self*: i. 8. 6: ii. 2. 14; 6. 25: iv. 3. 31.

‡ ὅπλισις, εως, ἡ, *warlike equipment*, ii. 5. 17.

†ὁπλῑτεύω, εύσω, ὡπλίτευκα, *to serve as a hoplite*, v. 8. 5.

†ὁπλίτης, ου, *a heavy-armed foot-soldier, man-at-arms, hoplite*. The ὁπλῖται, encased in metal and well trained in the use of arms, were the chief dependence of a Greek army, and were among the best soldiers the world has ever known. They carried a helmet, cuirass, shield, greaves, spear, and sword. i. 1. 2; 2. 3, 9.

‡ ὁπλῑτικός, ή, όν, *relating to* or *consisting of hoplites*: ὁπλιτικόν, sc. στράτευμα, *heavy-armed force, heavy infantry, hoplites*, iv. 8. 18: vii. 6. 26.

†ὁπλο-μαχία, ας, (μάχομαι) *the use of heavy arms*, the art of fighting with them; *infantry-practice;* ii. 1. 7.

ὅπλον, ου, *an implement*, esp. of war: pl. *arms*, esp. heavy arms; *armor;* the arms as stacked or deposited in an encampment (comm. in front of the men's quarters), *the place of arms*, or, in general, *the camp:* τὰ ὅπλα by metonymy for οἱ ὁπλῖται *the men at arms:* ἐν (τοῖς) ὅπλοις *in or under arms, armed:* i. 2. 2: ii. 2. 4, 20; 4. 15: iii. 1. 3, 33; 2. 28, 36; 3. 7. Der. PAN-OPLY.

†ὁ-πόθεν *whencesoever, whence;* (elliptically, 551 f) *anywhere whence, any place* or *source from which;* iii. 1. 32; 5. 3: v. 2. 2.

†ὅ-ποι *whithersoever, whither, wherever, where;* (elliptically, 551 f) *any place to which;* i. 9. 13 ? ii. 4. 19 s: iii. 5. 13, 17.

†ὁ-ποῖος, α, ον, *of whatever* or *what kind* or *nature, whatsoever, whatever* or *what* (in quality); *what kind* or *sort of;* such *as;* ii. 2. 2; 6. 4: iii. 1. 13: v. 2. 3; 5. 15; 6. 28 (550 d). [ὅ-πος an old rel. indef. pron., remaining in ὅπου, ὅπῃ, &c.]

‡ ὁ-πόσος, η, ον, *how much* or *great* (soever), as much or large *as:* ὁπόσον, sc. χωρίον, *as far as:* iii. 2. 21; 3. 10: iv. 4. 17: pl. *how many* (soever), *whatever* (in number), as many *as*, often preceded by the pl. of πᾶς, 550 f, i. 1. 6; 2. 1; 8. 27; v. 8. 10.

‡ ὁπότ-αν or ὁπότ' ἄν, = ὁπότε ἄν, w. the subj., 619 b, ii. 3. 27 : v. 7. 7 s.

‡ ὁ-πότε *whenever, when; at whatever time, as soon as;* at a time *when*, 550 b; *since:* ἦν ὁπότε [there was when] *sometimes:* ὁπότε γε at least when, *if indeed, since:* i. 2. 7; 6. 7: iii. 2. 2, 15 s, 36 : iv. 2. 27 : vii. 6. 11.

‡ ὁ-πότερος, α, ον, *whichsoever* or *which*, of two persons, parties, courses, &c., iii. 1. 21, 42 ; 4. 42 ; vii. 7. 18.

‡ ὅ-που *wherever, where*, to or in a place *where:* ὅπου μή [where not] *except where:* οὐκ ἦν ὅπου *there was no place where:* i. 3. 6; 5. 8 s: iii. 2. 9, 34: iv. 5. 30 s; 8. 26 : vi. 3. 23.

ὀπτάω, ήσω, ὤπτηκα, (akin to ἕψω) *to bake, roast*, A., v. 4. 29.

‡ ὀπτός, ή, όν, (shortened for ὀπτητός) *baked, burnt*, as brick, ii. 4. 12.

ὅ-πως* adv., *in whatever* or *what way, how, as;* conj., *in order that, so that, that;* i. 1. 4, 6; 6. 11; 8. 13: vi. 5. 30 : οὐκ ἔστιν ὅπως [there is not how] *it cannot be that*, 4. 3: ὅπως ἔσεσθε [sc. ὁρᾶτε] *see that you be*, 626, i. 7. 3 : οὐχ ὅπως *not only not*, 717 g, vii. 7. 8.

ὁράω,* ὄψομαι, ἑώρακα or ἑόρακα, ipf. ἑώρων, 2 a. εἶδον (ἴδω, -οιμι, -έ, -εῖν, -ών), a. p. ὤφθην, *to see* (including both sensation and perception, real or imaginary, and even mere mental discernment, while βλέπω is rather *to look*, of the outward sense, θεάομαι *to gaze upon a spectacle*, and σκοπέω *to look as a watchman* or *searcher*), *to behold, discern, perceive*, A. (often by attraction from a dependent clause, 474 b) P., CP., i. 2. 18 : iii. 1. 11 s, 15 ; 2. 8, 23 s, 29 : ὁρώμενος *seen, visible*, iv. 3. 5 : — 2 pf. οἶδα* (οἴδαμεν or ἴσμεν,

όργή 97 'Ορχομένιος

είδώ, είδείην, ίσθι, είδέναι, είδώς), 2 plp. ήδειν, f. είσομαι, [to have seen, hence] to know (in general presenting this result more simply than its synonymes, γιγνώσκω, επίσταμαι, &c.), to understand, be acquainted with, be assured, A. (sometimes by attraction from a dependent clause, 474 b) P., CP., i. 3. 5, 15 ; 8. 21: ii. 1. 13 ; 5. 13 : iii. 5. 11: iv. 1. 22 : χάριν είδέναι to [know] recognize or feel an obligation, D. G., i. 4. 15 : vii. 6. 32 : είδώς knowing, from certain knowledge, with certainty, i. 7. 4 : έκασταχόσε είδέναι [to be acquainted] to know the country in every direction, iii. 5. 17: οίδ' ότι parenthetic, I know, 717 b, v. 7. 33. Der. PAN-ORAMA.

όργή, ής, anger, i. 5. 8 : ii. 6. 9.

†όργίζω, ίσω ιώ, to make angry, enrage; M. w. a. p., to be angry, wroth, or enraged, D., i. 2. 26 ; 5. 11: vi.1.30.

†όργυιά, άς, the extent of the outstretched arms, a fathom, about 6 feet (= 4 πήχεις), i. 7. 14: iv. 5. 4.

όρέγω,* έξω, (akin to Lat. rego) to stretch or reach out, present, vii. 3. 29.

όρεινός, ή, όν, or όρειος, α, ον, (όρος) mountainous; of the mountains, mountain : οί όρεινοί the mountaineers : v. 2. 2 : vii. 4. 11, 21.

†όρθιος, α, ον, s., straight up, steep (cf. πρανής); τό όρθιον [sc. χωρίον] the steep ground; όρθιον ίέναι to go up a steep ascent: of a military company, [straight up towards the enemy] in a column, i. e. with narrow front, and much greater depth (cf. φάλαγξ): i. 2. 21 : iv. 2. 3, 11 ; 6..12 ; 8. 12 s.

όρθός, ή, όν, (akin to όρνυμι and Lat. orior) erect, upright, straight; right; ii. 5. 23 : vi. 6. 38. Der. ORTHO-DOX.

‡όρθρος, ου, ό, the rising of the morning light, dawn, daybreak, ii. 2. 21.

‡όρθώς rightly, right, properly, correctly, justly : ό. έχω (q. v.) to be proper: i. 9. 30 : iii. 2. 7 ; 3. 12.

όρίζω, ίσω ιώ, ώρικα, (όρος a bound) to bound, separate ; to define, determine; A.: M. to set up for one's bound, A.: iv.3.1 : vii.5.13 ; 7.36. Der. HORIZON.

όριον, ου, (όρος a bound) a boundary, bound: ch. pl., borders, confines, frontier, iv. 8. 8 : v. 4. 2 : vi. 2. 19.

όρκος, ου, ό, (akin to είργω to restrain) an oath : οί θεών όρκοι the oaths [of the gods as their keepers] by the gods : ii. 5. 3, 7 s : iii.1.20,22. Der. EX-ORCISM.

όρμάω, ήσω, ώρμηκα, (όρμή) to start quickly, rush, hurry, hasten, I., έκ, είς, &c. : όρμάν όδόν to start on or commence an expedition : M. to start, set forth, make incursions, άπό, έξ : i. 1. 9 ; 2. 5 ; 8.25 ; 10.1 : iii.1.8 ; 4.33,44.

όρμέω, ήσω, (όρμος) to be moored, lie at anchor, i. 4. 3, 6.

όρμή, ής, (akin to όρνυμι) the start or point of starting; motion, movement, impulse; ii. 1. 3 : iii.1.10; 2. 9.

†όρμίζω, ίσω ιώ, to moor or anchor (trans.), A.: M. to anchor (intrans.), come to anchor, moor one's vessel, είς, παρά : iii. 5. 10 : vi. 1. 15 ; 2. 1 s.

[όρμος, ου, ό, (είρω to tie) a place where vessels are fastened, anchorage, haven.]

†όρνεον, ου, a bird, vi. 1. 23.

†όρνίθειος, α, ον, of a bird, bird's : κρέα όρνίθεια fowl, iv. 5. 31.

όρνις,* ίθος, acc. όρνιν & όρνίθα, ό ή, (akin to όρνυμι) a bird, fowl, esp. domestic ; cock or hen; iv. 5. 25. Der. ORNITHO-LOGY.

[όρνυμι, όρσω, όρωρα, to rouse, raise : M. orior, to rise.]

'Ορόντας or 'Ορόντης, ου or α, Orontas or -es, a Persian nobleman of the royal family, condemned to death for treason against Cyrus, i. 6. 1, 3 s. — 2. Satrap of Armenia, married to Rhodogūne, daughter of the king, but afterwards disgraced for misconduct in the war against Evagoras of Cyprus, ii. 4. 8 s : iii. 5. 17.

όρος, εος (g. pl. όρέων & όρών both found), τό, (akin to όρνυμι) a mountain, i. 2. 21 s, 24 s. Der. OREAD.

όροφος, ου, ό, (έρέφω to cover) a roof, vii. 4. 16.

†όρυκτός, ή, όν, dug, dug out, excavated ; of a ditch, artificial; i. 7. 14 : iv. 5. 25.

όρύττω,* ύξω, όρώρυχα, to dig, quarry, A., i. 5. 5 : v. 8. 9.

όρφανός, ή, όν, orbus, bereft of parents, as an ORPHAN, vii. 2. 32.

όρχέομαι, ήσομαι, (όρχος row) to dance, v. 4. 34. Der. ORCHESTRA.

‡όρχησις, εως, ή, a dance, dancing, vi. 1. 8, 11.

‡όρχηστρίς, ίδος, ή, a female dancer, vi. 1. 12.

'Ορχομένιος, ου, an Orchomenian, a man of Orchomenus ('Ορχομενός), an ancient city in eastern Arcadia, of ὅς 98 ὅτι

early importance (πολύμηλος *rich in flocks*, Il. B. 605), ii. 5. 37. ‖Kalpáki.
ὅς, ἥ, οἵ, αἵ, as forms of the art., see ὁ : i. 8. 16 : iii. 4. 47 : vii. 6. 4.
ὅς, ἥ, ὅ,* rel. pron., qui, *who, which, what, that;* often referring to an antecedent understood or expressed in the same clause, often attracted in case to its antecedent, and sometimes used as complem., 551, 554, 563 ; i. 1. 2 ; 2. 1 s, 20 ; 3. 16 s ; 9. 25, 28. Forms of ὅς are often used adverbially ; or an adv. or conj. may be used in translating them : οὗ [sc. τόπου or χωρίου] *in which place, where, to the place where* [sc. ἐκεῖσε], i. 2. 22 : ii. 1. 6 : ᾗ [sc. ὁδῷ or χώρᾳ] *in what way, direction,* or *place, as, where, on the route by which;* iii. 4. 37 : iv. 5. 34: ᾗ ἐδύνατο τάχιστα [what way he could most quickly] *as rapidly as possible, with all possible speed* (some translate, *by the quickest route*), ᾗ δυνατὸν μάλιστα *as strictly as possible,* 553 c, i. 2. 4 ; 3. 15 ; so ᾗ τάχιστα vi. 5. 13 : δι' ὅ *on which account, wherefore,* i. 2. 21 : οὗ ἕνεκα *on what account, why,* vii. 4. 4. See ἀπό, ἐν, ἐξ, ἐπί, μέχρι· εἰμί.

ὅσιος, α, ον, *pious, religious, conscientious,* ii. 6. 25 : v. 8. 26.

ὅσος,* η, ον, rel. pron. of quantity, also used as complem., 563, (ὅς) quantus, *as much, great,* or *large as, how much* or *great;* pl. comm. = quot, as many *as, how many:* often translated by the simpler *who, which, that, what,* esp. when preceded by πᾶς or a numeral, 550 d, f; sometimes by *whoever* or *whatever, such as, so great that* (& pers. pron.), &c.: i. 1. 2 ; 2. 1 : ii. 1. 1,11,16 : iii. 1. 19 : ὅσον χρόνον *whatever time, as long as,* ii. 4. 26 : ὅσῳ w. compar., *by how much, the, according as,* 468, i. 5. 9 : iv. 7. 23. The neut. ὅσον is greatly and variously used, often as an indecl. adj. or subst., or as an adv., 507 e, 556, *as much as, as large as, as far as, as many as;* hence, *about* (w. numerals and words of measure, i. 8. 6 : iv. 5. 10); *enough* (esp. w. inf., iv. 1. 5 : vii. 3. 22, cf. 20); *so far that, as this that, as that, that;* iii. 1. 45 ; 3. 15 : iv. 8. 12 : vi. 3. 14 : vii. 3. 9 : w. superl., *as . . as,* e. g. ὅσον ἐδύναντο μέγιστον *as loud as they could,* 553 c, iv. 5. 18 : ἐφ' ὅσον *over as much ground as,* vi. 3. 19 : ὅσον οὐ tantum *non, as much only as not, only not, almost,* vii. 2. 5.

‡ὁσοσ-περ, ηπερ, ονπερ, strengthened fr. ὅσος, *just* or *even as much* or *many as,* &c., i.7.9 : iv.3.2 : vii.4.19; 7.28.

ὁσ-περ, ἥπερ, ὅπερ, strengthened fr. ὅς, *who* or *which indeed, which very, just who* or *which ; οὖπερ just where, ᾗπερ just as* or *where ;* &c.; i. 4. 5 : ii. 3. 21 : iii. 1. 34; 2. 10, 29 : iv. 8. 26.

ὅσπριον, ου, ch. pl. *legumes, pulse,* esp. *beans,* iv.4.9 ; 5.26: vi.4.6 ; 6.1.

ὅσ-τις,* ἥτις, ὅ τι, (g. οὗτινος or ὅτου, d. ᾧτινι or ὅτῳ, g. pl. ὧντινων or ὅτων, the shorter forms much prevailing in the Anab.) rel. indef. pron., also complem., *whosoever, whoever, which(so)ever, what(so)ever; one* or *any one who, a man who, anything which ; who, which, what, that;* sometimes referring to a definite antecedent, and often in the sing. referring to the pl., 501, 550b,f; i. 1. 5 ; 3. 5, 11s, 18 ; 6. 7 : ii. 5. 39 : iii. 2. 4 : ὅστις = *that he,* 558, ii. 5. 12, 21 : w. fut., denoting purpose, 558 a, i. 3. 14 : ὅτου δὴ παρεγγυήσαντος *some one indeed* [whoever it might have been] *having suggested it,* iv. 7. 25 ; cf. v. 2. 24 : ὅ τι ἐδύνατο [whatever] *as far as he could,* vi. 1. 32. See εἰμί, ἐξ.

‡ὁσ-τις-οῦν, ἡτισοῦν, ὁτιοῦν, *whoever then, whatever then,* &c. : μηδ' ὁντιναοῦν μισθόν *not any pay whatever* [then it might be], vii. 6. 27.

ὀσφραίνομαι,* ὀσφρήσομαι, *to perceive by smell, smell of,* G., v. 8. 3.

†ὅταν = ὅτ' ἄν or ὅτε ἄν, w. subj., *when, whenever,* iii. 3. 15 ; 4. 20.

ὅτε, by apostr. ὅτ' or ὅθ', adv. of time, (ὅς) quum, quando, *when, while,* i. 2. 9 : iii. 1. 37 : w. opt., *when, whenever, as soon* or *often as,* ii. 6. 12 : iv. 1. 16. See εἰμί.

ὅτι* conj., (fr. neut. of ὅστις, cf. quod) complem., *that;* more positive, direct, or actual than ὡς, 702 a (sometimes even used before direct quotation or the inf., 644, 659 e, i. 6. 8 : ii. 4. 16 : iii. 1. 9 ?): causal, *because:* i. 2. 21 ; 3. 7, 9 s : ii. 3. 19 : v. 6. 19 (repeated) : — as an intensive adv., w. superl., = quam, 553 c, as ὅτι ἀπαρασκευαστότατον(πλείστους)*as unprepared* (*many*) *as possible,* i. 1. 6 : cf. iii. 4. 5. Words logically following ὅτι sometimes precede it for greater emphasis,

ὅ τι, ὅτου, ὅτῳ, ὅτων, see ὅστις.

οὐ* (before a smooth vowel οὐκ, before an aspirated vowel οὐχ, and sometimes prolonged to οὐχί), not, the objective neg. adv., esp. denying fact, and ch. used with the ind., opt., and pt., 686 (sometimes by litotes, 686 i), i. 2. 11 : ii. 1. 13 ; 5. 21 : iii. 1. 13 : πλοῖα οὐκ ἔχομεν we have [not] no boats, ii. 2. 23 : οὐκ ἔφασαν ἰέναι they said that they would not go, they refused to go, 662 b, 686 i, i. 3. 1, cf. 8 : οὐ μή in strong denial of the future, 627, vi. 2. 4. In introducing a question, οὐ, or ἆρ' οὐ, implies that an affirmative answer is expected, 687, iii. 1. 18, 29. Οὐ has similar uses in compos.; where it is often repeated without doubling the negation, i. 3. 5 ; 8. 20 ; 9. 13 : iii. 1. 38. See μή.

οὗ whose ; as adv., where ; see ὅς.

οὗ, οἷ, ἕ,* encl., sui, sibi, se, pl. σφεῖς, &c., of him or himself, of her or herself, &c.; 3d pers. pron., comm. reflexive, but ch. yielding its place to other pronouns, 539 a, b, f. Of the sing., only the dat. occurs in the Anab. i. 1. 8 ; 2. 8 : iii. 5. 16 : v.7. 18, 25.

[†οὐδ-αμός, ή, όν, (old ἁμός = εἷς), = οὐδ-είς.] Hence the adverbs, οὐδαμοῦ nowhere, i. 10. 16 : οὐδαμόθεν from no place or quarter, ii. 4. 23 : οὐδαμῇ or -μῇ nowhere, in no wise, iv. 6. 11 ? v. 5. 3 : οὐδαμοῖ to no place, vi. 3. 16 ?

οὐ-δέ, by apostr. οὐδ', conj., and not, but not, nor, neither, nor yet (cf. οὔτε); used after a neg. clause, as καὶ οὐ after an affirmative one ; i. 2. 25 ; 6. 11 : cf. i. 4. 7 : v. 8. 25 : — emphatic adv., ne . . quidem, not even or also, certainly not, by no means, neither, i. 3. 12, 21 ; 6. 8 : οὐ . . οὐδέ not by any means, ii. 2. 16. For its compounds οὐδείς, &c., the stronger forms οὐδὲ εἷς, &c., are also found, iii. 1. 2 ? vii. 6. 35.

†οὐδ-είς,* οὐδε-μία, οὐδ-έν (εἷς) not even one, no one, no, none : οὐδέν subst., nothing ; as adv., as to nothing, by no means, not at all : i. 1. 8 ; 2. 22 ; 3. 11 ; 6. 7 s ; 8. 20 : ii. 5. 1 : vi. 2. 10.

†οὐδέ-ποτε not even at any time, never, ii. 6. 13.

†οὐδέ-πω not yet indeed, not as yet, vii. 3. 24, cf. 6. 35.

οὐθ' by apostr. before an aspirated vowel, for οὔτε neither, nor, ii. 5. 7.

οὐκ, οὐχ, οὐχί, not, see οὐ, i. 4. 8.

†οὐκ-έτι no longer, no farther, no more, not now, i. 8. 17 ; 10. 1, 12, cf. 13: ii. 2. 12 (w. μή, see οὐ): vii. 5. 1.

†οὐκ-οῦν declarative, and οὐκ-οῦν interrog., not therefore, not then, certainly not. This distinction of accent is not observed by all. In οὐκοῦν, neg. interrogation sometimes passes into assertion, therefore, then, 687 c. i. 6. 7 : ii. 5. 24 : iii. 2. 19 ; 5. 6 : vi. 6. 14.

οὖν* (post-pos. adv.), as contr. fr. the impers. pt. ἐόν it being (fr. εἰμί), may signify this being so, or this being as it may ; hence comm., therefore, then, now, accordingly, in this state of things ; but sometimes, yet, however, be this as it may, however that might be, at any rate, certainly, esp. in δ' οὖν : i. 1. 2 ; 2. 12, 15 s, 22, 25 ; 3. 5 s ; 5. 14.

οὗ-περ as adv., just where, the very place where, iv. 8. 26 ; see ὅσπερ.

οὔ-ποτε n-unquam, n-ever, i. 3. 5.

οὔ-πω non-dum, not yet, not as yet, i. 5. 12 ; 8. 8 ; 9. 25 : cf. vii. 3. 35.

οὐ-πώ-ποτε (also written οὐ πώποτε) not yet at any time, never before, i. 4. 18.

οὐρά, ᾶς, the tail : of an army, the rear, iii. 4. 38, 42 ? vi. 5. 5 s.

†οὐρ-αγία, ας, the rear-command, rearguard, iii. 4..42 : v. l. οὐρά.

†οὐρ-αγός, οῦ, ὁ, (ἄγω) a rear-leader, the rearmost or last man in a file, who of course became the first when the direction of the file was reversed, iv. 3. 26, 29.

οὐρανός, οῦ, ὁ, heaven, the heavens, sky, iv. 2. 2. Der. URANUS.

οὖς,* ὠτός, τό, auris, an ear, iii. 1. 31 : vii. 4. 3 s. Der. PAR-OTID.

οὕς whom, which, see ὅς, i. 4. 9.

οὖσα, οὖσι(ν), see εἰμί, i. 4. 15 ; 5. 9.

οὔ-τε conj., by apostr. οὔτ' or οὔθ', ne-que, and not, nor : οὔτε . . οὔτε neither . . nor : οὔτε . . τε neque . . et, both not . . and. Οὔτε is commonly thus doubled in whole or part, as both primary and secondary connective, and is thus distinguished from the conj. οὐδέ (yet μὲν οὔτε . . δέ, vi. 3. 16). i. 2. 26 ; 3. 11 : ii. 5. 4, 7. Cf. μή-τε.

οὔ-τινος, see ὅστις, i. 4. 15.

οὔ-τοι certainly not, not by any means, vii. 6. 11 : v. l. οὔτι not at all.

οὗτος,* αὕτη, τοῦτο, demonst. pron.,

(ὁ αὐτός) hic, *this*, pl. *these;* sometimes *that, those;* comm. referring to that which precedes or is contained in a subordinate clause (so οὕτως, τοιοῦτος, &c., cf. ὅδε, &c., 543 s) : as a pers. pron., *he, she, it, they:* i.1. 7 s, 9,11; 3. 7 s : καὶ οὗτοι *these also, and these* or *those too,* καὶ ταῦτα *and that too,* 544 a, i.1.11; 4.12: ii.5. 21: τούτους *those* well known, 542 b, i. 5. 8 : ταῦτα *here,* 509 b, iii. 5. 9 ? *therefore,* 483 b, iv. 1. 21 : τοῦτο ἔστω *so be it !* i. 8. 17.

‡οὑτοσ-ί,* αὐτηΐ, τουτί, (paragogic -ί, Att. & deictic, 252 c) hic-ce, Fr. celui-ci, *this* here, *this* . . *here present,* i. 6. 6 : vii. 2. 24.

‡οὕτως,* comm. οὕτω before a consonant, 164, *thus, so, in this way or manner, to such a degree, so much or very, on this condition or supposition,* i. 1. 5, 9 s : ii. 6. 6 : iv. 7. 4 : οὗτως . . ὅστις *so* . . *that he,* 558, ii. 5. 12: vii. 1. 28. See οὗτος, ἔχω.

‡οὑτωσ-ί(ν), *in just this way, as follows,* vii. 6. 39 : v. l. οὐ τῷ Σιῴ.

οὐχ, οὐχί, *not,* see οὐ, iii. 1. 13.

ὀφείλω,* λήσω, ὠφείληκα, 2 a. ὤφε-λον, *to owe:* P. *to be owed, be due:* ὤφελον* *ought, O that! would that!* I., 638 g : i. 2. 11 : ii. 1. 4 : vii. 7. 34.

ὄφελος,* τό, in nom. & acc., (ὀφέλλω *to further*) *advantage, profit, good, use,* G., i. 3. 11 : ii. 6. 9.

ὀφθαλμός, οῦ, ὁ, (ὀπ- in ὄψομαι) *an eye:* ἔχειν ἐν ὀφθαλμοῖς *to have in or under eye, keep in sight:* i. 8. 27 : iv. 5. 12 s, 29. Der. OPHTHALMIC.

ὀφλισκάνω,* ὀφλήσω, ὤφληκα, 2 a. ὦφλον, (ὀφείλω) *to incur, be adjudged to pay,* v. 8. 1.

Ὀφρύνιον, ου, *Ophrynium,* a small town of Troas, near the southern end of the Hellespont, with a grove sacred to Hector, vii. 8. 5. ‖ Fren-Keui.

†ὀχετός, οῦ, ὁ, *a conduit* of water, *duct, ditch, channel,* ii. 4. 13.

ὀχέω, ήσω, (ὄχος carriage, fr. ἔχω) *to carry, bear:* P. *to be borne, ride,* ἐπί, iii. 4. 47.

‡ὄχημα, ατος, τό, *a vehicle, conveyance, support,* iii. 2. 19.

ὄχθη, ης, (ἔχω) *a high bank,* esp. of a river, iv. 3. 3, 5, 17, 23.

ὄχλος, ου, ὁ, (akin to vulgus, Germ. *Volk,* Eng. *folk*) *a crowd, throng, multitude, rabble,* esp. *the crowd* or *retinue of camp-followers;* hence, *annoyance,* *trouble:* ii. 5. 9 : iii. 2. 27, 36 ; 3. 6 ; 4. 26. Der. OCHLO-CRACY.

ὀχυρός, ά, όν, (ἔχω) *fit for holding, tenable, strong, fortified, secure:* pl. ὀχυρά *strong-holds:* i. 2. 22, 24 : iv. 7. 17 : cf. ἐχυρός.

ὀψέ adv., (akin to ἕπομαι · contr. fr. ὄπισθε ?) *late:* ὀψὲ ἦν (ἐγίγνετο) *it was (became) late:* ii. 2. 16 : iii. 4. 36.

‡ὀψία, ας, *a late hour, evening,* vi. 5. 31 ?

‡ὀψίζω, ίσω ιῶ, *to be or come late,* iv. 5. 5.

†ὄψις, εως, ἡ, *sight, appearance, spectacle,* ii. 3. 15 : vi. 1. 9.

ὄψομαι, see ὁράω. Der. OPTIC.

Π.

παγ-κράτιον, ου, (πᾶν κράτος) *a contest demanding the entire strength; the pancratium,* a severe "rough and tumble" exercise, in which wrestling and boxing were combined, iv. 8. 27.

παγ-χάλεπος, ον, (πᾶν) *very hard or difficult,* v. 2. 20 ?

‡παγ-χαλέπως *very hardly:* π. εἶχον *were very hard in their feelings,* πρός, vii. 5. 16.

παθεῖν, see πάσχω, i. 8. 20 ; 9. 8.

‡πάθημα, ατος, τό, *calamity, suffering, misery,* vii. 6. 30.

‡πάθος, εος, τό, *affliction, ill-treatment, affection, disease,* i. 5. 14 : iv. 5. 7. Der. PATHOS, PATHETIC.

παιανίζω, ίσω ιῶ, (παιάν a PÆAN, *war-song*) *to sing* or *chant the pæan* or *war-song,* i. 8. 17 ; 10. 10 : iii. 2. 9 ?

†παιδεία, ας, *education, training, discipline,* iv. 6. 15 s. Der. CYCLO-PÆDIA.

†παιδ-εραστής, οῦ, (ἔραμαι) *a lover of boys,* vii. 4. 7.

†παιδεύω, εύσω, πεπαίδευκα, *to bring up a child, train, educate,* A., i. 9. 2 s.

†παιδικά, ῶν, τά, *deliciæ;* as sing., *a darling, favorite, object of love;* ch. of a boy ; ii. 6. 6, 28 : v. 8. 4.

†παιδίον, ου, τό, dim., *a little* or *young child,* iv. 7. 13.

†παιδίσκη, ης, dim., *a young girl, maiden,* iv. 3. 11.

παῖς, παιδός, ὁ ἡ, *a child,* whether *son or daughter, boy or girl ; a youth, boy, lad ;* hence, *a page, waiter, servant* (cf. puer) ; i.1.1 ; 9.2 s : ii. 6. 12: iv. 5. 33 : see ἐξ. Der. PED-AGOGUE.

παίω 101 παραγγέλλω

παίω,* παίσω, πέπαικα, to strike, as w. the hand or anything in it, to smite, beat, wound; often joined w. βάλλω, in a sense clear:y distinct; A. AE.; i. 8. 26s; 10. 7: iii. 1. 29; 4. 49: v. 7. 21; 8. 12s, 16.
παιωνίζω, ίσω ιῶ, =παιανίζω, iii. 2. 9?
πάλαι adv., long ago, long since, long before; formerly, previously; i. 4. 12: iv. 5. 5; 8. 14: vii. 6, 9, 37.
‡παλαιός, ά, όν, c. παλαίτερος or παλαίτερος, old, ancient: τὸ παλαιόν anciently: iii. 4. 7: iv. 4. 9; 5. 35. Der. PALÆ-ONTO-LOGY.
†παλαίω, αίσω, πεπάλαικα l., to wrestle, iv. 8. 26. Der. PALÆSTRA.
πάλη, ης, (πάλλω to shake) wrestling, common in the Greek games, iv. 8. 27.
πάλιν adv., again, back again, back, i. 1. 3; 6. 7 s. Der. PALIN-ODE.
παλλακίς, ίδος, ἡ, (πάλλαξ a youth) a concubine, mistress, i. 10. 2.
παλτόν, οῦ, (πάλλω to brandish) a dart, javelin, or light spear, used by the Asiatics for both throwing and striking (like the modern jereed); whence two were often carried; i. 5. 15; 8. 3, 27: v. 4. 12, 25.
†παμ-πληθής, ές, (πλῆθος) very numerous, vast, countless, iii. 2. 11.
†πάμ-πολυς,-πόλλη, -πολυ,very much or great, very numerous, vast: pl. very many, a great many: ii. 4. 26: iii. 4. 13: iv. 1. 8; 6. 26: vii. 5. 12 (see ἐπί).
†παμ-πόνηρος, ον, all-depraved: of a man, a perfect villain, the worst of men, vi. 6. 25.
πᾶν neut. of πᾶς; in compos., παγ- before a palatal, and παμ- before a labial; iv. 2. 22. Der. PAN-ACEA.
‡πᾶν-ουργία, ας, (ἔργον) knavery, villany, vii. 5. 11.
‡πᾶν-οῦργος, ον, s., (contr. fr. πανό-εργος, fr. ἔργον) ready for all work, unprincipled, knavish, crafty, perfidious, treacherous, ii. 5. 39; 6. 26.
‡πάντ', before a rough breathing πάνθ', by apostr. for πάντα, see πᾶς.
‡παντά-πᾶσι(ν) adv., all to all, all in all, altogether, wholly, entirely, absolutely, at all, i. 2. 1 : ii. 5. 18, 21.
‡πανταχῇ or -χῂ, or πανταχοῦ, everywhere, in any or all places, anywhere, ii. 5. 7 ; 6. 7 : iv. 5. 30.
‡παν-τελῶς (τέλος) quite to the end, completely, entirely, wholly, ii. 2. 11.
‡πάντῃ or -τῃ everywhere, on all sides, throughout, i. 2. 22: ii. 3. 3; 5. 7: iii. 1. 2.
‡παντο-δαπός,ή,όν,(δάπεδον ground?) of every region or kind, all kinds of, various, i. 2. 22 : iv. 4. 9 : vi. 4. 5.
‡πάντοθεν from every quarter, on all sides, iii. 1. 12 : vi. 6. 3.
‡παντοῖος, α, ον, of all or various kinds, all or various kinds of, various, i. 5. 2 : ii. 4. 14.
‡πάντοσε in all directions, everywhere (= -whither), vii. 2. 23.
‡πάντως by all means; at all, once; vi. 5. 21 ? vii. 7. 43 ?
‡πάνυ adv., wholly, altogether, very, very much; at all; i. 5. 7; 8. 14: ii. 5. 19, 27 : vii. 6. 4.
πάομαι * (ch. poet., pres. not in use), πάσομαι, πέπᾶμαι, potior, to acquire: pf. pret. [to have acquired] to possess, have in possession, A., i. 9. 19 : iii. 3. 18 : vi. 1. 12 : vii. 6. 41.
παρά* prep., by apostr. παρ', beside: (a) w. GEN., comm. of person, from beside, from the side or sphere of, from, often implying some action or influence; hence sometimes w. pass. verb, by, 694. 9 ; i. 1. 5 ; 3. 16 ; 7. 2; 9. 1 : ii. 6. 14 : v. 2. 25 : — (b) w. DAT., comm. of person, at or by the side of, beside, near, about, with ; at the court of; in the house, service, care, or esteem of; i. 1. 5 ; 2. 27; 3. 7; 9. 29 : ii. 6. 26: vi. 2. 2 : τὰ παρ' ἐμοί the advantages in my service, i. 7. 4 :— (c) w. ACC. of person, to the side of, to, towards, i. 2. 12; 3. 7; 6. 3 :— of place (sometimes of person, &c.) through the space beside, along side of, along, beside, by, past, near, about, i. 2. 13, 24 ; 8. 5 : iii. 1. 32: iv. 7. 16 : παρ' ὀλίγον [alongside of a little] of little account, vi. 6. 11 : παρὰ πότον with drink, ii. 3. 15 :— of words expressing obligation, opinion, &c., [along by or beside] beyond, contrary to, against, in violation of, i. 9. 8 : ii. 1. 18 ; 5. 41 : v. 8. 17 : vii. 6. 36. Its uses in compos. are similar.
παρα-βαίνω,* βήσομαι, βέβηκα, 2 a. ἔβην, to go beyond, transgress, violate, break, A., iv. 1. 1.
παρα-βοηθέω, ήσω, βεβοήθηκα, to hasten [by other troops] forward to give aid, iv. 7. 24.
παρ-αγγέλλω, ελῶ, ἤγγελκα, a. ἤγγειλα, to send word to or along, pass the word, and thus to direct, command,

παράγγελσις 102 παρασκευάζω

order, bid; to summon; to give out or issue a password; D. I. (A.), CP., A., εἰς: κατὰ τὰ παρηγγελμένα *according to the instructions given* : i. 1. 6 ; 2. 1 ; 5. 13 ; 8. 3, 15 s : ii. 2. 8, 21 : iii. 4. 3.
† παρ-άγγελσις, εως, ἡ, *a word of command, summons,* iv. 1. 5.

παρα-γίγνομαι,* γενήσομαι, γεγένημαι & 2 pf. γέγονα, 2 a. ἐγενόμην, *to come to* or *near, come, arrive, to present one's self* or *be present, join,* D., εἰς, ἐν, i. 1. 11 ; 2. 3 ; 7. 12 : v. 6. 8.

παρ-άγω,* ἄξω, ἦχα, 2 a. ἤγαγον, *to lead* or *conduct by* or *along, bring up* or *forward,* A. εἰς, &c., iii. 4. 14, 21 : iv. 6. 6 ; 8. 8 : vii. 6. 3.

† παρ-αγωγή, ῆς, *conveyance* along the coast, *transport,* v. 1. 16. Der. PARAGOGIC.

παράδεισος, ου, ὁ, (fr. the Pers., first found in Xen.) *a park,* i. 2. 7 ; 4. 10 : ii. 4. 14. Der. PARADISE.

παρα-δίδωμι,* δώσω, δέδωκα, a. ἔδωκα (δῶ, δοίην, δός, δοῦναι, δούς), tra-do, *to give* or *deliver up* or *over, give, grant,* A. D. I., ii. 1. 8 s, 12 : iv. 5. 22.

παρα-δραμεῖν, see παρα-τρέχω.

παρα-θαρρύνω or -θαρσύνω, ὑνῶ, *to cheer* [along] *on, encourage,* A., ii. 4. 1 : iii. 1. 39.

παρα-θεῖναι, see παρα-τίθημι.

παρα-θέω,* θεύσομαι, *to run by* or *past,* A., iv. 7. 12.

παρ-αινέω,* έσω, ἤνεκα, (αἰνέω *to commend*) *to recommend, advise, exhort,* AE., i. 7. 2 : v. 7. 35 : vii. 3. 20.

παρ-αιτέομαι, ήσομαι, ᾔτημαι, *to beg from, intercede with,* περί, vi. 6. 29.

παρα-καλέω,* καλέσω, καλῶ, κέκληκα, a. ἐκάλεσα, a. p. ἐκλήθην, *to call* [along] *forward, summon, invite, exhort, urge, encourage, call to, call in,* A. I., ἐπί, i. 6. 5s : iii. 1. 24 : v. 6. 19.

παρα-κατα-θήκη, ης, (τίθημι) *a deposit* with another, v. 3. 7.

παρά-κειμαι,* κείσομαι, *to lie beside* or *near,* D., vii. 3. 22.

παρα-κελεύομαι, εύσομαι, κεκέλευσμαι, *to urge* along or forward, *exhort, encourage,* D. I., i. 7. 9 ; 8. 11.

† παρα-κέλευσις, εως, ἡ, *encouragement, cheering on,* G.? iv. 8. 28.

παρ-ακολουθέω, ήσω, ἠκολούθηκα, *to follow beside* or *near, accompany, attend,* iii. 3. 4 : iv. 4. 7.

παρα-λαμβάνω,* λήψομαι, εἴληφα, 2 a. ἔλαβον, *to take* or *receive* from another, *succeed to; to take* to or with one's self ; A., παρά : v. 6. 36 : vi. 4. 11 : vii. 2. 17 ; 7. 7.

παρα-λείπω,* ψω, 2 pf. λέλοιπα, 2 a. ἔλιπον, *to leave on* one side, *leave, omit,* A., vi. 3. 19 ; 6. 18.

παρα-λυπέω, ήσω, λελύπηκα, *to annoy* [along side] *by competition* or *interference :* οἱ παραλυποῦντες *troublesome rivals,* ii. 5. 29.

παρα-λύω,* λύσω, λέλυκα, *to loose from beside, take off, unship (M. for one's own benefit),* A., v. 1. 11. Der. PARALYSIS, PALSY.

παρ-αμείβω, ψω, *to interchange : M. to change one's self* or one's own (army, line of battle, &c.), εἰς, i. 10. 10 (acc. to some, *to pass by*).

παρ-αμελέω, ήσω, ἠμέληκα, *to pass by* in *neglect, to neglect, treat with neglect, disregard, violate,* G., ii. 5. 7 : vii. 8. 12.

παρα-μένω,* μενῶ, μεμένηκα, *to stay beside, stand by, remain steadfast,* ii. 6. 2 : vi. 2. 15.

παρα-μηρίδιος, ον, (μηρός) *along the thigh :* neut. subst., *a thigh-piece, cuisse,* i. 8. 6.

παρα-πέμπω,* ψω, πέπομφα, *to send by* or *along, despatch,* A. εἰς, iv. 5. 20 ?

παρα-πλέω,* πλεύσομαι, πέπλευκα, a. ἔπλευσα, *to sail by* or *along,* A., εἰς, ἐξ, v. 1. 11 ; 6. 10 : vi. 2. 1 ; 6. 3.

παρα-πλήσιος, α, ον, or ος, ον, *near by, similar, like,* D., i. 3. 18 ; 5. 2.

παρα-προ-πέμπω,* ψω, πέπομφα, *to send by to the front,* iv. 5. 20 ?

παρα-ρ-ρέω,* ῥεύσομαι, ἐρρύηκα, 2 a. p. or a. ἐρρύην, *to flow by, to* (melt and) *run down beside,* D., παρά, iv. 4. 11 : v. 3. 8.

παρασάγγης, ου, *a parasang* (Pers. *farsang*), the comm. Persian road-measure, equal, acc. to Hdt. (2. 6) and Xen. (ii. 2. 6), to 30 stadia, = about a league or 3 geographical miles, or nearly 3½ statute miles. It was usu. estimated, and of course variously acc. to the difficulty of the route and the time occupied. i. 2. 5 s, 10 s.

παρα-σκευάζω, άσω, pf. p. ἐσκεύασμαι, *to put things side by side, to arrange, prepare, procure,* A., ii. 6. 8 : — ch. M., *to prepare* one's self or one's own ; *to prepare, provide,* or *procure* for one's self or one's own ; *to make preparation, make ready ;* A., I., P.

παρασκευή   1C3   Πάριον

(w. ὡς), ὅπως, ὥστε, ἀπό, ἐπί, ὡς εἰς: i. 8. 1 ; 10. 6, 18 : iii. 1. 14, 36 ; 2. 24 : vii. 3. 35 : παρασκευάζεσθαι τὴν γνώμην to make up one's mind, vi. 3. 17 : οἴκαδε π. to prepare for home (to go home), vii. 7. 57.

παρα-σκευή, ῆς, preparation, i. 2. 4.

παρα-σκηνέω, ήσω, to encamp by or near, D., iii. 1. 28.

παρα-σχεῖν, -σχήσω, see παρ-έχω.

†παρά-ταξις, εως, ἡ, arrangement, line of battle, v. 2. 13 ?

παρα-τάττω, τάξω, τέταχα, to arrange side by side, draw up in order of battle or in battle-array, A.: pf. p. pt. παρα-τεταγμένος so drawn up, i. 10. 10 : iv. 3. 3, 5 ; 6. 25.

παρα-τείνω,* τενῶ, τέτακα, to stretch along, extend, A. ἐπί, παρά, &c., i. 7. 15 : vii. 3. 48.

παρα-τίθημι,* θήσω, τέθεικα, a. ἔθηκα (θῶ, &c.), to place beside or near, set before, A. D., iv. 5. 30 s : M. to p'ace by one's side, lay aside, A., vi. 1. 8.

παρα-τρέχω,* δραμοῦμαι, δεδράμηκα, 2 a. ἔδραμον, to run by, past, or along, A., εἰς, ἐπί, παρά, iv. 5. 8 ; 7. 6 s, 11.

παρα-χρῆμα adv., with the affair, on the spot, forthwith, vii. 7. 24.

†παρ-εγγυάω,* ήσω, ἠγγύηκα, to pass from hand to hand, pass along, as a word of command or request ; hence, to give or pass the word of command, to command, order, charge, exhort, request, propose, cheer on, I. (A.), AF., iv. 1. 17 : 7. 24s : vi. 5. 12 : vii. 1. 22.

παρ-εγγυή, ῆς, (see ἐγγυάω) a command, charge, request, vi. 5. 13.

παρ-εγενόμην, see παρα-γίγνομαι.

παρ-έδοσαν, see παρα-δίδωμι.

πάρ-ειμι,* ἔσομαι, (εἰμί, εἴην, εἶναι, ὤν, &c.) to be by, near, at or on hand, with, or present (esp. as a friend or assistant); hence, to have come, to come, arrive, attend, be ready, D.; εἰς, ἐπί, or πρός w. A., 704 a ; i. 1. 1 s ; 2. 2s : iii. 1. 46 : vi. 4. 15 ; 6. 26 : τὰ παρόντα (πράγματα) the present state of affairs, present occurrences or circumstances, i. 3. 3 : iii. 1. 34 ; [sc. χρήματα] possessions, property, estate, vii. 7. 36 : ἐν τῷ παρόντι at the present time, in the present crisis, ii. 5. 8 : πάρεστι(ν) impers., it is present to one, i. e. in his power, possible, feasible, iv. 5. 6 (abs. παρὸν, v. 8. 3). Have may be sometimes used in translating πάρ-

ειμι as well as εἰμί, 459, ii. 3. 9 : iii. 2. 18.

πάρ-ειμι,* ipf. ᾔειν, (εἶμι) to go or come by or along, pass by, in, or through, to pass ; to pass by to the front, come forward ; A., ἐπί, παρά : iii. 2. 35 : iv. 5. 30 : vi. 5. 12, 23, 25.

παρ-εῖχον, -έξω, see παρ-έχω.

παρ-εκλήθην, see παρα-καλέω.

παρ-ελαύνω,* ἐλάσω ἐλῶ, ἐλήλακα, a. ἤλασα, to ride or march by, past, or along, A., ἐπί, &c., i. 2. 16 s ; 8. 12, 14.

παρ-έρχομαι,* ἐλεύσομαι, ἐλήλυθα, 2 a. ἦλθον, to come or go by, past, along, or through ; to pass by, over, through, &c.; to pass in, enter ; to pass by to the front or place of speaking, come forward ; of time, to pass, elapse ; A., εἰς : i. 4. 4 s ; 7. 16, 18 : v. 5. 11, 24.

παρ-έσομαι, -έστω, see πάρ-ειμι.

παρ-έστηκα, -έστην, see παρ-ίστημι.

παρ-ετέτατο, see παρα-τείνω, i. 7. 15.

παρ-έχω,* ἕξω & σχήσω, ἔσχηκα, 2 a. ἔσχον, to have or hold by or near another ; hence, to hand to, offer, afford, supply, furnish, provide, present, give, render ; to cause or make for a person, and hence, to produce, excite, or inspire in him ; to give up, deliver up, surrender, yield ; A. D. I., εἰς : i. 1. 11 : ii. 1. 11 ; 3. 22, 26 s ; 4. 10 s : vi. 6. 16, 20 : M. to render or make for one's self ; to contribute or exhibit of one's own ; A.; ii. 6. 27 : vi. 2. 10.

παρ-ηγγύων, see παρ-εγγυάω.

παρ-ῄειν, see πάρ-ειμι (εἶμι), iv. 2. 19.

παρ-ήλασα, see παρ-ελαύνω, i. 2. 17.

παρ-ῆλθον, see παρ-έρχομαι, i. 7. 16.

παρ-ῆν, -ῇ, -ῆσθα, see πάρ-ειμι.

†Παρθένιον, ου, Parthenium, a small town in the southwest part of Mysia, not far from Pergamum, vii. 8. 15, 21.

†Παρθένιος, ου, ὁ, the Parthenius, a river on the usual boundary between Bithynia and Paphlagonia, said to have been named from the virgin Diana's bathing in it, v. 6. 9 : vi. 2. 1. ǁ The Bartan-Su.

παρθένος, ου, ἡ, a virgin, maiden, iii. 2. 25. Der. PARTHENON.

Παριανός, οῦ, (Πάριον) a Parian, a man of Parium, vii. 3. 16.

παρ-ιέναι, -ιών, see πάρ-ειμι (εἶμι).

παρ-ίημι,* ήσω, εἷκα, a. ἧκα (ὦ, εἴην, &c.) to send by, let pass, yield, allow, D. I., v. 7. 10 : vii. 2. 15 ?

Πάριον, ου, Parium, a commercial

παρίστημι 104 πεδίον

city near the southwest end of the Propontis, an Ionian colony, vii. 2. 7; 3. 20. ‖ Kamares, or Kemer.

παρ-ίστημι,* στήσω, έστηκα, 2 a. έστην, *to station near;* pf. and 2 a. *to stand near* or *by*, v. 8. 10, 21 : 1 a. *m. to place* or *station by one's side, bring forward, produce*, A., vi. 1. 22 : vii. 8. 3.

πάρ-οδος, ου, ή, a way by, *passage, pass*, i. 4. 4 s ; 7. 15 s : iv. 2. 24.

παρ-οινέω,* ήσω, πεπαρώνηκα, a. έπαρώνησα, (οίνος) *to act the drunkard, be abusive*, v. 8. 4.

παρ-οίχομαι,* οίχήσομαι, ώχημαι ?, *to pass* or *have passed by :* pt. *past*, ii. 4. 1.

Παρράσιος, ου, *a Parrhasian,* a man of Parrhasia (Παρρασία), a district of southwest Arcadia, about Mt. Lycæus, i. 1. 2 : vi. 2. 9 ; 5. 2.

Παρύσατις, ιδος, ιδι, ιν or ιδα, ι, *Parysatis* (= a Peri's daughter ?), half-sister and wife of Darius II., and mother of Artaxerxes II. and Cyrus, an ambitious, daring, imperious, intriguing, and cruel woman, of great influence over her husband and sons. Of the latter, Cyrus was her favorite, and she avenged his death cruelly. She even poisoned her daughter-in-law, the queen Statīra. i. 1. 1, 4 ; 4. 9.

παρ-ών, -οὖσα, -όν, see πάρ-ειμι.

πᾶς,* πᾶσα, πᾶν, g. παντός, πάσης, *all, every, the whole ; all kinds of, every kind of:* sing. comm., without the art., *every;* but w. the art., *whole* or *all :* pl. comm. *all* (also translated by *every* w. the sing.) : i. 1. 2, 5 : ii. 5. 9 : vi. 4. 6 : ὑμεῖς οἱ πάντες *you, the whole body*, v. 7. 27, cf. 6. 7 : subst. πᾶν *everything, all*, τὸ πᾶν *the whole*, πάντα *all things* (or *everything*), i. 9. 2, 16 : vi. 2. 12 ; ἐπὶ πᾶν ἔρχεσθαι *to* [come to everything] *resort to every means*, iii. 1. 18. See διά, διαπαντός, νικάω. Der. PAN-THEISM. Cf. omnis.

Πασίων, ωνος, *Pasion*, a Megarian general in the service of Cyrus, who took offence and deserted, i.2.3 ; 4.7 s.

πάσχω,* πείσομαι, 2 pf. πέπονθα, 2 a. ἔπαθον, patior, *to receive* any effect, whether good or evil (comm. the latter, unless otherwise stated), *to be treated* or *affected, suffer : εὖ* or *κακῶς* (ἀγαθὸν or κακὸν) π. *to receive for good* or *evil, to receive good* (*benefit, favor*, *pleasure*) or *suffer ill (harm, injury, pain), to be well* or *ill treated, benefited* or *harmed :* A. ὑπό : i. 3. 4 s ; 8. 20 : iii. 3. 7 : iv. 3. 2 : τὰ μὲν ἔπαθεν *he received some wounds*, i. 9. 6 : ἤν τι πάθῃ *if anything should befall him*, by euphemism for *if he should lose his life,* v. 3. 6. Der. PASSIVE, PASSION.

πατάσσω, άξω (ch. poet. exc. aor. ἐπάταξα, see 50 τύπτω) *to strike, smite, pierce*, iv. 8. 25 : vii. 8. 14.

Πατηγύας, ου or a, *Pategyas*, a Persian attendant of Cyrus, i. 8. 1 : *v. l.* Παταγύας.

πατήρ,* πατρός, ὁ, Sans. *pitar*, Zend *patar*, Lat. *pater*, Germ. *Vater*, a FATHER, i. 4. 12. Der. PATERNAL.

†**πάτριος,** a, ον, patrius, *of* or *from one's father* or *ancestors, paternal, ancestral ; according to ancestral usage;* iii. 2. 16 ? v. 4. 27 : vii. 8. 5 ?

†**πατρίς,** ίδος, ή, patria, *one's fatherland, native land* or *city, country*, i. 3. 3, 6 : iii. 1. 3 s : iv. 8. 4.

†**πατρῷος,** a, ον, *descending from one's father, paternal, hereditary*, i. 7. 6 : iii. 1. 11 ; 2. 16 ? vii. 3. 31.

†**παῦλα,** ης, *means of stopping, stop, stoppage, prevention*, G., v. 7. 32.

παύω,* παύσω, πέπαυκα, *to stop* (trans.), *make* or *cause to cease, put an end to, remove, relinquish*, A. P., ii. 5. 2, 13 : iv. 8. 10 : *M. to stop* (intrans.), *cease, desist*, PAUSE, *rest, leave off, give up, end, finish*, G., P., i. 2. 2 ; 3. 12 ; 6. 6 : iii. 1. 19 : iv. 6. 6 : v. 1. 2.

†**Παφλαγονία,** ας, *Paphlagonia*, a country on the north coast of Asia Minor, between the Halys and Parthenius, famed for its good horses and horsemen, vi. 1. 1 s, 14.

†**Παφλαγονικός,** ή, όν, *Paphlagonian :* ή Παφλαγονική [sc. γῆ] *the Paphlagonian country :* v. 2. 22 : vi. 1. 15.

Παφλαγών, όνος, *a Paphlagonian*, a man of the Paphlagones, described by the Greeks as a rude, ignorant, credulous, and superstitious people, i. 8. 5 (as adj.) : v. 6. 3 (the king).

†**πάχος,** εος, τό, *thickness*, v. 4. 13.

παχύς, εῖα, ύ, *thick, large, stout*, iv. 8. 2 : v. 4. 25. Der. PACHY-DERM.

πέδη, ης, (πούς) pedica, *a* FETTER, iv. 3. 8.

†**πεδινός,** ή, όν, c., *flat, level*, v. 5. 2.

πεδίον, ου, (πέδον ground, akin to πούς) *a plain, a flat* or *level region ;*

sometimes used in naming cities (cf. Lich-field); i. 1. 2; 2. 11, 21s; 5. 1.
†πεζεύω, εύσω, *to march on foot, proceed by land*, v. 5. 4.
πεζός, ή, όν, (πούς) *on foot, of infantry*, i. 3. 12 : vii. 3. 45 : subst. πεζός *a foot-soldier*, οἱ πεζοί *the infantry, foot*, i. 10. 12: iii. 3.15: adv. πεζῇ *on foot, by land*, i. 4. 18: v. 6.1.
†πειθ-αρχέω, ήσω, (ἀρχή) *to yield to authority, obey*, D., i. 9. 17.
πείθω,* πείσω, πέπεικα, (2 pf. pret. πέποιθα *to trust*), a. ἔπεισα, *to persuade, induce, prevail upon;* in pr. and ipf., *to try to persuade, use persuasion, advise, urge*, 594 ; A. I., CP.; i. 2. 26 : ii. 6. 2 : vi. 1. 19 : *P. & M. to be persuaded, believe, obey, submit, yield* or *listen to, comply, follow one's direction* or *advice*, D. I. (A.), i. 1. 3 ; 2. 2 ; 3. 6, 15 ; 4. 14s: vii. 8. 3 : πειθόμενος as adj., *obedient*, ii. 6. 27.
πεινάω * (ἄεις ῇs, &c.), ήσω, πεπείνηκα, (πεῖνα *hunger*, akin to πένομαι) *to hunger, be hungry*, i. 9. 27.
πεῖρα, as, *trial, proof, experience, acquaintance*, G. ὅτι, iii. 2. 16 : ἐν πείρᾳ γενέσθαι *to have been well acquainted with*, i. 9. 1 (cf. ἐμπείρως) : πεῖραν λαμβάνειν *to take* or *have experience, make trial*, v. 8. 15. Der. EM-PIRIC.
‡πειράω, άσω, πεπείρακα l., comm. *M., to try, endeavor, attempt; to make trial* or *proof of, test;* I., G., ὅπως : i. 1.7 ; 2. 21: iii. 2. 3, 38s ; 5. 7. Der. PIRATE, EM-PIRICAL.
πεῖσας, πεισθείς, -θῶ, see πείθω.
Πεισίδης, see Πισίδης, i. 1. 11 ?
πείσομαι, f. m. of πάσχω & πείθω, i. 3. 5 s, 15.
πειστέον ἐστίν, (πείθομαι) *one* (*we, they*, &c.) *must obey*, 682, D.: ὡς π. εἴη Κλεάρχῳ *that C. must be obeyed:* ii. 6. 8 : vi. 6. 14.
πελάζω,* πελάσω πελῶ, ch. poet., (πέλας *near*) *to come near, approach*, D., i. 8. 15 ? iv. 2. 3.
Πελληνεύς, έως, *a Pellenian*, a man of Pellēne (Πελλήνη), an ancient town of Achaia and the most easterly of its twelve cities, v. 2. 15. ǁ Tzerkoví near Zugrá.
†Πελοποννήσιος,a,ον,*Peloponnesian:* οἱ Πελοποννήσιοι subst., *the Peloponnesians*, who were in general accounted the best soldiers in Greece, and who often, especially from the more mountainous parts, carried their vigor and bravery to a foreign market : i. 1. 6 : vi. 2. 10.
Πελοπόννησος, ου, ή, (Πέλοπος νῆσος, the island of Pelops), *the Peloponnese* or *-ēsus*, so named from its being so nearly surrounded by water, and from the sovereignty exercised over it by Pelops, an ancient king of Pisa in Elis, who, with his family, formed the subject of many myths and tragedies. i. 4. 2. ǁ Morea.
πελτάζω, άσω, (πέλτη) *to carry a target, serve as a targeteer*, v. 8. 5.
Πέλται, ῶν, αἱ, *Peltæ*, a city in the western part of Phrygia, i. 2. 10. ǁ On or near the plain Baklan-Ováh.
†πελταστής, οῦ, *a targeteer, peltast*. The πελτασταί not only carried a lighter shield (πέλτη), but were in other respects more lightly armed than the ὁπλῖται ; and were therefore less adapted to the shock of arms, but better fitted for rapid movements. i. 2. 6, 9 ; 7. 10 ; 10. 7.
†πελταστικός, ή, όν, *relating to* or *consisting of peltasts :* πελταστικόν, sc. στράτευμα, *light-armed force, light infantry, targeteers*, i. 8. 5 : vii. 3. 37.
πέλτη, ης, *a target, targe,* or *pelta*, a small, light shield, often of crescent shape, more used by the Thracians and other barbarians than by the Greeks. It had comm. a wooden (often wicker) frame, covered with leather, and sometimes strengthened by a thin metallic front. i. 10. 12 (acc. to some, here = παλτόν, which Rehdantz substitutes) : v. 2. 29.
†πεμπταῖος, α, ον, *on the fifth day, five days dead*, vi. 4. 9.
πέμπτος, η, ον, (πέντε) *fifth*, iii. 4. 24 : iv. 7. 21.
πέμπω,* ψω, πέπομφα, *to send*, D. A. P. (esp. fut. 598 b), εἰς, παρά, πρός, &c., i. 1. 8 ; 3. 8, 14 : ii. 1. 2, 17. Der. POMP, POMPOUS.
†πένης, ητος, ὁ, adj., *poor :* subst., *a poor man :* vii. 7. 28.
†πενία, as, *poverty*, vii. 6. 20. Cogn. penūria, *penury*.
πένομαι, in pr. and ipf., *to toil for daily bread, be poor, live in poverty*, iii. 2. 26. [*hundred*, i. 2. 3s, 6.
†πεντακόσιοι, αι, α, (ἑκατόν) *five-* πέντε indecl., quinque, *five*, i. 2. 8, 11. Der. PENTA-GON.

LEX. AN. 5*

πεντεκαίδεκα 106 περιίστημι

†πεντε-καί-δεκα (or πέντε καί δέκα) indecl., *fif-teen*, i. 4. 1 : iv. 7. 16.
†πεντήκοντα indecl., *fifty*, i. 4. 19 ; 7. 12 : ii. 2. 6. Der. PENTECOST.
†πεντηκοντήρ, ῆρος, ὁ, *a commander of fifty*, or of half a lochus, iii. 4. 21.
†πεντηκόντ-opos, ου, ἡ, (ἐρέττω *to row*) *a fifty-oared vessel* [sc. ναῦς], v. 1. 15 : vi. 6. 5, 22 s.
†πεντηκοστύς, ύος, ἡ, *a body of fifty*, or half a lochus : κατά π. *by fifties*, iii. 4. 22.
πέπαμαι, see πάομαι, iii. 3. 18.
πέπονθα, see πάσχω, iii. 2. 8 : vi. 1. 6.
πέπρακα, -ᾱσομαι, see πιπράσκω.
πέπτωκα, see πίπτω, i. 8. 28.
πέρ * encl., (root or shorter form of περί, cf. Lat. per) orig. *through, throughout;* hence, *altogether, just, very, even, indeed, particularly, in particular;* often added to a relative or particle for strength or emphasis (comm. written as part of the same word, but sometimes separately) ; i. 3. 18 ; 7. 9 ; 8. 18 : see εἴπερ, ὅσπερ, &c.
†πέρᾱ adv., *across, beyond;* of time, *beyond, past, after, after this;* G., vi. 1. 28 ; 5. 7.
†περαίνω, ανῶ, (πέρας *an end*) *to finish, complete, accomplish, execute*, A., iii. 1. 47 ; 2. 32 : vi. 1. 18.
†περαιόω, ώσω, *to carry across : M. to go across, pass over*, εἰς, vii. 2. 12.
†πέρᾱν adv., *across, on the other side*, G. : τὸ πέραν *the other side :* i. 5. 10 : iii. 5. 2, 12 : iv. 3. 29, 33.
†περάω, άσω, πεπέρᾱκα, *to cross*, A., iv. 3. 21 : v. l. διαπεράω.
Πέργαμον or -ος, ου, τό or ἡ, *Pergamum* or -*us*, the chief city of Teuthrania in southwest Mysia, situated in the beautiful valley of the Caïcus. It later became the capital of a kingdom, and renowned for its great library, giving its name to a material which was here brought into use, *parchment* (charta Pergamēna). This was also the seat of one of the Apocalyptic churches. vii. 8. 8, 23. ‖ Bergama, still a place of some consequence.
πέρδιξ, ῐκος, ὁ ἡ, perdix, *a PARTRIDGE*, i. 5. 3.
περί * prep., (πέρ per) *through* the circuit, *around, about:* (a) w. GEN. of theme (that which discourse, thought, or action is concerned about), *about, concerning, respecting, in respect*

to, for, i. 2. 8 ; 5. 8 ? 6. 6 : ii. 1. 12, 21 s : expressing valuation, as, w. ποιεῖσθαι, περὶ παντός [concerning every interest] *of all* or *the utmost concern* or *moment, all-important*, περὶ πλείονος or πλείστου *of more* or *the most account, value,* or *consequence, of greater (higher)* or *the greatest (highest) importance,* i. 9. 7, 16 : v. 6. 22 : — (b) w. DAT. of a part of the body, *around, about,* i. 5. 8 : vii. 4. 4 : — (c) w. ACC., *around, about ;* sometimes translated *with, among, towards, against, on the banks of, in respect to, in behalf of,* &c. : of place, i. 6. 4 : iv. 4. 3 ; 5. 8, 36 : of person, i. 2. 12 ; 4. 8 ; 5. 7 s ; οἱ περὶ Ἀριαῖον A. *and those with him,* ii. 4. 2, cf. ἀμφί, 527 a, and iv. 5. 21 : of time, i. 7. 1 : of object of concern, relation, &c., iii. 2. 20 : v. 7. 33 : vi. 6. 31 ; εἶναι περί *to be busy about*, iii. 5. 7 : — (d) in compos. as above, and also denoting superiority (the greater surrounding the less). Cf. ἀμφί.

περι-βάλλω,* βαλῶ, βέβληκα, 2 a. ἔβαλον, *to throw one's arms around, embrace,* A., iv. 7. 25 : *M. to throw round one's self* or *one's self around, to surround,* A., vi. 3. 3 : vii. 4. 17.
περι-γίγνομαι,* γενήσομαι, γεγένημαι, 2 pf. γέγονα, 2 a. ἐγενόμην, *to become superior to, prevail over, overcome, conquer,* G.; *to come round, turn out, result,* ὥστε : i. 1. 10 : v. 8. 26.
περι-δέω,* δήσω, δέδεκα, *to tie round,* iv. 5. 36 : v. l. —
περι-ειλέω,* ἥσω, or περι-ίλλω, (εἰλέω or εἰλέω *to roll, wrap*) *to wrap* or *tie around,* iv. 5. 36 : v. l. περιδέω.
περί-ειμι,* ἔσομαι, (εἰμί) *to be superior, excel, surpass, exceed, prevail,* G., i. 8. 13 ; 9. 24 : iii. 4. 33.
περί-ειμι,* ipf. ᾔειν, (εἶμι) *to go round* or *about,* A., iv. 1. 3 : vii. 1. 33.
περι-έλκω,* ἕλξω, ipf. εἷλκον, *to drag round* or *about,* 2 A., vii. 6. 10 (περιεῖλε has robbed, Ed. C. H. Weise).
περι-έρχομαι,* ἐλεύσομαι, ἐλήλυθα, 2 a. ἦλθον, *to go around,* vi. 3. 14 ?
περι-έχω,* ἕξω or σχήσω, ἔσχηκα, 2 a. ἔσχον, *to surround, encompass, protect,* A., i. 2. 22.
περι-ῇν, -ῇσαν, see περί-ειμι (εἰμί).
περι-ιᾱσι, -ιόντες, see περί-ειμι (εἶμι).
περι-ιδεῖν, see περι-οράω, vii. 7. 40.
περι-ίστημι,* στήσω, ἔστηκα (2 pf. pt. ἑστώς), 2 a. ἔστην, *to station round :*

περικυκλόω 107 Περσικός

pf. and 2 a. *to stand round,* iv. 7. 2 : vi. 6. 6.

περι-κυκλόω, ώσω, κεκύκλωκα, *to encircle : M. to gather in a circle round, surround,* A., vi. 3. 11.

περι-λαμβάνω,* λήψομαι, είληφα, 2 a. έλαβον, *to throw one's arms around, embrace,* A., vii. 4. 10.

περι-μένω,* μενώ, μεμένηκα, a. έμεινα, *to stay about, remain, wait; to wait for, await,* A.; ii. 1. 3, 6 ; 4. 1.

†Περίνθιος, ου, ό, *a Perinthian,* vii. 2. 8 ; a man of

Πέρινθος, ου, ή, *Perinthus,* a flourishing city of Thrace on the north shore of the Propontis, a Samian colony, later renowned for its obstinate defence against Philip of Macedon, ii. 6. 2 : vii. 2. 8. || Eregli, from a later name Ἡράκλεια.

πέριξ adv., (περί) *round about, around,* G., ii. 5. 14 : vii. 8. 12.

περί-οδος, ου, ή, a *way round, circuit,* iii. 4. 7, 11. Der. PERIOD.

περι-οικέω, ήσω, ῴκηκα, *to dwell around,* A., v. 6. 16.

περί-οικος, ου, ό, *a provincial, one of the Periœci,* v. 1. 15: see Σπάρτη.

περι-οράω,* ὄψομαι, ἑώρακα or ἑόρακα, 2 a. είδον, *to look about, see with indifference, overlook, neglect, allow,* A. P., vii. 3. 3 ; 7. 40, 46, 49.

περί-πατος, ου, ό, (πατέω *to walk*) *a walk round, walk* (both the act and the place), ii. 4. 15. Cogn. PERIPATETIC.

περι-πεσεῖν, see περι-πίπτω, i. 8. 28.

περι-πέτομαι,* πτήσομαι, *to fly about,* vi. 1. 23 : *v. l.* πέτομαι.

περι-πήγνῡμι,* πήξω, πέπηχα 1., *to freeze about,* trans.: *P. to be frozen about* or *on the feet,* iv. 5. 14.

περι-πίπτω,* πεσοῦμαι, πέπτωκα, 2 a. έπεσον, *to fall* or *throw one's self about* or *upon, to fall on and embrace; to fall foul of;* D.; i. 8. 28 : vii. 3. 38.

περι-πλέω,* πλεύσομαι, πέπλευκα, *to sail round,* i. 2. 21 : vii. 1. 20.

περι-ποιέω, ήσω, πεποίηκα, *A. & M.* (as for one's self), *to work round, manage to procure, acquire, gain,* A. D., v. 6. 17.

περι-πτύσσω, ύξω, *to fold round, enfold, enclose,* i. 10. 9.

περι-ῥρέω,* ῥεύσομαι & ῥυήσομαι, ἐρρύηκα, *to flow round, encompass,* A., i. 5. 4 : 2 a. *p.* or *a.* περι-ἐρρύην *to*

drop off, as water flowing about an object, D., iv. 3. 8 ; *v. l.* —

περι-ῥρήγνῡμι, ῥήξω, ἔρρηχα 1., 2 a. *p.* ἐρράγην, *to break around,* trans.: M., w. 2 a. *p., to break around,* intrans., iv. 3. 8 : *v. l.* περιρρέω.

περι-σταυρόω, ώσω, *to fence* or *palisade about,* A., vii. 4. 14.

περιστερά, ᾶς, *a dove, pigeon,* held sacred by the Syrians from the tradition that the great queen Semiramis was nourished as an infant by doves, and at death changed into a dove, i. 4. 9.

†περιττεύω or περισσεύω, εύσω, *to reach beyond, outflank,* G., iv. 8. 11.

περιττός or περισσός, ή, όν, (περί) *over and above, superfluous, spare,* iii. 2. 38 : vii. 6. 31: οἱ περιττοί *the men* or *forces beyond,* iv. 8. 11 : τὸ περιττόν *the surplus, residue,* v. 3. 13.

περι-τυγχάνω,* τεύξομαι, τετύχηκα, 2 a. έτυχον, *to happen about, happen to be near, meet,* vi. 6. 7.

περι-φανῶς (περι-φανής *seen around,* fr. φαίνω) *conspicuously, evidently, manifestly,* iv. 5. 4.

περι-φέρω,* οἴσω, ἐνήνοχα, *to carry round,* A., vii. 3. 24. Der. PERIPHERY.

περί-φοβος, ον, *greatly alarmed, much terrified, in great alarm* or *terror,* iii. 1. 12.

Πέρσης, ου, ό, *a Persian,* one of a people early restricted to the country of Persis (Περσίς, in its native form *Parsa,* whence the modern *Fars*) northeast of the Persian Gulf and south of Media, but by successive conquests extending their power "from India even unto Ethiopia, over an hundred and seven and twenty provinces" (Esther, 1. 1), an empire far greater than any before presented in history. In the time of Xen., the Persians had lost their early simplicity and vigor, and soon after fell an easy prey to the arms of Alexander. After their unsuccessful attempts to conquer Greece in the reigns of Darius and Xerxes, they interfered in Greek affairs chiefly by their money, which they employed in subsidizing states and corrupting public men. i. 2. 20 (as adj.); 5. 8.

‡Περσίζω, ίσω ιῶ, *to speak Persian,* iv. 5. 34.

‡Περσικός, ή, όν, *Persian:* τὸ Περσικὸν [sc. ὄρχημα] ὀρχεῖσθαι *to dance*

Περσιστί 108 πλαίσιον

the Persian [dance], also called ὄκλασμα from the dancer's often sinking upon the knee: i. 2. 27; 8. 21: iii. 3. 16; 4. 17: vi. 1. 10.

‡Περσιστί adv., in the Persian language, in Persian, iv. 5. 10.

περυσινός, ή, όν, (πέρυσι a year ago) of the last year, last year's, v. 4. 27 ?

πεσεῖν, -ών, see πίπτω, iii. 1. 11.

πέταλον, ου, (πετάννῦμι to expand) a leaf, v. 4. 12. Der. PETAL.

πέτομαι,* πετήσομαι, usu. πτήσομαι, 2 a. ἐπτόμην & ἐπτάμην, to fly, i. 5. 3: vi. 1. 23 (v. l. περιπέτομαι).

†πέτρα, as, a rock ; a mass of rock, large stone ; i. 4. 4 : iv. 2. 3, 20 ? 7. 4, 10 ? 14. Der. PETRI-FY, PETR-OLEUM.

†πετρο-βολία, as, (βάλλω) the throwing of stones, stoning, vi. 6. 15.

πέτρος, ου, ὁ, a stone, iv. 2. 20 ? 7. 12 : vii. 7. 54. Der. PETER.

πεφ- in redupl. for φεφ-, 159 a.

πεφυλαγμένως (fr. pf. p. pt. of φυλάττω) guardedly, cautiously, ii. 4. 24.

πῆ, πῇ, πή, or πῄ, also encl., (πός) in some or any way, by any means; πῇ μὲν .. πῇ δέ, in one view or respect .. in another, on some accounts .. on others, partly .. partly: iii. 1. 12? iv. 8. 11 : vi. 1. 20 (δ' αὖ for πῇ δέ) ?

πηγή, ῆς, a fountain, spring, source, comm. in pl., i. 2. 7 s; 4. 10 : iv. 1. 3.

πήγνῡμι,* πήξω, πέπηχα l., (2 pf. πέπηγα am fixed), to make fast or solid, stiffen, freeze, benumb with cold, A., iv. 5. 3 : P. & M. to be frozen, freeze (intrans.), vii. 4. 3.

πηδάλιον, ου, (πηδόν an oar) a broad steering-oar or rudder (the Greek vessel comm. having two, one on each side of the stern, but often connected by a cross-bar), v. 1. 11.

πηλός, οῦ, ὁ, mud, mire, i. 5. 7 s : ii. 3. 11.

πῆχυς, εως, ὁ, a cubit, = 1½ Greek feet, iv. 7. 16.

Πίγρης, ητος, ὁ, Pigres, an interpreter to Cyrus, prob. a Carian, i. 2. 17; 5. 7; 8. 12.

πιέζω, έσω, to press, oppress, A.: P. to be hard pressed, pressed or crowded together, oppressed or weighed down, i. 1. 10 : iii. 4. 19, 27, 48 : iv. 8. 13.

πικρός, ά, όν, bitter, iv. 4. 13.

πίμπλημι,* πλήσω, πέπληκα, (πλέως full) to fill, A. G., i. 5. 10.

πίνω,* πίομαι (ῑ), πέπωκα, 2 a. ἔπιον, poto, to drink, A., iv. 5. 32 : vi. 1. 4; 4. 11. Der. POTATION, SYM-POSIUM.

πιπράσκω,* πέπρᾱκα, f. pf. πεπράσομαι, (pr. a. comm. supplied by πωλέω, and f. and aor. by ἀποδώσομαι, ἀπεδόμην) to sell, A. G. of price, vii. 1. 36 ; 2. 6 ; 7. 26 ; 8. 6.

πίπτω,* πεσοῦμαι, πέπτωκα, 2 a. ἔπεσον, to fall, εἰς : to fall in battle, be slain : i. 8. 28 : ii. 3. 18: iii. 1. 11: iv. 5. 7. Der. A-PTOTE, DI-PTOTE.

Πισίδης or Πεισίδης, ου, a Pisidian. The Pisidæ were a race of bold, tameless robbers, occupying the western range of Mt. Taurus, where, in their mountain fastnesses, they long maintained their independence, and annoyed their neighbors by their ravages. The important but difficult work of their subjugation seemed a proper object for an expedition by Cyrus. The present occupants of this region have a marked resemblance to them. i. 1. 11 ; 2. 1 ; 9. 14.

†πιστεύω, εύσω, πεπίστευκα, to trust, believe, confide in, rely upon, D. I. (A.), i. 2. 2 ; 3. 16 ; 9. 8 : vii. 7. 25.

πίστις, εως, ἡ, (πείθω) faith, confidence, trust ; good faith, fidelity ; a ground of confidence, an assurance, pledge ; i. 2. 26 ; 6. 3 : iii. 2. 8 ; 3. 4.

πιστός, ή, όν, c., s., (πείθω) that may be trusted, trusty, trustworthy, faithful, devoted ; trusted, confidential, in one's confidence ; D.: οἱ πιστοί, a special term for the trusty or confidential attendants or officers of a Persian prince : i. 4. 15 ; 5. 15 ; 6. 3 : ii. 5. 22 : πιστά subst., trustworthy things, tokens of good faith, pledges, assurances, solemn sanctions, I. (A.), i. 6. 7: ii. 3. 26 ; 4. 7 ; iv. 8. 7 s.

‡πιστότης, ητος, ἡ, faithfulness, fidelity, i. 8. 29.

πίτυς, υος, ἡ, pīnus, a pine-tree, pine, iv. 7. 6.

πλάγιος, α, ον, (πλάγος side) in a side direction, slanting, oblique : εἰς πλάγιον obliquely : εἰς τὰ πλάγια to or against the sides or flanks, to the right and left : i. 8. 10 : iii. 4. 14.

πλαίσιον, ου, (akin to πλατύς) a rectangle ; of troops, a square. This square, which could present a front to the enemy on each side, might be either hollow, or filled with troops, or, as was common on a harassed

πλανάομαι   109   ποθέν

march, occupied in the centre by the camp-followers and baggage. i. 8. 9: iii. 2. 36; 4. 19, 43.

πλανάομαι, ήσομαι, πεπλάνημαι, (πλάνη a wandering) to wander about, i. 2. 25: v. 1. 7. Der. PLANET.

πλάτος, εος, τό, (πλατύς) width, breadth, v. 4. 32. Cog. PLAT, PLATE.

πλάττω, πλάσω, πέπλακα 1., to mould, shape: M. to fabricate, frame, invent, e.g. falsehoods, 582 γ, A., ii. 6. 26. Der. PLASTIC, PLASTER.

πλατύς, εῖα, ύ, c. ύτερος, wide, broad, iii. 4. 22. Der. PLATY-PUS.

†πλεθριαῖος, α, ον, extending a hundred feet, i. 5. 4; 7. 15: iv. 6. 4.

πλέθρον, ου, a plethron or plethrum, a hundred feet (in our measure, about 101 ft., 1½ in.), i. 2. 5, 23: iii. 4. 9.

πλείων or πλέων more, πλεῖστος most, see πολύς, i. 1. 6; 3. 7.

πλέκω,* έξω, plecto, plico, to plait, braid, A., iii. 3. 18. Der. COM-PLEX.

πλεον-εκτέω, ήσω, πεπλεονέκτηκα, (πλέον ἔχω) to have or get more, have the advantage, gain the ascendency, G. D. of respect, iii. 1. 37: v. 4. 15.

πλευρά, ᾶς, a rib (pl. side or sides); a side or flank of an army: iii.2.36s: iv. 1. 18; 7. 4. Der. PLEURISY.

πλέω,* πλεύσομαι or -σοῦμαι, πέπλευκα, a. ἔπλευσα, to sail, go by sea, ἐν, πρός, &c., i. 7. 15; 9. 17: v. 1. 10.

πλέων, πλέον, see πολύς, i. 2. 11.

πληγή, ῆς, (πλήττω) plāga, a blow, i. 5. 11: ii. 4. 11. Der. PLAGUE.

†πλῆθος, εος, τό, fulness, abundance, multitude; great quantity, extent, or number; amount, total, number or numbers; the multitude, mass, main or common body; i. 5. 9; 7. 4; 8. 13: iii. 1. 37: iv. 4. 8: v. 5. 4.

πλήθω in pr. and fut, (πλέως full) to be full, i. 8. 1: ii. 1. 7: see ἀγορά, πίμπλημι. Der. PLETHORIC.

πλήν* (πλέον more than) adv. as prep., except, save, G., i. 1. 6; 8. 6: —conj., except, but; except that, save that; i. 2. 24: 8. 20, 25; 9. 29.

πλήρης, ες, (πλέως full) plēnus, full, com-plete, filled with, abounding in, G., i. 2. 7; 4. 9; 5. 1; 8. 9: ii. 3. 10: vii. 5. 5. Cog. PLENARY, PLENTY.

†πλησιάζω, άσω, πεπλησίακα, to come or draw near, approach, D., i. 5. 2: iv. 6. 6: vi. 5. 26.

[πλησίος, α, ον, poet., near:] hence adv. πλησίον, near, nigh, close by, G., i. 8. 1: v. 2. 11: also used w. the art. as an adj. (c. πλησιαίτερος, s. -αίτατος), near, neighboring, nearest, D., i. 10. 5: ii. 4. 16: iv. 8. 13: — fr. πέλας near.

πλήττω,* πλήξω, 2 pf. πέπληγα, 2 a. p. ἐπλήγην, to strike, smite, wound, A., v. 8. 2, 4, 12: vi. 1. 5 (stronger than παίω). Der. APO-PLEXY.

†πλίνθινος, η, ον, made or built of brick, iii. 4. 11.

πλίνθος, ου, ἡ, a brick, whether baked by fire or dried in the sun, ii. 4. 12: iii. 4. 7. Der. PLINTH.

πλοῖον, ου, (πλέω) a vessel, esp. a merchant or transport vessel, more oval in form than the ship of war (ναῦς or τριήρης) and chiefly propelled by sails; a ship of burden, transport; a boat, (as for fishing, crossing or bridging a river, &c.), canoe; i. 2. 5; 4. 7 s, 18; 7. 15: v. 4. 11: μακρὸν π. a long vessel, i. e. ship of war, in distinction from the rounder ship of burden, v. 1. 11.

πλόος, ου, contr. πλοῦς, οῦ, ὁ, (πλέω) a voyage, sailing; hence, sing. and pl., weather for sailing: G., εἰς, ἐξ: v. 7. 7: vi. 1. 33; 4. 2.

[-πλοος -fold, akin to πλέκω, 240. 4.]

†πλούσιος, α, ον, c., rich, wealthy, i. 9. 16: vii. 3. 18; 7. 28.

‡πλουσίως adv., in wealth, iii. 2. 26?

†πλουτέω, ήσω, πεπλούτηκα, to be or become rich, to possess or acquire wealth, G., i. 9. 19: ii. 6. 21: vii. 7. 9, 28, 42.

†πλουτίζω, ίσω ιῶ, πεπλούτικα, to make rich, enrich, A., vii. 6. 9.

[πλοῦτος, ου, ὁ, (πλέος full) wealth, riches. Der. PLUTUS.]

†πνεῦμα, ατος, τό, wind, breath, iv. 5. 4: vi. 1. 14; 2. 1. Der. PNEUMATICS.

πνέω,* πνεύσομαι, πέπνευκα, to blow, breathe, v. 5. 3. Der. DYS-PNŒA.

πνίγω,* ξω, to choke, drown, A., v. 7. 25.

πο-δαπός, ή, όν, (πός; & δάπεδον ground, or ἀπό) cujas? of what country? iv. 4. 17.

†ποδ-ήρης, ες, (ἀρ-) reaching to the feet, i. 8. 9.

†ποδίζω, ίσω ιῶ, to fasten by the feet, fetter, iii. 4. 35.

ποδός, ποδῶν, &c., see πούς, i. 2. 8.

πόθεν; (πός;) unde, whence? v. 4. 7.

ποθέν encl., (πός) from any place or quarter, vi. 3. 15.

†ποθέω, ήσω, πεπόθηκα 1., *to long, earnestly desire, be anxious,* I., vi. 4. 8.
πόθος, ου, ό, *fond desire, longing for,* G., iii. 1. 3.
ποί encl., (πός) *to some* or *any place, in any direction, some-* or *any-where* (= *-whither*), v. 1. 8: vi. 3. 10.
ποιέω, ήσω, πεποίηκα, *to MAKE* or *DO,* but translated variously acc. to the connection: thus, *to MAKE, form, construct, erect, appoint, render, iustitute, organize ; to cause, produce, secure, give, iuduce, influeuce, enable* (π. μή *to prevent*); to make in fancy, *suppose ;* A. D., 2 A. (or A. & adj.), I. (A.), ὥστε: i. 1. 2 ; 6. 2, 6 ; 7. 4, 7 : iv. 1. 22 : v. 7. 9 : vi. 4. 9 ; π. ἐκκλησίαν *to call an assembly,* i. 4. 12 ; φόβον π. *to strike terror,* i. 8. 18 : — *to DO, perform, accomplish, effect, execute ; to do* (good, evil, &c.), *bestow, inflict ; to act, proceed ;* AE. (esp. neut. adj.) A., D.; i. 1. 11 ; 5. 2, 7 ; 9. 11: iv. 2. 23; w. εὖ, κακῶς, &c., *to treat, serve, do* well or ill *by, do* good or evil *to, benefit, injure,* &c., A., i. 4. 8 ; 6. 9 : —— *M. to MAKE or DO for one's self, make one's own ;* in general like the act., but more subjective, and oftener used with an acc. as =. a verb cognate w. the acc. (ἐξέτασιν ποιεῖσθαι or ποιεῖν *to make a review, to review,* i. 2. 9, 14); A., 2 A.; i. 1. 6; 7. 2, 20 ; 9. 20 : iv. 5. 28 : σπονδὰς ποιεῖν *to offer a libation,* but σπονδὰς ποιεῖσθαι to offer a libation together, *to make a treaty* or *truce,* ii. 3. 8 : iv. 3. 14 : — *to cause to be made, have* or *procure made,* A., 581, v. 3. 5 : — *to put, place, bring, set, station, form,* ch. in expressing military position or arrangement, A., i. 6. 9 ; 10. 9 : vi. 5. 5 s, 18, 25 ; ὀρθίους ποιεῖσθαι or ποιεῖν *to form in columns,* iv. 8. 10, 12, 14 s ; τριχῇ ποιεῖσθαι *to form in three divisions,* iv. 8. 15 (cf. δίχα) ; ἐν ἀπορρήτῳ ποιεῖσθαι *to put under seal of secrecy,* vii. 6. 43 : — in expressing value, to make to one's self, *make of account, esteem, regard, account,* A., I. περί, παρά, i. 9. 7, 16 : ii. 3. 18 : vi. 1. 11 ; 6. 11. Der. POEM, POET.
‡ποιητέος, α, ον, to be or *that must be made* or *done* (one must make or do), D. A., i. 3. 15 : iii. 1. 18, 35 : vi. 4. 12.
ποικίλος, η, ον, *variegated, many-colored, embroidered, tattooed,* i. 5. 8.

ποῖος, α, ον, interrog., (πός ;) quālis ? *of what kind ? what kind* or *state of ? what ?* ii. 5. 7, 13 : iii. 1. 14.
† πολεμέω, ήσω, πεπολέμηκα, *to war, make* or *carry on war, be at war, perform in war,* D. AE., πρός or ἐπί, i. 1. 5, 8 s ; 3. 4 ; 6. 1, 6 : iv. 1. 1.
†πολεμικός, ή, όν, s., *warlike, skilled* or *able in war, fitted for war,* ii. 6. 1, 7 : τὰ π. *warlike affairs,* iii. 1. 38 : σημαίνειν τὸ π. *to give the signal for attack, sound the charge,* iv. 3. 29 : ἀνέκραγε πολεμικόν *gave a war-shout,* vii. 3. 33. Der. POLEMICS.
‡ πολεμικῶς, s. ὤτατα, *hostilely :* π. ἔχειν *to be hostile* or *on terms of hostility,* vi. 1. 1.
†πολέμιος, α, ον, c., s., *relating to war ; hostile, at war with ; belonging to an enemy, of enemies, the enemy's :* subst. πολέμιος *an enemy,* οἱ π. *the enemy,* ἡ πολεμία [sc. χώρα] *the enemy's country,* τὰ π. *the affairs of war* or *military affairs :* D., G.: i. 2. 19 ; 4. 5 ; 5. 16 ; 6. 1: iii. 3. 5 : iv. 7. 19s.
πόλεμος, ου, ὁ, (πολέω *to haunt*) bellum, *war, warfare,* πρός : τὰ εἰς τὸν π. ἔργα *warlike exercises :* ὁ θεῶν π. *the hostility of the gods :* i. 6. 6 ; 9. 5, 14 : ii. 5. 7 : iii. 2. 8 : iv. 4. 1.
†πολίζω, ίσω ιῶ, *to build up into a city, colonize,* A., vi. 6. 4.
†πολι-ορκέω, ήσω, (εἴργω) *to hem in a city, besiege, invest, beleaguer, blockade,* A., i. 1. 7; 4. 2 : iii. 4. 8: iv. 2. 15.
πόλις, εως, ἡ, (akin to πολύς) *a city, town,* comm. fortified, and often distinguished in the Anab. as inhabited or deserted (several cities on the route being in the latter condition from war or political changes); a body of citizens, *state ; a citadel* (the Acropolis at Athens being sp. so called); i. 1. 6, 8s : ii. 6. 13 : vii. 1. 27. Der. NA-PLES.
‡πόλισμα, ατος, τό, (πολίζω) that which is built up like a city, *a city, town,* usu. of the smaller size, iv. 7. 17.
‡πολιτεύω, εύσω, *to be a citizen, live* or *dwell* as a citizen, iii. 2. 26.
‡πολίτης, ου, *a citizen,* v. 3. 9 s. Der. POLITICS.
†πολλάκις *many times, often, frequently, repeatedly,* i. 2. 11: vii. 3. 41.
†πολλα-πλάσιος, α, ον, (πλάττω *to form*) *manifold, manifold more ; many times as much, many,* or *numerous :* πολλαπλάσιοι ὑμῶν *many times your*

πολλαχῇ 111 πορίζω

own number: i. 7. 3 : iii. 2. 14, 16 : vii. 7. 25, 27.

†πολλαχῇ or -χῇ *in many places or cases, often,* vii. 3. 12.

†πολλαχοῦ *in many places, on many occasions, often,* iv. 1. 28.

†πολυ-άνθρωπος, ον, *populous,* ii. 4.13.

†πολυ-αρχία, ας, (ἄρχω) *a command vested in many, multiplicity of command, many commanders,* vi. 1. 18.

†Πολυ-κράτης, εος, *Polycrates,* a trusted and useful lochage from Athens, iv. 5. 24: *v. l.* Πολυβώτης or -βάτης.

†Πολύ-νῖκος, ου, *Polynicus,* an envoy to the Cyreans from the Spartan commander Thibron, vii. 6. 1, 39.

†πολυ-πραγμονέω, ήσω, (πρᾶγμα) to *be busy about many things. meddle, intrigue,* A.E.: π. τι *to engage in some intrigue,* v. 1. 15.

πολύς,* πολλή, πολύ, c. πλείων or πλέων, s. πλεῖστος, (akin to πλέως *full) much; many or numerous,* ch. in pl.; also, acc. to the subject, *large, great, in great quantity or numbers, in abundance, abundant, plentiful, extensive, long, deep, loud,* &c.; i. 1. 6 ; 2. 18 ; 3. 2, 7, 14 ; 7. 4 : sometimes pleonastically used or followed by καί q. v., 702 c, ii. 5. 9 ; 3. 18 : iv. 6. 27 (cf. iii. 5. 1): πολλοί *many,* οἱ πολλοί *the many, the most, the majority,* iii. 1. 3, 10 : πολλή, sc. ὁδός, *a long way or journey,* vi. 3. 16 : οἱ πλεῖστοι or πλεῖστοι (533 e) plurimi, *the most* (also π. *very many*), i. 5. 2, 13 : — πολύ subst. or adv., *much, a great part, greatly, very, a great distance, far, long; so* πολύ or πολλῷ often w. the compar.; ἐκ πολλοῦ, sc. διαστήματος, *from a distance;* i. 5. 2 s: ii. 5. 32 : iii. 3. 9 : iv. 1. 11 : see ἄξιος, ἐπί : τὸ πολύ *the much, the* [great] *greater part, the most,* i. 4. 13 : vii. 7. 36 : ὡς ἐπὶ τὸ πολύ *as things are for the most part, commonly,* 711, iii. 1. 42 s ? πολλά *many things, much, often, διὰ πολλά for many reasons,* i. 9. 22 : iv. 3. 2 : — πλεῖον or πλέον plus, subst. or adj. (often as indecl. 507 e), or adv., *more,* i. 2. 11 ; 4. 14 (by pleonasm) : ἐκ πλείονος *from a greater distance, sooner,* i. 10. 11 : — πλεῖστον or πλεῖστα subst. or adv., *the most, farthest; very much;* most or very plentifully: ii. 2. 12 : iii. 2. 31 : vii. 6. 35 ; 7. 1. See ποιέω. Der. POLY-GON, POLY-GLOT.

‡Πολύ-στρατος, ου, *Polystratus,* an Athenian, father of Lycius, iii. 3. 20.

‡πολυ-τελής, ές, (τέλος) *expensive, costly, rich,* i. 5. 8.

πόμα or πῶμα, ατος, τό, (πίνω) *a drink,* iv. 5. 27.

πομπή, ῆς, (πέμπω) *a sending forth, a solemn procession,* v. 5.5. Der. POMP.

†πονέω, ήσω, πεπόνηκα, *to labor, toil, incur toil, undergo hardship; to obtain by toil,* A.: i. 4. 14 : 9. 19 : ii. 6. 6 : vii. 6. 10, 41.

†πονηρός, ά, όν, *causing toil or hardship* (or in this sense πόνηρος); hence *bad, evil, disastrous, mischievous, wretched, worthless, troublesome, dangerous; base, vile, villanous, wicked, unprincipled, evil-disposed,* πρός : ii. 5. 21 : iii. 4. 19, 35 : vii. 1. 39 ; 4. 12.

†πονήρως or πονηρῶς, *with toil or difficulty,* iii. 4. 19.

πόνος, ου, ὁ, (πένομαι) *toil, labor, hardship, trouble, difficulty:* οἱ ἡμέτεροι π. *the fruits of our toil:* ii. 5. 18 : iii. 1. 12 : vii. 6. 9. Der. GEO-PONICS.

πόντος, ου, ὁ, *a sea or sea-basin* (while θάλαττα signifies rather the water of the sea, or the body of sea-water); hence, even *the region about a sea,* as its basin : ὁ Πόντος *the Pontus,* sp. used for ὁ Πόντος Εὔξεινος *the Euxine or Black Sea,* or its basin or surrounding region, iv. 8. 22 : v. 1. 1 ; 6. 15 s, 19 s. Der. PONTIC.

†πορεία, ας, *a journey, march, passage, course, route, way, mode of travelling:* τὴν π. ποιεῖσθαι *to make the march, pursue one's journey, to march, proceed:* i. 7. 20 : ii. 2. 10 : iii. 1. 5 ; 4. 36, 44 : iv. 4. 18 : v. 6. 12.

†πορευτέος, α, ον, *necessary to be passed or crossed, which one must cross,* D.: πορευτέον (ἐστίν) *it is necessary to march or proceed, one must,* &c., A.E.: ii. 2. 12 ; 5. 18 : iv. 1. 2 ; 5. 1.

πορεύω, εύσω, a. p. as m. ἐπορεύθην, (πόρος) *to make go, convey: M. to go, proceed, march, advance, set forth, journey, travel,* esp. by land, A.E., διά, ἐπί, παρά, πρός, &c., i. 2. 1, 4 ; 3. 4, 7 : ii. 2. 11 s, 14 : iii. 4. 46 : v. 3. 1.

πορθέω, ήσω, πεπόρθηκα, (πέρθω *to ravage) to ravage, lay waste, plunder,* A., v. 7. 14 : vii. 7. 3, 12.

†πορίζω, ίσω ιῶ, πεπόρικα, *to provide, supply, furnish, bestow,* A. D., ii. 3. 5 : iii. 3. 20 ; 5. 8 : — *M. to provide for one's*

πόρος 112 πρέσβυς

self, supply one's self with, procure, A., ii. 1. 6 : iii. 1. 20. Der. PORISM.
πόρος, ου, ὁ, (πέρα) a way across or through, passage, ford; hence, a resource, provision, means, πρός: ii. 5. 20: iv. 3. 13, 20. Der. PORE.
πόρρω (later for πρόσω, old Att. πόρσω, 104, 157) far from, G., 1. 3. 12.
πορφύριος, έα, εον, contr. οὖς, ᾶ, οὖν, (πορφύρα the purple-fish) purpureus, purple, i. 5. 8. Cog. PORPHYRY.
[πός an old indef. and interrog. pron., remaining in πού, ποῦ, πή, πῆ, &c.]
ποσί, see πούς, i. 5. 3.
πόσος, η, ον, interrog., (πός;) quantus? how much? how large or great? ii. 4. 21 : vii. 8. 1 : in exclam., vi. 5. 20 : πόσον; how far? vii. 3. 12.
ποταμός, οῦ, ὁ, (ποτός, as if drinkable water) a river, i. 2. 5, 7 s : see 522 i. Der. MESO-POTAMIA.
ποτέ encl. indef. adv., (πός) at some or any time, once, ever; sometimes strengthening a direct or indirect interrog., as ὅποι ποτέ where in the world; i. 5. 7 (δή π., also written δήποτε); 9. 6 : iii. 4. 10 (cf. 7) ; 5. 13.
πότερος, α, ον, (πός;) which of two? hence adv., πότερον or πότερα in inquiry between two suppositions (the second, which is connected by ἤ, being sometimes understood), whether, usu. expressed in Eng. in indirect question only (cf. Lat. utrum .. an), i. 4. 13 : ii. 1. 10, 21 ; 5. 17 : v. 8. 4.
‡ποτέρως in which way or on which supposition of two? εἰ .. ἤ εἰ, vii. 7. 30.
†ποτήριον, ου, a drinking-cup, vi. 1. 4.
ποτός, ή, όν, (πο- in πίνω) drinkable, POTABLE, to drink: subst. ποτόν or -ά drink: i. 10. 18 : ii. 3. 27 : iv. 5. 8?
‡πότος, ου, ὁ, a symposium or banquet, drinking, ii. 3. 15 : vii. 3. 26. Der. POTATION.
ποῦ interrog. adv., (πός;) ubi? where? ii. 4. 15 : v. 8. 2.
πού encl. indef. adv., (πός) somewhere, anywhere; hence, as a general indef., perhaps, I suppose; i. 2. 27 : ii. 3. 6: iv. 8. 21 (of time)? v. 7. 13.
πούς,* ποδός, ὁ, pes, Sans. pad, a FOOT: ἐπὶ πόδα ἀναχωρεῖν to retreat [stepping back upon the foot] facing the foe or without turning. As a measure of length, the standard Greek foot (the Olympic) was about ⅓ of an inch longer, while the Roman was about ⅓ of an inch shorter, than our own. i. 2. 8 ; 5. 3 : iv. 6. 12 : v. 2. 32. Der. ANTI-PODES, TRI-POD, POLY-PUS.
πρᾶγμα, ατος, τό, (πράττω) a thing done, deed, affair, event, occurrence, circumstance, case, matter: pl. affairs, state of affairs, business, troublesome business; hence, trouble, annoyance, difficulty: i. 1. 11 ; 3. 3 ; 5. 13 : iv. 1. 17 : vi. 3. 6. Der. PRAGMATIC.
‡πραγματεύομαι, εὔσομαι, πεπραγμάτευμαι, to be busy about, labor to effect, A., vii. 6. 35.
πρᾳέων, see πρᾶος, i. 4. 9.
πρανής, ές, (πρό) prōnus, inclined forward, PRONE; steep in descent: τὸ π. the steep, slope, place or ground below: i. 5. 8 : iii. 4. 25 : iv. 8. 28.
πρᾶξις, εως, ἡ, (πράττω) transaction, business, undertaking, enterprise, i. 3. 16, 18 : vi. 17. Der. PRAXIS.
πρᾶος (or πρᾷος),* πραεῖα, πρᾶον, gentle, tame, i. 4. 9.
πράττω, πράξω, πέπραχα, (περάω) to pass through an action, incident, or course of conduct or fortune ; to do, transact, PRACTISE, perform, effect; to manage, bargain, negotiate; to take or pursue a course; AE. διά, περί, &c.; i. 6. 6 : ii. 5. 21 : vii. 2. 12 :— to exact, DEMAND, require, 2 A., vii. 6. 17 :— to do for one's self, fare, succeed, eὖ or καλῶς, κακῶς, οὕτω, ἀγαθά, τάδε (as follows), &c., i. 9. 10 : iii. 1. 6 ; 4. 6 : vi. 3. 2 : ἃ πράττοι how he was succeeding, vii. 4. 21. Ποιέω refers rather to the effect produced, and πράττω to the occupation through which it is produced ; while ποιέω refers more to the effect produced upon another than πράττω. To express definite acts, ποιέω is more used ; but to express a course of action or fortune, πράττω. Der. PRACTICAL.
πρᾴως or πρᾴως, (πρᾶος) mildly, calmly, i. 5. 14.
πρέπω, έψω, to suit, become, beseem, ch. impers., D., I., i. 9. 6 : iii. 2. 7, 16.
†πρεσβεία, as, an embassy, vii. 3. 21.
†πρεσβευτής, οῦ, an ambassador, envoy, vi. 3. 10 : v. l. πρεσβύτης.
†πρεσβεύω, εύσω, πεπρέσβευκα, to be an ambassador or envoy, or to go, come, or act as one, D., παρά, ii. 1. 18 : vii. 2. 23 ; 7. 6.
πρέσβυς,* εως, υν, υ, pl. εις, ὁ (in sing. poet., 238 a), c. ὕτερος, s. ὕτατος,

πρεσβύτης 113 προέχω

(πρέπω?) old; as subst., (since old men were ch. so sent) an ambassador, envoy, deputy : c. older, elder, elderly; subst., an elder: s. oldest, eldest: i. 1. 1 s; 9. 5 : ii. 1.10 : iii. 1. 14, 28, 34. Der. PRESBYTER, PRIEST.
‡πρεσβύτης, ου, an old man, vi. 3. 10?
πρίασθαι, &c., to buy, see ὠνέομαι.
†πρίν* adv. or conj., prius, before, before that, ere, sooner than, until, even used after words already expressing precedence (πρόσθεν, φθάνω, &c.); commn. w. a finite mode after negation, but otherwise I.(A.), 703a; i. 1. 10 ; 2. 2, 26 ; 4. 13, 16 ; 8. 19 : ii. 5. 33 : iv. 5. 1 (πρὶν ἤ?), 30.
πρό* prep. w. gen., (cf. præ, pro) before : local, before, in front of (to protect, r. as a defence against, &c.), i. 2. 17; 4. 4 : vii.8.18 : — temporal, before, i.7.13 : — causal, &c., in behalf of, for, vii. 6. 27, 36 ; cf. vi. 1. 8. In compos., before, beforehand, previously, forward, forth, publicly, in behalf or defence of. — Hence, c. & s. adjectives πρό-τερος, (πρό-ατος) πρῶτος, q. v., 262 d ; cf. præ, prior, primus, fore, former, foremost or first. Der. PROPHET, PRO-EM.
προ-αγορεύω, εύσω, ἠγόρευκα, (commn. f. ἐρῶ, pf. εἴρηκα, 2 a. εἶπον) to say or announce before others, proclaim, publish, communicate publicly, A. D., ὅτι, i. 2. 17 : ii. 2. 20 : vii. 7. 13.
προ-άγω,* ἄξω, ἦχα, 2 a. ἤγαγον, to lead or proceed forward, advance, A., iv. 6. 21 : vi. 5. 6 s, 11.
προ-αιρέω,* ήσω, ἤρηκα, 2 a. εἷλον, to take before: M. to choose before, select, A., vi. 6. 19.
προ-αισθάνομαι,* θήσομαι, ἤσθημαι, 2 a. ἠσθόμην, to perceive or discover beforehand, A. P., i. 1. 7.
προ-αν-ᾱλίσκω,* -ᾱλώσω, -ηλωκα, to spend in advance, A., vi. 4. 8?
προ-απο-τρέπω,* έψω, τέτροφα, 2 a. m. ἐτραπόμην, to turn back previously, P., vi. 5. 31.
προ-άρχομαι, ἄρξομαι, ἦργμαι, to begin first or before the rest, I., i. 8. 17?
προ-βαίνω,* βήσομαι, βέβηκα, 2 a. ἔβην, to step or go forth or forward, advance, proceed, iii. 1. 13 : iv. 2. 28?
προ-βάλλω*, βαλῶ, βέβληκα, 2 a. ἔβαλον, to throw before: M. to throw before one's self; to bring forward, propose ; A.; π. τὰ ὅπλα to throw forward or hold forth one's arms, to present arms ; προβεβλημένος, sc. τὴν ἀσπίδα, having thrown his shield before, πρό· i. 2. 17: iv. 2. 21 : vi. 1. 25; 2. 6. Der. PRO-BLEM.
†προβάτιον, ου, dim., a small sheep, vi. 3. 22 : v. l. πρόβατον.
πρόβατον, ου, (προ-βαίνω) usu. pl., animals that go forth to pasture, cattle; ch. of small cattle, esp. sheep; ii. 4. 27 : iii. 5. 9 : vi. 3. 3, 32 ? 4. 22.
προ-βολή, ῆς, (προ-βάλλω) the presentation of arms, a charge, vi. 5. 25 ?
προ-βουλεύω, εύσω, βεβούλευκα, to plan in advance or behalf of another, lead in counsel, G., iii. 1. 37.
πρό-γονος, ου, ὁ, (γίγνομαι) a forefather, ancestor, iii. 2. 11, 13 : vii. 2. 22. Cog. PRO-GENITOR.
προ-δίδωμι,* δώσω, δέδωκα, a. ἔδωκα (δῶ, &c.), to give forth, give up, surrender, betray, desert, forsake, abandon, A. D., i. 3. 5 : iii. 1. 2, 14 ; 2. 2.
προ-διώκω,* ξω or ξομαι, δεδίωχα, to follow forth, advance in pursuit, iii. 3. 10 : v. l. διώκω.
†προ-δότης, ου, a betrayer, traitor, ii. 5. 27 : vi. 6. 7.
προ-δοῦναι, -δούς, see προ-δίδωμι.
προ-δραμών, see προ-τρέχω, i. 5. 2.
‡προ-δρομή, ῆς, a running forth, outrun, sally, iv. 7. 10.
προ-δῶ, -δώσω, see προ-δίδωμι.
προ-ειλόμην, see προ-αιρέω, vi. 6.19.
πρό-ειμι,* ipf. ᾔειν, (εἶμι) to go forward or before, go on, advance, proceed, precede, ἀπό, εἰς, &c., i. 2. 17 ; 3. 1 ; 4. 18 : ii. 1. 2, 6, 21? 2. 19.
προ-εῖπον, 2 a. to προ-αγορεύω or προ-λέγω, i. 2. 17.
προ-ειπεῖν, see προ-ίστημι,i. 2.1?
προ-ελαύνω,* ἐλάσω ἐλῶ, ἐλήλακα, to ride forward or before, push on or forward, advance, i. 10. 16 : vi. 3. 14.
προ-ελήλυθα, ελθών,see προ-έρχομαι.
προ-εργάζομαι,* άσομαι, εἴργασμαι, to work out or earn before or previously, A., vi. 1. 21.
προ-έρχομαι,* ἐλεύσομαι, ἐλήλυθα, 2 a. ἦλθον, to go, come, or march forward or before, to advance, proceed, A. of extent, εἰς, ii. 3. 3 : iii. 3. 6 ; 4. 37.
†προ-ερῶ, f. to προ-αγορεύω or προ-λέγω, vii. 7. 13 : cf. 3.
προ-έσθαι, -έμενος, see προ-ίημι.
προ-εστήκειν, see προ-ίστημι, i. 2. 1?
προ-έχω,* ἕξω, ἔσχηκα, to have one's

LEX. AN. H

self before another, *to surpass, have the advantage of*, G. or r. A., iii. 2. 19.

προ-ηγέομαι, ήσομαι, ήγημαι, *to lead forward*, AE., vi. 5. 10 : vii. 3. 42 ?

προ-ηγορέω, ήσω, (προ-ήγορος an advocate, fr. αγορά) *to speak in behalf of* others, v. 5. 7.

προ-ήειν, see πρό-ειμι, i. 8. 14.

προ-ήλθον, see προ-έρχομαι, ii. 3. 3.

προ-θέω,* θεύσομαι, *to run* or *hurry on before* or *forward*, v. 7. 21 ? 8. 13.

†προ-θυμέομαι, ήσομαι, a. προύθυμήθην, *to be eager, earnest, zealous, very desirous, anxious ; to desire* or *seek earnestly* or *ardently, urge* ; I. (A.) : *to be closely attentive, observe* or *watch closely*, εἰ : τὸ προθυμεῖσθαι *eagerness:* i. 9. 24 : ii. 4. 7 : iii. 1. 9 : vi. 4. 22 ?

†προ-θυμία, as, *readiness, good-will, alacrity, eagerness, zeal,* περί, i. 9. 18 : vii. 6. 11 ; 7. 45.

πρό-θυμος, ον, c., s., *having a forward mind, with good-will, willing, forward, ready, prompt, earnest, eager, zealous*, i. 3. 19 ; 4. 15 ; 7. 8 : iii. 2. 15.

‡προ-θύμως, c. ότερον, *willingly, readily, earnestly, eagerly, zealously,* i. 4. 9 ; 10. 10 : iii. 1. 5 : v. 2. 2.

προ-θύομαι, ύσομαι, *to direct a sacrifice*, vi. 4. 22 : v. l. προθυμέομαι.

προ-ίδοιμι, -ίδωμαι, see προ-οράω.

προ-ιέναι, -ιών, see πρό-ειμι, i. 3. 1.

προ-ίημι,* ήσω, εἶκα. a. ήκα (ὥ, &c.), *to send forth, send* or *grant to one*, D. I., vii. 2. 15 ? *M. to give up one's self* or *one's own, surrender, commit, intrust ; to bestow first* or *freely ; to give up, betray, desert, abandon ;* A. D., i. 9. 9 s, 12 : v. 8. 14 : vii. 3. 31 ; 7. 47.

προ-ίστημι,* στήσω, ἕστηκα, *to place before* : pf. pret., *to stand* or *be at the head of* or *in command of, preside over, lead, rule, command,* G., i. 2. 1 : vi. 2. 9 ; 6. 12 : vii. 1. 30 ; 2. 2.

προ-καίω & Att. κάω,* καύσω, κέκαυκα, *to burn* or *kindle before,* A. πρό, vii. 2. 18 : v. l. καίω.

προ-καλέω,* καλέσω καλῶ, κέκληκα, ch. M., *to call forth* to one's self, A. ἐκ, vii. 7. 2 : v. l. προσκαλέω.

προ-καλύπτω,ύψω,(καλύπτω *to cover*) *to place a covering before, cover, veil,* A., iii. 4. 8.

προ-κατα-θέω,* θεύσομαι, *to* [run along] *make an excursion in advance,* vi. 3. 10 : v. l. καταθέω.

προ-κατα-καίω & Att. κάω,* καύσω, κέκαυκα, *to burn* [down] or *destroy in advance* or *before* others, i. 6. 2.

προ-κατα-λαμβάνω,* λήψομαι, εἴληφα, 2 a. ἔλαβον, pf. p. εἴλημμαι, a. p. ἐλήφθην, *to seize* or *occupy in advance* or *beforehand,* or *before* or *against* others, *to pre-occupy, secure,* A. D., i. 3. 14, 16 : ii. 5. 18 : iii. 4. 38.

πρό-κειμαι,* κείσομαι, *to lie forth, jut out, ἐν,* vi. 4. 3.

προ-κινδυνεύω, εύσω, κεκινδύνευκα, *to incur danger* [before] *in defence* or *behalf of* another, vii. 3. 31.

Προ-κλῆς, έους, *Proc'es,* a descendant of the Spartan Damarātus, and prince of Teuthrania in Asia Minor, who befriended the Cyreans, ii. 1. 3.

προ-κρίνω,* κρῖνῶ, κέκρῖκα, a. p. ἐκρίθην, *to select* before, *prefer,* A., vi. 1. 26.

προ-λέγω,* λέξω, *to tell, bid,* or *warn publicly,* vii. 7. 3. Der. PROLOGUE.

προ-μαχεών, ῶνος, ὁ, (μάχομαι) propugnaculum, *a rampart, battlement,* vii. 8. 13 : v. l. προμαχών.

προ-μετωπίδιον, ου, (μέτ-ωπον *forehead,* fr. ὤψ *eye*) *a covering for the forehead, frontlet, head-piece,* i. 8. 7.

προ-μνάομαι, a. ἐμνησάμην, ipf. προύμνώμην, (μνάομαι* *to sue*) *to solicit* or *plead for* another, AE., vii. 3. 18.

προ-νοέω, ήσω, νενόηκα, also M., *to think* or *consider for, take thought* or *provide for* or *in behalf of,* G. AE., vii. 7. 33, 37.

πρό-νοια, as, (νόος) *forethought, kind* or *provident care,* vii. 7. 52.

προ-νομή, ῆς, [an arranging forth] *a regular foray* or *foraging party,* v. 1. 7 : for σὺν π., v. l. συμπρονομεῖν.

†προ-ξενέω, ήσω, προὐξένηκα, *to act as* a πρόξενος *in setting forth an entertainment ; hence, to set before,* A. D., vi. 5. 14.

πρό-ξενος, ου, ὁ, *a public guest-friend* or *agent,* a citizen of one state, who acted as a *patron* or *agent,* and *entertainer,* for the citizens or ruler of another state, receiving privileges and honors in return, v. 4. 2 ; 6. 11.

‡Πρόξενος, ου, *Proxenus,* a Cyrean general from Thebes in Boeotia, and an intimate friend of Xenophon, who writes his eulogy without concealing his defects as a commander, i. 1. 11 ; 5. 14 : ii. 1. 10 ; 6. 16 : iii. 1. 4.

προ-οίμιον, see προ-ίημι, i. 9. 10.

προ-οράω,* ὄψομαι, ἑώρᾱκα or ἑόρᾱκα,

προπέμπω 115 προσελαύνω

2 a. είδον, to see in front or before one, perceive beforehand, see coming, i. 8. 20 : so M., vi. 1. 8 ?

προ-πέμπω,* πέμψω, πέπομφα, to send before, forward, or forth ; to attend, accompany, escort; A.; ii. 2. 15 : iv. 4. 5 : vi. 1. 23 : — M. to send forward, as if intending to follow, A., vii. 2. 14.

προ-πίνω,* πίομαι (ῐ), πέπωκα, 2 a. ἔπιον, to drink first, then passing the cup to another, the usual Greek method of drinking his health ; hence, to drink to one, drink one's health, A. D., iv. 5. 32 : vii. 2. 23 ; 3. 26s.

προ-πονέω, ήσω, πεπόνηκα, to labor in advance or behalf of another, lead in toil, G., iii. 1. 37.

πρός* (πρό, 689 i) prep., (a) w. GEN., in front of (esp. w. the idea of some action or influence proceeding from), in sight of, before, by, from, on the part of, i. 6. 6 : ii. 5. 20 : hence to express agency, w. pass., &c., i. 9. 20 : ii. 3. 12 ? 18 : in adjuration, as πρὸς (τῶν) θεῶν by the gods, ii. 1. 17 : iii. 1. 24 :—in the direction fronting, in the direction of, on the side of, towards, iv. 3. 26 ; πρὸς τοῦ τρόπου in [the direction of] accordance with the character, i. 2. 11 : — (b) w. DAT., in front of, on the frontier of, face to face with, near, by, at, beside; besides, in addition to ; i. 2. 10 ; 8. 4, 14 : ii. 3. 4 : iii. 2. 33 : iv. 5. 9, 22 : — w. dat. om., as adv., 703 b, besides [this], moreover, further, iii. 2. 2 : — (c) w. ACC. of PERSON (so esp. used), sometimes of PLACE, TIME, or THING, to the front of, towards, to, before, at, near, against, upon, with, (πρός w. acc. often = dat., esp. w. words of motion, of address, or of friendly or hostile action or relation), i. 1. 3, 5 s ; 2. 1 ; 3. 4, 9 ; 4. 11 ; 5. 7, 13 ; 9. 22 : ii. 4. 25 ; 6. 12 : iv. 5. 21 :—hence, in general, of the object to or towards which anything is directed or related in view, thought, feeling, purpose, &c., in view of, in respect to, concerning, about, for, to, in comparison or accordance with, i. 4. 9 ; 10. 19 : ii. 3. 11 s ; 5. 20, 29 : vii. 7. 41 ; πρὸς ταῦτα in view of or in reply to these things, in respect to this, to or upon this, thereupon, accordingly, i. 3. 19 s : ii. 3. 21 ; τὰ πρὸς σέ, as to the things concerning you, towards you, vii. 7. 30 : — (d) in compos., to,

towards, against, besides. Der. PROSELYTE, PROS-ODY. See φιλία.

προσ-άγω,* ἄξω, ἦχα, 2 a. ἤγαγον, to lead to or against, bring forward, introduce, apply, urge, A. εἰς, πρός : w. acc. om., as intrans., to advance : i. 10. 9 : iv. 1. 23 ; 8. 11 : vi. 1. 14.

προσ-αιτέω, ήσω, ἤτηκα l., to ask in addition or besides, ask for more, 2 A., i. 3. 21 : vii. 3. 31 ; 6. 27.

προσ-αν-αλίσκω,* -αλώσω, -ήλωκα, to expend besides, A., vi. 4. 8 ?

προσ-αν-ειπεῖν, as aor. of προσ-αναγορεύω, εύσω, to [speak up] proclaim or announce besides, CP., vii. 1. 11 : see φημί.

προσ-βαίνω,* βήσομαι, βέβηκα, to step against or upon, πρός, iv. 2. 28 ?

προσ-βάλλω,* βαλῶ, βέβληκα, 2 a. ἔβαλον, to throw or strike against, to [throw one's self] advance against, assault, attack, make an attack, πρός, iv. 2. 11 ; 6. 13 ; 7. 2 : v. 2. 4 : vi. 3. 7.

προσ-βατός, ή, όν, (βαίνω) accessible, iv. 3. 12 ; 8. 9.

προσ-βολή, ῆς, (βάλλω) an attack, assault, charge, iii. 4. 2 : vi. 5. 25 ?

προσ-γίγνομαι,* γενήσομαι, γεγένημαι & 2 pf. γέγονα, 2 a. ἐγενόμην, to be added, joined, or attached to, to join, esp. as an ally, D., iv. 6. 9 : vii. 6. 29.

προσ-δανείζω, είσω, δεδάνεικα, (δανείζω to lend) to lend in addition : M. to borrow an additional sum, 581, vii. 5. 5.

προσ-δέω,* δεήσω, δεδέηκα, to need in addition : impers. προσδεῖ there is need besides, there is further or additional need, G., iii. 2. 34 : v. 6. 1 :— M. to need or desire as an addition or beyond what one has, G., vi. 1. 24.

προσ-δίδωμι,* δώσω, δέδωκα, to give besides or in addition, to add, A., i. 9. 19.

προσ-δοκάω, ήσω, δεδόκηκα l., (akin to δοκέω, the simple δοκάω not used) to think towards, expect, look or wait for, A., I. (A.), iii. 1. 14 : vii. 6. 11.

προσ-δραμών, see προσ-τρέχω.

προσ-είληφα, see προσ-λαμβάνω.

πρόσ-ειμι,* ipf. ἦειν, (εἶμι q. v.) to go or come to or towards, come up or on, come near, approach, advance, D., εἰς, πρός, i. 5. 14 ; 7. 5 ; 8. 11 : ii. 4. 2.

προσ-ελαύνω,* ἐλάσω ἐλῶ, ἐλήλακα, to ride or march to, towards, up, forward, or against, i. 5. 12 ; 7. 16 : vi. 3. 7.

προσ-έρχομαι,* ἐλεύσομαι, ἐλήλυθα, 2 a. ἦλθον, to come or go to or towards, come up or near, eome in or forward, approaeh, advance, D., εἰς, i. 3. 9 ; 8. 1 : iv. 4. 5 ; 8. 2, 4. Der. PROS-ELYTE.
προσ-ετάχθην, see προσ-τάττω.
προσ-εύχομαι, εὔξομαι, εὖγμαι or ηὖγμαι, to pray to, D., vi. 3. 21.
προσ-έχω,* ἕξω, ἔσχηκα, 2 a. ἔσχον, to [hold to] apply, A. D.: προσέχειν (τὸν νοῦν) to apply or direct the mind or attention, give thought or heed, give or pay attention, show regard, be intent upon, i. 5. 9 : ii. 4. 2 : v. 6. 22.
προσ-ῄειν, -ῄεσαν or -ῇσαν, see πρόσ-ειμι, i. 8. 11 : iii. 3. 7.
προσ-ήκω, ἥξω, ἧκα 1., to come, extend, appertain, or belong to, be related to, D., ἐπί, i. 6. 1: iii. 1. 31 (he has nothing to do with): iv. 3. 23 :— προσ-ήκει it belongs to, befits, beeomes, behooves, is fitting or proper, D. I. (A.), iii. 2. 11, 15 s : vii. 7. 18.
προσ-ήλασα, see προσ-ελαύνω.
προσ-ῆσαν or -ῄεσαν,-ῆτε, see πρόσ-ειμι, i. 8. 11 : vii. 6. 24.
πρόσθεν adv. of PLACE and oftener TIME, (πρό, πρός) before, in front of, previously, formerly, i. 3. 18 ; 6. 1 : πρόσθεν .. πρίν [previously .. before] before that, before, until, (w. neg.) 703 ζ, i. 1. 10 : iii. 2. 29 : iv. 3. 12 : πρόσθεν .. ἤ sooner than, before, ii. 1. 10 :— ὁ π. the previous, preceding, foregoing, or former, i. 3. 19 : ii. 3. 1, 22 : οἱ π. [those in] who were in front, v. 8. 16 : τὰ π. the [things in] front, the van, iii. 2. 36 : εἰς τὸ π. to the front, in advance, forward ; in front of, G.; i. 10. 5 : iii. 1. 33 ; 4. 38 :— τὸ π. as adv., previously, before, i. 10. 10 s.
προσ-θέσθαι, see προσ-τίθημι, i. 6. 10.
προσ-θέω,* θεύσομαι, to run to, towards, or up, v. 7. 21 ? vii. 1. 15.
προσ-ίᾶσι(ν), -ιών, see πρόσ-ειμι, i. 5. 14 : iv. 8. 12 s.
προσ-ίημι,* ἥσω, εἷκα, to let go to, permit to approaeh, ad-mit to, A. πρός, iv. 5. 5 :— M. to let eome to one's self, receive, adnnit, permit, A., iii. 1. 30 (εἰς ταυτόν tō the same plaee, rank, or office, to companionship): iv. 2. 12 : v. 5. 3.
προσ-καλέω,* καλέσω καλῶ,κέκληκα, to call to, summon, invite, A., i. 9. 28 : — M. to call to one's self, A. ἐκ, vii. 7. 2 (v. l. προκαλέω).

προσ-κτάομαι, ήσομαι, κέκτημαι, to gain or aequire additional, A. D., v. 6. 15.
προσ-κυνέω, ήσω, -κεκύνηκα 1., (κυνέω* to kiss) to kiss the hand to, salute, worship, adore, do homage or reverence to, bow down or (in oriental fashion) prostrate one's self before, A., i. 6. 10 ; 8. 21 : iii. 2. 9, 13.
προσ-λαμβάνω,* λήψομαι, εἴληφα, 2 a. ἔλαβον, to take, receive, or obtain besides, in addition, or as an aid; to take hold besides, take part ; A. πρός : i. 7. 3 : ii. 3. 11 s : vii. 6. 27, 32.
προσ-μένω,* μενῶ, μεμένηκα, to wait for, await, A., vi. 6. 1 : v. l. ἀναμένω.
προσ-μίγνυμι,* μίξω, to mingle or join with, join or come up to, iv. 2. 16.
πρόσ-οδος, ου, ἡ, access, approach ; approach or procession for worship, act of worship, πρός · income, revenue, gain, profit, reditus ; i. 9. 19 : v. 2. 3 : vi. 1. 11 : vii. 1. 27 ; 7. 36.
προσ-όμνῡμι,* ὀμοῦμαι, ὀμώμοκα, a. ὤμοσα, to swear besides or in addition, I., ii. 2. 8.
προσ-ομολογέω, ήσω, ὡμολόγηκα, to come to terms, submit, surrender, vii. 4. 24.
προσ-περονάω, ήσω, (περόνη a pin) to pin or skewer to, A. πρός, vii. 3. 21.
προσ-πίπτω,* πεσοῦμαι, πέπτωκα, to fall towards, rush to, D., vii. 1. 21.
προσ-ποιέω, ήσω, πεποίηκα, to make over to : M. to make over to one's self, to take to one's self what does not so belong, pretend, feign, make a feint, make as if one would, profess, I., i. 3. 14 : ii. 1. 7 : iv. 3. 20 ; 6. 13.
προσ-πολεμέω, ήσω, πεπολέμηκα, to war or prosecute a war against, A.? i. 6. 6.
προσ-σχών, see προσ-έχω, vii. 6. 5.
†προστατεύω, εύσω, to manage, use one's influence, bring it about, ὅπως, v. 6. 21.
†προστατέω, ήσω, to preside over, manage, G., iv. 8. 25.
προστάτης, ου, (προ-ίστημι) a leader, chief, manager, G., vii. 7. 31.
προσ-τάττω, τάξω, τέταχα, a. p. ἐτάχθην, to appoint to or enjoin upon any one, eommand, A. D., i. 6. 10.
προσ-τελέω, τελέσω τελῶ, τετέλεκα, to pay besides, A., vi. 6. 30.
προ-στερνίδιον, ου, (στέρνον) a breastplate, breast-piece, for a horse, i. 8. 7.

προσ-τίθημι 117 Πυθαγόρας

προσ-τίθημι,* θήσω, τέθεικα, 2 a. m. ἐθέμην, to add to: M. to add one's self to, accede to, agree to, concur in, D., i. 6. 10.

προσ-τρέχω,* δραμοῦμαι, δεδράμηκα, 2 a. ἔδραμον, to run to, run up to, D., iv. 2. 21 ; 3. 10 : vii. 4. 7.

προσ-φέρω,* οἴσω, ἐνήνοχα, to bring to, apply, A., v. 2. 14 :— M. to bear or conduct one's self towards, to address one's self or apply to, D., πρός, v. 5. 19 : vii. 1. 6.

προσ-χωρέω, ήσω, κεχώρηκα, to go or come to, surrender, submit, v. 4. 30.

πρόσ-χωρος (v. l. πρό-χωρος), ον, neighboring, v. 3. 9.

πρόσω adv., c. προσωτέρω, s. -τάτω, (πρό, πρός) forward(s), forth ; forth from, far from, far off, at a distance, at the outposts, G.; far into, G., 420a; ii. 2. 15: iv. 1. 3 ; 3. 28 : vii. 3. 42 : τοῦ πρόσω (430 a) or εἰς τὸ πρόσω [for or to the region forward] forward, in advance, farther, i. 3. 1: v. 4. 30 :— c. farther, farther off, iv. 3. 34 : vii. 7. 1 :— ὅποι ἐδύναντο προσωτάτω as far as they could, 553 c, vi. 6. 1.

προσ-ώμοσα, see προσ-όμνυμι, ii. 2. 8.

πρόσ-ωπον, ου, (ὤψ) the face, countenance, looks ; so plur., ii. 6. 11. Der. PROSOPO-PŒIA.

προ-τελέω, τελέσω τελῶ, τετέλεκα, to pay beforehand or in advance, A. D., vii. 7. 25.

†προτεραῖος, α, ον, preceding : τῇ π., sc. ἡμέρᾳ, on the day before, ii. 1. 3.

πρότερος, α, ον, (πρό q. v.) prior, former, preceding, previous; with adv. force (509 a), or (τὸ) πρότερον as adv., before, sooner, previously, G.; i. 2. 25 s; 4. 12 ; 7. 18 : iv. 4. 14 : vii. 8. 22.

προ-τιμάω, ήσω, τετίμηκα, f. m. τιμήσομαι (ch. as p., 576 a), to honor before or above others, prefer, select, esteem, i. 4. 14 ; 6. 5.

προ-τρέχω,* δραμοῦμαι, δεδράμηκα, 2 a. ἔδραμον, to run forward or before, outrun, G., ἀπό, i. 5. 2 : iv. 7. 10 : v. 2. 4.

πρού- by crasis for προ-ε, v. 8. 9.

προὐδεδώκειν, see προ-δίδωμι, iii. 1. 2.

προ-φαίνω,* φανῶ, πέφαγκα, to show before or forth : M. to appear before or beforehand ; to appear in front, in the distance, or in prospect ; to come in sight, make one's appearance : D.; i. 8. 1 : ii. 3. 13 (v. l. φαίνω).

†προφασίζομαι, ἰσομαι ἰοῦμαι, to plead or urge as an excuse, A., iii. 1. 25.

πρό-φασις, εως, ἡ, (φημί) a pre-text, pretence, excuse, G., I., i. 1. 7 ; 2. 1 : ii. 3. 21 : vii. 6. 22.

προ-φύλαξ, ακος, ὁ, a sentinel in front, advanced or outer guard, outguard, vedette ; pl. an outpost, picket, &c.; ii. 3. 2; 4. 15 : iii. 2. 1 : vi. 4. 26.

προ-χωρέω, ήσω, κεχώρηκα, to go forward, advance, prosper, succeed ; to be favorable or useful, suit one's convenience or be for his advantage ; D.; i. 9. 13 : vi. 4. 21 : vii. 3. 26.

πρύμνα, ης, (Ep. πρυμνός hindmost) the stern of a vessel, v. 8. 20.

πρωΐ adv., c. πρωϊαίτερον, contr. πρῴ, πρῳαίτερον, (πρό) early in the morning, ii. 2. 1 : iii. 4. 1 (earlier than usual, very early, 514): vi. 5. 2.

πρῷρα, ας, (πρό) prōra, the forepart of a vessel, PROW, bow, v. 8. 20.

†πρῳρεύς, έως, ὁ, the commander in the prow, prow-officer, v. 8. 20.

†πρωτ-αγός, οῦ, ὁ, a van-leader, ii. 2. 16 : v. l. πρῶτος.

†πρωτεύω, εύσω, πεπρώτευκα 1., to be first, hold the first place, παρά, ii. 6. 26.

πρῶτος, η, ον, (πρό q. v.) prīmus, first, in place, rank, or time, foremost, chief, earliest ; often w. adverbial force (509) ; i. 3. 1 ; 6. 9 : ii. 2. 12, 16 ? 6. 17, 26 :— τὸ πρῶτον subst., the first ; ἀπὸ or ἐπὶ τοῦ πρώτου from or at the first, iv. 3. 9 ; (τὸ) πρῶτον as adv., or as an appositive to a sentence, first, at (the) first, in the first place, as the first thing, i. 2. 16 ; 9. 2, 5, 7 ; 10. 10 : ii. 5. 7: iii. 2. 1 : vi. 3. 23, 25 : so πρῶτα, iii. 2. 27 ? Der. PROTO-TYPE.

πταίω, πταίσω, ἔπταικα, (akin to πίπτω) to fall, strike, or dash against or upon, iv. 2. 3 : v. l. παίω.

πτάρνυμαι,* 2 a. a. ἔπταρον, to sneeze, iii. 2. 9.

πτέρυξ, υγος, ἡ, (πτερόν wing, fr. πέτομαι) the wing of a bird ; a flexible skirt or flap at the bottom of the Greek corselet, usu. of leather strengthened by metallic plates ; i. 5. 3 : iv. 7. 15 (v. l. dim. πτερύγιον).

πυγμή, ῆς, (πύξ) pugnus, the fist ; boxing (rendered more severe among the Greeks by the use of the cestus), iv. 8. 27. Der. PYGMY.

Πυθαγόρας, ου, Pythagoras, a Spartan admiral, i. 4. 2. The commander of this fleet is named Σάμιος or Σάμος in Hel. 3. 1. 1 ; Diod. 14. 19.

πυκνός, ή, όν, (πύκα closely, cf. πύξ) close or near together, dense, thick, compact, firm, in close array : πυκνά adv., often : ii. 3. 3: iv. 8. 2: v. 2. 5.

πύκτης, ου, (πύξ) pugil, a boxer, PUGILIST, v. 8. 23.

πύλη, ης, one fold of a double gate: comm. pl., gate or gates ; hence, entrance, puss, passage, esp. a narrow entrance or pass into a country, sometimes really barred by gates ; as πύλαι τῆς Κιλικίας καὶ τῆς Συρίας the Gates of Cilicia and Syria, the Syro-Cilician Gates, a narrow pass between Mt. Amānus and the Gulf of Issus, barred by two walls with gates, of which those on the Syrian side are specially called αἱ Σύριαι πύλαι ; i. 4. 4s: v. 2. 16, 23 ; 5. 19s : vi. 5. 1 : vii. 1. 15s. Der. THERMO-PYLÆ, PYL-ŌRUS. So ‡Πύλαι, sc. αἱ Βαβυλώνιαι, the [Babylonian] Gates, Pylæ, a pass into Babylonia, on the north side of the Euphrates and, as some think, through the Median Wall, i. 5. 5. — The Cilician Pass (πύλαι τῆς Κιλικίας), over Mt. Taurus into Cilicia, "perhaps," says Ainsworth, "one of the most remarkable and picturesque mountain-passes in the world," while Chesney adds that it is one of the longest and most difficult, is mentioned, i. 2. 21 ; now Golek-Bogház.

πυνθάνομαι,* πεύσομαι, πέπυσμαι, 2 a. ἐπυθόμην, to learn by inquiry, hear, ascertain ; to ask, inquire, inquire into ; G. CP., A. P., I. (A.), περί ; i. 5. 15 ; 7. 16 : iv. 6. 17 : vii. 6. 11.

πύξ adv., with the fist, v. 8. 16.

πῦρ,* πῠρός, τό, FIRE : pl., Dec. 2, πυρά, -ῶν, -οῖς, fires, esp. watch-fires : ii. 5. 19 : iv. 1. 11. Der. EM-PYREAN.

‡**πυρά**, ᾶς, a funeral PYRE or mound, vi. 4. 9 : om. by some.

‡**πῡραμίς**, ίδος, ή, a flame-shaped structure, a PYRAMID, iii. 4. 9. One of the most prominent objects among the Ninevite ruins is the pyramid or conical mound here mentioned, situated at the northwest corner of the great platform on which the wonderful palaces of Nimrúd were erected, and still, after the wear of so many centuries, about 150 feet high. It was once a lofty tower 167 feet square

at the base, erected doubtless as a sepulchral or religious monument.

Πύραμος, ου, ὁ, the Pyramus, the largest river of Cilicia, rising in Cataonia, breaking through Mt. Taurus, and carrying so much alluvium through its fertile plain, that Strabo quotes an oracle that at length its deposits would unite Cyprus to the mainland, i. 4. 1. ǁ The Jeihûn, about 160 miles long.

†**πυργο-μαχέω**, ήσω, (μάχομαι) to assault or storm a tower, vii. 8. 13.

πύργος, ου, ὁ, a tower, castle, vii. 8. 13.

πυρέττω, έξω, πεπύρεχα, (πυρετός fever, fr. πῦρ) to have or be in a fever, vi. 4. 11.

†**πύρινος**, η, ον, made of wheat, wheaten, iv. 5. 81.

πυρός, οῦ, ὁ, (πῦρ, fr. the color?) comm. pl., wheat, i. 2. 22 : iv. 5. 5.

Πυρρίας, ου, Pyrrhias, an officer from Arcadia, vi. 5. 11.

πυρρίχη, ης, (fr. Πύρριχος or Πύρρος, the inventor ?) the Pyrrhic or war dance, in which armed dancers imitated the movements of attack and defence, keeping time with music, vi. 1. 12.

πυρσεύω, εύσω, (πυρσός torch, fr. πῦρ) to light torches, kindle beacon-fires, or make signals by them, vii. 8. 15.

πώ encl. adv., (orig. dat. of πός : by any means) yet, up to this time, hitherto ; used w. a neg. (often written w. it as one word, cf. dum), not yet, never yet, &c. ; i. 2. 26 ; 5. 12.

πωλέω, ήσω, (πέλω to be in business) to sell, A. D., i. 5. 5 : v. 7. 13 : vii. 3. 3 ; 7. 56. Der. MONO-POLY.

πῶλος, ου, ὁ ἡ, a colt, filly, young horse, iv. 5. 24, 35. Cf. pullus, FOAL.

Πῶλος, ου, Pōlus, a Spartan admiral, successor to Anaxibius, vii. 2. 5.

πῶμα, drink, see πόμα, iv. 5. 27 ?

πώ-ποτε ever yet, ever, at any time, stronger than ποτέ : comm. w. a neg. (sometimes written w. it as one word, cf. unquam), i. 4. 18 ; 9. 18s : v. 4. 6 ?

πῶς interrog. adv., (πός ;) quomodo ? how ? in what way, manner, or condition ? i. 7. 2 : ii. 5. 20 : iii. 2. 27 ? 4. 40 : — in exclamation, quam ! how ! vi. 5. 19 ?

πώς encl. indef. adv., (πώς) in some

or *any way* or *manner, by any means, somehow;* hence, *for some reason, somewhere, nearly, perhaps:* ὧδέ πως somehow thus, *to this effect:* i. 7. 9 : ii. 3. 18 ; 5. 2 ; 6. 3 : iv. 1. 8 ; 8. 21 ? vi. 2. 17. See ἄλλως, τεχνικῶς.

P.

ῥᾴδιος, α, ον, c. ῥᾴων, s. ῥᾷστος,* *easy,* I., ii. 6. 24 : iv. 6. 12 ; 8. 13.
†**ῥᾳδίως**, c. ῥᾷον, s. ῥᾷστα, *easily, readily,* iii. 5. 9 : iv. 6. 10 : vi. 3. 7.
Ῥαθίνης, ου, *Rhathines,* a general of the Bithynian satrap Pharnabazus, vi. 5. 7. He afterwards made a successful attack on the cavalry of Agesilāus, Hel. 3. 4. 13.
†**ῥᾳθυμέω**, ήσω, *to live at ease, lead a life of ease* or *indolence,* ii. 6. 6.
†**ῥᾳθυμία**, ας, *indolence, sloth, a life of ease,* ii. 6. 5.
†[**ῥᾴ-θυμος**, ον, *of easy mind, indolent.*]
ῥᾷον, ῥᾷστον, see ῥᾴδιος, iv. 6. 12.
↓**ῥᾳστώνη**, ης, *love of ease, indolence, laziness, sluggishness,* v. 8. 16.
ῥέω,* ῥεύσομαι & ῥυήσομαι, ἐρρύηκα, 2 a. a. or p. ἐρρύην, (cf. ruo, *rush*) fluo, *to flow, run* (of water), ἀπό, διά, &c., i. 2. 7 s, 23 ; 4. 4 ; 7. 15 ; vi. 4. 4. Der. RHEUM, DIAR-RHŒA.
ῥήτρα, ας, (ῥε- *to say*) *a saying, precept, ordinance, agreement,* vi. 6. 28.
ῥῖγος, εος, τό, frīgus, 141, *the cold, frost,* v. 8. 2. Cf. rigeo, rigidus.
ῥίπτω & **ῥιπτέω**,* ῥίψω, ἔρρῖφα, a. ἔρριψα, *to throw, cast, hurl, throw off* or *down, throw over* or *about*, A. D., εἰς, i. 5. 8: iii. 3. 1 : iv. 7. 13 : vii. 3. 22 ?
ῥ'ς, ῥινός, ἡ, *the nose,* vii. 4. 3. Der. RHINO-CEROS.
Ῥόδιος, α, ον, *Rhodian:* **Ῥόδιος** subst., *a Rhodian,* a man of Rhodes (Ῥόδος, from ῥόδον *rose ?*), a large and important island near the southwest coast of Asia Minor, colonized by the Dorians, and having a city of the same name (built B. C. 408), at the entrance of whose harbor stood the famed Colossus. The Rhodians were famed as slingers. iii. 3. 16 s ; 5. 8.
ῥοφέω, ήσω or ήσομαι, *to sup up, suck,* iv. 5. 32.
ῥυθμός, οῦ, ὁ, (cf. ῥέω, & ῥυ- *to draw*) RHYTHM, *musical time, a regular movement* or *tune:* ἐν ῥυθμῷ *in time* or

rhythm, πρός: v. 4. 14 : vi. 1. 8, 10 s : vii. 3. 32.
ῥῦμα, ατος, τό, (ῥυ- *to draw*) *a drawing, shot:* ἐκ τόξου ῥύματος *from the distance of a bow-shot,* iii. 3. 15.
†**ῥώμη**, ης, *strength,* a military *force,* iii. 3. 14. Some compare Rōma.
[**ῥώννυμι**,* ῥώσω l., pf. *p.* ἔρρωμαι, *to strengthen ;* see ἐρρωμένος.]
Ῥωπάρας, ου or α, *Rhoparas,* satrap of Babylonia, vii. 8. 25 : perhaps the same with Gobryas, i. 7. 12.

Σ.

σά, see σός, vii. 7. 44. — **σᾶ** or **σῶα,** see σῶς, v. 1. 16.
σάγαρις, εως, ἡ, (fr. Pers.) *a battle-axe, halberd, bill,* iv. 4. 16 : v. 4. 13.
σακίον or **σακκίον**, ου, (dim. of σάκος saccus, a SACK) *a small bag, a wrapper* of sackcloth, iv. 5. 36.
Σαλμυδεσσός, οῦ, ὁ, *Salmydessus,* the Thracian coast of the Euxine from the Bosphorus to the Thynian cape, dangerous from its shoals, lack of harbors, and predatory wreckers, and contributing largely to the early ill-repute of this sea, vii. 5. 12. The name was also given to a town on this coast, now Midia.
†**σαλπιγκτής** or **σαλπικτής**, οῦ, *a trumpeter,* iv. 3. 29, 32 : vii. 4. 19.
σάλπιγξ, ιγγος, ἡ, tuba, *a trumpet, trump,* usu. of bronze and straight, while the κέρας (cornu, *horn*) was curved. It was greatly used in Greek armies to direct and inspirit their movements. iii. 4. 4 : iv. 2. 7 s : vii. 3. 32.
↓**σαλπίζω**,* σαλπίσω l., a. ἐσάλπιγξα, *to sound* or *blow* with a trumpet, AE. : ἐπεὶ ἐσάλπιγξε, sc. ὁ σαλπιγκτής, *when the trumpeter blew, at the sound of the trumpet,* 571 b : i. 2. 17 : vii. 3. 32.
Σάμιος, ου, ὁ, *a Samian,* a man of Samos (Σάμος), one of the most important islands in the Ægēan, colonized by the Ionians, and early famed for its arts, commerce, and maritime power, standing with the neighboring Milētus and Ephesus at the head of the Ionian states. Its chief city and harbor had the same name. It was the birthplace of Pythagoras. Its patron deity was Hēra (Jūno), who had here her greatest temple. i. 7. 5. ‖ Samo.

Σαμόλας, ου or α, *Samolas*, a Cyrean officer from Achaia, v. 6. 14.

Σάρδεις, εων, αἱ, *Sardes* or *Sardis*, an ancient city on the Pactōlus, the capital of Lydia, the luxurious residence of Crœsus, the chief city of the dominions of Cyrus the Younger, and later the seat of one of the early churches; still showing, in its ruins, traces of its former magnificence; i. 2. 2 s, 5; 6. 6: iii. 1. 8. ‖ Sart.

Σάρος *v. l.* for Ψάρος, i. 4. 1.

†σατραπεύω, εύσω, *to be a satrap, to rule or govern as satrap*, G., A., 472 d, i. 7. 6: iii. 4. 31.

σατράπης, ου, (fr. Pers.) or SATRAP, a Persian *viceroy* or *governor* of a province, ruling at the pleasure of the king, but with largely discretionary power over life and property. Acc. to Hdt. (3. 89), Darius I., the great organizer of the Persian Empire, divided it into 20 satrapies. i. 1. 2; 9. 7.

Σάτυρος, ου, ὁ, a *Satyr*, a fabulous being combining the forms of a man and a goat, an attendant upon Bacchus, and devoted to the pleasures of sense, i. 2. 13.

σαυτοῦ, -ῷ, -όν, see σεαυτοῦ.

σαφής, ές, *clear, plain, manifest, evident*, iii. 1. 10.

‡σαφῶς *clearly, plainly, manifestly, evidently, certainly*, i. 4. 18: ii. 5. 4.

σέ te, *thee, you*, see σύ, ii. 5. 3 s.

‡σε-αυτοῦ,* ῆς, contr. σαυτοῦ, ῆς, refl. pron., *of thyself* or *yourself;* in gen. often = tuus, *your own:* ἡ σεαυτοῦ, sc. χώρα, *your own country:* i. 6. 7: ii. 5. 16: vii. 2. 37; 7. 23; 8. 3.

Σελινοῦς, οῦντος, ὁ, (σέλινον *parsley*) *Selīnus*, the name of a small river flowing by the temple of Diāna at Ephesus; and of another (now the Crestena) flowing through the grounds consecrated to her at Scillus; v. 3. 8.

σέσωσμαι, see σώζω, v. 5. 8.

Σεύθης, ου, *Seuthes* II., a Thracian prince, son of Mæsades and descendant of Teres, assisted by the Cyreans to recover his paternal dominion, but far better to promise than to bestow a recompense. He afterwards sent 500 troops to aid Dercyllidas in Bithynia; and had later, B. C. 390, a quarrel with his former patron Medocus, which Thrasybūlus reconciled, bringing both into friendship with Athens. v. 1. 15.

Σηλυβρία or Σηλυμβρία, ας, *Sely[m]bria*, a Megarian city on the north shore of the Propontis, vii. 2. 28; 5. 15. ‖ Selivri.

σημαίνω, ανῶ, σεσήμαγκα l., a. ἐσήμηνα or -άνα 152 c, (σῆμα *sign*) *to make* or *give a sign* or *signal; to indicate* or *show* by an omen or other sign, *signify, give notice;* often referring to ὁ σαλπιγκτής implied, as ἐσήμηνε [the trumpeter gave the signal] *the signal was given*, 571 b; AE., D. I. (W. ὡς), CP.; ii. 1. 2; 2. 4: iii. 4. 4: iv. 3. 29, 32: vi. 1. 24, 31; 3. 15: vii. 2. 18.

σημεῖον, ου, (σῆμα *sign*) *signum, a sign, mark, signal, standard*, i. 10. 12: ii. 5. 32: vi. 2. 2.

†σησάμινος, η, ον, *made from sesame*, iv. 4. 13.

σήσαμον, ου, SESAMÉ, *oil-seed*, sing. and pl., the seed of the sesamum, an oriental leguminous plant still much cultivated for the food and the excellent and abundant oil furnished by its seed, i. 2. 22: vi. 4. 6.

†σιγάζω, άσω, l. exc. in pres., *to try* or *endeavor to silence*, A., vi. 1. 32 ?

†σιγάω, ἡσομαι, σεσίγηκα, *to be* or *remain silent, keep silence*, v. 6. 27.

σιγή, ῆς, *silence*, i. 8. 11: ii. 2. 20.

σίγλος, ου, ὁ, (akin to Heb. *shekel*) a *siglus*, = 7½ Attic oboli, or about 25 cents, i. 5. 6.

†σιδηρεία, as, *the working in iron*, v. 5. 1.

†σιδήρεος, έα, εον, contr. οῦς, ᾶ, οῦν, *made of iron* or *steel*, v. 4. 13.

[σίδηρος, ου, ὁ, ferrum, *iron*.]

Σικυώνιος, ου, ὁ, a *Sicyonian*, a man of Sicyon (Σικυών), a very ancient city, with a small territory, on the northern coast of the Peloponnese, between Achaia and Corinth. It was conquered by the Dorians; but retained a large Ionian element, and varied in its political relations and form of government. It was famed for its schools of painting and sculpture; and in general for the arts of peace, rather than for energy in war, or the maintenance of liberty. iii. 4. 47. ‖ Vasiliká.

Σιλανός, οῦ, *Silānus*, a soothsayer from Ambracia in Epirus, more shrewd than trustworthy, i. 7. 18: v. 6. 16 s. — 2. A youthful trumpeter from Macistus in Triphylian Elis, vii. 4. 16.

σίνομαι,* Ion. σινήσομαι, to harm, do harm or damage, inflict injury, iii. 4. 16.

†Σινωπεύς, έως, ό, a Sinopean, iv. 8. 22: v. 3. 2; 6. 1: vi. 1. 15: a man of

Σινώπη, ης, Sinōpe, a Milesian colony on the Paphlagonian coast, the most prosperous and powerful city on the shores of the Euxine. It had a great commerce and valuable fisheries, and sent out itself several colonies. It was the birthplace of the Cynic Diogenes, and of Mithridātes the Great. v. 5. 7 : vi. 1. 15. ‖ Sinub, still of some consequence from its excellent harbor.

Σιός Laconic for θεός : τὠ Σιώ the twin gods, Castor and Pollux, by whom, as natives of Lacedæmon, the Spartans were wont to swear, vi. 6. 34: vii. 6. 39 ? see οὑτωσί.

σῖτ-αγωγός, όν, (σῖτος, ἄγω) carrying corn, for the conveyance of grain, i. 7. 15.

Σιτάκη, ης, see Σιττάκη.

Σῖτ-άλκας, ου, the Sitalcas, a martial song of the Thracians, prob. in honor of a prince Sitalcas, vi. 1. 6. See 'Οδρύσης.

†σῖτευτός, ή, όν, (σιτεύω to feed, fatten) made fat, very fat, v. 4. 32.

†σῖτηρέσιον, ου, money for buying bread, provision-money, vi. 2. 4.

†σῖτίον, ου, bread, food, i. 10. 18: pl. provisions, supply of food, vi. 2. 4 ?

σῖτος, ου, ό, corn or grain, esp. wheat, whether unground, simply ground, or cooked; hence, flour or meal, bread, and, in general, food; i. 4. 19; 5. 5 s, 10 : ii. 1. 6 : iii. 1. 3 : — pl. σῖτα (τά, 226 b) victuals, provisions, food, ii. 3. 27 : iii. 2. 28 : — ἡμέρας σῖτος a day's subsistence or supply of food, vii. 1. 41 ; so pl. vi. 2. 4 (v. l. σιτία). Der. PARA-SITE.

Σιττάκη, ης, Sittace, a large and populous city on the west bank of the Tigris, ii. 4. 13 : v. l. Σιτάκη. ‖ Near Akbara or, acc. to some, Sheriat-el-Beidha.

σιωπάω, ήσομαι, σεσιώπηκα, (σιωπή silence) to be or remain silent, keep silence, i. 3. 2 : v. 8. 25.

σκεδάννυμι,* σκεδάσω σκεδῶ, a. ἐσκέδασα, pf. p. ἐσκέδασμαι, to scatter or disperse, trans., iii. 5. 2.

σκέλος, εος, τό, a leg, iv. 2. 20 ; 7. 4 : v. 8. 10. Der. ISO-SCELES.

σκέπασμα, ατος, τό, (σκέπη shelter) a covering, tent-cover, i. 5. 10 ?

†σκεπτέος, α, ον, necessary to consider : σκεπτέον ἐστί impers., one or we must consider, ὅπως, i. 3. 11 : iv. 6. 10.

σκέπτομαι, comm. σκοπέω* (-έομαι v. 2. 20), σκέψομαι, ἔσκεμμαι, a. ἐσκεψάμην, specio, to look intently, observe closely, view, see, discern, examine, spy, reconnoitre, explore, ascertain ; to look out or for, look out for, keep a lookout, watch, provide ; to look or see to, consider, regard ; A., CP., πρός : i. 9. 22 : ii. 4. 24 : iii. 1. 13 ; 2. 20 : v. 1. 9 ; 7. 32. Der. SKEPTIC, MICRO-SCOPE.

†σκευάζω, άσω, to prepare, dress up, equip, vi. 1. 12.

†σκευή, ῆς, equipment, attire, dress, iv. 7. 27.

σκεῦος, εος, τό, an article of furniture, equipment, or baggage, utensil : pl. baggage, luggage, iii. 1. 30 ; 2. 28.

‡σκευοφορέω, ήσω, to carry baggage, be a porter, iii. 2. 28 ; 3. 19.

‡σκευο-φόρος, ον, (φέρω) carrying baggage : subst. -ος a baggage-carrier, porter ; -ον, sc. κτῆνος, a common beast of burden : τὰ σκευφόρα the baggage-animals, baggage-train, baggage ; i. 3. 7 ; 10. 3, 5, 17 : iii. 2. 28, 36 ; 3. 19.

†σκηνάω, ήσω, = σκηνέω, v. 3. 9 ? vii. 4. 12 ?

†σκηνέω, ήσω, & σκηνόω, ώσω, ἐσκήνωκα, to pitch or to occupy a tent (the former sense belonging rather to σκηνόω, and the latter rather to σκηνέω), encamp or be encamped, quarter or be quartered, lodge, ἐν, κατά, &c., i. 4. 9 : ii. 4. 14 : iv. 4. 14 ; 5. 23, 33 ; 7. 27.

σκηνή, ῆς, a tent : αἱ σ. the tents, camp : i. 2. 17 s ; 4. 3. Der. SCENE.

‡σκηνόω, ώσω, see σκηνέω, iv. 5. 23.

‡σκήνωμα, ατος, τό, a tent : pl. tents, quarters, encampment, ii. 2. 17.

†σκηπτός, οῦ, ό, a thunderbolt, iii. 1. 11.

†σκηπτοῦχος, ου, ό, (σκῆπτρον a staff, SCEPTRE, ἔχω) a sceptre-bearer, wand-bearer, usher, a Persian household-officer, comm. a eunuch, i. 6. 11.

[σκήπτω, ήψω, to lean, fall, dart.]

Σκιλλοῦς, οῦντος, ό, (σκίλλα SQUILL), Scillus, once a city of Triphylian Elis, near Olympia. It joined Pisa, B.C. 572, in warring with the Eleans, but the latter conquered and destroyed both cities. Long after, the Spartans took

σκίμπους 122 σπάνιος

the territory of Scillus under their control, and here gave Xenophon a delightful rural residence under their protection, about 393 B.C. This continued till the Eleans regained possession, after the battle of Leuctra (B. C. 371); and during this quiet period, the works of Xenophon were doubtless for the most part written or revised. He spent his time, says Laërtius, in hunting, entertaining his friends, and writing histories. The visit of Megabyzus to Olympia, prob. in the year 392 B. C., gave him a new object of interest. Pausanias, more than 500 years after, found the temple of Diana still at Scillus, and upon a tomb near it, a marble statue, which the inhabitants said was Xenophon's. v. 3. 7 : see Ξενοφῶν. ‖ In the vale of Rasa.

σκίμ-πους, ποδος, ὁ, (σκίμπτω = σκήπτω) a low *couch*, a *litter*, vi. 1. 4 ?

σκληρός, ά, όν, (σκέλλω to dry) *hard, rough*, iv. 8. 26. Der. SCLEROTIC.

‡σκληρῶς *in hardship, with difficulty*, iii. 2. 26 : v. l. ἀκλήρους.

σκόλοψ, οπος, ὁ, *a stake, pale, palisade*, v. 2. 5.

σκοπέω in pr. & ipf., see σκέπτομαι.

σκοπός, οῦ, ὁ, (σκέπτομαι) *a scout, spy, sentinel*, ii. 2. 15 : vi. 3. 11. Der. SCOPE.

σκόροδον, ου, *garlic*, pl. vii. 1. 37.

†σκοταῖος, α, ον, *in the dark, before morning* or *after nightfall*, ii. 2. 17 : iv. 1. 5, 10.

σκότος, εος, τό, *darkness, the dark*: ἐστί or γίγνεται σκότος *it is* or *becomes dark*: ii. 2. 7 ; 5. 7, 9 : iv. 5. 17.

Σκύθης, ου, a *Scythian*, one of the nomadic barbarians who occupied the most northern known parts of eastern Europe and western Asia. From their skill as bowmen, their name was applied by the Greeks to a kind of archers armed and trained in Scythian fashion : Σκύθαι τοξόται, or Σκυθο-τοξόται, *Scythian archers*. iii. 4. 15 (as adj.): om. by some.

‡Σκυθῖνοί, ῶν, οἱ, *the Scythini*, or *-inians*, a mountain tribe, not far from the southeast shore of the Euxine, perhaps of Scythian origin, iv. 7. 18 ; 8. 1 : v. l. Σκυθηνοί, Σκυθῖνοι.

‡Σκυθο-τοξότης, ου, *a Scythian archer*, iii. 4. 15 ? See Σκύθης.

σκυλεύω, εύσω, (σκῦλον *spoil*) *to despoil, strip off* the arms of an enemy, A., vi. 1. 6.

σκύταλον, ου, (ξύω ? see ξέω) a *staff, club, cudgel, mace*, vii. 4. 15.

σκύτινος, η, ον,(σκῦτος a *hide*) *made of leather, leathern*, v. 4. 13.

σμῆνος, εος, τό, a *bee-hive, a swarm of bees*, iv. 8. 20.

Σμίκρης, ητος, *Smicres*, an Arcadian commander, vi. 3. 4 s.

Σόλοι, ων, οἱ, *Soli*, an important maritime city of Cilicia, built by Argives and Rhodians ; who at length spoke such bad Greek, from mingling with the native Cilicians, as to give rise to the term *solecism* (σολοικισμός). It was the birthplace of the Stoic Chrysippus and the poet Arātus; and was later named Πομπηϊούπολις from Pompey the Great, who here settled a colony of reformed pirates. i. 2. 24. ‖ Eski-Shehr (i. e. *old city*) near Mezetli.

σός, σή, σόν, (σύ) *thy, your*: φιλίᾳ τῇ σῇ *love to you*, 538 d : τὰ σά *your affairs* or *interests*: vii. 7. 29, 44.

Σοῦσα, ων, τά, (Pers. *susan, lily*) *Sūsa* (Shushan, Neh. 1. 1) chief city of the province of Susiāna (Elam, Dan. 8. 2), and one of the capitals of the Persian Empire, comm. occupied by the king, from its genial climate, in the winter or spring, ii. 4. 25 : iii. 5. 15. ‖ Extensive ruins at Sûs, where the remains of the great palace of Darius I. have been lately disinterred.

†Σοφ-αίνετος, ου, *Sophænetus*, from Stymphālus in Arcadia, one of the oldest of the Cyrean generals. As his name does not appear after the Cyreans reached the Bosphorus, it is probable that he took this opportunity of leaving the army, perhaps displeased with his fine or thinking his age too little respected, and that Phryniscus was appointed in his place. He may have written a history of the expedition to justify himself, since we find a Sophænetus mentioned as the author of such a history. i. 1. 11 : v. 8. 1.

†σοφία, ας, *wisdom, skill*, i. 2. 8. Der. SOPHIA, PHILO-SOPHY.

σοφός, ή, όν, *wise, intelligent, clever, gifted, accomplished*, i. 10. 2.

†σπανίζω, ίσω ιῶ, *to lack, want, be in want of*, G., ii. 2. 12 : vii. 7. 42.

†σπάνιος, α, ον, *scarce, scanty*, i. 9. 27.

σπάνις, εως, ή, scarcity, scantiness, want, G., vi. 4. 8 : vii. 2. 15.

Σπάρτη, ης, Sparta (on the west bank of the Eurōtas, now the Iri), also called Λακεδαίμων, the capital of Laconia, and that city of Greece in which its military spirit and prowess, and the subordination of the individual to the state culminated. It was the especial residence of the Dorian conquerors of Laconia, a great military and land-holding aristocracy (οἱ ὅμοιοι the peers, iv. 6. 14), owning estates throughout the province, which were chiefly cultivated by the conquered people reduced to a state of serfdom under the name of Helots. Still a third class, the Perioeci (περίοικοι, dwelling around the capital in rural villages), were personally free, but without political power, neither serfs nor citizens. The trade and mechanic arts of the country were chiefly in the hands of these. The Spartan citizens were so few in comparison with their slaves and subjects, that they could hope to maintain their ascendency only by a thorough system of military and political training. Hence they submitted to the rigid and peculiar laws of Lycurgus, observed great simplicity in their personal habits, subordinated domestic to public life, accounted luxury, ease, and self-indulgence as crimes, disdained the protection of walls, and lived at Sparta as in a camp. At the head of the state were two kings and five ephors. In the government of their subject states, the Spartans were commonly disliked; because they here applied to so great an extent the arbitrary, selfish, unconciliatory, and inhuman principles, and the haughtiness of manner, which were observed at home in the government of their helots; sometimes combining with these a self-indulgence and deceit which at home they would not dare to practise, and covetousness, even to the taking of bribes. At the time of the Cyrean expedition, the Spartans, having so recently conquered their great rival, Athens, were the undisputed masters of the Greek world, and exercised their power arrogantly, wantonly, and cruelly. ii. 6. 4. ‖ New

Sparta (near Mistra), lately built to cherish the memory of ancient greatness.

†Σπαρτιάτης, ου, a Spartan, a man belonging by birth to the class of Spartan citizens, iv. 8. 25 : vi. 6. 30.

σπάρτον, ου, (σπεῖρα a twisted cord) a cord, rope, iv. 7. 15.

σπάω, άσω, ἔσπακα, pf. p. ἔσπασμαι, to draw : M. to draw one's own, A.; ἐσπασμένοι τὰ ξίφη with drawn swords; i. 8. 29 : vii. 4. 16. Der. SPASM.

σπείρω,* σπερῶ, ἔσπαρκα l., spargo, to scatter seed, sow, vi. 1. 8. Der. SPERM.

σπένδω,* σπείσω, ἔσπεικα l., a. ἔσπεισα, libo, to make or offer a libation, to pour, iv. 3. 13 s : — M. to make or agree to a treaty, peace, or truce (since in this mutual libations were common), D., πρός, ἐπί, i. 9. 7 s : iii. 5. 16 : iv. 4. 6.

σπεύδω, σπεύσω, ἔσπευκα l., to hasten, make haste, press on, be in haste, be eager, I., i. 3. 14 ; 5. 9 : iv. 8. 14.

Σπιθριδάτης, ου, a general of the Bithynian satrap, Pharnabazus. He afterwards took offence, and left his service for that of Agesilāus, but left the latter again from a new offence. vi. 5. 7.

σπολάς or στολάς, άδος, ή, (στέλλω) a leathern waistcoat, worn under or instead of the metallic θώραξ, iii. 3. 20 : iv. 1. 18. The form σπολάς appears to be Dor., 168. 2 : see λοχαγός.

σπονδή, ῆς, (σπένδω q. v.) a libation, drink-offering : pl. libations, hence comm., a treaty, truce, or armistice, peace, i. 9. 8 : ii. 3. 4 s : iv. 3. 14.

†σπουδάζω, άσομαι, ἐσπούδακα, to be busy, zealous, or in earnest, to work zealously or hard, ii. 3. 12.

†σπουδαιο-λογέω, ήσω, (σπουδαῖος earnest, λόγος) A. & M. to engage in earnest conversation, converse seriously, i. 9. 28.

σπουδή, ῆς, (σπεύδω) haste, speed, expedition, earnestness, i. 8. 4 : iv. 1. 17.

†στάδιον, ου, pl. οἱ στάδιοι & τὰ στάδια, a stadium, stade, nearly a furlong; the [stopping-place] length of the footrace-course, which at Olympia (the comm. standard) was = 600 Greek, or 606¾ Eng. feet : hence, the common or short foot-race itself, as in σ. ἀγωνίζεσθαι to contend in the short race or course : i. 4. 1, 4 ; 8. 17 : iv. 8. 27.

σταθμός 124 στράτευμα

†σταθμός, οῦ, ὁ, statio, *a* STATION or *stopping-place*, esp. at night ; hence, *a day's journey or march* (averaging in the Anab., acc. to vii. 8. 26, about 5½ parasangs, or 160 stadia), *a stage ;* i. 2. 5 s ; 7. 14 ; 8. 1 ; 10. 1 : ii. 2. 6.

σταίην, στάς, see ἵστημι, v. 2. 16.

‡στασιάζω, άσω, ἐστασίακα, *to form a party* or *excite faction* against, *be factious* or *contentious, be at variance* or *divided into parties, contend* or *quarrel*, D., πρός, ii. 5. 28 : vi. 1. 29, 32 : vii. 1. 39 ; 2. 2.

‡στάσις, εως, ἡ, [the standing up against] *faction, dissension*, vi. 1. 29. Der. APOSTASY.

‡στασιώτης, ου, *an opposer*, vi. 6. 6?

‡σταυρός, οῦ, ὁ, *a stake, pale*, or *palisade*, usu. crossing others, v. 2. 21: vii. 4. 14, 17.

[‡σταυρόω, ώσω, *to palisade*.]

‡σταύρωμα, ατος, τό, *a paling, line of palisades*, v. 2. 15, 19, 27. [28.

‡στέαρ, στέατος, τό, *tallow, fat*, v. 4.

†στέγασμα, ατος, τό, (στεγάζω *to cover*) *a covering, tent-cover*, i. 5. 10?

στέγη, ης, ἡ, (στέγω *tego, to cover, shelter*) *a roof, shelter* under a roof, *cover, covered house, cottage*, iv. 4. 14.

‡στεγνός, ή, όν, (στέγω) *covered, roofed*, vii. 4. 12.

στείβω (v. l. στίβω), ψω 1., (cf. stipo) *to tread, beat*, or *press down*, as a road, mattress, &c.; hence, *to frequent* a road ; A.; i. 9. 13.

στέλλω,* ελῶ, ἔσταλκα, pf. p. ἔσταλμαι, *to equip, accoutre, fit out, despatch, send*, A. ἐπί : *M. to* [send one's self] *set forth, proceed, journey, go*, ἐπί, κατά : iii. 2. 7 : v.6.5. Der. APOSTLE.

στενός, ή, όν, c. ώτερος or ότερος, 257 b, *narrow, strait : ἐν τῷ στενῷ* or τοῖς στενοῖς in angustiis, *in the narrows* or *defile, in the narrow space, road*, or *pass :* i. 4. 4 : iii. 4. 19, 22 : iv. 1. 14 ; 4. 18. Der. STENO-GRAPHY.

‡στενο-χωρία, ας, (χῶρος) *a narrow place, spot, road*, or *pass*, i. 5. 7.

στέργω,* στέρξω, 2 pf. Ion. ἔστοργα, *to love* (in the higher sense), *regard with affection*, A., ii. 6. 23. Cf. φιλέω.

στερέω & στερίσκω,* στερήσω, ἐστέρηκα, *to deprive*, A. G., ii. 5. 10 : — P. & *M.* στέρομαι (v. l. στερέομαι), στερήσομαι, ἐστέρημαι, n. ἐστερήθην, *to be deprived of, lose, want*, G., i. 4. 8 ; 9. 13 : ii. 1. 12 : iii. 2. 2 : iv. 5. 28.

στέρνον, ου, (στερεός or στερρός *firm*, whence STEREO-TYPE) *the breast*, i. 8. 26 : vii. 4. 4. Der. STERNUM.

στερρῶς (στερρός *firm*) *firmly, steadfastly, resolutely*, iii. 1. 22.

στέφανος, ου, ὁ, (στέφω *to encircle*) *a crown, garland, wreath*, common among the Greeks as a prize of victory, as a mark of honor, and as a festal or sacred ornament, i. 7. 7 : iv. 5. 33 : vi. 4. 9. Der. STEPHEN.

‡στεφανόω, ώσω, ἐστεφάνωκα, pf. p. ἐστεφάνωμαι, *to crown*, A.: *M. to crown one's self :* iv. 3. 17 ; 5. 33 : vii. 1. 40.

†στήλη, ης, *a pillar, post*, v. 3. 12 : vii. 5. 13.

στῆναι, στῆσας, see ἵστημι, i. 2. 15.

†στιβάς, άδος, ἡ, *a bed of straw* or *leaves, a mat, mattress*, vi. 1. 4 ?

†στίβος, ου, ὁ, *a trodden* or *beaten way* or *path, a track* (made by many *ἴχνη*, or single footsteps), i. 6. 1.

στίβω v. l. for στείβω, i. 9. 13.

στίζω, ίξω, pf. *p. ἐστιγμαι*, (cf. Lat. in-stigo, Germ. stechen, Eng. *stick, sting*) *to prick, tattoo*, A. AE., v. 4. 32. Der. STIGMA.

στίφος, εος, τό, (στείβω) *a throng, mass, dense* or *compact body*, of men, i. 8. 13, 26 : vi. 5. 26.

στλεγγίς, ίδος, ἡ, *a strigil, fleshcomb, scraper*, such as were used by bathers to cleanse the skin ; or, as some think, an ornamental *comb* for the head, such as even men wore on some sacred occasions ; i. 2. 10.

στολάς, see σπολάς, iii. 3. 20 ?

στολή, ῆς, (στέλλω) *an equipment, dress, garment, robe*, i. 2. 27 : iv. 5. 33 ; 7. 13 : vi. 1. 2. Der. STOLE.

στόλος, ου, ὁ, (στέλλω) *an equipment, preparation ; an armament, armed force, army ; an expedition, march, journey, voyage ;* i. 2. 5 ; 3. 16 : ii. 2. 10, 12 : iii. 1. 9 s ; 2. 11 ; 3. 2.

στόμα, ατος, τό, *the mouth* of a person, river, sea, pit, &c.; *the outlet* or *entrance ;* of an army, *the front* or *van ;* iii. 4. 42 s : iv. 5. 25, 27 : vi. 2. 1 ; 4. 1. Der. STOMACH.

†στρατεία, ας, *a campaign, expedition*, iii. 1. 9 : v. 4. 18.

†στράτευμα, ατος, τό, *a body led to war, an army, host ; a military force* (whether larger or smaller, an entire army or a division of it), for which στράτευμα is the most general term.

στρατεύω 125 συγγενής

Of στράτευμα, στρατιά, and στρατός, the first is far the most used in the Anab., and the last but once. i.1.7s; 2. 1, 14, 25 ; 5. 11s ; 7. 1s : v. 6. 17.

†στρατεύω, εύσω, έστράτευκα, to lead to war, make war, engage in war, make an expedition, march, ch. of leaders or commanders, έπί, είς, ii. 1. 14; 3. 20; 4. 3; 6. 29 :—M. (oftener, and of both leaders and followers) to take the field, make or engage in war, make an expedition or take part in one, march, serve in arms or as a soldier, έπί, είς, σύν, &c., i. 1. 11; 2. 2s; 9. 14 : ii. 1. 1 : iii. 1. 10 : v. 4. 34.

†στρατηγέω, ήσω, to be general or commander ; to lead, command, direct, or manage, as general ; to take command ; G. AE.: στρατηγείν διεπράξατο he obtained command of : στρατηγείν στρατηγίαν to undertake a command : τούτο ύμας πρώτον ήμών στρατηγήσαι that your first act in taking command of us should be this: i. 3. 15 ; 4. 3 : ii. 2. 13 ; 6. 28 : iii. 2. 27 : vii. 6. 40. Der. STRATAGEM.

†στρατηγία, as, generalship, military command ; mode of leading an army, plan of operations or management of affairs in war ; i. 3. 15 : ii. 2. 13 : v. 6. 25 : vii. 1. 41. Der. STRATEGY.

†στρατηγιάω, άσω, (desiderative, 378 d) to desire or seek military command, vii. 1. 33.

†στρατ-ηγός, ού, ό, (άγω) a leader or commander of an army or of one of its larger divisions, a general ; the commander of the troops of a Persian province (also termed κάρανος), according to the theory of the empire a different person from the satrap for the sake of mutual restraint, but in practice often the same ; G. In mercenary service, the pay of a general appears to have usu. been four times that of a private. i. 1. 2 ; 2. 15 : vii. 6. 7.

†στρατιά, άς, an army, host, comm. of an entire army, or of its mass in distinction fr. the officers or fr. an excepted part (hence ή στρατιά = πάν τό στράτευμα, vi. 6. 2, 27) ; also used as a collective, = στρατιώται soldiers; i. 2. 12, 27 ; 3. 20 ; 4. 5 : iii. 2. 13 : v. 2. 30 : vi. 3. 19 ; 6. 26 : see στράτευμα.

†στρατιώτης, ου, a soldier, esp. a private or common soldier, i. 1. 9 ; 2. 17 ; 3. 7s, 21 : iii. 2. 2 : vii. 2. 36.

†Στρατο-κλής, έους, Stratocles, from Crete, the commander of a serviceable body of archers, iv. 2. 28.

†στρατο-πεδεύω, εύσω, έστρατοπέδευκα, to make a camp : comm. M. to encamp, be encamped ; pf. to lie in camp ; άνά, έν, είς, παρά, &c.: i. 3. 7: ii. 2. 15 ; 4. 1, 10 : vi. 4. 7 : vii. 6. 24.

†στρατό-πεδον, ου, (πέδον ground) the ground occupied by an encamped army, a camp, encampment; by meton. for the army encamped ; i. 10. 1, 5 : iv. 8. 23 : vi. 4. 27 : so pl. vii. 3. 34.

στρατός, ού, ό, (akin to στρώννυμι sterno, STREW ? cf. strātus) a body of men encamped, hence, an army, host, = στρατιά q. v., i. 5. 7: see στράτευμα.

στραφείς, see στρέφω, i. 10. 6.

†στρεπτός, ή, όν, twisted, wreathed: subst. στρεπτός, sc. κύκλος, torquis, a wreath, necklace, collar, chain, i. 2. 27 ; 5. 8 ; 8. 29.

στρέφω,* έψω, έστροφα l., pf. p. έστραμμαι, 2 a. p. έστράφην, (τρέπω) to turn, twist, wreathe, braid, plait, A., iv. 7. 15 : — A. intrans. & M., w. 2 a. p., of soldiers, to turn, wheel, face about, πρός, i. 10. 6? iii. 5. 1 : iv. 3. 26, 32. Der. STROPHE, CATA-STROPHE.

στρουθός, ού, ό ή, a field-bird, esp. sparrow ; an ostrich (fully σ. ό μέγας the great bird), i. 5. 2, 3.

στρωματό-δεσμος or -ον, ου, ό or τό, (στρώμα bed) a bed-sack, in which the bed-clothes were carried or kept, v. 4. 13.

στυγνός, ή, όν, (στυγέω to hate) hateful, repulsive, gloomy, stern : τό στυγνόν the gloom or sternness: ii. 6. 9, 11.

Στυμφάλιος, ου, ό, a Stymphalian, a man of Stymphālus, a city near a lake of the same name in northeastern Arcadia. It was one of the fabled labors of Hercules to destroy the monstrous birds which haunted this lake. i. 1. 11. ‖ Ruins in the vale of Zaraká.

σύ * (σού, σοί, σέ, encl.), pl. ύμείς, tu (tui, tibi, te), vos, THOU, YOU, i. 3. 3s ; 6. 6s : ii. 1. 16s : vii. 7. 30s.

συγ- or ξυγ-, the form which σύν takes in compos. before a palatal, 150.

†συγγένεια, as, relationship, kin, vii. 3. 39.

συγ-γενής, ές, (γένος) joined by birth, of the same race, related, akin : pl. συγγενείς subst., relatives, relations, kinsmen, kinsfolk : i. 6. 10 : vii. 2. 31.

συγ-γίγνομαι,* γενήσομαι,γεγένημαι & 2 pf. γέγονα, 2 a. ἐγενόμην, to come to be with, *have intercourse, acquaintance,* or *an interview with; to be with, associate* or *confer with, become acquainted with; to be under one's instruction; to come together, meet;* D.; i. 1. 9; 2. 12, 27: ii. 5. 2; 6. 17.

συγ-κάθ-ημαι,* καθήσομαι, *to sit together,* v. 7. 21.

συγ-καλέω,* καλέσω καλῶ, κέκληκα, a. ἐκάλεσα, *to call together, convoke, convene, assemble,* A. εἰς, i. 4. 8; 6. 4.

συγ-κάμπτω, κάμψω, (κάμπτω *to bend*) *to bend together, to bend up,* A., v. 8. 10: *v. l.* συν-ανα-κάμπτω.

συγ-κατα-καίω & Att. -κάω,* καύσω, κέκαυκα, *to burn up with* them, A., iii. 2. 27.

συγ-κατα-σκεδάννυμι,* σκεδάσω σκεδῶ, A. or M. *to sprinkle* or *throw down with* another, A. G.? vii. 3. 32?

συγ-κατα-στρέφω,* ἔψω, ἔστροφα l.; M. *to assist in subduing* or *reducing,* D., ii. 1. 14: see κατα-στρέφω.

συγ-κατ-εργάζομαι,* άσομαι, εἴργασμαι, εἰργασάμην, *to assist in gaining,* A. D., vii. 7. 25: *v. l.* κατεργάζομαι.

σύγ-κειμαι,* κείσομαι, (as pass. of συν-τίθημι) *to be laid down mutually, to be agreed upon*: εἰς τὸ συγκείμενον, sc. χωρίον, *to the place agreed upon, to the rendezvous,* vi. 3. 4: τὰ συγκείμενα the [things agreed on] *agreement,* vii. 2. 7.

συγ-κλείω, είσω, κέκλεικα, *to shut together* (e. g. the two leaves of a double gate), *to close,* A., vii. 1. 12.

συγ-κομίζω, ίσω ιῶ, κεκόμικα, *to bring together, collect* : so M. (for one's own benefit), A., vi. 6. 37?

συγ-κύπτω, κύψω, κέκυφα, *to bend together* or *towards each other, approach, converge,* iii. 4. 19, 21.

συγ-χωρέω, ήσω, κεχώρηκα, *to go with, concur, assent, acquiesce,* v. 2. 9.

σύειος, α, ον, (σῦς) *obtained from swine,* iv. 4. 13 : *v. l.* σύϊνος, &c.

Συέννεσις, ιος, *Syennesis,* a king of Cilicia, who tried to pursue such a course that he should not lose his crown, whether Cyrus or Artaxerxes prevailed. Diodōrus states (14. 20) that he secretly sent a son to the king to assure him of his fidelity, to report the doings of Cyrus, and to say that whatever he had himself done for the latter, had been done through compulsion. Syennesis appears to have been a common name of the Cilician kings. i. 2. 12, 26 s: vii. 8. 25.

σῦκον, ου, *a fig,* vi. 4. 6; 6. 1. Der. SYCA-MORE, SYCO-PHANT.

συλ- or ξυλ-, the form which σύν takes in compos. before λ, 150.

συλ-λαμβάνω,* λήψομαι, εἴληφα, 2 a. ἔλαβον, *to take by bringing the hands together, seize, arrest, apprehend, capture,* A., i. 1. 3 ; 4. 8 ; 6. 4 : iii. 1. 2, 35 : iv. 4. 16. Der. SYL-LABLE.

συλ-λέγω,* λέξω, εἴλοχα, pf. *p.* εἴλεγμαι, 2 a. *p.* ἐλέγην, (λέγω lego, *to* LAY, *gather*) *to gather together, collect, levy, assemble, convene,* trans., A., i. 1. 7, 9 : ii. 4. 11 : iii. 1. 39 :— M., w. 2 a. *p., to assemble, congregate, come* or *get together, collect, gather, convene,* intrans.; *to be assembled,* &c.; iv. 1. 10 s; v. 5. 1, 12 ; 8. 9: v. 7. 3 : vi. 3. 6.

†συλλογή, ῆς, *an assembling, levy,* i. 6.

†σύλλογος, ου, ὁ, *a gathering, assembly, assemblage, meeting,* v. 6. 22 ; 7. 2 (not summoned, cf. ἐκκλησία). Der. SYLLOGISM.

συμ- or ξυμ-, the form which σύν takes in compos. before a labial, 150.

συμ-βαίνω,* βήσομαι, βέβηκα, 2 a. ἔβην, *to come together, meet, occur, happen, result,* iii. 1. 13.

συμ-βάλλω,* βαλῶ, βέβληκα, 2 a. ἔβαλον, *to cast, dash,* or *bring together, collect,* A., iii. 4. 31:— M. (of mutual or joint action) *to contribute, give a suggestion* or *hint, agree upon, contract,* A. D., περί, i. 1. 9 : iv. 6. 14 : vi. 3. 3 ; 6. 35. Der. SYMBOL.

συμ-βοάω, ήσομαι, βεβόηκα l., *to call aloud* or *shout to* each other, A., vi. 3. 6.

συμ-βοηθέω, ήσω, βεβοήθηκα, *to help together* or *in a body, join in assisting, hasten to add assistance,* ἐξ, iv. 2. 1 : vii. 8. 17.

συμ-βολή, ῆς, (συμ-βάλλω) *a dashing together, encounter in arms,* vi. 5. 32.

†συμ-βουλεύω, εύσω, βεβούλευκα, *to plan with, counsel, advise,* D. A., I. (A.), i. 6. 9 : ii. 1. 17s : iii. 1. 5 :— M. *to consult* or *confer with, ask* one's *advice,* D. CP., i. 1. 10 ; 7. 2 : ii. 1. 16 s.

συμ-βουλή, ῆς, *consultation, counsel, advice,* v. 6. 4, 11.

σύμβουλος 127 σύν

†σύμβουλος, ου, ὁ, a counsellor, adviser, i. 6. 5.

συμ-μανθάνω,* μαθήσομαι, μεμάθηκα, 2 a. ἔμαθον, to become familiar with or accustomed to, iv. 5. 27.

†συμμαχέω, ήσω, (σύμμαχος) to be or become an ally, form an alliance with, v. 4. 30.

†συμμαχία, as, (σύμμαχος) an alliance, offensive and defensive, v. 4. 3, 8 : vii. 3. 35.

συμ-μάχομαι,* μαχέσομαι μαχοῦμαι, μεμάχημαι, to fight together, with, or by one's side, D., v. 4. 10 : vi. 1. 13.

†σύμμαχος, ον, fighting with, auxiliary, allied, in alliance with ; τὰ σύμμαχα the aids, advantages, or resources, in war : σύμμαχος subst., an ally; auxiliary: D., G., ἐπί: i.3. 6 ; 7. 3 : ii. 4. 6 s ; 5. 11 : v. 4. 9.

συμ-μετ-έχω,* ἔξω, ἔσχηκα, 2 a. ἔσχον, to partake or have a share in with others, G., vii. 8. 17 : v. l. μετέχω.

συμ-μίγνῡμι or -ύω,* μίξω, μέμιχα l., to mingle or unite with (trans. or intrans.), join, form a junction with, meet (as friends or enemies), join battle with, D. ἐν, εἰs, ii. 1. 2 ; 3. 19 : iv. 6. 24 : vi. 3. 24 : vii. 8. 24.

συμ-παρα-σκευάζω,άσω,to co-operate by preparing, providing, or procuring, A., v. 1. 8, 10.

συμ-παρ-έχω,* ἔξω, ἔσχηκα, 2 a. ἔσχον, to join in giving, producing, or procuring, A. D., vii. 4. 19 ; 6. 30.

σύμ-πᾶς, ᾶσα, ἄν, all together, the whole together, entire, in all : τὸ σύμπαν adv., altogether, throughout : i. 2. 9 ; 5. 9 : iv. 3. 2 : vii. 8. 26.

συμ-πεδάω, ήσω, (πέδη) to fetter, confine, iv. 4. 11 : v. l. συμ-ποδίζω.

συμ-πέμπω,* πέμψω, πέπομφα, to send or despatch with another, A. D., i. 2. 20 : iii. 4. 42s : v. 5. 15 : 6. 7, 21.

συμ-περι-τυγχάνω,* τεύξομαι, τετύχηκα, to [fall in with round about] succeed in surrounding, D., vii. 8. 22?

συμ-πίπτω,* πεσοῦμαι,πέπτωκα, 2 a. ἔπεσον, to fall together, fall in, collapse; to meet in close conflict, grapple or close with ; i. 9. 6 : iv. 8. 11? v. 2. 24. Der. SYMPTOM.

σύμ-πλεως, ων, (πλέως * full) [filled together] quite or very full of, filled with, abounding in, G., i. 2. 22 : v. l. ἐμ-πλεως.

συμ-ποδίζω, ἴσω ιῶ, (πούς) to tie the feet together, confine, encumber, impede, A., iv. 4. 11 : v. l. συμ-πεδάω.

συμ-πολεμέω, ήσω, πεπολέμηκα, to war or make war with as an ally, assist in war, D. ἐπί, πρός, i. 4. 2.

συμ-πορεύομαι, εὐσομαι, πεπόρευμαι, to proceed or march with, take part in an expedition, i. 3. 5 ; 4. 9.

συμποσί-αρχος, ου, ὁ, (ἄρχω, συμπόσιον banquet, fr. πίνω) rex convivii, the president of a banquet, a symposiarch; an office for which Spartans were more rarely selected, from their lack of social vivacity ; vi. 1. 30.

συμ-πράττω, άξω, πέπρᾱχα, to cooperate with, assist, aid ; to assist in effecting or obtaining ; to join in arranging, agree ; D. AE. περί, ὥστε : i. 1. 8 : v. 4. 9 ; 5. 23 : vii. 4. 13 ; 8. 23.

συμ-πρέσβεις, εων, οἱ, (πρέσβυς *) fellow-ambassadors, colleagues in an embassy, v. 5. 24.

συμ-προ-θυμέομαι, ήσομαι, ipf. προυθυμούμην, to join in urging, add one's influence or efforts, I. (A.), AE., ὅπως, iii. 1. 9 : vii. 1. 5 ; 2. 24.

συμ-προ-νομέω, ήσω, (νέμω) to forage together, v. 1. 7: v. l. σὺν προνομαῖς.

συμ-φέρω,* οἴσω, ἐνήνοχα, a. ἤνεγκα or -ον, pf. p. ἐνήνεγμαι, to bring together, gather, collect, contribute ; to contribute good, be advantageous, beneficial, suitable, or suited, sometimes impers.; to bear or share with ; A. D., ἐπί, πρός, ii. 2. 2 : iii. 2. 27 ; 4. 31 : vi. 4. 9 : vii. 3. 37 ; 6. 20 ; 8. 4.

σύμ-φημι,* φήσω, to [say with another] assent to, acknowledge, A., v. 8. 8 : vii. 2. 26.

σύμφορος, ον, (συμ-φέρω) advantageous, beneficial, useful, D., vii. 7. 21?

σύν * prep., old Att. ξύν 170, cum, with, together with, at the same time with, in company or connection with, with the help or favor of, under the command of; w. DAT. of person (companion, helper, counsellor, commander, military force, &c.), instrument, dress, circumstance, feeling, means, manner, &c., i. 1. 11 ; 2. 15 ; 3. 5 s ; 8. 4 : ii. 1. 12 : iii. 1. 23 ; 3. 1 s, 14. In compos. (συγ- before a palatal, συμ- bef. a labial, συλ- bef. λ, συρ- bef. ρ, συ- or συσ- bef. σ, 150, 166), con-, with, at the same time, together, altogether, sometimes strengthening such an idea already in the simple verb.

συν-αγείρω, pf. άγήγερκα l., a. ήγειρα, to assemble together, collect, A. D., i. 5. 9.

συν-άγω,* άξω, ήξα, 2 a. ήγαγον, to bring together, collect, assemble, convene; to bring together or join the edges of, close; A. έξ : i. 3. 2, 9 ; 5. 10: iii. 5. 14 : iv. 4. 19 : vi. 2. 8.

συν-αδικέω, ήσω, ήδίκηκα, to commit injustice with another, join in wrongdoing, be an accomplice in evil deeds, D., ii. 6. 27.

συν-αθροίζω, οίσω, ήθροικα, to gather together, collect, esp. troops, A., vii. 2. 8 : — M. to flock together, vi. 5. 30.

συν-αιθριάζω, άσω, (αίθρία) to bivouac together in the open air, iv. 4. 10 ?

συν-αινέω,* έσω, (αίνέω to speak) to agree with, promise, concede, grant, A. D., vii. 7. 31.

συν-αιρέω,* ήσω, ήρηκα, 2 a. εΐλον, to take together, com-prehend: ως συνελόντι είπεΐν, sc. λόγω, to speak in comprehensive language, to say all in a word, iii. 1. 38 : see ώς f.

συν-ακολουθέω, ήσω, ήκολούθηκα, to go in company with, follow closely, accompany, D., ii. 5. 30, 35 : vii. 7. 11.

συν-ακούω,* ούσομαι, άκήκοα, to hear mutually, G., v. 4. 31.

συν-αλίζω, a. ήλισα, a. p. ήλίσθην, to gather together, collect, A., vii. 3. 48.

συν-αλλάττω,* άξω, ήλλαχα, a. p. ήλλάγην, (άλλάττω to change, fr. άλλος) to change so as to bring together, reconcile: M., w. 2 a. p., to become reconciled, come to an agreement, make peace, πρός, i. 2. 1.

συν-ανα-βαίνω,* βήσομαι, βέβηκα, 2 a. έβην, to go up with, D., i. 3. 18.

συν-ανα-κάμπτω, κάμψω, to bend up together, v. l. for συγ-κάμπτω, v. 8. 10.

συν-ανα-πράττω, άξω, πέπράχα, to join in exacting or requiring what is due, A. παρά, vii. 7. 14.

συν-αν-ίστημι,* στήσω, έστηκα, 2 a. έστην, to raise up with: M., w. pf. and 2 a. act., to rise or stand up with, vii. 3. 35.

συν-αντάω, ήσω, ήντηκα, (άντάω to meet, fr. άντί) to meet [and speak with], i. 8. 15 : vii. 2. 5.

συν-άπ-ειμι,* ipf. ήειν, (είμι) to depart or return with, ii. 2. 1.

συν-απο-λαμβάνω, λήψομαι, είληφα, to receive at the same time what is due, vii. 7. 40.

συν-άπτω, άψω, to fasten together; to join (battle), engage in, A. D., i. 5. 16.

συν-άρχω, άρξω, ήρχα, to be associated in command with, D., vi. 1. 32.

σύν-δειπνος, ου, ό, (δεΐπνον) a tablecompanion, guest at table, ii. 5. 27.

συν-δια-βαίνω,* βήσομαι, βέβηκα, 2 a. έβην, to cross with others, vii. 1. 4.

συν-δια-πράττω, άξω, πέπρᾶχα, to accomplish with : M. to negotiate with, ύπέρ, iv. 8. 24.

συν-δοκέω,* δόξω, to seem good in like manner, be likewise approved, D., vi. 5. 10.

συν-δραμοῦμαι, see συν-τρέχω.

σύν-δυο indecl., two together, two by two, vi. 3. 2.

συν-ε-: for augmented forms thus beginning, look under συγ- before a palatal, συμ- bef. a labial, συλ-, συρ-, bef. λ, ρ, and συ-(σ) bef. σ, 151, 166.

συν-εγενόμην, see συγ-γίγνομαι.

συν-έδραμον, see συν-τρέχω, v. 7. 4.

συν-είδον, -ειδέναι, see συν-οράω.

συν-είλεγμαι, see συλ-λέγω, iv. 3. 7.

συν-είληφα, -είλημμαι, see συλ-λαμβάνω, iii. 1. 2, 35.

σύν-ειμι,* έσομαι, (είμί) to be with, associate with, D.: οί συνόντες associates or followers: ii. 6. 20, 23 : vi. 6. 35.

σύν-ειμι,* ήειν, (είμι) to go or come together, come or advance for an encounter, P., i. 10. 10 : iii. 5. 7 ?

συν-ειπόμην, see συν-έπομαι, v. 2. 4.

συν-εισ-έρχομαι,* έλεύσομαι, έλήλυθα, 2 a. ήλθον, to enter together with, πρός . . είς . . σύν, iv. 5. 10.

συν-εισ-πίπτω,*πεσοῦμαι, πέπτωκα, 2 a. έπεσον, to fall, rush, or plunge into together with others, είσω . . σύν, v. 7. 25 : vii. 1. 18.

συν-εκ-βαίνω,* βήσομαι, βέβηκα, to go forth together with, έπί, iv. 3. 22.

συν-εκ-βιβάζω, βιβάσω βιβῶ, to join in lifting out, assist in extricating, A., i. 5. 7.

συν-εκ-κόπτω, κόψω, κέκοφα, to join in cutting down, A., iv. 8. 8.

συν-εκ-πίνω,* πίομαι (?), πέπωκα, 2 a. έπϊον, to drink with another to the bottom of the cup, vii. 3. 32.

συν-εκ-πορίζω, ίσω ιῶ, πεπόρικα, to aid in procuring or supplying, A. D., v. 8. 25 : v. l. συνεξευπορέω, &c.

συν-έλαβον, see συλ-λαμβάνω, iii. 2. 4.

συν-έλεξα, -ελέγην, see συλ-λέγω.

συν-ελήλυθα, -ελθεῖν, see συν-έρχομαι, ii. 1. 2 : iii. 1. 36.
συν-ελόντι, see συν-αιρέω, iii. 1. 38.
συν-έμιξα, see συμ-μίγνῦμι, ii. 3. 19.
συν-ενεγκών, -ενήνεγμαι, see συμφέρω, iii. 4. 31: vi. 4. 9.
συν-εξ-έρχομαι,* ελεύσομαι, ελήλυθα, to go out with, join in an excursion, D., vii. 8. 11.
συν-εξ-ευ-πορέω, ήσω, (πόρος) to aid in procuring relief, A. D., v. 8. 25 ?
συν-επ-αινέω,* έσω, ήνεκα, (αίνέω to speak) to join in approving, A., vii. 3. 36.
συν-επ-εύχομαι, εύξομαι, εύγμαι or ηύγμαι, to vow moreover at the same time, I., iii. 2. 9.
συν-επι-μελέομαι, ήσομαι,μεμέλημαι, to take or have the joint charge of, G., vi. 1. 22.
συν-επι-σπέσθαι, see συν-εφ-έπομαι.
συν-επι-σπεύδω, εύσω, to assist in hastening forward, A., i. 5. 8.
συν-επι-τρίβω, τρίψω, τέτρῑφα, (τρίβω to rub) to crush together, destroy utterly, ruin, A., v. 8. 20.
συν-έπομαι,* έψομαι, ipf. ειπόμην, to follow with or closely, follow, accompany, attend, D., i. 3. 9 ; 4. 17.
συν-επ-όμνῦμι,* όμοῦμαι, ὀμώμοκα, to swear at the same time yet further, to add the further oath, I., vii. 6. 19.
συν-εργός, όν, (έργον) working with: συνεργός subst., a co-worker, assistant, helper, coadjutor, D. G., i. 9. 20 s.
συν-ερρύην, -ερρυήκειν, see συρ-ρέω.
συν-έρχομαι,* ελεύσομαι, ελήλυθα, 2 a. ήλθον, to go or come together, assemble, convene, meet, παρά, ως P., ii. 1. 2; 2. 8; 3. 21; 5. 3: iii. 1. 33 s.
συν-εσ-: for most words thus beginning, look under συ-σ-: e. g.,
συν-έσπων, see συ-σπάω, i. 5. 10.
συν-εστάθην, -έστην, -έστηκα, see συν-ίστημι, iii. 1. 8 : vi. 5. 28, 30.
συν-εφ-έπομαι,* έψομαι, ipf. ειπόμην, 2 a. έσπόμην, to follow close upon, follow closely, accompany, D., iii. 1. 2 (v. l. συν-έπομαι) : iv. 8. 18: vii. 4. 6.
συν-έχω,* έξω, έσχηκα, to hold or keep together, A., vii. 2. 8.
συν-εώρων, see συν-οράω, iv. 1. 11.
συν-ήγαγον, see συν-άγω, i. 3. 2.
συν-ήδομαι, f. p. ησθήσομαι, to rejoice with, con-gratulate, D. ότι, v. 5. 8 : vii. 7. 42; 8. 1.
συν-ῄειν, see σύν-ειμι (ειμι), i. 10. 10.

συν-ῆλθον, see συν-έρχομαι, ii. 2. 8.
συν-θεάομαι, άσομαι, τεθέᾱμαι, to join in inspecting, A., vi. 4. 15.
συν-θέμενος, -θέσθαι, see συν-τίθημι, ii. 5. 8 : v. 1. 12.
‡σύν-θημα, ατος, τό, an agreement or thing agreed upon, token, watchword, password, i. 8. 16 : iv. 6. 20: vi. 5. 25.
συν-θηράω, άσω, τεθήρᾱκα, to hunt with another, join in the chase, v. 3. 10.
συν-θοῖτο or -θεῖτο, see συν-τίθημι.
συν-ιδεῖν, see συν-οράω, i. 5. 9.
συν-ίημι,* ήσω, είκα, ipf. ίην or ίειν, to put together, understand, A., vii. 6. 8.
συν-ίστημι,* στήσω, έστηκα, 2 a. έστην, a. p. εστάθην, to [bring together as friends] present or introduce to, A. D., iii. 1. 8 : vi. 1. 23 :—M., w. act. 2 a. & pf. (pret.), to stand together or in a body ; to assemble, gather, collect, combine, unite, intrans.; to exist in a body, be embodied or organized ; επί, &c.; v. 7. 2, 16 : vi. 2. 9, 11s; 5. 28, 30 : vii. 6. 26. Der. SYSTEM.
σύν-οδος, ου, ἡ, a way or coming together, meeting, encounter, shock of arms, εἰς, i. 10. 7 : vi. 4. 9. Der. SYNOD.
σύν-οιδα, see συν-οράω, i. 3. 10.
συν-οίσω, see συμ-φέρω, vii. 8. 4.
συν-ολολύζω, ύξομαι,(ὀλολύζω ululo, HOWL) to join in a loud cry, iv. 3. 19.
συν-ομολογέω, ήσω, ὡμολόγηκα, to agree upon with another, agree with or to, assent to, concert, A. D., iv. 2. 19: v. 7. 15 : vii. 5. 10 ; 8. 3.
συν-όντων, see σύν-ειμι (ειμί), ii. 6. 23.
συν-οράω,* όψομαι, εώρᾱκα or εόρᾱκα, ipf. εώρων, 2 a. είδον, to see at the same time, mutually, or in a comprehensive view; to observe, keep an eye upon, or watch each other ; to perceive ; A., P.; i. 5. 9 : iv. 1. 11 : — 2 pf. pret. σύν-οιδα (inf. συν-ειδέναι, &c.) conscius sum, to know or be cognizant with another, be conscious to one's self, D. P., εἰ, i. 3. 10: ii. 5. 7 : vii. 6. 11, 18.
συν-ουσία, ας, (εἰμί) the being together, an interview, conversation, conference, ii. 5. 6.
συν-τάττω, τάξω, τέταχα, pf. p. τέταγμαι, to arrange together, form or draw up in military order (esp. order of battle), array, marshal, A., i. 2. 15 : συντεταγμένοι drawn up, in battle-array, i. 7. 14 : iv. 2. 7 : — M., of a leader, to draw up his own troops, A.;

LEX. AN. 6* I

of soldiers, *to draw themselves up, array themselves, form* in military order (intrans.), ἐξ, ὡς εἶς· i. 3. 14; 8. 14; 10. 5, 8: iv. 4. 1: vi. 3. 21: vii. 1. 35 (= *v. l.* συντίθεμαι). Der. SYNTAX.

συν-τίθημι,* θήσω, τέθεικα, 2 a. m. ἐθέμην (θείμην or θοίμην, θέσθαι, &c.), *to put together: M.* to put together mutually, *arrange* or *agree with* any one, *agree upon, make an agreement* or *compact*, A., D. I. (A.), i. 9. 7: ii. 5. 8: iv. 2. 1s: vii. 1. 35? Der. SYNTHETIC.

σύν-τομος, ον, s., (τέμνω) con-cīsus, cut so as to come closer together, *concise, short*, ii. 6. 22.

συν-τράπεζος, ον, = ὁμο-τράπεζος q. v., i. 9. 31.

συν-τρέχω,* δραμοῦμαι, δεδράμηκα, 2 a. ἔδραμον, *to run together*, v. 7. 4.

συν-τρίβω, ίψω, τέτρῖφα, (τρίβω *to rub*) *to rub* or *crush together : συντετριμμένοι σκέλη καὶ πλευράς with legs and ribs crushed* or *broken*, iv. 7. 4.

συν-τυγχάνω,* τεύξομαι, τετύχηκα, *to happen* or *fall in with, happen upon, meet with, find*, D., i. 10. 8: vii. 8. 22?

συν-ωφελέω, ήσω, ὠφέληκα, *to join in benefiting*, AE. εἶς· σ. οὐδέν *to contribute no benefit* or *service*, iii. 2. 27.

Συρᾱκόσιος, or Συρᾱκούσιος, ου, ὁ, *a Syracusan*, a man of Syracuse (Συράκουσαι), the greatest city of Sicily, founded upon the east coast by a Corinthian colony, B. C. 734, and having two excellent harbors. It was the birthplace of Theocritus and Archimēdes, and was famed for two sieges, in one of which it repelled the Athenians (B. C. 413), but in the other, after long, brave, and ingenious resistance, was taken by the Romans under Marcellus (B. C. 212). i. 2. 9; 10. 14. || Siracusa.

†Συρία, ας, *Syria* (Aram, Numb. 23. 7), a great country in Asia, of remarkable interest in both sacred and profane history, lying east of the Mediterranean and north of Arabia, and in its early extent reaching even to the Tigris (later bounded by the Euphrātes). It was chiefly inhabited by the Semitic race. i. 4. 4: vii. 8. 25.

†Σύριος, α, ον, *Syrian*, i. 4. 5.

Σύρος, ου, ὁ, *a Syrian*, i. 4. 9.

συρ-ρέω,* ῥεύσομαι & ῥυήσομαι, ἐρρύηκα, 2 a. a. or p. ἐρρύην, (σύν) *to flow, run*, or *flock together*, εἶς, iv. 2. 19 : v. 2. 3.

σῦς, σύός, or ὗς, ὑός, ὁ ἡ, 139, 141, sus, *a* SWINE, *hog, boar*, SOW, v. 2. 3; 3. 10 s; 7. 24.

συ-σ- or ξυ-σ-, the form which, in compos., the prep. σύν takes with σ followed by a consonant, 166.

συ-σκευάζω, άσω, *to collect baggage : — M. to collect one's own baggage, pack up, make ready for a start*, A.; sometimes pf. or aor. pt., *all packed up, ready for a start;* i. 3. 14 : ii. 1. 2; 2. 4 ; 3. 29 ; iii. 4. 36 ; 5. 18 : vii. 1. 11.

σύ-σκηνος, ου, ὁ, (σκηνή) con-tuberālis, *a tent-companion, tentmate, comrade*, v. 7. 15 ; 8. 5 s.

συ-σπάω, άσω, ἔσπακα, *to draw together, sew together*, A., i. 5. 10.

συ-σπειράω, άσω, pf. p. ἐσπείραμαι, (σπεῖρα *a coil*, SPIRE) *to coil together, draw up in close order : συνεσπειραμένοι in close array*, i. 8. 21.

συ-σπουδάζω, άσομαι, ἐσπούδακα, *to join in earnest effort*, ii. 3. 11.

συ-στάς, see συν-ίστημι, v. 7. 16.

συ-στρατεύω, εύσω, ἐστράτευκα, *to join in making war : — M. to take the field, march, campaign, carry on war*, or *serve as soldiers* WITH ; *to join an expedition, take part in a campaign;* D., ἐν, ἐπί, σύν· i. 4. 3 : v. 6. 24 : vii. 3. 14.

συ-στράτηγος, ου, or -στρατηγός, οῦ, ὁ, *a fellow-general, colleague in command*, ii. 6. 29 : v. l. στρατηγός.

συ-στρατιώτης, ου, ὁ, *a fellow-soldier, comrade* in war, i. 2. 26.

συ-στρατοπεδεύομαι, εύσομαι, ἐστρατοπέδευμαι, *to encamp together*, σύν, ii. 4. 9.

συ-στρέφω,* έψω, ἔστροφα l., 2 a. p. ἐστράφην, *to turn together : M.*, w. 2 a. p., *to turn to each other, rally*, i. 10. 6 : v. l. στρέφω.

συχνός, ή, όν, (συν-εχής *continuous?* fr. ἔχω) *considerable* in quantity, length, number, &c., like πολύς, but less strong ; *much, long:* pl. *many, not a few, quite a number of, quite numerous :* συχνόν, sc. χωρίον, at *quite a distance, at considerable distances* or *intervals:* i. 8. 8, 10 : v. 4. 16.

†σφαγιάζω, άσω, A. & oftener M., *to slay a victim, to sacrifice, offer sacrifice*, D., εἶς, iv. 3. 18 ; 5. 4 : vi. 4. 25.

†σφάγιον, ου, *an animal sacrificed, victim* : τὰ σφάγια *the omens* or *indications from victims* (esp. fr. their motions, while τὰ ἱερά refers rather to

σφάζω 131 σωφρονίζω

act the omens fr. the entrails), the appearance of the victims, i. 8. 15: iv. 3. b 19: vi. 5. 8, 21.

σφάζω & later Att. σφάττω,* άξω, to cut the throat, esp. in sacrifice; hence, in general, to kill, slay, slaughter; A. εἰs: ii. 2. 9 : iv. 5. 16 ; 7. 16.

σφαιρο-ειδής, ές, (σφαῖρα ball, SPHERE, εἶδος) ball-shaped, having a ball, G. of material ? v. 4. 12.

σφάλλω,* αλῶ, ἔσφαλκα l., 2 a. p. ἐσφάλην, (cf. fallo, Eng. fall, fail) to trip up, throw down: P. & M. to be thrown down, fall, fail, meet with a reverse or mishap, AE., vii. 7. 42.

σφάττω, see σφάζω, iv. 7. 16.

σφεῖς, σφῶν, σφίσι (encl.), σφᾶς, they, themselves, comm. reflex., pl. to οὗ q. v., i. 7. 8 ; 8. 2 : iii. 5. 16 : iv. 3. 28 : v. 4. 33 ; 7. 18 : vii. 2. 16 ; 5. 9.

†σφενδονάω, ήσω, to sling, use or discharge the sling, throw or hurl with a sling, D. of missile, iii. 3. 7, 15 s.

σφενδόνη, ης, funda, a sling; by meton., the missile of a sling (stone, leaden ball, &c.); iii. 3. 16, 18 ; 4. 4.

‡σφενδονήτης, ου, funditor, a slinger, iii. 3. 6 s, 16, 20 ; 4. 2, 26.

σφίσι(ν) encl., see σφεῖς, i. 7. 8.

σφοδρός, ά, όν, vehement, exceeding, extreme, severe, pressing, i. 10. 18 : —

σφόδρα (neut. pl. w. accent changed) adv., vehemently, exceedingly, extremely, greatly, very much, very, implicitly, closely, ii. 3. 16 ; 4. 18 ; 6. 11.

†σχεδία, as, a temporary structure, esp. a raft or float, i. 5. 10 : ii. 4. 28.

†σχεδόν adv., of distance, time, number, or degree, close at hand, nearly, almost, about, mostly, i. 8. 25 ; 10. 15 : iii. 2. 1 : iv. 7. 6 ; 8. 15.

σχεῖν, σχήσω, see ἔχω, iii. 5. 11.

‡σχέτλιος, α, ον, holding out, unsparing, cruel, outrageous, vii. 6. 30.

‡σχῆμα, ατος, τό, habitus, form, shape, figure, i. 10. 10. Der. SCHEME.

σχίζω, ίσω, pf. p. ἔσχισμαι, a. p. ἐσχίσθην, scindo, to split, cleave, divide, A., i. 5. 12 : vi.3.1. Der. SCHISM.

†σχολάζω, άσω, ἐσχόλακα, to be at leisure, ii. 3. 2. Der. SCHOLASTIC.

†σχολαῖος, α, ον, leisurely, slow, iv. 1. 13.

‡σχολαίως, c. ὅτερον, slowly, tardily, leisurely, i. 5. 8 s.

σχολή, ῆς, (σχ- in ἔχω) leisure, spare time, I.: σχολῇ at leisure, slow-

ly: i. 6. 9 : iii. 4. 27: iv. 1. 16 : vi. 1. 9. Der. SCHOOL, SCHOLAR.

σῷ or σῴοι, see σῶς, ii. 2. 21.

†σώζω,* σώσω, σέσωκα, pf. p. σέσωσμαι or σέσωμαι, a. p. ἐσώθην, to save, rescue, preserve, keep safe, conduct safely, A., i. 10. 3 : iii. 2. 4, 10, 39 : — P. & M. to be saved, rescued, preserved, &c.; to save one's self, escape, arrive or return safely; pf. to have been saved, to be safe ; εἰς, ἐξ, ἐπί, &c.; ii. 1. 19 ; 4. 6 : iii. 2. 3, 11 : vi. 3. 16 ; 4. 8.

†Σω-κράτης, εος, Socrates, an Athenian philosopher, eminent for wisdom and virtue, teacher of Xenophon, Plato, &c. He drank the fatal hemlock, B. C. 399, a short time only before the probable return of Xenophon from the Cyrean expedition. iii. 1, 5, 7. — 2. An Achæan general in the Cyrean army, of good repute, but not of great prominence, i. 1. 11 : ii. 6. 30.

†σῶμα, ατος, τό, (σῴζω, as that which is recovered of the slain, in Hom. corpse) the body ; also translated person or life (σώματα ἀνδρῶν by periphr. for ἀνδρας, iv. 6. 10); i. 9. 12, 23, 27.

σῶς,* σῶν, pl. σῷ, σᾶ (contr. fr. σάος, ον, οι, α), or σῶος, α, ον, salvus, SAFE, ii. 2. 21 : iii. 1. 32 : v. 1. 16 ; 2. 32 ; 8. 4 : vii. 6. 32.

‡Σῶσις, ιος, or Σωσίας, ου, Sosis or Sosias, a Syracusan, who brought 300 hoplites to Cyrus. In which division these were incorporated does not appear, nor is his name again mentioned. i. 2. 9 : v. l. Σωκράτης, &c.

‡σωτήρ, ῆρος, ὁ, (σῴζω) a preserver, savior, deliverer, a surname of Ζεύς q. v., i. 8. 16 : iii. 2. 9 : iv. 8. 25.

‡σωτηρία, as, safety, preservation, deliverance, ii. 1. 19 : iii. 1. 26 ; 2. 8 s.

‡Σωτηρίδας or -ης, ου, Soteridas or -es, a Sicyonian, properly rebuked by Xen. and his own comrades, iii. 4. 47.

‡σωτήριος, ον, saving,salutary, promising or indicative of safety: σωτήρια, sc. ἱερά, thank-offerings for safety or deliverance: ii. 6. 11 : iii. 2. 9 ; 3. 2.

†σωφρονέω, ήσω, σεσωφρόνηκα, to be wise, prudent, or discreet, AE.: σ. τὰ πρός to perform discreetly one's duties towards: v. 8. 24 : vii. 7. 30 (v. l. φρονέω).

†σωφρονίζω, ίσω ιῶ, to bring to reason, teach discretion, reform, correct, be effectual in correcting, A., vi. 1. 28 : vii. 7. 24.

†σωφροσύνη, ης, practical wisdom, discretion, self-control, i. 9. 3. [σώ-φρων, ον, g. ονος, (σῶς, φρήν mind) of sound mind, discreet, wise.]

T.

τ' or θ', by apostr. for τέ, i. 3. 9. [τ- the, that, a great pronominal root, of which the regular stem τός is not found in use.]

‡τά, τά-δε (τάδ'), ταῖς, ταῖσ-δε, see ὁ, ὅδε, i. 1. 6 s; 4. 13; 6. 9.

τά- by crasis for τὰ ἀ- or τὰ ἑ-: as τἀγαθά = τὰ ἀγαθά, iii. 2. 26.

τάλαντον, ου, (ταλα- in τλάω to bear up) talentum, a TALENT, = 60 μναῖ or 6000 δραχμαί: acc. to the Att. standard, as a weight, = about 57 lbs. avoirdupois; as a sum of money, the value of this weight of silver (unless otherwise stated), = about $1200; G.; i. 7. 18: ii. 2. 20: vii. 1. 27; 7. 53.

τἆλλα or τἄλλα = τὰ ἄλλα, i. 8. 29.

ταμιεύω, εύσω, (ταμίας distributer, steward, fr. τέμνω) to be a steward: M. to carve or divide off as a steward, parcel out, determine, A. or CP., ii. 5. 18.

Ταμώς, ώ, or Ταμῶς, ῶ, an Egyptian from Memphis, who was, in the year 412 B. C., governor of Ionia under Tissaphernes; but afterwards went over to Cyrus, as did most of the Ionian cities, and was appointed his admiral. He returned from Cilicia, to take the charge, intrusted to him during the absence of Cyrus, of these cities and the neighboring coast; but on the approach of Tissaphernes after the death of Cyrus, he put his treasures and his children except Glūs into triremes, and sailed to Egypt, whose king Psammitichus was under obligation to him. But the ungrateful king slew both him and his children, in order to obtain possession of the treasure and fleet. i. 2. 21: ii. 1. 3.

τἀναντία = τὰ ἐναντία, iv. 3. 32.

†ταξί-αρχος, ου, ὁ, (ἄρχω) a commander of a division (τάξις), a taxiarch, iii. 1. 37: iv. 1. 28.

τάξις, εως, ἡ, (τάττω) arrangement, order, good order, discipline; esp. military arrangement or order (pl. tactics, ii. 1. 7), battle-array, rank and file, ranks, line; the post or proper place of a soldier; a rank or line of soldiers; a division, corps, body, or band of troops, usu. larger than a λόχος: i. 2. 16, 18; 8. 3, 8, 21: ii. 2. 21: iii. 2. 17, 38; v. 4. 20. Der. SYN-TAX.

Τάοχοι, ων, (Τάοι, Diod. 14. 29, the ending -χοι perhaps originating as in Καρδοῦχοι q. v.) the Taochi or -ians, a mountain tribe of Armenia, dwelling in strongholds, independent and warlike. Recent travellers in this region have recognized remains of their name and habits. iv. 4. 18.

†ταπεινός, ή, όν, lowly, humble, submissive, D., ii. 5. 13.

‡ταπεινόω, ώσω, τεταπείνωκα 1., to humble, abase, A., vi. 3. 18.

τάπις, ιδος, or ταπίς, ίδος, ἡ, tapes, a carpet, rug, often elaborately wrought, vii. 3. 18, 27. Der. TAPESTRY.

τἀπιτήδεια = τὰ ἐπιτήδεια, ii. 3. 9.

ταράττω, άξω, τετάραχα 1., pf. p. τετάραγμαι, a. p. ἐταράχθην, turbo, to disturb, disorder, trouble, make trouble, throw into disorder or confusion, A., AE., ii. 4. 18: iii. 4. 19: vi. 2. 9.

‡τάραχος, ου, ὁ, disturbance, agitation, i. 8. 2.

ταρῑχεύω, εύσω, (τάριχος preserved meat) to preserve by salting, smoking, drying, &c., to pickle, A., v. 4. 28.

Ταρσοί, ῶν, οἱ, or Ταρσός, οῦ, ἡ, Tarsi or Tarsus, a city of very ancient fame, the capital of Cilicia, situated on both sides of the Cydnus, in a fertile plain at the foot of Mt. Taurus. It became later a great seat of Greek learning and philosophy, vying with Athens and Alexandria; and was much favored by the Roman emperors. It was the birthplace of not a few eminent men, the Apostle Paul at their head. i. 2. 23. ‖Ταρσύς.

τάττω,* τάξω, τέταχα, pf. p. τέταγμαι, a. p. ἐτάχθην, to arrange, order, appoint, assign, place or station in order; esp. to arrange, draw up, form, post, or station in military order, to array, marshal; A. 1., ἐπί, εἰς, κατά, πρό, &c.: τεταγμένοι drawn up, appointed, in order, assigned to their places, &c.; τὰ τεταγμένα the arrangements made: M. to station one's self, take one's station or post; to arrange or station as one's allies, A. ἐπί: i. 2. 15 s; 5. 7; 6. 6; 7. 9, 11: iii. 2. 36;

ταῦρος 133 Τεμενίτης

act 3. 18 (ἐν τῷ τεταγμένῳ in the place assigned; v. l. ἐντεταγμένῳ) : iv. 3. 30 ;
ar' 8. 10 s : v. 4. 22. Der. TACTICS.
be' ταῦρος, ου, ὁ, taurus, a bull, ii. 2.9.
ταῦτα, ταύτας, ταύταις, ταύτης, &c., see οὗτος, i. 2. 4 ; 9. 14.
ταὐτά, ταὐτό or ταὐτόν (199a), ταὐτῷ, = τὰ αὐτά, τὸ αὐτό, τῷ αὐτῷ, i. 5. 2 : ii. 1. 22 s. Der. TAUTO-LOGY.
ταύτῃ dat. of οὗτος : as adv., sc. ὁδῷ or χώρᾳ, in this or that way, direction, or respect, by this or that way or route, thus ; in this or that place, here, there ; i. 10. 6 : ii. 6. 7 : iii. 2. 32 : iv. 2. 4 ; 3. 5, 20 ; 5. 36 ; 8. 12.
ταφείην, see θάπτω, v. 7. 20.
‡τάφος, ου, ὁ, a grave, tomb, i. 6. 11. Der. EPI-TAPH.
‡τάφρος, ου, ἡ, a ditch, trench, i. 7. 14 s : ii. 3. 10 ; 4. 13.
ταχ- in ταχθῆναι, -είς, see τάττω.
†τάχα adv., quickly, forthwith, presently, soon ; perhaps ; i. 8. 8 : v. 2. 17.
†ταχέως, oftener ταχύ, adv., c. θᾶττον, s. τάχιστα, quickly, rapidly, speedily, suddenly, soon, i. 2. 4, 17 ; 5. 3, 9 : iii. 4. 15, 27 : — ὡς τάχιστα as soon as, as soon (quickly, &c.) as possible (so ὅτι τάχιστα), 553 b, c, i. 3. 14 : iv. 2. 1 ; 3. 9, 29 : ὅπῃ δύναιντο τάχιστα in whatever way they could most rapidly, as rapidly as possible, iv. 5. 1 : ἐπεὶ (ἐπὰν, ἐπειδὰν) τάχιστα, as soon as, 553 b, iii. 1. 9 : iv. 6. 9 : vi. 3. 21. See βάδην, ὅς, ὅτι, ὡς.
†τάχος, εος, τό, swiftness, speed, ii.5.7.
ταχύς,* εῖα, ύ, c. θάττων, s. τάχιστος, swift, rapid, speedy, quick : τὴν ταχίστην, sc. ὁδόν, in the quickest way, as quickly or soon as possible, most speedily, immediately : i. 2. 20 : ii. 6. 29 : iii. 3. 15 s : iv. 4. 22. See διά.
τέ,* by apostr. τ' or θ', post-pos. & encl. conj., (cf. et, -que) and, both : τὲ . . τέ, and stronger τὲ . . καί, both . . and (stronger, and also, and even, &c.), as well . . as, not only . . but also (even, especially, &c.) ; but τέ sometimes not translated (esp. where other connectives might have been used, 705, i. 8. 8 : ii. 1. 7): i. 1. 3 ? 5 ; 5. 14 : iv. 5. 12 ; 8. 13 : τέ followed by δέ, v. 5. 8 : vii. 8. 11. When joined with other words, τέ has in Att. its own connective force, except in ἅτε, οἷός τε, ὥστε, and ᾧτε, 389 j. See καί, ἐάν, εἴτε, μήτε, οὔτε.

τεθ- in redupl. for θεθ-, 159 a.
τέθνηκα, -νατον, -νᾶσι, -νάναι, -νεώς, see θνήσκω, i. 6. 11 : iv. 1. 19 ; 2. 17.
τεθραμμένος, see τρέφω, v. 4. 32.
τέθρ-ιππον, ου, (τέτταρες, ἵππος) a four-horse chariot, iii. 2. 24.
τείνω,* τενῶ, τέτακα, tendo, to stretch, push on, pursue one's way, continue, iv. 3. 21. Der. TONE, TONIC, TUNE.
†τειχίζω, ἴσω ιῶ, τετείχικα, to wall, fortify, vii. 2. 36.
τεῖχος, εος, τό, (akin to τεῦχος) a wall, walls, esp. for defence ; a walled town, castle, fortress ; i. 4. 4 : iii. 4. 7, 10 : vii. 3. 19 : see Μηδία. — Νέον τεῖχος Neontichus (New-castle), a fortified harbor on the Thracian shore of the Propontis, vii. 5. 8. ǁAinadsjik.
τεκμαίρομαι, αροῦμαι, (τέκμαρ sign) to infer from a sign, judge, conjecture, iv. 2. 4.
‡τεκμήριον, ου, a sure sign, evidence, proof, i. 9. 29, 30 : iii. 2. 13.
τέκνον, ου, τό, (τεκ- in τίκτω to beget, bring forth ; cf. bairn and bear) a child, i. 4. 8 : iv. 5. 28 s.
†τελέθω in pr. and ipf., poet., to arise, become, be, be favorable, iii. 2. 3 (v. l. ἐλθεῖν) : vi. 6. 36 (v. l. ἐθέλει γενέσθαι).
†τελευταῖος, α, ον, final, last, hindmost, rearmost : οἱ τ. the rear : iv. 1. 5, 10 ; 2. 16 ; 3. 24.
†τελευτάω, ήσω, τετελεύτηκα, to end, finish ; to finish life, die : τελευτῶν making an end, finally, at last : i. 1. 3 ; 9. 1 : ii. 1. 1, 4 : iv. 5. 16 : vi. 3. 8.
†τελευτή, ῆς, the end, termination ; one's end, death ; i. 1. 1 : ii. 6. 29.
†τελέω, έσω ῶ, τετέλεκα, to finish, complete, fulfil ; to fulfil an obligation, pay ; A. D.; iii. 3. 18 : vii. 1. 6 ; 2. 27.
τέλος, εος, τό, (τέλλω to accomplish) the accomplishment, completion, fulfilment, end, conclusion, close, result ; the completion of civic rank, authority, pl. by meton. the authorities, rulers (at Sparta, the Ephors) : τ. ἔχειν to have or come to an end, to close : τέλος adv., at the end, at last, finally : i. 9. 6 ; 10. 13, 18 : ii. 6. 4 : v. 2. 9 ; 6. 1 : vi. 5. 2 ; 6. 11 : see διά. Der. TELIC.
τέμαχος, εος, τό, (τέμνω) a slice, esp. of fish, v. 4. 28.
Τεμενίτης, ου, a Temenite, a man of Temenus (Τέμενος), a place in Sicily, afterwards included in Syracuse, iv. 4. 15 : changed by some editors to

τέμνω 134 τίθημι

Τημνίτης, a man of Τῆμνος, an Æolian town of Asia Minor, near the mouth of the Hermus; and by others to Τημενίτης, a man of Τημένιον, a small town at the head of the Argolic Gulf.

τέμνω,* τεμῶ, τέτμηκα, 2 a. ἔταμον or ἔτεμον, *to cut*, v. 8. 18. Der. A-TOM.

τέναγος, εος, τό, (τείνω?) *a shoal*, vii. 5. 12.

τερεβίνθινος or **τερμίνθινος**, η, ον, (τερέβινθος or τέρμινθος *the terebinth* or *turpentine tree*) *from the terebinth, of turpentine*, iv. 4. 13.

τεσσ- v. l. for later Att. **τεττ-**.

τετ- in redupl. forms : as, **τεταγμένος** (τάττω), i. 2. 16 ; **τέτηκα** (τήκω), iv. 5. 15 ; **τετραμμένος** (τρέπω), iii. 5. 15 ; **τετρωμένος** (τιτρώσκω), ii. 5. 33.

†**τέταρτος**, η, ον, *fourth*, iii. 4. 31.

†**τετρακισ-χίλιοι**, αι, α, (τετράκις *four times*) *four thousand*, i. 1. 10 ; 2. 3.

†**τετρακόσιοι**, αι, α, (ἑκατόν) *four hundred*; so sing. w. ἀσπίς, 240 a ; i. 4. 3 ; 7. 10.

†**τετρα-μοιρία**, ας, (μοῖρα *share*) *a fourfold portion, four times as much*, vii. 2. 36 ; 6. 1.

†**τετρα-πλόος**, όη, όον, contr. οῦς, ῆ, οῦν, *quadruple, fourfold*, vii. 6. 7.

†**τετταράκοντα** indecl., *forty*, i. 5. 13.

τέτταρες,* ρα, g. ρων, quatuor, *four*, i. 2. 12, 15. See ἐπί. Der. TETR-ARCH.

Τευθρανία, ας, *Teuthrania*, a district in the southwest part of Mysia, about the Caïcus, including a town of the same name. Its chief town, however, was Pergamum. ii. 1. 3.

τεύξομαι, see τυγχάνω, i. 4. 15 : iii. 2. 19.

τεῦχος, εος, τό, (τεύχω *to make*) *a receptacle, vessel, pot, jar, chest*, v. 4. 28 : vii. 5. 14. Der. PENTA-TEUCH.

†**τεχνάζω**, άσω, *to use art, practise artifice* or *concealment, dissemble, deceive*, vii. 6. 16.

τέχνη, ης, (τεκ- in τίκτω *to produce*) *art, device, means :* πάσῃ τέχνῃ καὶ μηχανῇ *by every art and device, by all means*, iv. 5. 16. Der. TECHNICAL.

‡**τεχνικῶς** *artfully, skilfully :* τ. πως *in a certain artful way, quite artistically*, vi. 1. 5.

τέως adv., (τ-) *for a while, for some time ; up to this* or *that time, until then, previously ;* iv. 2. 12 : vii. 5. 8, 13.

τῇ, τῇδε, dat., sometimes as adv.; see ὁ, ὅδε : iv. 8. 10 : vii. 2. 13.

τήκω,* τήξω, *to melt*, THAW, trans. ; but 2 pf. τέτηκα intrans., iv. 5. 15.

Τηλεβόας, ου or α, *the Teleboas*, an Armenian affluent of the Eastern Euphrātes, iv. 4. 3. ‖ The Kará-Su, in the district of Mûsh.

Τημεντίτης or **Τημνίτης**, see Τεμενίτης, iv. 4. 15.

τήμερον adv., (τ-, ἡμέρα) *on this day, to-day :* ἡ τήμερον ἡμέρα *the present day :* i. 9. 25 : iii. 1. 14 : iv. 6. 8 s.

τηνικαῦτα adv., (τηνίκα fr. τ-, αὐτός) *at that very time, just then*, iv. 1. 5.

Τήρης, εος or ου, *Teres*, a king of the Odrysæ about 500 B. C., who made this kingdom powerful, and an ancestor of Seuthes, vii. 2. 22 ; 5. 1 (here, acc. to some, a later prince).

Τηρίβαζος, ου, see Τιρίβαζος, iv. 4. 4.

τί ; τί encl., see τίς, τίς, i. 6. 8.

τιάρα, ας, tiāra, *the tiara*, a Persian cap, erect and high as worn by the king, but flexible as worn by his subjects, ii. 5. 23.

‡**τιᾱρο-ειδής**, ές, (εἶδος) *shaped like a tiara*, v. 4. 13.

Τιβαρηνοί, ῶν, *the Tibarēni*, a tribe inhabiting the coast of the Euxine about Cotyōra. They were of milder spirit than most of the tribes found by the Cyreans, and were characterized as great laughers. v. 5. 1 s : vii. 8. 25.

Τίγρης, ητος, (also **Τίγρις**, ιδος) ὁ, *the Tigris* (i. e. *the arrowy stream*, from its swiftness ; the Hiddekel, Dan. 10. 4), an important river of western Asia, flowing by the sites of the great cities of Nineveh, Seleucīa, Ctesiphon, and Bagdad (the seats, through so many ages, of oriental empire), uniting with the Euphrātes below Babylon, and discharging its waters into the Persian Gulf after an estimated course of 1150 miles. It was the guide of the Greeks through much of their retreat. i. 7. 15 : ii. 2. 3. ‖ Dijleh. — In iv. 4. 3, an eastern branch of the Tigris is meant, now Bitlís-Su.

τίθημι,* θήσω, τέθεικα, a. ἔθηκα (θῶ, θείς, &c.), 2 a. m. ἐθέμην, *to put, place, set, institute*, A., i. 2. 10 ; 5. 13 : — *M. to place one's own* or *upon one's own :* τίθεσθαι τὰ ὅπλα *to ground arms* ; either, in line of battle, to rest the shield and spear upon the ground, ready to be instantly taken up for action (hence, *to rest arms, stand in arms, halt under arms,* the commander being sometimes said to do what he orders his men to do); or, for purposes of rest, to deposit one's arms upon the ground, as in a special part of the camp, &c. (hence, *to stack* or *pile arms, to lay aside one's arms*): Α., εἰς, ἐν, ἐπί, κατά, &c.: i. 5. 14, 17; 6. 4; 10. 16: ii. 2. 8, 21: iv. 2. 16; 3. 17: vii. 3. 23. Der. THEME, THESIS.

†**Τιμασίων**, ωνος, *Timasion,* an exile from Dardanus in Troas, chosen successor to Clearchus, and with Xenophon the youngest of the Cyrean generals; a gallant officer, but not always consistent in his course of proceeding. He had served in Asia Minor, under Clearchus and Dercyllidas, before the Cyrean expedition. iii. 1. 47; 2. 37.

†**τιμάω**, ήσω, τετίμηκα, *to honor, esteem, value, prize; to bestow honor, to favor, reward;* Α. ΑΕ. or D. of the honor, διά: i. 3. 3; 9. 14. Der. TIMO-THY.

τιμή, ῆς, (τίω *to pay,* esp. honor) *honor, reward, price,* i. 9. 29: ii. 1. 17; 5. 38: vii. 5. 2; 8. 6.

‡**Τιμησί-θεος**, ου, *Timesitheus,* a Trapezuntian who befriended the Cyreans, v. 4. 2 s.

‡**τίμιος**, α, ον, *honorable, precious, honored,* i. 2. 27; 3. 6.

‡**τιμωρέω**, ήσω, τετιμώρηκα, (τίμωρός [taking pay] *avenging,* fr. τιμῇ & αἴρω) *to avenge: M. to avenge one's self* upon, *take vengeance* on, *punish,* Α. G., ὑπέρ, i. 3. 4; 9. 13: vii. 1. 25; 4. 23: — *P. to be punished,* ii. 5. 27; 6. 29.

‡**τιμωρία**, ας, (see τιμωρέω) *vengeance, punishment,* ii. 6. 14.

τινός encl. **τίνος**; see τὶς, τίς.

Τιρίβαζος, ου, *Tiribazus,* a satrap of western Armenia, and high in the favor of Artaxerxes II. It was through his influence, acc. to Plutarch, that the king was induced to renounce his purpose of retreating before Cyrus into Persia, and to risk the battle of Cunaxa. He was afterwards satrap in the west of Asia Minor, and greatly influential in establishing the peace of Antalcidas. Accused by Orontes of misconduct in the war against Evagoras of Cyprus, he was honorably acquitted. But enraged by Artaxerxes' twice promising him a daughter in marriage, and twice marrying that daughter himself, he engaged with the young prince Darius in a plot against the king's life and thus lost his own. iv. 4. 4, 7: vii. 8. 25: *v. l.* Τηρίβαζος.

τὶς,* τί, g. τινός or τοῦ, d. τινί or τῷ, indef. pron., post-pos. & encl., (cf. quis) *some, any, a, a certain, a sort of, so to speak,* i. 2. 20; 5. 8; 8. 8: iii. 1. 4, 12: vi. 5. 20: — τὶς subst., *some* or *any one* or *person, a certain one, one, a person, each one,* i. 3. 12; 5. 2, 8 s, 12; 8. 18: ii. 2. 4; sometimes in place of a definite expression, as for Κῦρος, ὑμεῖς, or ἡμεῖς, i. 4. 12: iii. 3. 3; 4. 40: — τὶ subst., *something, anything, somewhat, some* or *any part, a certain part* (the context often supplying or suggesting a more specific noun, as ὑποσχέσθαι τι *to make any promise*), i. 8. 18; 9. 7: iv. 1. 14; often as adv. or acc. of spec., *somewhat, at all, in any respect,* iii. ¶. 23 (see δέω): iv. 8. 26. With some adjectives or adverbs, τὶς has an indefinite force which may be variously translated, or rather felt than expressed: οἱ μέν τινες *some few,* οἱ δέ τινες *some others,* iii. 3. 19: ii. 3. 15: εἴς τις *any single one,* ii. 1. 19: πόση τις *about how large,* ii. 4. 21: ὁποῖόν τι *whatever without exception,* ii. 2. 2; *what kind of an omen,* iii. 1. 13: ὁποῖοί τινες *what sort of persons,* v. 5. 15 (cf. vii. 6. 24): τοιαύτη τις *somewhat like this,* v. 8. 7: ὀλίγοι τινές *some few, but few,* v. 1. 6? ἕκαστός τις *every individual,* vi. 1. 19? ἧττόν τι *at all the less,* v. 8. 11: οὐδέν τι *not in the least,* vii. 3. 35: οὐ πάνυ τι *by no means whatever,* vi. 1. 26: σχεδόν τι *pretty nearly,* vi. 4. 20.

‡**τίς**,* τί, g. τίνος or τοῦ, interrog. pron. (always orthotone), quis? *who? which? what? what kind of?* τί as adv., [on account of what, *or* as to what] *why? how? τί γάρ;* quid enim? *what indeed? τί οὖν; what then?* i. 4. 13 s: ii. 1. 11; 2. 10; 4. 3: iii. 2. 16, 36; 5. 14: v. 7. 10; 8. 11: vii. 6. 4.

Τισσαφέρνης,* (εος) ους, ει, ην, η, *Tissaphernes,* satrap of Caria, and commander of a fourth part of the king's forces; one of the ablest of his officers, but wily, deceitful, and treacherous. From his first command in the west of Asia Minor, B. C. 414, he showed these qualities in his dealings with the Greeks; and no less afterwards in his conduct towards Cyrus and the Cyreans, where he appears as the διάβολος of the narrative. After his return to Asia Minor, invested with the authority which had before belonged to both Cyrus and himself, he was engaged in war with the Spartans as friends of the Ionian cities; but with so little success that at length Artaxerxes, dissatisfied, and urged on by Parysatis, sent out Tithraustes to put him to death and succeed him in his government, B. C. 395. He was slain in his bath, and his head sent to the king, a punishment deserved for his many crimes. Tithraustes was himself succeeded by Tiribazus, B. C. 393. i. 1. 2s, 6, 8; 2. 4s: ii. 5. 3, 31.

τιτρώσκω,* τρώσω, τέτρωκα l., pf. p. τέτρωμαι, a. p. ἐτρώθην, to wound, hurt, inflict wounds, ͬA. διά, εἰς, i. 8. 26: ii. 2. 14; 5. 33: iii.3.7: iv.3.33s.

τλήμων, ον, g. ονος, (τλάω to bear) suffering, wretched, miserable, iii. 1. 29.

τό, τό-δε, τόν-δε, τοῖς, see ὁ, ὅ-δε.

τοί* adv. post-pos. & encl., (old form of σοί, ethical dat., 462 e) in truth, indeed, truly, surely, certainly, ii. 1. 19; 5. 19: iii. 1. 18, 37.

‡τοι-γαρ-οῦν, for indeed therefore, therefore, accordingly, so for example, i. 9. 9, 15, 18: ii. 6. 20.

‡τοί-νυν post-pos., indeed now, therefore, then, now, accordingly; moreover, further; ii. 1. 22; 5. 41 : iii. 1. 36s; 2. 27, 39: iv. 8. 5: v. 1. 2, 8, 13.

[τοῖος, α, ον, demonst. pron. of quality, (τ-) tālis, such.] Hence,

‡τοιόσ-δε,* άδε, όνδε, usu. prospective, such as follows, of this kind, the following, as follows, i. 3. 2, 9; 7. 2: v. 4. 31. — Much oftener,

‡τοιοῦτος,* τοιαύτη, τοιοῦτον or -το, (αὐτός) usu. retrospective, referring to what has been already stated or implied, such, of this kind, the same or like in kind, as precedes, as above, thus; of such a character, such in rank, position, influence, conduct, &c., παρά, περί : i. 3. 14: ii. 6. 8: iii. 1. 30: vii. 6. 38 : εἰς τὰ τοιαῦτα for such services or emergencies, iv. 1. 28 : ἐν (τῷ) τοιούτῳ in such a situation or crisis, i. 7. 5: v. 8. 20.

τοῖχος, ου, ὁ, (akin to τεῖχος) the wall of a building, vii. 8. 14.

τολμάω, ἡσω, τετόλμηκα, (τόλμα courage, fr. τλάω to bear) to dare, venture, bc bold enough, presume; to have the courage, boldness, heart, or hardihood ; I.; ii. 2. 12: iv. 4. 12: vii. 7. 46.

‡Τολμίδης, ου, Tolmides, an Elean, a herald of unsurpassed excellence, ii. 2. 20 : iii. 1. 46 : v. 2. 18.

†τόξευμα, ατος, τό, that which is shot, an arrow, i. 8. 19: iii. 4. 4: iv. 2. 28.

†τοξεύω, εύσω, to use the bow, shoot with a bow, shoot arrows, A., ἀπό, διά, εἰς: P. to be shot with an arrow : i. 8. 20: iii. 3. 7, 10: iv. 1. 18; 2. 12, 28.

†τοξικός, ή, όν, relating to the bow: subst. τοξική, sc. τέχνη, the use of the bow, bowmanship, archery, i. 9. 5 : [τοξικόν toxicum, poison, orig. for arrows, whence IN-TOXICATE, i. e. to poison.]

τόξον, ου, arcus, the bow, the comm. weapon of more distant warfare among the ancients, as the gun among the moderns ; but used more by the barbarians than by the Greeks or Romans. Among the Greeks, the Cretans were the most famed for archery, and were fabled to have been taught the art by Apollo. iii. 3. 15 ; 4. 17 : iv. 4. 16.

‡τοξότης, ου, a bowman, archer. As archers had not the left hand at liberty to carry the shield, they were lightly armed for rapid advance and retreat, and were often covered by the heavy-armed. i. 2. 9 ; 8. 9 : iii. 4. 2, 15, 26. See Σκύθης.

τόπος, ου, ὁ, a spot, place, district, region, i. 5. 1 : iv. 2. 19 ; 4. 4; 6. 2 : v. 7. 16. Cf. χώρα. Der. TOPIC, U-TOPIA.

τορός, ά, όν, (τείρω to vex) sharp, smart, ready-tongued, vi. 6. 28 ?

[τός the, that, not in use, see τ-.]

[‡τόσος, η, ον, demonst. pron. of quantity, tantus, so much, so great; pl. tot, so many.] Hence,

‡τοσόσ-δε,* ήδε, όνδε, more deictic, so much or great as you see; pl. so many as you see, so many only or so few, ii. 4. 4 : vi. 5. 19. — Much oftener,

‡τοσοῦτος,* τοσαύτη, τοσοῦτον or -το, (αὐτός) more emphatic (usu. retrospective or explained by a dependent clause), just or only so much, so much as above, so much, so great, so large, so long ; pl. so many ; ὅσος, ὡς, ὥστε, &c.; i. 9. 11 : ii. 1. 16 ; 5. 15, 18 : iii. 5. 7: iv. 1. 20 : — neut. τοσοῦτο(ν) so much, so much space, so great a dis-

tance, so far, only so much or far as this, i. 3. 14; 8. 13 : iii. 1. 45 ; 4. 37 (cf. iv. 8. 12): — τοσούτῳ w. compar., by so much, so much the, the, i. 5. 9.

τότε adv., (τ-) tum, tunc, at that time, then, i. 1. 6 ; 3. 2 ; 6. 10 : οἱ τότε the men of that time, ii. 5. 11 : — with accent changed, τοτὲ μὲν .. τοτὲ δέ at one time .. at another, now .. and now, vi. 1. 9.

τοῦ- by crasis for τὸ ἑ- or τὸ ὁ- : τοὐλάχιστον = τὸ ἐλάχιστον, v. 7. 8 ; τοὔμπαλιν = τὸ ἔμπαλιν, i. 4. 15 ; τοὔνομα = τὸ ὄνομα, v. 2. 29 ; τοὔπισθεν = τὸ ὄπισθεν, iii. 3. 10.

τοῦ, τούς, τοῦ-δε, τοῦσ-δε, see ὁ, ὅ-δε: τοῦτο, τούτου, τούτῳ, τούτω, τούτων, τουτου-ί, τουτον-ί, &c., see οὗτος, οὑτοσ-ί.

τράγημα, ατος, τό, (τραγ- in τρώγω to eat without cooking) a dainty; pl. dainties, dried fruit, dessert, sweetmeats, ii. 3. 15 : v. 3. 9.

Τράλλεις, εων, αἱ, Tralles, a strong and wealthy city in the south of Lydia (sometimes assigned to Caria), between Mt. Messōgis and the Mæander, i. 4. 8. ‖ Ruins by the modern and flourishing town of Aidín.

Τρανίψαι, ῶν, the Tranipsæ, a people in the eastern part of Thrace, perhaps the Νιψαῖοι of Hdt. (4. 93), vii. 2. 32 : v. l. Θρανίψαι.

τράπεζα, ης, (τέτταρες, πέζα foot) a table, as so often four-footed, iv. 5. 31 : vii. 2. 33 ; 3. 22s. Der. TRAPEZIUM.

†Τραπεζούντιος, ου, ὁ, a Trapezuntian, iv. 8. 23 : v. 1. 15 ; 4. 2 : a man of

‡Τραπεζοῦς, οῦντος, ἡ, Trapezus, an important commercial city (as even at the present time) on the southeast coast of the Euxine, a Sinopean colony. From 1204 to 1461 A. D., it was the capital of a fragment of the Greek Empire (called the Empire of Trebizond). iv. 8. 22 : v. 2. 28 ; 5. 14. ‖ Trebizond (or Tarabozán).

τραποίμην, see τρέπω, vii. 1. 18.

τραῦμα, ατος, τό, (τιτρώσκω) a wound, i. 8. 26 : iv. 6. 10. [5. 8 : vii. 4. 9.

†?τράχηλος, ου, ὁ, the neck, throat, i.

τραχύς, εῖα, ύ, (akin to ῥήγνυμι to break) rough, harsh, ii. 6. 9 : iv. 3. 6 ; 6. 12. Der. TRACHEA.

τρεῖς,* τρία, g. τριῶν, tres, Sans. tri, Germ. drei, THREE, i. 1. 10.

τρέπω,* ἔψω, τέτροφα, pf. p. τέτραμμαι, a. p. ἐτρέφθην, verto, to turn, di-

vert, change the direction of, direct, drive back, A. ἀπό, πρός, iii. 1. 41 ; 5. 15 : v. 4. 23 : τ. εἰς φυγήν in fugam vertere, to put to flight, i. 8. 24 : — M., w. 2 a. ἐτραπόμην, to turn (intrans.), turn aside, betake one's self, take to flight, resort, have recourse to, indulge in ; w. 1 a. ἐτρεψάμην, to turn from one's self, drive back, put to flight, rout, A.; εἰς, ἐξ, ἐπί, πρός · ii. 6. 5 : iii. 5. 13 : iv. 5. 30 ; 8. 19 : v. 4. 16 : vi. 1. 13, 18. Cf. IN-TREPID.

τρέφω,* θρέψω, τέτροφα, pf. p. τέθραμμαι, 2 a. p. ἐτράφην, to nourish, nurture, rear, bring up, support, maintain, A. D., ἀπό, ἐξ, i. 1. 9s : iii. 2. 13 : iv. 5. 25, 34 : v. 1. 12 : — M. to feed one's self, subsist, D. of means, vi. 5. 20.

τρέχω,* δραμοῦμαι, δεδράμηκα, 2 a. ἔδραμον, curro, to run, εἰς, ἐπί, περί, i. 5. 2, 8, 13 : iv. 5. 18 ; 8. 26 : cf. θέω, more frequent in pres. Der. TROCHEE.

τρέω, ἔσω, (cf. terreo, and τρέμω tremo, to tremble) ch. poet., to tremble at, be afraid of, shrink from, A., i. 9. 6.

τρία, τριῶν, τρισί, see τρεῖς, i. 4. 1.

‡τριάκοντα indecl., triginta, thirty, i. 2. 9, 11 ; 4. 5 ; 10. 4.

‡τριακόντ-ορος, ον, (ἐρέττω to row) thirty-oared : ἡ τ., sc. ναῦς, thirty-oared galley, v. 1. 16 : vii. 2. 8.

‡τριακόσιοι, αι, α, (ἑκατόν) trecenti, three hundred, i. 1. 2 ; 2. 9.

τριβή, ῆς, (τρίβω to rub) constant practice or exercise, v. 6. 15.

†τρι-ήρης, ες, (ἀρ-, or ἐρέττω to row) triply fitted, or rowed : ἡ τ., sc. ναῦς, tri-rēmis, the trireme, the chief war-vessel of the Greeks, a galley with three banks of oars, which gave it great swiftness, and made it, like the modern steamer, independent of the wind ; while it could yet take advantage of this by its sails. It had a sharp metallic-pointed beak, which was often driven with great force against other vessels and thus sunk them. Some vessels were also fitted as triremes for the rapid transport of troops or of military supplies. i. 2. 21 ; 3. 17 ; 4. 7 s : vi. 2. 13 s.

‡τριηρίτης, ου, a ship-man, a man belonging to a trireme, esp. as oarsman or soldier, vi. 6. 7.

†τρί-πηχυς, υ, g. εος, three cubits long, iv. 2. 28.

τριπλάσιος 138 ὑβρίζω

†τρι-πλάσιος, α, ον, (πλάττω to form) three-fold, triple, thrice as great, vii. 4. 21.

†τρί-πλεθρος, ον, (πλέθρον) three plethra (300 ft.) long or wide, v. 6. 9.

†τρί-πους, ουν, g. ποδος, three-footed: masc. subst., a TRIPOD, a three-footed table, stool, or vase, vii. 3. 21.

τρίς adv., (τρεῖς· also for τρεῖς in compos.) ter, THRICE, three times : εἰς τρίς to thrice, even to the third time, vi. 4. 16, 19. See

‡τρισ-άσμενος or τρὶς ἄσμενος, η, ον, thrice happy, very glad, most gladly, iii. 2. 24.

‡τρισ-καί-δεκα indecl., or τρεῖς καὶ δέκα, thirteen, i. 5. 5.

‡τρισ-μύριοι, αι, α, thirty thousand, vii. 8. 26.

‡τρισ-χίλιοι, αι, α, three thousand, i. 6. 4 ; 7. 18.

†τριταῖος, α, ον, on the third day, 240. 3, v. 3. 2.

τρίτος, η, ον, (τρεῖς) third: τὸ τρίτον, as adv., the third time: τῇ τρίτῃ, sc. ἡμέρᾳ, on the third day: ἐπὶ τῷ τρίτῳ, sc. σημείῳ, on the third signal: i. 6. 8 ; 7. 1, 19 : ii. 2. 4 : iv. 5. 3.

τρίχα or τριχῇ adv., (τρεῖς) in three parts or divisions, iv. 8. 15 : vi. 2. 16.

τρίχινος, η, ον, (θρίξ,* g. τριχός, hair) made of hair, hair, iv. 8. 3.

τρι-χοίνικος, η, ον, (τρίς, χοῖνιξ) containing three chœnices, three-quart, vii. 3. 23.

Τροία, ας, Troja, Troy, v. l. for Τρῳάς, and used in the same sense, vii. 8. 7.

†τρόπαιον, ου, tropæum, a TROPHY, a memorial of the defeat of an enemy, usu. made ch. of captured arms, G., iii. 2. 13 : iv. 6. 27 : vi. 5. 32 : vii. 6. 36.

τροπή, ῆς, (τρέπω) the turning or flight of an enemy, defeat, rout, i. 8. 25 : iv. 8. 21. Der. TROPIC.

τρόπος, ου, ὁ, (τρέπω) the turn, direction, way, manner, method, disposition, temper, character, or habit of a person or thing; often in the modal dat. or adv. acc.; i. 1. 9 ; 2. 11 (see πρός); 9. 22 : ii. 2. 17 ; 6. 8 : ἐκ παντὸς τρόπου [from] by every way, at any rate, no matter how, iii. 1. 43 : vii. 7. 41 : κατὰ πάντα τρόπον by all means, vi. 6. 30. Der. TROPE.

τροφή, ῆς, (τρέφω) nourishment, support, sustenance, subsistence, i. 1. 9 : v. 6. 32 : vii. 3. 8. Der. A-TROPHY.

τροχάζω, άσω, (τρέχω) to run forward, vii. 3. 46.

τρῡπάω, ήσω, (τρῦπα a hole) to bore, A., iii. 1. 31. Der. TREPAN.

Τρῳάς or Τρωάς, άδος, ἡ, (Τροία) Troas or the Troad, a district in the northwest of Mysia, including the site of "Old Troy, — long since perished, but immortal in verse," v. 6. 23 s.

τρωκτός, ή, όν, (τρώγω to eat raw) eatable, edible ; as applied to trees, instead of their fruit, productive for eating or of edible fruit, v. 3. 12.

τρωτός, ή, όν, (τιτρώσκω to wound) vulnerable, liable or exposed to wounds, iii. 1. 23.

τυγχάνω,* τεύξομαι, τετύχηκα, 2 a. ἔτυχον, to happen or chance upon, meet with, find, hit, obtain, attain, acquire, receive, 2 G., A. (ταῦτα vi. 6. 32), παρά, i. 4. 15 : ii. 6. 29 : iii. 2. 19 : v. 5. 15 ; 7. 33 : — oftener w. a pt., to happen, chance, the pt. being usu. translated by the inf., 658. 1 (παρὼν ἐτύγχανε happened to be present, i. 1. 2); or else by a finite verb, and τυγχάνω by an adv. or adverbial phrase, as by chance, perchance, just then or now, just, then, now, 677 e (ἐτύγχανον λέγων I was just saying, iii. 2. 10, the idea of chance being expressed far oftener in Greek than in Eng.); while the pt. is sometimes understood, ch. ὤν, 677 d (ἐτύγχανεν chanced to be or to rest, iii. 1. 3) ; i. 5. 8, 14: ii. 1. 7 s ; 2. 14, 17 : — pt. τυχόν abs., it happening so, hence, as adv., perchance, perhaps, vi. 1. 20.

Τυραῖον, Τυριαῖον, or Τυριάειον, ου, Tyraium (-iœum, -iaëum) a town in the southeast of Phrygia (or in Lycaonia), i. 2. 14. || Ilghûn.

τῡρός, οῦ, ὁ, a cheese ; pl. ii. 4. 28.

τύρσις, ιος, ει, ω, pl. εις, 218, ἡ, turris, a TOWER, castle, TURRET, iv. 4. 2 : v. 2. 5, 27 : vii. 2. 21 ; 8. 12 s.

τυχεῖν, -ών, -όν, see τυγχάνω, ii. 3. 2.

τύχη, ης, fortūna, fortune, luck, chance, ii. 2. 13 : v. 2. 25.

τώ, τῷ, τῷ-δε, τῶν, see ὁ, ὅ-δε, i. 1. 1 s : — τῷ encl. = τινί, see τὶς, i. 9. 7.

Υ.

†ὑβρίζω, ἴσω ιῶ,"ὕβρικα, to be insolent, wanton, audacious, abusive, or so to

ὕβρις 139 ὑπερβαίνω

act or *treat another; to insult, abuse, maltreat, outrage*; A. AE.; iii. 1. 13, 29 : v. 8. 1, 3, 22 : vi. 4. 2.

ὕβρις, εως, ἡ, (ὑπέρ? cf. super-bus) *insolence, wantonness, abuse*, iii. 1. 21.

†ὑβριστής, οῦ, ὁ, as adj., *insolent, wanton, audacious, abusive*; c. & s.

ὑβριστότερος, ὑβριστότατος, 259 a (yet referred by some to a rare ὕβριστος), v. 8. 3, 22.

ὑγιαίνω, ανῶ, (ὑγιής sanus, *healthy*) *to be healthy, sound, strong, in full vigor*, or *in good condition* (of body), iv. 5. 18.

ὑγρότης, ητος, ἡ, (ὑγρός *moist*) *moisture, suppleness, perspiration*, v. 8. 15.

†ὑδροφορέω, ήσω, *to carry water*, iv. 5. 9.

†ὑδρο-φόρος, ου, ὁ ἡ, (φέρω) *a water-carrier*, iv. 5. 10.

ὕδωρ,* ὕδατος, τό, ("ὕω *to rain*) *water*: ὕ. ἐξ οὐρανοῦ *rain*: i. 5. 7, 10 : iv. 2. 2. Der. HYDRANT, HYDRO-GEN.

†υἱδέος, ου, contr. υἱδοῦς, οῦ, ὁ, (also υἱιδοῦς or υἱδοῦς) *a son's son, grandson*, v. 6. 37 : v. l. υἱός.

υἱός,* οῦ, ὁ, filius, *a son*, iv. 6. 1.

"ὕλη, ης, (cf. silva) *wood, a wood* or *forest, bushes, shrubbery*, i. 5. 1 : iii. 5. 10 s : v. 2. 31.

'ὑμεῖς, -ῶν, -ῖν, -ᾶς, ΥΟΥ, see σύ.

↓'ὑμέτερος, α, ον, *your, yours*: οἱ ὑμέτεροι *your subjects* or *countrymen*: τὰ ὑμέτερα *what belongs to you, your property, money*, or *affairs*: ii. 1. 12s : v. 5. 19 : vii. 3. 19 ; 6. 16, 18, 33.

ὑπ', ὑφ', by apostr. for ὑπό, i. 3. 13.

ὑπ-άγω,* ἄξω, ἦχα, *to lead under the pressure of followers, keep out of the way of others, keep ahead, lead* or *press on* (acc. to some, *to lead on slowly*), iii. 4. 48 : iv. 2. 16 : — *M. to lead, urge*, or *suggest insidiously* or *craftily*, AE., A. I., ii. 1. 18 ; 4. 3.

ὑπ-αίθριος, ον, (αἰθρία) *under the sky, in the open air*, v. 5. 21 : vii. 6. 24.

ὑπ-αίτιος, ον, (αἰτία) *under blame*: ὑπαίτιόν τι *a ground of censure, πρός*, iii. 1. 5 : v. l. ἐπ-αίτιος.

ὑπ-ακούω,* ούσομαι, ἀκήκοα, *to hear under the call of another, obey, pay attention, regard, listen, hearken*, G., iv. 1. 9 : vii. 3. 7.

ὑπ-ανα-τείνω,*τενῶ,τέτακα,*to stretch up* [under] *for the blow*, A., vii. 4. 9 ?

ὑπ-ανα-χωρέω, ήσω, κεχώρηκα, *to retreat somewhat* or *slowly*, εἰς, iii. 5. 13 ?

ὑπ-αντάω, ήσω, ἤντηκα, & ὑπ-αντιάζω, άσω, (ἀντάω & ἀντιάζω *to meet*, fr. ἀντί) *to come to meet and sustain, come to assist, come to the relief, come up*, iv. 3. 34 : vi. 5. 27.

ὑπ-αρχος, ου, ὁ, (ἄρχω) *a lieutenant* either in the command of an army or of a satrapy, *a vice-satrap* (ruling over a district, but under the satrap), *provincial governor, prefect, chief officer*, i. 2. 20 ; 8. 5 : iv. 4. 4.

ὑπ-άρχω,ἄρξω,*to begin* beneath or as a foundation, *take the initiative, commence*, P.; hence, *to be already a support for, to support, favor*, D.; *to be on hand to begin with* or *rely upon* (while εἰμί is simply *to be*), *be* or *exist already, be present, exist, be* (*have*, cf. εἰμί), D. εἰς : ἐκ τῶν ὑπαρχόντων *from the means at hand*: i. 1. 4 : ii. 2. 11 ; 3. 23 : vi. 4. 9.

ὑπ-ασπιστής, οῦ, (ἀσπίς) *a shield-bearer, armor-bearer*, an attendant not only upon commanders, but also upon some privates ; cf. the *esquire* of mediæval chivalry ; iv. 2. 20.

ὑπ-είκω, εἴξω, α. εἶξα, (εἴκω *to yield*) *to submit to*, D., vii. 7. 31.

ὑπ-ειμι,* ἔσομαι, ipf. ἦν, *to be* or *lie underneath*, iii. 4. 7 : v. l. εἰμί, &c.

ὑπ-ελαύνω,* ἐλάσω ἐλῶ, ἐλήλακα, a. ήλασα, *to ride up* to a superior, ὡς, i. 8. 15 : v. l. πελάζω.

ὑπ-ελήλυθα, see ὑπ-έρχομαι, v. 2. 30.

ὑπέρ,* prep., (akin to ὑπό, both marking vertical relation, cf. altus, high, deep) super, Germ. über, OVER: — (a) w. GEN., *over* in place, *above, from above*, i. 10. 12, 14 (ὑ. τοῦ λόφου *seen from above the hill*, i. e. *beyond it*): ii. 6. 2 : iv. 7. 4 : v. 4. 13 (ὑ. γονάτων *not reaching below the knee*) : — *over to protect, in defence of, in behalf of, on account of, in the name of, for the sake of, for*, i. 3. 4 ; 7. 3 ? 8. 27 : iv. 8. 24 : v. 5. 13 ; 6. 27 s : — (b) w. Acc., [going over] *beyond, above* (= *beyond*), of place, oftener of number, measure, age, &c., i. 1. 9 (v. l. ὑ. Ἑλλησπόντου): v. 3. 1 : vi. 2. 10 ; 5. 4. In compos., as above. Der. HYPER-.

ὑπερ-άλλομαι,* ἁλοῦμαι, *to leap* or *jump over*, A., vii. 4. 17.

ὑπερ-ανα-τείνω,* τενῶ, τέτακα, *to stretch up over another*, A., vii. 4. 9 ?

ὑπερ-βαίνω,* βήσομαι, βέβηκα, 2 a. ἔβην, *to go* or *pass over, cross*, A. εἰς, παρά, vii. 1. 17 ; 3. 43 ; 8. 7.

ὑπερ-βάλλω, 140 ὑπολαμβάνω

ὑπερ-βάλλω,* βαλῶ, βέβληκα, 2 a. ἔβαλον, to throw one's self over, to cross or pass over, A., κατά, πρός, iv. 1. 7 ; 4. 20 ; 5. 1 : vi. 5. 7 : vii. 5. 1.
‡ὑπερ-βολή, ῆς, a crossing, mountain passage or pass, G., εἰς, i. 2. 25 : iii. 5. 18 : iv. 6. 5 s. Der. HYPERBOLE.
ὑπερ-δέξιος, ον, over or above the right (hand, wing, &c.), iii. 4. 37 : iv. 8. 2 (v. l. ὑπὲρ δεξιῶν) : v. 7. 31.
ὑπερ-έρχομαι,* ἐλεύσομαι, ἐλήλυθα, 2 a. ἦλθον, to pass over or beyond, cross, A., iv. 4. 3.
ὑπερ-έχω,* ἕξω, ἔσχηκα, to be, rise, or project above, D.; to overhang ; iii. 5. 7 : iv. 7. 4.
ὑπερ-ήμισυς, εια, υ, above half, vi. 2. 10 : v. l. ὑπὲρ ἥμισυ.
ὕπερθεν adv., (ὑπέρ) from above, above, i. 4. 4.
ὑπερ-κάθημαι * pf. m. pret., f. pf. ἥσομαι 1., plp. ἐκαθήμην or καθήμην, to be seated or posted above, G., ἐπί, v. 1. 9 ; 2. 1.
ὑπερ-όριος, ον, or ος, α, ον, (ὅρος a bound) beyond the boundaries, foreign : ἐκ τῆς ὑπερορίας, sc. γῆς, from our foreign territory or from abroad, vii. 1. 27.
ὑπερ-ύψηλος, ον, exceeding high, very lofty, iii. 5. 7.
ὑπ-έρχομαι,* ἐλεύσομαι, ἐλήλυθα, to go under pursuit, retreat, A. of distance, v. 2. 30.
ὑπ-εσχόμην, see ὑπ-ισχνέομαι.
ὑπ-έχω,* ἕξω, ἔσχηκα, 2 a. ἔσχον, to have one's self under, submit to, undergo, A. D., v. 8. 1, 18 : see δίκη.
ὑπ-ήκοος, ον, (ὑπ-ακούω) obedient, submissive, subject : masc. subst., a subject, vassal : D. G. : i. 6. 6 : v. 4. 6.
ὑπ-ῆν, see ὑπ-ειμι, iii. 4. 7 : v. l. ἦν.
†ὑπ-ηρετέω, ήσω, ὑπ-ηρέτηκα, to serve, do or render service, supply, D. AE., i. 9. 18 : ii. 5. 14 : iii. 5. 8 : vii. 7. 46.
ὑπ-ηρέτης, ου, (ἐρέτης rower, fr. ἐρέττω to row) an under-rower ; hence (among so commercial a people), in general, a servant, attendant, assistant, i. 9. 18, 27 : ii. 1. 9 ; 5. 14.
ὑπ-ισχνέομαι,* ὑπο-σχήσομαι, ὑπ-έσχημαι, (ἔχω or ἴσχω) to hold one's self under obligation, to promise, engage, D. A., I (A.), CP., i. 2. 2 ; 7. 5, 18 : ii.3.20 : v.6.35s : vii.2.25 ; 7.46.
ὕπνος, ου, ὁ, somnus, sleep, iii. 1. 11. Der. HYPNOTIC.

ὑπό * prep., by apostr. ὑπ' or ὑφ', sub, under : (a) w. GEN., from under in place, from beneath, as ὑπὸ ἁμάξης from under [a wagon] the yoke, vi. 4. 22, 25 ; — usu., from under the effect or influence of, by (esp. w. pass. verbs, or equivalent verbs or phrases, 586 d, 575), by reason of, through the effect of, through, from, of, with, i. 1. 10 ; 3. 4, 13 ; 5. 4s : iii. 1. 3 : vii. 6. 15, 33 : ὑπὸ μαστίγων under (the compulsion of) the scourge, iii. 4. 25 : — (b) w. DAT., under (of situation or of subjection), beneath, i. 2. 8 ; 8. 10 : vi. 4. 4 : vii. 2. 2 : — (c) w. ACC., under or beneath, with the idea of motion or extension, i. 8. 27 ; 10. 14 : iii. 4. 37 : vii. 4. 5, 11 ; 8. 21 : — (d) in compos., under, beneath ; sometimes expressing diminution, inferiority, privacy, secrecy, or action under the pressure or influence of others, somewhat, a little, underhand, behind, &c. Der. HYPO-.
ὑπο-δεής, ές, (δέω to want) somewhat wanting ; found in c. ὑποδεέστερος inferior, lower in rank, i. 9. 5.
ὑπο-δείκνυμι,* δείξω, δέδειχα, to show somewhat, begin to show, give indications, threaten, v. 7. 12.
ὑπο-δέχομαι, δέξομαι, δέδεγμαι, to receive under one's roof or protection, welcome, A., i. 6. 3 : vi. 5. 31.
ὑπο-δέω,* δήσω, δέδεκα, to bind beneath, shoe, A.: ὑποδεδεμένοι with their shoes on, iv. 5. 14.
‡ὑπό-δημα, ατος, τό, a protection for the foot, shoe, sandal, iv. 5. 14.
ὑπο-ζύγιον, ου, (ζυγόν jugum, YOKE, fr. ζεύγνυμι) an animal under the yoke, beast of burden or draught ; pl. baggage cattle or animals, as oxen, asses, &c. ; i. 3. 1 ; 7. 20 : ii. 1. 6 ; 2. 4, 15.
ὑπο-κατα-βαίνω,* βήσομαι, βέβηκα, 2 a. ἔβην, to descend somewhat, go a little lower, vii. 4. 11.
ὑπο-κρύπτω, ύψω, κέκρυφα, to hide under : M. to conceal one's own, hoard, i. 9. 19 : v. l. ἀπο-κρύπτω.
ὑπο-κύπτω, κύψω, κέκυφα, to stoop under or before another, bow low, iv. 5. 32 : v. l. κύπτω or ἐπι-κύπτω.
ὑπο-λαμβάνω,* λήψομαι, εἴληφα, 2 a. ἔλαβον, to take under one's protection, A.; sc. τὸν λόγον, to take [under one's direction] up the discourse, reply, answer, retort : μεταξὺ ὑ. to interrupt another in the midst : i. 1. 7 : iii. 1. 27, 31,

ὑπο-λείπω,* ψω, λέλοιπα, 2 a. ἔλιπον, pf. p. λέλειμμαι, a. p. ἐλείφθην, to leave behind, A.: P. & M. to be left behind, fall or lag behind, remain behind, G., i. 2. 25 : iv. 5. 15 : v. 4. 22.
ὑπο-λόχᾱγος, ου, ὁ, a sub-lochage, lieutenant, v. 2. 13 (cf. iii. 4. 21).
ὑπο-λύω, λύσω, λέλυκα, to loosen below: M. to untie or take off one's shoes or sandals, iv. 5. 13.
ὑπο-μαλακίζομαι, f. p. ισθήσομαι l., (μαλακὸς soft) to soften under or somewhat, stoop to or act a less manly part, curry favor, lose courage, ii. 1. 14.
ὑπο-μένω,* μενῶ, μεμένηκα, a. ἔμεινα, to remain behind or in place, halt, await an attack, make a stand, stand one's ground; to wait for, A.; iii. 4. 21: iv. 1. 16 s, 21 ; 4. 21 : vi. 5. 29.
ὑπό-μνημα, ατος, τό, (μιμνήσκω) a private or suggestive reminder or memorial, reminiscence, i. 6. 3.
†ὑπό-πεμπτος, ον, sent covertly or insidiously, iii. 3. 4?
ὑπο-πέμπω,* πέμψω, πέπομφα, to send covertly, artfully, or under a false pretext, A., ii. 4. 22.
ὑπο-πίνω,* πίομαι (ῐ), πέπωκα, to drink somewhat freely, vii. 3. 29 : v. l.
ὑπο-πίπτω to fall back or withdraw a little.
†ὑπ-οπτεύω, εύσω, ipf. ὑπ-ώπτευον, su-spicor, to suspect, apprehend, mistrust, be suspicious or apprehensive, A., I. (A.), μή, i. 1. 1 ; 3. 1 : ii. 3. 13 ; 5. 28 : iii. 1. 5 : iv. 2. 15.
ὕπ-οπτος, ον, (ὑφ-οράω) suspicious, to be suspected, iii. 3. 4?
ὑπο-στῆναι, -στάς, see ὑφ-ίστημι.
†ὑπο-στρατηγέω, ήσω, to command under, be lieutenant-general to, D., v. 6. 36.
ὑπο-στράτηγος, ου, (v. l. ὅς, οῦ) ὁ, a lieutenant-general, iii. 1. 32.
ὑπο-στρέφω,* ἑψω, ἔστροφα l., 2 a. p. ἐστράφην, to make an unobserved, adroit, or sudden turn, to avoid a snare, ii. 1. 18: vi. 6. 38: so 2 a. p. as m., vii. 4. 18.
ὑπο-σχεῖν, see ὑπ-έχω, v. 8. 1.
ὑπο-σχέσθαι, see ὑπ-ισχνέομαι.
ὑπουργός, όν, (ὑπό, ἔργον) working under another, assisting, contributing, or conducive to, D., v. 8. 15.
ὑπο-φαίνω,* φανῶ, πέφαγκα, to show a little, begin to dawn or appear, dawn, iii. 2. 1 : iv. 2. 7 ; 3. 9.

ὑπο-φείδομαι, φείσομαι, πέφεισμαι l., (φείδομαι to spare) to spare somewhat, εἰ, iv. 1. 8.
· ὑπο-χείριος, ον, (χείρ) under the hand or power of, in the hands of, subject to, D., iii. 2. 3 : vii. 6. 43.
ὑπ-οχος, ον, (ἔχω) held under, subject to, D., ii. 5. 7.
ὑπο-χωρέω, ήσω, κεχώρηκα, to go under the pressure of others, retire before, make way for, retreat, D., i. 4. 18 ; 7. 17 : iv. 5. 20.
ὑπ-οψία, ας, (ὑφ-οράω) suspicion, mistrust, distrust, apprehension, ὅτι, i. 3. 21 : ii. 4. 10 ; 5. 1 s, 5 : iii. 1. 21.
'Υρκάνιος, α, ον, ('Υρκᾱνοί the Hyrcāni) Hyrcanian, pertaining to Hyrcania, a rude province of the Persian Empire, southeast of the Caspian, whose men were excellent horsemen, vii. 8. 15.
ὗς, ὑός, a swine, see σῦς, v. 2. 3.
†ὑστεραῖος, α, ον, following in time, subsequent, next : often (esp. in dat.) ἡ ὑστεραία, sc. ἡμέρα, the following or next day, i. 2. 21 : ii. 3. 25 : iii. 5. 13.
†ὑστερέω, ήσω, ὑστέρηκα, to be or come too late for, arrive after, G., i. 7. 12.
†ὑστερίζω, ίσω ῶ, to be or arrive too late, be behindhand, vi. 1. 18.
ὕστερος,* α, ον, (referred as c., with s. ὕστατος last, to ὑπό) post-erior, later, behind, afterwards, after, subsequently, 509, G., i. 5. 14 : iii. 4. 21 : vi. 4. 9 :— so neut. ὕστερον as adv., i. 3. 2 ; 5. 16 ; 6. 7 ; 8. 8 : iv. 3. 34.
ὑφ' by apostr. for ὑπό, before an aspirated vowel, i. 3. 10.
ὑφ-εῖμαι,-είμην, see ὑφ-ίημι, vi. 6. 31.
‡ὑφειμένως submissively, humbly, softly, vii. 7. 16.
ὑφ-έξω, see ὑπ-έχω, vi. 6. 15.
ὑφ-ηγέομαι, ήσομαι, ἤγημαι, to lead forward moderately or with others close behind, iv. 1. 7 : vi. 5. 25.
ὑφ-ίημι,* ήσω, εἷκα, a. ἧκα (ᾧ, &c.), 2 a. m. εἵμην, sub-mitto, to submit, admit, concede, give up, A. I., iii. 5. 5 : — M. to submit or give up one's self, submit or surrender (intrans.), yield, give way, be remiss or spiritless, D. I., iii. 1. 12 ; 2. 3 : v. 4. 26 : vi. 6. 31 ?
ὑφ-ίστημι,* στήσω, ἕστηκα, 2 a. ἔστην, to place under, station men covertly : — M. (w. pf., plp., and 2 a. act.) to stand up under an attack,

ὑφοράω   142   Φᾶσις

responsibility, &c.; *to withstand*, D.; *to under-take*, A.; *to volunteer; to post one's self eovertly, stand aside, ἐν* · iii. 2. 11 : iv. 1. 14, 26 s : vi. 1. 19.

ὑφ-οράω,* ὄψομαι, ἑώρακα or ἑόρᾱκα, su-spicor, to look under lest some mischief be hidden, *to suspect*, A., ii. 4. 10.

†ὑψηλός, ή, όν, s., *high, lofty:* τὸ ὑψηλόν, sc. χωρίον, *the high ground, height:* ἄλλεσθαι ὑψηλά *to leap high* (leaps): i. 2. 22 : iii. 4. 24 s : vi. 1. 5.

ὕψος, εος, τό, (ὕψι *on high*, akin to ὑπέρ) *height, altitude*, ii. 4. 12 : iii. 4. 7, 9 s: cf. εὖρος.

Φ.

[φα-, Sans. bha-, Lat. fa-, *to enlighten*.]
φαγεῖν, 2 a. of ἐσθίω, *to eat*, ii. 3. 16 : iv. 5. 8. Der. SARCO-PHAGUS.

φαιδρός, ά, όν, (φα-) *bright, brightly shining, beaming, animating, cheering*, ii. 6. 11.

φαίην, see φημί *to say*, i. 3. 7.
φαίνω,* φανῶ, πέφαγκα, a. ἔφηνα, 2 a. p. ἐφάνην, *to bring to light, show, reveal*, A., iv. 3. 13 : — P. & M. *to be brought* or *come to light, appear, be seen, show* or *present one's self, be in prospect* or *pretended*, D., I., P., ἐν, &c. (the pt. here implying reality, but not the inf., 657 k ; as φαίνεται εἶναι *he appears to be*, though he may not be; but ὤν φ. [being he so appears] *he appears to be*, as he really IS, *he is seen* or *shown to be, he evidently* or *manifestly is;* while both εἶναι and ὤν are often om., esp. before an adj. or appositive), i. 3. 19 ; 6. 1, 11 ; 9. 19 : iii. 1. 24 ; 4. 2 : v. 4. 29 : vii. 6. 37. Der. PHENOMENON, PHASE, FANCY.

φάλαγξ, αγγος, ἡ, *the line of battle*, in which the front was extended, and the depth comm. small (of 4 men i. 2. 15, of 8 men vii. 1. 23) ; a body of troops (esp. hoplites) so arranged, *a line, main line* or *body*, PHALANX (cf. κέρας *a body in column*, ὄρθιος) : ἐπὶ φάλαγγος, κατὰ or εἰς φάλαγγα, *in* or *into line of battle*. In open order, it was usual to allow each hoplite a space 6 feet square ; but in close array, as for a battle charge, only 3 feet square. i. 2. 17 ; 8. 17 s : ii. 1. 6 ; 3. 3 : iii. 3. 11 : iv. 3. 26 ; 8. 9 s.

Φαλῖνος, ου, *Phalīnus*, a Greek from the island *Zacynthus* (now Zante), in the service of Tissaphernes, ii. 1. 7.

φανείς, -ῆναι, -οῦμαι, see φαίνω.

‡φανερός, ά, όν, *apparent, visible, conspicuous, manifest, evident, plain*, i. 7. 17 ; 9. 6 : often in personal for impers. constr., w. a pt., 573, as στέργων φανερὸς ἦν (he was apparent loving] *it was apparent that he loved*, or *he evidently loved*, ii. 6. 23 ; cf. i. 6. 8 ; 9. 11, 16 ; and δῆλος : ἐν τῷ φανερῷ *in publie, openly*, i. 3. 21 : εἰς τὸ φ. *into a conspicuous position*, vii. 7. 22.

‡φανερῶς *openly*, i. 9. 19.

φαρέτρα, ας, (φέρω) pharetra, *a quiver*, comm. of leather, with a lid, and slung behind the shoulder or on the left side, iv. 4. 16.

φάρμακον, ου, *a drug*, whether healing or poisonous, *medicine*, vi. 4. 11. Der. PHARMACY.

‡φαρμακο-ποσία, ας, (πίνω) *the drinking of drugs, taking medicine* or *physic*, iv. 8. 21.

Φαρνάβαζος, ου, *Pharnabazus*, satrap of Bithynia and Lesser Phrygia, or of the northwest part of Asia Minor (as early as B. C. 412), a man of far higher character than his neighbor Tissaphernes, and at length honored with the hand of Apama, the king's daughter. He rendered valuable aid to the Spartans during the later years of the Peloponnesian War. After the Cyrean expedition, he was somewhat involved in the war with the Spartans, and was engaged in unsuccessful expeditions for the reconquest of Egypt, — the last B. C. 374. v. 6. 24.

φασί(ν), φατέ, φάναι, see φημί.

†Φασιᾱνοί, ῶν, *the Phasiāni*, or *Phasians*, a people dwelling about the river Phasis, iv. 6. 5 : v. 6. 36.

Φᾶσις, ιδος or ιος, ὁ, *the Phasis* (now Pasin-Su, thought by some the Pison of Gen. 2. 11), called in its lower course the Araxes (now Arás), a river of Armenia, uniting with the Cyrus (now Kûr) and flowing into the Caspian, iv. 6. 4. — 2. A noted river of Colchis, anciently regarded as the boundary between Asia and Europe, now called Rión or Faz. Xenophon seems to have regarded the Armenian Phasis as the upper part of this river, and calls the dwellers upon both Φασιᾱνοί. The name of the river was also given

φάσκω 143 φιλία

to a Milesian trading settlement near its mouth, and to the surrounding region. The pheasant is said to have been brought from this region by the Argonauts, and hence to have derived its name (ὄρνις Φασιανός the Phasian bird). v. 6. 36; 7. 1, 7, 9.

φάσκω (a strengthened pres. for φημί* q. v.) *to say, state, declare, affirm, allege,* ch. used in the pt., I., iii. 5. 17 : iv. 4. 21 ; 8. 4 : v. 8. 1.

φαῦλος, η, ον, (cf. paulus) *trifling, of small account,* vi. 6. 11 s.

φέρω,* οἴσω, ἐνήνοχα, a. ἤνεγκα or -ον, a. p. ἠνέχθην, fero, *to* BEAR, *carry, bring, endure, produce* (of land), *carry off* (hence, *receive as pay*), A. D., ἐπί, πρός, &c., i. 2. 22 ; 3. 21 : ii. 1. 17 : iii. 1. 23 ; 4. 32 : *to carry* one, hence of a road or entrance, *to lead,* ἐπί, εἰς, iii. 5. 15 : ὁ φέρων *the bearer,* i. 9. 26 : χαλεπῶς φέρειν ægre ferre, *to bear up with difficulty, to be dejected, deeply concerned* or *afflicted,* or *greatly excited,* D. 456, i. 3. 3 : see ἄγω, βαρέως: — P. or M. *to be borne, carried, &c.; to be borne on, thrown, hurled,* or *sent, to rush, fly* (of missiles); i. 8. 20 : iii. 3. 16 : iv. 7. 6 s, 14 : — *M. to bring in for one's own use,* A., vi. 6. 1 : vii. 4. 3. Der. PERI-PHERY, META-PHOR.

φεύγω,* φεύξομαι & φευξοῦμαι, 2 pf. πέφευγα, 2 a. ἔφυγον, fugio, *to flee, fly, take to flight, run away, retreat,* A., ἀπό, διά, εἰς, ἐξ, ἐπί, &c.; *to flee one's country, be* or *become an exile, go into exile, be banished:* οἱ φεύγοντες *the fugitives, exiles:* i. 1. 7 ; 2. 18 ; 3. 3 ; 10. 1 : iii. 2. 35 ; 3. 9, 19 ; 4. 35. **Φεύγω** denotes rather an attempt to escape by open flight ; and **διδράσκω** (only in compounds), by secret departure or concealment. Cf. ἀποφεύγω, ἀπο-διδράσκω. Der. FUGITIVE.

φημί* (pres. encl., exc. 2 sing. φής or φῄς) & strengthened **φάσκω** q. v., φήσω, ipf. ἔφην (usu. as aor.; 2 sing. ἔφησθα), rarer a. ἔφησα, (φα-) *to say, state, declare ; to affirm, assent, say yes,* (cf. aio): w. οὐ (which comm. modifies rather a dependent verb, 662 b), *to say that . . not, say no, deny, refuse* (see οὐ, and cf. nego) : I. (A., sometimes without the inf., which may yet be understood), OP. (r., vii. 1. 5) ; but often placed parenthetically and sometimes pleonastic, 574 (cf. *quoth*):

i. 2. 25 s ; 3. 1, 7 s, 18 ; 6. 6 s : ii. 1. 9 s ; 5. 24 s : v. 8. 5. — To φημί are usu. referred the f. ἐρῶ, pf. εἴρηκα, εἴρημαι, and 1 a. εἶπα (ind. 2 sing., and imv. exc. 2 sing., esp. used), oftener (exc. as above) 2 a. εἶπον (εἴπω, -οιμι, -έ, -εῖν, -ών); but these often correspond in their use more closely to λέγω or ἀγορεύω (hence also, *to mention, tell, bid, advise, propose,* &c.; and A. D., CP., &c., 659 h⁷) : i. 2. 5 ; 3. 5, 7, 14 : ii. 1. 15, 21 ; 3. 2 : εἴρητο *charge had been given,* D. I., iii. 4. 3 s. Cf. fāri, fāma, FAME.

φθάνω,* φθάσω & φθήσομαι, ἔφθακα, 1 a. ἔφθασα, 2 a. ἔφθην, *to anticipate, get the start of, be* or *get before another, arrive before, outstrip, surprise,* A. P. (often translated by a finite verb, and φθάνω by such expressions as *before, first, previously, beforehand, sooner, too soon, by anticipation* or *surprise,* 677 f), πρίν : φ. καταλαβόντες *to anticipate in getting possession,* or *to get possession first,* i. 3. 14 : φθάσαι πρὶν παθεῖν *to* [get the start] *act before suffering,* ii. 5. 5 : φθάσαι πρῶτος *to* [outstrip, so as to] *be foremost,* 509 d, iii. 4. 20 : ἁρπάσαι φθάσαντας *to take by surprise,* 677 f, iv. 6. 11 : see, also, iii. 4. 49 : iv. 1. 4, 21 : v. 7. 16.

φθέγγομαι, ἐγξομαι, ἔφθεγμαι, *to utter a sound* (esp. a loud, clear sound), *raise a cry, cry out, shout, scream, sound, make one's self heard,* D., i. 8. 18 : iv. 5. 18 : vi. 1. 23 : vii. 4. 19. Der. DI-PHTHONG, APO-PHTHEGM.

φθείρω,* φθερῶ, ἔφθαρκα, *to destroy, lay waste,* A., iv. 7. 20.

φθονέω, ήσω, (φθόνος envy) *to envy,* D., i. 9. 19 : v. 7. 10.

φιάλη, ης, patera, *a broad, shallow cup* or *bowl, saucer,* for drinking or libation, iv. 7. 27. Der. PHIAL, VIAL.

φιλαίτερος c. of φίλος, i. 9. 29 ?

†**φιλέω,** ήσω, πεφίληκα, *to love,* with a pure love, as of friendship ; more emotional in sense than ἀγαπάω, less passionate than ἐράω, and less strong than στέργω · A.; i. 1. 4 ; 9. 25, 28.

‡**Φιλήσιος,** ου, *Philesius,* an Achæan, chosen as successor to Menon, and one of the oldest of the Cyrean generals, but not one of the most prominent or highly esteemed, iii. 1. 47.

†**φιλία,** as, *friendship, attachment, affection, love,* G. or possessive pron.,

φιλικός 144 φοινίκεος

both subjective and objective (cf. *love of*), 444, 538 d, i. 3. 5 : ii. 5. 8, 24 : v. 6. 11: vii. 7. 29 (*love to you*) : — πρὸς φιλίαν [in accordance with friendship] *in a friendly manner, in peace* or *friendship*, i. 3. 19 (or *to a friendly country*, see φίλιος). See διά.

†φιλικός, ή, όν, *befitting a friend, of a friendly nature, friendly*, iv. 1. 9 : v. 5. 25 (*v. l.* ἐπιτήδειος). See φίλιος.

‡φιλικῶς *in a friendly manner, on friendly terms, as a friend*, ii. 5. 27 : vi. 6. 35.

†φίλιος, α, ον, *of a friend* or *friends, friendly, in amity* or *at peace*, esp. opposed to πολέμιος, and often applied to places (as φιλικός rather to acts, and φίλος to persons), D.: διὰ φιλίας τῆς χώρας *through the country as friendly* or *in peace*, 523 b : i. 3. 14 ; 6. 3 (of a person): ii. 3. 26 ; 5. 18 : v. 7. 13 s, 33 : φιλία, sc. χώρα or γῆ, *a friendly country, region*, or *land*, ii. 3. 27 : vi. 6. 38 : vii. 3. 13. See φιλία.

†φίλ-ιππος, ον, s., *fond of horses*, i. 9. 5. Der. PHILIP, PHILIPPIC.

†φιλό-θηρος, ον, s., (θήρα *hunting*) *fond of hunting* or *the chase*, i. 9. 6.

†φιλο-κερδέω, ήσω, (κέρδος) *to love, seek*, or *be greedy of gain*, i. 9. 16.

†φιλο-κίνδυνος, ον, s., *fond of danger, venturesome, adventurous*, i. 9. 6.

†φιλο-μαθής, ές, c. έστερος, s. έστατος, (μανθάνω) *fond of learning, eager to learn*, i. 9. 5. Der. PHILOMATH.

†φιλο-νεικία, ας, (νεῖκος *strife*) *love of strife, rivalry, emulation*, iv. 8. 27 : v. l. φιλο-νικία, ας, (νίκη) *eagerness for victory*.

†Φιλό-ξενος, ου, *Philoxenus*, a good soldier from Pellēne in Achaia, v. 2.15.

†φιλο-πόλεμος, ον, *fond of war, warloving, passionate for war*, ii. 6. 1, 6.

φίλος, η, ον, c. & s. φιλαίτερος or φίλτερος, -τατος,* amicus, *friendly* (cf. φίλιος), *well-disposed, attached:* subst. φίλος, ου, *a friend, adherent, favorite:* D. (as subst., also w. G.) : i. 1. 2, 5 ; 3. 6, 12 ; 4. 2 ; 6. 6 ; 7. 6 s ; 9. 10, 20 s, 27 s, 29 (c.), 31 : iv. 4. 4. Der. PHILO-, PHIL-.

‡φιλό-σοφος, ον, *fond of wisdom:* subst. φιλόσοφος, ου, a PHILOSOPHER, ii. 1. 13.

‡φιλο-στρατιώτης, ου, *a friend to the soldiers, the soldiers' friend*, vii. 6. 4, 39.

‡φιλοτῑμέομαι, ήσομαι, πεφιλοτίμημαι, a. ἐφιλοτιμήθην, (φιλό-τιμος *honor-loving, ambitious, jealous*, fr. τιμή) *to be jealous, piqued*, or *resentful, to resent it*, i. 4. 7.

‡φιλο-φρονέομαι, ήσομαι, a. ἐφιλοφρονησάμην or -ήθην, (φιλό-φρων *friendly-minded*, fr. φρήν *mind*) *to be kindly disposed, express good-will* or *friendship, show kindness* or *favor; to treat* or *greet as a friend*, A.; ii. 5. 27 : iv. 5. 29, 32, 34.

Φλιάσιος, ου, ὁ, *a Phliasian*, a man of Phlius (Φλιοῦς), a city with a small territory in the northeast of the Peloponnese, on the Asōpus (now the St. George). It was commonly jealous of its neighbor Argos, and in alliance with Sparta. vii. 8. 1. ‖ Ruins near the village of St. George.

†φλυαρέω, ήσω, (φλύαρος) *to talk nonsense, speak absurdly*, iii. 1. 26, 29.

φλυαρία, ας, (= φλύαρος *babbling*, fr. φλύω bullio, *to bubble up*) pl. nūgæ, *idle talk, absurdities, fooleries, mere trifling, nonsense*, i. 3. 18.

†φοβερός, ά, όν, s., *frightful, fearful, alarming, terrible, formidable, to be feared*, D. I., μή, ii. 5. 9 : iii. 4. 5 : v. 2. 23 ; 5. 17 ; 7. 2.

†φοβέω, ήσω, *to frighten, terrify, scare*, A., iv. 5. 17 :— φοβέομαι, ήσομαι, πεφόβημαι, a. ἐφοβήθην, *to be frightened, terrified, alarmed, afraid, apprehensive*, or *under the influence of fear; to fear;* A. μή, I., περί, διά · τὸ φοβεῖσθαι τὴν τιμωρίαν *the fear of punishment*; i. 3. 17 ; 8. 13 : ii. 4. 18 ; 5. 5 ; 6. 14, 19 : v. 5. 7 : vii. 1. 2 ; 8. 20.

φόβος, ου, ὁ, (φέβομαι *to flee*) *fear, dread, fright, alarm, panic, terror*, G., I., CP., ii. 2. 19 ; 4. 3 : iii. 1. 18 : vii. 4. 1 : pl. *terrors, fearful threats*, iv. 1. 23 : τὸν ἐκ τῶν Ἑλλήνων εἰς τοὺς βαρβάρους φόβον *the terror* [struck from the Greeks as the source, into the barbarians] *with which the Greeks struck the barbarians*, i. 2. 18 ; cf. vii. 2. 37. Der. HYDRO-PHOBIA.

†φοινίκεος, έα, εον, contr. φοινῑκοῦς, ῆ, οῦν, *purple-red, purple* or *crimson*, a color early prepared by the Phœnicians from the murex of the neighboring sea, and chosen by the Greeks for war-garments from its brilliant effect and its disguising blood, i. 2.16: v. l. φοινικός, φοινίκιος.

†**Φοινίκη**, ης, *Phœnicia* or *Phenice*, a narrow strip on the Syrian coast of the Mediterranean, peopled by a Semitic race, illustrious for their early commerce, arts, inventions, and colonies. They founded Carthage, "Rome's great rival," and imparted letters to Greece. i. 4. 5 ; 7. 12 : vii. 8. 25.

†**φοινικιστής**, οῦ, purpurātus, *a purple-wearer:* φ. βασίλειος *a wearer of purple at the king's court* from his high rank, i. 2. 20. Some translate (after Zonaras) *a dyer of purple*, or (as Larcher) *a bearer of the purple standard.*

Φοῖνιξ or **Φοίνιξ**, ικος, ὁ, *Phœnician:* subst., *a Phœnician*, i. 4. 6. Hence, ὁ **φοίνιξ** *the date-palm, date-tree, palm*, as bearing *the Phœnician fruit*, since dates were brought in commerce from Phœnicia to Greece (yet some explain rather **Φοινίκη** as *the date-land*), i. 5. 10. Of this tree, so great an ornament to the country where it grows, and so invaluable to the inhabitants, Strabo says that a Persian poem sang the uses to the number of three hundred and sixty. Der. PHŒNIX.

Φολόη, ης, a mountain range on the boundary between Elis and Arcadia, fabled as the scene of a battle of Hercules with the Centaurs, and as named by him from one of them who was here buried, Pholus, v. 3. 10. ‖ Mauro Bouni, or Xiria.

φορέω, ήσω, πεφόρηκα 1., (φέρω) iterative, *to carry habitually, wear; to bring* in successive loads ; A.; i. 8. 29 : v. 2. 26 : vii. 4. 4.

φόρος, ου, ὁ, (φέρω) *tribute*, v. 5. 7.

φορτίον, ου, (φέρω) *a burden, load*, v. 2. 21 : vii. 1. 37.

φράζω,* άσω, πέφρακα, *to TELL*, *bid, direct, state, declare, mention*, D. I., A. CP., i. 6. 3 : ii. 3. 3 ; 4. 18 : iv. 5. 29, 34 : vi. 6. 20. Der. PHRASE.

‡**Φρασίας**, ου, *Phrasias*, an officer from Athens, vi. 5. 11.

φρέαρ, φρέατος, τό, *a well, cistern*, iv. 5. 25.

φρονέω, ήσω, πεφρόνηκα, (φρήν *mind*) *to think, understand, perceive, discern, be wise* or *sagacious*, A. of neut. adj., ii. 2. 5 : μέγα φ. *to think* [big] *loftily, to be high-minded, elated*, or *proud*, ἐπί, iii. 1. 27 : v. 6. 8 : πλέον φ. *to be superior in wisdom*, vi. 3. 18.

‡**φρόνημα**, ατος, τό, *thought, spirit, confidence*, iii. 1. 22 ; 2. 16.

‡**φρόνιμος**, ον, *thoughtful, prudent, discreet, sensible, judicious, sagacious, self-possessed*, i. 10. 7 : ii. 5. 16 ; 6. 7.

‡**φροντίζω**, ίσω ιῶ, πεφρόντικα, (φροντίς *thought, solicitude*) *to take thought, be anxious* or *solicitous ; to consider, devise, contrive*, ὅπως : ii. 3. 25 ; 6. 8.

†**φρούραρχος**, ου, ὁ, *the commander* or *commandant of a garrison*, i. 1. 6.

†**φρουρέω**, ήσω, *to guard, keep under guard*, A., i. 4. 8 : v. 5. 29.

†**φρούριον**, ου, dim. in form only, *a garrisoned post, fortress, garrison*, i. 4. 15 : v. l. **φρουρά**, ᾶς, *a garrison*.

φρουρός, οῦ, ὁ, (προ-οράω, 159 g, hʳ) *a watcher, guard, garrison-soldier*, vii. 1. 20 ; 8. 15 (om. by some).

φρύγανον, ου, (φρύγω frīgo, *to parch*) *a dry stick*, or *twig ;* pl. *firewood, fagots*, &c., iv. 3. 11.

Φρυγία, ας, (Φρύξ) *Phrygia* (Great, or *Proper*) a large inland country, the western part of the great table land of Asia Minor. It appears to have been the native region of the flute-music (which early vied with that of the lyre, see Μαρσύας), and of some of the rites of Bacchus and Cybele. i. 2. 6 s ; 9. 7. — 2. *Lesser Phrygia*, a name given to the northern part of Mysia, extending along the coast of the Propontis to the Hellespont, with the Troad sometimes included. This was part of the satrapy of Pharnabazus, while Great Phrygia was given to Cyrus, and afterwards to Tissaphernes. v. 6. 24. — See Φρύξ.

Φρυνίσκος, ου, *Phryniscus*, an Achæan, appointed general during the latter part of the retreat, prob. in place of Sophænetus, vii. 2. 1s ; 5. 10.

Φρύξ, υγός, ὁ, *a Phrygian*. The Phrygians were an ancient people, of quiet agricultural and pastoral habits, who, according to some, had crossed from Thrace into Asia Minor. i. 2. 13.

†**φυγάς**, άδος, ὁ, *a* FUGITIVE, *exile*, i. 1. 9, 11 ; 7. 5 : iv. 2. 13.

†**φυγή**, ῆς, fuga, *flight ; banishment, exile ;* i. 8. 24 : iv. 2. 12 : vii. 7. 57.

φύγω, -οιμι, -εῖν, -ών, see φεύγω.

†**φυλακή**, ῆς, *watch* (whether act, time, place, or persons engaged, 363 h) *guard, ward, custody, guard-station, garrison, sentinels*, G., πρός. The

Greeks usu. divided the night into three watches, as the Romans into four. i. 1. 6 ; 4. 4 : ii. 4. 17 ; 6. 10 : iv. 1. 5 ; 5. 21, 29 : v. 8. 1 : vii. 6. 22.

†φύλαξ, ακος, ὁ ἡ, *a guard* (the individual, as φυλακή the company), *watcher, sentinel, custodian ;* pl. *a guard* (collectively), *body-guard, garrison,* &c.; i. 2. 12: iv. 2. 5s: vi. 4. 27; 5. 4 : λόχος φύλαξ (as adj.) *a company on the watch* or *of reserve,* vi. 5. 9.

φυλάττω, άξω, πεφύλαχα, *to guard, watch, garrison, keep, keep guard* or *watch,* A. D., AE., ἐπί · φυλακὰς φυλάττειν *to keep, maintain,* or *stand guard ;* i. 2. 1, 21 s ; 4. 4 s : ii. 6. 10 : v. 1. 2 ; 3. 4 : — M. *to guard one's self against another, be* or *keep on one's guard against, beware of, guard against, keep watch upon, guard* or *keep guard* for one's own *safety, take care,* A. (of object guarded against), AE., μή, ὡς, ὥστε, i. 6. 9 : ii. 2. 16 ; 5. 3, 37: vii. 3. 35 ; φ. πᾶσαν, sc. φυλακήν, *to take every precaution, to be on the strictest guard,* vii. 6. 22. Der. PHYLACTERY.

φῦσάω, ήσω, a. p. ἐφυσήθην, (φῦσα *a blast, bellows*) *to inflate, blow up,* A., iii. 5. 9.

Φύσκος, ου, ὁ, *the Physcus,* a stream by Opis, ii. 4. 25. || The canal Katur, or Nahr-Awán ; acc. to some, the river Adhem.

†φυτεύω, εύσω, πεφύτευκα l., (φυτόν *a plant*) *to plant,* A., v. 3. 12.

φύω (ῠ),* φύσω, πέφυκα, 2 a. ἔφυν, *to bring into being, produce,* A., i. 4. 10 : but in pf. and 2 a., *to come into being,* cf. fui. Der. PHYSICS, PHYSICIAN, PHYSIO-LOGY.

Φωκαΐς, ἴδος, ἡ, *a Phocæan woman,* from Φώκαια, *Phocæa* (now Foggia or Fokia), an Ionian city of great commercial enterprise and great prosperity until its capture by the army of the elder Cyrus, when a large part of its inhabitants, embarking in their vessels, sought new homes in the distant west (among others, Marseilles). The Phocæan mentioned in i. 10. 2 was named Milto from her brilliancy of complexion, but by Cyrus Aspasia after the favorite of Pericles. She had been brought up by her father Hermotimus in poverty and without a mother's care ; and when brought by force to Cyrus, won his affection by her wisdom and virtue, even more than by her remarkable beauty. After his death, she became also a favorite of Artaxerxes, who, it is stated, had specially ordered her capture ; but when he had associated with himself upon the throne his son Darius, the latter asked that he would also grant him Aspasia. Artaxerxes promised to do this, since, according to usage, the first request of a successor elect could not be denied ; but, instead of fulfilling his promise, made her a priestess (acc. to Plutarch, of Anītis, the Persian Diāna). This so enraged the disappointed son that he joined with Tiribazus in seeking his father's life, but lost his own. i. 10. 2.

φωνή, ἧς, (φα-) vox, *a sound* of the voice, *voice, speech, language,* ii. 6. 9 : iv. 8. 4. Der. PHONETIC, EU-PHONY.

φῶς, φωτός, τό, (φα-) *light* of day, a fire, &c., iii. 1. 12 : vii. 4. 18 : φῶς ἐγένετο *daylight came, it became light,* vi. 3. 2. Der. PHOTO-GRAPH.

X.

χαίρω,* χαιρήσω, κεχάρηκα, *to rejoice,* P., vii. 2. 4 : *to take leave, depart* (from the common expression in leave-taking, χαῖρε *farewell*); hence, ἐᾶν χαίρειν *to let go, bid farewell to,* vii. 3. 23 : χαίρων *rejoicing, with impunity,* v. 6. 32.

Χαλδαῖοι,ων,οἱ,*theChaldæi,*or-*æans,* a warlike and independent people of Armenia, perhaps the remains in their early seat of the powerful tribe that conquered Babylonia, and becoming effeminate were themselves conquered by the Medes and Persians. They seem to have been also called Χάλυβες ; and Xenophon uses both names, apparently for the same tribe. iv. 3. 4 : v. 5. 17 : vii. 8. 25. See Χάλυψ.

†χαλεπαίνω, ανῶ, *to be severe, angry, indignant, displeased, provoked, incensed,* or *enraged,* D. G., ὅτι, i. 4. 12; 5. 11, 14 : vii. 6. 32 : so a. *p.* as *m.* ἐχαλεπάνθην, iv. 6. 2.

χαλεπός, ή, όν, c., s., *HARD* to do, bear, take, &c.; *difficult, irksome, troublesome ; grievous, severe, stern, harsh, violent, bitter, cross, fierce,* cruel, dangerous: τὸ χαλεπόν the severity, harshness, fierceness: I.: i. 3. 12: ii.6.9,11s: iii.1.13; 4.35: v.1.7.

‡χαλεπῶς hardly, with difficulty, grievously, severely: χ. ἔχειν to be grievously affected, deeply concerned, or greatly distressed: see φέρω: i. 3. 3: iii. 3. 13; 4. 47: v. 7. 2: vi. 4. 16.

χαλῑνόω, ώσω, κεχαλίνωκα 1., (χαλῑνὸς a bridle) to bridle, A., iii. 4. 35.

†χάλκεος, έα, εον, contr. χαλκοῦς, ῆ, οῦν, brazen or rather bronze, of brass or bronze, i. 2. 16: v. 2. 29.

†Χαλκηδονία, or Καλχηδονία, ας, Chalcedonia, the territory about the city of Chalcēdon and belonging to it, vi. 6. 38.

†Χαλκηδών, or Καλχηδών (167 b), όνος, ἡ, Chalcēdon, a city in Bithynia, founded by the Megarians, B. C. 674, on the Propontis at the entrance of the Thracian Bosphorus. Though it became a considerable city, it was sometimes called the "City of the Blind," because its founders overlooked the superior advantages of the nearly opposite site of Byzantium. vii. 1. 20; 2. 24, 26. ǁ Kadi-Keui.

χαλκός, οῦ, ὁ, æs, copper; but more commonly bronze, an alloy of copper and tin (usu. about ⅞ copper to ⅛ tin) greatly used by the ancients, and admitting a harder temper than the more modern brass, an alloy of copper and zinc. The latter term is, however, common in translation. Χαλκός τις ἤστραπτε [some bronze glistened] there was a gleaming of brass or brazen armor, i. 8. 8.

‡χάλκωμα, ατος, τό, a brazen (or bronze) utensil, iv. 1. 8.

Χάλος, ου, ὁ, the Chalus, a river in Syria. i. 4. 9. ǁ The Koweik, the river of Aleppo.

Χάλυψ, υβος, ὁ, a Chalybian, or one of the Chalybes, a people so skilled in working iron that they either gave their name to steel (χάλυψ, as if Chalybian iron), or were themselves named from it: cf. οἱ σιδηροτέκτονες Χάλυβες, Æsch. Prom. 714. Some of the Chalybes (also called Χαλδαῖοι, v. 5. 17) were the bravest people found by the Cyreans; while others, west of Trebizond, were few in number and subject to the Mossynœci. iv. 4. 18; 6. 5; 7. 15: v. 5. 1: vii. 8. 25. Der. CHALYBEATE.

χαράδρα, ας, (χαράττω to cut, furrow, whence CHARACTER) a ravine, gorge, usu. furrowed by water, iii. 4. 1.

χαράκωμα, ατος, τό, (χάραξ stake, fr. χαράττω to cut) a paling, palisading, line of palisades, v. 2. 26.

†χαρίεις, ίεσσα, ίεν, g. ίεντος, ιέσσης, gratiōsus, graceful, agreeable, pleasing, clever, ingenious, iii. 5. 12 (v. l. χάριεν).

†χαρίζομαι, ίσομαι ιοῦμαι, κεχάρισμαι, gratificor, to grant one a favor, gratify, favor, oblige, please, indulge, D. AE., i. 9. 24: ii. 1. 10; 3.19: vii.1.25.

χάρις,* ιτος, ἡ, (χαίρω) gratia, grace, favor; obligation for a favor, gratitude, thanks: χάριν εἰδέναι (see ὁράω) to recognize a favor or obligation, esteem it a favor, be grateful: χάριν ἔχειν to have gratitude, feel grateful: D. G.: i. 4. 15: ii. 5. 14: iii. 3. 14: vi. 1. 26: vii. 4. 9; 6. 32. Der. EU-CHARIST.

Χαρμάνδη, ης, Charmande, a large city on the Arabian side of the Euphrates, thought by most to be the city called by Hdt. Ἴς, now Hit, remarkable for its bitumen springs, which furnished cement for the walls of Babylon, and which still seem inexhaustible, i. 5. 10. The Euphrates and Tigris are still crossed in the manner here stated by Xenophon.

Χαρμῖνος, ου, Charminus, an envoy from the Spartan commander Thibron to the Cyreans, vii. 6. 1, 39.

χειμών, ῶνος, ὁ, (χέω to pour, cf. χιών) hiems, winter, wintry weather, storm, cold, i. 7. 6: iv. 1. 15: vii. 3. 13.

χείρ,* χειρός, d. pl. χερσί, ἡ, the hand: εἰς χεῖρας ἰέναι or ἔρχεσθαι to come to [hands] blows or to close encounter or combat, but w. dat., [to come into hands to any one] to put one's self in the hands or power of any one : περὶ ταῖς χερσίν about the [hands] wrists: ἐκ χειρὸς βάλλειν to throw [from] with the hand merely, as darts (but ἐκ χ., v. 4. 25, hand to hand, = close combat): i. 2. 26; 5. 8, 15: iii. 3. 15: iv. 7. 15: vi. 3. 4: see δέχομαι. Der. CHIRO-GRAPHY, SURGEON.

‡Χειρί-σοφος, ου, Chirisophus, a general sent from Sparta to Cyrus with auxiliary troops, in return for the zealous and liberal aid which he had rendered in the Peloponnesian War. He was the chief leader of the van in the retreat, and was at one

time chosen sole commander of the Cyreans. After the death of Clearchus, he was considered the first of the generals in dignity, as Xenophon was first in influence; and the two worked together with great harmony for the salvation of the army. i. 4. 3.

‡**χειρο-πληθής**, *ές*, (πλήθω) *filling the hand, as large as can be held in the hand*, iii. 3. 17.

‡**χειρο-ποίητος**, *ον*, (ποιέω) *made by hand*, iv. 3. 5.

‡**χειρόω**, *ώσω*, *A.* and oftener *M.*, *to handle, master, overpower, subdue*, vii. 3. 11.

‡**χείρων**,* *ον*, (c. referred to κακός, s. χείριστος) *worse, inferior*: χείρόν ἐστιν αὐτῷ it is worse with him, *he is less to be prized* or *worth less*, πρός: v. 2. 13: vii. 6. 4, 39.

Χερρό-νησος, *ου*, *ή*, later Att. for χερσό-νησος (χέρσος νήσος *a shore-island*), *a peninsula*, vi. 2. 2. — 2. In a special sense, *the Chersonese*, a long, fertile peninsula on the Thracian side of the Hellespont. This was early colonized by the Greeks (especially the Athenians), who were often at war with the Thracians or with each other for its protection or possession. It was at length defended by a wall built across its isthmus. i. 1. 9: ii. 6. 2: vii. 1. 13. ‖ Peninsula of the Dardanelles.

χηλή, *ῆς*, *a hoof*; hence, from some resemblance, a sloping structure of stone to protect a wall from the violence of waves, *a breakwater, mole*, or *pier*, vii. 1. 17.

χήν, χηνός, ὁ ή, anser, Germ. *Gans*, *a goose*, i. 9. 26.

χθές adv., YESTER-*day*, vi. 4. 18?

χίλιοι, αι, α, *a thousand*, i. 2. 3, 6, 9; 6. 2: ii. 2. 6. Der. CHILIAST.

χίλος, οῦ, ὁ, *grass* cut for feeding animals, *fodder, forage*: ξηρὸς χ. *dry grass, hay*: i. 5. 7; 9. 27: iv. 5. 33.

‡**χιλόω**, ώσω, *to feed* with cut grass, *to fodder*, Λ., vii. 2. 21.

χίμαιρα, *ας*, (χίμαρος *a goat of the first year*; fr. χεῖμα *winter*, as if a *winter's kid*?) *a she-goat of the first year, female kid*, iii. 2. 12. Der. CHIMERA.

Χίος, *ου*, *ὁ*, *a Chian*, a man of Chios (Χίος, now Scio), one of the larger islands of the Ægean, near the coast of Ionia. It was colonized by the Ionians, and formed a powerful maritime state, until its conquest and cruel devastation by the Persians, B. C. 493. On recovering its liberty through the battle of Mycale, B.C. 479, it became for a long period one of the closest allies of Athens. It has since repeatedly suffered the evils of war, and most severely from its brutal desolation by the Turks in 1822 A. D. Of the many places that claimed the birth of Homer, Chios, except perhaps Smyrna, seems best entitled to the honor: "The blind old man of Scio's rocky isle" (Byron). iv. 1. 28.

χιτών, ῶνος, ὁ, tunica, *a tunic, frock*, the common under- or working-garment of the Greeks and Romans, ch. of wool, and often short or drawn up by the girdle; hence, in general, *a garment* worn next the skin; i. 2. 16; 5. 8: v. 2. 15: vii. 4. 4 (where the term is extended to the Thracian breeches or trousers).

‡**χιτωνίσκος**, *ου*, *ὁ*, dim., *a small* or *short tunic*, v. 4. 13.

χιών, όνος, ἡ, (χέω *to pour*) *snow*, iv. 4. 8, 11; 5. 3 s. Cf. χειμών; and Hima-laya, *the abode of snow*.

χλαμύς, ύδος, ἡ, *a short cloak* or *mantle*, esp. worn by horsemen, vii. 4. 4.

χοῖνιξ, ικος, ἡ (*v. l.* ὁ) *a chœnix*, or *a quart* very nearly, 1/48 of a μέδιμνος. This was a common daily allowance of corn to a soldier. i. 5. 6. Some reduce the χοῖνιξ to 1/64 of the μέδιμνος.

†**χοίρειος**, α, ον, *of swine*: κρέα χοίρεια *swine's flesh, pork*, iv. 5. 31.

χοῖρος, ου, ὁ ἡ, porcus, a tame *swine*, esp. *young, a pig*, vii. 8. 5.

†**χορεύω**, εύσω, κεχόρευκα, *to dance*, esp. in a choir, iv. 7. 16 : v. 4. 17.

χορός, οῦ, ὁ, *a* CHOIR, *band, troop*, or *row of dancers*, v. 4. 12. Der. CHORUS, CHORAL.

χόρτος, ου, ὁ, *fodder, forage, grass, herbage*, i. 5. 5: ii. 4. 11: see κοῦφος.

χράω* (άεις ῆς, &c., 120 g), ήσω, κέχρηκα, *to supply need*: hence, — (a) *M*. χράομαι, ήσομαι, κέχρημαι, a. ἐχρησάμην, ūtor, to supply one's own need by using what is required, *to use, employ, make use of, make useful* or *of use, have the use* or *service of; to experience, enjoy, find; to treat, manage, practise upon, take advantage of;*

D. (and appositive or adj., w. or without ὡς or ὥσπερ) AE., εἰς, ἀντί : i. 3. 5 ; 4. 8, 15 ; 5. 3 ; 9. 5, 17 : ii. 1. 6, 12 ; 6. 25 : iv. 4. 13 : χρῆσθαί τι *to make any use of, use* or *employ for any service, use* or *treat in any way*, i. 3. 18 : ii. 1. 14 : vi. 6. 20 : πολεμίᾳ ἐχρῆτο *experienced* [as hostile] *the hostility of*, ii. 5. 11 ; so πειθομένοις (πιστοτάτῳ) ἐχρῆτο *received obedience (the most faithful service) from*, ii. 6. 13 : iv. 6. 3 : μαχαίρᾳ χ. *to flourish a sword*, vi. 1. 5 : ἀγορᾷ χ. *to subsist by a market*, vii. 6. 24. — (b) impers. χρή* (χρῦ, χρείη, χρῆναι, χρεών), f. χρήσει, ipf. ἐχρῆν or χρῆν, *it supplies need, it is useful* or *necessary, it must* or *ought to be*, one *must, should*, or *ought*, I. (A.), i. 3. 11 ; 4. 14 : iii. 1. 7 ; 2. 24, 36. Der. CHRESTO-MATHY.

χρῄζω, ήσω not Att., (χρεία *usus, use, need*, akin to χράω) *to need, want, wish, desire*, I., i. 3. 20 : iii. 4. 41.

†**χρῆμα**, ατος, τό, *a thing* used (cf. πρᾶγμα) ; usu. pl. *things* of value, *goods, possessions, effects, booty, spoil, property, wealth*, esp. *money;* i. 1. 9 ; 3. 14 ; 4. 8 ; 10. 3 : ii. 4. 27 ; 6. 5 s.

‡**χρηματιστικός**, ή, όν, (χρηματίζομαι *to make money*) *money-making, promising wealth, indicative of gain*, vi. 1. 23.

χρῆναι, χρῆσθαι, see χράω, i. 4. 14 s.

‡**χρήσιμος**, η, ον, s., *useful, of use* or *value, serviceable*, D., i. 6. 1 : ii. 5. 23.

†**χρῖμα** or **χρῖσμα**, ατος, τό, *ointment, unguent*, iv. 4. 13. Der. CHRISM.

χρίω, ἴσω, κέχρῖκα l., *to anoint:* M. *to anoint one's self*, iv. 4. 12. Der. CHRISTIAN.

χρόνος, ου, ὁ, *time*, i. 3. 2 ; 8. 8 : πολλοῦ χρόνου [within] *for a long time*, i. 9. 25 : ἡμίσει χρόνῳ [with, by means of] *in half the time*, i. 8. 22 : χρόνῳ *by time, by protracted siege*, iii. 4. 12. See νῦν. Der. CHRONIC, CHRONICLE, CHRONO-LOGY.

†**χρύσεος**, έα, εον, contr. **χρῡσοῦς**, ῆ, οῦν, *of gold, golden, covered* or *plated with gold, gilded*, i. 2. 10, 27 ; 10. 12.

†**χρῡσίον**, ου, dim., *gold* in small pieces for money, *gold money*, amount of gold, i. 1. 9 ; 7. 18 : vii. 8. 1.

†**Χρῡσό-πολις**, εως, ἡ, *Chrysopolis*, a town of Chalcedonia, on the Thracian Bosphorus, opposite Byzantium ; said to have been so named, because the Persians made it a place of deposit for gold collected from Europe as tribute or booty. vi. 3. 16. ‖ Scutari.

χρῡσός, οῦ, ὁ, *gold*, iii. 1. 19. Der. CHRYSO-LITE, CHRYSALIS.

‡**χρῡσο-χάλῑνος**, ον, (χαλῑνός *bridle*) *with gold-studded bridle*, i. 2. 27.

χρῶμαι, -μενος, see χράω, i. 4. 8.

†**χώρα**, ας, *a place*, esp. *a country, region, province, district, territory, land; a place, position*, or *post*, in military disposition (see κατά) ; i. 1. 11 ; 5. 5, 9 ; 8. 17 : iii. 4. 33 : pl. i. 9. 14 : iv. 8. 15 : see φίλιος : — so of position in respect to rank, influence, &c., as ἐν ἀνδροπόδων χώρᾳ *in the condition of slaves*, v. 6. 13 ; ἐν οὐδεμιᾷ χώρᾳ ἔσονται *will be nowhere* or *of no account*, v. 7. 28. A country sometimes borrows the name of its inhabitants : τὴν χώραν εἶναι Χάλυβας *that the country was*, i. e. *belonged to the Chalybes*, iv. 5. 34. Χώρα and τόπος are related to each other much as, in Eng., *place* and *spot;* but their uses blend, since there is no dividing line between the larger and the narrower sense.

†**χωρέω**, ήσω or ἤσομαι, κεχώρηκα, *to give room, make room for others;* hence, *to move on, advance, march, proceed, go, pierce*, διά, ἐπί : *to give room for the reception of, contain, hold*, A. : i. 5. 6 : 10. 13 : iv. 2. 15, 28. Der. AN-CHORET.

†**χωρίζω**, ίσω ιῶ, (χωρίς) *to separate, detach*, A. I., vi. 5. 11 : κεχωρισμένος *separated, removed, differing*, G., v. 4. 34.

†**χωρίον**, ου, dim., *a limited space, extent*, or *distance;* esp. a particular *place* or *spot*, as a *stronghold* (so often), *hold, town, height, pass*, military *position, tract of land* (pl. *lands, surrounding country, region), landed estate, domain;* i. 2. 24 ; 4. 6 : ii. 5. 18 : iii. 3. 9, 15 ; 4. 24, 37 : iv. 5. 15 ; 7. 1 s, 6, 20 : v. 3. 7 s : vi. 4. 3 s, 27.

†**χωρίς** adv., *apart* (so as to leave room), *separately, singly, by one's self; apart from*, G. ; i. 4. 13 : iii. 5. 17 : vi. 6. 2.

χῶρος, ου, ὁ, *room, space*, open *ground, field; place*, esp. *country place* or *estate, country* in distinction from city ; rare in Att. prose, exc. Xen. ; v. 3. 11, 13 : vii. 2. 3 : see κατά. Der. CHORO-GRAPHY.

Ψ.

Ψάρος, ου, ὁ, *the Psarus*, one of the chief rivers of Cilicia, rising north of Mt. Taurus, breaking through this range, and entering the sea southeast of Tarsus, i. 4. 1 : *v. l.* Σάρος, Φάρος. ‖ Seihûn.

ψέγω, ψέξω, *to blame, censure, reproach*, A., vii. 7. 43.

ψέλιον or **ψέλλιον**, ου, (ψάω *to rub*) *a bracelet, armlet*, a favorite ornament among the Persians, worn even by men, i. 2. 27 ; 5. 8 ; 8. 29.

†**ψευδ-ενέδρα**, ας, *a false* or *pretended ambush* or *ambuscade*, v. 2. 28.

†**ψευδής**, ές, *false:* ψευδῆ subst., *falsehoods, lies :* ii. 4. 24 ; 6. 26.

ψεύδω, ψεύσω, pf. p. & m. ἔψευσμαι, a. p. ἐψεύσθην, a. m. ἐψευσάμην, *to cheat, deceive, disappoint*, A. AE., i. 8. 11 : iii. 2. 31 : — *M. to be* or *prove false, speak* or *act falsely, misstate, falsify, deceive, lie, promise falsely, break one's word, disappoint*, A. AE., πρός, περί, i. 3. 5, 10 ; 9. 7 : ii. 6. 22, 28 : v. 6. 35. Der. PSEUD-ONYM.

†**ψηφίζω**, ίσω ιῶ, ἐψήφικα, *to reckon:* — *M. to vote* (by casting a pebble into the urn, raising the hand, &c.), and thus *to resolve, decide, determine, decree*, A., I. (A.), εἰ, i. 4. 15 : iii. 2. 31, 33 : v. 1. 4 : vii. 6. 14 ; 7. 18.

ψῆφος, ου, ἡ, (ψάω *to rub*) a worn stone, *pebble*, often used as a counter or ballot ; hence, *a ballot, vote, sentence, decree*, v. 8. 21 : vii. 7. 57.

ψιλός, ή, όν, (akin to ψάω *to rub*, as if rubbed bare) *bare*, not covered by armor, vegetation, &c. ; hence, *unprotected* or little protected by armor (as the head *without a helmet*, but merely covered with the tiara), *light-armed ; without* or *bare of vegetation ;* i. 5. 5 ; 8. 6 : iii. 3. 7. Der. E-PSILON.

‡**ψιλόω**, ώσω, *to make bare, strip, clear, separate from*, A. G., i. 10. 13 : iv. 3. 27.

†**ψοφέω**, ήσω, ἐψόφηκα, *to resound, ring*, iv. 3. 29.

ψόφος, ου, ὁ, *a noise, sound*, iv. 2. 4.

ψυχή, ῆς, (ψύχω *to breathe*) anima, spiritus, *the breath, life, soul, spirit, heart*, iii. 1. 23, 42 ; 2. 20 : vii. 7. 43. Der. PSYCHO-LOGY.

ψῦχος, εος, τό, (ψύχω *to blow* and thus *cool*) *the cold ;* pl. frigora, *frosts, cold ;* iii. 1. 23 : iv. 5. 12 : vii. 4. 3.

Ω.

ὦ O, the familiar interjection of address, used far more in Greek than in Eng., and hence often untranslated, i. 4. 16 ; 6. 7. — ὦ subj. of εἰμί, i. 3. 6. ᾧ dat. sing. of ὅς, i. 3. 12.

ὧδε adv., (ὅ-δε q. v.) *thus, so, as follows, in this* or *the following manner*, usu. referring to what follows, i. 1. 6 ; 5. 10 ; 6. 5 : ii. 5. 15: see πώς.

ᾠδή, ῆς, (ᾄδω) *a song, chant*, iv. 3. 27. Der. ODE, MEL-ODY, PROS-ODY.

ᾤετο, ᾠήθην, see οἴομαι, i. 4. 5.

ὠθέω,* ὤσω, ἔωκα 1., *to push, shove, thrust*, trans. — *M. to push* or *thrust another*, in order to take his place, A. ἐξ· *to force one's way, push*, intrans.; iii. 4. 48 : v. 2. 18 (*v. l.* εἰσωθέω).

‡**ὠθισμός**, οῦ, ὁ, (ὠθίζω = ὠθέω) *a pushing, crowding, pressing*, v. 2. 17.

ᾠκοδομήμην, see οἰκο-δομέω, iii. 4. 7.

ᾤκουν, ᾠκούμην, see οἰκέω, iii. 4. 7.

ᾤκτειρον, see οἰκτείρω, i. 4. 7.

ὦμεν, see εἰμί *to be*, iv. 8. 11.

†**ὠμο-βόειος**, α, ον, or ὠμο-βόϊνος, η, ον, (βοῦς) *of raw* or *untanned ox-hides: δέρματα ὠ.* raw *ox-hides:* iv. 7. 22, 26.

ὠμός, ή, όν, *raw*, as uncooked or untanned ; hence, unsoftened in character, *unfeeling, harsh, cruel ;* ii. 6. 12 : iv. 8. 14.

ὦμος, ου, ὁ, humerus, *the shoulder* with the upper arm, vi. 5. 25.

ὤμοσα, see ὄμνυμι *to swear*, ii. 2. 8 s.

ὤν, see εἰμί, i. 1. 8. — ὤν, see ὅς, i. 1. 8.

ὠνέομαι,* ἤσομαι, ἐώνημαι, (ὦνος price) 2 a. ἐπριάμην (akin to πιπράσκω), *to buy, purchase:* ὠνούμενος *buying, by purchase:* A. D., G. of price, ἐξ, ὑπό : i. 5. 6 : ii. 3. 26 s : iii. 1. 20 : v. 3. 7.

ὤνησα, see ὀνίνημι, vi. 1. 32.

ὤνιος, α, ον, (ὦνος *price*) *to be bought, for sale :* τὰ ὤνια *the articles for sale, goods, wares, vendibles*, i. 2. 18.

ᾠόμην or **ᾤμην**, see οἴομαι, iv. 2. 4.

*****Ὦπις**, ιδος, ἡ, *Opis*, a large city of Assyria, on the Physcus, not far from the Tigris, ii. 4. 25. ‖ Near Eski-Bagdad (i. e. *Old Bagdad*) or, acc. to some, Kaim.

ὥρα, ας, hōra, *season, proper* or *fitting time, time* (of year, day, &c.),

ὡραῖος 151 ὥσπερ

HOUR, D. I. (w. ἐστί often om.): ἡνίκα or ὁπηνίκα τῆς ὥρας at what or whatever point of [the] time: i. 3. 11 s; 4. 10: ii. 3. 13: iii. 4. 34, 40; 5. 18: iv. 8. 21. Der. HORO-SCOPE.

✝ὡραῖος, a, ον, at the proper season (of life, the year, &c.), in the prime or bloom of youth, ripe, ii. 6.28 : v.3.12: τὰ ὡραῖα the produce of the season, ripe fruits, v. 3. 9.

ὥρμημαι, -ησα, -ώμην, see ὁρμάω.

ὡς * proclitic, (ὅς) ut, quam, quod, &c., as, how, that, so that, &c.: — 1. REL. ADV. (a) expressing MANNER, and hence circumstance, degree, occasion, time, cause, &c., AS, like as, as if, as it were, as much as, as far as, when, as soon as, since, inasmuch as, i. 1. 4; 4. 5, 7 : vv. 7. 8, 12 : in some of these uses, regarded by some as a temporal or causal conj. Ὡς, like our as, is used in many elliptical forms of expression, 711, i. 2. 4; 5.8; often performing the office of — (b) an APPROXIMATE ADV., w. expressions of quantity, esp. numerals, as it were, about, 711 b, i. 2. 3 s: vi. 5. 11 : — (c) an ADV. OF DEGREE, w. the superl., as .. as (the comparison being made with possibility, if not otherwise stated, and ὡς thus becoming intensive, cf. quam), 553 b, c, d ; e. g. ὡς τάχιστα ἕως ὑπέφαινεν as soon as the dawn began to appear, iv. 3. 9 (cf. i. 3. 15); ὡς ἐδύνατο τάχιστα as rapidly as he could, iii. 4. 48 ; ὡς τάχιστα as quickly or soon as possible, i. 3. 14 ; ὡς ἂν δύνηται πλείστους as many as he could, i. 6. 3; ὡς πλεῖστοι as many as possible, iii. 2. 28 : — (d) a PREP. = πρός, to, w. acc. of person, 711 c, ὡς βασιλέα i. 2. 4: cf. vii. 7. 55?

— or (e) a MODAL SIGN, as, as if, as though, for, considering (but not always translated), bef. a modifier, 65 d; as bef. an appositive or adj., i. 1. 2; 6. 3; bef. a prepositional phrase, i. 2. 1; 8. 1, 23 : v. 4. 2 : ὡς ἐν τοῖς ὄρεσιν [considering it was among the mountains] as or for mountaineers, iv.3.31. This modal use of ὡς is esp. frequent before the PARTICIPLE (even if abs.), to express appearance, pretence, opinion, purpose (w. pt. fut.), cause, &c.; and here is also translated apparently, on pretence of or that, on the ground that, in view of, for the purpose of, with

the design of, since, inasmuch as, that, &c.; while the pt. is often translated by an inf. or finite verb ; e. g. ὡς ἀποκτενῶν [as about to put] with the intent to put him to death, 598 b, i. 1. 3 ; ὡς ἐπιβουλεύοντος T. on the ground that T. was plotting, ὡς βουλόμενος [as if wishing] on pretence that he wished, ὡς ποιλεμήσων pretending that he was about to make war, i. 1. 6, 11 ; ὡς ἀπηλλαγμένοι inasmuch as they were delivered, iv. 3. 2 (cf. i. 2. 19); ὡς ὀλίγοι ὄντες [as they were few] being so few, vi. 5. 28 ; ὡς ἐμοῦ ἰόντος that I shall go, i. 3. 6 (cf. ii. 1. 21); see 68o. — (f) Hence, also, the use of ὡς bef. the INFINITIVE, with an office like that of a final or consecutive conjunction bef. a finite verb, in order to or that, so that, so as to (yet sometimes not translated), 671 ; e. g. ὡς συναντῆσαι in order to meet or that he might meet, so as to meet, to meet, i. 8. 15, cf. 10 ; ὡς μὴ δύνασθαι so that they could not, ii. 3. 10 ; βραχύτερα ἢ ὡς ἐξικνεῖσθαι [shorter than so as to reach] too short a distance to reach, 513 d, iii. 3. 7 ; ὡς ἀναπαύεσθαι for or as if for resting, ii. 2. 4 ; see συναιρέω. — (g) This rel. adv. is also used as COMPLEM. (563), how, in what manner or degree, i. 6. 5 : ii. 1. 1; 3. 11 : iii. 1. 40 : vi. 6. 32.

II. CONJ. (h) Complem., that, less positive, direct, or actual than ὅτι, 702 a, i. 1. 3 ; 3. 5 : vii. 5. 8 (bef. inf.? 659 e): — (i) Final, in order that, so that, that, i. 3. 14; 6. 9 : ii. 5. 16 ; ὡς μή that not, lest, iii. 1. 47 : vii. 6. 23 : cf. f : — (j) Causal, as, since, inasmuch as, ii. 4. 17 : v. 8. 10 : cf. a : — (k) Consecutive, so that, ὡς ἐδόκει, vi. 1. 5 (v. l. inf.); cf. f.

ὥς definitive adv., (ὁ) = οὕτως, thus, so, in this way or case, in these circumstances, then; used after οὐδέ not even, i. 8. 21: iii. 2. 23 : vi. 4. 22.

✝ὡσ-αύτως (ὁ αὐτός the same) in the same or like manner, like-wise, just so, iii. 2. 23 : iv. 7. 13 : v. 6. 9 (also, by tmesis, ὡς δ' αὕτως): vii. 3. 22.

ὡσ-εί as if, about, iii. 4. 3 : v. l. ὅσον.

ὥσθ' for ὥστε, by apostr. bef. an aspirated vowel, ii. 3. 25.

ὥσι(ν), see εἰμί. — ὡσί(ν), see οὖς.

ὥσ-περ * rel. adv., (ὡς strengthened, in its more direct rel. uses) just as, even as, as indeed, as, much used in

ὥστε   152   ὤψ

comparisons; *just as if, as if, as though*, esp. w. a pt. (sometimes abs.; ὥσπερ ἐξὸν *as if it were permitted*, iii. 1. 14); *as it were, like, apparently*; i. 3. 9, 16; 5. 1, 3, 8; 8. 8, 29: iv. 3. 11. ὥσ-τε * conj. & rel. adv., (ὥς τε *and so*), by apostr. ὥστ' or ὥσθ', (a) w. the IND. (r. OPT.), *so that, that, and so, consequently*, usu. of an actual consequence, i. 1. 8: ii. 4. 5 s; 5. 15: iii. 4. 37:— (b) w. the INF. (often translated by the ind. or potential), *so as to, so that, that, as,* of a consequence that, from the nature of the leading action, would, should, or might follow, whether actually following or not, 671, i. 1. 5; 4. 8 (ὥστε ἑλεῖν *so as to take, so that I can take,* or *for taking*); 5. 13: ii. 2. 17. (c) Ὥστε is sometimes used w. the inf. where it seems not to be required, and is not always translated; as ἐποίησα ὥστε δόξαι *I made* [so that it should seem] *it seem best,* i. 6. 6, cf. 2, & 7. 4; ὥστε μὴ ὀλισθάνειν σχήσει *will keep* [so that you should not slip] *you from slipping,* iii. 5. 11. (d) As used w. the inf. in expressing anticipated result, it sometimes marks a purpose or condition; πονεῖν ὥστε πολεμεῖν *to toil* [so as to be] *for the sake of being in war,* ii. 6. 6; ὥστε ἐκπλεῖν [so that they should or would sail out] *to secure* or *on condition of their departure,* v. 6. 26. (e) Ὥστε ἔχειν καλῶς [so as to have itself well] *favorably, satisfactorily,* v. 8. 26: εὔπορα ὥστε ἀποχωρεῖν *easy for retreat*, vi. 5. 18. ὦτα, ὦσί, see οὖς *ear*, iii. 1. 31. ᾧτε (also written ᾧ τε, dat. sing. neut. of the relative ὅσ-τε *who, which*) in the phrase ἐφ' ᾧτε (= ἐπὶ τούτῳ ὥστε, 557 a) *on this condition* or *for this purpose that, in order to,* and hence taking an inf., 671 a, vi. 6. 22: see ἐπί b.
ὠτειλή, ῆς, (οὐτάω *to wound;* ὠ- Dor. for οὐ-, see λοχαγός) *a wound, mark* from a wound, *scar*, i. 9. 6. ᾧ-τινι, see ὅσ-τις, ii. 5. 32. ὠτίς, ίδος, ἡ, (οὖς *ear*) a kind of *bustard* with long ear-feathers, prob. the *Great Bustard*, Otis Tarda, Fr. *outarde*, a large bird, far better in running than flying, and still hunted for its meat, i. 5. 2 s. ὤφελε *O that!* see ὀφείλω, ii. 1. 4. ὠφελέω, ήσω, ὠφέληκα, (ὄφελος) *to benefit, be of service* or *advantage to, aid, assist, help,* A. AE., ἀντί, i. 1. 9; 3. 4, 6: v. I. 12; 6. 30: vii. 6. 11. ↓ὠφέλιμος, ον, r. ος, η, ον, *advantageous, useful, serviceable, expedient,* i. 6. 2: iv. 1. 23. ὤφθην a. p., see ὁράω *to see*, vi. 5. 10. ὦφλον, see ὀφλισκάνω, v. 8. 1. ᾠχόμην, see οἴχομαι, ii. 6. 3. [ὤψ, ὠπός, ὁ or ἡ, (ὀπ-, see ὁράω) *the face, countenance.* Hence perhaps ἄνθρωπος, as one who has ἀνδρὸς ὦπα, *the outward form of a man,* though he may not be a true ἀνήρ.]

POSTSCRIPT. **Καΰστρου** (i. 2. 11) may be the name of a small stream (-ος, ου, ὁ, *the Caÿster,* now perhaps the Akkars-Su), on or near which was **Καΰστρου Πεδίον,** i. e. *Caÿster-field.* — **Κεραμῶν** (i. 2. 10) may be the name of a people (-οι, ων, οἱ, *the Cerami* or *-ians*), unless with some we read by conjecture **Κεράμων Ἀγοράν** (κέραμος, ου, ὁ, *clay, a tile*), *Tile-market:* cf. New-market. — For ἀνέῳγον, look under ἀνοίγω; and for δύω, in the place belonging to δύνω and δύομαι. — To the words cited from various readings may be added ἐπι-ζεύγνυμι = ζεύγνυμι, i. 2. 5 : μειζόνως (fr. μείζων) *with greater fame,* vi. 1. 20 : ναύσταθμος, ου, ὁ, or -ον, ου, *a naval station,* or here = ναῦλον, v. 1. 12 : σταφίς, ίδος, ἡ, or σταφίδιον, ου, = ἀ-σταφίς, iv. 4. 9.

THE END.

NOTES.

PREFACE.

THE present volume is issued under somewhat peculiar circumstances. The distinguished and lamented scholar, whose name appears on the title-page, had, for several years past, been purposing to publish an edition of the Anabasis, with Notes, Lexicon, and whatever else might be desired to illustrate a favorite classic. He was spared long enough to complete the Lexicon to the Anabasis, and to bring his Greek Grammar and other works to the highest point of the advanced scholarship of the present day; but he was removed from the scene of all earthly labors ere he could complete his plans and purposes in respect to the edition of the Anabasis, which was announced last year as nearly ready for the press.

On Professor Crosby's death, in the spring of the present year, the undersigned was asked by Mrs. Crosby to undertake the putting into shape for the printers, and seeing through the press, the work as left by the deceased. All the manuscripts and material for the purpose were placed in the undersigned's hands; and although the task has been a delicate as well as difficult one, he has endeavored to discharge the duty of an Editor, under these circumstances, with a conscientious regard to what is due to the reputation of one of the foremost of American scholars as well as to a warm-hearted and most estimable friend.

It was found on examination that the notes on the first four books were in a tolerable state of completeness, although not yet quite fitted for publication. The fifth and sixth books had also been annotated to a considerable extent.* In a number of instances Professor Crosby seems not to have determined finally upon critical points, whether as to readings or interpretation, but to have held in reserve various matters for a last revision of his manuscript, before sending it to the printers. It became consequently the duty of the undersigned to exercise his best judgment, and to use whatever discretion he possesses, in dealing with all matters of the kind. He has scrupulously refrained from altering or attempting to improve upon Professor Crosby's notes and criticisms; only here and there, as need required, a palpable oversight or mistake has been corrected; and he has felt more and more deeply, the more he has looked into the work of the departed, how profoundly to be regretted by all lovers of ancient lore is the loss of one who was so thorough and accomplished a student and so enthusiastic an admirer of Xenophon's writings.

In getting the volume ready for the press, the additions made have been simply in accordance with what is known

---

* It seems proper to state here, in regard to the edition containing notes on all the books of the Anabasis, that the undersigned is to be held responsible for those on the last three books. He has added to the matter contained in Professor Crosby's manuscript on the fifth and sixth books, and has supplied the accompanying notes on the seventh book. He trusts that what he has done will be found to be in harmony with, and similar in character to, Professor Crosby's own work in the notes on the first four books.

PREFACE. v

to have been Professor Crosby's wish, namely, to make it as useful as possible in every respect, and such material as he had prepared for this part of his work has been here introduced. These additions are, a Map (taken from Macmichael's Anabasis); an enlarged Introduction; a Record of the Marches, etc., during the Anabasis and Katabasis of the Greeks; together with headings to the books and chapters, and some valuable geographical matter in the Appendix. It would hardly be worth while to make this statement here, were it not that evident propriety demands that Professor Crosby be not held responsible for matter which has been supplied by another hand.

In concluding this Preface, the undersigned may be allowed to express the conviction, arising from an examination of the notes and papers of Professor Crosby, that the present work will be found to be a real and positive addition to the several excellent editions of the Anabasis already in print. The notes are full (especially on the first four books), as the author held that they ought to be, in a work such as the Anabasis is; they are, too, thoroughly analytical, and continually refer to the grammar for exact and complete information on philological points; they are also very instructive, particularly in the occasional paragraphs of enlarged comment and criticism, such as young students need and appreciate, as well towards rendering the author's meaning more clear as towards impressing the valuable lessons taught by this, and in fact all history, ancient and modern.

It deserves further to be stated, that the Lexicon to the Anabasis by Professor Crosby is by far the most full and complete of any in the English language, and evidences the patient care, thorough scholarship, and superior judgment and skill of the lamented author. The Lexicon for the first four books was prepared by the author, and is the same in all respects with the full Lexicon, except in the omission of words and names which occur only in the last three books. The Table of Citations from the Anabasis, contained in Crosby's Greek Grammar, was prepared expressly for this edition, and will be found to be of great service to the student who possesses and uses that admirable work.

J. A. SPENCER,
College of the City of New York.

November 25th, 1874.

INTRODUCTION.

XENOPHON was the son of Gryllus, an Athenian of the tribe Ægeis, the demus or subdivision Erchea, and the order of Knights. The date of his birth is unsettled. Some place it as early as B. C. 444. The probabilities are, however, that he was born some fourteen or fifteen years later, i. e., about B. C. 430. He lived to a very advanced age, being, it is said, ninety years old when he died.

He was remarkable for the singular attractiveness of his personal appearance; and one day in early life, as he was meeting Socrates in a narrow lane of the city, the philosopher, who had a keen eye for natural as well as intellectual and moral beauty, was so much struck with his fine form and expressive features, that he put out his staff across the pass and stopped him for conversation. He began, after his peculiar method, by asking the youth where he would purchase the various articles required for the sustenance of the body. The questions were answered with intelligence and promptness. "And where," continued the sage, turning the conversation, as he was wont to do, from the natural to the moral, — "where do men become honorable and virtuous? (Ποῦ δὲ καλοὶ κἀγαθοὶ γίγνονται ἄνθρωποι;)" The youth hesitated. It was a new question to him. "Follow me, then," said the philosopher, "and learn ("Επου τοίνυν καὶ μάνθανε)." From that hour, Xenophon became the companion, disciple, and bosom friend of Socrates.

An anecdote is related by Strabo and Diogenes Laërtius which I would fain believe to be essentially true, although I am one of those who cannot admit that Xenophon was born early enough for the occurrence of the incident where they place it, at the battle of Delium (B. C. 424). No one, it seems to me, can read carefully the history of the Expedition of Cyrus, without the conviction that the author was at that time in the bloom of early manhood. The anecdote is this. The youthful Xenophon fought in the battle on horseback. His teacher, poorer in worldly goods, served among the footmen, where he showed himself no less a hero than a philosopher. The Athenians are defeated; and, as they are flying, Socrates sees his young friend, thrown from his horse, and lying disabled upon the ground. He snatches him up, and, heroically protecting him from all pursuers, bears him upon his shoulders from the battle-field.*

From the society of Socrates, and the refined leisure of Athens, Xenophon was called away by a letter from an intimate friend (ξένος ἀρχαῖος), Proxenus the Bœotian, who had attached himself to the fortunes of the younger Cyrus. He urged Xenophon to come and join him, assuring him that he would make him a friend of Cyrus, whose friendship he regarded as worth more to himself than anything he could obtain in his native land. Xenophon, having read the letter, conferred with Socrates respecting its contents. The prudent philosopher, apprehensive that he would incur the displeasure of his fellow-citizens by joining a prince who had so zealously assisted the Spartans against them, and yet, as it would seem, not wishing to oppose directly the adventurous ardor of his young friend, advised him to consult the oracle at Delphi in regard to the measure. Xenophon went to the prophetic shrine, but simply asked to which of the gods he should sacrifice and pray, in order that he might accomplish most honorably and successfully the enterprise which he was proposing, and return safe with the acquisition of glory. He

---

* Plutarch (*Alcibiades* 7) tells the story of Socrates having saved the life of Alcibiades at Potidæa. He also relates that Alcibiades on his part protected Socrates in the retreat after the defeat at Delium. If Plutarch is to be relied on, the strongest argument in favor of B. C. 444 for Xenophon's birth is taken away. Curtius, *Hist. of Greece*, v. 156, adopts B. C. 431 as the date of Xenophon's birth.

received an answer to his inquiry, being directed to sacrifice especially to "Zeus the King." On returning to Socrates, he was blamed by his teacher for deciding himself the great question whether he should go or remain at home, and merely referring a minor point to the wisdom of Apollo. "But since," said he, "you so inquired, you must follow the directions of the god." Having sacrificed accordingly, he set sail, and found Proxenus and Cyrus at Sardis, on the point of setting forth upon their fatal expedition. Cyrus himself united with Proxenus in urging him to accompany them, informing him that the expedition was against the Pisidians, and assuring him that, as soon as it was over, he would send him home. Xenophon was persuaded, and joined the army rather as the friend of Proxenus than as holding any definite military rank.

Of the Expedition itself and the Retreat of the Ten Thousand it is not necessary here to speak. The Anabasis will probably always retain the high estimate which both the ancients and succeeding generations have placed upon it as a memorial of Xenophon's skill and ability as a soldier and a writer. His subsequent history may be briefly told. After handing over the army to the Spartan general Thibron, B. C. 399 (*Anab.* vii. 6. 1; 8. 24), it is supposed by some that he returned to Athens for a short period; by others it is stated, with more probability, that, as he was about to return home, a decree of banishment was passed against him at Athens because of his having joined Cyrus and fought against Artaxerxes, who was at that date considered to be a friend of Xenophon's native city. However this may be, as to his visiting Athens at this time, he seems not long after to have entered the army again, and to have served under Dercyllidas (B. C. 398), and then under Agesilaus, whom he greatly admired (B. C. 396). Two years later he returned with Agesilaus from Asia, and was present (though probably not a combatant) at the battle of Coronea. Xenophon next settled himself at Scillus, in Elis, near Olympia (B. C. 393 or 392), and for some twenty years or more occupied himself in literary and congenial pursuits. He was compelled to leave his pleasant home at Scillus after the battle of Leuctra (B. C. 371), and took up his residence in Corinth. The decree of banishment against him was, about the year B. C. 369, repealed, and it is supposed by Grote and others that he returned to Athens, and spent some of the remaining years of his life in the home of his youth. This is certainly not improbable; at the same time it is every way likely that Diogenes Laërtius is correct in his statement that Xenophon died at Corinth.

Beside the Anabasis, which, according to the view here maintained, was written out and published during his residence at Scillus, Xenophon wrote numerous other works. Among these may be mentioned, (1) "The Memorabilia of Socrates," in four books, a defence of his revered master and friend against the wicked charges under which he was compelled to drink the cup of hemlock; (2) "The Cyropædia," in eight books, which professes to give an account of the education and training of Cyrus the Elder, but is in reality little more than a political and moral romance; (3) "The Hellenica," or "Historia Græca," in seven books, covering a space of forty-eight years, from the time when the history of Thucydides ends to the battle of Mantinea, B. C. 362. It is not, however, regarded by critics as a work of much merit. Passing by, for the present, his minor works, a word or two deserves to be said as to Xenophon's style as a writer. It has uniformly been praised by critics, ancient and modern. Diogenes Laërtius, in speaking of him, says, ἐκαλεῖτο δὲ καὶ 'Αττικὴ Μοῦσα, γλυκύτητι τῆς ἑρμηνείας, and more recent judges have been equally lavish in commendation. So that, without claiming for him the lofty genius of Plato, or the keen, critical insight of Thucydides, it may safely be affirmed that, among the writings of antiquity which have come down to us, there are none which are more valuable, all things considered, than those of Xenophon.*

The PERSIANS were raised to the dominion of Western Asia, by the military and political talents of the great CYRUS (B. C. 559),

* See under Ξενοφῶν, Lexicon at the end of the volume.

seconded by their native valor and hereditary discipline. Crœsus, the rich and powerful monarch of Lydia, was defeated and taken prisoner, according to the chronology of Clinton, 546 years before Christ; Babylon, the magnificent capital of the luxurious Labynetus, in sacred history Belshazzar, was taken, notwithstanding its impregnable walls, by a diversion of the Euphrates, B. C. 538; and in the year 536 Cyrus succeeded his uncle Cyaxares, in sacred history Darius the Mede, upon the throne of the Medo-Persian empire, the sovereignty thus passing from the more refined Medes to the more energetic Persians.

Cyrus, who was slain in Scythia, was succeeded, B. C. 529, by his son CAMBYSES, who added Egypt and Libya to his before vast empire. After his death by an accident, B. C. 522, the Magian usurper who claimed to be SMERDIS, the younger son of Cyrus, reigned for seven months. He was detected in his imposture, and was slain by a conspiracy of seven Persian noblemen, one of whom, DARIUS, the son of Hystaspes, was raised to the throne, according to an agreement among themselves, by the first neighing of his horse, B. C. 521. This able monarch, notwithstanding his want of success against the Greeks and the Scythians, both greatly extended and strengthened the empire during his long reign, and left it at the acme of its power and prosperity to his son XERXES, who was probably the Ahasuerus of the Book of Esther, B. C. 485.

The accession of Xerxes to the throne formed a precedent in regard to the law of descent, which served as a pretext for the ambitious claims and enterprise of the younger Cyrus. Two sons of Darius had preferred claims to their father to be appointed his successor: Artabazanes, his oldest son, born while the father was yet in a private station; and Xerxes, the firstborn after his accession to the throne, and the son of Atossa, the daughter of Cyrus. Through the entire influence which this princess exercised over her husband, Xerxes was appointed successor, upon the pretext, that, although Artabazanes was the first-born of Darius *the man*, yet Xerxes was the first-born of

Darius *the king*, and that sovereignty could not be transmitted by birth before it was possessed.

The disastrous expedition of Xerxes against Greece was the chief event in the reign of this effeminate monarch. He was assassinated, B. C. 465, by Artabanus, the commander of the royal guard, who for his own ambitious purposes raised to the throne a younger son of the murdered king, ARTAXERXES, surnamed Longimanus (Gr. Μακρόχειρ), from the unusual length of one or both arms. This prince secured himself upon the throne by putting Artabanus to death, and during his long reign displayed many good qualities, but was not able to prevent the incipient decline of the empire. Upon his death, B. C. 425, he left the sceptre to his only legitimate son, XERXES the Second, who was murdered, after reigning forty-five days, by his bastard brother SOGDIANUS.

He, in turn, after a reign of six months, was slain by OCHUS, another illegitimate son of Artaxerxes, who ascended the throne, B. C. 424, under the name of DARIUS, to which historians add, for distinction, the surname Nothus (νόθος, *bastard*). Darius the Second married his half-sister, the artful, ambitious, and cruel Parysatis, by whom he had two sons conspicuous in history, ARTAXERXES, the eldest, who succeeded him, and CYRUS, the second, but the first-born after the accession of his father to the throne. Plutarch mentions two other sons, Ostanes and Oxathres. Artaxerxes was a prince of mild and amiable disposition, but of no great strength either of intellect or of character. He was chiefly remarkable for his great memory, on account of which he has been surnamed, by historians, Mnemon (μνήμων, *having a good memory*). His mother's favorite was the active, spirited, ambitious Cyrus, who, with her encouragement, early conceived hopes that, as the first-born of Darius *the king*, he might, after the example of Xerxes, succeed his father upon the throne.

At the early age of sixteen, B. C. 407, Cyrus was appointed, through his mother's influence, to the command, both civil and

LIFE OF CYRUS.   xiii

military, of the richest and most important provinces of Asia Minor (cf. i. 1. 2, Note), and intrusted with the charge of co-operating with the Lacedæmonians against the Athenians. In this co-operation, he deserted the astute and prudent policy of his predecessors in command, who had aimed to hold the balance of power, and so to assist either party as to sustain the protracted strife which was weakening both. His object was not so much to protect the interests of Persia as to bring the Lacedæmonians, whose assistance would be the most valuable to him, under the greatest possible obligation to aid him in his ambitious designs. He assured Lysander and the Spartan ambassadors, that he would leave nothing undone in their behalf; that he had brought with him five hundred talents for their aid; that if this sum should prove insufficient, he would add his own private revenue; and that, if that should fail, he would cut up the very throne upon which he was sitting, and which was of massive gold and silver.

At the same time he assumed the state which belonged to the heir of the throne; and even put to death two of his cousins, sons of his father's sister, because upon meeting him they did not observe a point of etiquette in regard to the covering of the hand with the sleeve, which was enforced only in the presence of the king. Upon the complaint of their parents, Darius recalled him, after two years' absence, the rather that the state of his own health warned him that he must make preparation for leaving his kingdom to a successor. Before his departure, Cyrus sent for Lysander, the Spartan admiral, gave him all the money which he had above the sum required for his journey, and placed at his disposal all the revenue of the province which belonged to himself personally; charging him to remember how deep a friendship he had borne, both to the Spartan state and to Lysander individually.

During his residence in Asia Minor, Cyrus held his court chiefly at Sardis; and an anecdote is related by Xenophon in his Œconomicus (iv. 20), upon the authority of Lysander, which gives so pleasing a view of his habits of life while there, and such a relief in the midst of scenes of blood and projects of criminal ambition, that I cannot withhold it. Cyrus was showing Lysander his park; and the Spartan, admiring the beauty of the trees, the symmetry of the plan, the exactness of the lines and angles, and the rich combinations of odors which met the delighted sense, said to his host, "Much as I admire these beauties, I admire yet more the artist that devised and arranged them for you." "But," replied Cyrus, gratified with the compliment unintentionally paid him, "I have been my own gardener; the plan is all mine; and I can show you some of the trees which I planted with my own hands." Lysander gazed upon the beauty of his perfumed robes, upon the magnificence of his jewelled wreaths and bracelets, and upon his other princely ornaments, and exclaimed with astonishment, "What do you say, Cyrus? Did you really plant any of these trees with your own hands?" "Does this excite your surprise, Lysander?" replied the prince; "I protest to you, by Mithras, that, when in health, I never dine till I have drawn forth the sweat by some military or gymnastic exercise, or by some work of husbandry." The Spartan grasped his hand, and warmly congratulated him upon the possession of habits so favorable to virtue and true happiness.

Cyrus returned to be present at his father's death, B. C. 405, and to witness the sceptre, which had glittered before his young imaginings, transferred to the hand of his elder brother. The last words of Darius deserve to be remembered. Artaxerxes, having received the sceptre, approached the bedside of his dying father, that he might obtain from his quivering lips the great secret upon which the stability of the throne depended. "By what observance," was his question, "have you maintained through life your power and prosperity? Tell me, that I may follow your example." "By observing the dictates of justice and religion," was the reply of the expiring monarch, whose reign had not been greatly inconsistent with these words, except as he had been misled by his unprincipled queen and by intriguing favorites.

Cyrus was simply appointed satrap of Lydia and of the adjacent provinces which he had before governed. Disappointed that his mother's influence, and his own superiority to his brother in every kingly attribute, had not won for him the crown, it was with no cordial feelings that he accompanied his brother to Pasàrgadæ, the royal city and the burial-place of the great Cyrus, for the coronation. Among the peculiar ceremonies of the coronation, Plutarch, in his life of Artaxerxes, mentions the new monarch's putting off his own robe and putting on that of the great Cyrus, and his partaking of figs, turpentine, and sour milk, — rites designed perhaps to teach him that he must put on the virtues of the founder of the empire, and that sovereignty blends with the sweet, the bitter, and the sour.

These ceremonies were on the point of commencing, when Tissaphernes, the wily and unscrupulous satrap of Caria, whose ambitious plans Cyrus stood in the way of, and whom Cyrus had taken with him· upon his journey to his father, more, as it would seem, because he was unwilling to leave him behind, than because there was any real friendship between them, brought to Artaxerxes a Magian who had been a teacher of Cyrus. This man accused the young prince of designing to assassinate his brother at the moment when he was taking off his own robe and putting on that of the founder of the empire. The ambition of Cyrus, although excessive, appears to have been of too elevated and open a character to allow us to give much credit to the charge. Yet his well-known disappointment, the utterly unprincipled character of his mother, and the past history of the Persian court, gave so much color to it, that Artaxerxes apprehended him with the design of putting him to death. As the sentence was on the point of being executed, Parysatis rushed frantic to her favorite, clasped him in her arms, threw about him her long tresses, and so entwined his neck with her own, that the same blow must sever both. She then, by her prayers and tears, prevailed upon her elder son to spare his life, and to send him back to his remote government in Asia Minor.

Cyrus returned, feeling that he owed his life to his mother's tears, and not to his brother's confidence; and stimulated by a sense of danger, as well as of disappointment and disgrace, he determined to wrest, if possible, the sceptre from his brother's hands. The expedition which he undertook for this purpose, after three years of preparation, B. C. 401, and the return of the Greeks who served in his army, form the subjects of the history before us, which was written by an eye-witness and an important actor in the scenes which he describes. "This expedition, taken in all its parts," says Major Rennell, "is perhaps the most splendid of all the military events that have been recorded in ancient history; and it has been rendered no less interesting and impressive, in the description, by the happy mode of relating it."

What would have been the effect upon the subsequent history of Greece and Persia, and indirectly, though in an important degree of the civilized world, had Cyrus been successful in dethroning and killing his brother, must of course be a matter of pure conjecture. However much our natural sympathies might incline us to lean towards the high-spirited and able prince, we can hardly think that the effect of his success would have been for good; and we agree in general with the summing up of Grote, "that Hellas, as a whole, had no cause to regret the fall of Cyrus at Cunaxa. Had he dethroned his brother and become king, the Persian empire would have acquired under his hand such a degree of strength as might probably have enabled him to forestall the work afterwards performed by the Macedonian kings, and to make the Greeks in Europe as well as those in Asia his dependants. He would have employed Grecian military organization against Grecian independence, as Philip and Alexander did after him. His money would have enabled him to hire an overwhelming force of Grecian officers and soldiers, who would (to use the expression of Proxenus, as recorded by

Xenophon, *Anab.* iii. 1. 5) have thought him a better friend to them than their own country. It would have enabled him also to take advantage of dissension and venality in the interior of each Grecian city, and thus to weaken their means of defence while he strengthened his own means of attack. This was a policy which none of the Persian kings, from Darius, son of Hystapes, down to Darius Codomannus, had ability or perseverance enough to follow out: none of them knew either the true value of Grecian instruments, or how to employ them with effect. The whole conduct of Cyrus, in reference to this memorable expedition, manifests a superior intelligence, competent to use the resources which victory would have put in his hands; and an ambition likely to use them against the Greeks, in avenging the humiliations of Marathon, Salamis, and the peace of Kallias." *

* Grote's "History of Greece," Chap. LXIX. Part II.

ABBREVIATIONS USED IN THE NOTES.

Grammatical references, by numerals, are to Crosby's Greek Grammar, revised edition (1871).

abs., absolute.
acc., accus., accusative.
acc. to, according to.
act., active.
adj., adjective.
adv., adverb, adverbial.
Æsch., Æschylus.
Ainsw., Ainsworth.
Anab., Anabasis.
aor., aorist.
apost., apostrophe.
appos., apposition.
Ar., Aristophanes.
Arr., Arrian; An., Anabasis of Alexander.
art., article.
asynd., asyndeton.
attr., attraction, attracted.
aug., augment.

bef., before.
Born., Bornemann.
Breit., Breitenbach.

Cæs., Cæsar; B. C., Bellum Civile; B. G., Bellum Gallicum.
cf., confer, *compare, consult.*
cog., cognate.
comm., common, -ly.
complem., complementary.
compos., composition.
cond., conditional.
conj., conjunction.
const. præg., constructio prægnans.
contr., contracted.
corresp., corresponding.
Ctes., Ctesias.
Curt., Curtius (Quintus).
Cyr., Cyropædia.

dat., dative.
dec., declension.
dep., deponent.
der., derivative.
Dind., Dindorf.
Diod., Diodorus Siculus.
dir., direct.

e. g., exempli gratia, *for example.*
ell., ellipsis.
emph., emphatic.
esp., especially.
etc., et cætera, *and so forth.*

eth., ethical.
Eur., Euripides.
exc., except, -ion.
foll., following.
fut., future; fut. pf., future perfect.
fr., from.

gen., genitive.
gend., gender.
gov., governed.

Hdt., Herodotus.
Hel., Hellenica of Xenophon.
Hom., Homer; Il., Iliad; Od., Odyssey.
Hor., Horace.

impers., impersonal.
i. e., id est, *that is.*
impf., imperfect.
imv., imperative.
ind., indicative.
inf., infinitive.
Ion., Ionic.
ipf., imperfect.

Küh., Kühner.
Krüg., Krüger.

Lex., Lexicon to Anabasis (Crosby's).
Liv., Livy.
Lucr., Lucretius.

Matt., Matthiæ.
McMich., McMichael.
MSS., manuscripts.

N., note.
neg., negative.
nom., nominative.
numb., number.

obj., object.
obs., observe.
Œcon., Œconomicus.
om., omitted, omission.
opp., opposed.
opt., optative.
orig., originally.
Ov., Ovid.

paron., paronomasia.
part., participle.
pass., passive.
periph., periphrasis.

Pers., Persian, Persic.
pers., person, -al, -ally.
pf., perf., perfect.
pl., plur., plural.
pleon., pleonastically.
plp., plup., pluperfect.
Plut., Plutarch; Artax., Artaxerxes; Apoph., Apophthegms; Lyc., Lycurgus.
Polyb., Polybius.
Pop., Poppo.
pos., position.
poss., possessive.
pred., predicate.
pres., present.
prep., preposition.
pret., preteritive, -ly.
prob., probably.
pron., pronoun.
prop., proper, -ly.

q. v., quod vide, *which see.*

refl., reflexive.
Rehdz., Rehdantz.
rel., relative.

s., sequens, *and the following.*
Sans., Sanskrit.
sc., scilicet, *namely, understand.*
Schn., Schneider.
Soph., Sophocles.
Stob., Stobæus.
subj., subjunctive.
subj. acc., subject accusative.
sync., syncopated.

Tac., Tacitus: Ann., Annals; Hist., History.
Thuc., Thucydides.
trans., transitive, -ly.

usu., usually.

v. l., varia lectio, *various reading.*
Virg., Virgil; Æn., Æneid; Ecl., Eclogue; G., Georgics.
voc., vocative.
Voll., Vollbrecht.

w., with.
wt., without.

Xen., Xenophon.

NOTES.

Ξενοφῶντος Κύρου 'Αναβάσεως (434 c) A' (= Λόγος Πρῶτος, or Βίβλιον Πρῶτον, 91 a). *Xenophon's Expedition of Cyrus* (into the interior of Asia; see Lex. ἀναβαίνω, ἀνάβασις). The whole work takes its name from the leading event, though six books of the seven are occupied with the return (κατάβασις, see Lex.) of the Greeks who took part in the Expedition. — The division of the Anabasis into books, and the summaries prefixed to most of them (see Book II., III., etc.), are so old that they are referred to by Diogenes Laërtius, about 200 A. D.; yet they are not believed to have been the work of Xenophon himself, but of some scholar who saw the need of such a division.

BOOK I.

EXPEDITION OF CYRUS AGAINST HIS BROTHER ARTAXERXES.
— BATTLE OF CUNAXA. — DEATH OF CYRUS.

CHAPTER I.

CYRUS SECRETLY RAISES AN ARMY FOR THE EXPEDITION.

PAGE 1. — 1. Δαρείου: for the case see 412; for the position, 719 c. — γίγνονται (719 ʃ), historic present, esp. frequent in Greek, 609 a. Observe the frequent interchange, in the narrative, of past tenses and the historic present: ἀναβαίνει...ἀνέβη, § 2, etc. — παῖδες δύο, dual and plural, 494. Only two of the children are here mentioned, as no others were related to the following history. According to Ctesias (*Persica* 49), who derived his information from Parysatis herself, there were in all thirteen, of whom only five survived infancy. — πρεσβύτερος [sc. παῖς], *the older* [child], partitive apposition, 393 d. The article is omitted in the comparison of the two, 533 f, g; yet we might translate, *an older.* — ἠσθένει, pos. 719 ϛ; tense 592 s. — τελευτήν (art. om. 533 c) τοῦ βίου, *the termination of his* (530 e) *life.* — τὼ παῖδε, *the two children,* or *sons,* case 666.

2. μὲν οὖν, pos. 720 a. — παρὼν ἐτύγχανε, 573 b, 658. 1, 677. — Κῦρον, pos. 719 θ; art. om. 533 a, cf. ὁ Κῦρος below, 522 g. — μεταπέμπεται, voice 579. — ἦς, sc. ἀρχῆς, 505 a, 551 c; pos. of rel. clause 523 g. — σατράπην, predicate appos. 393 b, 480 a. For the extent of his satrapy, see i. 9, 7. — ἐποίησε, ἀπέδειξε, tense 605. 3, c. — καὶ στρατηγὸν (Lex. = κάρανον) δέ (adv. 703 c), 480 a; in continuation of a rel. clause, 561 d, 562. Observe here, as below and elsewhere, the esp. emphatic word placed between καί and δέ. So between καί and αὖ, i. 1. 7. — πάντων ὅσοι, *of all* [as many as] *who,* 550 d, f. — εἰς, inasmuch as the mustering *in* a plain implies the coming *into* it, 704 a. — Καστωλοῦ : The Plain of Castolus appears to have been the muster-ground of the imperial (as distinguished from the mere provincial) troops in the western part of Asia Minor (Xen. *Hel.* i. 4. 3). The command of these troops gave the youthful Cyrus precedence over the neighboring satraps, and that general management of affairs along the Ægean and with Greece, which had before been committed to Tissaphernes (called στρατηγὸς τῶν κάτω, in Thuc., viii. 5). Discontent with this change has been supposed to have been the motive which incited the latter, while professing friendship to Cyrus, to seek his destruction (§ 3). — ἀθροίζονται, for annual review, before inspectors appointed by the king (Xen. *Œcon.* 4. 6). — λαβών...ἔχων, tense 592. — ὡς φίλον, modal appos. 393 c. — τῶν Ἑλλήνων, *of Greeks,* art. 522 a (or *of the Greeks* in his service, 530); case 418. — ὁπλίτας : these were doubtless before in the service of Cyrus, and were now taken by him as a special guard for his person; since he had well learned the vast superiority of the Greeks to the Persians in valor, prowess, and integrity. — ἀνέβη : observe the change of tense, and the chiastic arrangement (71 a); both of which are so common in Greek. — αὐτῶν, case 407.

3. ἐτελεύτησε, in Babylon acc. to Ctesias (*Pers.* 57), *had died* (tense 605 c). — κατέστη (577 b) εἰς (704 a) τὴν (530 c) βασιλείαν, *was established in the kingdom,* or *on the throne.* — Τισσαφέρνης διαβάλλει (Lex.) τὸν (522 g) Κῦρον πρὸς τὸν (530 e) ἀδελφὸν (as 702 a) ἐπιβουλεύοι (opt., as following the historic pres., 643 a) αὐτῷ (505 a, 540 g). Tiss. maliciously accuses Cyrus to his brother [that he was plotting against him] of a design upon his life. Acc. to Plutarch (*Artax.* 3) the Persian rites of coronation were not complete till the new monarch had repaired to the ancient capital Pasargadæ, and had there learned the lesson of primitive simplicity by putting off in the temple of the goddess of war his own rich vesture and putting on the plain dress which the elder Cyrus wore before he became king, and by an humble repast of dried figs, turpentine, and sour milk. Tissaphernes here brought to Artaxerxes a priest who had been a tutor of Cyrus, and who accused the young prince of designing to hide himself in the temple and assassinate his brother during the exchange of garments. — αὐτῷ, case 455 f. — Ὁ δέ (518 a)...Κῦρον, order 718 n, 720. — ὡς ἀποκτενῶν, apparent intention, 598 b, 680 a. — ἐξαιτησαμένη

BOOK I. CHAP. I. 5

(Lex.), acc. to Plut. (*Artax.* 3), by profuse tears and passionate entreaties, enfolding him in her arms, wrapping her tresses around him, and holding his neck to her own. — αὐτόν, double relation, 399 g.

4. Ὁ, the common subject of ἀπῆλθε and βουλεύεται. — ὡς ἀπῆλθε, tense 605 c. — βουλεύεται ὅπως μήποτε (686 b) ἔσται (624 b) ἐπὶ (691) τῷ ἀδελφῷ, [considers how] *resolves that he will never in future be in the power of his brother.* — ἢν δύνηται, βασιλεύσει (631 c, 633 a). — ἀντ' (696) ἐκείνου (536 e), *in his stead.* — μήτηρ, direct appos. 393 a. — Κύρῳ, case 453. — φιλοῦσα, expressing cause, 674. — μᾶλλον ἢ (511) τὸν βασιλεύοντα (525). Cyrus had evidently much more of his mother's intellect, energy, and ambition, than the mild but weak Artaxerxes.

5. Ὅστις s, order 718 o. — ἀφικνεῖτο, mode 641 e; tense of repeated action, 592. — τῶν παρὰ βασιλέως (533 b), [of those from the king, 527] *from the king's court,* referring esp. to *the king's envoys* (οἱ ἔφοδοι, *Cyr.* viii. 6. 16), sent annually, acc. to custom, to inspect the satrapies and report upon their condition and upon the spirit and conduct of the satraps. — πάντας, number 501. — ὥστε...εἶναι, [as to be] *that they were,* 671 a, e. — αὐτῷ, case 456. — βαρβάρων, case 474 c, 432 d. — εἴησαν, mode 624 c. Both εἴησαν and εἶεν are freely used; otherwise, this long form in -ίησαν is rare, 293 a. — εὐνοϊκῶς ἔχοιεν (Lex.) 577 d. For so young a prince Cyrus certainly showed great tact and shrewdness in making his preparations.

6. ὡς...ἐπικρυπτόμενος, 553 c, 674 b. — ὅτι ἀπαρασκευαστότατον, *as unprepared as possible,* ὅτι πλείστους, 553 c. — ἐποιεῖτο (Lex.) τὴν συλλογήν, *he made* [the levy for himself] *his levy.* — ὁπόσας, *whatever,* complem. or rel. with an antecedent understood in the gen. governed by φρουράρχοις. — πόλεσι : it appears from what follows that the Ionian cities were here esp. intended. So i. 2. 1. — φρουράρχοις, case 452 a. — ὡς ἐπιβουλεύοντος Τισσαφ., 680 b. — Καὶ γάρ (Lex.), [and he would naturally so plot, for] *for indeed,* 709. 2. — Τισσαφέρνους, case 443 a. — τὸ ἀρχαῖον, adv. 483 a. — ἐκ, w. agent of pass. 586 d. ἐξ is not common in this use, but may be employed with verbs of giving, from the conception of the gift as passing *from* the giver. This gift to Tissaph. deprived Cyrus of his former ready access to the sea and communication with the Greeks. — Μιλήτου, case 406 a; cf. 8. 6. A glance at the map will show that it was far more important to this commercial city to be on good terms with the satrap of Caria than with that of Lydia; and that it was under the easy control of the former.

7. Ἐν Μιλήτῳ : with this immediate emphatic repetition of the name after πλὴν M., compare i. 8. 6. — τὰ αὐτὰ ταῦτα (489 d) βουλευομένους [sc. τινάς, or αὐτούς with general reference to the citizens, 472 b], *that some* (or *they*) *were meditating this same course* (namely, ἀποστῆναι πρὸς K., though many regard this explanation as the marginal note of a grammarian, which at length crept into the text), 658. 1, 677. — τοὺς...ἐξέβαλεν, 419 a, 518 d. — K. ὑπολαβών (674 a, d) τοὺς φεύγοντας (678), συλλέξας (605 a) στράτευμα, (*Lat.* exercitu collecto, 658 b) ἐπολιόρκει (595 a). — M. καὶ κατὰ γῆν (689 m)...κατάγειν, order 718 l, m. Observe the parti-

ciples ὑπολαβών, συλλέξας, without an intervening conjunction, a frequent construction in Greek. Cf. i. 2. 17 ; 3. 5. — For φεύγω and ἐκπίπτω used as passives to ἐκβάλλω, see 575 a. — αὕτη...πρόφασις (524 c) ἦν αὐτῷ (459) τοῦ (664 a) ἀθροίζειν (444 b), *this again was another pretext with him* (or he had as another pretext) *for assembling.*
8. πέμπων ἠξίου, as not a single act. — ὧν ἀδελφὸς (without art.), *since he was a brother of his,* 674. — αὐτοῦ δοθῆναι οἱ (586 c, 537. 2, b, 788 c) ταύτας τὰς (524 b) πόλεις (666). — αὐτῷ, case 699 a, f. — πρὸς, 696. — ἑαυτόν, 505 a ; dir. refl. 537 a. — ἐπιβουλῆς, case 432 b. — ᾐσθάνετο, ἤχθετο, mode 671 d. — Τισσαφέρνει, case 455 f. — πολεμοῦντα, *because at war,* 674.
— οὐδέν, stronger than οὐ (adv. acc. 483 a, 471). — αὐτῶν πολεμούν-
3 των (case 661 b), *he was* [as to nothing] *not at all displeased* [they being] *with their being at war.* — καὶ γάρ (Lex.), *and the rather because,* 709. 2. — δασμούς : Hdt. states (iii. 90, s) the tax which, acc. to the assignment of Darius Hystaspis, the imperial treasury drew from each province. The satrap also collected other sums for himself and for the provincial expenses. — βασιλεῖ, case 450 b. — ἐκ...ἔχων, a deferred detail, modifying γιγνομένους, 719 d. — ὧν (Attic attr. 554 a) Τ. ἐτύγχανεν ἔχων, *which T.* [happened previously having] *had previously possessed,* the ipf. rather than the plf., to express continuance, 604 a. The idea of chance is expressed far oftener in Greek than in Eng.
9. Ἄλλο, without art. 523 f. — αὐτῷ (case 460). — συνελέγετο (tense 592), *was collecting for him.* — Χερ. τῇ (523 a, 3) καταντιπέρας (526) Ἀβύδου (445 c) τόνδε τὸν (524 b) τρόπον (adv. acc. 483). — Κλέαρχος, τούτῳ. Asyndeton is less frequent in Greek than in Eng. In Xen., it occurs chiefly in connection with a demonstrative pron. or adv. — τούτῳ, αὐτόν, 536 d, e ; order 719 θ, 718 k. — ἡγάσθη (as mid. 576 b, a), conceived an admiration for, *came to admire him* (592 d), esp. for his military talents and passion, which might be made so serviceable. — καὶ δίδωσιν : the change, in a sentence, from a past tense to the hist. pres. is more frequent than the reverse (as in i. 1. 2). — συνέλεξεν...ἐπολέμει, tense 592. — ἀπό, 695. — τοῖς Θρᾳξὶ (accent 778 c) τοῖς, 523 a, 2). — ἑκοῦσαι, *voluntarily,* 509 c. — ἐλάνθανεν, 677 f. — τὸ στράτευμα, supplied after its logical place, 719 d.
10. οἴκοι, 469 b, 526. — αὐτόν, case 480 c. — εἰς δισχιλίους ξένους, as object of αἰτεῖ, 706. — μηνῶν, case 445 a). — ὡς...ἄν, 658 a. — τῶν ἀντιστασιωτῶν, case 407. The history of rude Thessaly was strongly marked by such contests of aristocratic families. — δεῖται αὐτοῦ, *requests* [of] *him,* 434 a. — αἰτεῖ αὐτὸν (480 c) εἰς δισχιλίους ξένους (706, cf. 8. 5) καὶ τριῶν μηνῶν (445 a) μισθόν : the readiest version here seems to be, *asks him for two thousand mercenaries and three months' pay for them,* making εἰς δισχιλίους ξένους an object of αἰτεῖ, and translating in like manner the next sentence. But Cyrus, who was straining every nerve to increase his Greek force, could not have been willing to send back so large a force already levied into Greece and risk them in a Thessalian civil war. If then we thus translate, we must understand, by *giving Aristippus four thousand*

BOOK I. CHAP. II.   7

troops, little more than *granting him the privilege and means of levying them*. That, indeed, he levied this number seems doubtful; for Cyrus does not appear to have received more than fifteen hundred troops from this source (i. 2. 6). Some therefore prefer to connect εἰς...ξένους with μισθόν, and to translate, *asks of him pay for two thousand mercenaries and for three months*. — μὴ πρόσθεν καταλῦσαι...πρίν, not to [previously] *make peace, before*, 703 d, ʄ. Cf. i. 2. 2. — ἄν...συμβουλεύσηται, subj. after pres. δεῖται, 641 d, 619. 2, d.

11. εἰς Πισίδας...στρατεύεσθαι, to make an expedition [into the land of the Pisidians (Lex. εἰς, χώρα)] *against the Pisidians*. — Πισίδας, upon whom Cyrus had before warred (i. 9. 14). — ὡς βουλόμ., *stating that he wished*. — ὡς πράγματα παρεχόντων Π. (680 b) τῇ ἑαυτοῦ (538 f) χώρᾳ, *on the ground that the P. were giving trouble to his own country*. Cf. negotium facessere. — τούτους, 505 b, 393 h. — πολεμήσων: observe with this verb the difference between the simple dative and the dative with σύν. — οὕτως οὗτοι, 719 e, 544, 547.

4

CHAPTER II.

MARCH OF CYRUS AND HIS ARMY FROM SARDIS TO TARSUS IN CILICIA.

1. ἐδόκει, subject 571 f. — αὐτῷ (case 454), ἄνω, position 719 d. — μέν: the corresponding clause with δέ, stating the real object of the expedition, is not expressed, though it is implied iu § 4 (Lex.). — ὡς...βουλόμενος, [as if wishing], *that he wished*, 680 c. — ἐκ, 689 a. — ὡς ἐπὶ τούτους, ellipsis of verb, 711. — τὸ βαρβαρικόν, sc. στράτευμα, *his barbarian force*, 506 c. The τό is repeated before Ἑλληνικόν, because this refers to different persons from βαρβαρικόν, 534. 4. ὡς is often used before a prep. to express view or purpose, either real or pretended. Cf. 9. 23; iv. 3. 11, 21. — ἐνταῦθα καί, *then...also*, or *thither...also* (i. e. to the place of rendezvous). The τὸ Ἑλληνικόν preceding refers to the Greek force in the dominions of Cyrus; and Kühner and many other editors express this by reading thus: καὶ τὸ Ἑλληνικὸν ἐνταῦθα στράτευμα· καὶ παραγγέλλει. — Κ. λαβόντι (*having taken* = *with*, 674 b), Α. συναλλαγέντι, constructed acc. to 667 b; while λαβόντα below, removed from Ξενίᾳ, agrees with a pronoun understood, acc. to 667 e. — ὅσον ἦν αὐτῷ στράτευμα = τοσοῦτον στράτευμα ὅσον ἦν αὐτῷ, [as large a force as he had], *whatever troops he had*, or *his whole force*, 551 c, f. — ἀποπέμψαι...στράτευμα, 551 c, 661 a. Aristippus sent, under the command of Menon, as many troops as he chose to spare, § 6: ii. 6. 28. — αὐτῷ, case 460. — ἐν ταῖς πόλεσι, position 523 a, 1. — ξενικοῦ, case 407, 699 f. — πλὴν [τοσούτων] ὁπόσοι, 551 f, 406.

2. Ἐκάλεσε...ἐκέλευσε, λαβόντα, chiasma 71 a. — φυγάδας...στρατεύεσθαι, 666 b. — ἐφ' ἃ ἐστρατεύετο, (sc. τὰ πράγματα, or ταῦτα), *the objects for which he was making war, taking the field*. — παύσασθαι (some prefer the reading παύσεσθαι, 659 g, 660 d ; but παύσασθαι is the common reading of the MSS.). — καταγάγοι, 641 b, d. — αὐτῷ, case 456. For the grounds of this confidence, see i. 9. 7, s. — παρῆσαν εἰς Σάρδεις, [were present, having come to, arrived at], *came to S.*, const. præg., 704 a.

3. τοὺς ἐκ τῶν πόλεων λαβών = τοὺς ἐν ταῖς πόλεσιν ἐκ τῶν πόλεων λαβών, const. præg. 704 a. — ὁπλίτας, position 719 d. — εἰς τετρακισχιλίους, adj. 706. — γυμνῆτας, mostly, without doubt, targeteers (see Lex.).

5 — ὡς πεντακ., 711 b. — ἦν δέ, 163 b ; zeugma, 495, 497 b. — τῶν ...στρατευομένων, *of those who were serving*, 678 ; gen. partitive as an appositive 422.

4. Οὗτοι μέν : while others joined him at Colossæ, etc., § 6, 9. Cf. 1. 9 N. as to Κλέαρχος. — αὐτῷ, case 450 a. — Τισσαφέρνης : according to a less likely account by Ephorus (Diod. xiv. 11), the informant was Pharnabazus, who had learned the design of Cyrus from Alcibiades, and, lest the latter should himself inform the king, put him to death. Cf. ii. 3. 19. — μείζονα...ἢ ὡς ἐπὶ Π., *greater than as* [it would be] *if against the P.* (a small, though warlike tribe), i. e. *too great to be aimed at the P. merely*, 513 d. — ὡς βασιλέα, 711 c. — ᾗ...τάχιστα (Lex. ὅς), 553 c. — ἱππέας ἔχων (= *with*, 674 b) ὡς πεντακοσίους, order 719 d.

5. ἔχων οὕς εἴρηκα, 551 c. — ὡρμᾶτο ἀπὸ Σ., 688 : ἀπό, rather than ἐκ, since the army was doubtless mainly encamped about the city, 689 a, b. Cf. vi. 1. 23. — ἐξελαύνει, *he* [moves forth his army] *advances* or *marches :* cf. ἐξήλαυνε τὴν στρατιάν, Hdt. vii. 38, 577 c. Some supply ἵππον or ἅρμα : see Lex. ἐλαύνω. — διά, 689 a. — ἐπί, Lex. — σταθμούς, παρασάγγας, case 482 d. — εἴκοσι καὶ δύο, 242 a. — τὸν Μαίανδρον ποταμόν, 393, 522 i. — Τούτου...πλέθρα, 395 c. Observe how common asyndeton is in the itinerary, esp. with ἐνταῦθα and ἐντεῦθεν, § 6, 7. — ἐζευγμένη πλοίοις ἑπτά, *formed by the union of seven boats*, 466 ; a pontoon-bridge. For ἐζευγμένη applied to the stream itself, see ii. 4. 13. So, in Lat. pontem jungere, and amnem jungere.

6. διαβάς, 605 a, 674 e. — Κολοσσάς. Cyrus commenced his march eastward from Sardis, by the southern route through Colossæ and Celænæ, the same which Xerxes took in his march against Greece (Hdt. vii. 26 s) eighty years before. An especial motive to this was doubtless the desire to keep up as long as possible the pretence that he was proceeding against the Pisidians. It is also probable that he had on this route, as against those troublesome neighbors, troops stationed and supplies deposited, which he may have wished to take with him or put to present use. Such supplies and his princely residence at Celænæ would also make that a convenient place for his long delay in waiting for essential reinforcements. — πόλιν s, (Lex.) 504 a. — ἔμεινεν, the aor. because a simple view is taken of the stay as a whole, 591. — ἡμέρας, 482 a. The halt of so many days was probably to await the arrival of Menon, who came, we may suppose, by the direct route from Ephesus to Colossæ. — καί (= ἐν αἷς, § 10) ἧκε (for aor., which was only late, not then in use as aor. 603, c, β). — Μένων (§ 1 N) ὁ (525)

BOOK I. CHAP. II. 9

Θ. ὅπ. ἔχων (674 b). — Δόλοπας καὶ Αἰνιᾶνας, mentioned by Hom., *Il.* ix. 484; ii. 749.

7. τῆς Φ., 522 g. — ἐνταῦθα...πλήρης, 459, 504 a; order 719 θ, λ, μ. — βασίλεια, pl. 489 a. — ἦν, sing. 569. — θηρίων, case 414 a. — ἅ, not attr., because not limiting or defining the antecedent, 554 a; cf. οὕς, 4. 9. — ἐθήρευεν...βούλοιτο, sometimes called the iterative opt. See 5. 2; 641 b. — ἀπὸ ἵππου (Lex.), his attacks being made from his position on the horse. Cf. ex equo pugnabat, Liv. i. 12. — διὰ μέσου δὲ τοῦ παραδείσου, *and through the midst of the park*, 508 a. — ἐκ τῶν βασιλείων, *within the palace* (flowing out of it), const. præg. 704 a. This situation of the palace secured a supply of water. — Κελαινῶν, 395 c, 446 N. Apposition seems the harder of the two constructions, on account of τῆς, though the other is rather poetical.

8. μεγάλου βασιλέως (Lex.), 533 b: the Persian empire was far greater in extent than any before presented in history. — οὗτος, position, 719 δ. — ἐμβάλλει, sc. ἑαυτόν (Lex.), 577 c. — εἴκοσι...ποδῶν, sc. εὖρος, [a breadth of] *twenty-five feet*, 395 c, 440. — λέγεται (573 a)...οἱ, 537. 2, b, 539 a; case 455 f. See the account of Hdt. (vii. 26), who names the stream Καταρράκτης (*clashing stream*, cf. CATARACT); and also Diod. iii. 59; Liv. xxxviii. 13. — ὅθεν (550 e) αἱ πηγαί, sc. εἰσιν, 572.

9. τῇ μάχῃ, *the* famous *battle* of Salamis, B. C. 480, at which Xerxes was present, 530 a. — ἔμεινε: Cyrus may have been detained not only by waiting for his right arm, Clearchus, and others, but also by preparations required before leaving his Phrygian capital, esp. to check the incursions of the Pisidians. — Θρᾶκας, Κρῆτας, adj. 506 f. — Σῶσις (gen. -ιος, or, later, -ιδος, 218. 1). Sosis is not again mentioned, and seems, therefore, not to have commanded as a general; and Sophænetus has been before mentioned as joining Cyrus with his one thousand hoplites at Sardis (§ 3). The most probable explanation here is perhaps this: It was essential to Cyrus to keep the landing at Ephesus secure, and the way through Colossæ open for his reinforcements, and therefore to prevent the seizure of these cities by his dangerous neighbor Tissaphernes. Hence Xenias left Sosis at Ephesus with three hundred hoplites; and Cyrus on his march left at Colossæ the old and trusted Sophænetus. But when Cyrus learned of the departure of Tissaphernes, and the arrival at Ephesus of the last force expected there, he directed Sosis to accompany Clearchus to Colossæ, and that Sophænetus should there join them. The second mention of the arrival of Sophænetus led some copyist, who did not observe the repetition, to insert καὶ χίλιοι below, so that all the numbers mentioned might be included in the total. The removal of these words makes it easier to reconcile the numbers here with those in 7. 10, and elsewhere. The troops brought by Sosis would fall naturally into the division of Xenias. — Κῦρος...ἐποίησεν, 475 a. — πελτασταί: Greek light-armed troops were sometimes in general called πελτασταί, from the predominant class. Yet the total here stated is made out without including the archers of Clearchus, or all the γυμνῆτες of Proxenus. The summary stands thus: —

Xenias,	4000 ὁπλῖται,			= 4000
Proxenus,	1500 "	500 γυμνῆτες,		= 2000
Sophænetus,	1000 "			= 1000
Socrates,	500 "			= 500
Pasion,	300 "	300 πελτασταί,		= 600
Menon,	1000 "	500 "		= 1500
Clearchus,	1000 "	800 "	200 τοξόται,	= 2000
Sosis,	300 "			300
Totals,	9600 ὁπλῖται,	2100 πελτ., etc.,	200 τοξόται,	= 11900

As the enumeration is only given in round numbers, we cannot wonder that the sums do not agree precisely with the totals in thousands, as stated in the text. For a small body of cavalry in the division of Clearchus, see 5. 13. — ἀμφὶ (692. 5) τοὺς (531 d) δισχιλίους, 706 a.

10. Πέλταs. Having accomplished the objects of his visits to Celænæ, Cyrus turns back to the common, easier, and better supplied route from Sardis to Cilicia. Along this route he had doubtless stationed portions of his barbarian force, and deposited supplies, in part perhaps under the pretext that they were designed for action or protection against his enemies, the Mysians. This would explain the necessity of his visit to the Market of the Ceramians, the nearest city on the route to the Mysian territory, and hence an important military post. On his way thither he stopped three days at Peltæ, probably to gratify the many Arcadians in his army through the celebration, on the neighboring plain, of their national festival and games in honor of Lycæan Jove. — τὰ Λύκαια ἔθυσε (Lex.), 478, 507 c. This was an especial festival of the Arcadians, celebrated annually with sacrifices and games in honor of Lycæan Zeus and Pan, whom some regard as essentially the same deity, claimed as a native of Arcadia (born or reared on Mt. Lycæus). According to Plutarch, it was related to the Roman Lupercalia, the introduction of which into Italy has been ascribed to the Arcadian Evander. — στλεγγίδες, pred. appos., 393 b ; on account of which ἦσαν is the rather plur. 569 a, 500. — καὶ Κῦρος, pos. 719 δ. The especial antipathy of the Persians to idol-worship rendered this a greater compliment. — Κεραμῶν Ἀγοράν : Bornemann and others have conjectured Κεράμων (the MSS. all accenting on the ultima), which might be translated *Tile-market*. (Cf. New-market. · See postscript to Lex.) Cyrus here reached the great eastern imperial road ; and, instead of remaining at this frontier place to make in person any arrangements that might be necessary during his absence, pushed forward with a rapidity nowhere else equalled on the march. So much of the army as could not keep up with him (perhaps all the heavy-armed troops and most of the baggage) had time for rejoining him during the five days' halt at Caÿstri Campus. The motive to this extraordinary haste was probably the hope of meeting Epyaxa and receiving the supply of money expected from Cilicia before the Greek troops should be clamorous for their quarter's pay.

11. στρατιώταις, case 454 d. — πλέον (= πλειόνων)...μηνῶν, *for more than three months*, 507 e. — ἐπὶ τὰς θύρας, *to his door* or *quarters*. —

BOOK I. CHAP. II. 11

ἐλπίδας (Lex. 479) λέγων (677) διῆγε (Lex.), 577 c, *passed the time expressing hopes*, was constantly feeding them on hope. — δῆλος ἦν ἀνιώμενος, 573 c, 677 g. — πρός (Lex.), 696. — ἔχοντα, sc. αὐτόν, 667 e, *when he had the means*.

12. Ἐνταῦθα...Κῦρον, 719 d, 393 h. — Συεννέσιος, Ion. gen. 218. 2. Why hereditary king here, see Voll., note. — Κύρῳ δοῦναι χρήματα, order 718 i. This money, we may suppose, had been promised by the politic Syennesis ; as Cyrus would have been insane to start on such an expedition with so little money, unless he had expected a supply by the way. His long detention at Celænæ appears to have prevented his meeting the queen as early and as near Cilicia as he had expected. — δ' οὖν, *and accordingly*, or, *but at any rate*, however that might be. δ' οὖν, often used as here in passing from the questionable to the unquestionable (as to fact, in distinction from mere report or supposition), cf. § 22, 25 ; 3. 5. — στρατιᾷ, Greek army. — ἡ Κίλισσα, sc. γυνή or βασίλεια, 506 b. — συγγενέσθαι : reference here to *illicit intercourse* is mere camp-scandal, we may hope. If not so, it shows to what an extreme of complaisance the Cilician king and queen were ready to go to secure the favor of Cyrus. It was the policy of the Persians, in the extension of their empire, not to dethrone native princes, if they readily submitted and faithfully performed the duties of vassals. In this class were the kings of Cilicia ; and the present king was determined not to lose his throne, whichever of the rival brothers prevailed. He therefore sent his queen to meet Cyrus, from whom the danger was the nearest, with the large sum of money which this prince needed so much, and apparently with the charge to secure his favor, no matter by what means, and to learn his plans and resources. According to Diodorus (xiv. 20), he promised to assist Cyrus in the war, and sent one son and an armed force to serve with him ; but secretly sent another son to the king with pledges of unswerving fidelity, information respecting the hostile forces, protestations that whatever he had himself done for Cyrus had been done through compulsion, and assurances that he should seize the first opportunity of deserting Cyrus and fighting on the side of the king.

13. Ἐντεῦθεν. At Caÿstri Campus several important roads met ; and Cyrus here took the great thoroughfare from the Propontis to Cilicia. Henceforth he pressed on towards Babylon, without turning aside or voluntary delay. — παρὰ τὴν ὁδόν, the acc. rather than dat. from the fountain's flowing along the way, or the movement of the army by the fountain. — κρήνη ἡ Μίδου καλουμένη, *a fountain* [that called Midas's] *which was called the fountain of Midas*, 523 i. — τὸν Σάτυρον, THE (well-known) *Satyr*, Silenus, 530 a. — οἴνῳ, case 550 a. Compare Virg. *Ecl.* vi. (Eng. idiom, *wine with it*.) Κεράννυμι implies closer union than the more general μίγνυμι.

14. δεηθῆναι (576 b)...Κύρου, case 434 a : not merely for the spectacle, we must suppose, but also to display the strength of the army ; while Cyrus was, of course, glad to send a vivid impression of this strength to the Cilician king. There is a plain near Ilghún adapted to the review of an army. — τῶν Ἑλλ...τῶν βαρβ., 534. 4.

15. ὡς νόμος αὐτοῖς [sc. ἦν, or ἐστιν, since this is far oftener omitted than ἦν, 572] εἰς μάχην [τάττεσθαι], as their custom was for battle: 572, 459. — ἕκαστον [στρατηγὸν] τοὺς ἑαυτοῦ, 506 a. — ἐπὶ (Lex.) τεττάρων, 692. 5. A line eight deep was more common; cf. vii. 1. 23. — δεξιόν, εὐώνυμον, μέσον, 506 c. In this mere parade the first place was given to the ambitious Menon; afterwards, in real service, to the older and abler Clearchus. The wings were more exposed than the centre; hence, the more reliable commanders and troops were placed upon them, and they were accounted posts of honor. So, from the place of the shield, the right was more exposed, and consequently more honorable, than the left. — ἐκείνου, for distinction from αὐτῷ above.

16. Ἐθεώρει, proceeded to survey. — κατ' ἴλας καὶ κατὰ τάξεις, by troops (of horse) and battalions (of foot); cf. turmātim et centuriātim. — παρελαύνων. In this way their firm front of glistening metal was better shown; and the small depth, which enabled them to make a greater display, was less exposed. It is possible also that a compliment to the Greeks was designed. — καὶ τὰς ἀσπίδας ἐκκεκαθαρμένας (v. l. ἐκκεκαλυμμένας, see Lex.), and their shields burnished.

17. ἐκέλευσε s, to show their manner of advancing upon a foe. — ἐπιχωρῆσαι = ἐπιέναι. — ὅλην τὴν φάλαγγα, 523 e. — ἐπεὶ ἐσάλπιγξε, 571 b. — ἐκ...προϊόντων, and upon this [they advancing] as they kept advancing more rapidly, 592. For the gen. abs. agreeing with αὐτῶν understood (675, 676 a, b; cf. 6. 1) the dat. agreeing with στρατιώταις could have been used. — ἀπὸ τοῦ αὐτομ., 507 d. — δρόμος...στρατιώταις, 459. — ἐπὶ τὰς σκηνάς, upon the camp (mostly occupied by barbarians), as if for attack and plunder. Within or close by was the camp-market.

18. βαρβάρων, case 415. — φόβος, sc. ἐγένετο or ἦν. — ἔφυγεν ἐκ τῆς ἁρμ., fled from her carriage, as this slow vehicle, drawn by mules or oxen, would not take her quickly enough out of the reach of danger. — οἱ ἐκ... ἔφυγον, const. præg. 704 a. — τὴν τάξιν τοῦ στρατεύματος, 523 c. — ἐκ τῶν s, ἐκ less common than ἀπό. Cf. vii. 2. 37, where the more frequent ἀπό is used, and ex duce metus, Tac. Ann. i. 29. — φόβον (Lex.).

19. χώραν, the object of both ἐπέτρεψε and διαρπάσαι, or of the latter only.

20. τὴν Κιλικίαν, cf. § 21, 522 g, 533 a. — ὁδόν, 482 d, or 479. — αὐτῇ, case 699 a. It suited the plans both of the queen and of Cyrus that she should carry her report to the king before the arrival of Cyrus. By sending the division of Menon as an escort, he not only provided for her safety and honor, but secured the introduction into Cilicia of a considerable force, which might act, if necessary, in his favor. The shorter mountain route taken by Menon would have been very difficult for the whole army encumbered by its baggage. Cyrus seems to have made the way from Iconium to Dana (or Tyana) longer than necessary, in order that he might himself accompany the Cilician queen to the foot of the mountain pass, and perhaps that he might also give the army a better opportunity of plundering Lycaonia. The delay at Dana allowed time for Menon to reach

BOOK I. CHAP. II. 13

the Cilician plain, and also for making the necessary preparations before attempting the Cilician pass. — στρατιώτας οὕς, agreeing with 554 c in respect to the omission of the art. — καὶ αὐτόν, and Menon *himself*, 540 f. — μετά, see 2. 4. — ἐν ᾧ, sc. χρόνῳ, in *which* (time), 506 a. — ἀπέκτεινεν, as a man is said to do that which he causes others to do. Cyrus was unhesitating in the infliction of punishment. Cf. 9. 13. — αἰτιασά- μενος ἐπιβουλεύειν, having charged [that they were plotting] *them* **9** *with plotting*, 658. 1.

21. εἰσβάλλειν εἰς, 699 c. — εἰσβόλη, the Tauri Pylæ of Cicero, *Ad Att.* v. 20. 1. See Lex. Πύλαι. — ἁμαξιτός. In some places the width for a carriage has only been gained by cutting into the rock. — ἰσχυρῶς, 685, emph. position. — ἀμήχανος εἰσελθεῖν (663 g) στρατεύματι (453), *impracticable for an army to enter* = which it was *impracticable to enter* (ἦν ἀμή- χανον ἦν εἰσελθεῖν), the adj. agreeing with εἰσβολή by attraction instead of being in the neut. with εἰσελθεῖν. Cf. 573. — ἐν τῷ πεδίῳ. This spot directly in front of the pass is termed by Arrian, τὸ Κύρου τοῦ ξὺν Ξενοφῶντι στρατόπεδον, *An.* ii. 4. Alexander marvelled at his good fortune in making the passage here with like freedom from opposition. — ἐκώλυεν, tried to hinder. — λελοιπὼς εἴη, mode 643; form 317 a. We cannot suppose that Syennesis had any real design of defending the entrance; but he wished to be able to claim, if necessary, that he had made the attempt. The arrival of Menon in his rear gave him the excuse which he desired for leaving the pass. — ᾔσθετο...ἦν, 657 a. Ἦν is used rather than εἴη, as expressing a perceived *fact*, 644 s. — ὁρέων, case 445 c. — καὶ ὅτι, and *because*. Ὅτι, like the Lat. quod, is both a complementary and a causal conjunction, 701 i, j. — τριήρεις, the obj. of ἔχοντα, as Ταμών of ἤκουε. For the order see 719 d. Cf. ἔπεμψε δέκα τριήρεις ἔχοντα Ἐτεό- νικον, *Hel.* ii. 5. — ἤκουε...Ταμὼν ἔχοντα, he *heard* [of T. having] *that T. had*, 677 b. This use of the part. w. ἀκούω here implies certainty that the report heard was true, which the inf. would not; 657 k; cf. 3. 20. For the arrival of this fleet see 4. 2. Some prefer to regard τριήρεις περι- πλεούσας as immediately depending upon ἤκουε, and Ταμὼν ἔχοντα as a parenthesis similarly depending: he *heard* [of triremes sailing round, of Tamos having such] *that triremes were sailing round under the charge of Tamos*. — τὰς Λακ., sc. τριήρεις. — αὐτοῦ, cf. vi. 3. 5.

22. οὐδενὸς κωλύοντος, 675. — τὰς σκηνάς: these may have been rather huts than movable tents; or the term may be a general one for a camp or post. This was probably over the pass, in a convenient place for crushing invaders with stones. The conjectural substitution of εἷλε for εἶδε by Muretus and others seems, therefore, groundless. — οὗ οἱ Κίλικες ἐφύλατ- τον, *where the Cilicians were previously keeping guard*, or *had been keeping guard*, 604 a. Cf. ἐτύγχανεν ἔχων, 1. 8. — εἰς πεδίον, 689 a. — δένδρων, case 414 a. The plain of Cilicia is still remarkable for its fertility and beauty. — Ὄρος s: for the order see 719 d. This mountain defence consists of the united chains of the Taurus and the Amanus. See Map.

23. Καταβὰς...Ταρσούς, *and having descended he advanced through*

this plain to Tarsus four stations, twenty-five parasangs (from the last stopping-place). This explanation is required, since, acc. to Ainsworth, the march on the plain itself would occupy only one day. — ἦσαν, plur. 569 a. — μέσης δὲ τῆς πόλεως, 508 a, 523 b, 4. — ὄνομα, εὖρος, case 481; art. om. 533 c. — δύο, 240 c. — πλέθρων, modifying ποταμός, 440 a.

24. Ταύτην τὴν (524 b) πόλιν ἐξέλιπον, 605. — εἰς [to go to], for. — χωρίον, identified by some with the Castle of Nimrud in the adjacent mountains. — ὄρη, accus. on account of the preceding verb of motion. — πλὴν ...ἔχοντες, these remaining for the profits of trade, and to take from the Cyreans the excuse of necessity for further plundering; doubtless by the command or with the consent of Syennesis. So the inhabitants of Issus; and (with reference to the fleet) those of Soli.

25. προτέρα Κύρου, 509 a, 408. — τῶν εἰς τὸ πεδίον, sc. καθηκόντων (cf. 4. 4), reaching, or descending to the plain. Reiske and some others conjecture τῇ agreeing with ὑπερβολῇ. — ὑπολειφθέντας, for plunder, probably. — καὶ οὐ...οὐδέ (Lex.). — τὸ ἄλλο στράτευμα, 508 a, 523 f. — ἦσαν δ' οὖν...ὁπλῖται, but, however (they perished), these were one hundred hoplites lost to the army (these λόχοι being smaller than usual, or, as Küh. thinks, not wholly destroyed).

10

26. Οἱ δ' ἄλλοι (721 b), the rest of Menon's force. — διήρπασαν, seizing eagerly this pretext for plundering so wealthy a city before the arrival of their comrades; and Menon, doubtless, encouraging and profiting most by the crime. See ii. 6. 27. — ὀργιζόμενοι, infuriated, in pretence. — τὰ ἐν αὐτῇ, sc. ὄντα, 523 a, 2, 526, 678 c. — μετεπέμπετο (as introductory, 595 a) τὸν Σ. [sc. ἰέναι, 668 b] πρὸς ἑαυτόν, sent for S. to come to him, 583 : cf. 579. — ὁ δ' οὔτε (οὐ joined with ἔφη, though prop. modifying ἐλθεῖν) πρότερον οὐδενί (713 a) πω κρείττονι ἑαυτοῦ (408) εἰς χεῖρας ἐλθεῖν ἔφη, οὔτε τότε Κύρῳ ἰέναι ἤθελε, but he both replied that he had never yet [aforetime] put himself into the hands of any one stronger than himself, and refused then to go to Cyrus [sc. εἰς χεῖρας, to put himself into his hands]. Ἔρχομαι and εἶμι are comm. construed with prepositions, but with such expressions as εἰς χεῖρας, εἰς λόγους, may take a personal modifier in the dat., 450 b (or the phrases taking the dat. acc. to 455, 452 a, or perhaps 464). — ἔλαβε, sc. Συέννεσις, as the leading subject.

27. ἀλλήλοις, 583. — ἃ νομίζεται (sing. 569) παρὰ βασιλεῖ τίμια, which are [accounted honorable] special marks of honor at the king's court, where the three gifts first mentioned were allowed to no one, unless presented by the king, Cyr. viii. 3. 8. Cyrus thus assumed royal state. — καὶ ..καὶ, 707 j. — ἀκινάκην χρυσοῦν, a gilt poniard, as one simply of gold would be of very little service. — στολὴν Περσικήν, the candys (i. 5. 8), borrowed by the Persians from the Medes; and, as a royal robe, of purple and embroidered with gold. Compare the modern caftan. — τὴν χώραν μηκέτι ἀφαρπάζεσθαι, that the country should no longer (more) be pillaged, an object of ἔδωκε. — ἀνδράποδα, ἥν που ἐντυγχάνωσιν (for opt., 653 a, 633 a), ἀπολαμβάνειν, that they (the Cilicians) should recover their slaves, if they should anywhere find any. These inf. clauses are direct objects of ἔδωκε, understood with Κῦρος.

CHAPTER III.

THE GREEK TROOPS, SUSPECTING THE REAL OBJECT OF THE EXPEDITION, REFUSE TO ADVANCE; BUT ARE PERSUADED BY CYRUS, THROUGH CLEARCHUS, TO MARCH AS IF AGAINST ABROCAMAS ON THE EUPHRATES.

1. ἔμεινε, zeugma 497 b.—οὐκ ἔφασαν ἰέναι (as fut. Lex.) τοῦ πρόσω, *they said that they would not go any farther* [for that which is farther on, 430 a], or *they refused to go forward*, 662 b, 686 i.—ἐπί, 689 g.—μισθωθῆναι, 588. From Tarsus Cyrus would of course march westward, if his expedition were against the Pisidians, as pretended. An attempt to march farther eastward would therefore naturally alarm the Greeks. The Greeks were familiar with the sea and seacoast; but before this expedition, had a natural dread of the long and untried march into the interior of the great Asiatic continent and the mighty Persian empire.—πρῶτος, *first* or *foremost* of the generals, since § 7 seems to imply that Xenias and Pasion displeased their soldiers by a similar urgency. The v. l. πρῶτον would signify *first* or *at first*, in distinction from *afterwards*. See 509 f.—ἐβιάζετο, etc., tenses 594. This prompt resort to compulsion suited well the harsh nature of Clearchus (ii. 6. 9 s); while his subsequent tears might well have excited wonder.—αὐτόν τε, *both himself*, τε throwing distinctive emphasis upon αὐτόν, 540 f.

2. μικρόν, [a short distance only] *narrowly*, the accus. of extent here passing into the adv. acc., 483a.—ἐξέφυγε, etc., tense 594.—μή, 713 d.—δυνήσεται, 607 a, 643 h.—ἐκκλησίαν, an assembly duly called, in distinction from spontaneous gatherings (σύλλογοι v. 7. 2).—χρόνον, case 482 a.—ἐδάκρυε...ἑστώς [standing 46,320 d], *he stood and wept* (674 d) tears, we may suppose, even more of policy than of chagrin.—τοιάδε [such things as the following], *as follows*, 547. Τοιάδε and τοιαῦτα, talia, do not claim as much exactness for the report as τάδε and ταῦτα, hæc; yet they are sometimes interchanged with these: cf. § 7, 9, 12. Clearchus speaks throughout with great art. Discourses, like his, in which the real was opposite to the apparent purport, were termed by the Greek rhetoricians λόγοι ἐσχηματισμένοι, orationes figuratæ. Cf Agamemnon's speech, *Il.* ii. 110 s; Antony's oration over the body of Cæsar in Shakespeare.

3. Ἄνδρες στρατιῶται, 393 e, 484 g.—μὴ θαυμάζετε, 628 c, e, 686 a.—χαλεπῶς φέρω (Lex.) τοῖς παροῦσι (Lex.) πράγμασιν, *I am deeply afflicted at the present state of affairs*, 456.—με...τά τε ἄλλα (480 b) ἐτίμησε, καί, *both favored me in all else, and in particular, or as an especial favor*, τὲ... καί giving more emphasis to the second part than τέ...τέ (Lex.).—ἐμοί, 537 a; emph. in contrast with ὑμᾶς.—κατεθέμην...ἐδαπάνων, the aor. expressing the simple and absolute denial of the action as a whole, the ipf. presenting it as continued or as a course of conduct, 591 s.

NOTES.

4. ἐπολέμησα, *I engaged in war*, inceptive aor. 592 d. — τῆς Ἑλλάδος, 522 g. — τῆς Χερρονήσου, 522 h. — μεθ' ὑμῶν, *with you* as partakers in the work, *with your co-operation*, more complimentary than σὺν ὑμῖν (σύν simply denoting *connection*, while μετά with the gen. goes further, and implies *participation*). — Ἕλληνας τὴν γῆν, 485 d. — ἐπειδή s, order 718 o, p, q. — ἐκάλει, tense 595 a. — εἴ τι (478 a) δέοιτο, ὠφελοίην, 633 a. — ἀνθ' ὧν (elliptic attr. 554 a N.) εὖ ἔπαθον (Lex.) ὑπ' (since ἔπαθον is akin to a pass. Lex.) ἐκείνου, *in return for the favors which I had received from* HIM. The student will observe the distinctive emphasis of ἐκείνου, while αὐτόν is unemphatic, 536 d, e, 540 g.

5. ἀνάγκη δή μοι, 459, 572. — προδόντα, 667 e. — φιλίᾳ, case 466 b. — μεθ' ὑμῶν εἶναι, *to remain associated with you*, see § 4. — αἱρήσομαι... πείσομαι, emphasized by the chiastic order, which is so frequent in Greek, 71 a. — σὺν ὑμῖν, remaining *with you, in your company*: μεθ' ὑμῶν would have signified that they would likewise suffer, which he more delicately leaves them to infer. — ὅ τι ἂν δέῃ, sc. πάσχειν, *whatever* [it] *may be necessary* [to suffer], 551 a, 641 a. — οὔποτε s, 713 a, 719 a. — ὡς, rather than ὅτι, *inasmuch as, since*, to express the idea that he spurns the thought, 702 a. — Ἕλληνας, not definite,...τοὺς Ἕλληνας, definite from previous mention, 530 a.

6. ἐμοί, case 455 g. — ἐμοί, ἐγώ, emphatic, strongly distinctive, 536 a, e. — πείθεσθαι οὐδὲ ἕπεσθαι, "illud animi, hoc corporis est." Kühn. — σὺν ὑμῖν ἕψομαι, *I will* [follow with, as a companion] *accompany you*. To follow a guide or leader is expressed by ἕπομαι without σύν, § 17, iii. 1. 36. — νομίζω, a stronger word than οἶμαι, (Lex.). — εἶναι, 480 a, N. — πατρίδα, since he was an exile. Compare *Il.* vi. 429 s; Eur. *Hec.* 281. — καί...καί...καί, making the three accusatives all emphatic (Lex.), 701, 1. — ἂν οἶμαι εἶναι τίμιος, 621 e, f, 657 f, 658 a. — ὑμῶν, case 414 b. — οὐκ ἂν ἱκανός s, 714. 2, 622 a. — ὡς ἐμοῦ οὖν ἰόντος, 680 c. — ὑμεῖς, sc. ἴητε, 572 a.

7. οἵ (accent 787) τε αὐτοῦ ἐκείνου, 540 d. — ὅτι s, appos. 58 h. — οὐ φαίη, 662 b or 686 i; mode 643. — παρά, 689 d. παρά denoting *to* or *towards* with the accus. here derives from the connection the idea *against*. In this sense ἐπί and πρός are more common.

8. τούτοις, case 456; cf. 5. 13. — μετεπέμπετο, 595. The idea of repetition does not here suit the person or the narrative. — στρατιωτῶν, case 418. — αὐτῷ, case 450 b. — ἔλεγε, bade, i. e. through the messenger; see 659 h. — ὡς καταστησομένων τούτων [on the ground that], *since these things would result*, 680 b, c. — μεταπέμπεσθαι, *to keep sending*, or *send again for him*, 592. — αὐτὸς δὲ οὐκ ἔφη ἰέναι, *but for himself he said* (in the message sent to Cyrus) *that he should not go;* αὐτός emphatic subject of ἰέναι, in appos. with subject of ἔφη, 667 b. The course pursued by Clearchus manifested great adroitness, though he loved better to employ force where this was possible.

9. τῶν ἄλλων (case 419 d) τὸν βουλόμενον, 678 a. — τὰ μὲν δὴ Κύρου (523) δῆλον ὅτι (717 b) οὕτως ἔχει πρὸς ἡμᾶς, ὥσπερ τὰ ἡμέτερα (506 c) s,

BOOK I. CHAP. III. 17

certainly the relation of Cyrus to us is manifestly the same [has itself so] *as ours to him,* obligation and friendship having ceased on both sides, so that no favor is to be expected. — οὔτε γάρ s, 719 e, f. — ἐπεί γε, *of course since.* — ἡμῖν, case 454 e.

10. ἀδικεῖσθαι νομίζει, *he thinks that he is wronged,* the subject of the inf. being the same with that of the governing verb, 667 b. — καὶ μεταπεμπομένου αὑτοῦ, *even though he is sending for me again and again,* concessive, 674 f. — οὐκ ἐθέλω ἐλθεῖν, 598 a. — τὸ μὲν μέγιστον, αἰσχυνόμενος, *as the chief reason, ashamed,* or *chiefly from shame.* τὸ μέγιστον is in appos. with the incorporated clause following, 396 a, or it may be explained as an acc. of specif. or adv. acc. — σύνοιδα ἐμαυτῷ (699) πάντα (478 or 481) ἐψευσμένος (657 j, 677 a) αὐτόν, *I am conscious* [with or to myself] *of having* [or that I have] *disappointed him in everything.* — ἔπειτα (Lex.) μέν. — δεδιὼς μή, *fearing lest,* or *that,* 625 a. — δίκην...ὧν [= τούτων ἅ, 554 a, N.] νομίζει...ἠδικῆσθαι (586 c, 480 b), *the penalty of those wrongs which he thinks he has received.*

11. ὥρα, subject of δοκεῖ : [the time seems not to be] *it seems to be no time.* — ἀμελεῖν ἡμῶν αὐτῶν, 432 d, 537. — χρὴ ποιεῖν (598 a) ἐκ τούτων (Lex. ἐξ, cf. ἐκ τούτου). — ἕως...μένομεν, *while we are remaining here.* Ἕως signifies *while* before a verb implying continuance, but otherwise *until;* hence comm. *while* before a definite tense, but *until* before the aor. Μένομεν is in the ind. as denoting that which was actually going on. — σκεπτέον μοι δοκεῖ εἶναι, ὅπως, *it seems to me that we must consider, how,* 682. — ἄπιμεν (Lex. εἶμι), 603 c, 609 c. — τούτων, case 405 a. — στρατηγοῦ, 412.

12. Ὁ...ἀνήρ [sc. ἐστιν], *the man,* not an expression indicative of friendship, cf. 8. 26. — πολλοῦ...ἄξιος, *worth much, of great value,* 431 b. — ᾧ ἂν φίλος ᾖ, *to whomsoever he may be a friend,* 456, 641 a. — χαλεπώτατος δ' ἐχθρὸς (Lex.), ᾧ ἂν πολέμιος ᾖ, *but a most bitter hater to whomsoever he may be a foe.* — δοκοῦμέν μοι, for courtesy (Lex. δοκέω), 654. — αὐτοῦ, case 405 a, the close vicinity implying danger. — ὥρα λέγειν, sc. ἐστίν, 572. — ἐπαύσατο, voice 582 b.

13. Ἐκ τούτου, (Lex. ἐξ). — οἱ μὲν...οἱ δέ, (Lex. ὁ), 518 d. — λέξοντες, *to say,* purpose, 598 b. — οἷα (Lex.), *how great.* — εἴη, mode 643.

14. Εἶς δὲ δὴ εἶπε, *and one* [indeed] *in particular,* so proposing means of return, as to suggest throughout difficulties and dangers; εἶπον, signifying *to command, bid, advise,* is followed by the inf., 659 h. — ὡς τάχιστα (Lex.), 553 c. — ἑλέσθαι, ἀγοράζεσθαι (a more continued act), voice 579. — βούλεται, tense 607 a, 645. — ἡ δ' ἀγορά...στρατεύματι, a note of the historian, showing the dependence of the Greeks upon Cyrus for supplies. — αἰτεῖν (of course through deputies), w. 2 acc. 480 c. — ὡς ἀποπλέοιεν, mode 624 c. — ἐάν...μὴ διδῷ, *if he* [*do nothing towards giving,* stronger than aor. δῷ, 594 a] *refuse these.* διδῷ, ἀπάξει, etc., the modes appropriate to the present rather than the past time, and to direct rather than indirect discourse, 645, 653; blending of forms; greater vivacity, animation by this. — φιλίας (Lex.), 523 b, 4. — συντάττεσθαι, more continued than πέμψαι. —

2

—τὴν ταχίστην, 483 d. — προκαταληψομένους [sc. τινάς or ἄνδρας], purpose, 598 b. — τὰ ἄκρα, the heights of Mt. Taurus, which they must cross in return by land, as they had done in advance. — φθάσωσι, 677 f; syllepsis 496 e. — ὧν, partitive with πολλούς, but possessive with χρήματα, *from whom we have seized and still hold many captives and much property*, 679 b; even the person of direct discourse being here used, 644. 1. The position of ἀνηρπακότες gives special emphasis to the pillage by which they had so incurred the enmity of the Cilicians. — τοσοῦτον, emphatic, *only so much*, simply *this much*, and no more, here prospective.

15. Ὡς μὲν στρατηγήσοντα s, 659 c, 675 e, 680 c. — στρατηγήσοντα... στρατηγίαν (Lex.), 477. 1. — ἐμοὶ (458) τοῦτο οὐ ποιητέον, sc. ἐστίν, *I must not do this*, 572. — ᾧ, attr. 554 a. — πείσομαι, observe the double form of const. after λεγέτω. The λεγέτω understood agrees with a pronoun implied in μηδείς, *let him say;* so often in Eng. and other languages. — ᾗ (Lex. ὅς) δύνατον μάλιστα, 553 c. — ἵνα εἰδῆτε, 624 a. — καὶ ἄρχεσθαι ἐπίσταμαι, ὥς τις καὶ ἄλλος μάλιστα ἀνθρώπων, *I know also how to submit to authority* [no less than to exercise it] *quite as well as any other man in the world*, 553 a. But see 8. 12 s, ii. 6. McMich. compares "non ut magis alter," Hor. *Sat.* i. 5. 33. The expression τίς ἄλλος is emphasized by the position of καί (*even, also*) between the pronouns.

16. ἄλλος: Halbkart thinks that this was Xenophon himself. But Xen. accompanied the expedition as the friend of Proxenus, and would not have taken part in the deliberation of the soldiers of Clearchus. — ὥσπερ πάλιν τὸν στόλον Κύρου μὴ ποιουμένου, *as though Cyrus* [were not for making again, pres. for fut.] *would not resume his march;* for whether this were westward against the Pisidians, the pretended aim, or eastward, as they feared, in either case he would require his vessels as tenders to his army; 680 b. — ἐπιδεικνὺς δὲ, ὡς εὔηθες (emphatic repetition) εἴη, ἡγεμόνα αἰτεῖν παρὰ (693. 6) τούτου, ᾧ (464) λυμαινόμεθα, 644 b. — πιστεύσομεν, fut. as subj. — ᾧ (attr. 554 a) ἂν Κῦρος διδῷ, *whom C. may offer*, or be disposed to give, 594. — τί κωλύει καὶ τὰ ἄκρα ἡμῖν (rather than ἡμῶν governed by πρό in compos. 463, cf. iii. 4. 39) κελεύειν Κῦρον προκαταλαμβάνειν; *what hinders Cyrus* [also to command men to preoccupy the heights for us] *from also issuing orders for the occupation of the heights in advance of us?* Some make the question ironical, "What hinders our also asking Cyrus to preoccupy the heights in our behalf?"

17. Ἐγὼ (emph. 536. 1) γὰρ ὀκνοίην...ἄν, *for I should be reluctant*, 636. — δοίη, mode 641 b, 661 a. — μὴ ἡμᾶς αὐταῖς ταῖς τριήρεσι καταδύσῃ (650 a, 624): Most MSS. have this reading, which gives the sense, *lest he should sink us triremes and all* (see Lex. τριήρης), pursuing with his swift galleys our slow transports; cf. 4. 7 s. Others omit αὐταῖς, and render, *lest he should sink us with his triremes.* — ἀγάγῃ, 650 a; redupl. 284 g. — ὅθεν, sc. ἐκεῖσε or εἰς χωρίον, *to a place from which*, 551 c, f. — ἄκοντος ἀπιὼν Κύρου, *departing* [C. being unwilling, 676 a] *against the will of C.*; cf. ii. 1. 19. This ellipsis of the part. with ἑκών and ἄκων is common, because they so resemble participles themselves. — λαθεῖν αὐτὸν ἀπελθών, 677 f, 444 a.

18. With δοκεῖ are construed several infinitives with ἄνδρας or ἡμᾶς as subject: ἐρωτᾶν, ἔπεσθαι, ἀξιοῦν, ἀναγγεῖλαι, etc. — οἵτινες (sc. εἰσίν), *whoever are*, or such as are. — ἐπιτήδειοι, σὺν Κλεάρχῳ, deferred details, 719 d. — τί (complementary 563, 564; case 478) βούλεται ἡμῖν (case 466 d) χρῆσθαι, *what use he wishes to make of us*. — παραπλησία οἵᾳπερ (= τοιαύτῃ οἵᾳπερ, such as, 554, a N., 560)...ἐχρῆτο, *similar to* [such as] *that for which he employed*. χρῆσθαι πρᾶξιν, like χρῆσθαι χρῆσιν, but bolder (as χ. πρὸς or εἰς π. would be more common), 477, 479. For the service referred to, see 1. 2. — ξένοις, case 466 b. — τούτῳ, *with this same man*, stronger than αὐτῷ, 536 e.

19. μείζων, in the pos. of emphasis, from contrast with παραπλησία, 719 a a. — τῆς πρόσθεν, sc. πράξεως, *the previous undertaking* or *service*, 526; cf. 4. 8. — πείσαντα, esp. by larger pay. Cf. § 21. — φιλίαν (Lex.). — ἑπόμενοι = εἰ ἐποίμεθα, 635. — ἄν...ἐποίμεθα, 631 d, 621 b. — αὐτῷ, a common object of φίλοι and ἐποίμεθα, 399 g.

20. ἔδοξε (Lex. 2). Such asyndeton, with the verb leading, is frequent in expressing a decision; cf. iii. 2. 33, 38 : iv. 2. 19. — ἠρώτων s, 595. — τὰ δόξαντα τῇ στρατιᾷ, [the things which had seemed best to the army] *the questions approved* (or voted) *by the army*, 528 a; 2 acc. 480 c. — ἀκούει, tense 612; mode 644 a. For ἀκούω with εἶναι, see note to 2. 21, not implying certainty, 657 k. — ἄνδρα, Lex. — ἐπὶ τῷ...ποταμῷ, 689 g. — δώδεκα σταθμούς, case 482; made by Cyrus sixteen to Dardas. Why may the distance have been designedly understated?— πρὸς τοῦτον, *to him*, i. e. *against him*, πρός implying here hostility, but less decidedly than ἐπί would have done; cf. below, § 21, 2. 4. Abrocomas appears to have been both satrap of Phœnicia and commander (στρατηγός or κάρανος) of the army in the southwest part of the Persian Empire. It was his especial duty, unless otherwise ordered, to interpose his great army for arresting the onward march of Cyrus. — βούλεσθαι, 659 d. — κἂν (= καὶ ἐὰν) μὲν ᾖ, 631 c. — τὴν δίκην (Lex.), *the punishment due;* 530 d; cf. § 10. — ἡμεῖς...βουλευσόμεθα, expressed with winning courtesy.

21. τοῖς δέ, 459. — ἄγει, 645 a; cf. ἄγοι below. — πρὸς βασιλέα, 689 i. — προσαιτοῦσι, *they ask additional:* some read προσαιτοῦσι δὲ μισθὸν ὁ Κῦρος, making προσ. a participle. — ἡμιόλιον, 242 e, ἐ, 416 b. — οὗ = τούτου ὅ, or τοῦ μισθοῦ ὅν, 554 a. — ἡμιδαρεικά (242 e) τοῦ (522 b) μηνός, 433 f. — ὅτι δέ s, order 721 a. — ἔν γε τῷ φανερῷ, 507 d. The Greeks could now have had no doubt of the nature of the enterprise; but they saw as much danger in going back as forward, besides the loss of pay.

CHAPTER IV.

MARCH FROM TARSUS TO THE EUPHRATES. — CROSSING THE RIVER.

1. οὗ τὸ εὖρος στάδιον, 572. — ἐσχάτην (sc. τὴν 533 e) πόλιν ἐπὶ τῇ θαλάττῃ (689 g) οἰκουμένην, *the last inhabited city by the sea,* or upon the sea-coast.

NOTES.

2. αἱ ἐκ Π. νῆες, see 2. 21. Double dealing of Lacedæmonians (Diodorus, xiv. 21). — **τριάκοντα καὶ πέντε,** 242 a. — **ἐπ' αὐταῖς** (dat.), *over them* in command, while ἐπὶ τῶν νεῶν (gen. § 3) is simply local, *on board the vessels;* cf. iv. 3. 3. N. — **ἡγεῖτο δ' αὐτῶν** : some read αὐταῖς (463), which would mean that Tamos led the way for them, *conducted them*, not implying command, as the gen. here implies (407). — **Κύρου,** which belonged to Cyrus, without implying that those before mentioned so belonged, 567 e. — **ἐπολιόρκει,** ipf. see ἐτύγχανεν, 1. 8 ; ii. 1. 6. — **συνεπολέμει,** connected by καί to ἐπολιόρκει, both referring to Tamos : 1. 7. To whom does αὐτόν refer ?

3. ὦν (case 407) **ἐστρατήγει,** *which he* henceforth *commanded*, 604 b. Observe in this section the varied use of παρά : παρὰ Κύρῳ, [at the side of] *with C.* ; παρὰ Κῦρον, [to the side of] *to C.* ; παρὰ τὴν...σκηνήν, [through the space beside] *alongside of the tent :* παρ' Ἀβροκόμα, [from beside] *from A.*, gen. for dat. by const. præg. : the Greek mercenaries with A. having revolted from him, 704 c. Yet some have παρ' Ἀβροκόμᾳ.

4. πύλας, as prop. name, without art., 533 a. — **Ἦσαν** (569 a) **δὲ ταῦτα,** 500. According to Ains., remains of these walls are still found. — **τὸ...ἔσωθεν πρὸ τῆς Κιλικίας,** *the inner one in front of Cilicia* (to protect this country from invasion), 523 k, 526. The MSS. here omit τό after ἔσωθεν, but almost all insert it after ἔξω below. — **Σ. εἶχε καὶ Κιλίκων φυλακή,** *S. held* [and] *with a guard of the Cilicians*, not in person. — **διὰ μέσου** (Lex.) art. om. 533 d...**τούτων,** [through the midst of] *between these.* — **ὄνομα, εὖρος** (481) **πλέθρου,** 440 ; cf. 2. 23. N. — **τὸ μέσον τῶν τειχῶν** (445 b ; cf. iii. 4. 20) **ἦσαν,** 500. — **παρελθεῖν οὐκ ἦν βίᾳ** (466. 1), *it was not possible to pass them by force* (Lex. εἰμί), cf. 571 f. — **ἐπὶ τοῖς τείχεσιν,** [resting against, 689 g] *in the walls.* — **ἐφειστήκεσαν,** *stood*, plp. as ipf., 268, 46 d. — **πύλαι,** *gates* in the literal sense. So Thermopylæ had anciently a wall and gates, Hdt. vii. 176. The marginal figure illustrates the general topography of the pass. There was another pass. Why Cyrus chose this ? He could descend to the mouth of the Orontes, if necessary. Other objects : to bring and protect transports in conveying supplies, and to act upon Syennesis.

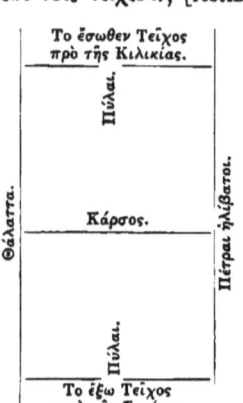

5. Ταύτης ἕνεκα τῆς παρόδου, case 436 d ; order 721 c. — **ἀποβιβάσειεν,** mode 624 c. — **πυλῶν,** case 445 c ; i. e. between and beyond the walls, so as to attack Abrocomas from different points. — **παρέλθοιεν,** i. e. Cyrus and his troops. See a like change of number in § 19. — **φυλάττοιεν,** mode 633 a. — **ἔχοντα,** [having] *as he had*, 674. — **ὄντα,** 677 b. See 3. 20, N. **εἶναι.** — **τριάκοντα μυριάδας στρατιᾶς** (Lex.), *thirty myriads of soldiers*, 418.

6. ἐμπόριον δ' ἦν s, 534. 3. That which was observed in the past, even

BOOK I. CHAP. IV. 21

though it may continue to the present, is often expressed narratively in the Greek, as in other languages, by a past tense, 611. Cf. ἐνόμιζον, εἴων, § 9. — ὁλκάδες, more oval than ships of war, and (except as sometimes towed) chiefly propelled by sails.

7. ἔμειναν, doubtless to land and dispose of the supplies brought by the fleet, which was now to return, and to procure in this mart other necessaries for the long inland march through the interior. — τὰ πλείστου ἄξια, [the things worth most, 431 b] *their most valuable effects*. — ἀπέπλευσαν, availing themselves of their last opportunity to desert safely. Cyrus was probably well content that the forces of so efficient a commander as Clearchus should be increased; and even if he intended to compel the return of those who had left, Xenias and Pasion, he may not have thought it safe to make the attempt till he had left the sea-coast, where desertion was so easy. This freedom in passing from one commander to another is spoken of, ii. 6. 11 s, as if not unusual with mercenaries. Cleanor and Agias, who have not been heretofore mentioned, but are hereafter introduced as generals (ii. 1. 9 s; 5. 31), appear to have succeeded the deserting commanders. — ὡς μὲν τοῖς πλείστοις ἐδόκουν (personal for impers. const., 573 d), *as indeed* [they] *it seemed to most*. As the opinions of others are not mentioned, the μέν is not followed by its corresponding δέ. — στρατιώτας, ἔχειν, both positions emph. See 3. 7. — ὡς ἀπιόντας, [as going to return] *so that they might return*, 598 b, 680. — καὶ οὐ πρὸς βασιλέα, sc. ἰόντας, drawn from ἀπ-ιόντας; an example of rhetorical zeugma, 68 g, 572 b. Cf. vii. 4. 20. Why is Κλέαρχον repeated? — ἦσαν ἀφανεῖς, *were gone* (from sight), or *had disappeared*. — διώκει, *was pursuing*, 645 a. — ὡς δολίους ὄντας αὐτοὺς ληφθῆναι, *that they might be taken* [as being treacherous], *since they were traitors*. Some have δειλούς, *since they were cowards*. — ᾤκτειρον s, 633 c, 643 e; from C.'s usual severity in punishment, 9. 13; 2. 20. But clemency was here more politic.

8. ἀπολελοίπασιν (Lex. ἀπό); numb. 496 a. — ἀλλ' εὖ γε (strengthening εὖ) μέντοι (a more general confirmative, *certainly* or *however*) ἐπιστάσθωσαν, *but, however, let them at least know full well*. — οὔτε ἀποδεδράκασιν ..., οὔτε ἀποπεφεύγασιν, *they have neither escaped by stealth* (as a fugitive slave)..., *nor have they escaped through speed* (as a flying enemy); they have neither got beyond my knowledge, nor beyond my reach. — ὅπῃ οἴχονται, *which way they have gone*, 612. — ὥστε ἑλεῖν, [so as to take, i. e.] *so that I can take*, 671 a. — θεούς, case 476 d. — οὐκ ἔγωγε αὐτοὺς διώξω, *I for my part will not pursue them*, NOT I, whatever others have done; so ἐγώ emph. .below. — παρῇ, mode 641 a. — καὶ αὐτούς (540 f; numb. 501) κακῶς ποιῶ, καὶ τά (530 e) χρήματα (480 c) ἀποσυλῶ, *both maltreat them personally, and despoil them of their property*. — ἀλλὰ ἰόντων, εἰδότες, *let them go, conscious*. — καὶ τέκνα καὶ γυναῖκας, art. om. 533 f. — φρουρούμενα, zeugma, the Persian, from the natural influence of polygamy, placing children before wives, unless, indeed, both wives and children are here regarded as things, articles of property. — στερήσονται = pass. 576 a. — ἀπολήψονται, sc. αὐτούς, 536 c. In Greek, if two closely connected verbs

have a common object, this is more comm. expressed but once, and in the case required by the nearer verb; cf. 399 g. — τῆs πρόσθεν (cf. 3. 19) ἕνεκα, pos. 721 c.

9. εἴ τις καί, *even if any one.* — ἀθυμότερος, 514. — σταθμούς, doubtless by the pass of Beïlaw, over Mt. Amanus. The passage, though not picturesque, presented no difficulties or incidents which Xen. deemed worthy of mention. The Πύλαι Ἀμανίδες, by which Darius III. crossed this mountain into Cilicia before his disastrous defeat at Issus, were farther north. — πλέθρου, case 440 a. — ἰχθύων (Lex.): This river is said still to abound in fish, acc. to Ainsw. — οὖς (not limiting antecedent, 554 a; cf. ἅ, 2. 7)... θεούς, 2 acc. 480 a. — ἀδικεῖν, sc. τινά, 667 h. (Lex.) — τὰς (522 a) περιστεράς, sc. ἀδικεῖν...εἴων. — Παρυσάτιδος (case 443) ἦσαν; hence prob. spared from ravage. — ζώνην (Lex.). The MSS. have chiefly εἰς ζωήν, *for her subsistence.* The vast empire of the Persian kings made this an easy mode of providing for their pensioners or favorites. So Artaxerxes I. (Thuc. i. 138) gave Themistocles Lampsacus to supply him with wine; Magnesia, with bread; and Myus, with accompanying dishes.

10. Δάρδητος (Lex.). Xenophon writes as if he supposed the Dardas to have been a river with springs so copious that it began as a broad stream. — ἦσαν, numb. 569 a. — τοῦ Συρίας ἄρξαντος, *who had ruled over Syria as satrap,* but had now, it would seem, retired before the approach of Cyrus, — perhaps with the army of Abrocomas. The prince therefore treated his palace and park as those of an enemy. — ὅσα, numb. 550 f. — ὧραι, without art., 533 d. — αὐτὸν (referring to παράδεισον) ἐξέκοψε, by the hands of others, 581.

11. ἐπὶ τὸν Εὐφράτην, *to the ford of the Euphrates;* since, according to the common opinion, the preceding three stations were all in the valley of this river. Kiepert says σταδίων should be πλέθρων; but see Ainsw. — ὀνόματι, case 467 b, 485 e, γ: one of the MSS. has ὄνομα, the more common form. — ἡμέρας πέντε: the longer, doubtless, from the necessity of negotiating anew with the Greeks, since it was no longer possible to conceal the object of the expedition, and a conference had been promised here; cf. 3. 20. — ἔσοιτο, 643 h. Concealment was, of course, now no longer possible. — πρός, with name of person, but εἰς with name of place (see Lex. Explan. 6). — βασιλέα μέγαν, see 2. 8.

12. ἐχαλέπαινον, the anger feigned, doubtless, in part, to draw forth larger bounties. — κρύπτειν, *had been concealing,* 604 a; in truth, only Clearchus, acc. to iii. 1. 10. — οὐκ ἔφασαν. See 3. 1. — τις, *some one,* i. e. Cyrus, whom it was less delicate to name, 548 g. — χρήματα, *a largess* of money in addition to their pay. — διδῷ, what reg. mode? — ὥσπερ, sc. δοθῆναι, or ἐδόθη, *even as* had been given. — προτέροις, 509 a. See 1. 2. — καὶ ταῦτα, *and this too,* sc. was given or done, 544 a. — οὐκ...ἰόντων, [the not going, 676 a, sc. ἐκείνων, cf. 2. 17] *though they did not go.* One of the MSS. has ἰοῦσιν agreeing with τοῖς ἀναβᾶσι, an admissible but weaker construction, 676 b. — ἰόντων, ἀλλὰ καλοῦντος, chiastic order.

13. δώσειν, tense 659 g. — πέντε...μνᾶς = about $100, but in purchas-

BOOK I. CHAP. IV. 23

ing value at that time nearer $1000. — ἀργυρίου, case 435, 446 e. — ἥκωσι, καταστήσῃ, mode 641, 645, 650. — τὸν μισθὸν ἐντελῆ, without reduction on account of the donative, or reducing to the original terms of engagement, 3. 21. See 523. — τὸ...πολύ, 523 f. — Μένων, ever ready to gain advantage for himself, ii. 6. 21 s. — πρὶν...εἶναι, 703 d, β. — τί, complem. 563. — ποιήσουσιν, mode 650, 645. — πότερον, 701 i, n. — ἄλλων, case 405 a; pos. 718 h.

14. μοι, case 455 g. — οὔτε s, *without incurring either danger or toil.* — τῶν ἄλλων...στρατιωτῶν, pos. 719 d, ν. — πλέον προ-, emph. pleonasm; cf. 511 a. Kühn. weakens the sentence by regarding πλέον as also modifying κινδυνεύσαντες and πονήσαντες. — προτιμήσεσθε (= pass. 576 a). — τί οὖν s, rhetorical question; cf. vii. 6. 20. — Νῦν, emph. pos. — ὑμᾶς χρῆναι διαβῆναι, *that* [it is proper that you cross] *you ought to cross.* — ὅ τι, complem. 563, cf. τί § 13.

15. ἄρξαντες (674) τοῦ διαβαίνειν, *having commenced the crossing,* or *by being the first to cross,* 663 f, 425. — ὑμῖν, case 454 d. — ἐπίσταται, sc. χάριν ἀποδοῦναι [knows how to do this], *he understands this;* i. e. the requital of favors. —εἴ τις καὶ ἄλλος, *if* [even] *any other man in the world;* cf. 3. 15 N. — ψηφίσωνται, *shall have voted* (617 d), more idiomatically, *vote* or *shall vote.* — ἄπιμεν, as fut. — πιστοτάτοις χρήσεται, *he will employ most* [trust] *confidentially,* cf. 509. — ἄλλου (for which we might have ἄλλο as an obj. of τεύξεσθε) οὕτινος, *whatever else* = anything else which, ἄλλου falling into the relative construction, 553. — ὡς φίλοι τεύξεσθε Κύρου (case 434 a), *you will obtain it as friends from* (so generous a man as) *Cyrus.* There is an emphasis in the repetition of the name, instead of employing a pronoun, while the position is also emphatic. Others have φίλου in apposition with Κύρου, and some regard ἄλλου as depending directly on τεύξεσθε, acc. to 427, less probably, but cf. v. 7, 33.

16. ἐπείθοντο καὶ διέβησαν, tense 595. — ᾔσθετο διαβεβηκότας, *perceived that they had crossed,* 677. — τῷ στρατεύματι, *to the division* of Menon, comm. obj. of πέμψας and εἶπεν. — ἐγὼ μέν (685 b) s, 536. — ὅπως... ἐπαινέσετε, 624 b. — Why ἐμέ, but με below? — ἐμοί, case 457. — μηκέτι με Κῦρον νομίζετε, *no longer think me Cyrus,* 393 b, 480 a; it was his especial principle, pride, and policy to reward most liberally faithful service, 9. 11, 14, 18. Krüger cites the parallel from Cic.: "Noli oblivisci te Ciceronem esse."

17. στρατιῶται, of Menon. — εὔχοντο αὐτὸν εὐτυχῆσαι, *prayed* [that he might succeed] *for his success,* or *wished him success.* — Μένωνι, μεγαλοπρεπῶς, emphatic positions. — διέβαινε, *began to cross,* 594. — διέβαινε and συνείπετο, brought together by chiastic arrangement, from their close relation, while ἅπαν is also made emphatic by its pos. — τῶν διαβαινόντων, gen. partitive w. οὐδείς. — μαστῶν, case 408.

18. ἔλεγον (repeated), with oriental flattery, even more regardless of truth than occidental. — γένοιτο, mode 643. — ἀλλά, *but only,* sc. μόνοις, cf. iii. 2. 13. — ἃ τότε s, language of the historian. — κατέκαυσεν, tense 605. — διαβῇ, mode 650. — ὑποχωρῆσαι, *made way for,* or *submitted to.*

24 NOTES.

— Κύρῳ, case 455 g. — ὡς βασιλεύσοντι, as [about to reign] *the future king.*

19. διὰ τῆς Συρίας (Lex.); through the region afterwards more commonly called Mesopotamia, from its situation between the Euphrates and Tigris, — in Hebrew, Aram-Naharaim, the Syria of the two rivers, Judg.

20 iii. 8.— ἐνταῦθα ἦσαν s, order 719 b, ʃ, 718 f, g.— σίτου, case 414 a; of especial value, when such a desert lay before them. The abundance of provisions here is one of the proofs that Abrocomas, who did not care to arrive till the question of sovereignty was settled, took a different route from that of Cyrus, doubtless farther north and less direct, but furnishing more subsistence. The route of Alexander from Thapsacus was also much farther north. Cyrus took the more direct desert route from his haste, his confidence in his supplies (which yet proved inadequate, § 6), and perhaps the fear that he might find yet greater scarcity if he followed in the track of Abrocomas.

CHAPTER V.

MARCH THROUGH A DESERT REGION, NEAR THE EUPHRATES.

1. Ἀραβίας (Lex.). On the left bank of the Euphrates, Xen. makes the Araxes the dividing line between Syria and Arabia (so called because occupied of old, as now, by tribes of roving Arabs, the Ἄραβες Σκηνῖται of Strabo). — ἐν δεξιᾷ (Lex.), 506 b ; art. om. 533 d. — ἐρήμους (Lex.). The eighteen desert marches between the Araxes and Pylæ were greatly forced, being much beyond the general average and without any intermission. Had they been otherwise, the army would have been much reduced in men and animals from lack of supplies. See § 5 s, 7 s, 9. — ἦν μὲν ἡ γῆ πεδίον ἅπαν, *the land* or *ground was an entire* or *unbroken plain.* For ἅπαν agreeing with πεδίον, ἅπασα agreeing with γῆ might have been expected : *the country was all a plain.* See 500 ; and cf. iv. 4. 1. To make, with some, ἅπαν an adv. modifying ὁμαλές would give a false sense. — ἀψινθίου : McMich. cites "Tristia per vacuos horrent absinthia campos." Ov. *Pont.* iii. 1. 23. — εἰ (Lex. 639 a) δέ τι καὶ ἄλλο ἐνῆν ὕλης, *and if there was there* [anything else also] *any other kind of bush* or *shrub,* cf. εἴ τι ἄλλο, 6. 1. — ἅπαντα (numb. 501) ἦσαν εὐώδη : "Arabia, odōrum fertilitate nobilis regio." Curt. v. 1.

2. θηρία, sc. ἐνῆ. — ὄνοι ἄγριοι, the wild ass was noted in Western Asia as a free, swift ranger of dry and rocky pasture-ground. See Job xxxix. 5-8. It is now rare in this region. — στρουθοί : from στρουθός, through the Lat. *avis struthio,* come from the Fr. *autruche,* the Eng. *ostrich,* etc. A later name, from its camel-like neck, was στρουθοκάμηλος, Diod. ii. 50. — διώκοι, πλησιάζοιεν, mode 641 b. Sometimes termed the iterative opt. Krüg. — ἔστασαν (plp. pret.), ἔτρεχον, ἐποίουν, habitual, 592. — πολύ... θᾶττον, *much swifter,*—so placed for emph.—ἵππων, case 408.—ταὐτό(ν),

BOOK I. CHAP. V.

by crasis for τὸ αὐτό, 199 a. — οὐκ ἦν (571 f.) λαβεῖν, *there was no taking them*, εἰ μὴ...θηρῷεν (634, b, d), *unless the horsemen, stationed at intervals, pursued the chase* [succeeding each other with their horses] *with relays of fresh horses*.

3. ἀπεστᾶτο φεύγουσα, *it outstripped them in its flight*. — τοῖς μὲν ποσὶ (466 b) δρόμῳ (467), ταῖς δὲ πτέρυξιν (αἴρουσα) ὥσπερ ἱστίῳ (393 c) χρωμένη, *using its feet in* (or *for*) *running, and its wings* (*lifting them up*) *as a sail*. — ἄν τις ταχὺ ἀνιστῇ (631 c), *if one start them suddenly*. — ἔστι, accent 788 f. What example of chiastic arrangement?
4. Μάσκαν, dec. 227 b. — πλεθριαῖον, 440 a. — ὄνομα δ᾽ αὐτῇ (459) Κορσωτή, sc. ἦν, and [there was to it as a name C.] *its name was Corsote.* — περιερρεῖτο, pass. 586 a. — κύκλῳ (469 b, or 467), strengthening περιερρεῖτο. The Mascas, with the Euphrates, made the circuit complete. — ἐπεσιτίσαντο: How can it be explained that Corsote was deserted, and yet had provisions for the great army of Cyrus? By supposing that its governor pursued a crafty policy like that of Syennesis and Abrocomas; that, as if loyal to Artaxerxes, and perhaps by his command, he withdrew the inhabitants upon the approach of the king's enemy; and yet, as if friendly to Cyrus, left a supply of provisions for his army. In this way, he may also have best secured the people and the city from injury by the invading army. But whence had the city such greatness and abundance in the midst of this desert region? It was situated at the bend of the Euphrates, where the great route through the desert to Tyre, Palestine, and Egypt left the river. Hence it became a great depot of supplies and place of exchanges (like "Tadmor in the wilderness" farther west, 2 Chron. viii. 4) for the merchant caravans upon this route.

5. τρεῖς καὶ δέκα, 240 e, v. l. τρισκαίδεκα. — Πύλας (Lex.). — ὑποζυγίων, case 419 b. — ὑπό (Lex.), with ἀπώλετο, as pass. in force. — ἄλλο, *besides* (Lex. a), 567 e; cf. 7. 11. — ὄνους. The name of the ass passed to the millstone which he so often turned. Compare, in Eng., the extension of the word *Jack*. Ains. says that in this region there is found "a gritty silicious rock alternating with iron-stone, and intercalated among the marles, gypsum, and limestones of the country, capable of being used as a millstone."

6. ὁ σῖτος, art. 522 a. — Λυδίᾳ (Lex.). The Lydians, forbidden the use of arms, devoted their attention to trade, which the Persians despised. See 3. 14. — τὴν καπίθην, obj. of πρίασθαι understood, *the capithe*, as a common measure, 530 a. — ἀλεύρων, case 446 e. — σίγλων, case 431 a. — δύναται, *is equivalent to*, (Lex.) 472 f. — Ἀττικούς, zeugma 497. When Archelaus invited Socrates to come to his court and be rich, the philosopher replied that four choenices of barley-meal cost only an obolus at Athens (Stob. 97. 28). The famine price in the army of Cyrus was sixty times as great. At this rate, how many times his whole pay would a Greek soldier expend for bread, his allowance being a choenix of corn a day? — κρέα...ἐσθίοντες...διεγίγνοντο, *subsisted by eating flesh*, obtained on the march to supplement the deficiency of bread.

7. Ἦν (570) δὲ τούτων τῶν σταθμῶν (521 a), sc. τινές, *there were some of these marches;* cf. 559 a, oftener ἦσαν οἵ, (as) erant qui. — οὓς (477) πάνυ μακροὺς (509 d) ἤλαυνεν, *which he* [marched] *made very long,* or, *pushed very far.* — διατελέσαι (sc. τὴν ὁδόν), *to complete the distance,* 476. 2. This region, according to Ains., is "full of hills and narrow valleys, and presents many difficulties to the movement of an army." He himself, he says, "had to walk a day and a night across these inhospitable regions, so that he can speak feelingly of the difficulties which the Greeks had to encounter." — καὶ δή ποτε, *and on one occasion in particular.* — στενοχωρίας, abs., sc. φανείσης, 497, 675, *when there presented itself a narrow pass.* — ἁμάξαις, case 458. — στρατοῦ, case 423.

8. ὥσπερ ὀργῇ, *as in anger,* real or feigned, case 467 a; ell. 711. — συνεπισπεῦσαι : observe the difference in force between this aor. and the pres. συνεκβιβάζειν, 594. — ῥίψαντες s: observe the animation of the narrative. — ἵεντο, [sent themselves as one would send a dart] *darted,* or *rushed forward.* — ὥσπερ ἂν δράμοι τις περὶ (694) νίκης, 635, in the foot-race. — καὶ μάλα κατὰ πρανοῦς s, *and even down a very steep hill.* μάλα (as πολύ, etc., cf. iii. 1. 22) is often separated from the word which it modifies, and even by a preposition, becoming thus more emphatic. — τούτους, 542 b. It may refer also, by zeugma, to ἀναξυρίδας, 497. — ἀναξυρίδας, "οὓς καλοῦσι βράκκας" (Tzetzes, Lat. braccæ, A. Sax. bræc, Scott. brecks, Eng. breeches). Such coverings, now an essential part of civilized costumes, were accounted by the Greeks and Romans *barbarian,* inasmuch as they distinguished the dress of most other nations from their own. Euripides ridicules them as θυλάκους ποικίλους, *party-colored bags.* — θᾶττον ἢ ὥς, 711. — ἂν ᾤετο, *would think* (believe, suppose), if he did not see it, 636. 631 b. — μετεώρους (Lex.) ἐξεκόμισαν, *they lifted up and brought out.*

9. Τὸ δὲ σύμπαν, *and* [as to the whole together] *in general,* 483 a. — δῆλος ἦν Κῦρος ὡς (680, though not comm. after δῆλος) σπεύδων, *C.* [was manifest as hastening] *was evidently hastening.* — πᾶσαν τὴν ὁδόν, order 523 e ; case 482 d, or 472. — ὅσῳ...τοσούτῳ, 468, 485 e, β, quanto...tanto, *the...the.* — ὅσῳ μὲν θᾶττον s, *the more rapidly he* [should advance, 641 b, 643 e] *advanced* [he would fight with the king so much the more unprepared], *the less prepared he would find the king for battle.* — σχολαιότερον : so mss. ; Dind. -αίτερον ; 258 d, 259 a. — συναγείρεσθαι, the pres. rather than the fut., because the assembling was now in progress. — καὶ συνιδεῖν (663 g) δ' ἦν τῷ προσέχοντι (678) τὸν νοῦν ἡ βασιλέως ἀρχὴ (573),...ἰσχυρὰ οὖσα (677), *and indeed to the* [person applying his mind] *attentive observer, the empire of the king was* [to behold being] *manifestly strong,* or, *the attentive observer might perceive that the empire,* etc. — πλήθει, *in* (its) *abundance,* 467. — τῷ διεσπάσθαι τὰς δυνάμεις, *in* [that its forces were dispersed] *the dispersion of its forces.* — διὰ ταχέων, 695, 507 d. — ποιοῖτο, 634 a, b; *v. l.* ἐποιεῖτο. History however shows that the military weakness of the Persian Empire did not lie in the difficulty of promptly assembling troops, but in the inferiority of those troops in comparison with the Greeks. Despite the great effort of Cyrus to take his brother by surprise,

BOOK I. CHAP. V. 27

the latter had, acc. to Xen., 900000 men assembled to meet the attack. But these 900000 could not withstand the 10000 Greeks. The last Darius found it easy to gather hosts against Alexander; but these hosts were powerless before the Macedonian phalanx.

10. ποταμοῦ, case 445 c. — ἐκ, const. præg. 704 a. —σχεδίαις (case 466) διαβαίνοντες ὧδε (place 719 κ). — στεγάσματα, modal appos. 394 b. —χόρτου, case 414 a. — ὡς μὴ (686 c) ἅπτεσθαι (mode 671) τῆς κάρφης (case 426) τὸ ὕδωρ (subj. acc. of ἅπτεσθαι). Skins stuffed or inflated are still so used on the Euphrates and Tigris, either singly to support individual swimmers, or collectively under wooden platforms. Layard even used 600 in a raft for transporting heavy monuments. — οἶνον, a wine still used in the East. Cf. ii. 3. 14. — τῆς...τῆς, 523 a 2. Observe the distinction between ἐκ, from the inside or contents of, and ἀπό, from the outside of, 689 a, b. — μελίνης, case 412. — τοῦτο, referring to σῖτον or μελίνης, as a thing without life, 502 b. Some would supply βρῶμα, food, or φυτόν, plant. Cf. ii. 3. 16. How many days the army halted opposite Charmande to obtain supplies is not stated.

11. Ἀμφιλεξάντων...τι, having [disputed somewhat] had some quarrel, 478. — ἀδικεῖν, to have done wrong, be in the wrong, 612. — τὸν τοῦ M., the particular soldier chiefly concerned. The incident here related illustrates well the character of Clearchus and Proxenus. — ἐνέβαλεν, in Spartan fashion, — arbitrary and severe; prob. on the spot, with his own truncheon. Cf. ii. 3. 11. — Κλεάρχῳ, case 456.

12. Τῇ δὲ αὐτῇ, 540 b; case 469 a. — ἀγοράν, where the provisions brought from Charmande were sold. — ἑαυτοῦ, 537 a. — σὺν ὀλίγοις τοῖς περὶ αὐτόν, with [those about him few] few attendants, 523 b, 4. — ἧκεν, tense 612 (observe the different force in προσήλαυνε). For an aorist force, see i. 2. 6 ; 5. 15. — ἵησι τῇ ἀξίνῃ, [lets fly, throws at him with his axe] throws, or, aims at him with his axe, 466 ; where ἵησι τὴν ἀξίνην, hurls his axe at him, might have been rather expected. — αὐτοῦ, case 405 a. — λίθῳ, sc. ἵησι. Observe the elliptic vivacity of the narrative. — εἶτα, 703 c ; cf. εἶτα δέ, i. 3. 2, 703 c.

13. παραγγέλλει [sc. ἰέναι, 668 b] εἰς τὰ ὅπλα, summons to arms, cf. κελεύσαντες ἐπὶ τὰ ὅπλα, Hel. ii. 3. 20 ; conclamatur ad arma, Cæs. B. C. i. 69. — αὐτοῦ, there, on the spot. — ἀσπίδας (Lex.). Cf. obnixo genu scuto. Nepos, Chab. 1. 2. — Θρᾷκας, i. 2. 9. — ἱππέας : this small body was not specified in 2. 9. — οἱ ἦσαν αὐτῷ, qui ei erant, of whom he had, 459. — ὥστ' ἐκείνους ἐκπεπλῆχθαι, 599 b (pret. 268), so that they were amazed, or alarmed, in the condition of those who have been struck out of their self-possession ; cf. ii. 4. 26. — αὐτὸν M., 540 c. — τρέχειν, more pictorial than δραμεῖν. — οἱ δὲ καὶ ἔστασαν, and they also stood, after taking their arms, as well as the hoplites of Clearchus. — οἱ δέ, but others, as if οἱ μέν had preceded. Others translate, and others also. Cf. vii. 4. 17. — ἀποροῦντες τῷ πράγματι, being perplexed at the affair, or at a loss what to do in the case, 456 ; cf. 3. 8.

14. ὕστερος, 509 a ; cf. προτέρα, 2. 25. — εὐθὺς οὖν, immediately then,

οὖν referring to the state of things stated in the parenthesis, and being used here, as not unfrequently in resuming a discourse so interrupted. Cf. Lat. igitur. — αὐτῷ, case 450 a. — μέσον (Lex.). — ἀμφοτέρων, case 445 b. — ἔθετο, Lex. τίθημι. — Κλεάρχου, case 434 a. — μὴ ποιεῖν ταῦτα, *not to* [be doing] *do this*, which, as the pres. implies, he was then doing; *not to persist in doing this*. — ὀλίγου (414 b) δεήσαντος, 573 e. — τέ: Xen. chiefly uses τέ in correspondence with καί; not often τέ...τέ, or τέ alone.

15. Ἔν (Lex.). — παλτά (Lex.). The Persian horsemen usually carried two: παλτὰ δύο, ὥστε τὸ μὲν ἀφεῖναι, τῷ δ', ἂν δέῃ, ἐκ χειρὸς χρῆσθαι. *Cyr.* i. 2. 9. — σὺν τοῖς παροῦσι τῶν πιστῶν (Lex.), 419, 678.

16. Κλέαρχε s, 484 b. — καί [sc. ὑμεῖς] οἱ ἄλλοι, 401. 3, 485 a. — τῇδε brings the danger more vividly near than ταύτῃ would have done, 545. — κατακεκόψεσθαι, tense 601 b. — ἐμοῦ, case 408. — ἐχόντων (Lex.). — οὗτοι οὓς ὁρᾶτε, 523 g, 544. — πολεμιώτεροι, for the sake of restoration to the king's favor, to prevent the weight of the king's displeasure from falling upon themselves, or from envy towards the specially favored Greeks. The weak faith which Cyrus had in the fidelity of his Persian adherents appears again in 6. 4.

17. ἐν, const. præg. 704 d. — ἐγένετο (Lex. γίγνομαι); cf. ἐν σαυτῷ γενοῦ, Soph. *Phil.* 950. This figure is common to many languages. So in Eng., he was beside himself with passion, he came to himself; Lat. ad se rediit; Germ. er ging in sich. — κατά (Lex.).

CHAPTER VI.

TREACHERY OF ORONTES. — TRIAL AND CONDEMNATION.

1. Ἐντεῦθεν, from their halting-place opposite Charmande. — προϊόντων, sc. αὐτῶν, *as they were advancing*, 676 a. — ἐφαίνετο, *there appeared* (continuously). — ἵππων, place, 719 d, μ. — ὡς δισχιλίων, 711 b. — οὗτοι, referring to ἱππεῖς implied in ἵππων. Cf. vii. 3. 39. — εἴ τι, 639 a. Cf. 5. 1. — Πέρσης, as adj., 506 f; cf. 8. 1. — γένει, cf. γένος, v. 2. 29, 485. — τὰ πολέμια, case 481. — Περσῶν, case 419 c, 511.

2. Κύρῳ, case 452 a. — δοίη, κατακάνοι, 643 c. How in dir. discourse? — ὅτι, pos. 719 b, η: cf. ii. 2. 20.—κατακάνοι (50, καίνω) ἄν, 622 b. Observe the varied position of κατακάνοι, ἕλοι, κωλύσειε, etc. — τοῦ καίαν, case 405 a; art. 663 f, 664 a; pres. because the burning goes on. Cf. i. 5. 14. — ποιήσειεν ὥστε, [effect that] *bring about such a result that;* cf. § 6. The inf. is thus expressed as the result of the action denoted by ποιεῖν; while in the more frequent construction without ὥστε (7. 4; v. 7. 27), it is expressed simply as the direct object or effect. — ἐκέλευσεν: a decisive order seems best expressed by the aor., as in § 3 a simple request by the ipf. ἐκέλευεν. — ἡγεμόνων, case 419 a.

3. νομίσας, nearly = νομίζων, but strictly, *having come to the belief*, 592 d. — παρά [= πρὸς] βασιλέα, [to send] *to the king*. — ἥξοι, 649 d. — ὡς

BOOK I. CHAP. VI.   29

ἄν s, 553 c. — δύνηται, mode 645 b, 650. — ἀλλά, expression of opposition to the natural apprehension that his approach might be hostile. — ἱππεύ-σιν, whom he would naturally first meet, as they were scouring the region between the two armies. — τῆς πρόσθεν, cf. 3. 19 ; 4. 8. — ὑπομνήματα, pos. 719 d, μ.
4. Περσῶν s, order 719 d, ν, 523 k. — ἑπτά, *seven* in number, a deferred detail made prominent by its pos. The Persian king had **25** *seven* chief counsellors (Esth. i. 14; Ezra vii. 14), either from the dignity and sacredness of this number, or, as some think, from the number of the noblemen who slew the usurper Smerdis. — θέσθαι, 579. — τὴν αὐτοῦ (*v. l.* αὐτοῦ) σκηνήν, 538 g. Cyrus reposed but weak faith in the fidelity of his Persian adherents; cf. 5. 16 ; and on this occasion the rank and popularity of Orontes may have demanded especial caution.
5. σύμβουλον, 394 b. — ὅς (558 a) γε καὶ s, *since indeed he seemed both to him and to the rest* (the seven counsellors) *to* [be the most honored before others, 69] *hold the first position among the Greeks.* And hence, as so esteemed by the Greeks themselves, it seemed to them that he might be called in from the generals around the tent without exciting dissatisfaction or envy among the rest. The change by some editors of αὐτῷ to αὑτῷ is needless, and, if this is referred to Clearchus, injures the sense. — τὴν κρίσιν, prolepsis 474 b, 71 b. — ἀπόρρητον ἦν, sc. ὡς ἐγένετο, 491 a. — ἄρχειν (Lex.), w. gen. 425 : to open the conference. McMich. Cf. primus ibi ante omnes. Virg. Æn. ii. 40.
6. Παρεκάλεσα implies the superiority of Cyrus, and that the final decision would rest with him, as συνεκάλεσα would not have implied. — ὅ τι, acc. to some, rel. referring to τοῦτο (551 c); acc. to others, complem. connecting ἐστι to βουλευόμενος. — πρός, *before, in the sight of* (Lex.). — πράξω, subj. 624 a, the preceding aor. having the force of our perf., 605. — τουτοῦ (Lex. 252 c, d) ; pos. 719 a. — ὁ ἐμὸς πατήρ, 524 a. — ὑπήκοον, prob. as a military officer under Cyrus, who was then κάρανος in Western Asia, 1. 2 N. — ἐμοί, case 454 e and 455 g. — ταχθείς, showing, if true, the unfriendly relations between Cyrus and his brother, and giving C., if he had not himself provoked this action, some excuse for revolt. But is it not quite possible that this order from Artaxerxes was a mere fiction of the mischief-making Tissaphernes ? — ἐμοί, 455 f. — ἔχων...ἀκρόπολιν. It was the policy of the Persian monarchs to garrison some of the most important strongholds with royal troops under commanders of their own appointment, as a check upon the satraps. It is not strange that collisions sometimes took place. — αὐτόν, regarded by some as the object of προσπολεμῶν (instead of the more familiar dative), and by others as the obj. of ἐποίησα by anticipation (474 b), or with anacoluthon (Xen. having commenced as though he intended to write αὐτὸν ἐποίησα παύσασθαι, *I made him cease*). The introduction of ὥστε δόξαι represents it as a freer act, and thus more exposes the inconsistency and treachery of Orontes. — ὥστε δόξαι, 671 b ; cf. § 2. — πολέμου, case 405 a. — δεξιάν s, a pledge of esp. solemnity among the Persians : Τὴν δεξιὰν ἔδωκε ['Αρταξέρξης] τῷ Θετ-

ταλίωνι· ἔστι δ' ἡ πίστις αὕτη βεβαιοτάτη παρὰ τοῖς Πέρσαις. Diod. xvi. 43. Cf. ii. 3. 28; 4. 1.

7. ἔστιν ὅ τι, 549 b, 559 a; case 480 b. — ὅτι οὐ [= οὐκ ἔστιν or οὐδέν ἐστιν], "*No*" or "*Nothing.*" — αὐτὸς σύ, 540 d, e. — οὐδέν, case 586 c. — Μυσούς (Lex.), cf. 9. 14. — ὅ τι ἐδύνω (sc. ποιεῖν), [whatever you were able to do] *as far as you were able*, to the extent of your ability. — Ἔφη ὁ Ὀρόντης, 668 b. — δύναμιν, i. e. its inferiority, inadequacy to the contest. — Ἀρτέμιδος βωμόν, doubtless the world-renowned altar at Ephesus, a sanctuary for fugitives, which was respected by the Persians as well as the Greeks. Ἄσυλον μένει τὸ ἱερόν, Strab. xiv. 1. Τιμᾶται γὰρ καὶ παρὰ τοῖς Πέρσαις ἡ θεὸς αὕτη διαφερόντως, Diod. v. 77. See Acts xix. 27. — μεταμέλειν σοι, te poenitere, [that it repented you] *that you repented*, 572 d; case 457.

26 **8.** Τί, constructed like οὐδέν above and below. For its connection with a part., see 566 a. The Eng. would prefer, "What wrong have you suffered, that you now," etc. — φανερὸς γέγονας; *have you* [become manifest] *been found*, or *been manifestly?* 573. Cf. 2. 11; 9. 11, 16. — ἀδικηθείς, sc. γέγονε, or γέγονα, etc. — περί, 697. — [Ὁμολογῶ, 708 c], ἡ γὰρ ἀνάγκη (Lex. sc. ἐστὶν ὁμολογεῖν), [I do confess it] *Yes, for indeed it is inevitable*. Cf. 3. 5. — ἔτι οὖν s, 636 b. — ὅτι s, 644 a. — γενοίμην, δόξαιμι, mode 631 d. Why is σοί so placed and followed by γέ? The highminded frankness of Orontes inclines us to regard him as perhaps a loyal servant of the king, whose chief fault lay in not observing enforced agreements made with Cyrus. The tribute of reverence which was boldly paid him on the way to death speaks loudly in his favor; nor did Cyrus venture on a public execution.

9. Πρὸς ταῦτα (Lex. πρός), 697. — τοιαῦτα (case 478) μὲν πεποίηκε (tense 599 a), τοιαῦτα δέ. Μέν and δέ often distinguish words so repeated. — ὑμῶν, gen. partitive, 418. — ἀπόφηναι γνώμην, *express* [an, or see 533] *your opinion;* voice 579. For the om. of the art. with γνώμην, cf. v. 5. 3; 6. 37. What reasons may Cyrus have had for first applying to Clearchus? — ἐγώ, why expressed? — τὸν ἄνδρα τοῦτον, 524 b. — ἐκποδὼν (Lex.) ποιεῖσθαι, rather mid. than pass. — δέῃ, ἤ, why subj.? — φυλάττεσθαι, voice 579. — σχολὴ ᾗ ἡμῖν, observe the repetition of sound, permitted by the Greek ear. — τὸ κατὰ τοῦτον εἶναι, 665 b. Observe the pointed and perhaps contemptuous repetition of τοῦτον. — τοὺς ἐθελοντάς (also accented ἐθέλοντας, as a part.)...εὖ ποιεῖν, *to benefit these your willing friends.* — τούτους appears to be emphatically added for an effect upon those present; see 505 b.

10. γνώμῃ, case 699 g. — προσθέσθαι (Lex.). — ἔφη, who? — ζώνης, case 426 a. — ἐπὶ θανάτῳ (Lex.). This was a sign among the Persians of a death-sentence, Diod. xvii. 30. (Cf. the Eng. custom of putting on the black cap.) This action on the part of Cyrus alone was enough; but he chose to require the others to join, perhaps as a test of their fidelity. — οἷς (551 f) προσετάχθη (as impers., sc. ἄγειν), *those to whom it was appointed*, the executioners. — προσεκύνουν, tense 592. Often among the

Persians, as familiarly now in the East, by prostration to the earth, and touching this with the forehead, or even kissing it. — καίπερ εἰδότες, 674 f, 685 b. — ἄγοιτο, why opt.?

11. σκηπτούχων. In *Cyr.* vii. 5, 59 s, the reasons are stated which induced Cyrus the Elder to select eunuchs as his personal attendants and body-guards, a custom followed by his successors, and still so extensively retained in Oriental courts and harems. — εἰδώς (Lex. ὁράω), cf. 7. 4. — ἔλεγεν, εἴκαζον, ἐφάνη, double chiasma. — ἄλλοι ἄλλως (Lex. ἄλλος c), 567 d. — τάφος s. The execution and burial seem to have taken place within the tent. It is not unlikely he was buried alive, as the Persians had this mode of execution. See Hdt. vii. 114; Περσικὸν δὲ τὸ ζῶντας κατορύσσειν.

CHAPTER VII.

MARCH THROUGH BABYLONIA. — REVIEW OF THE TROOPS.

1. Ἐντεῦθεν, 5. 5. The scene of the trial of Orontes seems to have been at or near Pylæ. — σταθμῷ, sense? — Ἑλλήνων, case 27 444 a. — μέσας νύκτας, 508 a; pl. 489; cf. iii. 1. 33, art. om. 533 d. — ἐδόκει, *he thought* (Lex. 1). — μαχούμενον, tense 598 b. — ἐκέλευε, διέταξε, tense 595. — κέρως, *wing* of the Greeks; case 407. The whole Greek force was placed upon the right of the army. See 2. 15 N. In the sense *to command*, ἡγέομαι has regularly the gen.; but in the more literal sense, *to lead* or *guide*, often the dat.; cf. ii. 2. 8; iii. 2. 20. — τοὺς ἑαυτοῦ, *his own men*, in distinction from the Greeks.

2. ἡμέρᾳ, case 450 a. — βασιλέως: the Greek repeats the noun, instead of substituting a pronoun, more freely than the Eng. — λοχαγούς, 386 c. In a mercenary Greek force, the lochagi had an especial independence and importance, as they commonly engaged the men primarily, and came with them to the standard of the general. Hence we shall find them often in councils of war, ii. 2. 3; iv. 1. 12. — πῶς (complem. 563 s) ἂν τὴν μάχην ποιοῖτο, *how he should fight the battle* (if there should be one, 636 a). — αὐτὸς παρῄνει θαρρύνων (674 b, d) τοιάδε (478), *he himself exhorted and encouraged them as follows*.

3. A brief speech, admirably adapted to produce the effect desired. — οὐκ ἀνθρώπων (see case 414 b) ἀπορῶν βαρβάρων, order 719 a, β. — ἀμείνονας (Lex.) καὶ κρείττους, 211. Cf. λῷον καὶ ἄμεινον, vi. 2. 15. — ὅπως s, 626. — ἐλευθερίας ἧς, case 431 b, 554 a. How sweet the sound upon the Greek ear! and with what flattering emphasis does Cyrus repeat it! — κέκτησθε, 280 b; pret. (Lex. κτάομαι). — ὑπέρ, here inserted, though not usual with εὐδαιμονίζω, to distinguish this use of ἧς from the preceding. — ἴστε, mode? — ἑλοίμην ἄν, 636 a. How gratifying to the honest pride of the Greeks. The subjects of an absolute monarch are all slaves; cf. 9. 29; ii. 5. 38. The aor. here makes the expression more decided; *that I would unhesitatingly choose*, 594 s. — ἀντὶ ὧν ἔχω πάντων, 554 a N., 553.

4. Ὅπως, connecting εἰδῆτε to διδάξω, 624 a. — οἷον, complem. 563 (so οἵους); cf. vii. 4. 1. — κραυγῇ, 698 a. — ἐπίασιν, as fut. (Lex. εἶμι), 603 c. — ἄν, *if*, 619 a. — ταῦτα, the throng and the outcry. — τὰ ἄλλα, *as to all else*, 481. — καὶ αἰσχύνεσθαί μοι (537) δοκῶ (Lex.) οἵους ἡμῖν (eth. dat. 462 e) γνώσεσθε τοὺς ἐς τῇ χώρᾳ ὄντας ἀνθρώπους, *I* [seem to myself even to be ashamed] *may well be ashamed what sort of men for us you will find those in the country to be*. Ὄντας seems to be rather complem. after γνώσεσθε (677 b), than definitive with τούς, as some consider it; and ἀνθρώπους, though placed at the end for strong and contemptuous emphasis, to be directly constructed with οἵους rather than with τούς. Αἰσχύνεσθαι implies *thinking* or *considering*. — ἀνθρώπους, ἀνδρῶν (Lex.), how differing? cf. πολλοὶ μὲν ἄνθρωποι..., ὀλίγοι δὲ ἄνδρες, Hdt. vii. 210 (of the Medes at Thermopylæ). — καὶ εὐτόλμων γενομένων, *and having proved yourselves heroes*. Rehdz. has καὶ εὖ τῶν ἐμῶν γενομένων, *and my affairs having prospered*. — ἐγὼ ὑμῶν, pos. 719 b, ε. — ὑμῶν...ἀπιέναι, *any one of you that wishes to return home*; part. 678 a. — τοῖς οἴκοι (Lex. case 458) ζηλωτόν (Lex.). — τὰ παρ᾽ ἐμοὶ s, 528 a.

28

5. εἶπε, illustrating the freedom which Cyrus permitted in the Greeks, though Gaulites, who is spoken of as "in the confidence of Cyrus," probably spoke simply to draw from him a stronger statement for the assurance of others. — διά...κινδύνου (416 a) προσιόντος, *on account of your being in such* [an emergency of the danger approaching] *imminent danger;* order 719 d, ν. Most MSS. have τοῦ before προσιόντος, which would then simply define the danger; with its omission, the danger is affirmed as approaching; 523. 2, 5. — ἂν εὖ γένηταί τι, *if* [aught shall have resulted well, 617 d] *you gain any success.* — οὐ μεμνῆσθαι, prophetic pres. for fut. 609 b; *v. l.* μεμνήσεσθαι, 686 c. — μεμνῷο, 317 c.

6. Ἀλλ᾽ ἔστι μὲν (Lex.) ἡμῖν, *but there certainly is for us* (extending afterwards implied). — πρὸς μὲν μεσημβρίαν, πρὸς δὲ ἄρκτον, order 720 a; art. om. (so καῦμα, ἄνθρωποι) 533 d, c. — μέχρι οὗ, 557. — διὰ καῦμα, 694. — τά...πάντα, *all the parts between these* limits (or extremes); case 472 d; cf. iii. 4. 31.

7. ἡμᾶς (489 b) δεῖ τοὺς ἡμετέρους (538 a) φίλους τούτων (407) ἐγκρατεῖς ποιῆσαι, *we must make our friends masters of these* domains. — δέδοικα (671 d) μὴ (625 a) οὐκ (686 h) ἔχω. — ὅ τι δῶ, *what* [I may give] *to give*, 642 a; cf. ii. 4. 19, 20. — ὑμῶν, pos.? — στέφανον...χρυσοῦν, a reward in Greece for eminent public services. Compare the lavish promises of Cyrus to the Spartans, Plut. *Artax*. 6.

8. Οἱ δέ, *and they*, i. e. the generals and captains, who reported to their men. — Εἰσῄεσαν, into his tent for more personal and private interviews, which Cyrus was not now in a condition to refuse them. — Ἑλλήνων, case 419 a, 418 b. — σφισιν, 539 a; case 459. — ἔσται, κρατήσωσιν: what the reg. mode? — ἐξήγγελλον, εἰσῄεσαν, ἀπέπεμπε, παρεκελεύοντο: why the ipf.? What arrangement do you here observe? — Ὁ δέ s, 536 b, c. — γνώμην, numb. 488 d; cf. ἐκπλῆσαι τὰς γνώμας αὐτῶν, *Hel.* vi. 1. 15.

9. μάχεσθαι, personally. — ἑαυτῶν, case 445 c. — οἴει (297 f) γάρ, 708 e.

BOOK I. CHAP. VII. 33

— μάχεῖσθαι, i. e. prob., in person. "Why should you so expose yourself, *for do you think that your brother will come out to meet you?*" Some think that giving battle in general is all that is here meant. — νὴ Δία, 476 d. — ἐμὸς ἀδελφός, 538 a. How does this differ from ὁ ἐμὸς ἀδελφός, 6. 8? — οὐκ ἀμαχεί s, *I shall not carry off this prize without fighting for it.* — ταῦτ', to what does this refer? In a military despotism the sovereign must not be suspected of wanting personal valor. Plut. ascribes to Cyrus this reply to the prudent advice of Clearchus: "What do you mean, Clearchus? Do you bid me, in seeking the throne, to show myself unworthy of it?" *Artax.* 8.

10. Ἐνταῦθα δή, *here indeed*, or *thereupon:* δή, time past. — ἐξοπλισίᾳ, either in the night (§ 1), or more prob. during the next day, when preparations for the expected battle could be made more completely and more favorably than during a night alarm. — ἀριθμὸς ἐγένετο, [a numbering took place] *the number was taken,* viz. — ἀσπίς (by meton. for the shield-bearers, Lex. 70 h), πελτασταί, etc., specifications in appos. w. ἀριθμός, 393 d, 395. — μυρία, numb. 240 a. The total of hoplites stated in the note to i. 2. 9 was 9600. If to this number we add the 700 brought by Chirisophus and the 400 who deserted Abrocomas (4. 3), and then subtract the 100 lost by Menon (2. 25), and 200 more for the various casualties of the march, we have the number here given, 10400. The total of lighter troops in the same note was 2300. This number is now increased to 2400, or, acc. to some MSS., to 2500. This increase, unless arising from a different mode of enumeration, may be accounted for by supposing that the hoplites of Chirisophus, according to Spartan usage, had lighter-armed attendants which it was not deemed important to mention (cf. 5. 13 N.), or that some of the baggage-men, as supplies diminished, and the hour of fighting approached, were enlisted into the lighter companies. — μυριάδες, 241, III. — ἀμφὶ τὰ εἴκοσι, 706, 531 d.

11. ἑκατὸν καὶ εἴκοσι μυριάδες, a reported and prob. exaggerated statement. Ctesias, the king's surgeon, stated the number of his troops in the battle as 400000 (Plut. *Artax.* 13); and the historian Ephorus, as quoted in Diod. xiv. 22, as "not less than 40 myriads." The inclusion of camp-followers in the larger and not in the smaller number would make the discrepancy less. — Ἄλλοι, *besides* (Lex.), 567 e; cf. 5. 5.

12. ἄρχοντες καὶ στραγηγοὶ καὶ ἡγεμόνες. Xen. may have used these different terms to show and emphasize the power of these great commanders; or some of them, as Weiske and others suppose, may have crept into the text from explanatory glosses. In general, Abrocomas seems to have commanded the troops of the southwestern part of the empire, Tissaphernes of the northwestern, Gobryas of the southeastern, and Arbaces of the northeastern. — μάχης, case 408. — ἡμέραις s, case 468. The tardiness of Abrocomas was perhaps simply caused by his longer route; but was prob. intentional. The king may have himself suspected this, since he did not think it worth while to wait for him. A reinforcement from the east also came too late; see ii. 4. 25.

NOTES.

13. πρὸς Κῦρον, this is prob. used with ἤγγελλον for the comm. dat. (ii. 3. 19), through the influence of αὐτομολήσαντες, which it also modifies in sense; cf. 399 g; ii. 27. Some, by a harder const., regard it as a direct adjunct of αὐτομολήσαντες, notwithstanding its position. — οἱ αὐτομολήσαντες, 678 a. — ἐκ, παρά, how do these prepositions differ in force? — πρό, μετά, 690. — οἱ...τῶν πολεμίων, gen. partitive w. οἵ, 553. — Difference between ταὐτά and ταῦτα? — What do you observe in the general arrangement of this section? Xen., differing from Ctesias, states his authority.

14. ἐξελαύνει, perhaps on the second day after the night-review, as a single day would give scanty time for the council of war, the private interviews (§ 2, 8), and this march with the defiling of so great an army through a narrow pass (§ 14 s). — τῷ στρατεύματι (case 467), why not with σύν, as in § 1? The prep. is less needed on account of the participle συντεταγμένῳ. — μέσον τόν, 508 a, 523 b, 4. — εὖρος, case 481. — ὀργυιαί, 395 c. The dimensions of Plut. and Diod. are less probable.

15. Μηδίας (Lex.). For a description of this wall see ii. 4. 12. The trench seems to have been dug to this wall from the canal-system mentioned below, and to have received its water from the latter. — διώρυχες. The general statement, ancient and modern, represents the canal-system here connecting the two rivers as flowing from the Euphrates to the Tigris. There is reason for supposing that the canals may have been filled from the Euphrates at the time of its flood (see Appendix at end of vol.); and that, as the rivers sank, flood-gates were closed to retain the water for purposes of irrigation. Hence, the trench may have been connected with the canals rather than with the river, which was now too low to supply it with water. We may add that the flowing of the water from the west end of the canal-system into the trench would present to the eyes of Xen. the appearance of its flowing from the Tigris; and hence, that statement of its direction, which has led so many to question the genuineness of the passage, Ἔνθα δή εἰσιν...γέφυραι δ' ἔπεισιν, is rather an evidence in its favor, since a student adding this would not have been likely to differ from the general account. Cf. the rivers of Babylon, Ps. cxxxvii. See Owen, ii. 4. 13. — τέτταρες, the present number of the main canals from river to river in this region (Nahr-Malcha, or King's Canal, etc.). — διαλείπουσι ἑκάστη (393 d), and [leave each as an interval] *are distant from each other*. — παρασάγγην, 472 or 482. — πάροδος, prob. left to prevent the escape of the water into the river, and perhaps with the intent to occupy the space with a wall, which there was not time to construct. — ποταμοῦ, case? — ποδῶν, case?

16. ποιεῖ, πυνθάνεται, use of tense? — προσελαύνοντα, 677. — παρῆλθε, ἐγένοντο, 495. Cf. iv. 2. 22. — τάφρον, case?

17. Ταύτῃ μέν: no δέ corresp. before § 20. — ὑποχωρούντων, emphat. pos. 719. — ἦσαν, number 569 a. Cf. ἤγοντο, § 20.

18. τῇ ἑνδεκάτῃ ἀπ' (Lex.) ἐκείνης τῆς ἡμέρας (524 b), or ἀπ' ἐκείνης ἡμέρᾳ, reckoning back. Most MSS. show the first ellipsis, but β' the second.

BOOK I. CHAP. VIII. 35

This sacrifice may have taken place during the halt at Charmande, where Cyrus was doubtless aware of the preparations which the king seemed to be making for a standat the trench. — μαχεῖται (mode?) δέκα ἡμερῶν, 433 a. — Οὐκ, why first in the clause? — εἰ ἐν ταύταις οὐ μαχεῖται (631 a) ταῖς ἡμέραις. Many MSS. have here the more regular εἰ μὴ ἐν ταύταις ταῖς ἡμέραις μαχεῖται, 686 b. If οὐ μαχεῖται is genuine, it is an emphatic, perhaps contemptuous, repetition of the words of Silanus, 686 k. εἰ οὐ also vii. 1. 28; vi. 6. 16. — ἀληθεύσῃς, 617 d. — ὑπισχνοῦμαι, a form of expression referring to the future, 631 c. — δέκα τάλαντα, a money of account, = how many darics? = how many dollars? A most lavish gift for a successful prediction, even at the present value of money.

19. ἐκώλυε, tense 594. — τοῦ μάχεσθαι, case 699 f, 405 a (acc. also admissible). The conclusion of Cyrus was natural, as the king had made no opposition at Pylae, and then had relinquished a line of defence prepared with so much labor. Yet, in truth, a narrow pass, unless defended by a strong wall, was the very last place for Persians to risk an encounter with Greeks, as they could not there offset by their superiority of numbers the superior personal prowess of the Greeks. Their best chance for success was in an open plain, which they could scour with their cavalry, and where they could amass their hosts on all sides against the Greeks. — ἠμελημένως, some read ἠμελημένος. — μᾶλλον, 685, 510.

20. πορείαν ἐποιεῖτο (Lex.), 475. — αὐτῷ, for him, i. e. of his army, 463. — στρατιώταις, case 460, 463.

CHAPTER VIII.

BATTLE OF CUNAXA. — DEATH OF CYRUS.

1. ἦν, 571 d. — ἀγοράν, cf. ii. 1. 7. — ἔνθα (550 e) ἔμελλε, 598 a. **31** — καταλύειν, for breakfast; see 10. 19. — ἀνήρ, without art., 525 a. He had been sent forward for observation or some preparation. — ἀνά (Lex.), 695. — ἱδροῦντι τῷ ἵππῳ, case 467 a; order 523 b, 4. — οἷς, numb. 550 f. — ἐνετύγχανεν, ἐβόα, tense? — ὡς εἰς s, 711; cf. § 23; 9. 23. The battle here described was fought, acc. to Plut. (*Artax.* 8), at a place called Κούναξα, 500 stadia from Babylon (but 360 stadia, ii. 2. 6). This may have been the name of the station at which the army of Cyrus was to halt, or of the village mentioned in 10. 11, or these may possibly have been the same place.

2. αὐτίκα, pos.? what modifying? — καί...δέ (Lex.), cf. 1. 2. — σφίσιν, case 699 g. — ἐπιπεσεῖσθαι, subject?

3. Why aorists, and afterwards imperfects? — τοῦ, τόν, τά, τάς, 530 e. — ἵππον, according to Plut., a noble horse, but hard to manage and fierce, named Pasacas (γενναῖον, ἄστομον δὲ καὶ ὑβριστήν, *Artax.* 9).

4. Κλέαρχος: to whom was unfortunately given the chief command of the Greeks in the battle, — prob. the only general who would have there disobeyed Cyrus, ii. 6. 15. — δεξιά, numb. 489 a. — τοῦ κέρατος, *of the wing*, since the whole Greek force formed only the right wing of Cyrus's army. — Πρόξενος δὲ ἐχόμενος (Lex.), and *next Proxenus*, with whom doubtless was Xenophon. — [καὶ τὸ στράτευμα], and *his division*, if the words are genuine. They are certainly not required. — εὐώνυμον s, next to the Persian main body.

5. βαρβαρικοῦ, pos.? — εἰς χιλίους, 692. 5, 706; cf. 1. 10. — ἐν τῷ δεξιῷ, on the right of the Greeks, to join in the pursuit, after the enemy should have been routed. So apparently beyond them, the targeteers, who could operate closer to the river than the cavalry. — ἐν τῷ εὐωνύμῳ, *on the left* of the Greeks, yet constituting the main body of the army.

6. Κῦρος, ἱππεῖς (sc. ἔστησαν), here specially mentioned for the description of their armature, which was rather Greek than Persian. Cyrus was doubtless in or near the centre of the barbarian host (§ 22); and some editors, without MSS. authority, insert κατὰ τὸ μέσον, citing the statement of Diod., Κῦρος ἐτέτακτο κατὰ μέσην τὴν φάλαγγα, xiv. 22. — ὅσον (Lex.), 507 f. — θώραξι, case 466. — μὲν αὐτοί, *indeed themselves*, corresponding to οἱ δ' ἵπποι, in § 7; μέν here preceding the contrasted word, that it may come earlier in the sentence, 720 a. — Κῦρου, case 406 a; cf. 1. 6. — ψιλήν (523 b, 4), *unarmed*, i. e. simply covered with the erect tiara, which he proudly wore as a sign of distinction and dignity, asserting in itself his claim to the throne. This, however, might be so thickly and so firmly fitted as to afford considerable protection. Cf. Ἀποπίπτει δὲ τῆς κεφαλῆς ἡ τιάρα τοῦ Κύρου, Ctesias's account of the battle in Plut. (*Artax.* 11). — [Λέγεται] (cf. 573 a) s, a general statement (corresponding to those in Hdt. v. 49 and vii. 61, and Strabo xv. 3) now thought by many to have crept into the text from a gloss. If genuine, Xen. writes as if from the information of others.

7. οἱ μετὰ Κύρου, *in Cyrus's body-guard*. — μαχαίρας, better shaped for striking, as the ξίφος for piercing. — Ἑλληνικάς, pos.?

8. A description brief, but graphic. — μέσον, δείλη, art. om.? — ἡμέρας, case 416 a. — ἡνίκα δὲ δείλη (533 d) ἐγίγνετο, *but* [when the afternoon was coming on, 594] *early in the afternoon*. — ἐφάνη, *came into sight*, incept. aor. 592 d. — λευκή, μελανία, from the different manner in which the sunlight struck or was reflected from the long cloud of dust. — χρόνῳ (case 463) δὲ συχνῷ ὕστερον, *and a considerable time after*, the period of intent and excited watching doubtless seeming long. Some needlessly conjecture οὐ συχνῷ. — ἐπί (Lex. c). — ἐγίγνοντο, ἤστραπτε, tense? — χαλκός (Lex.) τις, "etwas wie Erz." Rehdz.

9. λευκοθώρακες, *white-mailed* (Lex.). — ἐχόμενοι δὲ τούτων, *and next to these*; case 426. — γερροφόροι, the common Persian infantry, well armed for Oriental warfare, but not for a shock with the iron-clad Greeks, while from their political institutions and habits of life they were no less deficient in spirit, discipline, and physical training. Cf. *Cyr.* i. 2. 13; Hdt. vii. 61. These were bowmen, acc. to Grote. — ποδήρεσι, 722 d. — Αἰγύπτιοι (Lex.). — ἄλλοι s, *and other horsemen and also bowmen*, or,

BOOK I. CHAP. VIII. 37

and others, horsemen and bowmen, 567 e. The asyndeton renders the enumeration less formal, 68 d. — κατά (Lex.), 692. 5. — ἕκαστον τὸ ἔθνος, v. l. ἕκαστον ἔθνος, 522 b, as usual in armies composed of different nationalities. Cf. Hdt. vii. 60. — ἐπορεύετο, uumb. 501 a.

10. ἅρματα, subject of ἐπορεύοντο or ἦσαν understood, to which εἶχον is connected by δέ. Numb. of verb? — διαλείποντα, cf. 7. 15. — ἀπ' ἀλλήλων, 689 b. — δή, *indeed, namely.* — εἰς πλάγιον (sc. μέρος or χωρίον), [to a side quarter] *sideways* (comm. with the idea of obliqueness), *obliquely* (oftener slanting or curving). — ἀποτεταμένα, [extended] *extending* or *projecting* (about two cubits in length acc. to *Cyr.* vi. 1. 30), to mow down standing troops, and sometimes attached to the wheel so as to revolve swiftly. — ὑπό, 689 j. — δίφροις, these were high, to protect the driver, who was also defended by armor so that only his eyes were exposed. — εἰς γῆν βλέποντα, to mangle those who had been thrown down by the rush of the horses. Such a chariot had long axles, that it might be in less danger of being overturned in passing over corpses ; and its driver was protected, as just stated. See *Cyr.* vi. 1. 29 s. — ὡς διακόπτειν, expresses purpose, 671 e. — ὅτῳ, 253. 1 ; case 699 f, 450 a. — γνώμη ἦν, ὡς...ἐλῶντα (sc. ταῦτα), *the plan was* [as though they were going to drive] *that they should drive,* 680 c, 675 d. — διακόψοντα, sc. ταῦτα. Cf. 4. 8.

11. ῟Ο, rel. referring to τοῦτο. — εἶπεν, i. 7. 4. — καλέσας, object? Cf. the fuller, but less frequent, form of expression in 7. 18. In Greek, if two closely connected verbs have a common object, this is usually expressed but once and in the case required by the nearer verb ; cf. 399 g, 536 c. — ἐψεύσθη τοῦτο (case 478 or 481, 586 c), *in this he was mistaken.* — κραυγῇ, case 467 a. — ὡς ἀνυστόν (sc. ἦν 572), *as far as* [was] *possible.* — ἐν ἴσῳ (sc. βήματι, *step*), (Lex.), 695 ; pos. 718 e.

12. ἐν (Lex.), 690. — αὐτός s, simply *himself with P.*, without his body-guard, 540 c, 541 a. — Κλεάρχῳ, case 452. — ἐβόα, tense 595 a. — ἄγειν...εἴη, 659 c, 643 c. — μέσον τό, 523 a, 3. — κἂν τοῦτ' s, 644 b. — νικῶμεν, mode ? — πάνθ' ἡμῖν (case 461) πεποίηται (tense 610 a) = *our work is all done.*

13. 'Ορῶν, ἀκούων, ἔχων, concessive, = *though he saw,* etc., 674. 1, f. — 'Ορῶν, pos. ? — ὁ Κλέαρχος, the subj. of ἤθελεν, yet repeated after the parenthesis, and ἀλλ' ὅμως used as if a finite verb had preceded ; cf. 70 t. — τὸ μέσον στῖφος, order 523 b. The king's horse-guards would be esp. conspicuous, 7. 11. — Κύρου, case 434 a ; cf. 10. 5. — ὄντα, part. ? — εὐωνύμου, case 445 c. Some needlessly omit Ἑλληνικοῦ, as rendering the statement less strong than that below. The truth appears to be that Xen. was so absorbed in the contest between the Greeks and Persians, and esteemed so lightly the barbarian forces of Cyrus, that he leaves the latter mostly out of account in describing the battle, and sometimes seems to speak in general of the army of Cyrus as the Greek army, and of that of the king as the barbarian army ; see § 10, 14, 19, 24. — τοσοῦτον, 485 e, β, 483 ; used rather than the dat., on account of πλήθει, 487 b. — πλήθει, case 467 b. — μέσον τὸ ἑαυτοῦ, *his own centre,* i. e. the centre of his army. — Κύρου, gen. poss. — μὴ κυκλωθείη, 625 a. — ὅτι αὐτῷ μέλοι (v. l. μέλει, 645 a), ὅπως καλῶς ἔχοι (Lex. 624 c), *that he himself was taking care* (even more arrogant than *that he would take care*) *that* [it should have itself well] *all should go well*. The self-willed and insubordinate course pursued by Clearchus to secure himself and the Greeks, left Cyrus with his Persian force to contend with several times the number of similar troops, and made his destruction almost certain. Ὁ δ' αὐτῷ μέλειν εἰπών, ὅπως ἕξει κάλλιστα, τὸ πᾶν διέφθειρεν, is the language of Plutarch, who is esp. severe upon the selfish caution, the folly, and faithlessness of Clearchus. *Artax.* 8. Cyrus prob. understood the reply of Clearchus as expressing an intent to follow his direction, and supposed that all would be well.

14. βαρβαρικὸν στράτευμα, *the Persian host* of the king. Born. and Dind. say "of Cyrus," but it was very unlikely that he would lead his inferior Persian host to the encounter, before the Greeks, upon whom he placed his main reliance, were ready; cf. § 13 N. See Grote's remarks on Clearchus. — αὐτῷ (Lex.). — συνετάττετο s, *was forming from those who were still coming up*, and successively deploying into line. — παρελαύνων, returning from the extreme right, where Clearchus was posted. — πρὸς αὐτῷ s, 541 e, *at a considerable distance even from his own army*. — κατεθεᾶτο ἑκατέρωσε, *took a survey on each side*. What a season of observation, excitement, and suspense!

15. Ξενοφῶν Ἀθηναῖος, wt. art. 525 a; the first mention of the author. Whether he was with his friend Proxenus, or with Clearchus as a mounted aid, or with the few cavalry of the latter, is not stated. His horse, freedom of movement, and relations to Cyrus and the generals, made the service which he now rendered both convenient and fit for him. — ὑπελάσας ὡς συναντῆσαι, 671 a, e. — εἴ τι παραγγέλλοι, *if* [he would command anything] *he had any commands to give*, 648 a. — ἐπιστήσας, McMich. compares "having pulled up." Cf. στήσας τὸ ἅρμα, 2. 17. — ὅτι καὶ τὰ ἱερὰ καλά (sc. εἴη) s, *that both the sacrifices* [esp. the omens from the entrails] *were auspicious, and all the attendant circumstances* [esp. the movements of the victims]. For the generally accepted distinction between ἱερά and σφάγια, see Lex. In such sacrifices, to which both the Greeks and the Romans attached a vital importance, every appearance of the victim had its significance, the manner in which it approached and stood at the altar and received the fatal blow, its fall and dying groans and struggles, the burning of parts upon the altar, and esp. the forms and condition in which the entrails (eminently the vital organs) were found. — καλά, repeated in emphatic confirmation.

16. θορύβου, case 432 a, i; cf. ὁ θόρυβος, 530 a. — τίς, ὅ τι, complem. 563. — εἴη, mode? — [Ξενοφῶν.] If Κλέαρχος, the reading of some MSS., is correct, then this general must also have left the line for conversation with Cyrus; but this seems quite improbable after the previous interview, § 12 s. — τὸ σύνθημα, *the password* for distinguishing friends from foes, in two parts: the sign Ζεὺς Σωτήρ, and the countersign Καὶ Νίκη. Cf. vi. 5. 25; Lat. *tessera*, Virg. *Æn*. vii. 637. — παρέρχεται, παραγγέλλει (mode?).

BOOK I. CHAP. VIII. 39

— δεύτερον: the password was repeated in a low tone by each soldier, from the commander to the end of the line, and then back again, to secure its correct transmission, from the end of the line to the commander; see *Cyr.* iii. 3. 58. It was usually, as here, both religious and animating. — Καὶ ὅς (518 f) ἐθαύμασε, as it should not have been given out without his concurrence; the tense denoting the momentary expression of surprise, rather than the continuous feeling of wonder; but Clearchus was autocratic.

17. Ἀλλά (Lex.). — δέχομαι, *I accept it,* I hail it as a good omen. Cf. accipio, Virg. *Æn.* xii. 260. — τοῦτο ἔστω, [let this be] *so let it be,* = may the result be in accordance with these auspicious words. — οὐκέτι...στάδια (case 482) διειχέτην (568) τὼ (234 e, 492 c) φάλαγγε s, *the two lines* [were no longer distant] *were within three or four stadia of each other.* About what part of a mile? — ἐπαιάνιζον (Lex.). The Greeks were wont to sing the pæan to one or more of the gods (Apollo, Mars, etc.), both before a battle, in anticipation of victory (παιὰν ἐμβατήριος), and after a successful battle, in thanksgiving (παιὰν νικητήριος). — ἀντίοι (Lex.), 509. — πολεμίοις, case 455 f.

18. πορευομένων, sc. αὐτῶν, 676 a. — ἐξεκύμαινε, a metaphor, imitated and commended for its expressiveness and beauty by the ancients; nearly expressed by our *undulated,* more closely by *billowed forth.* — τι (sc. μέρος) τῆς φάλαγγος, some part of the line, 418 b. — δρόμῳ 34 (Lex. case 467 a) θεῖν, *to run* [with running] *outright, to hasten upon the run,* differing from the simple ἔθεον below, not so much in what it expresses, as by its fuller and more emphatic expression, partaking of pleonasm, 69. — ἐφθέγξαντο, *gave a shout.* — οἱόνπερ, case 468 (sc. φθέγμα, *cry*) or 483. — ἐλελίζουσι, from ἐλελεῦ, one form of the war-cry, as ἀλαλάζω (iv. 2. 7) from another form; cf. ὀλολύζω, and our *to whoop, huzza,* etc. — ἔθεον, tense and order? It was for the interest of the Greeks thus to shorten the period of exposure to missiles, and to come as soon as possible to close quarters. — Λέγουσι, Xen. writes here, as elsewhere, as if he had not been present. — ἐδούπησαν, stem 344; cf. iv. 5. 18. So Alexander's soldiers, Arr. i. 6 (where the expression seems to us more natural: τοῖς δόρασι δουπῆσαι πρὸς τὰς ἀσπίδας).— φόβον ποιοῦντες τοῖς ἵπποις (460), [causing terror to] *striking terror into the horses;* acc. to some, seeking to terrify the horses (598 c, 594); esp. those of the scythe-armed chariots.

19. ἐξικνεῖσθαι (Lex.), mode, 703 d, β; i. e. *before they came within bow-shot.* — ἐκκλίνουσιν, ἐδίωκον, ἐβόων, tense? — κράτος (Lex.). — μή, why rather than οὐ? — ἐν (τῇ) τάξει, without art. 533 c. — θεῖν...ἕπεσθαι, order?

20. τὰ μέν, appos. 393 d. — ἡνιόχων (case 414 b), such frightened cowards that they had deserted their chariots, and fled with the rest. Cf. *Cyr.* viii. 8. 25. — προΐδοιεν, mode? cf. 5. 2. — διίσταντο. Alexander bade his soldiers do the same at Arbela, Curt. iv. 13. — ἔστι (Lex.) δ' ὅστις (ἦν δέ τις ὅς, 553, 559 a), *but there was one at least who.* This seems to express the force of this indefinite form of expression, which does not affirm of more than one, and yet does not confine the statement to one. — ἔφασαν, subject 571 c. — οὐδὲ...δέ, neg. corresponding to καί...δέ affirm. (Lex. δέ). — οὐδείς s, neg. tripled? — τις, *a certain one*. The precision of statement here used seems to show that τίς is used to denote a single person, and not vaguely for one or two, or a small number.

21. τό, sc. πλῆθος, μέρος, or στράτευμα. — οὐδ' ὥς (Lex.). — συνεσπειραμένην, pos.? — ποιήσει, mode? — καὶ γάρ (Lex.), 1. 6, 8. — αὐτόν, case 474 b; cf. κρίσιν, 6. 5.

22. μέσον...τὸ αὐτῶν, *their own centre* (i. e. of their own army); gen. poss. 443; cf. 538 a. — ᾖ, χρήζοιεν, mode? — ἄν, 618 c, 658 a. — ἡμίσει χρόνῳ, [by means of] *in half the time*, 466, 469 e.

23. αὐτῷ, case 455 f. — ἀντίου (Lex.). — αὐτοῦ, governed by ἔμπροσθεν: cf. πόρρω, iii. 4. 35. — ὡς εἰς κύκλωσιν, *as if for surrounding* the enemy, 511; cf. § 1; 2. 1.

35

24. δή, force? — τὸ Ἑλληνικόν: Xen. was intent upon the fortunes of the Greeks. Cyrus must have seen that the king's manœuvre would place himself and his barbarian army between two vastly superior forces, and expose them to almost certain destruction. As the Greeks were too much occupied in their petty victory, and too far removed to render him the needed support, his only hope seemed to lie in a bold effort to arrest the king's movement, and bring the battle to a decision by a direct charge upon him. Cyrus has been blamed for his rashness; but his desertion by Clearchus and the Greeks left him no alternative. He must snatch the crown by his personal prowess, or atone for his ambition by death. He almost won. — ἐλαύνει ἀντίος (Lex.), 509; with a general advance, no doubt, of his barbarian troops. — ἑξακοσίοις, § 6. — ἑξακισχιλίους, 7. 11, emphatically added, as showing the great disparity of number. — ἔτρεψε: after the vivid description by the hist. pres. (ἐλαύνει, νικᾷ), the aor. better represents the feat as accomplished. Observe in the graphic account below the repeated interchange of present and past tenses. — αὐτὸς...ἑαυτοῦ, 541 h. — Ἀρταγέρσην, who, acc. to Plut., advanced against Cyrus with insulting and threatening words, and hurled his javelin against him with great force. The javelin which Cyrus sent in return pierced Artagerses through the neck.

25. In the all-absorbing excitement of hand-to-hand fighting, it was natural for each soldier to press on as he could; and a commander lost, in great measure, the power of directing and controlling the movements of his men. — ὁμοτράπεζοι, see Voll. and Rawlinson.

26. τὸ ἀμφ' ἐκεῖνον στίφος, *the crowd about him;* i. e. his more immediate attendants, as ὁμοτράπεζοι, etc., gathering close about him for his protection. — ἡνιόχετο, aor., since all was here momentary (Lex. ἀνέχω). — Τὸν (530 a) ἄνδρα ὁρῶ, tense 603 a. — ἵετο, not perhaps mere impulse in the heat of the engagement, since it was almost certain that he would be overwhelmed in the ocean of the opposing army, unless he could gain a personal victory over the king. (On παίει, vii. 4. 9 w. 6.) — τιτρώσκει, with a spear two-fingers'-breadth deep, acc. to Ctesias (Plut. *Artax.* 11), the king having first hurled his javelin in vain at Cyrus. Ctesias adds

BOOK I. CHAP. IX. 41

that the king fell from his horse, and that he himself, with others, attended him out of the fight. — καί, a loose connection by co-ordination, instead of a closer by subordination, which indeed Cobet gives by inserting ὅς before καί. — ἰᾶσθαι (660 c) αὐτὸς (case 540 e, 667 b). — φησι, order?

27. τις, Mithridates, a young Persian, acc. to Ctesias. Wounds added by others made it doubtful who slew Cyrus. Artaxerxes himself jealously asserted the honor, and when Mithridates and a Carian claimed it, gratified the vengeance of Parysatis by giving them up to a death of lingering tortures. A like fate befell Masabates (Bagapates in Ctes. *Pers.* 59), a faithful eunuch, who by order of the king cut off the head and right hand of Cyrus, and whom Parysatis artfully won from the king in a game of dice. See Plut. *Artax.* 14 s. This hand-to-hand fight of the two brothers has been compared to that of Eteocles and Polynices, the sons of Œdipus, for the crown of Thebes. — μαχόμενοι (mode 580) βασιλεύς, left without a finite verb, and independent, through anacoluthon, 402 a, 675 f. What case with the part. would have here given a regular construction? Some would rather refer the construction to 395. — ἀπέθνησκον (one after another), ἀπέθανε, tense? Diod. states that more than 15000 of the king's army were slain in this battle, mostly by the Greeks; and that of the barbarian force of Cyrus about 3000 fell; but of the Greeks not one perished, and only a few were wounded. — ἔκειντο, i. e. in death; so often κεῖμαι, jaceo, *lie*, etc.

28. ὁ πιστότατος αὐτῷ (453) s, *the* [attendant most faithful to him] *most devoted attendant of his wand-bearers.* — περιπεσεῖν αὐτῷ, case 450 a; cf. 699 g. Cf. super amici corpus procubuit, Curt. viii. 11; Virg. *Æn.* ix. 444.

29. Κύρῳ, 699 a. — ἑαυτόν, 583; with the idea seemingly implied, here and before, of immolation to the dead (Lex. σφάζω). Cf. *Cyr.* vii. 3. 11 s. — σπασάμενον, voice 579. — χρυσοῦν, *a gilt* poniard. — στρεπτόν, etc. cf. 2. 27.

CHAPTER IX.

XENOPHON'S PANEGYRIC ON CYRUS.

1. μέν (Lex.). — παρά (Lex.), 586 d, 694. 9; an acknowledgment being regarded as proceeding from the speaker; cf. ἐκ (ii. 6. 1). — **36** Κύρου...ἐν πείρᾳ, [in the knowledge of Cyrus by experience] *personally acquainted with Cyrus.* Κύρου is governed by πείρᾳ (Lex.); observe the order.

2. μέν, corresp. to the first δέ in § 6 or in § 7. — πάντα, case 481; order 719 b, ϵ. Observe the use of the definite tenses in the description of character in this chapter (and in ii. 6. 25; 592 a), a description which seems in general correct of Cyrus, as he appeared in his ambition for the throne. How he would have shown himself in the actual possession of it, is, perhaps fortunately for his reputation, an unwritten chapter of history. — κράτιστος, hence regarding himself as more worthy to reign than his brother.

3. ἐπὶ ταῖς βασιλέως θύραις, *at the king's court*, kept there largely as hostages for their fathers' loyalty. — καταμάθοι ἄν, *might learn*, 636 a. — αἰσχρόν, ἔστι, pos.? — οὔτ' ἀκοῦσαι οὔτ' ἰδεῖν ἔστι, [it is possible neither to] *one can neither hear nor see anything base*, or, *there is nothing base to be either heard or seen*, 633 g, — a picture belonging, acc. to Xenophon's own statement in Cyropædia (viii. 8. 12 s), to the early rather than the later Persian court, though we may hope that the gross corruptions of the later Persian court were in large measure hidden within from the youthful pages. Cf. the early system of Persian education in *Cyr.* i. 2. 2 s.

4. ἀκούουσι, *hear of.* — εὐθὺς (Lex.) ; cf. ii. 6. 16 ; iv. 6. 14. — μανθάνουσιν (mode 671 d), in this atmosphere of absolute authority and unquestioning obedience, so different from that which surrounded the Athenian boy. Abuse of freedom in Athens inclined Xen. to see the advantages of a more arbitrary government.

5. αἰδημονέστατος (pos.?)...τῶν ἡλικιωτῶν, [the most respectful of his equals] *more respectful than any of his equals*, 515. — μέν, corresponds to what? — τοῖς τε πρεσβυτέροις (case 455 g) καὶ τῶν ἑαυτοῦ (case 408) s, *and to be more obedient to his elders than those even who were lower in rank than himself.* — ἵπποις, case 466 b. — Ἔκρινον, subject, 571 c. — εἰς τὸν πόλεμον, [tending into war] *preparatory to war, for war*, 694. — ἔργων (Lex.) ; gen., obj. w. φιλομαθέστατον and μελετηρότατον, 444 a. — τοξικῆς, art. om.?

6. Ἐπεὶ δὲ τῇ ἡλικίᾳ (case 453) ἔπρεπε, i. e. when he had passed from the class of παῖδες, *boys*, into that of ἔφηβοι, *youths, young men*, which was usually, acc. to *Cyr.* i. 2. 8, at the age of 16 or 17, but must have been earlier in the case of the precocious Cyrus. — ἄρκτον, not necessarily a *she-bear*, as the word is comm., epicene, 174 a. — ἐπιφερομένην (Lex.), 578 a. — τὰ μέν (sc. πάθη), *some* [*injuries*, or *hurts*], 478 ; not followed by τὰ δέ, as there is a change in the form of expression : τέλος δέ s. — πρῶτον, adj. or adv.? — πολλοῖς (case 458) μακαριστόν (Lex.) ; cf. τοῖς οἴκοι ζηλωτῶν, 7. 4. N.

7. Explain use of tenses in this section. — στρατηγὸς...ἀπεδείχθη, voice, 586 c ; cf. 1. 2. — μέν, to which the first δέ in § 11 may correspond. — αὐτόν, case 474 b ; cf. i. 8. 21. — περὶ (Lex., 692. 4) πλείστου ποιοῖτο (Lex.), voice 579. — ποιοῖτο, σπείσοιτο, mode ? — συνθοῖτο, 315 c (v. l. συνθεῖτο) ; not implying, like σπείσοιτο, previous hostility. — τῷ = τινι, 253. 1. — μηδὲν ψεύδεσθαι, *to* [falsify nothing, 478] *prove false in nothing*.

8. Καὶ γάρ (Lex.) οὖν, introducing a consequence in confirmation of what has been before stated. — αἱ πόλεις (generic, 522 a ; so the contrasted οἱ ἄνδρες) ἐπιτρεπόμεναι, *cities, on being committed* (or committing themselves) *to his charge*, nearly = the cities which were committed (by the king, or committed themselves) to his charge. — ἐπίστευον δ' οἱ ἄνδρες (sc. ἐπιτρεπόμενοι), *and individuals reposed full confidence* in him. Observe the emphatic repetition of ἐπίστευον.

9. Τοιγαροῦν and καὶ γὰρ οὖν have nearly the same force ; though

BOOK I. CHAP. IX. 43

strictly the connective power is somewhat more prominent in the former, and the confirmative power in the latter. — ἐπολέμησε, *had engaged in war*, inceptive 592 d. — αἱ πόλεις, the Greek cities in his neighborhood, those of Ionia; see 1. 6. — τοὺς φεύγοντας, 1. 7; the partisans of Cyrus, who had been banished by Tissaphernes and his partisans. — ἐφοβοῦντο, 582 β; apprehending the revenge which he might take in their behalf.
10. Καὶ and καί may correspond as *both, and: for he both showed by his conduct and expressly declared.* — προοῖτο, form 315 c; mode?—ἐπεὶ ἅπαξ... ἐγένετο, *after he had once become*, ind. as referring to a definite fact; cf. 641. Observe the distinction between the definite ἅπαξ, *once for all*, and the indefinite ποτέ, *at any time*. — μείους, *fewer* in number. — ἔτι (emph. repeated) δὲ κάκιον πράξειαν (Lex.), *and should be still less fortunate.*
11. Φανερός (Lex., 573) δ' ἦν, καὶ..., νικᾶν πειρώμενος, *he* [was apparent] *showed himself...endeavoring to outdo.* — ἦν, ποιήσειεν, modes 634 d, b. — ἀγαθόν, αὐτόν, case 480 b. — εὐχήν (pos.?) δέ τινες αὐτοῦ ἐξέφερον, ὡς (702 a) εὔχοιτο (mode 643, tense?), *some indeed* [brought out from his society] *reported a prayer of his, how he prayed.* "Similes orationis redundantias in deliciis habent Græci." Kühn. — τοσοῦτον χρόνον, emphatically pleonastic. — χρόνον, case? — ἔστε νικῴη (form 293 c; mode 641 d; tense 612)...ἀλεξόμενος, *until he* [should have outdone, requiting] *had outdone by requital*; ἀλεξόμενος, properly of requiting evil, but here, by zeugma (68 g), of returning both evil and good. The returning of good for evil has found little place even in the theory of heathen morality. Would that it were not so limited in the practice even of Christians! How many, while they praise the Gospel rule, follow the worst part of the precept of Isocrates (1. 26): Ὁμοίως αἰσχρὸν εἶναι νόμιζε, τῶν ἐχθρῶν νικᾶσθαι ταῖς κακοποιΐαις, καὶ τῶν φίλων ἡττᾶσθαι ταῖς εὐεργεσίαις. But Cyrus, from his ambition, failed signally of making a due return for the mildness and forgiveness of his brother.
12. πλεῖστοι (art. om. 533 e) δὴ αὐτῷ, ἑνί γε ἀνδρὶ (512 c, 393) τῶν ἐφ' (Lex. a, 690) ἡμῶν, ἐπεθύμησαν...προέσθαι, *the greatest number certainly desired to intrust to him, at least for a single individual* [of those] *in our time*; cf. § 22. — δή, often with superl.
13. Οὐ μὲν (Lex.) δὴ οὐδὲ (713 c) τοῦτ' (544) ἄν τις εἴποι (mode 636 a), *not indeed surely could any one say even this.* — τούς, not repeated, as the adjectives together describe a single class, 534. 4. — πάντων, case 420 c. — ἦν ἰδεῖν, [it was possible to see (Lex. εἰμί), 571 f] *one might see;* cf. 5. 2. The Persians were exceedingly rigid and severe in punishment; and a young ruler, with his limited knowledge of the springs of human conduct, is in danger of relying too exclusively upon the principle of rewarding the good and punishing the bad. Cf. Cæs. *B. G.* vii. 4, at end. — ποδῶν, *of feet*, one or both; τῶν ποδῶν, *of their feet*, would have implied both. — ἐγένετο (Lex. γίγνομαι), 571 f. — "Ελληνι, case 459. — μηδὲν (686 d) ἀδικοῦντι (Lex.), *if he did no wrong*, condition, 635, 674. — τις, [any one] *he*. In general reference the Greek often uses an indef. where the Eng. prefers a pers. pron.; cf. i. 9. 18. — προχωροίη, agreeing w. ὅ τι, or impers.

NOTES.

w. ἔχειν understood (Lex.); mode 641 b; form 293 c. There seems to be esp. reference here to valuable articles of traffic, the conveyance of which is attended with special risk.

38 **14.** γέ (Lex.); cf. γὲ μήν, § 16, 20. — ἀγαθούς, pos.? — ὡμολόγητο, pers. const. for impers., 573; it [had been acknowledged and settled] *was without dispute that he honored*, 599 b, c, 268; cf. vi. 3. 9. — πρῶτον μέν (Lex.), left without the regular sequence. If these directly modified ἐποίει, and ἦν αὐτῷ πόλεμος was changed to ὄντος αὐτῷ πολέμου, the correspondence with ἔπειτα δέ would be more regular. — καὶ αὐτός, *even in person*. — οὕς, as indef. 550 a; the relative clause preceding, 551 c. — ἑώρα, augm. 279 b. — ἧς, attr. 554 a. — χώρας, 551 c. — δώροις, case 466.

15. ὥστε s, *so that* (in the domain of Cyrus) *the brave appeared the happiest of men, and the cowardly were deemed fit to be their slaves*. — οἴοιτο, mode? — Κῦρον, more emphatic than the pronoun.

16. Εἴς (Lex.) γε (Lex.); cf. § 20, and γε μέντοι, § 14. — εἴ τις αὐτῷ (case 454 d) s, *if any one appeared to him desirous of exhibiting it*. — γένοιτο, ἐποιεῖτο, mode, etc., 634 b, d. — περί (Lex.). — τούτους, [these] *such persons*, numb. 501; cf. αὐτούς 4. 8. — ἐκ, denoting source, *from* or *by means of* (Lex. ἐξ), cf. ἐκ τοῦ δικαίου, § 19.

17. αὐτῷ, case 460. — τε (Lex.)...καί (Lex.), *both...and especially*. — διεχειρίζετο, pass., used of a series of measures, while ἐχρήσατο and ἔπλευσαν have reference to a single expedition, viewed as a whole, 591 s. — Καὶ γὰρ στρατηγοί s, *for indeed* (or both) *generals and captains did not sail to him* [for the sake of money] *for their mere wages, but* [since] *because they* (657 k) *knew that to serve Cyrus well was more gainful than the pay by the month*; cf. § 20.

18. Ἀλλὰ μήν (Lex.) εἴ τίς γέ (accent 787) τι (case 478), *nay truly, if indeed any one rendered any good service* [to him having commanded] *upon his command, he never left* [to any one the zeal, 460; cf. § 13 N. τις] *his zeal unrewarded*. — ὑπηρετήσειεν, mode? — εἴασε, aor. to deny a single instance, and not merely the habit; the more positive, because ἄν is not added, as in § 19 w. ἀφείλετο. — κράτιστοι δή, *the* [best certainly] *very best*; cf. § 12, πλεῖστοι δή. — ὑπηρέται παντὸς ἔργου, *supporters of*, or, *in every work*, 444. — Κύρῳ...γενέσθαι, *to* [have come to] *belong to Cyrus*, 459.

19. ὁρῴη, ἀφείλετο (616 c), προσεδίδου, 634 b, d, e. — δικαίου (Lex.). — ἄρχοι, mode 641 b (v. l. ἄρχει 651. 1). — χώρας, 551 c; cf. § 14 (sc. τὴν χώραν, 480 c). — οὐδένα ἂν πώποτε ἀφείλετο, *he would never take away from* [any one, cf. § 18] *him*; cf. ἔστασαν ἄν, 5. 2. — ἐπόνουν, i. e. his vassals, local administrators. — καί...αὖ, *and still further*. — ἥκιστα, *least of all*, or, *not at all*. — ἔκρυπτεν, sc. ταῦτα, 480 c. — πλουτοῦσιν, case 456. — ἐφαίνετο, *he showed himself not envying*, with impf., fact or not? — ἀποκρυπτομένων, tense? Observe the pairs of kindred words, φανερῶς... ἐφαίνετο, χρῆσθαι...χρήμασι. The Greek often seeks an echo of sound which in English would rather be avoided. We shall also find frequently that the near repetition of the same word, even if not specially emphatic, was more agreeable to the Greek ear than it is to the English.

BOOK I. CHAP. IX. 45

20. Φίλους, seems not so much the direct object of θεραπεύειν as the noun expressed in the relative clause (which here precedes, 551 c), and placed first for emphasis: [friends at least certainly as many as he might have made] *and certainly whatever friends he made.* The same noun, with τοσούτους or τούτους (cf. ὅσα...τούτων § 23), also belongs to the antecedent clause, where it is governed by θεραπεύειν. — ποιήσαιτο, voice? mode? — συνέργους εἶναι (sc. τούτου, cf. § 21). — ὅ τι τυγχανοι (Lex.) s, *co-workers* [of that whatsoever] *in whatever he* [might happen to] *desired to effect.* — πρός, w. pass., 586 d (rare in Att. prose). — ὁμολογεῖται, pers. 573. — κράτιστος...θεραπεύειν, *the best* [to cherish] *for, or, in cherishing,* 663 d or e.

21. αὐτὸ τοῦτο (481 b), *with respect to this very end,* explained by the appositive clause, ὡς συνεργοὺς ἔχοι. — οὕπερ αὐτὸς ἕνεκα φίλων s, *for the sake of which he thought that he himself needed friends,* 719 a, β. — ἔχοι, mode 624 c. — συνεργὸς τοῖς φίλοις (451 b, 699 f)...τούτου (case 444 a), *co-worker with his friends for that.* — ὅτου, case 432 e ; form ?

22. Δῶρα (pos. ?) s, 512 c. — οἶμαι, form 313 e. — διὰ πολλά (Lex.); the oriental usage of approaching the great with presents, combining with the attractiveness of his personal character the example of his own generosity, and the influence of his exalted prospects. — πάντων, case 420 c. — διεδίδου, tense? form 315 b. — τρόπους (*v. l.* τρόπον), 488 d. — καί (sc. πρὸς τοῦτο) ὅτου, case 414 b, c.

23. τῷ σώματι (460, so ἀνδρὶ below) αὐτοῦ (538 f) κόσμον (394 b), *as an equipment for his person.* — ἢ ὡς εἰς πόλεμον ἢ ὡς εἰς καλλωπισμόν, *either* [as he would send for war] *for use in war or for mere embellishment,* ὡς marking the purpose of the giver. Cf. 2. 1 ; iv. 3. 11. — τούτων, as antecedent of ὅσα, 550 d. — οὐκ ἂν δύναιτο, [would not be able, 636 a] *could not.* — κοσμηθῆναι, etc., see § 19 N. φανερῶς...ἐφαίνετο. — νομίζοι, w. 2 acc. 480 a.

24. τὸ μέν s, *that he surpassed his friends in conferring* [the] *great benefits is nothing wonderful.* — ἐπιμελείᾳ, case 467 b. — φίλων, case 491 c, 699 f. — ταῦτα, *this,* in appos. with τὸ περιεῖναι, 505 b ; numb. 491 c ; perhaps the plur. rather on account of the two particulars mentioned, or the many examples in his life.

25. ἔπεμπε, ἔπεμψε, tense ? Cf. διέφθειρον, διέφθειραν, iii. 3. 5. — λάβοι, mode ? — λέγων, through the messenger, to whose own words the construction changes in τοῦτον s. In Persia presents from the king's table were esteemed great honors, and esp. if he had himself partaken of the same dish. See *Cyr.* viii. 2. 4 ; iv. 5. 4. — οὕπω δή, [not as yet certainly] *certainly not.* — χρόνου, 433 a ; cf. δέκα ἡμερῶν, 7. 18. — οἴνῳ, case 450, 699 g. — σοί (σέ § 26), the accent renders the message more courteous. — σὺν οἷς s, 551 f.

26. ἡμίσεα, subst. (Lex.). — Τούτοις ἥσθη, *enjoyed these,* case 456. — τούτων, case ?

27. ἐδύνατο, force of ind. here ? — διὰ τὴν ἐπιμέλειαν, *through the care which he exercised,* or, as some think, through their care for him. — ὡς μὴ πεινῶντες...ἄγωσιν (mode 645 a, 650), [that they may not being hungry] *that hungry animals might not carry his friends.* "Love me, love my" horse.

28. Εἰ...ποτε, *if at any time,* = ὁπότε, whenever, 639 a. — πλεῖστοι, *very many.* — δηλοίη (mode? form?) οὖς (563) τιμᾷ, mode?—Ἑλλήνων, from οὔτε naturally connected as part. gen. w. οὐδένα. Some connect with πλειόνων.

29. τούτου, τόδε, 544. — παρά, 689 d. — δούλου ὄντος, [being] *though a slave,* or *subject,* since in an absolute government all the subjects are simply slaves; cf. 7. 3; ii. 5. 38. Τὰ βαρβάρων γὰρ δοῦλα πάντα πλὴν ἑνός. Eur. *Hel.* See *Œcon.* iv. — ἀπῄει, cf. ἀπῆλθον, 603 c; and observe chiasma. — καὶ οὗτος δή, ὅν (pos. 551 c) ᾤετο πιστόν οἱ,...ἑαυτῷ, 537; αὐτόν less emphatic than τοῦτον, the emphasis falling rather on ταχύ, 540 g; cf. οἱ... αὑτούς, ii. 5. 27. — φιλαίτερον, form 261 e; w. dat. 456. See 6. 3. — παρὰ δὲ...ἀπῆλθον, 699 c. — καὶ οὗτοι (554 a) s, *and these indeed men who were especially beloved by him* (the king). — τιμῆς, case?

30. τεκμήριον, pred. appos. 534. 3. — τῇ τελευτῇ τοῦ βίου (523 c). — αὐτῷ (460, 464) γενόμενον, *happened to him at the end of his life.* — ὅτι, connects its clause to τεκμήριον: for arrangement see 719 d. — τοὺς πιστούς s, art. 534. 4.

31. Ἀποθνῄσκοντος, ἀπέθανον, tense?— γάρ, *for* = *namely* (Lex.), 705 b. — αὑτοῦ, αὐτόν, Κύρου. Cf. 6. 11. — ὑπέρ, 693. 7. — ἔφυγεν, to the camp (see 10. 1); having before fought bravely, Diod. xiv. 24. — ἔχων = *with,* 674 d, b. — τὸ στράτευμα πᾶν, 523 e. The characteristics ascribed to Cyrus in this chapter are those of a young, talented, intelligent, energetic, generous, ardent, and ambitious prince, straining every nerve to win honor and popularity, and highly successful in gaining them. It is not wonderful that they were greatly fascinating to a knightly adventurer like Xenophon, beginning already to conceive a disgust at democracy; or that they should have obscured or palliated to his mind some faults, if not crimes, which Cyrus also pressed into the service of his ruling passion, ambition. To what lengths this passion would have carried him, had he reached the throne, we can only conjecture. He would, we must suppose, have been himself the ruler of his vast empire, governing it with an absolute sway, yet, in general, just and generous; he would have striven to enlarge its limits, and to put down all rebellion within them. He would have been a seducing and dangerous neighbor to the Greeks; and might have thrown far into the future, if he could not prevent, the conquest of Persia by Greece. He might have been in reality, as in name, a second Cyrus on the throne. It is evident, at least, that Xenophon took him as a model for the ideal character presented in the Cyropædia (see Introduction).

CHAPTER X.

CONTINUANCE OF THE FIGHT.—THE GREEKS REPULSE THE PERSIANS.

1. ἀποτέμνεται, zeugma, 497 b ; acc. to a law of the Persians, says Plut. (*Artax.* 13), i. e. the head that had plotted treason, and the right hand that had executed it. For the fate of the eunuch who cut them off by the king's order see 8. 27 N. The king is said to have seized the head by its abundant hair, and held it up to confirm his wavering followers and arrest those who were fleeing. The head and hand were afterwards exhibited on a pole, iii. 1. 17. — χεὶρ ἡ δεξιά, 523 a 2, 3 (*v. l.* ἡ χεὶρ ἡ δεξιά). — Βασιλεὺς δὲ καὶ οἱ σὺν αὐτῷ διώκων εἰσπίπτει, an unusual zeugma, in which καὶ οἱ σὺν αὐτῷ seems parenthetic, unless, with some, we regard it as inserted by mistake from § 2, where the plur. follows ; 497. — Κύρειον = Κύρου, 443 c. — οἱ μετὰ Ἀριαίου (those with A. =), *A. and his troops,* 527 a. — σταθμόν, the second night-station after passing the trench, § 19 s. — τέτταρες s, [there were said to be four parasangs of the way] *the distance was said to be four parasangs.*

2. τά τε ἄλλα πολλὰ διαρπάζουσι, *both plunder the other valuables to a large amount.* — λαμβάνει, *takes* for his harem. Why the change of number in the verbs ?

3. ἡ νεωτέρα, *the younger* of the two. Cyrus showed his preference for the Greeks, even in the selections for his harem, which, so far as appears, was very small for a Persian prince. Cf. Esth. ii. — ἐκφεύγει γυμνή (Lex.), *escapes out of their hands in her under-dress,* leaving with them her robe. — πρὸς τῶν Ἑλλήνων, [on the side of, or in view of] *towards the Greeks;* not *to them,* as πρός w. the acc. would denote, for they seem, upon the sight, to have left the baggage which they were guarding, and to have rushed forward in battle line to repel the invaders, and save their employer's favorite. Many supply τούτους before τῶν Ἑλλήνων, making a hard ellipsis, and impairing the sense ; (yet cf. Hdt. i. 110 ; *Hel.* v. 1. 11.) — ἀντιταχθέντες, *formed* (or as mid., *forming themselves*) *in opposing line.* — ἁρπαζόντων (Lex.). — οἱ δὲ καὶ αὐτῶν, and [others] *some of them also.* — μήν (Lex.). — ἄλλα ὁπόσα ἐντὸς αὐτῶν s, *whatever else was brought within their line, both property and persons.* — ἔσωσαν, a natural and somewhat emphatic repetition. The part which the Milesian had in bringing about this result is playfully exaggerated in vi. 1. 13.

4. διέσχον ἀλλήλων, case 405 a. How many miles ? — τε, not translated into Eng., since the pred. applies only jointly to the subject. — οἱ Ἕλληνες, the main body. — οἱ μὲν (518 d)...πάντας νικῶντες (Lex.), *these* (the Greeks) *pursuing the opposite wing, as if victorious over all* the king's troops ; by a mistake which cost Cyrus his life. In such cases, the sense must determine whether οἱ μέν refers to the nearer or more distant subject. — οἱ δ' ἁρπάζοντες s, *those* (the king and those with him, § 1 s, 499 e)

plundering, as if they were now all victorious (viz. the whole army). See 9. 19 N (at end).

5. ᾔσθοντο, *became aware;* perhaps through a distant view of the turmoil, perhaps through information from the nearer peltasts, § 7 s. — Τισσαφέρνους, case 434 a; cf. 8. 13. See § 8. — τὸ καθ' αὑτούς, sc. μέρος or στράτευμα. — εἰς τὸ πρόσθεν οἴχονται (612, mode ?) s, [are] *were gone forward in pursuit.* — πλησιαίτατος, of the generals, 8. 4; form 257 d. — πέμποιεν, mode 648 a. — ἀρήξοντες, purpose, 598 b.

6. Ἐν τούτῳ (Lex. ἐν), 506 a. — δῆλος ἦν προσιών, *was* [evident] *seen approaching.* — ὡς ἐδόκει, ὄπισθεν, *from behind* (i. e. to take them in the rear), *as it seemed.* — παρεσκευάζοντο, ὡς ταύτῃ προσιόντος (sc. βασιλέως, gen. abs., 676 a), *as though he would come that way,* καὶ δεξόμενοι, *and they would receive him,* 676 b, a strongly idiomatic passage, illustrating, as McMich. remarks, the power of ὡς with the part. "to express complex ideas with elegance, brevity, and precision." (See 1. 11.) Some have προσιόντες, prepared to advance this way and receive, etc. (Hickie.) — ὁ, to correspond better in form with οἱ μὲν Ἕλληνες, used from its familiar association w. δέ at the beginning of a clause; see 533 b: easier than βασιλεὺς δέ. — ἦγεν, voice 577 c. — ᾗ (sc. ὁδῷ, 467 a) δὲ παρῆλθεν ἔξω τοῦ εὐωνύμου κέρατος (case 445 c), ταύτῃ καὶ ἀπήγαγεν, *but by what route he passed beyond the left wing, by this he also* [led back] *returned;* cf. 8. 23. — ἀναλαβών, at or near the camp. — τοὺς...κατὰ τοὺς Ἕλληνας αὐτομολήσαντας, *those who deserted* [over against] *to the Greeks,* ii. 1. 6 ; regarding the battle, doubtless, as decided in favor of Cyrus.

7. διήλασε...Ἕλληνας (adj. 506 f) πελταστάς, [rode through] *charged along the river against and through the Greek peltasts.* — αὐτούς, *them,* i. e. Tissaphernes and his corps, 499 c; cf. § 4. — γενέσθαι, *to have proved himself.*

8. ὡς μεῖον (Lex.) ἔχων ἀπηλλάγη, *as he* [withdrew having the worst] *came off at disadvantage.* Cf. iii. 4. 18. — οὐκ ἀναστρέφει, which would have exposed him to further loss. See ii. 3. 19. — τὸ...τό, 523 a, 2.

9. κατὰ s, *near the left wing of the Greeks,* beyond it, or by its side, § 6; the left wing as before named, strictly the right as the men now stood. — μὴ (Lex.) προσάγοιεν s, *that they might make an attack upon the wing, and infolding it on both sides cut them* (the Greeks) *to pieces.* The Persians must have been already moving towards this, or their great army could not have been so soon in the position stated in § 10. — ἀναπτύσσειν τὸ κέρας, *to fold back the wing,* by counter-marching or a quarter-wheel, so that the line should be parallel to the river instead of being at right angles to it. — καὶ ποιήσασθαι ὄπισθεν τὸν ποταμόν, *and bring the river in their rear,* so that they could no longer be enclosed.

10. Ἐν (Lex. 557 a) ᾧ δὲ ταῦτα ἐβουλεύοντο, *but while they were planning these measures* of safety, though they had not yet reached their intended position on the river's bank. — παραμειψάμενος, *having changed to the same form,* or, *position,* i. e. having brought his line parallel to the river. — κατέστησεν ἀντίαν...συνῄει, *stationed his line opposite, just as at*

BOOK I. CHAP. X. 49

the first he came to the battle, i. e. the relative position of the two lines was the same, the direction of both having been similarly changed. Some connect εἰς τὸ αὐτὸ σχῆμα with κατέστησεν and ὥσπερ. — τὸ πρῶτον (529 a) μαχούμενος (purpose 598 b). — ὄντας, sc. αὐτούς, referring to φάλαγγα, 499 a. — προθυμότερον ἢ τὸ πρόσθεν (529 b), having proved their cowardice.

11. ἐκ πλέονος, sc. διαστήματος (Lex. πολύς). See 8. 19. — κώμης, not improbably the place which Plut. calls Cunaxa. The present identification of a mere village could not, of course, be expected.

12. γήλοφος : this "appears to have been one of the numerous artificial mounds, topes, or tels, sometimes sepulchral, sometimes heaps of ruins, which abound on the plain of Babylonia." Ains. — πεζοί, in appos. w. oἱ. — τῶν δὲ ἱππέων (case 586 c) ..ἐνεπλήσθη, by change of const. for ἱππεῖς δέ ὦν, to strengthen the expression, 716 c ; the infantry still fleeing, cf. § 15, while the array of cavalry hid from the Greeks the movements behind. — τὸ ποιούμενον, *what was doing.* — βασίλειον, 443 c, cf. Κύρειον, § 1. — ἀετόν (Lex.). The indef. τινα, *a certain,* or *kind of,* seems to imply that the representation was not very artistic, or was indistinctly seen : nearly = *what appeared to be a golden eagle*. The royal standard of Persia is described in *Cyr.* vii. 1. 4, as ἀετὸς χρυσοῦς ἐπὶ δόρατος μακροῦ ἀνατεταμένος. — ἐπὶ πέλτης ἐπὶ ξύλου, *on a target uplifted upon a pole*. Some give to πέλτης the unusual sense of spear, regarding ἐπὶ ξύλου as an explanatory gloss brought into the text.

13. λείπουσι, *begin to leave ;* ἐψιλοῦτο, *was gradually thinned ;* ἀπεχώρησαν, *had departed :* beginning, progress, end, order, chiasma. — ἄλλοι (Lex. ἄλλος c), 567 d ; ἄλλοθεν, *in different directions* (the Greek mode of conceiving direction was often the opposite of ours) ; or from different points of the hill, *one here and another there*.

14. ἀνεβίβαζεν, tense 594 a. — ὑπὸ αὐτόν, acc. on account of previous motion implied, 704 c. — Λύκιον, one of his few horsemen. — κατιδόντας τὰ (prolepsis, 474 b) ὑπὲρ (Lex. a) τοῦ λόφου, τί ἐστιν (sc. ταῦτα, 502, cf. ii. 1. 22), *having observed from above* [the things beyond the hill, what they are] *the condition of things beyond the hill*.

15. ἤλασε (Lex.), 476 2. — ἀπαγγέλλει, pres. more important. — ἀνά (Lex.). — ἥλιος, without art. 533 a.

16. ἅμα μέν...Καί (§ 17) (for ἅμα δέ), 716 b. — φαίνοιτο, mode 643 a. — ἀπό, not παρά. — καταληψόμενόν τι, *to seize some* [thing] *advantage*, 598 b.

17. αὐτοί, belongs in force with ἄγοιντο and ἀπίοιεν, rather than ἐβουλεύοντο, *and for themselves they consulted*. — τὰ σκευοφόρα ἐνταῦθα ἄγοιντο, *they should bring their baggage there* by a detachment sent for it, or, *should have their baggage brought there*, 579, 581. — αὑτοῖς, subject of ἀπιέναι, as well as indirect obj. of ἔδοξεν, 667 b ; and so used emphatically.

18. ἡμέρας, a day so fatal to the ambitious hopes of Cyrus and his Greeks, and ultimately to the Persian Empire by exposing so decisively its weakness even at home. How the great lesson of this battle was applied by Alexander is familiar to all. It is wonderful that the Persian kings had not anticipated him by applying it themselves to a new armature and discipline of their troops after the Greek model. With their vastly inferior arms of both defence and offence it was impossible that these should stand, however brave, against an iron-clad and iron-tempered host. — καὶ εἴ τι, *and especially whatever*, 639 a; cf. 5. 1. — σφοδρά, pred. adj. (v. l. σφόδρα), *in severe form*. — ἐλέγοντο, pers. const., 573 d. — καὶ ταύτας, *even these*, 505 b, c.

44

19. What examples of chiasma ? — μέν, corresp. to δέ, ii. 1. 2. — νύκτα, case 699 a.

BOOK II.

FROM THE DEATH OF CYRUS TO THE BREAKING OF THE TRUCE BY THE PERSIANS, AND THE TREACHEROUS SEIZURE OF THE FIVE GENERALS.

CHAPTER I.

THE GREEKS OFFER TO PLACE ARIÆUS ON THE THRONE. — DEMANDS OF THE KING. — ANSWER OF THE GREEKS.

45

1. Ὡς...ζῆν, subject of δεδήλωται. — Ὡς μὲν οὖν, *how*, or, *in what way, then,* since we have come to this point in the history (see page 3 of notes, as to divisions into books, summaries, etc.); μέν introduced by the writer of this section as a new correlative to δέ, § 2; see i. 10. 19 N. — Κύρῳ, for *Cyrus*, by various Greek commanders, 460. — ἐστρατεύετο, *was preparing an expedition*, 594. — τὰ πάντα, 478. — νικᾶν (Lex.). — Κῦρον, case 666. — τῷ ἔμπροσθεν (v. l. πρόσθεν), Lex. 526.

2. Ἅμα (Lex.). — πέμποι, χρή, mode ? v. l. πέμπει: see Rehdz. — πρόσθεν, i. 10. 5. — ἕως, *until*. — συμμίξειαν, mode 641 b; cf. i. 10. 16.

3. ὄντων, sc. αὐτῶν, 676 a; cf. i. 6. 1; 2. 17. — Προκλῆς, decl. 219 c. — ἀπό, 693. 6. Compare simple gen. of father (i. 1. 1), and gen. w. ἀπό of more remote ancestor. — Ταμώ (v. l. Ταμῶ), case 438 a; form ? — ἔλεγον, of course to the generals. — τέθνηκεν, "the ind., as *oratio recta*, puts the fact in its sad actuality; with the less important event the mood relaxes to the natural opt." Kendrick. — ὅθεν, 550 e. — λέγοι, ὅτι...ἀπιέναι φαίη (somewhat more positive than λέγοι), 659 h. — ἄλλη (Lex. ἄλλος).

46

4. ἀκούσαντες, [πυνθανόμενοι], tense ? — βαρέως (Lex.). — Ἀλλ' ...ἐστί: How characteristic of the unyielding Clearchus : ἀλλ', [but this is our reply] *well!* spoken sadly, but not dejectedly. — ὤφελε s, 611, 638 g. — ἡμεῖς γε (685 b) νικῶμεν (Lex.), 612. — εἰ μή s, 615 a, c. — ὑμεῖς, emphatic. — καθιεῖν, 305 a. — τῶν γὰρ μάχῃ νικώντων (443 a) s, *for to*

BOOK II. CHAP. I. 51

those who conquer in battle it also belongs to rule. How large a part of history is summed up in these few words!
5. Χαρίσοφον, his fellow-countryman, and from the leading state in Greece, i. 4. 3. — αὐτός, 540 c. — φίλος καὶ ξένος, *a friend and guest.*
6. Οἱ μέν, see i. 1. 9 N. — Κλέαρχος...περιέμενε, *waited* with the army for their return; cf. § 2 s. — κόπτοντες, numb. 449 a. — ξύλοις (394 b) δ' ἐχρῶντο, μικρὸν (Lex. 482 d) προϊόντες ἀπὸ τῆς φάλαγγος (sc. ἐκεῖσε, 551 f) οὗ (Lex. ὅς) ἡ μάχη ἐγένετο, τοῖς τε ὀϊστοῖς, *and, going forth a short distance from their line to the place where the battle was fought,* [as fuel they used] *they gathered for firewood both the arrows.* — ἐκβάλλειν (Lex.), lest they should do mischief in their rear or at the camp. — αὐτομολοῦντας, i. 10. 6. — πολλαὶ δὲ καὶ πέλται καὶ ἅμαξαι (cf. i. 10. 18) ἦσαν φέρεσθαι (depending on ἦσαν or ἔρημοι) ἔρημοι, *and there were also many deserted targets and wagons* [to be carried off] *which they could take,* apparently left at the camp by the fleeing troops of Ariæus, i. 10. 1. — κρέα, double relation, 399 g. — ἐκείνην τήν, 524 b.
7. ἀγοράν (cf. i. 8. 1) καί, 705 : *when it was now...there come ;* cf. i. 8. 8. — παρά, as sent by them. — οἱ ἄλλοι, in appos. w. κήρυκες, and then a distinct sentence, 716 c. — ἦν δ' αὐτῶν s, *but* [of them P. was one] *one of them was Phalinus, a Greek; but among* [of] *them there was one Greek, Phalinus.* If Ctesias was in the company, as he claimed, he did not make himself known; Plut. *Artax.* 13. — ἔχων (Lex.). — τῶν, case 432 b, cf. 444 a. — ὁπλομαχίαν, wt. art., 553 c.
8. ἰόντας (cf. i. 1. 7 N.) ἐπὶ τὰς βασιλέως θύρας εὑρίσκεσθαι ἄν [= ἐάν] τι δύνωνται ἀγαθόν, *to go* (as suppliants) *to the king's gate* 47 (his quarters or residence) *and find* (favor if they can find any) *whatever favor they can.*
9. τοσοῦτον, *simply this* (Lex.), 544, 547; assuming an air of superiority. — οὐ τῶν νικώντων εἴη τὰ ὅπλα παραδιδόναι : observe the emphatic arrangement of this brief and truly Spartan reply, one worthy of Leonidas: *not for conquerors is it their arms to surrender.* The following words were addressed aside to the other generals. — ὅ τι κάλλιστόν τε καὶ ἄριστον ἔχετε, [whatever you have to say that is both most honorable and best] *as you can most honorably and advantageously.*
10. Κλεάνωρ...πρεσβύτατος, of the generals present. Sophænetus, said to be the oldest of the generals (vi. 5. 13 ; v. 3. 1), was probably absent. — ἄν, 622 b. — παραδοίησαν, 293 a. —'Ἀλλ' ἐγώ, ὦ Φαλῖνε, θαυμάζω, order 718 a, b, c, d. — τί δεῖ (Lex., yet see 571 h) αὐτὸν αἰτεῖν (tense 595 a), καὶ οὐ λαβεῖν. To the demand of Xerxes at Thermopylæ, Πέμψον τὰ ὅπλα, Leonidas replied, Μολὼν λάβε, "*Come and take them.*" Plut. *Apoph. Lac.* 11 ; Wks. iii. 277, ed. Didot. — ἐὰν αὐτῷ ταῦτα χαρίσωνται, *if they grant him this favor.*
11. αὐτῷ, case 455 f; yet possibly 459. So placed for emphasis. — ἀρχῆς, case 430 a. — μέσῃ, 508 a ; cf. i. 2. 7 N. μέσον. — πλῆθος ... (sc. τοσοῦτον) ὅσον s, *a multitude so great* [as] *that you could not slay them, even if he should bring them to you* for that purpose.

NOTES.

12. Ξενοφῶν (v. l. Θεόπομπος: see the Lex. to 7 Bks. of Anab.). Diod. ascribes these words to Proxenus, Xenophon's friend, iv. 14. 25. — σύ, slightly emphatic, in distinction from ἡμῖν, 536. 1 ; cf. § 16. — οἰόμεθα ἂν (621 a)...χρῆσθαι, *we think that we could use.* — ὅπλα, first emphatic, then παραδόντες, making chiasma. — παραδόντες δ' ἂν (621 b). — παραδώσειν, sc. ἡμᾶς om. after ἡμῖν. — ἀλλὰ σὺν τούτοις, *nay, with these* to sustain us ; cf. ἔχοντες, § 20, iii. 3. 8.

13. φιλοσόφῳ (case 451 a), in discoursing of ἡ ἀρετή and τὰ ἀγαθά, said ironically and sneeringly. — οὐκ ἀχάριστα (Lex.), 478 ; cf. 686 i. — ἴσθι (form 320 a) μέντοι ἀνόητος ὤν, *but know that you are senseless* (or lacking in sense), 677 a. — οἴει, form ? — δυνάμεως, case ?

14. ἐγένοντο, mode 645 a. — βασιλεῖ (case 454 d) ἂν πολλοῦ (case 431 b) ἄξιοι γένοιντο, mode 631 d. — εἰ βούλοιτο, *if he chose.* — εἴτε θέλοι, *whether he wished* (Lex. ἐθέλω.). — ἄλλο τι χρῆσθαι, *to employ them for any other service* (Lex.), 478. — Αἴγυπτον (Lex.). — συγκαταστρέψαιντ' ἂν αὐτῷ, *they would* [subdue it with him] *aid him in his plans of conquest;* used with direct reference to the conquest of Egypt, cf. 68 g.

15. ἀποκεκριμένοι εἶεν, mode ? form ? — ὑπολαβών, *breaking in,* discourteously. — ἄλλος, appos. 393 d. — λέγει, numb. 501 a. — ἡμῖν εἰπὲ (accent, 781 d), τί λέγεις, *tell us, what* [you say] *is your reply.*

16. ἄσμενος (Lex.), 509 c. — οἶμαι, parenthetic. — σύ τε γάρ s, 497 b. — τοσοῦτοι (547)...σὺ (1. 12 N.) ὁρᾷς, *being* [so many] *so great a number as you see* for yourself ; said to impress him with the greater respect, cf. iii. 1. 36. — συμβουλευσόμεθά σοι, *we* [advise with you] *ask your advice.* — περὶ ὧν = περὶ τούτων ἅ, 554 a N.

17. συμβούλευσον, tense 592 b. — ἀναλεγόμενον, ὅτι, [being] *when it is recounted* [namely], *that;* ἀναλεγόμενον and the sentence following (as an appositive) agree with ὅ, in place of a more independent construction ; cf. 573, 676 b. — συμβουλευομένοις συνεβούλευσεν (cf. i. 9. 19 N.) αὐτοῖς τάδε (544), *upon their consulting him, advised them* [the following] *so and so* (as the narrator would proceed to state) : act., I counsel with another for his sake, advise him ; mid., I counsel with another for my own sake, consult him. — Οἶσθα, form 297 b, 46 a, e. — δέ = γάρ, cf. 705 a. — ἀνάγκη λέγεσθαι s, *whatever you may advise* [it is a necessity that it should be reported] *will of course be reported in Greece,* which was all the world to the honor-loving Greek.

18. αὐτὸν τὸν πρεσβεύοντα, *the very person who was acting as envoy,* 540 c, 678 a. — αὑτοῦ, pos. 538 f.

19. Ἐγώ, emphatic, and, as Voll. thinks, with perhaps a delay upon the word : *as to my opinion.* — τῶν μυρίων, 531 d. — μία τις (strongly expressed, sc. ἐλπίς)...σωθῆναι (sc. ὑμᾶς, 667 e) s, [any single] *a single chance* [to be saved] *of escaping in a war with the king.* — ἄκοντος βασιλέως, *against the will of the king,* 676 a, cf. i. 3. 17. — συμβουλεύω, μὴ παραδιδόναι, pres. with pres., as in § 18 aor. w. aor. — συμβουλεύω σώζεσθαι ὑμῖν ὅπῃ δυνατόν (sc. ἐστιν), *I advise you to save yourselves* [in what way it is possible] *in the only possible way.*

BOOK II. CHAP. II. 53

20. τάδε, in distinction from ταῦτα, though explained by a dependent clause, 544 ; so § 21. — εἰ μὲν δέοι, *if it should behoove us to be friends to the king*, if we are to be friends. — φίλοι, in appos. w. ἡμεῖς, the subject of εἶναι, 667 b. — πλείονος (case?) ἂν ἄξιοι εἶναι φίλοι (case 667 b), *that we should be* [friends worth more] *worth more as friends*. — πολεμεῖν, tense?

21. ὅτι μένουσι μὲν ὑμῖν αὐτοῦ σπονδαὶ εἴησαν, *that* [to you remaining here there is an armistice] *remaining here you have an armistice*. — προϊοῦσι καὶ (cf. ἡ § 23) ἀπιοῦσι, *advancing* [and] *or retreating*. — Εἴπατε, see use of aorists, Lex. φημί. In what forms is this first aor. most common? — ὡς πολέμου ὄντος, 680 c.

22. καὶ ἡμῖν ταὐτὰ δοκεῖ, ἅπερ καὶ βασιλεῖ, [the same things seem best to us also, which also seem best to the king] *we also are pleased with the same terms as the king*, 714. 2. — Τί οὖν ταῦτά ἐστιν ; 502. — ἔφη, Ἀπεκρίνατο, the asyndeton suits the quick interchange of rapid dialogue. — σπονδαί, sc. εἰσιν, borrowed from τί οὖν ταῦτά ἐστιν ; — ἀπιοῦσι, sc. ἡμῖν.

23. Σπονδαί...πόλεμος, order? — ποιήσοι, mode 643 a.   It is interesting in this specimen of ancient diplomacy to see how craft is met by craft. The first object on the king's side was to frighten the Greeks into an unconditional surrender ; the second, to induce them to remain where they were till the toils could be drawn around them ; the third, to learn their intentions. All these failed. On the other hand, Clearchus did not draw such advice as he wished, but could hardly have expected, from Phalinus.

CHAPTER II.

THE GREEKS JOIN ARIÆUS TO RETURN TO IONIA. — NIGHT PANIC.

1. Οἱ παρὰ Ἀριαίου ἧκον, [the men from A. came] *the envoys returned from A.* — δέ = γάρ, cf. 1. 17. — αὐτοῦ (Lex.), adv. explained by παρὰ Ἀριαίῳ. — ἔμενε, prob. to concert with his intimate Ariæus plans for their own private interest, 1. 5 ; 6. 28. — ἑαυτοῦ βελτίους, *superior to himself*, esp. in rank. — ἀνασχέσθαι, 659 b. — αὐτοῦ βασιλεύοντος, case 432 f, 461 b. — ἀλλ' εἰ βούλεσθε, 644 b. — νυκτός, case ? — εἰ δὲ μή, *but if you do not come*, otherwise (Lex. μή), 717 c.

2. Ἀλλ' οὕτω (rather than ὧδε, 544, 547) χρὴ ποιεῖν, *well, so it is proper to do*. — πράττετε ὁποῖον ἄν τι (Lex.) ὑμῖν s, 537 b.   There is hence a change in the form of construction.

3. ἡλίου, 675. — τοὺς στρατηγοὺς καὶ λοχαγούς, viewed as belonging to the single class of commanders, 534. 4 ; cf. 5. 25. — Ἐμοὶ θυομένῳ ἰέναι, [to me sacrificing for going] *when I sacrificed in respect to marching*. — οὐκ ἐγίνετο (Lex.). — ἐγώ, see σὺ ὁρᾷς, 1. 12. — νῦν πυνθάνομαι, *I now learn* = have learned, 612.   He had been wrongly informed, or supposed a canal to be the Tigris. — ἐν μέσῳ, *between* (Lex.). — Οὐ μέν (Lex.) ; cf. i. 9. 13. — οὐκ ἔστιν ἔχειν, [it is not possible to have] *we cannot have.* — ἰέναι, *for going*.

4. ποιεῖν, δειπνεῖν, sc. ὑμᾶς or ἡμᾶς. — **ἐπειδὰν δὲ σημήνῃ** (sc. ὁ σαλπιγκτής, 571 b; mode 641 a)..., **ὡς ἀναπαύεσθαι,** to deceive the enemy's scouts, 671 a. — **κέρατι** (Lex. κέρας, σάλπιγξ). — **τὸ δεύτερον,** sc. σημήνῃ. — **ἀνατίθεσθε,** sc. τὰ σκεύη. — **τρίτῳ** (Lex.), 506 e. The Romans, in like manner, used three signals in starting, Polyb. vi. 40. 2 s. — **ἔπεσθε τῷ ἡγουμένῳ,** follow your leader, i. e. the one who precedes you in the appointed order of the march. Some make τῷ ἡγ. neut., see Lex. — **πρὸς τοῦ ποταμοῦ,** for greater security. — **τὰ ὅπλα** (Lex.). — **ἔξω,** on the outside.

51 **5. τὸ λοιπόν** (Lex.), 485 e, ε, 482 a. — **ὁ μὲν ἦρχεν** s, he (Clearchus) commanded, and the rest obeyed, 518 d. — **ἔδει,** sc. φρονεῖν: some read δεῖ.

6. ἥν, case, 477. — **τῆς Ἰωνίας,** [of] in Ionia, 418 a. — **τρεῖς καί** s, 242 a. — **ἐλέγοντο,** pers. const. This section is thought by many to have crept into the text from a marginal note. The numbers correspond nearly, but not exactly, with the summary of those presented in the preceding book. — **εἰς Βαβυλῶνα,** Plut. states the number as 500.

7. Θρᾷξ (Lex.). — **ἱππέας,** the small body of cavalry in the division of Clearchus, all the Greeks had, and now esp. needed, i. 5. 13. — **εἰς,** i. 1. 10. — **ὡς,** i. 2. 3.

8. τοῖς ἄλλοις ἡγεῖτο, led [the way for] the rest, marched at their head, 463; cf. i. 7. 1 N. κέρως. — **πρῶτον,** in returning; see 1. 3. — **εἰς,** w. place, **παρά,** w. persons (Lex.). — **ἐκείνου στρατιάν,** his army, in distinction from the other, 542. — **μέσας νύκτας,** i. 7. 1. — **ἐν τάξει θέμενοι** s, resting arms in battle-array, for security, i. e. ordering their men so to do (Lex. τίθημι).

9. σφάξαντες, βάπτοντες, tense? — **λύκον** (Lex.) **καὶ κάπρον**: Some have objected to this statement the difficulty of procuring these wild animals for the occasion. But in ancient military operations sacrifices held such a place that proper victims were deemed an essential part of an army's outfit. It was a Greek usage to give special solemnity to an oath by a combined sacrifice of three animals (τριττύς, cf. the Roman su-ove-taur-ilia); and the Persians seem here to have added a fourth, — which, however, did not secure their good faith. — **εἰς ἀσπίδα,** [into] over a shield, so that the blood flowed into it (Lex. ἀσπίς), 704 a; cf. iv. 3. 18, and Æsch. Theb. 43. — **ξίφος, λόγχην,** thus consecrating their weapons to that union and mutual defence which was symbolized by the mingled sacrifice and confirmed by their oaths. Among the Scythians, acc. to Hdt. iv. 70, contracting parties dipped their weapons into their own mingled blood, and then drank it.

10. Ἄγε (Lex.), 577 c. — **καί,** 705 c. — **εἰπέ, τινά** s, 564. — **πότερον** (Lex.), 685 c. — **ἄπιμεν** (as fut. 603 c), (sc. τὴν ὁδόν, case?) **ἧνπερ,** shall we return by the same route as we came? — **ἐννενοηκέναι δοκεῖς;** do you think that you have devised? — **κρείττω,** emph.

11. Ἤν, sc. ὁδόν, cf. § 10. — **ἀπιόντες,** cond. 635. — **ὑπάρχει** (Lex.) γὰρ νῦν ἡμῖν (case 459) **οὐδέν** s, for we have now [on hand to start with] none of the needed supplies. — **σταθμῶν τῶν,** case 433 e; art. 523 a, 3; i. e. from

BOOK II. CHAP. II.   55

Corsote, i. 5. 4. — ἔνθα δ' εἴ τι ἦν, *and even if there was anything there.* Some adopt the needless conjecture of Schneider, ἔνθα δέ τι ἦν, and where there was anything. — μακροτέραν, sc. ὁδόν. — τῶν δ' ἐπιτηδείων s, *but* (one in which) *we shall not want supplies,* cf. 705.   **52**

12. Πορευτέον δ' (sc. ἐστίν, 572) ἡμῖν (case 478) τοὺς πρώτους σταθμοὺς (cuse 482 d) ὡς ἂν δυνώμεθα μακροτάτους (i. 2. 4), *we must* [march] *make the first stages as long as we can.* — ὡς πλεῖστον, *as far as possible,* 482 d. — ἢ τριῶν ἡμερῶν ὁδόν, 445 a, 482 d. — οὐκέτι μὴ δύνηται (*v. l.* δυνήσεται) βασιλεύς, *the king will certainly no longer be able* [there is no danger that, etc.], 627. — ἔγωγε, note triple emphasis.

13. Ἦν δὲ αὕτη ἡ στρατηγία οὐδὲν ἄλλο (case 472 f) δυναμένη (part. 679 a), ἢ (701 l) ἀποδρᾶναι ἢ (701 d) ἀποφυγεῖν s, *now this mode of leadership* [was equivalent to] *meant nothing else than to escape by stealth or by speed; but fortune* [led them more honorably] *proved a nobler general.* For she led them not only on their way and to villages, but still farther (ἔτι δέ) to the neighborhood of the king's army, over which they obtained a new and bloodless triumph. — ἐν δεξιᾷ...ἥλιον, prob. in a northeasterly direction, towards the Tigris, — for supplies, since the region of the Euphrates was exhausted. A simple northerly direction, which so many here understand, is not required by the text, and would not, in any probability, have brought them to the king's army. — ἅμα (Lex.) ἡλίῳ, cf. τῷ ἡλίῳ § 16, 533 a. — τοῦτο, cf. i. 8. 11 N. ἐψεύσθη.

14. Ἔτι δέ, *but moreover, but yet more,* with reference to ἐστρατήγησε κάλλιον. — ἀμφὶ δείλην (Lex.), *towards evening* is about as precise as the Greek. — ἔδοξαν s, *they thought they saw horsemen of the enemy.* — τῶν τε Ἑλλήνων, οἳ μὴ ἔτυχον...ὄντες, *both* [those] *such of the Greeks as happened not to be.* — μή, w. ind., in a conditional relative clause, 686 b, 641; cf. v. 7. 2.

15. Ἐν ᾧ, sc. χρόνῳ, [during what time] *while* (Lex. ὅς), 557 a. — ὡπλίζοντο, tense 593. — εἰσιν, νέμοιντο (numb. 569 a, i. 2. 23), mode 645 c. — ἐστρατοπεδεύετο, tense 646 b. — καὶ γὰρ καί (not a frequent combination; *v. l.* καὶ γάρ) s, *and the rather because smoke also appeared,* 709. 2.

16. μέν, emphasizing ἐπί : what corresponds to this μεν ? — ἀπειρηκότας, cf. i. 10. 16. — ὀψέ (Lex.), 571 d. — οὐ...οὐδέ (Lex.), *not at all, not even,* 713 c ; cf. i. 9. 13. — τῷ ἡλίῳ, cf. § 13. — εἰς, with κατεσκήνωσεν, which implies entrance into. — διήρπαστο, pos. 719 b, ς. The king's army, in its vast demand for supplies, had here quite anticipated the Cyreans. — αὐτὰ τά s, 540 c. — ἀπό, 704 a. The Eng. *from* may be used with the same const. præg.   **53**

17. τρόπῳ τινί, *in some fashion,* or, *with some method.* — ὕστεροι σκοταῖοι, 509 a. — ὡς ἐτύγχανον (sc. αὐλιζόμενοι) ἕκαστοι, ηὐλίζοντο, *lodged as they* [each happened] *severally chanced.* — ἕκαστοι, plur., as referring to each company rather than each individual. — κραυγὴν s, 671 d : to show the distinctive force of the inf., ἀκούειν might be trans. *could hear.*

18. ἐδήλωσε (Lex.), *showed itself.* — οἷς...ἔπραττε, *by what he did,* 554 a N., 466.

19. φόβος, *a panic*, so named from PAN, who was believed to send such terrors (e. g. into the Persians at Marathon). — (sc. τοιοῦτος, 495) οἷον εἰκὸς. (sc. ἐστι, 572) s, *such as* [it is natural should arise] *naturally arise upon the occurrence of a panic.*
20. κήρυκα s, *the best herald of* [the men or heralds of] *his time.* — τοῦτον, 505 c. — σιγὴν κατακηρύξαντα, the usual introduction to a proclamation. — ὅτι, needless, as the form of direct quotation follows, 644 a. — ὃς ἂν τὸν ἀφέντα s : Some editors prefer the reading ἀφιέντα as more pointed, and translate, that whoever will make known the man that is letting an ass loose among the heavy arms shall receive, etc. This joke of Clearchus has a keen double sense. It seems to refer to the presence of an ass among the deposited arms, but really to the presence of an ass's spirit among the men at arms (τὰ ὅπλα = οἱ ὁπλῖται, § 4). — ὅτι, pos. 719, b, η. Cf. i. 6. 2.
21. κενός, σῶοι, 523 b : chiasma. — εἰς τάξιν τὰ ὅπλα τίθεσθαι, *to stand to their arms in order* (εἰς, as coming into order). — ᾗπερ (469 b or 469) εἶχον, *just* [where they had themselves] *as they stood*, in the same relative position, i. 8. 4.

CHAPTER III.

NEGOTIATIONS BETWEEN THE PERSIANS AND GREEKS: TREATY CONCLUDED.

54 1. Ὃ δὲ δὴ ἔγραψα...τῷδε (case 466, *v. l.* τῇδε) δῆλον ἦν, *and now what I wrote* (2. 18) *was evident* [by] *from this.* — τῷδε...γὰρ s, 705 b. — ἐκέλευε : which effected nothing, 595 a.
2. τυχὼν (Lex.) τότε...ἐπισκοπῶν, *who was just then inspecting.* — σχολάσῃ, mode 641 d, 645 a : the tone of a superior, who was granting the interview as a favor.
3. ὥστε s, *so that it was in a fine condition to be seen* [as] *a compact line throughout.* — τε, τε, correspondence of each ? — τοῖς ἄλλοις στρατιώταις ταὐτὰ ἔφρασεν, *and directed* [the same to the other generals] *the other generals to do the same.*
4. ἀνηρώτα, force of the ipf.? — βούλοιντο, mode 643 a. — ἥκοιεν, ἔσονται, mode 645 b. — ἄνδρες, οἵτινες (550 b) s, *men duly empowered both to report the communications from the king to the Greeks.*
5. Ἀπαγγέλλετε τοίνυν, *report then*, roughly echoed to ἀπαγγεῖλαι. — μάχης δεῖ, 571 d. — ἄριστον (pos. ?) γάρ s, *for we have no breakfast.* — οὐδὲ ὁ τολμήσων, *nor is there* [he] *the man that will dare;* a threat even for the king himself. — μὴ πορίσας s, [not having provided] *until he has provided a breakfast*, 686 d. — ἄριστον...ἄριστον, pos. ? A sentence so returning to its first word was termed by the Greek rhetoricians κύκλος, *a circle*.
6. ᾧ, cf. τῷδε, § 1. — δῆλον, gend. 491 a. — ᾧ ἐπετέτακτο s, *to whom it had been committed to make these negotiations.* — ἔλεγον : which of the fol-

BOOK II. CHAP. III. 57

lowing finite verbs have the form appropriate to indirect discourse, and which to direct? — δοκοῖεν...βασιλεῖ, *seemed to the king*. — ἥκοιεν, i. e. the messengers. — αὐτοὺς...ἄξουσι (sc. ἐκεῖσε) ἔνθεν ἕξουσι, *would conduct them to a place from which they would obtain*. Cf. i. 3. 17, ὅθεν.

7. εἰ αὐτοῖς τοῖς ἀνδράσι (450 a) σπένδοιτο ἰοῦσι καὶ ἀπιοῦσιν, *whether he* [Clearchus] *was making a truce simply with the men* [who were] *coming and going*. A truce was sometimes simply so made for purposes of conference between contending parties. Cf. Thucyd. iv. 118. 6. — τοῖς ἄλλοις ἔσοιντο σπονδαί, *the truce should* [be] *extend to the rest*. — **55** τὰ παρ' ὑμῶν, cf. § 4.

9. ταχύ, emphatically repeated (from § 8). — ἔστ' ἂν ὀκνήσωσιν, *until they* [shall have] *become afraid ;* tense 592 d; mode? — μὴ (625 a) ἀποδόξῃ ἡμῖν...ποιήσασθαι, *lest we decide not to make*. How does ποιήσασθαι differ from ποιεῖσθαι above?

10. οἱ μέν, the Persian guides. — στράτευμα ἔχων ἐν τάξει, to guard against treachery. — τάφροις καὶ αὐλῶσιν (Lex.), see 4. 13 N. — ὡς μή, i. 5. 10. — ἦσαν ἐκπεπτωκότες, 679 a, β. — τοὺς δέ, for ἄλλους δέ: cf. i. 5. 13.

11. ἐνταῦθα ἦν Κλέαρχον (474 b) s, i. 6. 5, *there* [it was to observe] *was an opportunity of observing Clearchus*, who had now come to the front. — ἐπεστάτει, augm. 282 c. — τὸ δόρυ, art. 530 d. — βακτηρίαν, often used for discipline by Spartan officers. Cf. i. 5. 11. — εἴ τις s, 634. Cf. i. 9. 19. — πρὸς τοῦτο, *to this work*, viz. of bridging the streams. — ἔπαισεν ἄν, cf. i. 9. 19 N. — μὴ οὔ, 713 f.

12. πρὸς αὐτοῦ, some read πρὸς αὐτό. — οἱ τριάκοντα ἔτη (Lex.) γεγονότες, a loose form of expression, if the text is correct, for the men who were not more than thirty years old, from whom the most active service was required. Cf. vii. 3. 46.

13. μὴ ἀεὶ οὕτω πλήρεις...ὕδατος, *not always so full of water*, **56** especially at this season. — οὐ γὰρ ἦν ὥρα, οἵα τὸ πεδίον ἄρδειν, *for it was not* [such a time as was for irrigating] *a proper time to irrigate the plain ;* the period of summer irrigation having now past. — τούτου, referring to the preceding clause, which is the motive of ἀφεικέναι. It was the pride and policy of Clearchus, throughout this adroitly managed transaction, to act the conqueror, and to show the Greeks superior to any effort which the king could make.

14. ὅθεν, 550 e. — σῖτος, *food*, of grain, dates, etc. — οἶνος φοινίκων (case 412), *palm wine ;* cf. i. 5. 10.

15. ἔστιν ἰδεῖν, cf. i. 5. 2. — τὸ κάλλος καὶ τὸ μέγεθος, 481, 533 f (v. l. τοῦ κάλλους καὶ μεγέθους), *for beauty and size*, 429 b. — ἠλέκτρου (case 406 a) = τῆς ἠλέκτρου ὄψεως, 438 b. For the comparison of color it is indifferent in which of its two senses the word is here used, amber or an amber-colored metal. — τὰς δέ τινας (Lex.), *and certain others ;* v. 7. 16. — ἀπετίθεσαν, *were storing*. The Cyreans arrived at the time of the date harvest. — ἦν, for ἦσαν, on account of τραγήματα, 500 : *these were also a pleasant* [thing with, 502] *accompaniment to drink*, — in the symposium, which in ancient, as in modern times, so often followed a feast.

NOTES.

16. τὸν ἐγκέφαλον, see Lex.; *medullam*, Pliny, xiii. 9. — τοῦτο, 502; sc. βρῶμα; but cf. i. 5. 10 N. — ὅθεν (cf. § 14) ἐξαιρεθείη, mode ? — ἐξηναίνετο, 606 a; used with reference to the time of observation; *v. l.* ἀναίνετο.

17. ἧκε, numb. 497 b; tense, cf. i. 2. 6. — ὁ τῆς s, 523 a 1, 442. — γυναικός, Statira, daughter of Idernes, saved by the prayers and tears of her husband from the general execution of her family by Darius II. on account of the crime of her brother Terituchmes. She had much influence over Artaxerxes, and often opposed the schemes of the wicked Parysatis, by whom she was at length poisoned while sitting at the same table, and partaking of the same bird, — this having been divided by a knife smeared on one side (Ctes. *Pers.* 53 s, 61). — ἔλεγε πρῶτος, 509 f; and with consummate cunning.

18. ὦ ἄνδρες Ἕλληνες, 484 g; cf. i. 3. 3. — Ἑλλάδι, case 450 a, but gen. iii. 2. 4. — εἰς πολλά (Lex. 702 c) κακὰ καὶ ἀμήχανα, *into many and inextricable evils*, or, *difficulties*. Some editors omit κακά before καί. —

57 εὕρημα s, 633 d. — αἰτήσασθαι (cf. § 25, vii. 6. 30) δοῦναι ἐμοὶ ἀποσῶσαι ὑμᾶς, *obtain by entreaty* [that he would grant me to restore] *the privilege of restoring you safe*. Compare aor. αἰτήσασθαι with impf. § 19. — Οἶμαι γὰρ ἂν οὐκ ἀχαρίστως μοι ἕξειν, 620 b (*v. l.* ἔχειν), s, *for I think* [it would not have itself ungratefully] *there would be no lack of gratitude to me, both either from yourselves*.

19. ὅτι, ὅτι, different force? how differing ? — δικαίως ἄν μοι χαρίζοιτο, sc. εἰ χαρίζοιτο, should he do this, 636 b. — ἤγγειλα, mode ? cf. i. 2. 4; rare with part. — διήλασα, καὶ συνέμιξα, cf. i. 10. 7 s. — ἀπέκτεινε, tense ? — ἰδίωξα, coöperating with the king, cf. i. 10, 1, 5, 8. — τοῖσδε, deictic, 545. Observe the compliment to his associates, who are most fully in his confidence, and may therefore be received as representing him.

20. βουλεύσασθαι, ἐρέσθαι, order ? — τίνος ἕνεκεν, orat. recta. — μετρίως, less haughtily than Clearchus had before answered, § 5; i. 9, 20 s. — ἵνα μοι (case 458) εὐπρακτότερον ᾖ (sc. διαπράξασθαι, or impers.; mode 633 a), ἐάν τι δύνωμαι (mode ?) s, *in order that my work may be easier, if I may possibly obtain for you any favor from him. — ἐάν τι = ὅ τι.*

21. ἐβουλεύοντο, ἀπεκρίναντο, ἔλεγεν, tense 595, 592 a. — ὡς...πολεμήσοντες, cf. i. 1. 3. — οὔτ' ἐπορευόμεθα ἐπὶ βασιλέα, *nor did we set forth* [begin our march, 594] *against the king*. See iii. 1. 10. — εὕρισκεν, tense ? Cf. i. 2. 1; 3. 20. — οἶσθα, knowing the professed intent of Cyrus, i. 2. 4.

22. ᾐσχύνθημεν (Lex. αἰσχύνω), 472 f; w. inf. or part., 657 k. — παρέχοντες (604 a) ἡμᾶς αὐτοὺς (reflex.) εὖ ποιεῖν (663 g), [yielding, giving up ourselves for him to do well by] *having permitted ourselves to be the recipients of his favors*.

23. ἀντιποιούμεθα, cf. ii. 1. 11. — οὔτ' ἔστιν ὅτου ἕνεκα βουλοίμεθ' ἄν, *nor is there any* [thing on account of which] *reason why we should wish* (if we could, 636 a). — οὐδ'...ἂν ἐθέλοιμεν, 636 a. — εἴ τις, *if one* [more courte-

58 ous than *you*, 548 g] *should not molest us*. — ἀδικοῦντα, sc. τινα, cf. i. 1. 7; v. 4. 9. — σύν (Lex.) τοῖς θεοῖς, 696. — ἐὰν μέντοι τις ἡμᾶς καὶ εὖ ποιῶν ὑπάρχῃ, *but if any one shall take the lead by doing well*

BOOK II. CHAP. IV.

to us also, 714. 2 ; cf. ii. 1. 22. — καὶ τούτου (case 408) ... οὐχ ἡττησόμεθα, *we also will not* [be worse than he] *fall behind him.*
24. ἥκω, mode 641 d. — μενόντων, imperative.
25. εἰς, i. 7. 1. — ἐφρόντιζον, tense ? — ἔλεγεν, with the preliminary *buncombe (began by saying)* ; but εἶπε with the decisive proposition, § 26. — διαπεπραγμένος...δοθῆναι αὐτῷ, σώζειν *having obtained* [that it should be granted to him to save, 663 b] *the privilege of saving.* — καίπερ πάνυ πολλῶν ἀντιλεγόντων (674 f), ὡς...βασιλεῖ (case 454 d or 453), [even very many objecting] *though very many objected that it was not befitting the king.*
26. Τέλος, 483, 485 e, ε. — ἔξεστιν (Lex.), 571 f. — πιστά, i. 2. 26. — φιλίαν, pred. adj.: render *friendly*, etc. — ἦ μήν (Lex.) : cf. vi. 1. 31. — παρέξειν, supply ἡμᾶς as subject (from ἡμῶν). — ὅπου δ' ἂν μὴ ᾖ (impers. subj. of εἰμί) πρίασθαι, *and wherever there may not be an opportunity of purchasing.*
27. πορεύεσθαι, used as fut. Cf. 5. 18 ; vii. 3. 8. — φιλίας, sc. χώρας or γῆς, 506 b. Cf. i. 3. 14, 19. — ὠνουμένους, *by purchase*, 674 d. It is not strange that, in other respects, the Greeks, in their difficult position, thought it best to accept the offer of Tissaphernes, who had such strong motives for keeping good faith with them ; but we must wonder that with their scanty means they bound themselves to purchase, if they had opportunity, all their supplies during so long a march. The mistake was exposed by Xen., iii. 1. 20. There should have been also security against the delay of their march.
29. ἄπειμι, ἀπιών, as fut. (Lex.), 603 c. — ὡς βασιλέα, i. 2. 4 ; ii. 6. 1. — ἃ δέομαι (Lex.), 472 b, d ; i. 3. 4. — ἥξω s, *I will come prepared to conduct.* — ἀρχήν, Caria, and afterwards Lydia, etc., 5. 11.

CHAPTER IV.

THE GREEKS, SUSPECTING THE DESIGNS OF TISSAPHERNES AND ARIÆUS, BEGIN THEIR MARCH, PASS THE MEDIAN WALL, AND CROSS THE TIGRIS.

1. Ἀριαῖος, who had accompanied the Greeks in the movements of the preceding chapter, but without mention, through the intentness of Xen. on the fortunes of the Greeks. — ἀλλήλων, case ? — ἡμέρας s, during this time, which seemed to the Greeks so long, acc. to Diod. xiv. 26, the king returned to Babylon, where he awarded the highest prize of merit to Tissaphernes, adding to his satrapy the province of Cyrus and giving him his daughter in marriage. On the other hand Tissaphernes promised that if the king would furnish him with an army and become reconciled to Ariæus, he would effect the destruction of the Greeks. Hence the negotiations mentioned below. into which Ariæus and his officers entered, regardless of their solemn oath to the Greeks, 2. 8 s. — δεξιάς...φέροντες :

cf. dextras ferentem, Tac. *Hist.* ii. 8. Cf. 5. 3. — αὐτοῖς, case 456. — ἐπιστρατείας, case 429 a, *that the king would not remember against them their service with Cyrus.* — μηδέ s, *nor anything else of the* [things] *past.*

2. ἔνδηλοι ἦσαν...ἧττον s, [were evident paying] *evidently paid less attention to the Greeks,* 573 c. — οἱ περὶ 'Αριαῖον, 527 a. — καί, *also,* besides the suspicious visits, etc. — τοῖς μὲν πολλοῖς, corresponding to Κλέαρχος δέ, § 5. — προσιόντες ἔλεγον, tense ? notice change of subject.

3. Τί (Lex. τίς), 483 b. — ἡμᾶς ἀπολέσαι s, *would deem it of the utmost consequence to destroy us* (if he could, 636 a). — φόβος εἴη (*v. l.* ᾖ), 664 a ; mode 649 d. — μέγαν, here emphatic. — ὑπάγεται, *is craftily leading,* or, *inducing, is seducing.* — τό (663 f) διεσπάρθαι αὐτῷ, 464. — ἁλισθῇ, chiefly poetic. — οὐκ ἔστιν ὅπως (Lex.), iv. 5. 31.

4. ἀποσκάπτει τι, *he is* [trenching off something] *digging some trench.* — εἴη (*v. l.* ᾖ), mode 652. — Οὐ γάρ ποτε s, *he will never consent, at least willingly* (if he can prevent it). — τοσοίδε (Lex.), 545. — τόν, perhaps inserted for scornful emphasis. — ἐπὶ ταῖς θύραις αὐτοῦ, *at his palace-gates,* in the immediate vicinity of his capital. — καταγελάσαντες, *laughing him to scorn,* in triumph.

5. καί, i. 3. 15. — ἐπὶ πολέμῳ, *on the footing,* or, *terms of war.* McMich. — οὐδέ (τόπους) ὅθεν s, *nor* [whence] *places from which;* like the villages in which they then were, 3. 14. — ὁ ἡγησόμενος s, 678 a ; i. 3. 9. — ἅμα ταῦτα ποιούντων ἡμῶν, [we doing this, at the same time] *as soon as we do this.* — 'Αριαῖος ἀφεστήξει (319 b) ... λελείψεται, tense (Lex.) 601 c, mode 671 d, *Ariæus will* [stand off] *withdraw, so that no friend will be left us.*

6. Ποταμὸς (emph. pos.) δ' εἰ μέν τις καὶ ἄλλος ἄρα ἡμῖν (case 458) s, *and whether indeed there is also any other river, as might be expected, for us to cross.* Observe the force of each particle here ; ἄρα, *according to probability, as might be expected.* — δ' οὖν, i. 2. 12. — Εὐφράτην, obj. of διαβῆναι, or of ἴσμεν by prolepsis. — ἴσμεν, form 320 a. — ἀδύνατον, sc. ἐστί. — Οὐ μέν (Lex.) δή (see 2. 7) ἂν μάχεσθαί γε δέῃ, *nor yet indeed, if fight we must, have we cavalry to aid us; while the enemy have cavalry the most numerous* (in the world) *and serviceable.* — ὥστε s, this consecutive clause, for livelier effect, has first an interrogative and then a negative form. — νικῶντες, ἡττωμένων, 635. — τίνα, i. e. in the rout, where, in ancient battles, was the chief carnage. — οἷόν τε, sc. ἐστί or ἂν εἴη.

7. βασιλέα, prolepsis. — ὅ τι δεῖ (Lex.), *what need there is.* — πιστὰ ἄπιστα, from the Greek love of joining kindred but contrasted words, 719 ε ; as if we should say, make his faith faithless, or his credit discredited.

8. ὡς εἰς οἶκον ἀπιών, *as if setting out for home,* i. e. Caria. — 'Ορόντας (Lex. 2), cf. iii. 4. 13 ; 5. 17 ; Plut. *Artax.* 27 ; Diod. xv. 8 – 11. The northern route to Asia Minor and that to Armenia were, for a considerable distance, the same.

9. Τισσαφέρνει, case 450 a.

10. αὐτοί (541 h) ἐφ'-(Lex. 695) ἑαυτῶν ἐχώρουν, *marched* [themselves resting upon themselves] *by themselves.* — ἀλλήλων, case 699 f.

BOOK II. CHAP. IV. 61

11. ἐκ τοῦ αὐτοῦ (Lex.), sc. χωρίου.
12. τὸ Μηδίας καλούμενον τεῖχος, *the wall* [called the wall of Media] *so-called of Media*, 678 a. See i. 7. 15. Tissaphernes seems to have met the wishes both of the king and of the Greeks by commencing upon the direct route of the return-march, and to have passed beyond the line of the Median Wall, perhaps at a spot where it was so ruined that it was not recognized by Xen. The most probable reason for coming again within this line (i. e. on the side towards Babylon) was to obtain additional supplies before crossing the Tigris. — Ἦν δὲ ᾠκοδομημένον, 679 a, β. — πλίνθοις ὀπταῖς, [with] *of burnt brick*, as far stronger for a wall of defence than those dried in the sand. — εὖρος, case? — ποδῶν, case 440 a; sc. τεῖχος. — ἀπέχει...πολύ, thought by some a mere gloss, from the looseness of its statement.
13. ἐζευγμένην, junctum, *spanned*, or, *bridged over*. McMich. — ὀχετοί, *rivulets*, or, *channels*. Acc. to Schn. these were probably equivalent to the αὐλῶνες, 3. 10. — ᾗ ὄνομα Σιττάκη, 459.
14. παραδείσου, case 445 c. — δένδρων, case 414 a. The dat. of means is more common with δασύς, iv. 7. 6; 8. 2.
15. ἐν περιπάτῳ, *upon a walk.* — πρὸ τῶν ὅπλων (Lex.); hence in front of the encampment, upon the ground traversed by the sentinels. — τις, 548 c. — καὶ ταῦτα s, *and* [did] *that too, though he was from Ariæus*, 491 c, 544 a; bringing, of course, suspicion upon Menon.
16. ὅτι Αὐτός εἰμι, *I am the very person,* 540 e. — Ἔπεμψε, ὄντες, κελεύουσι, numb. 497 b. — πιστοί...εὖνοι, order? — ὄντες, tense 604 a. — δέ =γάρ, 705.
17. παρὰ τὴν γέφυραν, *along the bridge*, to occupy or man it, as it was liable to be severed in any part, § 24; v. l. ἐπὶ τὴν γέφυραν, *to* or *upon.* — ὡς, as used before διανοεῖται, and before μή?
18. ἐταράχθη καὶ ἐφοβεῖτο, tense?
19. Νεανίσκος, not improbably Xen., who was modest in representing himself as wiser than the commander-in-chief. — ὡς οὐκ s, *that the* [being about] *scheme, both to attack and to break up the bridge, was inconsistent.* — Δῆλον γάρ, what change in the discourse? — ἐπιθεμένους, [having attacked, it will be necessary that they either conquer] *if they attack us, they must, of course, either conquer or be conquered.* — τί δεῖ, cf. § 7, ὅ τι δεῖ. — ἔχοιμεν ἄν (636 a, 637 c) ὅποι s, *should we have* [whither] *any place to which we might flee and be safe*, 642 a.
20. οὐχ ἕξουσιν s, 642 a. — λελυμένης s, observe the emph. repetition.
21. πόση τις (Lex.). — χώρα ἡ, art. 523 a, 3. — πολλή, sc. ἐστι. — πολλαὶ καί, 3. 18.
22. ὑποπέμψαιεν. Compare the like means used by Themistocles to hurry Xerxes out of Greece, Hdt. viii. 110. — καὶ τῶν ἐργασομένων, abs. w. ἐνόντων: *while there were peasants there who would cultivate it* for them. — ἀποστροφή, *a place to turn back to*, suited to a marauding enemy, *a retreat*. McMich. How remarkably is the weakness of the Persian Empire, even at home, shown by this eagerness to hurry a mere handful of Greeks out of

Babylonia; and the apprehension that remaining they might form an independent state and hold out to a disaffected population a standard of rebellion against the king! Indeed in the Persian, as now in the Ottoman Empire, most of the nationalities simply submitted to the force of arms.

23. οὐδείς, 713 a.
24. ἕως, art. 533 d. — ὡς οἷόν τε μάλιστα, i. 2. 4 ; 7. 19 : vii. 7. 15. — παρά, const. præg., cf. i. 1. 5, *with Tiss.* — ὡς (rather than ὅτι ?) διαβαινόντων (sc. αὐτῶν), *while they were crossing.* For the gen. abs. here and below the dat. might be used : διαβαίνουσιν αὐτοῖς, 676 b. Cf. iii. 4. 1. — μέλλοιεν ἐπιθήσεσθαι, 598 a, sc. the Persians. — διαβαίνοιεν, mode? — ᾤχετο ἀπελαύνων, [riding off he was gone] *he forthwith rode away,* 679 d.
25. ᾗ s, cf. § 13. — πρὸς ἥν, *near which;* accus., as he was moving towards it.
26. εἰς (Lex.) : εἰς and ἐπί in such connections comm. refer to the narrower dimension, whether depth or width. — ἄλλοτε (Lex.), 567 c. — Ὅσον δὲ χρόνον τὸ ἡγούμενον...ἐπιστήσειε, *and as long a time as he halted the van,* 641 b. — ἐκπεπλῆχθαι, i. 5. 13.
27. Μηδίας, that part oftener called Assyria (Lex.). — ἐρήμους, i. 5. 5. — Παρυσάτιδος, cf. i. 4. 9. — Κύρῳ ἐπεγγελῶν, [insulting C.] *as an insult to the memory of C.,* to whom Parysatis had been so partial. — πλὴν ἀνδραπόδων, *with the exception of slaves.* The inhabitants were not to be so taken. Cf. i. 2. 27.
28. σχεδίαις διφθερίναις, still used here. Cf. i. 5. 10 (Lex. Χαρμάνδη). — ἄρτους s, asyndeton, 707 g, j.

CHAPTER V.

CRAFT AND TREACHERY OF TISSAPHERNES. — CLEARCHUS AND FOUR OTHER GENERALS ENTRAPPED AND MADE AWAY WITH.

1. Ζαπάταν, see Lex. — φανερά, pos.?
2. δύναιτο, mode ? — πρίν : why may the inf. here follow ? 703 d, β. — γενέσθαι, mode ? — ἐροῦντα, dicturum, fut. part., 598 b, 674 c.
3. Τισσαφέρνῃ, form, 225 d, i. 4. 2 ; 2. 4. — ἡμῖν, case ? by whom ? — φυλαττόμενον...ἀντιφυλαττομεθα, order ? — ἡμᾶς, case 472 f.
4. οὔτε δύναμαι σὲ αἰσθέσθαι, would have been more regular, but less emphatic. — σέ (case 472 b) πειρώμενον, part. 657 d. — λόγους (Lex.). — σοι, case 450 b ; see also 452 a. — δυναίμεθα, ἐξέλοιμεν, mode 633 a. — ἀλλήλων, case 699 a, f ; yet see 523 c (4).
5. ἐκ διαβολῆς, ἐξ ὑποψίας, 694. These causes are more prominent from their insertion, by a species of prolepsis, in the antecedent, rather than the relative clause where they properly belong. Some explain thus, that Xen. began the sentence as if the part. ποιήσαντας was to follow, and then avoided the aggregation of participles by changing this

BOOK II. CHAP. V. 63

into the rel. and finite verb. — φθάσαι (Lex.). — κακὰ τούς, case ? — μέλλοντας, sc. ποιεῖν.

7. Πρῶτον...μέγιστον, for [the] *first and greatest* [thing], 396 a. — οἱ θεῶν (made more emphatic by the insertion of ἡμᾶς, 719 a, β) ὅρκοι, *the oaths to the gods*, 444 b. — ὅστις δὲ τούτων (432 d) σύνοιδεν αὐτῷ παρημεληκώς, *and whoever is conscious* [with himself] *of having disregarded these*, the gods, as more emph. — Τὸν γὰρ s, *for the hostility of the gods I know not* [either] *through what speed any one could escape it by flight, nor into what darkness he could run for concealment*. — θεοῖς, case 455 g. — πάντων, case 407. Cf. acc. v. 6. 9 ; iii. 2. 19. This address, which has been greatly praised by ancients and moderns, is more in the style of the philosopher Xen. than of the rude soldier Clearchus. Indeed it is well known that the ancient historians, who had no short-hand reporters to aid and fetter them, exercised much freedom in shaping the speeches of their personages, especially when, as here, there was no one who had been present to correct them. Cf. with this fine passage, Psalm cxxxix.

8. μὲν δή, office here ? — θεῶν, ὅρκων, hendiadys, 69 e. — παρ' οἷς s (*v. l.* οὕς, motion toward being implied), *with whom* (the gods) *having contracted friendship, we have made it a sacred deposit*, i. e. *to whose keeping we have intrusted the friendship we have contracted*, as written contracts committed to a powerful third person for safe keeping and enforcement. — σὲ ἔγωγε, pos.? — παρόντι (Lex. πάρειμι). — νομίζω, formal and weighty.

9. πᾶσα μὲν ὁδός, 523 e. — μέν, μέν, μέν, correspondence ? — πᾶσα μὲν διὰ σκότους ἡ ὁδός, *the way is all* [through darkness] *in the dark*, 523 b, 4, e. — οὐδὲν γὰρ αὐτῆς, *nothing* [no part] *of it*. — αὐτῆς gen. partit., or of theme. — φοβερώτατον, gend. 502 ; pos.? — μεστὴ γὰρ s, *for it is* [full of much helplessness] *a most helpless condition*.

10. Εἰ δὲ s, *but even if we* [having become insane should slay] *should be so insane as to slay you*. — ἄλλο τι (sc. γένοιτο) ἂν ἤ...ἀγωνιζοίμεθα, [would anything else result than that we should have to contend] *should we not then of necessity have to contend?* 567 g. — τὸν μέγιστον ἔφεδρον (Lex.); a very impressive metaphor from the Greek games. The combatants in wrestling or boxing were usually paired by lot, and if an odd combatant remained, he was to *sit by* (an ἔφ-εδρος) till one was defeated, whose place he could take. Of course he engaged with great advantage against one who had already exhausted much of his strength. Some good MSS., instead of ἔφεδρον, *sitter by*, have ἔφορον, *looker on*, but with reference to the same custom. — οἴων ἂν ἐλπίδων, case 414 b. — ταῦτα, *this*, 491 c.

11. εὖ ποιεῖν (sc. τινά), ὃν βούλοιτο, 551 f. — τὴν σεαυτοῦ ἀρχὴν σώζοντα, *retaining your own province*. — ᾗ Κῦρος πολεμίᾳ ἐχρῆτο (Lex.), qua Cyrus hostili utebatur, *which was hostile to C.* — ταύτην, 2. 20.

12. Τούτων δὲ τοιούτων ὄντων, cf. quæ quum ita sint. — τίς οὕτω μαίνεται, ὅστις s, 558. Cf. vii. 1. 28. — ἐρῶ γάρ : in regular construction, either this γάρ, or that in § 13, should be omitted. Cf. iii. 2. 11.

13. οὓς νομίζω ἂν...παρασχεῖν, *whom I believe I could render*, 667 b. — Πεισίδας, sc. λυπηροὺς ὄντας. — ἔθνη πολλά : in the lax administration of

the Persian Empire there were not a few independent and predatory tribes. See iii. 2. 23 ; 5. 16 : vii. 8. 25. — εἶναι, how diff. from part.? — ἃ οἴμαι ἂν παῦσαι ἐνοχλοῦντα, *which I think I should stop from continually disturbing*, 677 b. — μάλιστα, pos.? — ποίᾳ δυνάμει...κολάσεσθε (v. l. κολάσαισθε), 620 b : κολάζω, seldom in mid. except in future, κολάσομαι ; yet see Dind. — τῆς, sc. δυνάμεως, *than* (by using) *the force*, 511 b.

14. ἔν γε τοῖς πέριξ οἰκοῦσι, *among those dwelling around*. — τῷ = τινι. — ὡς μέγιστος ἂν (applying also to ἀναστρέφοιο, 622 b) εἴης, *you would be the most powerful friend possible*, 553 c ; very strong language. — ἦς (v. l. ἦν), 554 a. — σοῦ σοί, pos.? *you at least*, thus suggesting the idea of the king himself, whom he would not venture to mention.

15. οὕτω is often emphatic by being separated from the word which it most directly modifies ; cf. § 21. — τό gives greater prominence and actuality to σέ. — ἡμῖν (case 456) ἀπιστεῖν, the subj. of δοκεῖ, 663 f, 664 b, *your distrust of us*. — ἥδιστ' ἂν ἀκούσαιμι (636 a) τὸ ὄνομα, τίς, *I should be most glad to hear the name, who there is of such power in speaking ;* i. e. *the name of one who is*, 566 a : Menon was the person suspected, § 28. — τοσαῦτα, ὧδε, 547. — ἀπημείφθη, "perhaps used as a high-flown word in irony," Boise. The answer of Tissaphernes is marked by consummate duplicity and affectation of virtue : but cf. § 7.

16. σου, *from you*, 434 a. — ἂν (620 c, 621) μοι δοκεῖς (573)...εἶναι, [*you seem to me that you would be*] *it seems to me that you would be*, or, *you would seem to me to be*. — 'Ὡς δ' ἂν μάθῃς, 624 a.

17. ἐβουλόμεθα, 631 b. — πότερά σοι s, [whether] *do we seem to you to want either*. — ὁπλίσεως, ἐν ᾗ, *warlike equipment, weapons*, or, *armature in which*, i. e. *with which*, referring to the missiles in which the Greeks were so deficient and with which they might be picked off with little power of retaliation. — κίνδυνος, sc. ἐστίν, or, ἂν εἴη.

18. ἐπιτίθεσθαι, tense ? — ἀπορεῖν ἄν σοι δοκοῦμεν, *do we seem to you* [*that we should want*] *likely to want*. Why ἄν here, and not with ἀπορεῖν above ? — Οὐ (687 b) τοσαῦτα. — ὑμῖν ὄντα (= εἶναι) πορευτέα, prob. pointing to the great mountain range along the north. — ταμιεύεσθαι (Lex.), 582 d ; by attacking a portion on one side, while the others are crossing. — εἰσὶ δ' αὐτῶν s, 421 a, 418 b.

19. ἡττώμεθα, (present indicative) *we are worsted*. — ὅν, object of κατακαύσαντες. — ὑμῖν (case 455) ἀντιτάξαι, *to array against you*, a bold metaphor.

20. ἄν...ἄν, 622 a, 621 c, d. — ἔχοντες, *if we have*, hence μηδένα, 686 d. — ἔπειτα, i. 2. 25. — ὃς μόνος s, order 719 e, f.

21. ἀπόρων ἐστί...οἵτινες, 558. — ἐχομένων (Lex.). — καὶ τούτων πονηρῶν, *and* [*those wicked*] *wicked men too*, 544 a. — ἠλίθιοι, a stronger term added for emphasis ; ἀλόγιστοι denying the fact of consideration, but ἠλίθιοι even the capacity for it.

22. ἐξόν (Lex. ἔξειμι), 675 b, c. — οὐκ ἐπὶ τοῦτο ἤλθομεν, *did we not* [go] *proceed to this?* cf. iii. 1. 18. — ὁ ἐμὸς ἔρως (sc. ἦν or ἐστί) τούτου (case 444 f) αἴτιος τὸ (664 c) τοῖς Ἕλλησιν ἐμὲ πιστὸν γενέσθαι,

BOOK II. CHAP. V. 65

καὶ ᾧ ἀνέβη ξενικῷ (551 c, 466. 1) s, *the cause of this was my ardent desire* [in respect to this] *that I might* [become trusted by] *secure the confidence of the Greeks, and that with the foreign troops with which Cyrus made his ascent, trusting them* [on account of payments] *from his payment of wages, with this I might descend* [go back to my satrapy] *strong in their attachment through my kindness.*

23. Ὅσα δέ μοι ὑμεῖς χρήσιμοι ἔσεσθε, *and* [as to how many things, 481] *in what respects you will be capable of serving me* (v. l. ἐστέ, you are, etc.). — τιάραν (Lex.). — ὀρθήν, *Cyr.* viii. 3. 13. — τὴν δ' ἐπί...ἔχοι (sc. ὀρθήν), *but that upon the heart, perhaps with your presence another also might easily so wear;* i. e. might have equally erectness of spirit and independence of feeling. Some see in this boldly figurative expression an intimation from Tissaphernes (the better to blind Clearchus), that he might himself wish with the aid of the Greeks to aspire to that sovereignty which Clearchus had already offered Ariæus.

24. ἔφη, 574. — τοιούτων ἡμῖν s, *when we have such inducements to friendship.* — τὰ ἔσχατα παθεῖν, extrema pati.

25. Καὶ ἐγὼ μέν γε, [and I for my part certainly] *yes, and I for my part;* καὶ...γε, as not infrequently in dialogue, implying assent, and μέν corresponding to δέ in § 26. — στρατηγοί and λοχαγοί, in appos. with ὑμεῖς understood.

26. ὅθεν, [whence] *from what source,* i. e. *from whom.*

27. μέν, after τότε, as corresponding with τῇ ὑστεραίᾳ, while its more regular place would be before Τισσαφέρνης. — δῆλός τ' ἦν πάνυ φιλικῶς οἰόμενος s, *both* [was evident thinking, 573 b] *showed that he thought* [that he was related in a very friendly way to T.] *himself on very friendly terms with Tissaphernes.* — χρῆναι ἰέναι s, *that* [it was proper that those should go] *those ought to go to T. whom he had invited.* — ἐξελεγχθῶσι, mode ? — τῶν Ἑλλήνων, case ? — ὡς προδότας αὐτούς, *as* [being] *themselves traitors.*

28. αὐτῷ, i. e. Clearchus. — ᾗ, mode ? § 36 : i. 4. 18.

29. ἅπαν τὸ στράτευμα (523 e, observe the different emphasis in τὸ στράτευμα ἅπαν, § 28) s, *that the whole army should* [have its mind towards himself] *be devoted to him.* — μηδὲ πιστεύειν, indef. subject.

30. κατέτεινεν : with the temper of Clearchus, the opposition of others only made him more vehement, while perhaps he regarded it as proof of machinations against him of which their authors feared the exposure. — διεπράξατο s, *he had so far succeeded that five generals* (including himself) *went,* i. e. all except Chirisophus, Cleanor, and Sophænetus. — ὡς εἰς ἀγοράν, *as for the market,* which they were in the habit of visiting for supplies (4. 9), and consequently unarmed and without apprehension.

31. ἐπὶ ταῖς θύραις, without art., vii. 3. 16. — Πρόξενος s : Menon feeling doubtless that at all events he was safe among the Persians, while it might endanger him among the Greeks to refuse to go ; and the others being misled or overpersuaded. Ctesias, prob. from Menon's own false claim at the court, represents the fatal visit of the generals as a plot of Menon's, against the better judgment of Clearchus, *Pers.* 60. The whole

number of lochagi in the army was not far from a hundred. — 'Αγίας, not before mentioned (Lex.).

32. πολλῷ, case 468, 485 e, β. — ἀπό, iv. 1. 5. — σημείου, acc. to Diod. xiv. 26, a red flag, the sign of blood, raised above the tent of Tissaphernes. — ξυνελαμβάνοντο, κατεκόπησαν, tense 595. — τινές, pos. 548 b, 719 d, ν. — ᾧτινι, numb. 550 f. — ἐντυγχάνοιεν, mode ?—ἔκτεινον: Xen. uses the simple verb here only. Hence Hartlein proposes ἀπέκτεινον.

33. ἠμφιγνόουν (v. l. ἠμφεγνόουν), 282 b. — πρὶν...ἧκε, 703 d, a, indic. denoting fact. — Νίκαρχος, one of the soldiers who visited the market, acc. to Diodorus.

34. αὐτούς, the cavalry mentioned in § 32. The extreme dread which the Persians had of the Greeks is strikingly shown by the fact that they did not avail themselves of this opportunity of making a general attack.

35. Κύρῳ, while he was living.

36. ἀπαγγείλωσι, mode ?— τὰ παρὰ βασιλέως, 3. 4.

37. φυλαττόμενοι, *with a body-guard*, or simply, *with due precaution*. — τὰ περὶ Προξένου, 528 a.

38. ἔστησαν εἰς (const. præg.). — ἐπήκοον (Lex.). — ὑμᾶς, ὅπλα, case 480 c. — ὁ βασιλεύς: ὁ expressing more formality. Hence fitting in this place : noster rex. — ἀπαιτεῖ, how diff. fr. αἰτεῖ?— ἑαυτοῦ, Κύρου, case 433, 437 a. — εἶναι, i. e. τὰ ὅπλα. — δούλου, pos.? cf. i. 9. 29.

39. ἀπεκρίναντο, ἔλεγε, expressing his honest indignation with great plainness and straightforwardness; cf. 1. 10. —'Ὦ κάκιστε, 484 d. — οἱ ἄλλοι, sc. ὑμεῖς. — θεούς, 3. 22. — οἵτινες (550 b), ὀμόσαντες...προδόντες ἡμᾶς...ἀπολωλέκατε, *you who, after giving us your oaths,...then betraying us,...have destroyed*. — ἡμῖν, comm. obj. of ὀμόσαντες and τοὺς αὐτούς. — τοὺς ἄλλους ἡμᾶς προδεδωκότες, *having given up* [us the rest] *the rest of us to destruction;* observe the passionate repetition. Most MSS. also introduce ὡς before ἀπολωλέκατε, as though the speaker in his intenseness of feeling had forgotten the previous connective οἵτινες.

40. γάρ, connecting this sentence to what ?

41. τούτοις, τάδε, 544. Contrast the cool, shrewd logic of Xenophon with the vehement outburst of Cleanor. — Πρόξενος, Μένων, emph. pos. before ἐπείπερ.

42. ἀλλήλοις, case 452.

CHAPTER VI.

XENOPHON'S ESTIMATE OF THE CHARACTER OF THE FIVE GENERALS.

1. ἀνήχθησαν, in chains: Ctes. *Pers.* 60; Diod. xiv. 27. There was especial curiosity at Babylon, says Ctesias, to see the Spartan prisoner; and he was himself, as court-physician, an instrument of Parysatis in doing much to relieve the imprisonment of the favorite general of her favorite son. Acc. to Ctesias, the weak Artaxerxes first promised Parysatis with an oath

that he would spare Clearchus; but was afterwards influenced by Statira to execute all except Menon. This same writer adds the marvellous story that when their bodies were thrown out to the birds and dogs, a whirlwind covered the body of Clearchus with a great mound which was speedily overgrown with palm-trees so that the king repented his execution as that of an evident favorite of the gods. Plut. *Artax.* 18. — ὡς (Lex. d). — ἀποτμηθέντες (587. 2) τὰς κεφαλάς (481), [cut off as to their heads] *having their heads cut off, beheaded;* except Menon, § 29. — εἰς (395 a). — μέν, corresponding to δέ, § 16. — ὁμολογουμένως (Lex.). — ἐμπείρως (Lex.) αὑτοῦ, 432 b. — δόξας γενέσθαι, *esteemed to have been.* — ἐσχάτως, pos.?

2. πόλεμος, the so-called Peloponnesian War. — ἐγένετο, B. C. 404. — ἀδικοῦσι, mode? — τοὺς Ἕλληνας, i. 3. 4; 1. 9, colonized on the coast of Thrace. — διαπραξάμενος ὡς ἐδύνατο, *having obtained* [as he could] *leave and supplies by what means he could.* — τοῖς, with dat. and with πρός, after πολεμέω. See McMich.

3. ἔξω, *without, abroad;* i. e. here, *at sea.* — ὄντος, for ὄντα, i. 2. 17 N. — Ἰσθμοῦ, so common a place of call in the coasting voyages along the eastern shore of Greece. — ᾤχετο πλέων, 4. 24. See Diod. xxiv. 12; Polyænus, ii. 2.

4. ἔρχεται, having been defeated by a Spartan force and shut up in Selybria, from which he made his escape by night, Diod. xiv. 12. — ἔπεισε Κῦρον, *persuaded Cyrus to aid him.* — ἄλλῃ, *elsewhere.* Whether Xen. referred to another work, or supposed he had written more fully in this, does not appear.

5. ἀπὸ τούτων, i. 1. 9. — ἔφερε καὶ ἦγε (Lex. ἄγω). — πολεμῶν διεγένετο, *continued at war*, 677.

6. φιλοπολέμου: brought out into greater prominence by the insertion of μοι δοκεῖ before ἀνδρὸς (719 a, β) ἔργα, *acts, ways, procedure, behavior.* — ὅστις...αἱρεῖται πολεμεῖν, [who prefers] *that he should prefer,* i. e. *to prefer;* cf. 5. 21. — ἐξὸν (Lex.) μὲν εἰρήνην ἔχειν, *when he might live in peace* (v. l. εἰρήνην ἄγειν, see Lex.). — βούλεται πονεῖν ὥστε s (Lex. ὥστε d), 671 a.

7. ταύτῃ, *in this,* or, *in these respects, herein.* — ἡμέρας καὶ νυκτὸς (433) ἄγων, *day and night alike* [leading] *ready to lead.* — πανταχοῦ πάντες, order?

8. ὡς δυνατὸν ἐκ, *as far as was possible* [from] *with such a temper,* which forbade his obtaining the affections of his men, § 12 s. — οἶον καὶ ἐκεῖνος εἶχεν, *as indeed* HE *had*, however strange it might seem in others. — Ἱκανὸς μέν...δέ, i. 3. 16. — ὥς τις καὶ ἄλλος, i. 3. 15. — αὑτοῦ, some read αὑτῷ, ethical dat. — ὡς πειστέον εἴη Κλεάρχῳ (emphatic), *that Clearchus must be obeyed*, 682 a, 455 g.

9. χαλεπός, case 667 c: Diod. xiii. 66. — ὁρᾶν στυγνὸς ἦν, καὶ τῇ φωνῇ τραχύς, 663 e, 467 b. — ἐκόλαζε...ἐκόλαζεν · ἀκολάστου, order, etc.? — ὥστε καὶ αὐτῷ (457) μεταμέλειν, *so that there were times when* [it even repented him] *he even himself repented,* 457; ἐνίοτε and ἔσθ' ὅτε here implying rarer occurrence than ἐνίοτε (see Lex. εἰμί, 559 a). — ἀκολάστου...ἡγεῖτο s, *for he thought there was no profit from* [of] *an unchastised army,* 472.

NOTES.

73 **10.** εἰ μέλλοι ἢ φυλακὰς φυλάξειν, *if he were either to keep guard,* or, *maintain his guard.*

11. ἤθελον αὐτοῦ ἀκούειν σφόδρα, *were willing to obey him implicitly,* 432 g ; order, 719 b, ϛ. — τὸ στυγγὸν (507 a) τότε φαιδρὸν s, *they said that the gloom in his countenance then appeared lustrous.* Some good MSS. have ἐν τοῖς ἄλλοις προσώποις, *that his gloom appeared lustrous among the other countenances.* — τὸ χαλεπὸν s, *and his harshness seemed to be energy against the foe.*

12. καὶ ἐξείη πρὸς ἄλλους ἀρχομένους (*v. l.* ἄρχοντας, Lex.) ἀπιέναι, *and* [it was permitted] *they were free to go to* (others to be commanded) *other commanders,* their engagement with him having expired. — τὸ γὰρ ἐπίχαρι οὐκ εἶχεν, *for* [the winning he had not] *he had nothing attractive.* — ὥσπερ παῖδες πρὸς διδάσκαλον : "it is to be hoped that boys nowadays will not understand this comparison." Boise.

13. εὐνοίᾳ, 466. 1. — τεταγμένοι, i. 6. 6. — ὑπὸ τοῦ δεῖσθαι, *through want.* — σφόδρα πειθομένοις ἐχρῆτο (Lex.), *from these he received implicit obedience.* Cf. iv. 6. 3.

14. μεγάλα ἦν τὰ...ποιοῦντα, [great were the things making] *there were powerful influences which made.* — τὸ ἔχειν, subject of παρῆν. — θαρραλέως (Lex.).

15. οὐ μάλα (Lex.) ἐθέλειν (litotes, 686 i), of which his disobedience to the Ephori, and his conduct at Cunaxa, presented striking examples. — τὰ πεντήκοντα, 531 d.

16. εὐθὺς (Lex. 662) μὲν μειράκιον ὤν, *from his very youth.* — ἔδωκε Γοργίᾳ ἀργύριον, *he* [gave money] *paid tuition to Gorgias.* Diod. xii. 53, mentions 100 minæ (= about $2000) as his price, — perhaps an extreme case, but enough to make Krüger exclaim, "The Greeks were — well, not Germans!"

74 **17.** μὴ ἡττᾶσθαι εὐεργετῶν, *not to be outdone in conferring favors,* even by those of high rank, 677.

18. οὐδὲν ἂν θέλοι, *if he must obtain it unjustly,* 635. — σὺν τῷ δικαίῳ καὶ καλῷ, [with that which is justice and honor] *justly and honorably,* 695, 507 a ; δίκαιος referring more to the essential character, and καλός more to the impression made (Lex. καλός). So below, καλῶν καὶ ἀγαθῶν, *honorable* or *estimable and good,* a frequent combination to express the Greek ideal of internal virtue united with external propriety. — μή, sc. τυγχάνειν, *by no means,* emph. from pos.

19. αἰδῶ...ἑαυτοῦ, *respect for himself.* — οἱ ἀρχόμενοι, *even those who were under his command,* emphasizing the unnatural state of things. — ἦν φανερός (Lex.), cf. § 21, 23. — στρατιώταις, case 457. — ἐκείνῳ, why rather than αὐτῷ?

20. ἴτων, case 437 a.

21. δῆλος (Lex.). — ἐπιθυμῶν, observe the emphatic repetition. — μέγιστα δυναμένοις (Lex.). — δίκην (Lex. 1).

22. διὰ τοῦ ἐπιορκεῖν, 663 f : τοῦ not repeated? — τὸ δ᾽ ἁπλοῦν s, 507 a, 451. — τῷ ἠλιθίῳ, case 451.

BOOK II. CHAP. VI. 69

23. Στέργων (stronger than φιλῶν, Lex.) δέ s, *he evidently had no real love for any one.* — φανερός, ἔνδηλος (Lex.), 573 c. — Στέργων...ἐπιβουλεύων, order ? — ὅτῳ, form 253. 1. — τούτῳ s, *against him it became evident that he was plotting.* — πολεμίου, case 699 a.

24. τὰ δὲ τῶν φίλων μόνος (677 b) ... ὃν (677) ἀφύλακτα (pred. adj., 523 b, 5), *he thought that he alone understood that it was most easy to take the property of friends as being unguarded;* at least he so acted. **75**

26. τῷ...δύνασθαι, case ? — τὸν μὴ (sc. ὄντα, 686 d) πανοῦργον, *the man who was not a villain,* or, *knave.* — τῶν ἀπαιδεύτων, *one of the ignorant, a mere simpleton.* — διαβάλλων (674 d)...κτήσασθαι (agreeing in subject with ᾤετο, notwithstanding the intervention of the impers. δεῖν, 667 c), *he thought he must win these by maligning those who held the first place.*

27. Τὸ δὲ πειθομένους τοὺς στρατιώτας...ἐμηχανᾶτο, *he contrived* [the rendering] *to render his soldiers obedient.* — συναδικεῖν, *so that they hoped for gain in pleasing him, and feared exposure if they displeased him.* — Τιμᾶσθαι δέ s, *and he thought himself entitled to be honored and courted, if he showed that he was able, and would be ready* (if there was occasion) *to inflict the greatest injuries.* — Εὐεργεσίαν δὲ κατέλεγεν, *and he charged it as a favor.* — αὐτοῦ ἀφίστατο, *was leaving him.* — αὐτῷ, αὐτόν, repeated for stronger expression : one of these would have been sufficient in unemphatic language.

28. τὰ μὲν δὴ ἀφανῆ s, *doubtful matters of course one might misstate;* with allusion probably to the charges of treachery made against him. Diod. is less reserved, and says that he was spared when the other generals were put to death : see § 29 N. — ἃ δέ s, *but the following is what all know.* — ἔτι ὡραῖος ὤν, στρατηγεῖν διεπράξατο, *while yet in the bloom of youth, he obtained* [to command] *the command of;* his youth leading to the belief that this was through dishonorable favoritism. — ἀγένειος ὢν γενειῶντα, *a bearded man, while himself beardless,* 719 b, ε. Reference is here made to the vice which the apostle exposes in Rom. i. 27. The age of Menon is not stated ; but he is represented as remarkably precocious in command, corruption, and villany. Krüg. regards this section as not by Xenophon.

29. οὐκ ἀπέθανε, for this reason, says Diod. xiv. 27, ἐδόκει γὰρ μόνος οὗτος στασιάζων πρὸς τοὺς συμμάχους προδώσειν "Ελληνας. — τὸν τῶν ἄλλων θάνατον στρατηγῶν, order 719 d, ν, 523 k. — τιμωρηθείς s, *he died* [punished by] *as a punishment from the king;* cf. below. — ζῶν αἰκισθείς, *having been tortured alive;* prob. because, through the weakness of the king, he fell into the hands of the vengeful Parysatis (Lex. Μένων); cf. i. 9. 13 ; 10. 1. — λέγεται τῆς τελευτῆς (case 427) τυχεῖν, added instead of continuing the construction with ἀπέθανεν. **76**

30. τούτω, 505 b. — Τούτων...κατεγέλα, 699 a. — ἐς φιλίαν, 697.

BOOK III.

HOSTILITIES BETWEEN THE PERSIANS AND GREEKS, AFTER THE BREAKING OF THE TREATY BY THE FORMER. — MARCH OF THE TEN THOUSAND TO THE CARDUCHIAN MOUNTAINS.

CHAPTER I.

GREAT DEJECTION AMONG THE TROOPS. — XENOPHON AROUSES THEM TO ACTION. — NEW GENERALS CHOSEN.

77 1. Ὅσα μὲν δή s, see p. 3, Notes, statement as to division into books, summaries, etc. — ἐτελεύτησε, tense 605 c.
2. οἱ στρατηγοί, the (five) generals. — μέν, anticipated, as often, from its strictly regular place after ἐπί. Observe the nine clauses introduced by ἐννοούμενοι ὅτι, to make up the gloomy and disheartening picture so graphically and impressively drawn ; and also the position of their prominent words. — ἦσαν, προυδεδώκεσαν, tense, etc., 646 b. — ἐπὶ ταῖς βασιλέως θύραις, i. e. in the heart of his dominions. Cf. ii. 2. 4. — πολλά (496 c), πολέμιαι (497), belong to both ἔθνη and πόλεις, each taking the gender of the nearest noun. — οὐ μεῖον (cf. 507 e) ἢ μύρια στάδια : ii. 2. 6. — νικῶντες s : cf. ii. 4. 6.

78 3. ἀθύμως ἔχοντες, 577 d ; sc. οἱ Ἕλληνες. — ὀλίγοι, few, ...πολλοί, 395 a. — εἰς τὴν ἑσπέραν, [into the] at evening. — σίτου, case 432 a. — ἐπὶ τὰ ὅπλα (Lex.), to the place of arms, which marked the men's quarters. — ἀνεπαύοντο, ἐτύγχανεν (Lex., sc. ὤν or ἀναπαυόμενος) numb. 501 a ; ii. 2. 17. — πατρίδων s, asynd. 707 g. — οὕς (masc. with reference to the persons), οὔποτ' ἐνόμιζον ἔτι ὄψεσθαι, whom they never expected to see [more] again, 662 b ; observe the same idiom in Eng. Muretus compares Virg. Æn. ii. 137 s.
4. τις...Ξενοφῶν Ἀθηναῖος, a certain Xenophon, an Athenian; what a modest introduction of the leading spirit of the subsequent retreat ! — ἀλλὰ Πρόξενος αὐτόν, instead of ὄν, 562. — αὐτός, emphasizing the subject of νομίζειν, cf. 662. — κρείττω ἑαυτῷ, worth more to himself, 453.
5. ἀνακοινοῦται, mid. of mutual conference, as by equals, 580 ; but act. below, of simple reference to a higher intelligence, as v. 9. 22. — Σωκράτει : Diogenes Laërtius gives an interesting account of the first meeting of teacher and pupil. (See Introduction to the present volume.) — τῷ Ἀθηναίῳ, why art. here, and not with Ἀθηναῖος, § 4 ? — ὑποπτεύσας μή, apprehensive [lest] that, 625 a. — τι, as adv. or with ἐπαίτιον. — πρός, i. 9. 20. — Κύρῳ φίλον, 456. — συμπολεμῆσαι, in the Peloponnesian War (B. C. 408-4),

chiefly by giving the Spartans, through Lysander, liberal supplies of money. Cf. Lex. Κῦρος. — ἐλθόντα, case 667 e : i. 2. 1.

6. Ἀπόλλω, 211 a. — ὁδόν, case 477. — ἐπινοεῖ, mode 645 b ; i. 9. 28. — θεοῖς οἷς, inverse attr., 554 c ; reference esp. to Ζεὺς Βασιλεύς, vi. 1. 22.

7. ἰτέον εἶναι, i. 3. 11. — ταῦτα...ὅσα, 550 d.

8. ἀνεῖλεν, sc. θύεσθαι or θύειν.

9. ὅτι...ἀποπέμψειν, 659 e. — Ἐλέγετο, position ?

10. οἱ πολλοί : a few may have sailed with Xenias and Pasion (i. 4. 7), or have deserted in some other way. — αἰσχύνην (Lex.) καὶ ἀλλήλων (case 444, cf. ii. 6. 19), lest they should seem cowardly in deserting their comrades, and ungrateful towards Cyrus ; nearly = *a sense of honor towards each other.*

11. μικρόν, adv. — ὕπνου, case 416 a. — ὄναρ, form 228 a. — Ἔδοξεν, 573 b, asynd. As often happens, the waking apprehension of danger in one form induced in sleep a vivid image of another form. For another impressive dream of Xen. cf. iv. 3. 8.

12. ἀγαθόν, from the familiar association in all ages of light and good. Cf. *Cyr.* iv. 2. 15. — Διός...βασιλέως, Jupiter (or Zeus), as king, was regarded as the special patron of kings (Διοτρεφέων βασιλήων, *Il.* i. 176); and, as the Greek representative of Ormuzd, he was claimed by the Persian monarchs as their paternal deity, the founder and upholder of their dynasty: Ζεὺς πατρῷος, *Cyr.* i. 6. 1. — κύκλῳ : one encircling might be regarded as the sign of another. Upon such doubtful and equivocal analogies the doctrine of omens has rested in all ages.

13. Ὁποῖόν τι (Lex.). It is easy to interpret an omen after the result. — τὸ τοιοῦτον, 531 c. — πρῶτον μέν, followed by ἐκ τούτου, § 15 ; cf. 2. 1 N. — ἡ δὲ νύξ, 705, cf. a. — εἰκός, sc. ἐστί, *it is probable,* 572. — ἐπὶ βασιλεῖ, cf. i. 1. 4. — τί ἐμποδών, μὴ οὐχὶ...ἀποθανεῖν, *what* [is in the way that we should not die] *prevents our dying* (713 g) [outraged] *miserably, after looking upon all that is most grievous.* — παθόντας, ὑβριζομένους, cf. i. 1. 7.

14. Ὅπως δ' ἀμυνούμεθα, *and* [how we shall defend ourselves, 624 b] *for defending ourselves.* — κατακείμεθα, ὥσπερ ἐξόν, 680 b. — Ἐγὼ οὖν s, [the general from what state then, am I looking for] *from what state, then* (rather than my own) *do I look for a general to do this ?* I, who am an Athenian, while no leading general survives ? His pride of country is well expressed by ποίας. — ἡλικίαν : Xenophon's age at this time is a matter of great uncertainty. Krüg. makes him to have been 44 ; other authorities, with more probability, give his age as about or under 30. — οὐ γάρ s, *for I shall never be any older.* — τήμερον, the Greek civil day beginning at sunset.

15. Ἐκ τούτου, i. 3. 11 ; 2. 17. — Προξένου, his intimate friend whom he had accompanied. — ὥσπερ, οἶμαι, οὐδ' (Lex.) ὑμεῖς, *as neither you, methinks.* — ἐν οἵοις, sc. πράγμασιν, *in what circumstances.*

16. δῆλον ὅτι, 717 b. Cf. § 35. — ἐξέφηναν (Lex.), *show forth what was before in the heart.* — πρότερον...πρίν, 703 d, ς ; cf. 1. 10. — καλῶς τὰ

ἑαυτῶν παρασκευάσασθαι, *that they had well arranged their* [affairs] *plans.* — οὐδέν, 478, or 483. — ὡς (Lex. c).

17. καὶ τεθνηκότος ἤδη : the Greeks regarded the mutilation of the dead with horror. — ἡμᾶς δέ s, *but we who have no intercessor* (while Cyrus had the queen-mother to plead for him) *made war.* — ἡμᾶς : cf. vii. 1. 30. — ἐστρατεύσαμεν δέ = οἱ δὲ ἐστρατ., 562. — δοῦλον, i. 7. 3 ; 9. 29. — ὡς ποιήσοντες, i. 1. 3. — τί ἄν (662 b) οἰόμεθα παθεῖν, *what* [do we think we should] *might we expect to suffer,* if we should fall into his hands? cf. τί οἰόμεθα πείσεσθαι above, 637 c.

18. Ἆρ' οὐκ ἄν ἐπὶ (Lex.) s, *would he not resort to every means?* — ἡμᾶς τὰ ἔσχατα αἰκισάμενος, *having outraged us to the uttermost,* 480 b. — τοῦ στρατεῦσαι, 664 a. — ὅπως...γενησόμεθα, 624 b. — πάντα ποιητέον, 682 a.

19. Ἐγὼ μέν (Lex.): use of each μέν in this section? Cf. i. 9. 28 ; 3. 17; vii. 6. 10. — αὐτῶν, case 413. Some supply τοῦτο or τάδε. — ὅσα, supply the ellipsis of this pron. with χρυσόν and ἐσθῆτα.

81

20. Τά...τῶν στρατιωτῶν, *the condition of our soldiers.* — ἐνθυμοίμην, mode? — ὅτι τῶν μὲν ἀγαθῶν πάντων (gen. part. w. οὐδενός) οὐδενὸς (421 a, 418 b) ἡμῖν (459) μετείη s, *that in all good things* (for the body) *we had no share, except by purchase.* Cf. ii. 3. 27 N. — ὅτου (case 431 a) δ' ὠνησόμεθα, ᾔδειν (mode ?) *and knew that few still had* [that for which] *the means of buying,* or, *wherewith to buy.* — ἄλλως (Lex.). — πορίζεσθαι...ὅρκους s, *that oaths now forbade us to obtain,* etc. — ταῦτ' οὖν λογιζόμενος, as repetition of preceding part of section.

21. ἐκείνων, ἡμετέρα, pos. 538 f. — Ἐν μέσῳ, as the prizes for athletes were displayed in the midst of the assembled crowds. The Greeks were esp. animated by allusions to their games. — ἆθλα (τούτοις or τούτων) ὁπότεροι, *prizes* [of whoever of us] *for those of us who may be the better men.* — τὸ εἰκός, sc. ἐστίν, 572.

22. αὐτούς, ii. 4. 7. — τοὺς τῶν θεῶν ὅρκους, ii. 5. 3, 7 s. — ὥστε ἐξεῖναι (sc. ἡμῖν), *so that methinks* [it is allowed us] *we may go.* — πολὺ...μείζονι, emphatically placed, as often ; so μάλα, i. 5. 8. Cf. i. 5. 2 ; ii. 2. 19.

23. τούτων, *than* [they] *theirs,* 438 b, 511 b ; ii. 3. 15. — ψύχῃ, numb. 489 a. — σὺν τοῖς θεοῖς, reverently inserted, since the gods might send a panic upon the bravest. — οἱ ἄνδρες : cf. 4. 40 ; ἄνθρωποι, iv. 2. 7. — τρωτοί : The Greeks had greater physical vigor and hardihood from their gymnastic exercises and mode of dress ; they had stouter hearts from their civil freedom ; and they were also better armed.

24. Ἀλλ', marking the transition from argument to earnest exhortation. — ταῦτ' ἐνθυμοῦνται, *and may get the start of us;* which would rouse Greek ambition (Townsend reads ταῦτά for ταῦτα). — πρὸς τῶν θεῶν : τῶν om. elsewhere in Anab., Rehdz., Krüg. — μὴ ἀναμένωμεν s, 628 a. — παρακαλοῦντας, fut. or pres. — τοῦ ἐξορμῆσαι, 425, 664 a. — στρατηγῶν, paron. 70 n.

82

25. ἀκμάζειν ἡγοῦμαι, ἐρύκειν, *I esteem myself at the very acme of life for warding off.* See § 14 N. on ἡλικίαν.

26. πάντες, so placed for immediate connection with πλήν. — βοιωτιάζων, the Bœotians spoke a coarse, broad variety of the Æolic, 82. — οὗτος

BOOK III. CHAP. I. 73

δ' = ὥς, 705. — λέγοι, some read λέγει, v. 6. 36. — ἄλλως πως...ἤ, see § 20. — λέγειν, the inf. used rather because he attempted in vain.

27. Ὦ θαυμασιώτατε, 484 d, 514. — οὐδὲ...οὐδέ s, *not even ..., nor yet,* familiar proverbial expression. — Ἐν ταὐτῷ...τούτοις, *in* [the same place] *company with these.* See ii. 1. 8. — μέγα φρονήσας (Lex.), 478.

28. παρεσκηνήσαμεν, ii. 3. 16 s. — τί οὐκ ἐποίησε, cf. § 18.

29. εἰς λόγους αὐτοῖς : see ii. 5. 4. — οὐ...οὐδὲ, 713 i; unable as so bound and guarded. *Was not this the result that they are now,* etc. — κεντούμενοι, Hdt. iii. 130 ; Thuc. iv. 47. 3. — οἱ τλήμονες, in appos. w. ἐκεῖνοι : observe its emph. pos. — καὶ (674 f, cf. i. 6. 10) μάλ', οἶμαι s, 313 e, 432 e. — Ἃ σὺ πάντα εἰδὼς,...φῄς ; *and knowing all this, do you say?* 561 b. — πείθειν, tense 594 ; cf. πείσας, § 26.

30. Compare ἄνδρες and ἄνθρωπον.— μήτε...τε, ii. 2. 8. — προσίεσθαι (Lex.). — ἀφελομένους, ἀναθέντας : see i. 1. 7. — ὡς τοιούτῳ χρῆσθαι, *that we should use him* [as such] *in that capacity,* i. e. as a mere baggage-carrier.

31. τούτῳ...τῆς s, *to this fellow there appertains nothing of Bœotia.* — τὰ ὦτα τετρυπημένον, *having his ears bored,* 587. 2 ; 481 ; a barbarian custom, which the Greeks scorned, as befitting slaves. This man had doubtless resided in Bœotia, but whether as a slave or a metic does not appear. — εἶχεν (Lex.) οὕτως, as an examination proved.

32. σῶος (v. l. σῶς), 236 d. — εἴη, mode 641 b, 634 b, d : cf. i. 2. 7. — ὑποστράτηγον, comm. a lochage who acted as first officer under the general, or supplied his place.

33. εἰς (const. præg.). — τὸ πρόσθεν (Lex.); an open place convenient and often used for this purpose, cf. § 3 ; ii. 4. 15. — ἐγένοντο, *amounted to.* — τούς, 531 d ; cf. i. 2. 9 ; ii. 6. 15.

34. βουλευσαίμεθα, δυναίμεθα, mode 633 a. — ἄπερ καί, i. 3. 16.

35. οὓς s, *have seized of us whom they could,* 551 f, 553. — ὡς, ἣν δύνωνται, ἀπολέσωσιν, 633 a. — Ἡμῖν...πάντα ποιητέα (sc. εἶναι or ἐστίν), 458, 682 a. — ἐπὶ...ἣν δυνώμεθα, cf. i. 1. 4, *if* [we can effect it] *possible.*

36. τοσοῦτοι s, [being so many] *so great a number as have now assembled,* there being here a source of encouragement. Cf. ii. 1. 16. — μέγιστον καιρόν, *grandest opportunity* of exerting an influence for good or evil. — ὑμῖν, case 450 a.

37. ὑμᾶς, ὑμεῖς, ὑμεῖς (turning, with asyndeton, to the other officers), etc. Observe the repetition in this emph. appeal. — τι (Lex.) τούτων, case ? — ταξίαρχοι, lochagi who took the command when their lochi were combined with others. — χρήμασι (Lex. λοχαγός and στρατηγός) ; cf. vii. 2. 36 ; 6. 7. — τούτων ἐπλεονεκτεῖτε, 408. — νῦν τοίνυν, 2. 39 ; vii. 2. 29. — ἀξιοῦν δεῖ ὑμᾶς αὐτούς, *you ought to deem yourselves* [fit persons] *bound to be.* Compare the precept of Cyrus the Elder : ἄρχειν δὲ μηδενὶ προσήκειν, ὃς οὐ κρείττων ἐστὶ τῶν ἀρχομένων : Plut. *Apophth.* — πλήθους...τούτων, 499 a.

38. οἴομαι ἄν s, 621 a. — ἀπολωλότων, ἀπολώλεκεν, 577 b. — ὡς μὲν συνελόντι εἰπεῖν (Lex. συναιρέω), 671 c. Some refer this expression to 462 c, d. — παντάπασιν, sc. οὐδέν, *nothing at all.* — σῴζειν δοκεῖ, [seems to

save] *tends to safety :* σώζει τὰ πολλὰ σώμαθ' ἡ πειθαρχία : ἀναρχίας δὲ μεῖζον οὐκ ἔστιν κακόν, Soph. *Ant.* 676, 672.

40. **ὡς** (Lex. g), *how*, modifying each. — **οὕτω γ' ἐχόντων,** *while they are in such a state* (or, affairs stand thus), *at least*, 676 a, b. — **ὅ τι ἄν τις χρήσαιτο αὐτοῖς,** *what use one can make of them,* or, *what service one can obtain from them.* — **δέοι τι,** sc. χρῆσθαι or χρήσασθαι.

41. **αὐτῶν,** gen. w. γνώμας : pos. 538 f.

42. **οὔτε πλῆθός ἐστιν οὔτε ἰσχὺς ἡ...ποιοῦσα** (= τό...ποιοῦν). — **σὺν τοῖς θεοῖς,** § 23 ; 2. 8. 11, 14. — **ὡς ἐπὶ τὸ πολύ** (Lex.). — **δέχονται,** *receive* to an encounter, *withstand* (Lex.).

43. **πᾶσι,** case 460. — **περὶ δὲ τοῦ καλῶς ἀποθνῄσκειν,** [about the dying honorably] *for an honorable death.* Cf. Hor. *Odes,* iii. 2. 13. Effugit mortem, quisquis contemserit ; timidissimum quemque consequitur, Curt. iv. 14. 25. — **τούτους ὁρῶ μᾶλλόν πως...ἀφικνουμένους** : οὗτοι...ἀφικνοῦνται, would have corresponded to the construction above. — **μᾶλλόν πως,** *in some way the rather.*

44. **παρακαλεῖν,** sc. ἄνδρας ἀγαθοὺς εἶναι, cf. iv. 3. 17.

45. **τοσοῦτον μόνον σε...ὅσον** [= ὅσον τοῦτο, ὅτι, 560] **ἤκουον** (612) **Ἀθηναῖον εἶναι** (657 k), *I knew you only so far as this, that I had heard that you were an Athenian.* The adv. use of τοσοῦτον μόνον and ὅσον may be referred to 478 or 482 ; cf. v. 8. 8. — **ἐφ' οἷς** = ἐπὶ τούτοις ἅ, 554 a N. — **βουλοίμην ἄν,** 636 a. — **ὅτι πλείστους,** i. 1. 6 ; 2. 4.

46. **μὴ μέλλωμεν,** § 24. — **οἱ δεόμενοι,** *you who need them* (ἀρχόντων). — **συγκαλοῦμεν,** cf. § 24.

47. **ἅμα ταῦτ' εἰπών,** 662 a. — **μέλλοιτο,** mid. or pass. *linger,* or, *be delayed.* — **Κλεάνωρ,** the troops of Agias joining the force which Cleanor before commanded; ii. 5. 37. — **Ὀρχομένιος,** some read Ἀρκάς.

CHAPTER II.

SPEECHES TO THE TROOPS BY THE NEW GENERALS, ESPECIALLY XENOPHON. — ORDER OF MARCH ADOPTED.

1. **ἡμέρα τε** s, *it was* [both] *nearly daybreak.* — **καὶ εἰς** (705) **τὸ μέσον,** 1. 46. — **καταστήσαντας,** sc. σφᾶς, 667 e ; voice 577 b. — πρῶτον μέν, followed by ἐπὶ τούτῳ, § 4 ; cf. 1. 13 N.

2. **ἄνδρες στρατιῶται, ἀνδρῶν στρατηγῶν** (Lex. ἀνήρ), 506 f. — **στερόμεθα,** i. 9. 13 ; 6. 2. — **λοχαγῶν,** order 719 d, *v.* — **πρός** (Lex. 703 b) **δ' ἔτι καί,** observe the pleonasm, 69 b. Some here recognize a tmesis of προσέτι, *yet further,* 388 c, 699 i. — **οἱ ἀμφὶ Ἀριαῖον,** ii. 4. 2.

3. **πειρᾶσθαι, ὅπως...σωζώμεθα,** *to strive* [so that we may save] *to save ourselves ;* "gravius dictum pro πειρᾶσθαι σώζεσθαι," Kühn.; cf. § 5. — **ἀποθνῄσκωμεν,** *let us die,* 628 a. Some regard it as constructed like σωζώμεθα. — **οἷα** s, *as may the gods bring upon our enemies !* cf. § 6.

BOOK III. CHAP. II.

4. ἐπὶ τούτῳ, *upon this*, or, *after him*, 690; deinceps, Kühn. — ὦ ἄνδρες, 484 g. — ὅστις, 550 b, ii. 3. 4. — λέγων.. ὁμόσας, tense? — εἴη, mode? — Ἑλλάδος, case 442 a : see ii. 3. 18, where dat. — περί (Lex.) πλείστου ἂν ποιήσαιτο, mode, and force of ἄν? — ἐπὶ τούτοις, [upon these declarations] *in accordance with*, or, *in addition to this*. — αὐτός, 540 c; observe the emphatic repetition (with asyndeton); and above, of ὁρᾶτε. — αὐτὸς ἐξαπατήσας συνέλαβε s, *then did himself* [having deceived] *seize the generals whom he had deceived*. — Κλεάρχῳ, case 451 b. See ii. 5. 27. — αὐτοῖς τούτοις, *by this very means*.

5. καί (sc. ᾧ) ἐδώκαμεν, 562; for the more comm. ἔδομεν, 306 b, c. — καὶ οὗτος, 685 b. — Κῦρον...ζῶντος, order? — ἐκείνου, case 442 a.

6. ἀποτίσαιντο, mode 638 d; cf. ποιήσειαν, § 3. — ὡς...κράτιστα, i. 6. 3; 2. 4. — τοῦτο...πάσχειν (Lex.), *meet that fortune* (whether good or evil) *which the gods may assign*.

7. Ἐκ (Lex. ἐξ). — κάλλιστα, Xen. was eminently fond of the beautiful (φιλόκαλος, Ælian. *Variæ Historiæ*, iii. 24). — τὸν...τῷ νικᾶν πρέπειν, *that the most beautiful attire befitted victory*. — ὀρθῶς ἔχειν, *that it was well*. — τῶν καλλίστων (431 b) ἑαυτὸν ἀξιώσαντα, *since he had deemed himself worthy of the most beautiful equipments*. — λόγου, case 425.

8. Τὴν μέν, the regular sequence having been interrupted by the sneezing. — λέγει, tense 612. — διὰ φιλίας, διὰ παντὸς πολέμου (Lex. διά). — στρατηγούς, prolepsis, 474, 657 : cf. i. 8. 21. — διὰ πίστεως, 694. — σὺν τοῖς ὅπλοις : cf. ii. 1. 12. — ὧν...δίκην = δίκην τούτων ἃ πεποιήκασι, [the penalty of those things which they have done] *vengeance for their deeds*. — πολλαὶ καί, ii. 3. 18. Cf. order in § 10.

9. πτάρνυται, a sudden, involuntary outburst of this kind was referred by the Greeks, as by so many other nations, to a divine interposition, indicating good or evil according to the circumstances (πταρμὸν τ' ὄρνιθα καλεῖτε, Ar. *Av.* 720). As the sign here fell upon σωτηρίας, Xen. interpreted it as promising safety, and proceeding from Ζεὺς Σωτήρ. — τὸν θεόν, the deity from whom the sign proceeded. Ζεῦ, σῶσον, *Jupiter (Zeus), be propitious*, was a common Greek exclamation when one in a company sneezed, as in Germ., "Gott helf," and in Eng., "God bless you." — ὅτῳ ...ἀνατεινάτω τὴν χεῖρα, a very common mode of voting among the Greeks, as with us. The Greeks naturally carried the usages, as well as the spirit, of their popular institutions into the field; and of this army in particular Krüg. says, that it was "civitatem perigrinantem," *a travelling commonwealth*. — τὰ τῶν θεῶν καλῶς εἶχεν, *the* [things of the gods were well] *religious rites had been duly performed*.

10. Ἐτύγχανον (Lex.) λέγων, i. e. when this omen came. — θεῶν, ii. 7. 5. — οὕτω δ' ἐχόντων, 676 a ; quæ cum ita sint. — οἵπερ ἱκανοί s. Cf. Ὁ θεὸς δέ, ὥς ἔοικε, πολλάκις χαίρει τοὺς μὲν μικροὺς μεγάλους ποιῶν, τοὺς δὲ μεγάλους μικρούς, *Hel.* vi. 4. 23.

11. γάρ, γάρ, in reg. const. one of these should be omitted. Cf. ii. 5. 12; 716 a. — ὑμᾶς, κινδύνους, 473 a. — ἀγαθοῖς...ἀγαθοί, order? — ὑμῖν, cf. 15, 661 b. — παμπληθεῖ στόλῳ, *in a vast array;* acc. to Nepos, 100000 infan-

try, and 10000 cavalry. Others increase this number, and Justin even to 600000 (of whom 200000 perished). — ὡς ἀφανιούντων s, *that they might bring Athens to nothing again*, 598 b. — ὑποστῆναι, at Marathon, B. C. 490; acc. to the comm. statement, 10000 in number, and aided only by 1000 Plataeans.

12. εὐξάμενοι, as if its subject followed in the nom., instead of the dat. αὐτοῖς w. ἔδοξεν, 402 a. — ἔδοξεν αὐτοῖς = ἐψηφίσαντο, [it seemed best to them] *they determined;* the dat. being used, by a change of const., for the nom. with which the sentence commences, cf. 402 a. — κατ' ἐνιαυτόν (692. 5) πεντακοσίας θύειν, upon her altar at Agrae upon the Ilissus; an annual sacrifice of 500, without limit of time, being substituted for an immediate payment of the whole number (6400 barbarians having fallen in the battle, acc. to Hdt. vi. 117). Plutarch mentions the thank-offering as existing even in his time, some 600 years after the battle.

13. τὴν ἀναρίθμητον στρατιάν, *that innumerable army*, so celebrated, 530 a. Hdt. (vii. 186) sets the entire host at 5283220 men, one half of whom were combatants. — ἐνίκων (tense? cf. ἐνίκησαν, § 11), at Salamis, B. C. 480, at Plataeae and Mycale, on the same day, B. C. 479, etc. — ῏Ων ἔστι (788 f) μὲν τεκμήρια (394 b) s, [as proofs of which one may see the trophies] *of which exploits we may behold proofs in the trophies* then erected. — ἀλλά, i. 4. 18. — προγόνων, case 412.

14. ἡμέραι, sc. εἰσίν, a comm. ellipsis in such expressions. — ἀφ' οὗ (Lex. ἀπό), 557 a (= ἀπὸ τοῦ χρόνου ὅτε). — ὑμῶν αὐτῶν, case 409. — ἐνικᾶτε (tense?), *were conquering.*

15. περὶ τῆς Κύρου s, [about] *in behalf of the sovereignty of Cyrus;* i. e. to make Cyrus king. — ἀγαθοί, πολύ, pos.? — ὑμᾶς, case 661 b; cf. § 11.

16. αὐτῶν, case? — τό τε πλῆθος ἄμετρον (sc. ὄν) ὁρῶντες, *and seeing the multitude* [to be] *immense*, 523 b, 5. — ἰέναι εἰς αὐτούς, *to go against them* [INTO them, stronger than ἐπὶ αὐτούς UPON them]. — θέλουσι...μὴ δέχεσθαι ὑμᾶς, *they are not willing to receive you* [will or choose *not* to receive, stronger than οὐ θέλουσι δέχεσθαι, do not will to receive].

17. Μηδὲ...δόξητε, as imv. 628 c. — μεῖον (Lex.). — εἰ, *if*, = ὅτι, *that*, 639 a. — Κυρεῖοι, cf. vii. 2. 7. — ἀφεστήκασιν, ii. 4. 2, 9 s. — ἔτι, pos.? — ἔφευγον, *they* [were fleeing] *fled.* The impf. presents more vividly than the aor. the scene when the army under Ariaeus showed its cowardice by running away and leaving the Greeks to their fate, i. 10. 1. The MSS. have πρός before ἐκείνους, but there does not appear to be any occasion on which the army of Ariaeus actually *fled to* the king's troops. The insertion came possibly from a copyist, who did not distinguish between ἀφεστήκασιν and ἔφευγον. — φυγῆς, case 425. — πολὺ κρεῖττον, sc. ἐστί.

18. τις...ἐνθυμήθητε, numb. 501. On value of cavalry, see ii. 4. 6. — οἱ μύριοι ἱππεῖς, 531 d, 534. 3: so in Eng. "your ten thousand horse." — ἄνθρωποι, pos.?

19. ἱππέων, case? — κρέμανται, [hang] *are placed aloft.* — μᾶλλον...τευξόμεθα, *shall better hit*, from our steadier aim. — Ἐνὶ μόνῳ, *in one respect alone*, 467 b. — ἡμᾶς, case 472 b. — φεύγειν s, 663 a. The

BOOK III. CHAP. II. 77

sportive and somewhat sarcastic tone of parts of this address was admirably adapted to raise the spirits of the soldiers.

20. μάχας, case 472 f. — ὑμῖν, ii. 2. 8 ; i. 7. 1. — τοῦτο, 483 b. — ἢ οὖς ...ἄνδρας, or (to have as guides) *whatsoever men* (553), *such men as*. — ἤν τι (478) περὶ ἡμᾶς ἁμαρτάνωσι (631 c), *if in aught they sin against us;* some read ὑμᾶς, *you*. — τὰς ἑαυτῶν ψυχὰς καὶ σώματα, *their own lives* (which may be taken) *and persons* (which may be beaten), 534. 4. Cf. "life and limb"; Germ., " Leib und Leben."

21. μικρά...πολλοῦ, in a kind of sarcastic antithesis. — μέτρα, in appos. w. ἐπιτήδεια, 395 a. — ἀργυρίου, case ? — μηδὲ...ἔχοντας, *as we no longer receive pay;* as they had been so long without pay. — μέτρῳ...ὁπόσῳ, *as large measure as*.

22. ταῦτα, prolepsis. — κρείττονα, sc. ἐστίν. — ἄπορον, ii. 5. 9; iv. 4. 11. — διαβάντες, *when you crossed them,* referring esp. to the passage of the Tigris, which was planned for the destruction of the Greeks, ii. 4. 24. — εἰ (complem.) ἆρα s, *whether indeed* (or, *after all*) *the barbarians* [have not done this even a most foolish thing] *have not here done a most foolish thing*, as they simply constrain us to make a longer march through the heart of their country. — πηγῶν, case ? — προϊοῦσι, *to* [persons proceeding] *those who proceed,* or, *if we ascend ;* case 458.

23. διοίσουσιν, some read διήσουσιν (δίημι, *allow to pass*). — οὐδ᾽ ὣς (Lex.). — φαίημεν βελτίους, [say are better] *admit to be better*. — βασιλέως, contemptuously repeated, to emphasize the king's inefficiency. Yet it seems quite possible that the first βασιλέως has crept into the text from a grammatical gloss, and that the true reading is οἱ ἄκοντος (so placed for emphasis) ἐν τῇ βασιλέως χώρᾳ. Hence in MS. Eton. οἱ ἐν βασιλέως χώρᾳ ἄκοντος. — Λυκάονας...εἴδομεν, in passing through Lycaonia, i. 2. 19 : cf. § 8, 29. — τούτων, the Persians or subjects of the king ; *v. l.* τούτου.

24. ἂν ἔφην, *I might say,* were it not for the reason mentioned in § 25. — χρῆναι...ὡρμημένους, *ought not to appear to have set out for home*. — ὁμήρους τοῦ ἀδόλως ἐκπέμψειν, *hostages* [of his being about to send] *that he would send them away faithfully*. — οἶδ᾽ ὅτι, [I know that he would] *I am well assured,* thrown in parenthetically, 717 b.

25. Ἀλλὰ γάρ, *but* [I do not so say] *for,* 709. 2. — μή, repeated after the conditional clause, 714. 2. Cf. εἰ...εἰ, § 35. — μεγάλαις, *tall or stately*. Physical prowess was so indispensable among the Greeks, that good size became an important element of female attractiveness. — ὥσπερ οἱ λωτοφάγοι, *as those who taste the lotus ;* μή πώ τις λωτοῖο φαγὼν νόστοιο λάθηται, *Od.* ix. 102. The poems of Homer were most familiar sources of illustration to the Greeks.

26. ἐξὸν (Lex.) αὑτοῖς (459) ...κομισαμένους (667 e) s, [it being in their power, having brought, etc.] *when, if they will bring hither the citizens that now live in want at home* (as being without estate) *they may behold them rich :* τοὺς πολιτεύοντας is the comm. object of κομισαμένους and ὁρᾶν.

27. ἵνα μὴ τὰ ζεύγη ἡμῶν (407) στρατηγῇ, *that our teams may not control* [us] *our march,* obliging us to go only by carriage routes. Cf. ii. 2. 13.

— ὄχλον μὲν παρέχουσιν ἄγειν, [give trouble] *are troublesome to carry*, 663 d, e. — οὐδέν, case 478.

28. τῶν ἄλλων...πλὴν ὅσα, *of our other effects let us dispense with the superfluous*, [all except what we carry] *whatever we do not carry*, etc. Cf. i. 2. 17. — Κρατουμένων (sc. τινῶν, 676), *if*, or, *when men are conquered;* Xen. would not here use the humbling and ill-omened ἡμῶν. — πάντα (sc. γίγνεται) ἀλλότρια, *everything becomes another's*.

29. Λοιπόν (Lex.) μοι, case 460. — 'Ορᾶτε γάρ, so v. 1. 8; 8. 11. — πρόσθεν...πρίν, cf. 1. 16; i. 1. 10. — ἄν...ἀπολέσθαι, 621 d. — ἀταξία, cf. 1. 38.

30. τοὺς νῦν τῶν πρόσθεν, order 719 b, ε; cf. νῦν ἢ πρόσθεν.

31. "Ην δέ τις ἀπειθῇ, ἣν ψηφίσησθε, *and in case any one is disobedient, if you would vote*. In the logical order the latter clause would precede the former, but the other is placed first in distinction from πειθομένους in § 30. — τὸν...ἐντυγχάνοντα, *any one of you who may be present at the time*. — ἀεί, see Lex. — σὺν τῷ ἄρχοντι κολάζειν, *should join with the commander in punishing him;* a measure more likely to be voted than well executed; cf. v. 8. 21 s. — πλεῖστον...ἔσονται, *will be most completely disappointed*. — Κλεάρχους (Lex.), 227. 1; i. e. rigid disciplinarians, ii. 6. 9 s. — οὐδ' ἑνί, *not a single man* (Lex. οὐδέ): v. l. οὐδενί. — κακῷ, [bad as a soldier] *remiss in duty*.

32. 'Αλλὰ γάρ (Lex.), 709. 2. — ἢ ταύτῃ [for ταῦτα], *than* [that things should be in this way] *this*. — ὁ ἰδιώτης, art. 522 a.

33. ψηφίσασθαι ἄριστον εἶναι, *to be best to vote*. — ἀνέτειναν, asynd. Cf. 2. 9.

34. (sc. ἐκεῖσε) ὅπου, 551 f; cf. οὗ, ii. 1. 6. — πλέον, case 482 d.

36. ποιησαμένους, cf. i. 2. 1. — τῶν ὅπλων, ii. 2. 4 N. — εἴη, ii. 4. 5. — τὰ πρόσθεν (Lex.). — ἑκατέρων, cf. i. 8. 27. — χρώμεθα...τεταγμένοις, *we could immediately put our marshalled men in action*.

37. ἄλλως ἐχέτω, *let it be otherwise*. — Χειρίσοφος: Chirisophus had before been kept in the shade by his older and abler countryman, Clearchus. — Λακεδαιμόνιος: the Spartans, now sovereign through Greece, were very jealous for their precedence; cf. vi. 1. 26, 32; 6. 12. — πλευρῶν, case? — πρεσβυτάτων, 418 c. — τὸ νῦν εἶναι, 665 b.

38. πειρώμενοι s, 432 b; but with any changes that may seem expedient from time to time; e. g. 4. 19 s. —"Εδοξε ταῦτα, asyndeton.

39. εἶναι, inf. 657 k. — τούτου τυχεῖν, *to obtain this* sight, 427. — τῶν μέν...νικώντων, 443 a. — Καὶ εἴ τις δὲ χρημάτων (case 432 e) ἐπιθυμεῖ, *and even if any one is desirous of wealth;* a lower motive presented thus conditionally. This peroration, though not observing strictly the law of climax, was admirably adapted to impress the hearers. Observe the emphatic repetitions, chiasms, etc.

CHAPTER III.

THE GREEKS CROSS THE ZAPATAS AND ADVANCE. — ANNOYED BY THE PERSIANS.

1. Τούτων s, 675. — ἀνέστησαν, the assembly having been before this seated. Cf. 1. 33; vi. 2. 5. — κατέκαιον, *engaged in burning.* Observe the imperfects to depict the scene, 592 a; cf. 2. 27 s.

2. πιστός, ii. 5. 35. — εὔνους, sc. εἰμί. — πρός με, accent, 788 e. — τί ἐν νῷ, 564. 2.

3. ἔλεγε, cf. ii. 3. 21. — ἦν μέν s; observe the close correspondence in form of the contrasted clauses. — τις, *one* (much like Fr. *on*, and Germ. *man*) = *if we are permitted*, with esp. but not sole reference to the king and Tissaphernes, whom he does not care to name; cf. i. 4. 12. — ἰᾷ, in what mode after ἦν? — τὴν χώραν, *his country*, or, *territory*, 530 e. — ἡμᾶς τῆς ὁδοῦ (405) ἀποκωλύῃ, *obstructs* [us from the way] *our passage.*

4. ἐγιγνώσκετο, [he] *it was perceived*, pers. or impers., 573; cf. ii. 4. 22. — τις, pos.? Cf. ii. 5. 32 N. — πίστεως ἕνεκα, [for the sake of assurance] *to secure his fidelity* to the king; cf. ii. 5. 35.

5. βέλτιον εἶναι, *to be* [better] *advisable.* Observe the succession of infinitives. — ἔστ', *as long as, whilst.* — διέφθειρον, διέφθειραν, sc. the enemy, fr. τῇ πολεμίᾳ: tense? — Νίκαρχον (Lex.). — ᾤχετο ἀπιών, 679 d. — νυκτός, prob. the preceding night, which afforded such opportunity for intrigue and desertion, 1. 3.

6. διαβάντες: the Greeks were encamped upon the southeast bank of the Great Zab, prob. by one of its lowest fords, ii. 5. 1. This is identified by Layard with the principal ford in this part of the river, about twenty-five miles from its junction with the Tigris. The χαράδρα mentioned 4. 1, 3 s, would then correspond with the dry bed of the torrent Bumadus, now Gazir-su; and the second day's march would bring the army to the Tigris at Larissa. The Greeks had made such preparations during the night that they were ready to cross at once, before the Persians, little suspecting such an efficient and rapid movement, were prepared to interfere. The final battle between Alexander and Darius III., commonly called the battle of Arbela, was fought on the plain. — Ζαπάταν, some read Ζάβατον: see Lex. — Οὐ πολύ, sc. χωρίον, expressed § 15. Cf. βραχύ, i. 5. 3, etc.

7. ἐτίτρωσκον, both archers and slingers. — Κρῆτες, i. 2. 9. — τῶν Περσῶν, who had not only esp. skill in archery, but very large and strong bows, 4. 17. — ὅπλων = ὁπλιτῶν. — ἀκοντισταί: the Greek peltasts were trained not only to use their light spears in the hand, but also to throw them (v. 2. 12); and were then specially called ἀκοντισταί. — βραχύτερα ἠκόντιζον, ἢ ὡς s, 513 d. — σφενδονητῶν, case?

8. διωκτέον εἶναι, 682. — ἐδίωκον, sc. οὗτοι : ii. 2. 14.

9. οἱ πεζοὶ τοὺς πεζούς, order? — ἐκ πολλοῦ (Lex.); cf. ἐκ πλέονος, i. 10.

NOTES.

11. — οὐχ οἷόν τε ἦν, 556 c ; lest they should be surrounded and destroyed by the cavalry.
10. εἰς τοὔπισθεν (Lex. ὄπισθεν), 125 a, 526 b, τοξεύοντες, *shooting backwards*, or, *behind;* "a dexterity which the Parthians exhibited afterwards still more signally, and which the Persian horsemen of the present day parallel with their carbines." Grote.

96 11. ἡμέρας, δείλης, case 433 a. — κώμας, mentioned above, 2. 34. — πολεμίους οὐδέν, two accus., 480. 2 b.
12. ᾐτιῶντο, μαρτυροίη, mode 651 a. — ἐν τῷ μένειν, *while keeping our places* in the appointed order.
13. ἀληθῆ...λέγετε, *you speak the truth*, briefly and forcibly, for the fact was as you say. — κακῶς...χαλεπῶς, order ?
14. θεοῖς χάρις, sc. ἔστω, *thanks* [be] *to the gods*. — μεγάλα, ii. 3. 23.
15. [sc. τοσοῦτον] ὅσον οὔτε, *as far as neither*, i. e. farther than either. — οἱ ἐκ χειρὸς βάλλοντες = οἱ ἀκοντισταί, § 7. — ἐξικνεῖσθαι, *hit, send*. — πολὺ...χωρίον, pos. 719 a, *v*. — πεζὸς πεζόν, cf. § 9. — διώκων...ἐκ τόξου ῥύματος (Lex.); if he had a bow-shot the start, as an archer would be likely to have.
16. Ἡμεῖς (emph. pos.) οὖν εἰ μέλλομεν s, *if then we are to check these men*. — μέλλομεν, some read μέλλοιμεν. — σφενδονητῶν, case 414 b. — τὴν ταχίστην, 483 d ; cf. i. 3. 14, 20. — ὧν...αὐτῶν, 562. — σφενδονῶν, 2.14 ; case 409.

97 17. χειροπληθέσι, pos. 523 b, 4.
18. αὐτῶν...τίνες, *who of them*, or see 413, and cf. 1. 19. — πέπανται (πάομαι), i. 9. 19. — τούτῳ, as if τίς had preceded, 501. — αὐτῶν, *for them*, i. e. the slings, 429 a. — ἐν τῷ τεταγμένῳ, *in the place assigned him:* pro in loco constituto, assignato. Poppo. — ἀτελείαν (Lex.).
19. τοὺς μέν τινας, 530 b. — τοὺς δὲ τῷ Κλεάρχῳ, *those that belonged to Clearchus* (v. l. τοὺς δὲ τῶν Κλεάρχου). — σκευοφόρα (Lex.), i. e. mules, asses, or oxen. — εἰς ἱππέας, *for* [horsemen] *cavalry* use.
20. ἐγένοντο, [came to be] *were provided*. — ἐδοκιμάσθησαν, a term for the annual examination and approval of the Athenian cavalry. — στολάδες, *v. l.* σπολάδες (see Lex.). — θώρακες αὐτοῖς s, 587 a, 454 e.

CHAPTER IV.

MARCH ALONG THE TIGRIS FROM THE VICINITY OF NINEVEH TO THE REGION OF THE CARDUCHIAN MOUNTAINS.

1. τῇ ἄλλῃ, 567 a. — πρωΐαίτερον (Lex. πρωΐ, v. l. πρωΐτερον). — χαράδραν, see 3. 6 N. — μὴ ἐπιθοῖντο, 624 c ; form 315 c.
2. τοσούτους s, 2 accus. 480, 2 c. — ἔλαβεν, ὑποσχόμενος, *had received them* [having promised] *on the promise*. Having been an adherent of Cyrus, Mithridates must, forsooth, commend himself to the confidence and favor

BOOK III. CHAP. IV. 81

of the king by an excess of zeal. — λάβῃ, mode 645 a. — πρόσθεν (v. l. ἔμπροσθεν, 706 b). **98**

3. ὅσον, about (Lex.), 556 d, 507 e. — Παρήγγελτο s, *instructions had been given, both who of the peltasts were to pursue*. — εἴρητο (Lex. φημί). — ὡς ἐφεψομένης s, *as* (or, *assured that*) *a competent force would follow* in their support.

4. ἐξικνοῦντο, [were reaching their aim] *could take effect*. Observe the force of each tense in this section. — ἐσήμηνε, i. 2. 17; ii. 2. 4. — οἱ δέ, often of enemy, iv. 3. 31; v. 2. 5.

5. βαρβάροις, case 464. — ἠκίσαντο: this, though provoked by the repeated treachery of the enemy, was so contrary to Greek usage that Xen. takes pains to say that it was done without orders; cf. 1. 17 N. — ὁρᾶν, 663 g; 1. 23; ii. 3. 3.

6. οὕτω πράξαντες, *having fared thus*. — τὸ λοιπόν, 482 a.

7. ὄνομα δ', see Lex. Λάρισσα, Μέσπιλα. — τὸ παλαιόν, 529 a: τὸ ἀρχαῖον, i. 1. 6; ii. 2. 5. — κύκλου ἡ περίοδος, order 523 c.

8. βασιλεύς, i. e. Cyrus the Elder. — ἥλιον δὲ νεφέλη προκαλύψασα ἠφάνισε, μέχρι s, *but a cloud veiling the sun hid it from sight, until the inhabitants abandoned the city* through superstitious terror from the unusual gloom. Some suppose that this tradition originated in an eclipse. Such is the common but conjectural text. The MSS., with great unanimity, read ἥλιος δὲ νεφέλην προκαλύψας ἠφάνισε, which seems to be a figurative account of the final effort and success of Cyrus: *and the Sun* (Cyrus, whose name has this meaning) *having brought a cloud as a veil* (a cloud of troops) *hid the city from sight, until the inhabitants left it* (coming forth to surrender). — οὕτως ἑάλω, voice 575 a. Even if the Greeks had been aware that they were passing by the remains of one of the mightiest cities in the world's history, they had no time to stop for their examination, or even to gather up carefully the traditions respecting them. But certainly Xenophon's slight notices are a striking illustration how complete was the desolation of "great Nineveh" to the mind as well as to the eye.

9. Παρά, *beside:* cf. i. 2. 13; 3. 7: παρά with *things* regularly takes the accusative, sometimes the dative, vii. 2. 25. See Lex. — πυραμίς (Lex.). **99**

10. τεῖχος ἔρημον μέγα, *a desolate wall* (or, *castle*) *of great extent*. — πρὸς τῇ πόλει κείμενον, *lying* (in ruins) *before its city*. This seems much like gloss, and is omitted by some editors. — Μέσπιλα, see Lex.

11. κύκλου: if, as some suppose, τεῖχος, in § 10, signifies an outlying fortress or castle, τοῦ κύκλου here must still refer to the enclosure of the city also. — καταφυγεῖν, 660 b.

12. ἐμβροντήτους ποιεῖ, *strikes with madness*, or, *with a panic*, perhaps through a terrific thunder-storm. Compare the word "Dunder-head." (Anthon.)

13. Εἰς τοῦτον...σταθμόν, *in this day's march*, intruding into or upon it, 704 a. — οὕς τε αὐτὸς ἱππέας ἦλθεν ἔχων = ἔχων τούς τε ἱππέας οὓς αὐτὸς ἦλθε ἔχων, *having both the cavalry which he* [himself came having] *brought*

6

with him from his own satrapy; i. 2. 4. — **'Ορόντου** (v. l. 'Ορόντα), ii. 4. 8.
— **οὓς Κῦρος ἔχων ἀνέβη βαρβάρους,** [what barbarians Cyrus having went up] *the barbarians with whom Cyrus made his ascent.* — **ἀδελφός,** ii. 4. 25.
— **ἐβοήθει,** tense?

14. The following diagram may perhaps sufficiently illustrate the relative position of the Greeks and Persians:

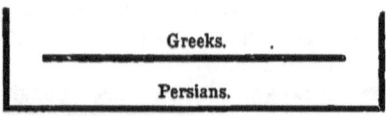

Observe the order of the four infinitives in this section, ἐμβάλλειν, etc.

100 15. **Σκύθαι τοξόται** (v. l. Σκυθοτοξόται): this term, not explained by Xen., appears to distinguish those of the archers who had obtained large bows (such as the Scythians carried), chiefly, we may suppose, by despoiling those who fell in the battle of the ravine, § 5 (since in the previous attacks the bows of the Greeks were inferior in power to those of their assailants). — **οὐδὲ γὰρ, εἰ πάνυ προθυμοῖτο** (v. l. προύθυμεῖτο) s, 632: in such a dense mass did the enemy stand. — **ἀπεχώρει, ἀπεχώρησαν,** tense?

16. **καὶ τῶν πλείστων τοξοτῶν,** *and than most of the archers could send their arrows.*

17. **Μεγάλα** s: yet the bows of the Persians were also large, so that the Cretans found their captured arrows of great use with the larger bows which they themselves now carried. Cf. Hdt. vii. 61. — **Κρησί,** case 453. — **διετέλουν** (Lex.) **χρώμενοι,** *were constantly using,* 677. — **ἄνω,** *into the air,* so that they might recover the arrows, as they could not afford to waste their small supply in the needed practice with new weapons. — **μόλυβδος,** sc. πολύς?

18. **μεῖον** (Lex.), i. 10. 8.

19. **κέρατα,** *the wings, flanks,* or, *sides,* = πλευραί, § 22. — **ἐκθλίβεσθαι** s, *that the hoplites should be pushed out of their places,* or, *ranks.* — **ἅμα μὲν πιεζομένους, ἅμα δὲ καί,** *being at the same time crowded, and* [at the same time] *not only crowded, but also,* etc. Cf. iv. 1. 4; vi. 2. 14, for this doubling of ἅμα, which the Eng. does not imitate. — **ὥστε δυσχρήστους εἶναι ἀνάγκη** (v. l. ἀνάγκῃ), *so that it is unavoidable that they should be,* or, *they are necessarily, useless.*

20. **κενὸν γίγνεσθαι...κεράτων,** *that the interval between the flanks should be open;* as in their confusion they could not at once take their places so

101 as to fill up the ranks. Cf. i. 4. 4; 445 b. — **ταῦτα πάσχοντας,** [suffering this] *so affected.* — **διάβασιν,** ii. 3. 10. — **φθάσαι** (Lex.). — **εὐεπίθετον** (Lex.) ...**πολεμίοις,** case 458; cf. iv. 8. 12.

21. **ἐποιήσαντο** (v. l. ἐποίησαν), by the selection of the most valiant, active, and reliable, for special service wherever they might be needed. — **ἀνὰ ἑκατόν,** 240 f, 692. 5. — **Οὗτοι δὲ πορευόμενοι,** 402 a. To avoid or soften the anacoluthon some needlessly conjecture the gen. for the nom., and

others οὕτω for οὗτοι. — ὑπέμενον ὕστεροι s, *the captains remained behind with their companies*; i. e. when stationed in the rear, as they seem at first to have been because the danger was from behind. Afterwards, when the danger was divided, half the companies were in front with Chirisophus, § 43. — τότε δὲ παρῆγον ἔξωθεν τῶν κεράτων, *and then led on their companies outside of* the line between *the two wings*, i. e. here, behind it, or apart from it.

22. κατὰ λόχους, *by companies:* in this way the companies were arrayed side by side, one enomoty in width and four in depth.

— κατὰ πεντηκοστῦς : the width was now doubled by bringing each pentecostys (or fifty) of the company into the line ; while in the arrangement κατὰ ἐνωμοτίας it was quadrupled by bringing each enomoty forward to the line. When each enomoty formed a square, the first arrangement would make of the six lochi a body 30 men wide and 20 men deep; the second, 60 wide and 10 deep ; and the third, 120 wide and 5 deep.

23. οἱ λοχαγοί, *the captains* of the army in general, who crossed in order under the protection of the six select companies. — εἴ που δέοι τι τῆς φάλαγγος (gen. w. που, 420 a), ἐπιπαρῆσαν (v. l. ἐπιπαρῆσαν), *if there was any need in any part of the phalanx, these* (the select companies) *were at hand* for support. — ἐπορεύθησαν, ἐπορεύοντο § 24, tense 593.

24. βασίλειον, a (satrap's) *palace,* § 31 ; cf. iv. 4. 2. — διά, [through] over. — ἡ κώμη, *the chief village,* containing the palace ; or perhaps the first appearance was that of a single village only, though the Greeks found that there were many.

25. ἀνέβησαν, κατέβαινον, tense ? — ἀναβαίνειν, mode 671 d. — εἰς τὸ πρανές (Lex.), *down the hill,* giving them a great advantage over the Greek missiles sent up the hill. — ἔβαλλον s, asyndeton. — ὑπὸ μαστίγων, 695. The Persian troops, even in battle, were treated as slaves. So at Thermopylæ, Hdt. vii. 223 : cf. Ctes. *Pers.* 23.

26. κατετίτρωσκον, ἐκράτησαν, tense 595 a. — γυμνήτων, case ? εἴσω τῶν ὅπλων, § 17 ; 2. 36 ; 3. 7.

27. Observe the tenses. — ἀπεπήδων, some read ἀνεπήδων.

28. στρατιώτας, see iv. 3. 22, and στρατιά, vi. 3. 19. — πρίν, conj. 703 d, a. — τὸ ὄρος, rising above the hills, § 24.

29. ἀποτμηθείησαν, 293 a ; cf. § 35. — αὐτῶν, case ? Observe the different reference of the second οἱ πολέμιοι from the first.

30. οἱ δέ, the targeteers, § 28 ; they passed along the mountain above the main army, and in a parallel direction. — ἰατρούς, i. e. soldiers who had most experience and skill in dressing wounds. A Greek army had not the fully and carefully appointed staff of modern times ; and the wounds from which they suffered were in general less difficult of treatment than those made by fire-arms.

31. εἶχον, for ἔχοντες, 716 c. — ἄλευρα s, asynd. 707 j. — τῷ σατραπεύοντι, case 460 (or 461 ?), chiefly for the support of the troops which he must maintain. Cf. Xen. *Œcon.* iv. 5 s.

103
33. αὐτοῖς, case? — διέφερον (Lex.).
34. πολεμίοις, case 460. — ἐπιθῶνται, mode? i. 8. 24.
35. Πονηρόν, ii. 5. 9; 4. 35: iii. 2. 22. Cf. *Cyrop.* iii. 3. 26 s. — αὐτοῖς, case 464. — ὡς ἐπὶ τὸ πολύ (Lex.). — τοῦ μὴ φεύγειν ἕνεκα (436 d, 664 d) εἰ λυθείησαν, *that they might not escape if they should be loosed*, or, *get loose*. — δεῖ, δεῖ, observe the emph. repetition and order. — ἀνδρί, dat. after δεῖ, for the more comm. acc. (subject of the inf., Lex. δέω), 453; yet below θωρακισθέντα, cf. i. 2. 1. — Ἑλλήνων, case 405; cf. 699 f.
36. ἐκήρυξε (Lex.), 571 b. — ἐπέσχον τῆς πορείας, *delayed their march*, 405 a (Lex. ἐπέχω).
37. ἀναζεύξαντες, *having [yoked] harnessed up*, or, *decamped*. They had beasts of burden, but had burned their wagons, 3. 1. — τῇ ὑστεραίᾳ, νυκτός,

104 case 469 a, 433. — ᾗ (Lex. ὅς). — ὑφ' ἦν, implying motion towards and under; cf. ὑφ' ᾧ, of rest beneath, § 24.
38. οὐρᾶς, cf. στόμα, § 42 s.
39. Ἔξεστιν ὁρᾶν, *you can see for yourself*. — ἡμῖν, *for us*, i. e. to prevent our passage, 462 e. Cf. i. 3. 16. — οὐκ ἔστι παρελθεῖν, *there is no getting by*.
40. ἔρημα, [without defenders] *unguarded*, or, *exposed*. — τις...ἀπελᾷ, [one] *we shall drive off*, 548 g.
41. τοῦ ὄρους, pos. 523 c. — ὑπὲρ αὐτοῦ τοῦ ἑαυτῶν (i. e. the Greeks implied in Ξενοφῶν, 499 e) s, *directly above their own army*, 541 e, or, *even above*, cf. i. 8. 14. — βούλει, form? — ἐγὼ δ', expressed in distinction from σὺ μέν, understood with the preceding imperative, but which it was more courteous to omit.
42. εἰπών, asynd. Cf. iv. 1. 20; 8. 6. — κελεύει, *requests* Chirisophus. — οἱ, dat. w. συμπέμψαι, 539 a. — στόματος, cf. οὐρά, § 38. — μακρὸν...ἦν, longum erat, "*it was too far to get them from.*" McMich.

105 43. ἔλαβε, took himself in their place. — ἐπιλέκτων, § 21.
44, 45. Observe emph. repetitious. — διακελευομένων, numb.?
46. λοιπήν (Lex.), 506 b; case?
47. ἴσου (Lex.), 691.
48. Καὶ ὅς, i. 8. 16. — ἀκούσας, καταπηδήσας, i. 8. 3. — ὠθεῖται καὶ ...ἐπορεύετο, tense? — ἔχων ἐπορεύετο, *marched on with it*, 674 b. — θώρακα (Lex. θώραξ, ἱππεύς). — παριέναι s, *to pass, though following with difficulty*, or, *while they followed with difficulty*.
49. Ὁ δέ, i. e. Xenophon. — βάσιμα ἦν [impers. 571 e, or sc. τὰ χωρία], sc. τῷ ἵππῳ, *the ground was passable* (fit for riding); cf. iv. 6. 17. — φθάνουσιν...πολεμίους, *outstrip the enemy in reaching the summit*.

CHAPTER V.

THE GREEKS RESOLVE TO FIGHT THEIR WAY ACROSS THE MOUNTAINS AND THROUGH THE CARDUCHIAN COUNTRY.

1. Οἱ δὲ ἀμφί, 527 a; cf. § 3; ii. 4. 2. — ὁδόν, case? ii. 2. 16; iii. 4. 26; i. 2. 20. — μεστῇ πολλῶν ἀγαθῶν, *full of various supplies*, unless the expression is pleonastic. **106**
2. διαβιβαζόμεναι, *in the act of being removed*, for security. — τὸ πέραν, 527.
3. τὰ ἐπιτήδεια, pos.? — μὴ (625 a) ... οὐκ ἔχοιεν, *lest they should have no source from which they could obtain*. Observe the change of subject.
4. ἀπῄεσαν ἐκ τῆς βοηθείας, *were returning from the rescue* of the men who were dispersed for supplies, § 2. — κατέβη, i. e. from the summit, height, 4. 49.
5. Ὁρᾶτε...ὑφιέντας, *do you see them conceding?* — ἃ γάρ...διεπράττοντο, *for as to what they stipulated*, ii. 3. 27. Cf. Cyrop. i. 4. 6. — μὴ καίειν, sc. ἡμᾶς, appositive of ἅ; more logically of its antecedent. The sentence closes as if it had commenced τὴν γὰρ βασιλέως χώραν, ἥν.
6. Playful remarks by the generals, to cheer the desponding.
7. σκηνάς, a general term for *quarters, camp*, the tents proper having been burned, 3. 1. — στρατηγοὶ δὲ καὶ λοχαγοί, art. om. **107** 533 f; cf. § 14. — ὄρη s, cf. iv. 1. 2. — ὑπερέχειν, sc. τοῦ ὕδατος. — πειρωμένοις, [for them testing] *when they tested*. The length of the common spear (say about 8 feet) much exceeded a man's height. — βάθους, case?
8. κατά (Lex.), 240 f.
9. ταῦτα [*v. l.* ταὖτα om.] πρόβατα, 509 b. — ἅ, gend. 496 c. — καὶ φυσηθέντα, *and* (their skins) *inflated*, that being referred in general to the animal, which belongs specially to its skin; see 70 j.
10. Observe multiplication of participles. — ὁρμίσας s, *having anchored each bag* (or, *skin*) *by attaching stones and dropping them*. — διαγαγών s, *having extended them across the stream and fastened them at each end to the bank*, — thus making a floating bridge, suggested by the floats made of skins, i. 5. 10 N.
11. ἕξει τοῦ μή (713 d) καταδῦναι, case 405 a. Cf. the different mode of expression below, ὥστε δὲ μὴ ὀλισθάνειν...σχήσει (the comm. fut. in this sense, Lex. ἔχω), *will keep you* [that you should not slip] *from slipping*.
12. τοῖς πρώτους, *the pioneers*, who were to cross and fasten the opposite end of this bridge.
13. ἡ πρὸς Βαβυλῶνα, *or towards Babylon*, apparently a gloss which crept into the text. — οὐ προσήλαυνον, as they were quite at a loss what the Greeks were intending, whether to submit to the king, or in their desperation to make offensive war. — ὅμοιοι ἦσαν, 657 j. — ὅποι ποτέ (Lex.). — τρέψονται, 643 h, 645 c.

14. ἤλεγχον s, *inquired in respect to the whole country round*, 474 b. — τίς ἑκάστη (sc. χώρα) εἴη, *what each region was*.
15. τὰ μὲν, sc. μέρη or χωρία. — τῆς ἐπὶ B. (sc. ὁδοῦ) εἴη, [belonged to, 443] *lay upon the route.* — ἡ δὲ πρὸς ἕω (sc. ὁδός) ... φέροι, *the route to the east led.* — θερίζειν καὶ ἐαρίζειν, obviously, from the climate of the two capitals, in chiastic order (the spring spent at Susa, etc.). Cf. *Cyr.* viii. 6. 22. — ἡ δὲ διαβάντι s, *the route* [for one crossing the river, 462 c] *across the river.* — ὅτι, repeated (though not in its proper place before ἡ δὲ διά, 719 η), giving prominence to this final statement of the route which was taken.
16. ἀνὰ τὰ ὄρη, 689 l. — βασιλέως, case 432 g. — ἐμβαλεῖν (Lex.), having στρατιάν as its subject ; an expedition of which nothing more is known. — σφῶν, sc. τινάς (421 b), *some of* [themselves] *their own people*, i. e. the inhabitants of the plain, this statement coming from them. — πρὸς ἐκείνους, *with them* (the Carduchi).
17. τοὺς...εἰδέναι, sc. τὴν ὁδόν, *those who professed to know the way to each quarter.* — οὐδὲν δῆλον ποιήσαντες, *giving no intimation.* — τούτους, gov. by διά. — ἔφασαν, sc. οἱ ἐαλωκότες, § 14. — πολλῆς, for πολλήν, 553.
18. Ἐπὶ τούτοις, *in respect to this* proceeding or course ; cf. i. 6. 10. — ὁπηνίκα (*v. l.* ἡνίκα) ... τῆς ὥρας (Lex.), 420 a. — ὑπερβολήν s, *they feared lest the pass over the mountains should be preoccupied*, 474 b. — δειπνήσαιεν, παραγγέλλῃ, mode ? order ?

BOOK IV.

FROM THE ENTRANCE OF THE GREEKS AMONG THE CARDUCHI TO THEIR ARRIVAL AT THE PONTUS EUXINUS.

CHAPTER I.

MARCH THROUGH THE MOUNTAIN REGION. — SUFFERING FROM ATTACKS OF THE ENEMY AND THE COLD.

1. Ὅσα μέν, etc. The first four sections, which are chiefly recapitulations, are regarded by some as not from the pen of Xenophon. Sections 2 - 4 are wanting in MSS. b, c, e (see p. 3, as to division into books, summaries, etc.). — ὅσα...ἐπολεμήθη, [how many things were performed in war] *what war was made.* — τοῦ Περσικοῦ στρατεύματος. This did not venture to follow the Greeks among the Carduchian mountains ; and ceased the pursuit, as if now certain of their destruction, Tissaphernes proceeding to Asia Minor, Orontas to Armenia, etc.
2. ἐδόκει δή, *v. l.* ἐδόκει δέ. Some editors bracket as doubtful §§ 2, 3, 4.

BOOK IV. CHAP. I. 87

3. τῶν ἁλισκομένων, case? tense? — εἰ διέλθοιεν...ἢν μὲν βούλωνται, διαβήσονται...περιίασι (as fut.), 633 b. — τοῦ Τίγρητος, for τῶν τοῦ Τ., 438 b; ii. 3. 15. — καὶ ἔστιν οὕτω στενόν, sc. τὸ διάστημα or χωρίον, and [it is so narrow] *so small is really the distance* here between the two rivers, the Tigris flowing from the southern side of Mt. Niphates, and the Eastern Euphrates from the northern side. Such is the text of the MSS. Most editions have now the conjectural reading of Abresch, καὶ ἔστιν οὕτως ἔχον, *and so it is*.

4. εἰς τοὺς Καρδούχους (Lex. εἰς, χώρα); cf. i. 1. 11. — ἅμα μέν s, *endeavoring both to steal away* (from the Persians), *and at the same time to* [anticipate before, etc.] *gain the heights, before the enemy* (the Carduchians) *should seize them*. 110

5. ἀμφὶ τὴν τελευταίαν φυλακήν (Lex.), i. e. *about 3 o'clock in the morning*. — ἐλείπετο s, 556 d. — σκοταίους, § 10; ii. 2. 17. — ἀπὸ παραγγέλσεως, *summons*, or, *word of command*, quietly passed from man to man. A trumpet-signal might have defeated their plan. — ἅμα (Lex.), 450 a.

6. στρατεύματος, case 407. — πορευομένων, i. 4. 12; 2. 7: ii. 4. 24.

7. ἐφείπετο δὲ ἀεὶ τὸ ὑπερβάλλον s, *and* [continually the crossing part of the army] *each part of the army, as it crossed* (the height), *followed on*.

8. τὰ δὲ...λαμβάνειν, *and then was an opportunity of taking provisions in abundance*. — χαλκώμασι : "The Kurds at the present day take great pride in their *copper* (not brass) utensils." Ainsworth. — ὑποφειδόμενοι, *sparing them somewhat*, or [covertly], *from policy*. — εἴ πως s, (to see) *if perchance the Carduchi would consent*, i. e. to ascertain whether, etc. (Lex. εἰ). — ὡς διὰ φιλίας τῆς χώρας, [as through the country friendly] *through the country as a friendly one*, 553; cf. i. 3. 14.

9. καλούντων, sc. αὐτῶν, case 432 g (or, as some prefer, 676 a).

10. σκοταῖοι, 509; § 5 : ii. 2. 17. — ὅλην τὴν ἡμέραν (482) ... αὐτοῖς ἐγένετο, [took place for them through the whole day] *occupied for them the whole day*. — ὀλίγοι τινές, 548 d.

11. πολύ, wt. art. 523 f. — οὕτως, *so, as has been stated*, § 8. 111 — συνεώρων ἀλλήλους, *watched each other* for their common safety.

13. Σχολαίαν, πολλά, πολλοί, etc., pos.? — ἐποίουν, pl., the subject including persons, 569 a. — πολλοὶ δὲ οἱ ἐπί...όντες, *and* [those who were over these, many in number] *many having charge of these*. — Δόξαν δὲ ταῦτα (sc. ποιεῖν, or see 502), *and this resolved on*, 675 c.

14. ἐν στενῷ, sc. χωρίῳ, *in a narrow pass*. — πλὴν εἴ τίς τι ἔκλεψεν, *except* [they did not comply, if] *perchance one smuggled something by*. — οἷον ...ἐπιθυμήσας, *as, for instance, from attachment to*. — γυναικὸς (432 e) τῶν εὐπρεπῶν (418 c). — τὰ μέν...τὰ δέ, 483 a, 518 d.

15. Εἰς s, i. 7. 1; iii. 4. 13. — χειμών : "A great storm arose in the very place to expect it, on the ascent of the highlands of Finduk." Ainsworth.

16 παρήγγελλεν, *sent along word* to the van. — ἐπικέοιντο, mode? 112

17. ὅτε παρεγγυῷτο, *whenever the word was passed*. — τότε δέ, *but* [this

time, of which an account is to be now given] *on one occasion*. — πρᾶγμά τι, *something important*. — ὀπισθοφύλαξι, case ?

18. στολάδος, *v. l.* σπολάδος (see Lex.). — διαμπερὲς εἰς τὴν κεφαλήν, i. e. *through* the helmet, *into*, etc. Some omit εἰς: if so, διαμπερές is followed by the acc., like simple διά, 699 a (or refer κεφαλήν to 481).

19. σταθμόν, *a stopping-place*. — ὥσπερ εἶχεν (Lex.). — φεύγοντες ἅμα μάχεσθαι, [fleeing] *to flee and fight at the same time*. — δύο καλώ τε s, "*two fine brave fellows*," McMich.; cf. ii. 6. 19. — ἀνελέσθαι, θάψαι, the Greeks regarded it as a sacred duty to take up and bury the dead.

20. Βλέψον, tense 592 b; see Lex. ὁράω. — ἔφη, 574. — Μία (pos.) δὲ αὕτη (deictic, 524 c) ὁδός, ἣν ὁρᾷς, ὀρθία (pos.), *there is that one steep path, which you see;* or, as some prefer, *that which you see is the only path* (and) *steep enough*: see 7. 4. — ὄχλον τοσοῦτον (deictic), [so great a] *that multitude*. — τὴν ἔκβασιν, *the egress* (from the valley in which the Greeks then were) by a mountain pass; hence τὴν ὑπερβολήν, § 21.

21. ταῦτα, case 483 b. — εἰ πῶς: § 8. — οὔ φασιν, cf. § 24; i. 3. 1.

22. ὕπερ, 491 b. — ζῶντας, sc. τινάς.

23. ἤλεγχον, sc. Chirisophus and Xenophon, with the cooperation, doubtless, of other generals. — οὐκ ἔφη, sc. εἰδέναι. — καὶ μάλα, i. 5. 8. — φόβων, ii. 5. 1. — ἔλεγεν, ἔλεξεν, § 24, tense, 594 a.

24. αὐτῷ τυγχάνει (sc. οὖσα) s, *he happened to have a daughter there, settled with a husband*. — δυνατήν, i. 2. 21; iii. 1. 21.

25. ὃ εἰ (561 a) μή τις (of the Greeks) προκαταλήψοιτο s, *which* [unless one should preoccupy] *must be first occupied, or it would be impossible to pass*.

26. λοχαγοὺς καὶ πελταστάς [= τῶν πελταστῶν] s, *the captains both targeteers and* [some of the] *heavy-armed*, πελταστάς in appos. w. λοχαγούς, while a different form of expression follows. — ἐθέλοι ἄν, *v. l.* ἐθέλει. — ὑποστάς, *having offered himself*.

27. Ὑφίστανται, *v. l.* ὑφίστανται, numb.? explain as punctuated. — Μεθυδριεὺς Ἀρκάς, *an Arcadian from Methydrium* (with this name compare Lat. Interamna). Some suppose the triple Ἀρκάς to have stolen into the text from marginal notes. If genuine, it emphasizes the bravery of the Arcadians. — ἀντιστασιάζων, cf. 7. 9; vi. 2. 11. — ἔφη ἐθέλειν s, 659 d, 503 a.

28. ἐθέλοι, mode? — πολλοῦ, case 431 b. — στρατιᾷ, case ?

CHAPTER II.

SEVERE FIGHTING AND LOSS IN STRUGGLING FORWARD.

1. οἱ, *they*, sc. the generals. — αὐτούς, i. e. the volunteers. — σημαίνειν, sc. τινά, *that a signal should be given*. — τὴν φανερὰν ἔκβασιν, i. 20, 23. — αὐτοί, i. e. the generals, with the main army. —

BOOK IV.   CHAP. II.   89

συμβοηθήσειν ἐκβαίνοντες, v. l. συμβολῆς ἕνεκεν βαίνοντες : συμβολή = conflict. See McMichael.

2. οὐρανοῦ, without article, 533 a.

3. χαράδρᾳ...ἣν ἔδει διαβάντας (674 d) s, *a ravine* (or torrent bed) *which they must* [having crossed go forth] *cross before climbing the steep ascent.* — φερόμενοι...πταίοντες, *dashing in their course against the rocks.* — τῇ εἰσόδῳ (case 450 a), *the entrance* to the mountain path.

4. εἰ μὴ ταύτῃ δύναιντο, sc. ἐκβαίνειν, mode 634 b, *by this* (i. e. one) *way*. — ἐπειρῶντο, ἐποίουν, tense ? — τεκμαίρεσθαι δ' (705) ἦν, *for this* [it was easy to infer] *we could tell : v. l.* τεκμήρασθαι.

5. τοὺς φύλακας, *the guards* of the height mentioned § 1 ; 3. 25 ; who were not, however, upon the summit. — ὡς...κατέχοντες, *as holding*, or, *supposing they held*, 680.

6. Οἱ δ', exception to 518 e. — ἡ στενὴ αὕτη ὁδός, order 524 b. Cf. v. 7. 29 ; vii. 3. 20.

7. ἔλαθον (Lex. λανθάνω). — ὀλίγοι, *but few* (οἱ ὀλίγοι, *the few*, 523 f) *of them*, 395 a, c, 417 a.

8. τῆς σάλπιγγος, i. e. *the signal* expected from the volunteers, § 1.

9. τοῖς προκαταλαβοῦσι, § 7. — τοὺς ἡμίσεις (= τὸ ἥμισυ), sc. ἄνδρας, 419 e, 418 b ; taking the gend. and numb. of the persons constituting the half. — [τῇ ὁδῷ] ᾗπερ, referred to in the next clause.

10. ἂν ἐπορεύθησαν, 636 a. Cf. iii. 2. 24. — οἱ ἄλλοι, 523 f, as stated in § 8.

11. ὀρθίοις (Lex., cf. φάλαγξ) τοῖς λόχοις, *with their companies in columns* (five in front, if the enomoty was square). — ἄφοδον..., εἰ βούλοιντο, 702 b.

12. ἐδύναντο ἕκαστος, 501 a. — Καὶ τοῦτον s, *and when the Greeks had passed by this, they see another.*

13. Ἐννοήσας μή, iii. 5. 3. — καί, *even*. — καὶ πάλιν, with this adv. use of πάλιν, Krüg. compares Ἀνὴρ ὁ φεύγων καὶ πάλιν μαχήσεται : Menander, *Frag*., γνῶμαι μονός. 45. — ἐπιθοῖντο, form ? — ἐπί (Lex.) πολὺ δ' ἦν, *formed a long train, were greatly extended.* — ἅτε, quippe quæ. — διὰ στενῆς τῆς ὁδοῦ : στενῆς, predicative, *was narrow.* — Κηφισόφωντος, case ? why father's name mentioned ? Krüg.

14. μαστός...φυλακῆς, § 5 s. — τῆς νυκτὸς ὑπὸ τῶν ἐθελοντῶν, deferred details ; note difference between ἐθελοντῶν and ἐθελόντων.

15. πᾶσι, case 458. — καὶ ὑπώπτευον, observe change to an independent constr. — πολιορκοῖντο : a compound sometimes becomes so familiar that it is treated as a simple, losing the distinct force of one of its elements. Hence πολιορκέω may even take πόλιν as an obj., vi. 1. 28. — ἄρα, *in truth*, or, *as it proved.*

16. ὑπάγειν, *to lead forward*, and not halt in the narrow path for Xen. to join them, since this would stop all behind them. — προσμίξειαν, *might march on to join them*, which could only be through their issuing upon a broader spot. Observe force of πρός. — τῷ ὁμαλῷ, *the level ground* to which the different passes through the heights led, § 22. Voll. refers ὁδόν to § 8.

17. πεφευγώς, *having escaped by flight.* — ὡς...ὅτι, 702 a. — τεθνᾶσι, form 50, θνήσκω, 320. — ὅσοι μή, [as many as did not] *all except those who.* — κατά, 689 m.

117
18. ἀντίπορον, *over against:* trajection, emph. — νέκρους, 1. 19 N (θάψαι).

19. ἐφ' ᾧ s, 557, 671 a. — Ἐν ᾧ (Lex. ἐν). — τὸ ἄλλο στράτευμα, *the rest of the division* under Xenophon. — οἱ ἐκ, constr. præg., i. 2. 18. — ἵσταντο, *were* [stationing themselves] *taking their position.* Note graphic effect of the imperfect.

20. ἤρξαντο, sc. Xenophon and those with him, § 16. — ἔνθα τὰ ὅπλα ἔκειντο (as pass. of θέσθαι, § 16), *where the arms were grounded,* i. e. *where they were resting under arms.* McMich. — ὁ ὑπασπιστής, an officer who was often mounted and required a servant to carry the shield which he might need when fighting on foot (Lex. ἱππεύς). In the hurry of the descent and avoidance of the stones Xenophon's shield-bearer was separated from him.

21. πρὸς τοὺς συντεταγμένους : see § 16.

23. διεπράξαντο : the exchange seems to have involved an armistice during the funeral obsequies, which, with the time occupied in the negotiation and in the collection of the bodies, appear from the statement of time (in 3. 1 s) to have occupied two days. The Greeks, from their favorable situation and need of rest, were probably in no haste. — ἡγεμόνα, § 1; 1. 24; 2. 1. — τοῖς ἀποθανοῦσιν, *for the slain,* in honor of them. — δυνατῶν (Lex.).

24. Τῇ ὑστεραίᾳ, *on the day following* the funeral obsequies. — ἐκώλυον τὰς παρόδους, [hindered the passing] *obstructed the passages.* But acc. of person, § 25.

25. τοῖς πρώτοις, case ? — τῶν κωλυόντων, case ? Observe the parallelism in § 25 and 26.

118
27. Ἦν...ὁπότε (Lex.), ii. 6. 9 ; i. 5. 7. — ἀναβᾶσι, § 25 s. — πάλιν καταβαίνουσιν, *when descending again.* — ἐγγύθεν, opp. to ἐκ πολλοῦ, iii. 3. 9. They could approach very near the Greeks and still escape.

28. Ἄριστοι τοξόται, *excellent bowmen :* jaculo bonus, Æn. ix. 572. — τριπήχη, διπήχη, form 213 d. — πλέον, 507 e, f. — πρὸς τὸ κάτω...προσβαίνοντες (v. l. προβαίνοντες), *stepping with the left foot against the lower part of the bow.* It is easy to understand how a bow of remarkable size and strength might be thus strained by the use of foot and hands. The question is how it was kept strained till it could be brought into position, aimed, and discharged. Some think, with Schn., that the bow was a kind of cross-bow ; Rehdz. is of opinion that the archer shot sitting, still using his left foot to keep the bow strained and guide the arrow. It is perhaps more natural to suppose, with Anthon, that when the bow had been bent with one end resting upon the ground, and the arrow adjusted, the strength of the arms (aided perhaps by the arrow) sufficed during the moment in which the bow was raised and discharged. — ἀκοντίοις, in apposition with αὐτοῖς, 394 b.

CHAPTER III.

SUCCESSFUL CROSSING OF THE RIVER CENTRITES INTO ARMENIA.

1. Ταύτην δ' αὖ τὴν ἡμέραν ηὐλίσθησαν s, *and* [through] *this day again they lodged at quarters in the villages:* ἡμέραν, acc., as the time of the march which led to these quarters, 482; αὖ, as their last quarters were in villages, 2. 22. — ταῖς, τοῦ, 523 a, 2. — τῶν ὀρέων...τῶν Καρδούχων, the latter governed by ὀρέων, deferred detail.
2. πολλὰ τῶν...πόνων μνημονεύοντες, [much remembering] *dwelling much upon their past toils.* Suavis laborum est præteritorum memoria; Cic. *De Fin.* ii. 32. — ὅσασπερ, 550 d. Acc. to chapters 1 and 2, they were strictly but five days on the march. For the other two days of the seven, sec 2. 23 N. — μαχόμενοι διετέλεσαν, *were constantly fighting:* with the exception of the time taken for burial of the dead. — ὅσα οὐδὲ τὰ σύμπαντα (in appos. with ὅσα), sc. ἔπαθον, [as many as they had not suffered] *more than they had suffered all together.* Yet these Carduchian mountains, as they turned back the Persian army, must be regarded as having saved the Greeks.
3. πού, [somewhere] *in some places, here and there,* as not fully discerned. — ἐπὶ ταῖς ὄχθαις, [upon] *in command of the upper banks* (the higher secondary banks); while ἐφ' ὧν (§ 5), *upon which,* denotes simply local position, as the idea of military occupation did not need to be repeated.
4. Ἦσαν, *belonged to,* or, *were troops of.* — Ὀρόντου, *Orontas* (see Lex. 2). — μισθοφόροι: from the sentence following this appears to be connected with Χαλδαῖοι only.
5. ἀπεῖχον: higher up however, it would seem, forming rocky bluffs directly over the river, § 11, 23. — ὁδὸς δέ...ἄνω, *there was only one way which was visible leading up.* — ταύτῃ, *here,* i. e. over against this road.
6. πειρωμένοις, [for them attempting] *on their making the attempt,* 462 c. — οὔτ' ἐν τῷ ὕδατι, corresponding to ἐπί τε τῆς κεφαλῆς. — τὰ ὅπλα, esp. their shields. — εἰ δὲ μή, *otherwise,* or, *else* (Lex. εἰ), 717 c. Cf. vii. 1. 8. — τις, γυμνοί, number?
7. Ἔνθα, *where,* 550 e. — πολλούς, *in great number.* — ὁρῶσι, obs. the emphatic repetition: i. 9. 10. — ἐπικεισομένους, *ready to fall upon.*
8. ἐν πέδαις, [in] *with fetters,* 695. — αὐτῷ, [for him] *from around him;* περιρρυῆναι, beautifully expressive of ease. — διαβαίνειν, *to stride,* seemed to promise διαβαίνειν, *to cross,* § 12, 15.
9. ὡς τάχιστα, 553 b. — πρώτου (Lex.). Some supply ἱερείου (expressed vi. 5. 2), which rather weakens the sense.
10. Ξενοφῶντι, αὐτῷ, case 699 g. — προσέτρεχον δύο νεανίσκω, numb. 494. — ἐπεγείραντα, sc. τινά. — ἔχοι, sc. εἰπεῖν. — τῶν πρὸς τὸν πόλεμον, *of matters relating to the war,* 526 a, b.
11. ὡς ἐπὶ πῦρ, [as] *for a fire:* see i. 2. 1. — ἐν πέτραις, *upon rocks*

extending down to the very river; belonging, it would seem, to a bluff connected with the heights mentioned in § 3, 5. See § 23 N.

12. οὐδὲ γάρ (stronger than οὐ γάρ, and the negative of καὶ γάρ) τοῖς πολεμίοις ἱππεῦσι (case ?) προσβατὸν (v. l. πρόσβατον) εἶναι κατὰ τοῦτο, *for indeed* [it was not accessible] *there was no access for the enemy's cavalry to this point;* though footmen, it would seem, could climb over the rocks. — ὡς νευσούμενοι, *in order to swim,* if necessary : (v. l. νευσόμενοι). — διαβαίνειν, διαβῆναι, tense ?

13. τοῖς νεανίσκοις ἐγχεῖν ἐκέλευε, καὶ εὔχεσθαι, *he commanded* [to pour in wine] *the cup to be filled for the young men* (to offer a libation), *and* [to pray] *prayer to be made.* ἐγχεῖν and εὔχεσθαι refer for their subject to the attendants or persons about Xen. If expressed, it would have been regularly in the acc. after ἐκέλευε : cf. 17. — τοῖς φήνασι θεοῖς (case 455, subject of ἐπιτελέσαι) τά τε ὀνείρατα, order 523 k, 719 d, ν. — ὀνείρατα, *the night-visions,* referring to the single dream of Xen., § 8. — τὰ λοιπὰ ἀγαθά, *the remaining benefits,* the favors still needed ; or ἀγαθά may be the adj. of effect (509 d), — *that they would also bring what remained to an issue* [as good] *of good.*

14. σπονδὰς ἐποίει = ἔσπενδε. Cf. ii. 3. 8.

16. ἐν ἀριστερᾷ s, of course ascending the river, about half a mile from their former position.

17. τὰς ὄχθας, the steep rocky banks close to the river, § 11 ; mentioned again § 23. — στεφανωσάμενος, a Spartan custom before battle, as if this were a festivity, Xen. *De Repub. Lac.* xiii. 8 ; Plut. *Lyc.* 22. The material was prob. taken from the bank on which they stood. See 5. 33. — ἀποδύς, *having stript off his outer garment,* for easier passage through the water (not, as Grote and others think, his wreath, which would have been very un-Spartan).

18. ἐσφαγιάζοντο s, to propitiate the divinity of the stream. So Alexander in crossing the Hellespont, and to Indian rivers. Arr. *An.* i. 11 ; vi. 3. Cf. Hdt. vi. 76 ; vii. 113 : *Il.* xxi. 131. — εἰς τὸν ποταμόν, so that the blood and entrails fell into the stream ; cf. ii. 2. 9.

19. συνωλόλυξαν : ὀλολύζω being esp. applied to the loud cries of women (chiefly in worship, oftener joyous), as ἀλαλάζω to those of warriors. Observe the parataxis.

20. ἐνέβαινε, into what ?— πόρον, § 5 s. — τοὺς...ἱππεῖς, § 17 ; to induce these to return and thus leave the way open for Chirisophus.

21. Οἱ δὲ πολέμιοι, referring to τοὺς ἱππεῖς, § 20. — μὴ ἀποκλεισθείησαν, opt. with hist. pres., 624 c, 625 a. — ὡς πρός, [as to] *that they might reach,* or, *aiming at.* — τὴν ἀπὸ τοῦ ποταμοῦ ἔκβασιν ἄνω, *the pass from the river upward.* ἄνω (which some omit) modifies the verbal idea in ἔκβασιν, 685 a. Some read τὴν τοῦ ποταμοῦ ἄνω (526) ἔκβασιν, *the pass above the river.* Rehdz. compares τὴν ˝Αλυος ποταμοῦ ἄνω ᾿Ασίην, Hdt. i. 103 ; and the place of ἔξω in 8. 12, 15 s. — κατὰ...ἐγένοντο, *arrived at,* or, *reached the road.*

BOOK IV. CHAP. III.

22. οἱ δὲ στρατιῶται s, *and the soldiers* (esp. the main body under Chirisophus) *shouted to them not to be left behind* by the enemy, *but to come out with them upon the mountain.* But the enemy with their good horse were too far in advance for this, § 25.

23. κατὰ τάς s, *went forth by the heights extending to the river* (§ 17 N.), i. e. climbing the rocky steep above the river so as to be at once, in an unlooked-for way, upon the range of hills occupied by the enemy's foot, § 3, 5. The Greek horse and targeteers appear to have emerged upon the plain to the left of this rocky steep.

24. The narrative would be more symmetrical, if § 24 and § 25 changed places.

25. τὰ ἄνω = τὰ ἄκρα, § 23. — τῶν σκευοφόρων τὰ ὑπολειπόμενα, *those of the baggage-animals that fell behind.*

26. ἀντία τὰ ὅπλα ἔθετο, [placed arms opposite] *took position in arms over against them;* the lochi being in columns, thus (the front being marked by a star, the rear by R):

```
  *    *    *    *
  □    □    □    □    □    □
  □
  □
  □
  R
```

— κατ' ἐνωμοτίας ποιήσασθαι ἕκαστον τὸν ἑαυτοῦ λόχον, *that each one should form his company by enomoties,* i. e. each enomoty brought to the front. A long and continuous line was thus made to prevent the Carduchi from anywhere molesting those who were crossing the river. — ἕκαστον, appos. παραγαγόντας, 501. — παρ' ἀσπίδας παραγαγόντας (501) s, *bringing the enomoty* [so that it should stand in, 704] *into line of battle by a movement to the left* (παρ' ἀσπίδας, *the shield-side,* viz. the left), i. e. into the following position (the foremost enomoty, of course, keeping its place):

```
  *
  □    □    □    □         □    □    □    □
  R
```

— τοὺς ἐνωμοτάρχας... ἰέναι, *that the enomotarchs should* [go] *take their positions towards the Carduchi.* — οὐραγούς s, *and that they should station rear-leaders towards the river;* for the sudden reverse movement, § 32.

27. τοῦ ὄχλου, case ? The Carduchi, at their distance, did not perceive that this separation rendered the rear-guard freer for action. — ᾄδοντες, cf. 7. 16. — τὰ παρ' αὐτῷ ἀσφαλῶς εἶχε, *his own condition was secure.* Cf. § 24.

28. διαβαίνοντας, *beginning to cross* (v. l. καταβαίνοντας). — μὴ διαβάντας, [not having crossed] *without crossing.* As this forms part of the command and involves an inf. idea (*and not to cross*), μή is used, 686 e. — αὐτοί, *they themselves,* Xenophon's party or division. — ἐναντίους ἔνθεν καὶ ἔνθεν σφῶν (539 a ; case 445 c) ἐμβαίνειν, *that they* (the peltasts, etc.) *should enter from the opposite bank on each side of* [themselves (Xenophon's men)] *their own track.* — ποταμοῦ, case 420 a.

29. ἐπειδὰν s, *whenever, as soon as, a sling* (stone) *should reach them, and a shield ring* (struck by a missile). — τὸ πολεμικόν, *the signal for charge* and not for retreat, to deceive the enemy and hasten their flight, § 32. — ἀναστρέψαντας, belonging to both οὐραγούς and πάντας. — ᾗ ἕκαστος εἶχεν, *where each one had his place,* each enomoty through its proper part of the river. — ὅτι (animated asynd.) s, saying *that he would be the best fellow who should be first across.* — γένηται, mode ?

31. ὡς (Lex. c). — ἱκανῶς..ἱκανῶς, order ?

32. ἔφευγον, ἔφευγον, θᾶττον, τάχιστα, vivid picture of the two armies running away from each other. — στρέψαντες, voice 577 a : vi. 6. 38.

33. οἱ μέν τινες, 530 b : v. 7. 16.

34. Οἱ δέ, the targeteers, etc. The passage of this rapid stream with an army in front, and another in their rear, was an admirable example of strategy.

CHAPTER IV.

MARCH THROUGH ARMENIA. — REACH THE TELEBOAS. — TRUCE WITH TIRIBAZUS.

1. συνταξάμενοι, to guard against sudden attack ; ii. 5. 18. — ἐπορεύθησαν διὰ τῆς Ἀρμενίας πεδίον ἅπαν s, *they pursued their way through Armenia, — entire plain and gentle* (or, *smooth*) *hills :* πεδίον and γηλόφους follow ἐπορεύθησαν, defining the journey, 479. The expression is condensed, and ἅπαν seems to agree by attraction with πεδίον (applying no less to γηλόφους) instead of agreeing with a word like ὁδόν : *by a route* [which was all] *consisting entirely of a plain and smooth hills.*

2. Εἰς δὲ ἣν ἀφίκοντο κώμην = ἡ δὲ κώμη, εἰς ἣν ἀφίκοντο, *but the village to which they came* by this long march, 551 c. — βασίλειον, cf. βασίλεια, § 7, 489 a. — σατράπῃ, i. e. Orontas. — τύρσεις, form 213. 2 ; as defences probably against the neighboring Carduchi.

3. περί (Lex.) τὸν ποταμόν, [about] *on.*

4. ἡ πρὸς ἑσπέραν, 526 a. — ὕπαρχος, as Orontas was satrap of all Armenia. — ὁ καί...γενόμενος, *who had also won the friendship of the king.* He showed his desert of this by the manly counsel which he gave the king on the approach of Cyrus (Lex. Τιρίβαζος); Plut. *Artax.* 7. — βασιλέα ἐπὶ τὸν ἵππον ἀνέβαλλεν (constr. changed from part. to finite verb, 716 c). Cf. regem in equum subjecit ; Liv. xxxi. 37. This was accounted a high honor.

5. εἶπεν, i. e. through the interpreter. — ἄρχουσι, case ? — εἰς ἐπήκοον, ii. 5. 38. — ἠρώτων (tense ?), τί θέλοι, 643 a.

6. ἐφ' ᾧ, *on these terms that.* — αὐτός, 667 c. — μήτε...τε, ii. 2. 8.

BOOK IV. CHAP. IV.

7. βασίλεια, perhaps of Tiribazus : cf. § 2. — πολλῶν...μεστάς, *supplied with provisions in abundance.*
8, and foll. For the sufferings during this march in Armenia from storm and cold, cf. Diod. xiv. 28 ; Curt. vii. 3.
9. πάντα τὰ ἐπιτήδεια...ἀγαθά, [all provisions as many as are good] *all kinds of good provisions.*
10. διασκηνοῦν, *to quarter* (their men) *apart.* — διαιθριάζειν, this would expose them more to attack in the villages, while it would remove an objection to their bivouacking together.
11. κατακειμένων γὰρ, ἀλεεινόν (gend. 502), ... ὅτῳ (460 or 699 a) μὴ παραρρυείη (mode ?), *for, as they lay, the snow having fallen was a warm covering* [to every one by whose side it did not run down] *on whom it rested without melting.* — ἐπιπεπτωκυῖα, *having fallen*, predicate.
12. γυμνός, *in his tunic*, prob. (Lex.); cf. i. 10. 3. — τις καὶ ἄλλος, *another one also.* — ἀφελόμενος, sc. τὴν ἀξίνην, or τὰ ξύλα. — ἐχρίοντο, to take the stiffness from their limbs, and for some protection against the cold.
13. χρῖσμα, μύρον, difference ? — ἐκ τῶν πικρῶν, 506 e. — Ἐκ...τῶν αὐτῶν τούτων, *from these same substances.*
14. εἰς στέγας, [into] *under shelter.* — τὸ πρότερον, 529 a (Lex.); for the time, see § 10. — ὑπὸ τῆς αἰθρίας, *in the open air*, 509 b : Dind. and others read ὑπὸ ἀτασθαλίας (connecting with ἐνέπρησαν), *out of recklessness.*
15. μὴ ὄντα...οὐκ ὄντα, *if things were not* so and so, he represented them *as not so.* Obs. use of μή and οὐ. McMich. — τὰ μὴ ὄντα ὡς, 686 d.
16. Πορευθείς, closely connected in sense with ἰδεῖν. — ἄνδρα s, *but he* [came leading] *brought with him a man whom he had taken, armed with.* Obs. the sequence of verbal forms. — αἱ Ἀμαζόνες, as represented in works of art.
17. ἔφη, tense 603 c. — τὸ στράτευμα, case ? — ἐπὶ τίνι, *for what purpose :* cf. ἐπὶ τούτῳ, i. 3. 1.
18. ὅτι Τιρίβαζος εἴη ἔχων, *that it was Tiribazus with*, 679 a. — παρεσκευάσθαι...ὡς...ἐπιθησόμενον, *that he was prepared to attack.* — ᾗπερ μοναχῇ, *by which way only.*
19. ἐπί : cf. i. 4. 2, ἐπ' αὐταῖς.
20. τὸ στρατόπεδον × τὸ στρατόπεδον, § 22. (For the sign × see 797.)
21. ὑπέμειναν × ἔμειναν, § 20. — ἥλωσαν, ἑάλω (279 b, more Attic ; cf. ἥλω, 5. 24), voice 575 a. — οἱ...φάσκοντες εἶναι, *those who said they were.* The state and luxury with which Persian commanders went to war are illustrated by Hdt. ix. 80 s.
22. ἐπίθεσις...τοῖς καταλελειμμένοις (case ?), the enemy wheeling back for this purpose.

CHAPTER V.

GREAT SUFFERING OF THE GREEKS IN THEIR ONWARD MARCH, FROM DEEP SNOWS, COLD, AND SCARCITY OF PROVISIONS.

1. ὅπῃ s (Lex. ταχέως). — πρὶν ἤ, 703 d, δ. — τὸ στράτευμα, what army? — τὰ στενά, ἔμελλεν, cf. 4. 18.

128   2. Εὐφράτην, the eastern branch, now the Murad : see Lex. — διέβαινον, tense?

3. διὰ χιόνος πολλῆς καὶ πεδίου, *through a plain of deep snow:* hendiadys, 69 c. — πεντεκαίδεκα, this rate of marching seems incredible. Some editors read πέντε (for πεντεκαίδεκα), which would be quite miles enough of travelling under such circumstances. — ἀποκαίων, *parching,* spoken of severe cold; see vii. 4. 3 : Lat. urere, adurere, torrere. (Virg. *Georg.* i. 92.) — παντάπασιν...πάντα, obs. the strength of expression.

4. εἶπε σφαγιάσασθαι, *bade them sacrifice,* 659 h : i. 3. 14, 8. — σφαγιάζεται, *the sacrifice is* immediately *offered,* impers.; while some supply ὁ μάντις. — ἔδοξε, note difference between this and ἐδόκει (as in i. 4. 18). — τὸ χαλεπόν, 507 a. — τοῦ πνεύματος : in their adoration of the great forces of nature the Greeks not only worshipped Æolus, the god of the winds in general, but also special winds. Boreas was honored at Athens with a temple and festival, cf. Hdt. vii. 189 ; and the Thurians adopted him as a citizen, Ælian, xii. 61. — ὀργυιά, doubtless in places only. The wind forbids our believing the depth uniform.

5. ἐν τῷ σταθμῷ, *at the station,* or, *halting place.* This region has since been so stripped of its wood that dried dung is used for fuel. — πυρούς (ὧν, § 6), case 472 b, 424. The acc. of that which is given ; the gen. of the whole of which a part is given.

6. ἕκαστοι, *each party.*

7. ἐβουλιμίασαν, *became* [ox-hungry] *faint with hunger.* — εἴη, mode 643 a.

129   8. αὐτῷ τῶν ἐμπείρων, pos.? — βουλιμιῶσι, φάγωσιν, mode? — διδόντας, *to give,* with a verb of motion, 598 c.

9. Πορευομένων, i. 2. 17. — ὑδροφορούσας, pos.? Cf. Gen. xxiv. 11 s ; Hdt. vi. 137. — ἐκ τῆς κώμης, connected with γυναῖκας and κόρας. — τῇ κρήνῃ, *the spring* of the village.

10. εἴη, ἀπέχοι (v. l. ἀπέχει). — ὅσον, 507 e ; i. 8. 6. — συνεισέρχονται s : observe the chiastic order in the explanatory repetition of the prepositions.

12. τὰ μὴ δυνάμενα, *those which were not strong,* or sc. πορεύεσθαι or διατελέσαι τὴν ὁδόν, from § 11. — ὀφθαλμούς, δακτύλους, case ?

13. ὀφθαλμοῖς (case 453) ἐπικούρημα τῆς χιόνος (case 405 a) ... τῶν δὲ ποδῶν (case 444 b), *a protection to the eyes from the snow ... but of the feet.* In ὀφθαλμοῖς, the dat. is used rather than the gen., to distinguish its office from that of χιόνος, 487 b, 464 c. — πορεύοιτο, v. l. ἐπορεύετο.

BOOK IV. CHAP. V. 97

14. "Οσοι, antecedent τοσούτων, understood with πόδας. — ἦσαν
...καρβάτιναι (accent, as properly an adj., 777. 2). **130**
15. τετήκει (v. l. ἐτετήκει), 284 c : see v. 2. 15 ; vi. 4. 11.
16. τελευτῶν, *finally, at last*, 509 a, 674 b, d. — δύνασθαι, sc. ἔφασαν, 669.
17. ἀμφί, with gen. rare in Attic prose ; Redhz. says, only in Xenophon.
18. ὅσον (Lex.).
19. οὐδέ, loose constr. — ἀνίστασαν, *endeavored to rouse them*, were for rousing them.
20. οὐχ ὑποχωροῖεν, § 11. — ἀπήγγελλον, ὅλον (pos.?). They seem not to have ascertained that the van was more comfortably **131** quartered, § 11.
22. πέμπει (sc. τινάς) τῶν (423) ... σκεψομένους, *sends some of his men from the village to see*. — κομίζειν, iii. 4. 42. — ηὐλίζετο × ηὐλίσθησαν, § 21.
23. ἕκαστοι, i. e. each *set* of officers belonging to each στρατηγία. McMichael. — τοὺς ἑαυτῶν, cf. i. 2. 15, τοὺς ἑαυτοῦ.
24. ἐκέλευσεν ἀφιέναι ἑαυτόν, *requested* [his commander to send him off] *leave to go forth*. — εἰς δασμόν : acc. to Strabo, xi. 14, the satrap of Armenia sent an annual tribute of 20000 horses. — ἑπτακαίδεκα, a number far too small for the distribution stated in § 35. A careless copyist may have changed it from ἑπτὰ καὶ ἑκατόν, which Bornemann suggests, p. xxiv.; less prob. from the numeral letter Σ′ (200) to ΙΖ′ (17), as suggested by Krüger. — ἐνάτην (article omitted, 533 e) ἡμέραν, case 482 c.
25. τὸ μὲν στόμα (in partitive appos. with οἰκίαι, 393 d, 395 a [sc. ὄν]) ὥσπερ φρέατος, [the mouth being] *with the mouth like that of a* **132** *well*. — ἐτρέφοντο, i. e. during the winter.
26. καί, καί, cf. asynd. in § 25. — οἶνος κρίθινος, [barley wine] *beer*, invented, according to the Egyptians, who made much use of it, by their god Osiris, Diod. i. 20, 34 ; Hdt. ii. 77. It has been a favorite beverage with the Germans from the days of Tacitus (*Germ.* 23). — αἱ κριθαί, some of the barley not strained out, but floating on the surface, which would be avoided, as well as the need of drinking-cups, by the use of reeds (the tubes between the joints).
27. συμμαθόντι, sc. τινί, *to one accustomed to it*.
28. στερήσοιτο, as pass. 576 a. — ἁπάσιν, § 10. — ἦν...ἐξηγησάμενος (Lex.), *if he should appear to have rendered a faithful service to the army*. — ἐν, const. præg.
29. φιλοφρονούμενος (Lex.), *to show his good-will*. — οἶνον, case 474 b : cf. § 34 ; 2. 22. — οὕτως, modifies what ? — ἐν φυλακῇ...ἐν ὀφθαλμοῖς, order ?
30. ἀφίεσαν, referring to τοὺς ἐν ταῖς κώμαις, their comrades. — αὐτοῖς (v. l. αὐτῷ), Xen. and his companions.
31. Οὐκ ἦν δ' ὅπου οὐ παρετίθεσαν, *and there was no place where they did not set forth*, i. e. everywhere, etc., nusquam non ; cf. ii. 4. 3. — ἄρνεια s, form 375 a : asyndeton.

7

NOTES.

133 32. ῥοφοῦντα, *sucking* through the reed. — ὥσπερ βοῦν, sc. δεῖ πίνειν, or rather by attraction for βοῦς πίνει, 715. Capital sport for the soldiers after their severe sufferings !

33. κἀκείνους σκηνοῦντας, *in their quarters*, feasting implied. — χιλοῦ, their only material, while its use might add to their merriment. Cf. 3. 17 N. — ἐδείκνυσαν, why ?

34. δασμός, appos. — χώραν...εἶναι Χάλυβας, metonymy (70 h), the people for the country, vii. 2. 32. — χώραν (Lex.). — ὁδόν, case 474 b; cf. § 29.

35. ἵππον...παλαίτερον (514), *a horse somewhat old*, which Xen. had taken on the route from necessity, though informed that it had been consecrated to the Sun ; and which he now feared might die on his hands to the displeasure of the deity. The religious character of Xenophon makes it probable that he was here acting sincerely and not deceptively. (The ind. ἤκουσεν expresses fact, not pretence.) For the sacrifice by the Persians of horses to the sun, see *Cyr.* viii. 3. 12. Some refer αὐτόν to *genus* (horses in general), but this interpretation is doubtful. — Ἡλίου, case 437 b. — τῶν πώλων, *some of the young horses*, 423.

36. πολύ, case 485 e, β; pos.? — σακία: these appear to have been slender bags of leather stuffed and then bent and made fast around the feet so as to enlarge the surface pressing upon the snow and answer the purpose of our snow-shoes.

CHAPTER VI.

MARCH THROUGH THE COUNTRY OF THE PHASIANI.

134 1. ὀγδόη (wt. art.). The comfort and abundance found in the villages had tempted the army to prolong their stay. — τὸν ἡγεμόνα, the village-chief, i. e. τὸν κωμάρχην. — τοῦ υἱοῦ τοῦ ἄρτι ἡβάσκοντος, *the son who was now approaching manhood*, in distinction from other sons, 523 a. — εἰς τὴν οἰκίαν s, § 28. — φυλάττειν, as κομίζειν, 5. 22.

2. αὐτοῖς, case 463. — ἤδη τε ἦν s, 705. — αὐτῷ, case 456. — οὔ, accent 786 b. The pause here forbids the change to οὐκ.

3. Ἐκ...τούτου (Lex. ἐξ). — ἀποδρὰς ᾤχετο, 679 d. — ἡ ἀμέλεια, appos. cf. ἔδησε δ' οὔ, § 2. — ἡράσθη, became attached to, inceptive aor., 592 d. — παιδός, case ? — πιστοτάτῳ ἐχρῆτο, *found him very faithful:* see ii. 6. 13.

4. ἀνά (Lex.). — τῆς ἡμέρας, 522 b. — παρά, *along* (Lex. c). — Φᾶσιν, see Lex.

5. Ἐντεῦθεν, *thence*, leaving the river which they found was carrying them too far east. — τὸ πεδίον, *the plain* of the next river perhaps.

6. εἰς, 692. 5. — κατὰ κέρας (Lex.), as was common on a march. — ἐπὶ φάλαγγος, opposed to κέρας, the one meaning *in column*, the other *in line:* see 2. 11. — παράγειν τοὺς λόχους, *to bring up their companies alongside*, i. e. to the front.

BOOK IV. CHAP. VI.

7. ἀγωνιούμεθα, 624 b.
9. ἐπάν (Lex.), iii. 1. 9. — τήμερον (Lex.), 526. — ἄλλους εἰκός **135**
(sc. ἐστί), ... πλείους προσγενέσθαι, [it is natural for others to join] *we must expect that others, still more in number, will join them.*
10. Ἐγὼ δ', 708 e. — τοῦτο δεῖ...μαχούμεθα, *we must provide for this, how we shall fight.* — ὡς ἐλάχιστα, *as few as possible.*
11. Τὸ...ὄρος...τὸ ὁρώμενον, *the mountain* [that seen] *in sight,* or, *so far as we see it.* — κρεῖττον...μᾶλλον ἤ, *better* ... [rather] *than,* 510 a. Observe in §§ 11, 12, the artistic antitheses. — τοῦ ἐρήμου ὄρους...τι, *some unoccupied part of the mountain.* — κλέψαι...λαθόντας s, 677 f, 674 b; for order, see 719 d, ν. — πειρᾶσθαι, subject of κρεῖττόν ἐστιν, and governing κλέψαι and ἁρπάσαι.
12. ὄρθιον (sc. χωρίον) ἰέναι, *to traverse steep ground,* case 477 s. — μεθ' ἡμέραν (Lex. μετά), 690. — ἡ τραχεῖα (sc. ὁδός) τοῖς ποσίν s, *the path that is rough to the feet is kinder to those that march without fighting.* **136**
— κεφαλάς, in antithesis to ποσίν : case ?
13. ἐξὸν δὲ (sc. ἡμῖν) ἀπελθεῖν τοσοῦτον, *and when we may go so far off from the post of the enemy.* — Δοκοῦμεν (573) δ' ἄν (621 a, 622 a) μοι... χρῆσθαι, *and it seems to me that we should find.* Cf. 2. 2. — μένοιεν, the force of ἄν continued, 622 b.
14. τί ; *why?* since any such suggestion to a Spartan is so needless. This lively sparring of the generals may have been simply playful to keep up the spirits of the army ; or it may have had a tinge of bitterness from their recent variance, § 3. — τῶν ὁμοίων (Lex. Σπάρτη), case 422. — κλέπτειν μελετᾶν, *to practise* [to steal] *theft.* The Spartan youths were thus trained, under their peculiar system of education, to stratagem in war.
15. ἄρα = *actually,* as if the statement were an extraordinary one in the speaker's judgment. McMichael. — τοῦ ὄρους, case 423 ; § 11.
16. δεινούς...κλέπτειν, *terrible fellows to steal,* or, *at stealing.* — δεινοῦ, adj. emphatically repeated. The penalties for this peculation were the restitution of double the amount, loss of citizenship, and sometimes even death. — τοὺς κρατίστους, to match τῶν ὁμοίων, § 14. — ὑμῖν...ἄρχειν, *to* [rule for you] *hold your offices.* Observe here the sarcasm upon the worthlessness of many of the Athenian office-holders, which was such an object for the keen satire of Aristophanes.
17. Xen. wisely proceeds to the practical, since he could neither deny nor outdo the sharp retort of Chirisophus. — τούτων, case ? Cf. ii. 5. 16.
— νέμεται (Lex.) αἰξί, case ? — βατά (sc. χωρία) s, *the ground will be feasible:* see iii. 4. 49.
18. ἡμῖν s, *to a level with us,* 451.
19. καί, 708 e. — ἀλλά, *on the contrary, nay rather ;* 4. 10 ; **137**
8. 12 ; v. 1. 7.
21. ὅπως...προσάξειν, *that he might* [seem as much as possible to be about to advance] *excite the strongest possible expectation of his advance in that direction.*
22. ἐγρηγόρεσαν, plup. used as impf., *kept watch.*

24. τοῖς κατὰ τὰ ἄκρα, § 23. — Πρὶν δὲ ὁμοῦ...τοὺς πολλούς, but before the main bodies had come together; cf. πολλοί, § 26, 523 f.
25. ἐκ τοῦ πεδίου, const. praeg., i. 2. 18 ; 1. 5. — οἱ πελτασταί, partitive appos. οἱ ἐκ τοῦ πεδίου. — βάδην (Lex.) ταχύ, pleno gradu, Liv. iv. 32.
26. τὸ ἄνω, sc. μέρος, § 24 : i. 8. 18. — γέρρα, which they threw away, for the more rapid flight.

CHAPTER VII.

ADVANCE THROUGH THE COUNTRY OF THE TAOCHI, CHALYBES, AND SCYTHINI. — FIRST VIEW OF THE SEA.

1. Ἐκ δὲ τούτων, sc. κωμῶν, 6. 27. — εἶχον s, 679 b.
2. συνεληλυθότες δ' ἦσαν, 679. — αὐτόσε, rather than οἷ or εἰς ὅ, 561 d, 562. — προσέβαλλεν, tense? — εὐθὺς ἥκων, immediately upon his arrival. — ἀλλὰ ποταμός : v. l. ἀλλ' ἀπότομον, which would seem to have been also true, § 13 s. — κύκλῳ (Lex.), leaving only a narrow access.
3. Εἰς καλόν, "in the nick of time." — ἥκετε, tense 612. — ἔστι, ληψόμεθα, tense 604 b, mode 653 c. — χωρίον, repeated and positive, iii. 2. 5.
4. μία αὕτη πάροδός ἐστιν s, there is one passage there, or, this which you see is the only entrance, 524 c. — ὑπέρ, 689 j.
5. ἄλλο τι ἢ s, 567 g (Lex. b), may we not be sure that nothing forbids ? — ὀλίγους τούτους ἀνθρώπους, a few men there.
6. βαλλομένους, exposed to their missiles: cf. "under fire." — ἀνθ' (Lex. 689 h) ὧν...πάσχοιεν, [against, as viewed from the position of Greeks] behind which if men should stand, what would they suffer ? — φερομένων, [borne on, here, through the air] flying, in distinction from κυλινδουμένων, while in § 7, 10, one verb seems to be used to express both ideas.
7. πολλοί, 523 b, 5. — εἴη, mode 637 b. — πορευώμεθα, mode? (sc. ἐκεῖσε). — ἔνθεν, [thither whence] to a spot from which : eo unde, cf. ii. 3. 6.
8. ἡγεμονία, acc. to Greek custom, taken by the captains in turn each day. — καθ' ἕνα, iii. 5. 8.
9. ἐφέστασαν, ἑστάναι, form 46 d, 320.
10. In the lively and graphic narrative following observe the interchange of modes. — προέτρεχεν, asynd. of explanation. — ἅμαξαι, ii. 2. 20.
11. Observe each clause preliminary to χωρεῖ. — Καλλίμαχον, 474 b. — πρῶτος, 509 f. — οὔτε...παρακαλέσας, without even calling. — αὐτός, 541.
12. αὑτοῦ, pos. 538 f. — ὕπνος, case 426. — οὗτοι, all Arcadians; cf. 1. 27; v. 2. 11. — ἀρετῆς, case 430 a.
14. πολλοί, pos., cf. vi. 3. 22.
15. ὧν, case 554 a, N. — πτερύγων (Lex.); cf. Xen. De Re Equest. xii. 4; v. l. πτερύγιον. — σπάρτα πυκνὰ ἐστραμμένα, cords [platted compact] firmly interwoven for protection.

16. μαχαίριον (cf. κράνη, 488 d, i. 7. 8 ; 5. 25) ὅσον ξυήλην [= τοσοῦτον ὅση ἐστὶ ξυήλη, 556 a], *a knife as large as a dagger.* — ἂν...ἔχοντες ἐπορεύοντο, *they would march with them.* Some extend the force of ἄν to ᾖδον and ἐχόρευον : but see 616 d. — πηχῶν, form 220 f. — μίαν λόγχην, while the Greek had also the σαυρωτήρ (Lex. δόρυ).

17. μαχόμενοι, *fighting ; v. l.* μαχούμενοι, *for battle.* — ἐν, const. præg., § 2. — λαμβάνειν, διετράφησαν, obs. change of structure ; cf. 671 d. — ἅ, exc. to 554 a. — ἐκ τῶν Ταόχων (Lex. ἐξ, χώρα).

18. "Αρπασον, the northern and chief branch of the Araxes. Ainsworth.

19. πρὸς πόλιν s, order ? — οἰκουμένην, *well inhabited, populous.* Some omit καί before οἰκουμένην. — διὰ τῆς ἑαυτῶν (cf. iii. 4. 41, case 442 or 436 ; .cf. ἑαυτοῖς, § 20, 455) s, *through the country of their own enemies.* — ἄγοι, after historic present.

20. ἡμερῶν, i. 7. 18. — ὅθεν, 550 e. — τεθνάναι (Lex. θνήσκω). — Ἑλλήνων, case 444 d.

21. τὸ ὅρος, i. e. χωρίον, § 20. Why article ?

22. ἄλλους (Lex. b) 567 b. — πολεμίους, cf. v. 4. 12. — δασειῶν βοῶν ὠμοβόεια [= ὠμῶν, by pleonasm] *of shaggy ox-hides untanned ; βοῶν* gen. of material, or in appos. with βοῶν contained in ὠμοβο. 394 c. — ἀμφὶ τά, i. 2. 9.

23. (sc. τοσούτῳ) ὅσῳ, *just as.* Observe the repetition of δή in § 23-25. — μεῖζον, [greater than usual, 514] *of unusual moment.*

24. ἐφ' ἵππον, 689 g. — στρατιωτῶν, case ? i. 8. 16. — Θάλαττα, case 401 b. Cf. Virg. Æn. iii. 523. There were so many Greek cities on the shores of the Euxine that they now felt almost at home. — παρεγγυώντων, *urging* others to hasten (make haste). — ἠλαύνετο, numb. 569 a.

25. στρατηγούς, without article. — ὅτου δή s, 551 h.

26. δερμάτων s, articles which they had obtained from the region to make a kind of trophy for their victory over it. — κατέτεμνε, that there might be no temptation to take them away for use.

27. ἀπὸ κοινοῦ, sc. χρήματος or ταμιείου, *from the common stock, property,* or, *store,* booty which had not been divided ; cf. v. 3. 4 ; or, *at common cost.* — ἑσπέρα, wt. art. 533 d. — νυκτός, as his way lay through a hostile region.

CHAPTER VIII.

MARCH THROUGH THE COUNTRY OF THE MACRONES TO TRAPEZUS ON THE PONTUS EUXINUS.

1. τρεῖς, the first occupied in part in reaching the Macrones. — ὤριζε, tense ? cf. ὁρίζει, 3. 1.

2. οἷον (Lex.), 556 a. — δι' οὗ, manifestly referring to ὁ ὁρίζων ποταμός. — δένδρεσι, cf. δένδροις, 7. 9, 225 f. — ἔκοπτον, in order to clear a way

through the thicket to the stream. This mountain branch could not need bridging, while the trees are not represented as suitable for this.

3. εἰς τὸν ποταμὸν ἐρρίπτουν, in the direction of the Greeks, to deter them from crossing. — οὔ, οὐδέν, pos. emphatic and chiastic.

4. Ξενοφῶντι, case 699 g. — πελταστῶν, case 418. — φάσκων (Lex.), changed to λέγων to avoid repetition; see 659 h. — ἐμὴν ταύτην s, without article 524 c = ταύτην εἶναι ἐμὴν πατρίδα, 524 c.

5. διαλέγου καὶ μάθε, tense 592. — αὐτῶν, case? — ἐρωτήσαντος, sc. αὐτοῦ, 676 a. — ἀντιτετάχαται, form 300 c.

6. Λέγειν, asynd. in dialogue, iii. 4. 42. — ποιήσοντες, sc. ἐρχόμεθα or ἔρχονται.

144 7. εἰ δοῖεν ἄν × εἰ δοεῖν. See 4. 20 N.; cf. i. 6. 2. — τὰ πιστά, *the proper pledges*. Cf. i. 6. 7. — διαδιδόασιν, *presented*, or, *handed over*. Cf. *Il.* vi. 230.

8. ὁδὸν ὁδοποιοῦν, cf. πόλιν πολιορκέω, 2. 15 N. — ὁδόν, the road through the river, and down and up its banks through the thickets. — διαβιβάσοντες: for the difference between this verb and βαίνω see Lex. — μέσοις, 508 a.

9. μέγα, wt. μέν. Cf. τὸ εὖρος, iii. 4. 7; iv. 6. 2. — ὡς...ἄξοντες, *as intending to advance in this way*, i. e. κατὰ φάλαγγα, in phalanx form. See McMichael. — ἀγωνιοῦνται, fut. indic.

10. ποιῆσαι (Lex.). Observe carefully Xenophon's various reasons for preferring the arrangement by columns. — τῇ μέν...τῇ δέ (Lex. ὁ), 518 d. — ὁρῶσιν, mode?

11. ἐπί (Lex.). — ἐπὶ πολλούς, accus. to show that a change would be required for this order, since they were now arranged ἐπ' ὀλίγων. — ἡμῶν, case? — χρήσονται, ὅ τι (case 478) ἂν βούλωνται (sc. χρῆσθαι), *they will make whatever use they may please*. — ὑπὸ ἀθρόων (pos.?) ...ἐμπεσόντων, *by many missiles and men falling thick upon us*.

12. ὀρθίους, pos.? cf. § 14, 15. — τοσοῦτον...λόχοις, *that standing apart we should occupy so much space with the companies*. — ὅσον = ὥστε, [as that] *that the outside companies should reach beyond*, etc. — κεράτων, case?

145 — λόχοι, appos. to ἡμεῖς subject of ἐσόμεθα, 393 d, 395 a; the rather from Xenophon's own position, § 16. — ὀρθίους ἄγοντες, *leading our troops in columns;* related alike to προσίασιν and ἄξει, which are joined by τε. — οἱ κράτιστοι s, *the best of us will be foremost in the advance* (not being confined to a uniform line of advance); while each company would have some freedom to choose the best place of ascent.

13. ὁ πλησίον, sc. λόχος. — οὐδεὶς μηκέτι μείνῃ, 627.

14. ἐπὶ τὸ εὐώνυμον, i. e. to his own position, as in the order of battle the van regularly took the right, and the rear the left. — ἡμῖν (case?) ἐμποδὼν τοῦ μή (713 d) ἤδη εἶναι, *in the way* [to us of the now being] *of our now being*. Cf. iii. 1. 13. Some read τὸ μὴ εἶναι. — ἐσπεύδομεν, tense? — ὠμοὺς δεῖ καταφαγεῖν, *we must eat up raw*, or, *devour alive*, a hyperbole to express fierceness of attack, apparently from *Il.* iv. 35, ὠμὸν βεβρώθοις Πρίαμον.

15. ἕκαστοι, i. e. the soldiers of each company. Cf. 5. 23 N.
16. εὔχεσθαι, cf. § 25. — **ἐπορεύοντο,** more rapidly than the heavier troops, as if to take the enemy in the flank.
18. κατὰ τὸ Ἀρκαδικόν, (in the centre) *beside the Arcadian division,* a body more purely of Arcadians, while there were also many Arcadians in other parts of the army. — ὧν, numb. 499 a. — **ἀνακραγόντες,** v. l. ἀνὰ κράτος. 146
19. ἤρξαντο, sc. οἱ πελτασταί. — **φυγῇ ἄλλος ἄλλῃ ἐτράπετο,** [turned in flight] *fled one this way and another that.*
20. τὰ μὲν ἄλλα, οὐδέν, 417 a. Some regard ἄλλα as acc. of specif. 481. — **ὅ τι καί** s, *which* [also] *excited their wonder,* as much as what follows, viz. the honey and its effects. — **κηρίων,** case 423. — **αὐτοῖς,** *for them.* — **ἐδηδοκότες, ἐῴκεσαν,** form 280 c, 279 d. — πολύ, sc. ἐδηδοκότες. — **ἀποθνήσκουσιν,** dat. pl. part.
22. ἐπὶ θάλατταν, [upon the sea] *to the seaside,* 689 g (Lex. ἐπί): cf. εἰς Τραπεζοῦντα. — **οἰκουμένην ἐν,** denoting not only situation, but also that the city was inhabited. — **ἐν τῷ Εὐξείνῳ Πόντῳ** (Lex.), *in the Euxine Pontus,* the basin of the Black Sea.
24. μάλιστα οἰκούντων, *especially those dwelling,* or, *who chiefly dwelt.* — ἦλθον, of things: cf. § 25. 147
25. ἀποθῦσαι s: the expression would have been more complete, if σωτήρια had been expressed with Σωτῆρι (iii. 2. 9), and τῷ Ἡγεμόνι (vi. 2. 15; 5. 25) with ἡγεμόσυνα. — **ἔφυγε,** *went into exile* (cf. i. 1. 7). Among the Greeks even involuntary homicide was thought to bring pollution requiring exile, at least for a time, and purification. See Smith's Dict. of Antiq. Banishment (Greek).
26. τὰ δέρματα s, to be distributed as prizes; cf. *Il.* xxii. 160; Hdt. ii. 91. — **ἡγεῖσθαι** (sc. ἐκεῖσε) ... **ὅπου,** *to lead to the place where.* — **πεποιηκὼς εἴη,** form 317 a; mode 641 b, or 643 c. — **δείξας, οὗπερ,** *pointing to the very spot where;* with Spartan disdain of ease and comfort. — **τρέχειν,** *for running,* 663 d. — **οὕτως,** emph. pos. — **Μᾶλλόν τι ἀνιάσεται,** *will suffer somewhat more,* a stimulus to make greater exertion.
27. στάδιον (Lex.), case 479. — **παῖδες...οἱ πλεῖστοι,** *boys* [of those taken captive the most] *chiefly captives.* — **ἕτεροι,** sc. ἠγωνίζοντο. — **κατέβησαν,** cf. descendat in campum: Hor. *Od.* iii. 1. 11. — **ἅτε,** quippe; 2. 13; v. 2. 1. — **ἑταίρων:** some few prefer ἑταιρῶν, but not well (see Lex. ἑταῖρος, ἑταίρα).
28. αὐτούς, i. e. the riders implied in ἵπποι. — **πρὸς τὸ...ὄρθιον,** [against] *up the exceedingly steep ground.* — **παρακέλευσις...αὐτῶν,** *cheering of them on.*

BOOK V.

FROM TRAPEZUS ALONG THE COAST TO COTYORA.

CHAPTER I.

PREPARATIONS FOR LEAVING TRAPEZUS AND FOR FURTHER ADVANCE.

148 1. Ὅσα μὲν δή s. See p. 3, Notes, as to division into books, summaries, etc. — μέχρι, *v. l.* μέχρις. — τὴν ἐν τῷ Εὐξ. Πόντῳ, iv. 8. 22. N. — εὔξαντο, iii. 2. 9 ; iv. 8. 16. — σωτήρια, 551 c ; iv. 8. 25 N. — ἀφίκοιντο, *v. l.* ἀφίκοντο. — δεδήλωται, the sentences beginning with ὅσα and ὡς form the subject of this verb.
2. Ἐγὼ μὲν τοίνυν, *I for my part then*, since this subject is proposed. — ἔφη, 574. — ἀπείρηκα (Lex. under ἀπαγορεύω). — καὶ...καὶ.. καὶ, etc. Observe how the wearisomeness is enhanced by the repetition. — φυλακὰς φυλάττων, ii. 6. 10. — ὥσπερ Ὀδυσσεύς, who was carried asleep by a Phæacian vessel to his native Ithaca ; *Od.* xiii. 74 s ; cf. iii. 2. 25 N.

149 4. πέμψητέ με, to Byzantium, where Anaxibius then was ; cf. vii. 1. 3. — ἂν ἐλθεῖν, aor. for fut. after the subjunc. πέμψητε, but somewhat less positive, 631 c, 649 c.
5. ἐπί, cf. ii. 3. 8 ; vi. 2. 2. — καιρός (Lex.).
6. ὅτου (431 a) ὠνησόμεθα, [of that for which we shall purchase] *of the means of purchase*, or, the wherewithal to purchase.
7. Ἀλλά, in opposition to what is conveyed in ἀμελῶς s ; cf. iv. 6. 19. — σὺν προνομαῖς, *v. l.* συμπρονομεῖν : cf. *Cyr.* vi. 1. 24 ; *Hel.* iv. 1. 16. — ἄλλως, *at random.* — ἡμᾶς, *we*, the generals. — ἔδοξε ταῦτα, asyndeton.
8. γάρ, 705 b ; cf. iii. 2. 29 ; vi. 4. 8. — καὶ ὅποι, sc. μέλλει ἐξιέναι. — ἀπειροτέρων, 514. — ἐγχαρῇ ποι, *make an attempt* [to go] *in any direction*, the idea of *going* implied ; *v. l.* ἐγχειρῇ τι ποιεῖν. — εἰδέναι, *to keep ourselves acquainted with*, i. e., to aid him through knowledge of the strength, etc. — δύναμιν [sc. τούτων] ἐφ' οὕς, 551 f. — ἴωσιν, number ?
9. λῃτζεσθαι [sc. ἡμᾶς], *to prey upon us :* cf. θηρᾶν περί, 689 f. — ἂν δύναιντο, cf. ἂν ἐλθεῖν, § 4 N.

150 10. ἠπιστάμεθα...ἂν ἔδει, 631 b ; πλοῖα ἱκανά, emph. pos. in participial clause. — νῦν δέ, *but as it is.* — αὐτόθεν, *from this very region.* — ἔλθῃ, ὑπαρχόντων [sc. πλοίων], *shall come*, bringing vessels, *while we have others here.* — ἀφθονωτέροις (Lex.). — πλευσούμεθα, *v. l.* πλευσόμεθα.
11. αἰτησάμενοι, *having* [asked for use] *borrowed.* — μακρά, *long* in proportion to the width, for greater swiftness. — παραλυόμενοι, [loosening from beside] *unshipping*, to prevent the secret escape of the crews. — ἕως

ἄν s, *until* [those about to convey become sufficient] *there should be enough to convey us.*

12. εἰ εἰκός, *whether it is not reasonable;* cf. iii. 2. 22 N. — ἀπὸ κοινοῦ, iv. 7. 27. — ὠφελοῦντες καὶ ὠφελῶνται, parataxis.

13. ἦν ἄρα, *if* [perhaps, or] *after all;* cf. iii. 2. 22. — ὁδούς, obj. of ὁδοποιεῖν : pos.? — ταῖς παρά s, *to enjoin upon the states which* [dwell beside the sea] *occupy the sea-shore.*

14. ἐπεψήφισε μὲν οὐδέν, *he put nothing to the vote;* cf. vii. 3. 14.

15. πεντηκόντορον, a long war-vessel, having 25 oarsmen on each side in a single row (the τριακόντορος having 15 ; § 16). — ᾗ, 699 g. — Λάκωνα περίοικον (Lex. Σπάρτη). The Periœci appear to have descended in part from the old Achæan inhabitants who made terms with the Doric conquerors, and in part from inferiors who accompanied these or later immigrants, etc. See Smith's Dictionary, Περίοικοι. — ᾤχετο, to Byzantium, to Anaxibus and Cleander, whom he endeavored to set against the Cyreans, especially Xenophon ; see vi. 1. 32 ; 6. 5 s. — ἀπέθανεν ὑπὸ Νικάνδρου (575 a), *died at the hands of Nicander.*

151

16. φύλακας : these were afterwards brought to account for some loss, cf. 8. 1. — εἰς παραγωγήν, in their plundering excursions, cf. 7. 15.

17. οἱ δὲ καὶ οὔ, cf. i. 3. 13 N ; Diod. xiv. 31.

CHAPTER II.

EXPEDITION AGAINST THE DRILÆ.

1. ἦν λαμβάνειν, 571 f, h. — στράτευμα, *v. l.* στρατόπεδον. — ἐξάγει, histor. pres. — Δρίλας, the Drilæ were, according to Arrian, the same as the *Sanni :* Kühner holds rather that the *Macrones* (iv. 8. 1) and the Sanni were the same people. — ἅτε, iv. 2. 13 ; 8. 27.

2. [sc. ἐκεῖσε] ὁπόθεν, *to places from which.* — αὐτοῖς, *to the inhabitants,* implied in ὁπόθεν ; cf. Hdt. ix. 1.

3. Δρίλαις, case 454 c. — εἰς τοῦτο, asyndeton.

4. προδραμόντες, obs. participles, and see i. 1. 7 ; 3. 5, 10. — ὁπλιτῶν, case ? — εἰς δισχιλίους s, as nom. 706 a.

152

5. ἀναβεβλημένη, [thrown up] *with the earth thrown up.* — οἱ δέ, i. e. the Drilæ.

6. ἐφ' ἑνός (Lex ἐπί), ii. 4. 26 N. — ἡ κατάβασις ἐκ, art. omitted, 523 d.

7. Ὁ δ' ἐλθών, *and* [he that came] *the messenger.* — ὅτι, i. 6. 7.

8. ἀπάγειν, *to lead back.* Some editors, following a few MSS., have here ἀναγαγεῖν, in the same sense. But, in such a connection as this, that use of the term would seem inappropriate : see κατάβασις, § 6, ἀπάγειν, § 9. MS. C. has ἀναγαγεῖν, corrected by ἀπαγαγεῖν. — καί, *also,* so that they should be beyond the ravine as well as the hoplites. — ὡς ἁλόντος s, *as if the place might thus be taken,* 680 b.

9. γάρ, introduces the reasons for the latter of the two courses. — οὐκ εἶναι, *not to be possible*. — ἀποδεδειγμένοι ἦσαν, plup. mid. — ἔσται (for ἔσοιτο), cf. i. 3, 14 N.

153 11. ἐκέλευσέ s, *he bade each of the captains to form his company in that way*, etc. — ἀντεποιοῦντο (cf. iv. 1. 27). The minutiæ of the arrangement, for the general order was determined by the nature of the place, might very safely be left to such men.

12. ὡς ἀκοντίζειν, *that they might shoot.* If the absolute impers. δεῆσον (which is bracketed by some editors) is retained, translate, *since they must shoot;* 675 (Lex. δέω). — σημήνῃ, i. 2. 17; iii. 4. 14. — γυμνῆτας (Lex.). The slingers, from the great freedom and energy of motion which they required, were even less encumbered than the peltasts and bowmen. Still, the term may here apply in general to any lightly clad men who had pouches (διφθέρας) to hold stones and slings or hands to throw them; see § 4, 14.

13. παρεσκεύαστο, *were ready*, 599 a. — οἱ ἀξιοῦντες s, *those who claimed that they were not inferior to these.* — παρεσκεύαστο, παρατεταγμένοι ἦσαν, ξυνεώρων, ἐπαιάνισαν (§ 14), distinguish force of the tenses; cf. iii. 4. 4; vi. 2. 8. — καί...μὲν δή, *and so*, etc., *et vero, et profecto*, Kühner.

14. ἐπεί, repeated after the parenthesis. The apodosis begins with ἅμα τε. — σφενδόναι, observe the asynd. and the polysyndeton in § 15; 707 j. — ἦσαν δὲ οἵ, *and there were those who;* cf. 559 a.

15. Ὑπό (Lex.), i. 5. 5. — ἄλλος ἄλλον εἷλκε, 567 c. — καὶ ἄλλος ἀνα-

154 βεβήκει, *and another had already climbed up of himself;* the sing., as before, for the plural, to render the description more graphic, 488. — καὶ ἡλώκει s, *and the place* [had been] *was now taken*, 599.

16. κατεκώλυε, v. l. κατεκώλυσε. — ἔξω, proleptic = ὥστε ἔξω (τοῦ χωρίου) μένειν: Küh., cf. iv. 2. 12.

17. τάχα δέ τις, *and presently one;* or, *and perhaps one or two*, τις not used as strictly singular, 548 c. — οἱ ἐκπίπτοντες, *those that were rushing out.* — ἔστιν, oratio dir.

18. νικῶσι...ὠθούμενοι, *those* (of the hoplites, § 16) *who were pressing in prevail over and force back those* (the lighter troops) *that were rushing out.*

19. ἐξεκομίσαντο, sc. τὰ ἀλόντα, prædam.

20. ἐσκόπουν, refers rather to the examination, σκοπουμένοις to what was subsequent on consideration, 582 γ.

21. ἕκαστοι, *each company*, iv. 5. 23 N; 8. 15. — διῄρουν, for freer egress. — ἀχρείους, camp-followers, calones.

22. ἔνδοθεν, *from within* the citadel. — κράνη, of leather thongs braided,

155 4. 13; Hdt. vii. 72. — ὁδοῦ, case? iv. 3. 28.

23. κατὰ τὰς πύλας, *along the passage*, or, *to* [the vicinity of] *the gates.*

24. Μαχομένων, i. 4. 12; 2. 17; ii. 4. 24. — θεῶν...σωτηρίας: these words form an undesigned iambic trimeter. — ὅτου δή s, 551 h, cf. iv. 7. 25. — οἱ ἀπό, const. præg., i. 1. 5; 2. 3.

BOOK V. CHAP. III.

25. παρά (Lex. a), Fortune regarded as a person, cf. Hdt. i. 126. — ἐνάπτειν, pos.? — ἐκέλευε, tense, 595 a. — ταχὺ ἐκαίοντο, *were quickly on fire.*
26. Οἱ...κατὰ τὸ στόμα, *those in front* towards the citadel. McM. says that this rendering is inconsistent with the narrative, and translates, "*only those about the entrance* (into the fort) *were still giving trouble.*" — δῆλοι ἦσαν, 573 a. — παραγγέλλει [sc. πάντας or πᾶσι]...ὅσοι, 550 f.
27. καὶ οἱ οἰκίαι, *both the houses;* cf. Cæs. *B. G.* viii. 15.
29. τοὔνομα τοῦτο : he may have been a slave, since slaves were often so named from their native lands : cf. οἰκέτης. — δέκα, v. l. τέτταρας ἢ πέντε. — τοὺς πολεμίους s, *to seek concealment from the enemy.* — χαλκαῖ, i. e. in front : see Lex. πέλτη.
30. ἐφοβοῦντο [sc. αὐτὰ] ὡς ἐνέδραν οὖσαν (500), *feared* [them] *as* [being] *as if there were a real ambuscade;* cf. 675 e. — τῷ Μυσῷ ἐσήμηνε, *a signal was given to Mysus* (Lex.). Some place the comma after Mysus, omitting it after ὑπεληλυθέναι. — καὶ ὅς, 518 f, i. 8. 16.
31. οἱ μὲν ἄλλοι Κρῆτες, *the others, the Cretans* (567 e), i. 5. 5. — ἁλίσκεσθαι, *that* [they were being caught] *the enemy were overtaking them.* — ἔφασαν, vii. 4. 15. — ἐκπεσόντες, iv. 5. 15. — κυλινδούμενοι, v. l. καλινδούμενοι, Kühner.
32. ἐβόα, i. 8. 12. — βοηθεῖν· καὶ ἐβοήθησαν, order? — ἐπὶ πόδα ἀνεχώρουν, *they retreated backwards,* facing the enemy. Cf. *Cyr.* vii. 5. 6.

CHAPTER III.

MARCH TO CERASUS. — DIVISION OF THE SPOIL. — XENOPHON'S DESCRIPTION OF THE TEMPLE OF ARTEMIS AT SCILLUS IN ELIS.

1. Χειρίσοφος, 1. 4. According to Diodorus (xiv. 30) the Greeks waited for him 30 days. — ἦν λαμβάνειν, 2. 1. — παῖδας καὶ γυναῖκας, *children and women,* not, however, without exception, 4. 33. — ἐπορεύοντο, sc. κατὰ γῆν, cf. 4. 1. — ὡδοπεποιημένη (form 283 a) ἦν, *was now repaired.*
2. Κερασοῦντα (Lex.). — τριταῖοι, *on the third day,* 509 a. Cf. i. 2. 11 ; 5. 1 ; ii. 2. 17.
3. δέκα, as still expecting Chirisophus. — ἀμφὶ τοὺς μυρίους, as gen. 706 a. Cf. v. 7. 9. — ἀπώλοντο ὑπό, voice 575 c. — εἴ τις νόσῳ, [if any one perished] except as any one may have perished by disease, or now and then one by disease or sickness.
4. τὴν δεκάτην, a frequent portion for religious consecration. Compare the *tithes* among Jews and Christians. — φυλάττειν, *to keep,* infin. of purpose, after giving, going, sending, etc.
5. Ἀπόλλωνος ἀνάθημα, [Apollo's gift] *the votive gift to Apollo.* Some work of art, statues, tripods, vases, were common gifts. — ποιησάμενος, *procuring to be made* (581), possibly upon his return to Athens directly

after the enlistment of the army under Thibron, while he had still the privileges of an Athenian (see INTRODUCTION, p. ix). — θησαυρόν, the Grecian states had each a treasury at Delphi for the reception of their offerings. Cf. Hdt. i. 14, 51.

6. Τὸ δὲ τῆς Ἀρτέμιδος (sc. ἀνάθημα), *but that* (portion or offering) *for Artemis*. — ἀπῄει...τὴν...ὁδόν (case 477), *departed upon the expedition* [into the country of] *against the Bœotians*. — κινδυνεύσων...ἰέναι, *he seemed to be going* [to incur danger] *on a perilous adventure*. — σώθῃ, mode ? — ἤν δέ τι πάθῃ (Lex.), *but if* [he should suffer anything] *aught should befall him;* the usual Greek euphemism.

7. ἔφευγεν, *when he was in exile; v. l.* ἔφυγεν. This latter, as McM. says, would imply that he was banished *after* serving against his country under Agesilaus at Coronea, B. C. 394. — τῇ θεῷ = τῇ Ἀρτέμιδι, § 4. — ὁ θεός, doubtless Apollo at Delphi.

8. Ἔτυχε, as the river had this name at the time of the purchase. — νεών, ναόν, § 9, 12 s. Observe use of both forms. — τῷ ἐν Σκιλλοῦντι χωρίῳ, the estate at Scillus. — πάντων, sc. θηρίων. — ἀγρευόμενα θηρία, *beasts of the chase*.

9. Ἐποίησε × ἐποίει ? cf. iii. 3. 5. — Παρεῖχε : through of course Xenophon her steward, whose security and popularity were thereby promoted, no less than the honor of the goddess. — τοῖς σκηνῶσιν, *to those who were tented for the feast; v. l.* σκηνοῦσιν.

10. τὰ μέν, sc. θηρία.

11. ἦ ἐκ Λακεδαίμονος...πορεύονται, [where they travel] *on the road from Lacedæmon or Sparta*. — ὡς εἴκοσι στάδιοι, in appos. with χώρα, 395 c. — ἔνι (Lex.), *there are in*.

12. ὡς μικρὸς [sc. ναὸς εἴκασται] μεγάλῳ. — χρυσῷ, *covered with gold*. Statements differ in respect to the material so covered.

13. γράμματα : the inscription was in capital letters, and hence is here so printed. An almost exact duplicate of this inscription was found on the island of Ithaca in 1758. — ΑΡΤΕΜΙΔΟΣ, case 437 b. — ΤΟΝ ΔΕ ΕΧΟΝΤΑ...[sc. δεῖ or χρή] ΚΑΤΑΘΥΕΙΝ, *and whoever occupies it must offer*, 670 a. — ΠΟΙΗΙ = ποιῇ. — ΤΗΙ ΘΕΩΙ ΜΕΛΗΣΕΙ (Lex.), 457.

CHAPTER IV.

MARCH THROUGH THE COUNTRY OF THE MOSSYNŒCI.

1. οὕπερ καὶ πρόσθεν, 3. 1.

2. Μοσσυνοίκων (Lex.), cf. Strabo xii. 3 ; also, μόσσυνι, § 26. — ὡς διὰ φιλίας...τῆς χώρας [= διὰ τῆς χώρας ὡς φιλίας, as through the country friendly], *through the country as friendly*.

3. εἰ (Lex.) βούλοιντο, *to see if they would be willing*, iv. 1. 8.

4. Μοσσυνοίκων, Ἑλλήνων, order ? — ἔλεγε, ἡρμήνευε, tense ? *v. l.* ἔλεξε.

BOOK V. CHAP. IV.

5. διασωθῆναι, *to go through safe:* cf. Hdt. vii. 208. — πρός, with accus. of place, for the more common εἰς, vi. 4. 8 ; *Cyr.* v. 4. 16. — οὖς ἀκούομεν, cf. ii. 5. 13.

6. ἠδικήκασι, *v. l.* ἠδίκησαν. — ὑμῶν, dat. vii. 7. 29. — εἶναι, with impers. ἔξεστι, though ἔχειν would here give a more systematic construction.

7. ἀφήσετε, *if you shall let us go* (without availing yourselves of our help), Krüg.

8. ὁ ἄρχων, who spoke for the rest, or, the head-chief. — δέχοιντο, *they accepted.*

9. Ἄγετε δή, *come now,* or, *well then.* — τί ἡμῶν δεήσεσθε χρήσασθαι, [what shall you want of us to employ us in] *what service shall you wish from us?* 661 d. Cf. *Cyr.* v. 2. 23 : see also vii. 2. 31. — ὑμεῖς, pos.? — τί οἱοί τε s, *what* [will you be able to do in co-operation with us] *assistance will you be able to render us?*

10. ὅτι ἱκανοί ἐσμεν, 644 a, 714, 3. — ἐκ τοῦ ἐπὶ θάτερα, *from the other,* or, *farther side.*

11. Ἐπὶ τούτοις, *hereupon,* or, *on these terms,* 695. — ὧν οἱ μὲν δύο...ὁ δὲ εἷς, *of whom* [the] *two...but the third,* 530 b. — εἰς τάξιν s, [put their arms into military position] *stood to their arms in order.*

12. οἱ μέν, *these,* who remained in the canoes. — μένοντες, to assist the Greeks. — Ἔστησαν ἀνὰ ἑκατόν, *they stood in two lines,* or *companies, of a hundred each.* — ὥσπερ μάλιστα χοροί s, *very much* [as] *like rows of dancers fronting each other.* Some read ἑκατὸν μάλιστα ὥσπερ, making μάλιστα qualify ἑκατόν = in round numbers, pretty nearly. — ὄπισθεν s, *having a ball of the wood itself,* in place of the Greek σαυρωτήρ : see δόρυ, iv. 7. 14.

13. πάχος ὡς λινοῦ στρωματοδέσμου (412), [as of a linen bed-sack as to thickness] *about the thickness of a linen bed-sack.* — κράνη, cf. 2. 22. — κρώβυλον, a tuft, prob. of the ends of leathern thongs used in making the helmet. Cf. Tacitus, *Germ.* 38.

14. τάξεων, *troops of peltasts and light armed,* McM. — διὰ τῶν ὅπλων, the place in the camp where the arms were deposited. Others (Matt., Vollb., etc.) make τάξεων...ὅπλων a hendiadys = *through the* [ranks and arms] *armed ranks;* expecting, doubtless, in their simplicity, that the Greeks would at once follow them.

15. Ὤικεῖτο, iv. 8. 22 ; *v. l.* ἔκειτο. — αὐτοῖς [to or for them] *their;* others translate *by them,* making it the dat. of the simple agent after passive verbs. McM. — τῶν Μοσσυνοίκων, *of the country of the Mossynæci.* — περὶ τούτου, referring to τὸ ἀκρότατον. — ἐγκρατεῖς...πάντων Μοσσ., case 407. — ἔφασαν, those of the Mossynæci with the Greeks. — τούτους, those in possession. — κοινὸν ὄν, [being] *though common property.*

16. μέχρι οὗ, 557.

17. νόμῳ τινὶ ᾄδοντες, *singing a kind of tune;* cf. ἐν ῥυθμῷ, § 14 ; Thucyd. v. 69.

18. ὅτι ἐπεποιήκεσαν, their allies ; see αὐτοῖς below. — ὅ, antecedent ?

19. μηδὲν ἀθυμήσητε, *do not become at all dejected;* the pres. imperat. would imply that they were now dejected, 628 c, e. — ἴστε, *be assured* (Lex. ὁράω).

20. ἡμῖν, case ! — τῷ ὄντι (Lex. εἰμί). — οἷσπερ...ἀνάγκη, *to whom* [it is unavoidable that we also should be enemies] *we also must be enemies*. — τῶν Ἑλλήνων, pos. ? see 523 c. — οἱ ἀφροντιστήσαντες s, *those who have made light of their orderly arrangement with us*. — ταὐτά, *v. l.* ταῦτα. — ἅπερ ξὺν ἡμῖν (ξύν omitted by some, 707 b), sc. ἔπραξαν, *as with us*. — δίκην (Lex. 1).

21. ὁμοίοις ἀνδράσι...νῦν τε καὶ ὅτε, *with the same kind of men* [both now and when] *now as when*, 705 c.

22. Observe the series of participles ; θύσαντες preceding in action ἀριστήσαντες : this preceding ποιησάμενοι and ταξάμενοι : and these, ἐπορεύοντο.

162 — κατὰ ταὐτά, *in the same way* (Lex. κατά). — ὑπολειπομένους... στόματος (case 406 b), *as they were not well protected from the missiles of the enemy*, § 23.

23. Ἦσαν οἵ, ii. 2. 14. Rehdz. — ἀνέστελλον, *endeavored to keep in check*. — πρῶτον μέν, cf. ἐπεὶ δέ, § 25. — οἱ βάρβαροι × οἱ βάρβαροι, § 24.

24. Observe the tenses, the interchange of impfs. and aorists, 592.

25. δή...ὁμοῦ δή, i. 8. 8 ; 1. 4. — ἄλλα, as in i. 5. 5, unless the πάλτα are regarded as a kind of δόρατα. — παχέα μακρά, an unusual asynd. — ἂν φέροι, *could carry*, cf. 7. 7. — ἐκ χειρός (Lex.).

26. αὐτοῦ μένοντα : the king lived in a seclusion, of which Oriental courts have presented many examples ; and, after the defeat of his forces, chose rather to die than to submit to the indignity of leaving it. The subordinate ruler in the place first taken (ὁ ἐν τῷ πρότερον s) made the same heroic, or stolid, choice ; cf. Diod. xiv. 30. — φυλάττουσιν, *v. l.* φυλάττονται. — μοσσύνοις, form 225 f.

27. ὡς ἔφασαν οἱ Μοσσ., referring to the usage stated in πατρίους. — ἦσαν δὲ ζειαὶ αἱ πλεῖσται, *the most of it was spelt* (conforming to ζειαί rather than regularly to σῖτος, 500 a) ; cf. i. 4. 4.

163 29. κάρυα s. These were afterwards distinguished as κάρυα καστάναια, the large chestnut of the Old World, nuces castaneæ, from, it is said, Κάστανα, a town of Pontus, or, according to others, of Thessaly. Ainsworth represents them as still abundant along this coast. — τὰ πλατέα, *of the broad kind*, 523 i. — τούτῳ (conforming to σίτῳ rather than κάρυα) καὶ πλείστῳ s, *this they used even as their chief food ;* τούτῳ, *v. l.* τούτων. — οἶνος : grapes are still found wild in this region, the Koran not allowing their culture for wine.

30. σὺν τοῖς πολεμίοις, [with] *on the side of the enemy.* — οἱ μέν...οἱ δέ, *some...others* of the enemy.

31. ἑτέραν...ἑτέρας ; not unusual with the Greeks ; compare with the natural order in English ; cf. vii. 4. 18, εἰς τὸ φῶς ἐκ τοῦ σκότους. — ὑψηλή, even with these advantages for the transmission of sound, a long distance for the combined shout of many men to reach.

32. οὐ πολλοῦ δέοντας ἴσους...εἶναι, [not lacking much to be] *not far from being equal.* — ποικίλους τὰ νῶτα, *having their backs party-colored* (case 481 ; so τὰ ἔμπροσθεν). In a rude state of society the natural love of distinction and ornament has led to this embellishment of the body itself.

BOOK V. CHAP. V. 111

This has the advantage over the civilized passion for dress, of being cheap and permanent. For this custom among the Thracians, see Hdt. v. 6. — ἐστιγμένους ἀνθέμιον (case 479), *tattooed in flower patterns;* Mossyni notis corpus omne persignant, Pomp. Mela, i. 19.

33. σφίσι, as reflexive, implies that they stated this.

34. Τούτους...βαρβαρωτάτους διελθεῖν, *that* [they passed through these the most barbarous] *these were the most barbarous of the tribes through which they passed.* — ἄνθρωποι, i. e. men in general. — ὅμοια...ἅπερ ἄν (sc. ποιήσειαν or πράξειαν, or ἄνθρωποι ποιήσειαν from above), *such things as they* (or, *men*) *would do,* 560. — διελέγοντό τε ἑαυτοῖς, 583, asynd. of explanation. — ἐφ' ἑαυτοῖς, *at* (or *by*) *themselves*; *v. l.* ἐφ' ἑαυτῶν, *by themselves.*

164

CHAPTER V.

ARRIVAL AT COTYORA. — PLUNDER OF THE NEIGHBORING COUNTRY.

1. ὀκτὼ σταθμούς : as to the time here noted, McM. suggests that "by σταθμούς is probably meant the whole time spent in fighting and negotiating, as well as marching." See i. 2. 23 N. — Χάλυβας : Strabo (xii. 3) regards the Chalybes as those referred to by Homer (*Il.* ii. 857), who calls them Alizonians, originally Alybians, from their metropolis Alyba. Cf. § 17 N. — Μοσσυνοίκων, case 432 g. — Τιβαρηνούς, "quibus in risu lusuque summum bonum est," Pomp. Mela, i. 19.

2. ἔχρῃζον, ἐδέχοντο, order? — προσβάλλειν...ὀνηθῆναι, change from act. to pass. construction ; cf. vii. 3, 3 ; ὀνηθῆναι, rare for ὄνασθαι : τι, case? — βουλεύσαιντο, mode 641 d.

3. ἀπεδείξαντο, thereby preventing a great crime. — προσίοιντο, form? cf. i. 9. 7. — ἀποίκους οἰκοῦντας, [colonists] *a colony dwelling*, 394 c; *v. l.* ἀποικίαν, ὄντας δ', 499 e ; ii. 1. 6.

4. ἡ στρατιά, the greater part, 3. 1. — Πλῆθος τῆς καταβάσεως τῆς ὁδοῦ : the latter word in appos. w. καταβάσεως, *the total of the descent of the march;* but Rehdz. & Krüg. govern καταβ. by ὁδοῦ. — ἐν Βαβυλῶνι (Lex. ἐν), iv. 8. 22.

5. ἔμειναν, still expecting Chirisophus, and uncertain about their future movements. — κατὰ ἔθνος ἕκαστοι τῶν Ἑλλήνων, [each body of the Greeks] *all the Greeks by tribes,* each tribe having its special religious rites.

165

6. Παφλαγονίας, bounded, in Hdt. i. 6, 72, on the east by the Halys ; but here regarded as extending under the powerful king Corylas, to the vicinity of Cotyora.

7. Κοτυωριτῶν, modifying both πόλεως and χώρας, 523 c. — φοβούμενοι, *apprehensive* with the rest of the Sinopeans ; φοβούμενοι, ἐκείνων, ἤκουον, referring in sense to the Sinopeans in general, whom the ambassadors represented. — ἔφερον, sc. Κοτυωρῖται : Greek colonies were always under

some obligations to the parent states in respect to precedence, alliance, etc.; but Sinope kept her colonies in more than usual subjection, cf. § 19. — δεινός...λέγειν: his reputed skill certainly failed him here.

8. τέ...ἔπειτα δέ (giving more distinctness and thus emphasis to the clause), 716 b. — νικᾶτε, *are victors over*, or, *have conquered*, 612. — πολλῶν τε καί, ii. 3. 18, Vollb. — ὡς ἡμεῖς ἀκούομεν, tense 612; ii. 1. 12; 2. 3.

9. "Ελληνες...'Ελλήνων, ἡμεῖς ὑμᾶς, order? — οὐδὲ γάρ, iii. 1. 16, Rehdz. — ὑπήρξαμεν, ii. 3. 23.

10. μέν, see δέ, § 11. — ἀφελόμενοι: for the cases with this verb, see 485 d. — ὅ τι s, order 718 o.

11. ὑμᾶς...ἐνίους, 417 a. — οὐ πείθοντας, *not* [persuading the owners] *by their consent.*

12. Ταῦτ'...ἀξιοῦμεν, *these proceedings we think not right*, i. e. we protest against, i. 1. 8, McM. — ποιήσετε, (stronger than the subjunc.) *will persist in doing.* — ἄλλον ὅντινα, i. 10. 3; 4. 15.

13. Ἡμεῖς δέ, iv. 6. 10. — ἀγαπῶντες, thankful, well content. Cf. Thucyd. vi. 36. — ἄγειν καὶ φέρειν, ii. 6. 5 N.

14. ἐν Τραπ. μέν, cf. Κοτυωρίτας δέ, § 19. — ἀνθ' ὧν (= ἀντὶ τούτων ἅ, 554 a, N.) s, *in return for the honors which they showed us, and* [they also bestowed gifts] *the gifts which they bestowed.* — τις, τούτων, 501, i. 4. 8. — ἡγοῦντο, mode?

15. ὁποίων τινῶν (Lex.), 548 d.

16. ἄν τε (Lex. ἐάν) εἰς βάρβαρον γῆν, sc. ἔλθωμεν.

17. Χαλδαίους, also called Χάλυβες, iv. 7. 15; οἱ νῦν Χαλδαῖοι, Χάλυβες τὸ παλαιὸν ὠνομάζοντο, Strabo xii. 3. — καίπερ, καὶ μάλα, in concession, 674 f.

18. τῶν ἐκείνων, sc. χρημάτων, *of their property;* see 524 b.

19. Κοτυωρίτας, inverse attr. to οὕς, 554 c; or to be explained by anacoluthon (e. g. as if ἀφῃρήμεθα were to follow instead of αὐτῶν εἰλήφαμεν) or synecdoche, 481 b. — τι αὐτῶν, *anything of theirs.* — ἁρμοστήν (Lex.), cf. vi. 2. 13; 4. 18; Thucyd. viii. 5.

20. Ὁ δὲ λέγεις, quod autem dicis, *as to what you say;* so ἅ δὲ ἠπείλησας, § 22. Ὁ is explained by βίᾳ παρελθόντας [sc. ἡμᾶς or ἐνίους, § 11] σκηνοῦν. — ᾗ ἡμᾶς s, *where the place itself admitted us* without force, it was so ill fortified. — δαπανῶντες (Lex.). — ἐφ' ἡμῖν ᾖ s, *it may be in our power to remove them.*

21. ὑπαίθριοι, 509 b.

22. ποιήσεσθε, ποιήσομεν, voice 585. — ἡμεῖς δέ, *we on the other hand,* or, *for our part.* — ὑμῶν, case? — τὸν Παφλαγόνα, *the Paphlagonian* king.

24. τῷ Ἑκατωνύμῳ χαλεπαίνοντες τοῖς εἰρημένοις, *displeased* [with Hecat., with what he had said] *with what Hecat. had said.* Some govern Ἑκατ. by σύν in compos. — παρελθών, used of public speakers. Cf. vi. 1. 31, 32. — ξενίοις, pos.?

25. πολλά τε καί (702 c) ἐπιτήδεια...τά τε ἄλλα [sc. διελέγοντο]...ἐδέοντο, *they conversed on many suitable topics* [both the others and] *and especially they made such careful inquiries as each party desired respecting*, etc.: ἐπιτήδεια, v. l. φιλικά.

CHAPTER VI.

THE GREEKS RESOLVE TO PROCEED BY SEA.—XENOPHON'S PLAN TO FOUND A CITY IN PONTUS.

1. αὐτοῖς...παρακαλέσαντας, cf. i. 2. 1 N. — Σινωπέας, with whom the generals had already conferred. — ἄν, ἄν, pos. 621 d, f. **168** — χρήσιμοι, it seemed that the Sinopeans would be useful as guides. — προσδεῖν ἐδόκει, there seemed to be still more need.

2. Ἕλληνας ὄντας Ἕλλησι, being Greeks to Greeks, i. e. being to them as Greeks should be to Greeks. Some regard Ἕλλησι as displaced by a violent parataxis, and as the object of εὔνους and συμβουλεύειν.

3. ἀπελογήσατο, a clumsy lie. — σφῶν, the Sinopeans.

4. πολλά...γένοιτο, may many blessings betide me, 638 d. How would the addition of ἄν to γένοιτο affect the sense? 638 f. — Αὕτη (509 b) γάρ ...παρεῖναι, for [that which is said to be sacred counsel] Sacred Counsel so called seems to me to be here present, as a goddess forbidding all falsehood on penalty of infamy. There seems to be here a reference to the proverb ἱερὸν ἡ συμβουλή, with rhetorical personification. — νῦν γάρ, refers to an omitted clause; and I have more than ordinary reason to give faithful counsel, for, etc. McM. — πολλοί...μέ, there will be many to praise me, both you and others.

5. κομίζησθε, pass. — ἡμᾶς, ὑμᾶς, in emphatic antithesis. — στέλλησθε, mid. (or, pass.?). — ὑμᾶς...εἶναι, you will have [to be the fighters] the fighting to do.

6. λεκτέα, sc. ταῦτά ἐστιν.

7. μέν, see δέ, § 8. — εὐθύς, protinus, gives emphasis to πρῶτον. **169** — οὐ γὰρ ἔστιν ἄλλῃ, ἢ ᾗ (observe the repetition of sound), for it cannot be in any other place than where. — ὁδοῦ, governed by ἑκάτερα (Lex.). — ἅ, the comm. obj. of κρατεῖν and κατέχοντες, 399 g; which a very few [occupying] occupants could hold. — οὐδ' ἄν...ἄν, 622 a. — οἱ πάντες ἄνθρωποι, all the men in the world, 523 e.

8. πεδία ὄντα (677), that there are plains, specially favorable to cavalry for harassing infantry. — μεῖζον φρονεῖ, thinks too much of himself, or, is too proud for this, 514 a; cf. iii. 1. 27; vi. 3. 18, ὁ ἄρχων, Corylas.

9. κλέψαι, ἢ φθάσαι λαβόντες, to seize by stealth or surprise. — πλεῖον, μεῖον, 507 e. — ἄλλως τε καί, especially, 717 a. — Ἄλυν, cf. Strabo xii. 3 for derivation of name. — ὡς δ' αὕτως (Lex. ὡσαύτως).

10. οὐ, not merely.

11. φιλίας ἕνεκα τῆς Κορύλα (object. gen.), order 721 c, 523 a, **170** 3. — ὡς δῶρα ληψόμενον, in expectation of receiving presents. — τὴν Σινωπέων χώραν κακόν τι, χώραν belonging, but not essentially, with τὴν Σινωπέων, and κακόν with τι, 719 d. — οἱ δ' οὖν, i. 3. 5; 2. 12.

H

12. οὕτω ἔχει (Lex.), ita se res habet, voice 577 c. — μέλλει...ἂν πλέοιμεν, mode? — ἕνα μή, stronger than μηδένα, and made still more emphatic by ἀριθμῷ; not [one in number] *a single individual*. Some editors, according to the conjecture of Weiske, place ἀριθμῷ after ὣς; but see Küh. in loc.
13. κρατῶμεν, δυναίμεθ' ἄν, mode? — ἐν...χώρᾳ, in loco et numero. Cf. 7. 8 : Krüger.
15. Ξενοφῶντι...αὐτῷ, 505 b. — παρεσκευάσθη, mode 631 b, 636 a, iv. 2. 10. — χώραν καὶ δύναμιν, an object not unworthy of the ambition of Xenophon. — προσκτήσασθαι, sc. αὐτούς.
16. αὐτῶν, v. l. αὐτῶν; cf. iv. 7. 19, Küh. — τοὺς περιοικοῦντας, successful in trade, but otherwise having no eminence. — ἐπὶ τούτοις, force of, cf. § 22, 27, 28 (περί). — εἰπεῖν, mode 703 d, β.

171
17. ἑαυτῷ...περιποιήσασθαι, referring, by a change of subject, to Xenophon.
18. ἔλαβε, see i. 7. 8. — Κύρῳ, indir. obj. of ἠλήθευσε or θυόμενος, or both.
19. ὅτι, ὅτι, cf. vii. 4. 5. — ἐκπλέοντας, numb.? — βουλεύεται γάρ, change?
20. ὡς...ὀνῆσαι, [so that you might benefit] *to benefit :* ὡς is omitted before ἔχειν, and in some MSS. here also. — τῆς...χώρας...ἐκλεξάμενοι, *having selected from* (or, of) *the country*, 699 f, or 423. — τὸν μέν s, *that whoever wishes may return.* — πλοῖα δ' ὑμῖν, *then you have vessels*, δ' introducing the apodosis, while the preceding infinitives depend on

172 βούλεσθε.
22. στρατιωτῶν ὄντων, 675. — προσέχειν...ποιεῖσθαι, pos.? — "Ελλαδος, pos.? — τινας, preferring not to name Xenophon ; cf. i. 4. 12.
23. νουμηνίας, the most frequent time of commencing service and of payment. — κυζικηνόν, a standard gold coin among the colonies about the Euxine, corresponding in general use to the daric, though somewhat more valuable ; cf. i. 3. 21 ; vii. 6. 1. — ἕκοντες, numb. and gend.?
24. Φρυγίας (Lex. 2).
25. αὖθις, v. l. εὐθύς. — στρατηγίας ἐμάχετο, thinking perhaps that, as a Bœotian, he ought to have succeeded Proxenus. — ὥστε τῷ βουλομένῳ ἐνοικεῖν, *so that whoever wished might settle there.* The dat. is here used for the accus. to agree with αὐτοῖς, 667 c, cf. ii. 6. 9 ; or, is governed by ἔσεσθαι, supplied from above.
26. ἔστε, change ? — ὥστε (Lex. d).

173
27. ὑπέρ, differs from περί, which Xen. uses § 28, in implying inclination ; cf. § 16, 22. — μὴ κοινούμενον. This forms part of a case here assumed upon the statement of others, and not affirmed, 686 ; cf. οὐ πείσας, § 29. — εἰς, with reference to the introduction of the subject ; so, εἰς ὑμᾶς, § 28, cf. § 37. — τὸ κοινόν, sc. πλῆθος, the general council of officers, 7. 17.
28. ταῦτα...ὁποῖα, 550 d. — Καὶ νῦν, cf. iv. 3. 11. — ἄρχεσθαι, *to* [begin] *undertake at all ;* an ingenious defence against the charge. — περί, cf. § 27, 16.

BOOK V. CHAP. VII. 115

29. τὸ μὲν μέγιστον, as to *the most important*, i. 3. 10. — ἐμοί, governed by ἐπιβουλή, 455 f, or φάνοιτο, 460. Cf. insidiæ consuli, Sallust. — οὐ πείσας : οὐ, not μή (§ 27) : οὐ represents πείσας as part of the *fact alleged*, viz. that "without having persuaded you I was purposing...," — μή would represent πείσας as part of the speaker's *thought*, —"I was purposing to do this without persuading you." οὐ πείσας is an adjunct of "I " as the subj. of διανοοίμην : μὴ πείσ. of "I" as the subj. of πράττειν : cf. *Cyr.* ii. 3. 5, διανοεῖται...μηδὲν καλὸν κἀγαθὸν ποιῶν...ἰσομοιρεῖν. McM.

30. ἑώρων...ἐσκόπουν, 631 b. — τοῦτ' ἂν ἐσκόπουν, ἀφ' οὗ ἂν γένοιτο, ὥστε, *I should be looking out for* [that from which it would result so that] *a measure which would so result that:* ὥστε, marking result, is not uncommon after γίγνομαι. — ὑμᾶς...τὸν μὲν βουλόμενον, 417 a. — τὸν μὴ βουλόμενον, sc. ἀποπλεῖν ἤδη.

31. πέμποντας, tense 594. The vessels had begun to come. — καλόν μοι...τῆς πορείας (*v. l.* σωτηρίας) λαμβάνειν, *it seems to me* [to be] *an admirable thing to be safely conveyed to the point we wish to reach, and then to receive* [the wages of the journey] *pay for our journey;* spoken with quiet sarcasm. Cf. vii. 6. 30.

32. ἐν γάρ, cf. iii. 2. 28. — κατὰ μικρὰ γενομένης, *resolved into fragments;* κατά distributive, as in i. 8. 9. **174**

33. ἅπερ ὑμῶν, sc. δοκεῖ. — 'Ανέτειναν, asynd., cf. iii. 2. 33.

34. λήψονται...ἐπιθήσοιεν, mode 645 b ; so μεταμέλοι...ἔστε, § 36.

35. τὰ δὲ χρήματα...ἐψευσμένοι ἦσαν τῆς μισθοφορᾶς (pos. 719 d), *but the money* [of the wages] *for the payment of wages they* [had falsified about] *withheld;* cf. ἐψεύστο τὴν συμμαχίαν, Thucyd. v. 83.

36. ἐκπεπληγμένοι ἦσαν, *were* [having been struck with surprise] *confounded*, 599 c, 600 a, b. — Φᾶσιν (Lex. 2).

37. Αἰήτου, mentioned as a king that was known. — αὐτῶν, case 442 a, 407. — εἴποι εἰς, cf. § 27. — ὑμεῖς δέ, change ? — μὴ ἐκκλησιάζειν, **175** 686 c ; *v. l.* οὐκ ἐκκλησιάζειν, a stronger expression in contrast to ἀλλά s, 686 k. — αὐτοῦ ἕκαστον, parataxis, 719, b, e.

CHAPTER VII.

CHARGES AGAINST XENOPHON. — ELOQUENT AND EFFECTIVE DEFENCE OF HIMSELF.

1. ἀνεπύθοντο = *got to know*. — πάλιν, *back;* i. e. towards the quarter from which they had just come ; used perhaps the rather from the confounding of two rivers (see Lex. Φᾶσις).

2. ξύλλογοι, *meetings* (i. e. for seditious purposes). — κύκλοι, cf. vi. 4. 20. — μάλα φοβεροὶ ἦσαν, μὴ ποιήσειαν, *they were greatly to be feared, lest they should do:* see 573. — τοὺς τῶν κήρυκας, § 17 s. — ἀγορανόμους, § 21 s.

3. ἀγοράν = ἐκκλησίαν, a use more Homeric than Attic.

NOTES.

4. τῶν μὲν στρατηγῶν (case 699 a)...αὐτόν, *did not charge the generals with coming to him.*

5. διαβάλλειν...ὡς, cf. i. 1. 3. — ἀκούσατε, tense 592 b. — θεῶν, ἥλιος § 6, βορέας and νότος § 7, without art. 533 c, a.

176 **6.** τοῦτο...ὑμᾶς (480 b) ἐξαπατῆσαι, *cheat you into this belief.* — ὡς ἥλιος...ἐντεῦθεν, *that* [whence] *where the sun* actually *rises, there on the contrary he sets; and where he sets, there* on the contrary *rises;* i. e. sets in the east, and rises in the west. Observe that δέ is used here twice as an adv. and once as a conj. Cf. Hdt. ii. 42.

7. βορέας, βορρᾶς, so the MSS. — ὡς καλοὶ πλοῖ εἰσιν, [there are favorable voyages] *it is fine weather for sailing.* — Τοῦτο (pos.? for constr. see § 6)...ἐξαπατῆσαν, *is there then* [how] *any way in which one could cheat you in this?*

8. Ἀλλὰ γάρ (709, 2), *but*, you say perhaps, this will not secure you, *for I shall make you embark*, etc. — ἐμβιβῶ = ἐμβιβάζω. — Πῶς ἄν s, order 621 c.

9. Ποιῶ δ᾽ ὑμᾶς...ἥκειν (612), *I* [make] *will suppose you to have come.* — καὶ δὴ καὶ ἀποβαίνομεν, *and now indeed we are even landing*, in supposition. — ἐγγὺς μυρίων, 445 c ; for a different constr. see iv. 2. 8 ; vii. 8. 18. — Πῶς ἄν οὖν...δίκην, *how then could a man more surely bring punishment upon himself.*

10. δύναται, sc. λέγειν. — Τί γάρ ; 564 c. — τινι, case 453. — Παρίημι, **177** ἀρχέτω· μόνον s, obs. the effect of the asynd. Thorax was a disappointed aspirant for the generalship, 6. 25, and perhaps Neon.

11. ἐμοί, pos.? — ἢ αὐτὸς (677 b) ἐξαπατηθῆναι ἄν (622 b) οἴεται ταῦτα (586 c) s, *thinks that he either could himself be deceived in these matters, or could deceive another in these,* viz. the points mentioned in § 6 s.

12. τούτων, case 414 a. — ἅλις, as subst. in acc. 706 a. — μὴ ἀπέλθητε, πρὶν ἄν ἀκούσητε, 641 d, 619 b. — ὃ εἰ ἔπεισι, [if which proceeds] *for if this proceeds,* 561 a. — ὑποδείκνυσιν, sc. ἔσεσθαι. — καὶ καταφρονηθῶμεν, omitted by some editors, bracketed by Rehdz. and others.

13. ὧν εἶχον, *of what they had.* — δοκοῦσι...τινες, *and I think that some of you.*

14. Τοῦτο (pos.?) καταμαθών...μικρὸν εἴη, *observing*, or, *learning* [this that it was] *that this was small.* — διὰ τὸ φίλιον νομίζειν εἶναι, *from the belief that it was on friendly terms with us.* — αὐτούς, numb.?

15. Διενενόητο, *he* [had formed the plan] *had intended.* — ἐλθεῖν, ii. 1. 1. — παραπλέοντες, some of the coasting party, 1. 16. — εἴ τι λάβοι, *whatever plunder he might have taken*, 639 a. — ἐκ τοῦ πλοίου, const. præg. cf. § 17.

16. Πορευόμενον...γενομένῃ, *but the dawning of the day surprises him* **178** *in his march*, 677 f. Cf. iii. 4. 49. — οἱ δέ τινες, ii. 3. 15.

17. ἐν τῇ ἡμέρᾳ, [sc. ἐν] ᾗ, 707 b ; see 4. 1. — ἀνηγμένοι, having put out to sea. — ἐκ, const. præg. § 15. — τρεῖς ἄνδρες, 418 c.

18. τί ἡμῖν δόξειεν, [why it seemed best to us] *what induced us.* — Ἐπεὶ μέντοι σφεῖς (v. l. σφᾶς) λέγειν (mode 659 b, *but* the Cerasuntians *said, that, when they themselves told them that the affair was not by public*

BOOK V. CHAP. VII. 117

authority, they (the barbarians) *were both gratified:* σφεῖς is here used (if it be the true reading) as having a kind of reflexive reference to the subject of ἔφασαν, 667 b: *v. l.* 'Επεὶ μέντοι ἔφασαν ὅτι, κ. τ. λ. — ὡς ἡμῖν λέξαι s, *that they might tell us what had taken place, and invite those who desired, themselves to take and bury the dead.*

19. Τῶν δ' ἀποφυγόντων, § 16. — τινές, pos. 548 b, cf. ii. 5. 32. — βαρβάρους, § 14. — τοῖς λίθοις, the stones at hand. — οἱ πρέσβεις, καταλευσθέντες, thus added to emphasize the enormity of the outrage, both from its manner and from the sacredness of the persons against whom it was committed.

20. πρὸς ἡμᾶς, i. e. to Cotyora. — ὅπως, *how.* — ταφείησαν, iii. 4. 29. Kühner.

21. ἔξωθεν τῶν ὅπλων, *outside of the place of arms,* a common place for consultation and for receiving visitors.

22. ὡς ἂν [sc. ἀποχωροῖεν] καὶ ἑωρακότες, [as they would naturally do having even seen] *as well they might having seen.*

23 s. Observe interchange of tenses. — μέν, to which δέ corresponding? **179**

25. καθ' αὑτούς, in their direction, *adversum*; ἐπί, expresses hostility, *in se.* — ἐπνίγετο, *was in danger of drowning,* 594.

26. δοκεῖτε (Lex.). Some here supply ποιῆσαι, or δρᾶσαι, or δεῖσαι. Cf. *quid illum censes.* Ter. *Andrian,* v. 2. 12. — 'Ηδίκουν, tense 612. — ἐμπεπτώκοι, form 317 b.

27. οἱ πάντες, *the whole body, collectively;* ἰδίᾳ, [by one's self] *individually.* — οὐκ...οὔτε, 713 b. — ἀνελέσθαι πόλεμον = πολεμῆσαι, governing the dat. 455 f. — ἐφ' ὅ τι ἂν ἐθέλῃ, *against whatever* place, people, etc.; or, *to whatever enterprise.* — τῶν λόγων, partit. gen. — τῶν...ἰόντων, gov. by λόγων.

28. χώρᾳ (Lex.), 6. 13.

29. οἱ αὐθαίρετοι οὗτοι στρατηγοί, more emphatic order; see **180** 524 b. — ἀδικεῖ, οἴχεται, 612. — ἀποπλέων, 679 d. — φεύγει, *he is a fugitive.*

30. διεπράξαντο...μὴ ἀσφαλὲς εἶναι, have [brought it about that it should not be safe] *rendered it unsafe.* — ἂν μή, *unless.* — κηρυκίῳ, often marked by wreaths, or figures of serpents (as on the caduceus of Mercury).

31. δοξάτω ὑμῖν, *let it* [seem good to you] *be so voted.* — ὡς τοιούτων ἐσομένων, *in the expectation of such acts.* — φυλακήν...τις, *each one may keep guard on his own account.* — ὑπερδέξια, doubtless looking or pointing to them.

32. ἡδέως, cheerfully, with confidence.

33. φιλίᾳ, predicatively, [as friendly] or, *to its friendship.* — περὶ τὰ μέγιστα...ἐξαμαρτάνοντες, *committing such sins* [in respect to the greatest matters, as the treatment of heralds] *against the highest obligations.* Some connect τοιαῦτα with τὰ μέγιστα. — Οὗ, *where,* i. e. in Greece, cf. vi. 6. 16, Krüg., Küh., etc. — πάντων (governed by ἐπαίνου), *from all,* 434 a, or, join οὗ with ἐπαίνου, [what praise] *the praise which.*

118 NOTES.

34. πάντες έλεγον : this statement must not be pressed. All concurred in this view, several speaking as their representatives. — τοὺς...τούτων ἄρξαντας, *those who had led in these things.* — δοῦναι, ἐξεῖναι, etc., infin. after ἔλεγον = ἐκέλευον. — τοῦ λοιποῦ [sc. χρόνου], Lex. 433 a. — τις...ἄγεσθαι

181 αὐτοὺς (numb.?) ἐπὶ θανάτῳ, *that they should be led out for death,* or, *punished with death.* — δίκας...καταστῆσαι, cf. δίκην ὑποσχεῖν, 8. 1. — τι ἄλλο, case 586 c, 480 b. — ἐξ οὗ (Lex. ἐξ), 557 a.

35. Παραινοῦντος...συμβουλευόντων, order? — καθῆραι (sacrifices, washings, etc.), especially to remove the stain incurred by the murder of the heralds, and thus, by these religious ceremonies, to avert the displeasure of the gods. (See Dictionary of Antiquities, κάθαρσις, lustratio.) The effect upon the discipline of the army may have been also considered.

CHAPTER VIII.

INVESTIGATION INTO THE CONDUCT OF THE GENERALS. — XENOPHON FULLY JUSTIFIES HIS COURSE.

1. The army, in the spirit of Greek institutions, proceeded as a little republic, entitled to call its rulers to account. Φιλήσιος μὲν ὦφλε καὶ Ξανθικλῆς, 497 b. — τῆς φυλακῆς, *for their* negligent *charge,* 429 a, 431 c. — ἄρχων αἱρεθείς, a *commander* of the transports, to take charge of the persons and property conveyed, 3. 1. — ὑβρίζοντος, *as guilty of wanton abuse.* Among the graver suits under the Attic law was the ὕβρεως δίκη, an indictment for wanton outrage to the person, where the penalty was often death. (See Dictionary of Antiquities.)

2. ποῦ καί, *where indeed.* — τῷ ῥίγει, iv. 5. 3 s.

3. [sc. τοιούτου] οἷον, 554 a. — ἐπιλελοιπότος, παρόν, 675. — οἴνου (case 432 a) δὲ μηδ' ὀσφραίνεσθαι παρόν (675), *and where it was not possible even to catch the scent of wine,* we were so destitute of it. — ὑπὸ τῆς ὕβρεως, *through their wanton spirit.* "Every one knows," says Spelman, "that asses, and mules, their offspring, have such an inbred viciousness that no fatigue can subdue it." Cf. εἰδέναι ὄνων ἁπάντων ὑβριστότατόν σε ὄντα, Lucian. *Pseudologista,* 3.

4. ἐκ τίνος, *on what account.* —'Ἀλλ' ἀπῄτουν, *well then* (after a silence which implied a negative), *did I make a demand?* — μαχόμενος, sc. ἔπαιόν σε. — ἐπαρῴνησα (Lex. παροινέω).

182 5. οὐκ ἔφη, sc. ὁπλιτεύειν, *he said* NO, 662 b. — οὐδὲ τοῦτ' ἔφη, *he did not even say this.*

6. μὰ Δί', case 476 a. — διέρριψας, a harsh term for the act; cf. διέδωκα, § 7.

7. τοιαύτη τις (Lex.). — σοι...σὺ ἐμοί, 536. — σὺ ἐμοὶ ἀπέδειξας s, *you had shown me the man* [back] *again,* i. e. produced him at the end of the day's march. Here ἀπό seems to have the same force as in ἀπολαβών and ἀπέδωκα (Lex. ἀπό). — ἄξιον, sc. ἀκοῦσαι.

BOOK V. CHAP. VIII. 119

8. κατελείπετο, *was being left behind.* — ὅτι = ὅσον τοῦτο, ὅτι, 560 ; cf. iii. 1. 45. — ἐγώ, cf. σύ, ii. 1. 12. — ἄνθρωπος, why rather than ἀνήρ?

9. ὀρύττοντα ὡς κατορύξοντα, parataxis, chiastic. — ἐπιστάς, adstans, Krüg. i. 5. 7.

10. 'Οπόσα γε βούλεται, *just as* [much as] *he pleases,* for aught I care about it. — εἰδότι ἐοικέναι, *to* [be] *act like one who knew.*

11. Τί οὖν ; 564 c. — ἧττόν τι s (Lex. τίς), 584 d. — Καὶ γάρ, the negation, " no," is here left to be implied.

12. Τοῦτον, pos.?—ὀλίγας, *too few* (Lex.), 515, case ? Cf. Luke xii. 47 ; Aristoph. *Nubes,* 968. — ἄλλους, ἕκαστος, numb. 501.

13. ὅσοις s, *as many as* [it contented] *were content.* — δι' ἡμᾶς ...ιόντων, 676 b. — αὐτοὶ δέ, 562. — τοῦτο ἐποιοῦμεν, *had behaved thus,* tense 604 a ; mode ?

14. Ἤδη δὲ καί, [and now also] *then also, so also,* ἤδη referring rather to the time of the acknowledgment, than to that of the action. — μαλακιζόμενόν τινα, *a man yielding to sloth,* not referring to a particular individual, 548 c. — προϊέμενον αὐτόν, 583 ; see iv. 5. 15 s. — κατέμαθον ἀναστάς, *found that I rose,* 677 a, i. 3. 10. — μόλις, pos. 719 d, μ.

15. Ἐν ἐμαυτῷ, *in my own case.*

16. Ἄλλον δέ γε ἴσως, [and indeed] *yes, and another one perhaps.* — ἡμᾶς, as Xenophon commanded the rear. — πύξ...λόγχῃ, order?

17. Xen. acutely shows that they owe their very ability to call him to account to the services which he had rendered them. — δίκαιον, δίκην, parataxis, or parachesis, Vollb. — ἐπί, cf. i. 1. 4 ; iii. 1. — τί μέγα...λαμβάνειν, *what outrage could they have suffered so great* [of which they would now be claiming to receive the penalty] *that they could now be claiming to receive satisfaction.*

18. ἐπ' ἀγαθῷ...ἐπ' ἀγαθῷ, cf. ii. 4. 5 N. — ἀξιῶ s, *I deem myself bound to render such an account as,* 7. 34.—Καὶ γάρ, *and so of others, for.*

19. θάρρω...μᾶλλον, *I have higher spirits.*—νῦν ἢ τότε, order? — εὐδίᾳ = ἡ ἄνευ ἀνέμων ἡμέρα, i. e. *security.*

20. θάλαττα (Lex.). Some regard μεγάλη as a pred. adj.; *the sea runs high.* See Rehdz. — χαλεπαίνει, obs. the parallelism of the two clauses. — πρωρεύς, "the command in the prow of a vessel was exercised by an officer called πρωρεύς, who seems to have been next in rank to the steersman, and to have had the care of the gear, and the command over the rowers." (Dict. of Antiq.)

21. οὔτε...ἐπαίετε, as was recommended and voted, iii. 2. 31, 33.

22. αὐτῶν, [of] *among them.* — Οἶμαι γάρ, prefixed without influencing the construction.

23. διεμάχετο...ἀσπίδα μὴ φέρειν, [fought through not to carry] *contended persistently for the privilege of not carrying his shield.* — νῦν δέ s, he is well enough to plunder by night, and carry off his booty. — ἀποδέδυκεν, (vestibus) spoliavit, Krüg.

24. τοῦτον τἀναντία...ποιοῦσι (571 c), [you will treat this man contrary than, etc.] *your treatment of this man will be the reverse of that given to*

dogs. — τοὺς μέν, v. 8. 24. — τὰς ἡμέρας, τὴν ἡμέραν, *through the day* [days], or, *by day.* — διδέασι (Lex. δίδημι): if we have here an extract from an old rhyming proverb, the use of this very rare poetic word might seem explained. Cf. iii. 4. 35.

25. 'Ἀλλὰ γάρ, *but,* one word more, *for.* — μέμνησθε, obs. how often Xen. repeats this word, in impressing his hearers with their faults of memory. — εἰ δέ τῳ (cf. τινι above) ἤ...ἐπεκούρησα, *but if I either* [relieved for any one a storm] *protected any one from a storm,* or the cold, wintry weather.

185 — τούτων οὐδείς s, 432 c. — οὐδέν, as i. 1. 8; v. l. οὐδέ, emphatically repeated from οὐδ' εἰ.

26. ἀνεμίμνησκον, *made mention* of his (Xenophon's) services. — περιεγένετο, [it came about so as to be well] *and all at length resulted well* or *happily.*

BOOK VI.

FROM COTYORA BY SEA TO CALPE. — THENCE TO CHRYSOPOLIS ON THE BOSPORUS OPPOSITE BYZANTIUM.

CHAPTER I.

TREATY WITH THE PAPHLAGONIANS. — VOYAGE TO SINOPE. — XENOPHON OFFERED THE CHIEF COMMAND.

186 1. As the usual recapitulation is here wanting, some editors (as Schneider, Krüg., etc.) attach this and the next chapter to Book V., and make Book VI. to begin at what is here numbered as Chapter III., which has a brief recapitulation. — διατριβῇ, at Cotyora. — 'Ἐκλώπευον, i. e. to keep or sell them as slaves. — εὖ μάλα (Lex.), *quite easily* or *adroitly,* scite admodum, Dind.

2. ἵππους καὶ στολάς, for presents. — τοὺς "Ἕλληνας s, i. e. to agree to these terms.

3. δικαιοτάτους (Lex.), cf. § 22, Thucyd. i. 41.

4. βοῦς τῶν, 418 c. — κατακείμενοι, according to custom, supported by the left arm and taking food with the right. — σκίμποσιν, v. l. στιβάσιν.

5. σπονδαί, the Greek dinner of luxury consisted regularly of two parts, the substantial meal and the symposium. The latter, in which came the wine and the dessert, was the part especially devoted to conversation, music, spectacles, and in general to pleasure and amusement. This part was always introduced, as for a blessing, by sacred libations, with the common addition of the singing of a pæan. (For a vivid picture of such an entertainment, see Becker's *Charicles,* Scene vi.) Both Plato and Xen. intro-

BOOK VI. CHAP. I. 121

duce Socrates at a symposium. — πρῶτον μέν, corresponding to
μετὰ τοῦτο, § 7, 9, etc. — πρὸς αὐλόν, *to* [a flute] *the music of the*
flute, 695. — ὠρχήσαντο, ἥλλοντο ὑψηλά (Lex. 477 b), ἐχρῶντο, tense
592 a. — ταῖς μαχαίραις ἐχρῶντο (Lex.), [used] *flourished*, or, *played with
their swords*. — ὁ ἕτερος τὸν ἕτερον, 567 c. — πεπληγέναι, transitive, acc.
to McM.

6. τὸν Σιτάλκαν, *the Sitalce-song*, in honor of a Thracian king of this
name. See Dind., Thucyd. ii. 29, Diod. xii. 50. — ἦν...πεπονθώς, *but he
was not at all harmed*, 679 a, β.

7. καρπαίαν, *the carpæan* or *farm dance* (from καρπός, fruits or crops,
Lex.) ; McM. calls it the *wrist dance* (from καρπός, *wrist*). See Dind.,
who quotes Max. Tyr. *Diss*. xxviii. 4.

8. παραθέμενος τὰ ὅπλα, as our forefathers did with the guns which
they carried to the field for protection against Indian attacks. Cf. Thucyd.
i. 6. — προΐδηται, *as soon as he sees him coming; προ-*, "in front," often
implies distance. Cf. *Cyr*. iv. 3. 21. So "*prospexi* Italiam," Virg. *Æn*.
vi. 357, 385, McM. — ἐποίουν, in pantomime. — τὸν ἄνδρα, the common
obj. of δήσας and ἀπάγει. — τὼ χεῖρε, case 481, 485 e.

9. μιμούμενος, *in pantomime*.

10. Περσικόν, sc. ὄρχημα, case 477 b (see Lex.).

11. Ἐπὶ δὲ τούτῳ ἐπιόντες, *and following him*. — αὐλούμενοι, *with the
flute playing* to the warlike movement. Cf. vii. 2. 30. —
προσόδοις, solemn processions. Cf. Schneider.

12. Ἐπὶ τούτοις, perhaps best connected with ἐκπεπληγμένους. — πυρρίχην ἐλαφρῶς, the Pyrrhic dance was practised with such rapidity as to
give its name to the quickest foot in prosody, 77, 740 c. It was especially
used as a preparation for war; to give strength, and to train to ease and
lightness of movement in arms. Byron taunted the modern Greeks with
retaining it as a mere entertainment : —

> "You have the Pyrrhic dance as yet;.
> Where is the Pyrrhic phalanx gone?
> Of two such lessons, why forget
> The nobler and the manlier one?"
> *Don Juan*, iii. 86.

13. αὗται καὶ αἱ τρεψάμεναι, obs. the repetition of final αι, and how the
influence of a woman (i. 10. 3) is exaggerated into the direct action of the
whole sex. The Greeks were intent upon astonishing the credulous and
simple-minded Paphlagonians.

14. μήτε ἀδικεῖν s, cf. § 2.

15. Σινώπης, [of] *belonging to Sinope*. Some regard the word as here
used to include the whole adjacent territory belonging to the city.

16. Χειρίσοφος, Ἀναξίβιος, v. i. 4 ; cf. Diod. xiv. 31. — ἐπαινοίη,
numb.?

17. εἰσῄει αὐτοὺς, ὅπως, [it entered] *the question occupied their
thoughts, how*, etc.

18. μᾶλλον ἄν.. στρατεύματι, *that the one could manage the army better* than if there were a multiplicity of command. — εἴ τι δέοι λανθάνειν...κρύπτεσθαι...ὑστερίζειν, if it were necessary that any measure should [lie hid] be kept secret, that it could better be concealed; and, on the other hand, if it were necessary that any measure should [anticipate] be carried by surprise, it would be in less danger of being too late; or, more personally, if there were any need that they should act in secrecy, they could more surely be hidden, etc. — τὸ δόξαν τῷ ἑνί, quod uni visum esset id perficiendum. — νικώσης, sc. γνώμης, i. e. the opinion of the majority.

20. πῇ μέν, corresp. to ὁπότε δέ, § 21. Cf. iii. 1. 12. — τὴν τιμήν... γίγνεσθαι, that so [the honor would be greater to him] he would be in higher honor. Some omit καί before πρὸς τοὺς φίλους, and translate, would be in higher estimation with his friends. — μεῖζον, [greater] with greater distinction. — τυχόν (Lex.), 483 a. — ἀγαθοῦ, case 444 f. — αἴτιος, case?

21. ἕξει, εἴη : it is only through the opt. in Greek, as through the potential in English, that the future tense can be carried back into the past; and it is only in indirect discourse, and in clauses partaking of its nature, that the fut. opt. is used. Yet even here the fut. indic. is very often preferred, and even though associate tenses may take the opt., 643 h.

22. Διαπορουμένῳ...διακρῖναι, being at a loss how to decide; v. l. ἀπορουμένῳ. — δύο ἱερεῖα, as was common, in order that a second sacrifice might be forthwith tried, if the first was unsatisfactory. — αὐτῷ, case 452 a: μαντευτὸς ἦν, for ὥπερ (θύειν)...μαντευτὸν ἦν: cf. i. 2. 21 N; iv. 1. 17. McM. — ἐκ Δελφῶν, by the response of Apollo, iii. 1. 6. — τὸ ὄναρ, iii. 1. 11. — ἀπὸ τούτου τοῦ θεοῦ, for ἀφ' οὗπερ, 562. — ἤρχετο s, he began to [set himself to] undertake the joint charge of the army.

23. Κύρῳ s, iii. 1. 8. — ἑαυτῷ...φθεγγόμενον, screaming [for or to him on the right] on his right. — δεξιόν, i. e. in the east, or the lucky quarter. The Greek augur faced the north, and had the east on his right hand; the Roman faced the south, and had the lucky omens on the left. Cf. Il. xxiv. 320; Cicero De Divin. ii. 39. See Dict. of Antiq. — ὥσπερ (v. l. ὄνπερ) s, as (or, of whom) the seer said. Obs. how minute analogies were caught up in the ancient system of divination. — μέγας s, as king of birds and favorite of Zeus: so to Tarquinius Priscus, Vollb. Cf. Il. i. 279; Odyss. xv. 160–178. — πετόμενον, v. l. περιπετόμενον, i. e. by flying about. McM. says that there is a prospective reference here to the narrative at vii. 7. 54; 8. 3.

24. Οὕτω θυομένῳ, § 22. — προσδεῖσθαι s, to desire additional command.
25. αἱρήσονται, mode 643 h; cf. § 21 N.
26. αἴτιον...[sc. με] γένεσθαι, 677 e. — Λακεδαιμονίου, sc. Chirisophus. — ὑμῖν...συμφέρον, case? pos. of ὑμῖν and ἐμοί? — ἀλλ' [sc. μοι δοκεῖ] ἧττον. — ἄν...τυγχάνειν, supply ὑμᾶς as the subj. and τούτου or τούτων (from εἴ τι) as the obj. of the verb. Breitenbach. — εἴ τι δέοισθε, case 478 a; cf. i. 3. 4. — οὐ πάνυ τι (Lex.), i. e. not at all.

27. πρόσθεν, πρίν, cf. i. 1. 10 N; iv. 3. 12. — ἐπαύσαντο πολεμοῦντες, part. 677 a. The great struggle between Athens and Sparta, the Peloponnesian war, lasted 27 years (B. C. 431–404), and resulted in the Athenians

BOOK VI. CHAP. II. 123

making a complete submission to the Spartans as their masters, sacrificing their famous long walls and their naval power, and promising τὸν αὐτὸν ἐχθρὸν καὶ φίλον νομίζοντας, Λακεδαιμονίοις ἕπεσθαι καὶ κατὰ γῆν καὶ κατὰ θάλατταν ὅποι ἂν ἡγῶνται, Hellen. ii. 2. 20. — αὐτῶν, numb.?

28. ἐπολιόρκησαν, iv. 2. 15 N. Cf. ὁδὸν ὁδοποίουν, iv. 8. 8. — ἐκεῖνο (472 or 481) ἐννοῶ, μὴ (625 a) λίαν ἂν s, *in respect to that, I apprehend that I should be very quickly brought to my senses:* ἂν is here retained without regard to the dependence of the clause on ἐννοῶ μή, 631 d, 633 a. Some editors reject it: ἐκεῖνο seems to be used for the sake of more marked contrast with ὁ δὲ ὑμεῖς ἐννοεῖτε, *but as to this which you have in mind* (§ 29). Some regard μή as here complem., *I consider whether I should not*, etc.

29. ἔλησθε, θαυμάσαιμι, εὕροιτε, mode 633 b. — εἴ τινα, sc. Chirisophus. **191**

30. ὅτι...αἱρῶνται, *that it were ridiculous, if it were so, if the Lacedæmonians would be angry should even banqueters coming together not elect*, etc.; i. e. if they insisted on supremacy in everything. Some MSS. have ὡς ὀργιοῦνται, *as then* (to carry out the principle) *the Lacedæmonians will be angry*, etc. — ὀργιοῦνται, mode? — συμποσίαρχον (Lex.). Cf. Dict. of Antiq.

31. ἐνδέον (Lex.) 677 c. — ὀμνύω (form 315 a) ὑμῖν θεοὺς (case 472 f) πάντας καὶ πάσας [sc. ὅτι]...ἐθυόμην εἰ (Lex.). — ᾐσθανόμην, tense? — ἰδιώτην, *a common person*, not a μάντις: cf. Thucyd. vi. 72.

32. οὐδ' ἂν ἔγωγε, *neither would I*, more than Xenophon, § 29. — οὐχ ἑλόμενοι, *in not choosing him;* οὐ, as *fact* is denoted, 686 n. —'Ο δ'...ἑαυτῷ, sc. Dexippus, who ascribed the preference of Clearchus's troops for Timasion (iii. 1. 47 ; 2. 37) above himself to the influence of Xen. The consequence attached to such a charge shows how jealous the Lacedæmonians were for their dignity. — Ὁ δ' ἔφη s, this part of the section seems not to have been spoken by Chirisophus, but to be an explanation by the author, and hence thrown into a parenthesis: Townsend takes this view; but most editors regard the words as part of Chirisophus's speech.

33. κατασχεῖν, sc. ναῦς, est *appellere*. Cf. Hdt. vii. 188, Krüg. See Küh. *in loc.* **192**

CHAPTER II.

THE GREEKS SAIL TO HERACLEA. — SERIOUS DISSENSIONS IN THE ARMY, AND DIVISION INTO THREE PARTIES.

1. παραπλέοντες, *in sailing along the coast*, referring to the whole voyage of the army from Cotyora to Heraclea. They had already passed all the places here mentioned as seen, except the mouth of the Parthenius. Hence some needlessly suppose that Xen. forgot the situation of the places, or that there is here an interpolation. — ἀκτήν, poetic form, see Lex. — Ἴριος, form 218, 2.

2. ἐπὶ τὸν Κέρβερον, *to fetch Cerberus.* Cf. v. 1. 5, ἐπὶ πλοῖα. Thucyd. i. 117. McM.

4. πορείαν...πορευθῆναι, case 477 : some join πορείαν with ἐβουλεύοντο, 474 b. — τῶν στρατηγῶν, case 432 f ; 474 c. — οὐ μὴ γένηται, 597, cf. ii. 2. 12 ; iv. 8. 13 N. — ὁπόθεν...οὐκ ἔστιν, *there is* [not whence] *no source from which we can obtain provisions for our journey;* cf. ii. 4. 5.

193

5. μυρίους, cf. v. 6. 35 : the Heracleotes had broken their promise of a month's pay. — ἡμῶν καθημένων, note the transition to oratio directa : cf. i. 3. 14 N ; vii. 1. 33 ; *Odyss.* i. 372.

6. ἔστι δ' οἵ, 559 a. — ἀναγκάζειν, sc. διδόναι. — ὅ τι μή, nisi quod.

7. ἐπαπειλεῖν, 632 c. — ποιήσοιεν, v. l. ποιήσαιεν.

8. ἀνεσκεύασαν, ἐκέκλειντο, tense 599 c, f. McM. calls attention to Donaldson's Greek Grammar for this particular usage of the pluperfect to denote "the *establishment of a state* of condition in past time." Cf. ὡμολόγητο, i. 9. 14 N.

9. οἱ ταράξαντες ταῦτα, *those who had made this trouble,* 478.

10. Οἱ...αὐτοῖς, *and their language was.* — Ἀθηναῖον (ἕνα rejected by some), sc. Xenophon, whom they regarded as the actual leader, notwithstanding 1. 32. — καὶ Λακεδαιμονίων, *and even Lacedæmonians.* — οὐδέν, *nothing,* or, *of no account.* — ὑπὲρ ἥμισυ, as nom. 706 a ; v. l. ὑπερήμισυ.

194

11. ἑαυτῶν, καθ' ἑαυτούς, order ? cf. 6. 18.

12. Χειρισόφῳ, case 464 ; cf. 3. 1. — ἀφ' ἧς = ἀπὸ ταύτης ᾗ (or, ἧς).

13. μετ' αὐτῶν, sc. the Arcadians and Achæans. — καθ' αὐτὸν πορεύεσθαι, but with the agreement, it would seem, that the two forces should meet at Calpe. — Χειρισόφου, case ?

14. μηδείς, i. e. of the rest of the army. — αὐτοί, viz. Neon, Chirisophus, and Xenophon. — αὐτῶν, pos. 538 g. — τοῖς γεγενημένοις, case ? — αὐτῷ, i. e. Neon, to whom, as his lieutenant, Chirisophus in disgust left the conduct of affairs. Some, with less reason, refer αὐτῷ to Xenophon, or the army.

15. ἔτι μέν, has been explained in two ways, *still further indeed* (a sense belonging to v. l. μὲν ἔτι) and *as yet indeed,* referring to a time continuing till what is afterwards stated with δέ. In this last sense, which is now generally preferred, it may be translated *at first,* or, *for a while.* Cf. *Hell.* ii. 4. 11 ; Plato *Protag.* 310 c. — λῷον καὶ ἄμεινον, a frequent pleonasm in consulting the gods ; cf. vii. 6. 44.

16. γίγνεται...τριχῇ, [comes to be in] *is divided into three parts.* — Ἀρκάδες, appos. 393 d. — Χειρισόφῳ, *for Chirisophus,* or supply εἰσί. — εἰς τετρακοσίους, as nom. 706 a. — Θρᾷκες, cf. i. 2. 9. It is not surprising that Chirisophus and Xenophon felt deeply this breaking up of the army which they had guided safely through so many perils ; the more because the movement was directed so personally against themselves. The small forces which they had rallied about them were mixed, including many inferior troops, and consisting only in part of their own soldiers, many of the best of whom had deserted them. Chirisophus, sick at heart and enfeebled

BOOK VI. CHAP. III. 125

in health, gave up the conduct of affairs to his lieutenant, Neon; and Xenophon, who had incurred no responsibility by enlisting troops for the army, and yet had done more than any other one to save the whole, saw now an opportunity, the great perils past, of honorable return to his native city Athens. He perhaps thought that the best measure for his present force was to unite it with that of Chirisophus: Timasion was the only other general who was not an Arcadian or Achæan; cf. 3. 14.

17. Ἀρκάδες, sc. καὶ Ἀχαιοί, the chief tribe only mentioned. — κατὰ μέσον πως, [somehow at] *about the middle of* [Thrace] *the Thracian coast.* — τῆς Θρᾴκης, *Asiatic* Thrace, i. e. Bithynia, 4. 1.

18. καὶ γὰρ ἤδη ἠσθένει, 709, 2. He therefore took the easiest and safest route, 3. 10. He died on the march, 4. 11.

19. μεσογαίας, where supplies could be more abundantly obtained.

CHAPTER III.

THE ARCADIANS ATTACK THE BITHYNIANS. — RESCUED FROM GREAT DANGER BY XENOPHON AND HIS COMPANY. — ARRIVAL AT CALPE.

1. The first section is rejected by many: cf. 1. 1 N. — τρόπον, case? — Χειρισόφου, 447 b.

2. Ἔπραξαν...τάδε, *fared as follows;* case 478. — μέν, corresp. to δέ, § 10. — Ἀρκάδες, 2. 17. — λάχος, v. l. λόχον. — ὁποία δὲ μείζων, but [whatever, cf. 641] *if any one seemed larger than usual,* or, too large for a single division, 514. — σύνδυο, 240 f. — ἦγον, sc. ἐπὶ ταύτην.

3. δέοι, mode 643 e.

4. ἡθροίζοντο, tense? — διέφυγον...ὁπλίτας s, *escaped from heavy armed troops, out of their very hands.* **196**

5. ἅμα (Lex.). — τρέπονται, sc. οἱ Θρᾷκες: cf. vii. 3. 3.

6. πράγμασιν, *trouble* or *difficulty* (Lex.), cf. iv. 1. 17. — εὐτύχημα, case 477: cf. i. 3. 17 N.

7. τοξότην, sing. × plur.? — οἱ δέ, i. e. the enemy. — ἐπίοιεν, sc. οἱ Ἕλληνες: cf. iv. 2. 15. — ἄλλοι δὲ ἄλλῃ s, *while others made an attack in another quarter.* Some explain according to 567 d.

8. τελευτῶντες, cf. iv. 5. 16 N.

9. οὐκ ἐδίδοσαν, *would not give,* 594, cf. i. 3. 1; vii. 1. 7. — ἐν τούτῳ ἴσχετο (Lex.), [on this] *here the matter stuck* or *hung.* **197**

10. Ξενοφῶντι...πορευομένῳ, [for Xen. marching] *as Xen. was marching;* cf. iii. 2. 22 N. — ἥσθηνται, v. l. ἥσθοντο. — ὄντος Ἑλληνικοῦ, *consisting of Greeks.*

11. νῦν ὅτι, order 719 b, η. What word thus becomes more emphatic? — πολιορκοῦνται, εἶεν, mode?

12. οὐδ', in indirect discourse, 686 c. — οὐδεμίαν: after verbs of "thinking," οὐ often takes the place of μή in an infinitive clause, when it is intended to give to the negative an emphasis which μή appears too weak to bear. McM. — ούτω...ούτω, anaphora, Vollb.

13. μόνοι...μόνοι, obs. emphasis of the repetition.

14. Rehdz. perceived that § 16-18 ought to precede § 14; and Schenkel so places them. Whether a copyist misplaced them accidentally, or in order that the words of Xen. might immediately precede ταῦτ' εἰπὼν ἡγεῖτο (§ 19), we can only conjecture. Rehdz. and Schenkel, from more regard to form than thought, place ταῦτ' εἰπὼν ἡγεῖτο between § 14 and 15. — ὅσον ἂν δοκῇ, [so far that, 557 a] s, *until it may seem to be time*, or, as far as it may *seem proper* to advance *before supper;* so as to make rapid progress. — Τιμασίων, 2. 16 N. — ἐφορῶν, *keeping us in sight.*

15. ἐκέλευε, and so also others, § 19. — καίειν ἅπαντα, ὅτῳ, 550 f., cf. § 19. For the purpose had in view, see § 19 s, 25.

16. οὐδαμοῦ, § 23; v. l. οὐδαμοῖ. — πολλή, sc. ὁδός ἐστι. — οὔτε...δέ, 716 b, v. l. τέ. — μένουσιν, sc. ἡμῖν. — αὐτοῦ, sc. at Calpe.

17. διακινδυνεύειν, [to risk ourselves through] *to meet all perils* of a march through the country. — τῆς σωτηρίας ἔχεσθαι (Lex.), case 426. — ἔστιν, *it is ours,* or, *in our power,* we have now an opportunity.

18. ὁ θεός (Lex.)...ούτως, *perhaps the deity thus directs;* cf. Hdt. vii. 8, 1. — ὡς πλέον φρονοῦντας (Lex.), cf. 2. 11; × μεῖζον φρονεῖ, v. 6. 8; cf. Hdt. vii. 10, 5. — ἀπὸ θεῶν ἀρχομένους (Lex.), *who began with the gods,* i. e. by consulting them. See 2. 15; cf. *Cyrop.* i. 5. 6. — ὡς ἄν, final ὡς (or ὅπως) is sometimes followed by ἄν, chiefly after a command (here implied in χρή), "you must apply your mind to this, in order that you may be able (or, how you may be able)." See ii. 5. 16; vii. 4. 2. In such cases, Donaldson says, ἄν expresses an *eventual* conclusion, i. e. one in which an additional hypothesis is virtually contained; i. e. "*if you do,* — *you will...*" See McM.

19. ἐφ' ὅσον (Lex.). — ἐπιπαριόντες (Lex.), marching by the side of the main army, § 15; cf. iii. 4. 30. — πάντα, ὅσα, 550 f, cf. § 15. — ἡ στρατιά (Lex.), *the* main *army;* οἱ ὁπλῖται, sc. ἔκαιον. Cf. Cæsar *B. G.* ii. 11. — παραλειπομένῳ, by the cavalry who preceded, § 14 s.

21. φυλακάς × φύλακας? — ὡς εἰς, iv. 3. 11; i. 8. 1; i. 2. 21.

22. τοὺς ἡγεμόνας, § 10 s. — ἐλάνθανον (Lex.). — ἐπολιορκοῦντο, [were previously] *had been besieged;* cf. i. 2. 22 N. — γραΐδια δὲ καὶ γερόντια, probably captives whom they did not think worth taking with them.

23. τί, cf. ii. 1. 10, Rehdz. — τῶν καταλελ., case? — εὐθὺς ἀφ' ἐσπέρας, *immediately* [from evening] *after nightfall;* cf. ἔωθεν, iv. 4. 8; v. 6. 23. — ὅπου, repeat οἴχεσθαι: ὅπου is for ὅποι (signif. præg.) the notion of arrival and rest being included in the verb of motion (οἴχεσθαι) "*where they were got to...*" Cf. iv. 7. 17. McM.

24. εἰς, [having come to, 704 a] *at.*

25. σχεδὸν ἀμφί, *nearly* [about] *at,* or *just about.*

26. ὁ χρόνος, *the time* requisite for such a march. — τὰ παρ' ἡμῖν, [the state of things with us] *our situation.* — ὑμῶν, case?

CHAPTER IV.

THE GREEKS AT CALPE. — ANOTHER EXPEDITION UNDER NEON. — XENOPHON AGAIN COMES TO THE RESCUE.

1. ἀρξαμένη...ἐστὶν ἀπὸ τοῦ στόματος...μέχρι Ἡρακλείας, *commencing at the mouth*...[is] *extends to Heraclea* (i. e. its territory, 2. 19). Obs. the two limits placed side by side, 719 b, ε. — εἰσπλέοντι, 462 c.

2. τριήρει...κώπαις ; from the uniformity of this motion in calm weather, a convenient mode of denoting distance by sea. See Hdt. iv. 86, where the voyage for a long day is set at 700 stadia (= about 80 miles), and for the night at 600 (= about 68 miles). Arrian's *Periplus*, in which the voyage from Byzantium to Calpe is reckoned at 870 stadia (= about 98 miles). — ἀλλά, cf. iii. 2. 13 N. — Θρᾷκες Βιθυνοί, cf. McM. *in loc.* — τοὺς "Ελληνας, for stronger expression rather than αὐτούς.

3. ἐν μέσῳ...Βυζαντίου, *lies* [in the middle] *midway of* [persons sailing from each place, from H. and B.] *the voyage between Heraclea and Byzantium.* Some regard πλεόντων as gen. absol. 676 a. — τὸ μέν, αὐχήν, τὸ δέ, 393 d. — ὁ αὐχήν: Krüg. quotes Pliny, iv. 5, as applying the term *cervix* to the Isthmus of Corinth. — μάλιστα, cf. v. 4. 12 N.

4. ὑπ' αὐτῇ τῇ πέτρᾳ, *beneath the very rock*, i. e. close beneath the rock. — τὸ πρὸς ἑσπέραν, 529 c. — ἄφθονος ῥέουσα, cf. πολὺς ῥέει = *multus fluit*, Virg. *Georg.* iii. 28.

6. χώρα, naturally connected with the harbor. — καὶ κριθὰς καὶ πυρούς s, cf. 6. 1 ; 707 j.

7. τὸ πόλισμα ἂν γενόμενον = τὸ χωρίον ὃ πόλισμα ἂν γένοιτο, *the spot which might have been made a city.* — βουλομένων : such a desire on Xenophon's part certainly shines through his description. He wishes, however, to show that he himself took no steps in that direction ; while the omens pointed very strongly that way, and seemed almost to forbid any other course.

8. Obs. the chiastic order of the participles. — ἦσαν...ἐκπεπλευκότες, *had sailed forth.* — οὐ σπάνει βίου...ἀλλά s, *not from the want of subsistence, but* [having heard] *from the report which they had received of the virtue of Cyrus.* — οἱ μὲν καὶ ἄνδρας ἄγοντες, especially the lochagi. — καὶ τούτων ἕτεροι, *and* [others than these, 406 a] *yet others.* — ἀποδεδρακότες, καταλιπόντες, tense 605 b : ἀποδιδράσκειν is here used as a transitive verb, taking the syntax of the equivalent notion φεύγειν. Cf. Thucyd.·viii. 102, ἐκπλεῖν πολεμίους : *egredi urbem*, Livy xxii. 55 : see vii. 8. 12. McM. — ὡς...πάλιν, [as to come again] *in the hope of returning with wealth acquired for them.* — τοὺς παρὰ Κύρῳ, cf. i. 4. 12. — πολλὰ καὶ ἀγαθὰ πράττειν, *were making* [for themselves many and good things, 702 c] *their fortunes,* or, *had done exceedingly well*, 604 a.

9. συνόδου, depends on ὑστέρα, 408; cf. i. 7. 12. — πεμπταῖοι (Lex.); cf. τεταρταῖος...ἐστι, St. John xi. 39. — κενοτάφιον, 722 a; cf. tumulum inanem, Virg. Æn. vi. 505. — αὐτοῖς, 460. — στεφάνους, for funeral crowns the Greeks commonly used parsley, if within reach.

202 10. Ἀγασίας τε Στυμφάλιος, v. l. Ἀγασ. ὁ Στυμφ. See Küh. for other readings.

11. δίχα (Lex.). — κατά (Lex.): the old arrangement of the army, recently broken up, was now restored: cf. 2. 12. — ἀπιέναι, depart for home. — τετελευτήκει, v. l. ἐτετελευτήκει, 284 c; cf. § 13, 20. — φάρμακον πιών, Xenophon seems to mention this as the cause of his death: cf. 2. 18. — τὰ ἐκείνου...παρέλαβε, succeeded to his command, 428 a; cf. v. 6. 36.

12. δῆλον ὅτι...ποιητέον, sc. ἐστίν, impers. 572, 682 a. — ἤδη, pos.? — Ἡμεῖς × ὑμᾶς?

13. What examples of chiasma? — ὁ Σιλανός, that Silanus, who had been the chief soothsayer of the army, 523 h; cf. v. 6. 18, 33 s. — μισθωσάμενος, voice 581. — ἐγίγνετο, (Lex.) cf. ii. 2. 3.

14. λέγειν, mode 666 b.

15. κηρύξας, some editions read Ξενοφῶν after this word. — παρεῖναι ἐπὶ τὴν θυσίαν, const. præg. cf. i. 2. 2. — μάντις, pos.? — ἔθυε...Θυομένων (§ 16), he proceeded to sacrifice: θυομένων expresses the subjective notion of consulting the gods by sacrifice, the matter on which they were consulted being expressed by ἐπὶ τῇ ἀφόδῳ. See v. 5. 3, vii. 2. 14, 15, where ἐθύετο follows ἔθυε τι (held a sacrifice), vii. 1. 37 N. McM.

203 16. ἃ ἔχοντες ἦλθον, which they had brought with them.

18. ὡς...ὅτι, anacoluthon, 716 a. — τινος, case? — ἐκ, for ἐν, const. præg.

19. σκηνήν...τὴν Ξενοφῶντος, art. 523 a 3, c. — μή, 686 d.

20. σχεδόν τι (Lex.). — διὰ τὸ μελεῖν, from its concerning all. — οὔ, pos.?

21. τῷ ἐρυμνῷ χωρίῳ, cf. § 3, 7.

22. ὡς οὐδὲν δέον, [as though there were] that there was no need, 680 c. Rehdz. supplies ἐστί, and Kendrick εἴη, with δέον. — ὑπό (Lex.) 689 k. — προθυμεῖσθαι...εἴη, to observe closely whether there was [anything in this] here anything favorable. Xen. seems to have so requested Cleanor, on account of the suspicion with which his own movements were regarded. — ἐγένετο, v. l. ἐγένοντο.

204 23. ἀνθρώπους, case? — ἡγεμόνος, sc. the Heracleot. — ἀσκοῖς s. The ἀσκός was rather for liquids, and the θύλακος for dry provisions, as meal, etc.

24. ὡς ἐπί, iv. 3. 11 N. — πρῶτοι, cf. § 26. — βεβοηθηκότες ἦσαν, § 8 N. — Βιθυνοῖς, cf. Hdt. iii. 89, and Xen. Hell. iii. 2. 2. — Φρυγίαν, which Phrygia? — μὴ ἐλθεῖν, 713 d. — οὐ μεῖον πεντακοσίους, 507 e, 511 c. — τὸ ὄρος, cf. § 5 s.

25. Ἐκ τούτου s, obs. order, 719 d. — οὐκ ἐγεγένητο, the sacrifice had not been offered owing to the want of victims, § 20. — ὑπό, § 22.

26. τοὺς λοιπούς, i. e. those who had escaped. — καὶ ἐξαπίνης, when suddenly, 705. — μέχρι, v. l. μέχρις.

27. ἐν δὲ τοῖς ὅπλοις, cf. iii. 1. 3 N.

CHAPTER V.

THE GREEKS ENCAMP AT CALPE. — SUCCESSFUL ATTACK UPON THE BITHYNIANS.

1. εἴποντο, having learned, however reluctantly, the necessity of this, from the incident in 4. 26 s. — ἅπαν, a distance of 400 feet, 4. 3.   **205**
2. ἐπὶ τοῦ πρώτου ἱερείου, [upon] *in the case of the first victim*, or, *upon the first sacrifice:* see ἐπί with gen. iv. 7. 10.
3. διαβάντες, sc. the generals.
4. τοῦτον, i. e. Neon with his division. — ἐπὶ τοῦ, cf. i. 4. 3 ; iv. 3. 3 N. — οἱ λοχαγοὶ καὶ στρατιῶται ἀπέλειπον (v. l. ἀπέλιπον) αὐτούς, *the captains and soldiers were leaving them* (i. e. the camp-followers with Neon) ; v. l. αὐτόν, *him*, i. e. Neon. — κατέλιπον, sc. the generals, substituting for Neon's division, which was unwilling to remain, the older soldiers from the army in general.
5. τὴν οὐράν...ποιησάμενοι s, *bringing the rear of the column* (in which they marched) *beside* (or into line. with) *the first*, etc. — ὁπόσους...κέρας, i. e. all on either side of the column from front to rear. The men simply stepped sidewise for their work, ready to fall into line upon any summons.
6. τρόπον, case 483, 485, e, a. They repeated this method as often as was necessary. — τῶν κωμῶν, 4. 23, 24.
7. ἡμέρας, case? — φάλαγγος: the army was now stretched out in line of battle, beyond the villages, to cover those that were gathering supplies. — δύναμιν, v. l. τὴν δύναμιν.   **206**
8. σφαγιάζεται, καὶ ἐγένετο, order ? — ἐπὶ τοῦ πρώτου (Lex.) ; some supply ἱερείου, cf. § 2. — σφάγια, not ἱερά, as above § 2 ; the two are distinguished § 21 : see i. 8. 15 N ; iv. 3. 18, 19.
9. φύλακας (Lex.). — οἱ πολέμιοι s, *the enemy in a state of disorder may encounter men in good order and fresh.* McM.
10. τήν, sc. ὁδόν. — ὡς μὴ ἑστήκωμεν (form 317 b), *that we may not be standing*, as if afraid to proceed. — πολεμίους, case 432 h.
11. ἥσυχοι, v. l. ἡσύχως. — ἀφελών, *having detached*. — ἀνά, cf. iii. 4. 21 N ; v. 4. 12. — ἀπολιπόντας, numb. and gender ? — τὴν δὲ μίαν, *and one other*.
12. τὸ ἡγούμενον, cf. ii. 2. 4 N.
13. ὅ τι τὸ ἰσχον εἴη, cf. iv. 5. 20 ; 7. 4. Rehdz. — βουλῆς οὐκ ἄξιον εἴη εἰ, *it was not worth consideration whether*, implying that the attempt would be hopeless.   **207**
14. ἐθελούσιον, with με, 509 c. Some join it with κίνδυνον, *a [voluntary] danger*, i. e. one which could be avoided. — δόξης...εἰς ἀνδρειότητα, *reputation for valor*.
16. Order ? — μεταβαλλομένους, *reversing them:* cf. i. 2. 17.

6*   I

17. οὐδενὶ καλῷ, neuter as ii. 6. 18. Born., following Sturtz, gives to ἔοικε the Homeric sense of *decere:* "honestum decet neminem." Cf. Plato *Legg.* ix. 16. McM. — τούτους, obj. of οἶδα, 474, or subj. of δέξασθαι and repeated in αὐτούς. — ἐλπίζετε, *expect.*

18. Τὸ δὲ διαβάντας s, *to cross and bring a difficult ravine in our rear.* — ἆρ' οὐχὶ καὶ ἁρπάσαι ἄξιον; *is not this an advantage even worth snatching at?* as obliging us to fight desperately. — ἡμᾶς...δεῖ διδάσκεσθαι, *it is well that we should be taught.* — μὴ νικῶσι, *unless we conquer,* 686 d.

19. τὸ νάπος, position ?

20. πόσον τι νάπος ὁ Πόντος; *what sort of a valley is Pontus* (to cross)? νάπος, properly a hollow between hills, glen, ravine, etc. (Lex.) is here the basin of the sea lying between its opposite coasts. Cf. McM. — ἦν θᾶττον, [if] *the sooner.*

21. τὰ ἱερά, § 2. — σφάγια, § 5. Cf. i. 8. 15 N. — πάντως, *v. l.* πάντας.

22. Καὶ ὅς, 518 f. Cf. i. 8. 16 N. — ᾗ...τοῦ νάπους, [where, 420 a] *at whatever part of the ravine.* — ἄν, modifies γένεσθαι, 621 e, f. — ἐξεμηρύοντο, (Lex. ἐκμηρύομαι).

23. ἐπὶ ταῖς θύραις τῆς Ἑλλάδος, cf. ii. 4. 4 N.

24. ἕπεσθε s, *follow Hercules as leader,* 523 b. — ὀνομαστί, cf. Homer, *Il.* x. 68. — ἀνδρεῖόν τι, *v. l.* ἀνδρὶ ὄντι. — εἰπόντα...παρέχειν, sc. τινά, 667 h. — μνήμην [sc. ἐν τούτοις, 551 f], ἐν οἷς ἐθέλει [sc. παρέχειν, etc.], *to secure a remembrance of himself among those he wishes.*

25. ποιησάμενοι, sc. the Greeks, especially the officers. — ἐπί, const. præg. i. 2. 2. — σημαίνοι, cf. ii. 1. 2; iv. 3. 29. — σύνθημα παρῄει, cf. Virgil, *Æn.* vii. 637; also i. 8. 16 N.

26. καλὸν ἔχειν τὸ χωρίον, *had* [their position favorable, 523 b] *a favorable position.*

27. Obs. the polysynd. and change of number. — ὑπηντίαζεν, note use of ὑπό with words denoting rapid movement. — ἐπαιώνιζον, *v. l.* ἐπαιδνιζον (Lex.); cf. i. 8. 17; iii. 2. 9.

28. ὡς ὀλίγοι ὄντες, [as being few] *with so small a number,* 2. 16. — ἅτε, iv. 2. 13.

29. τὸ ἱππικόν...τὸ τῶν πολεμίων, 523 a, 2; 719 d.

30. συνεστηκός, consistere, Dind., a compact, unbroken force. — ἀπειρήκεσαν...ἐδόκει, 705. — οὕτως ὅπως, *in such manner as;* ὅπως when used thus instead of ὡς or ὥσπερ implies distress or difficulty, as in ἔπλευσ' ὅπως ἔπλευσα. Cf. ii. 1. 6. McM. — ὡς μή...ἀναπαύσαιντο, ne hostes fiducia sumpta vires suas reficerent.

31. νάπος...αὐτοὺς ὑπεδέχετο, *a ravine received them* beneath, or, more freely, *lay in their way.* This prevented their retreat in order, while they hastened to effect their escape through or across it. — ὅ (comm. referred to the preceding sentence rather than to νάπος)...Ἕλληνες s, *which the Greeks were not aware of, but had turned back from the pursuit too soon to observe:* fortunately, perhaps, as otherwise they might have been tempted, late as it was, to follow on to the ravine, in the hope of harassing the enemy there.

32. ἔνθα, *v. l.* ἔνθα δή, cf. iv. 1. 2.

CHAPTER VI.

MUCH SPOIL OBTAINED. — CLEANDER ARRIVES, BUT DECLINES THE COMMAND. — MARCH TO CHRYSOPOLIS.

1. ἀμφί (Lex.). — προσωτάτω (Lex.). — Κλέανδρον, 4. 18. — ὡς ἥξοντα, [as about to come] *in expectation of their coming;* ἥξοντα agreeing with Κλέανδρον as most prominent, or with πλοῖα as nearest, 497. — ἑκάστης ἡμέρας, [in each day] *every day,* 433 a. ἀδεῶς, v. l. ἀδεῶς ἤδη. — πυροὺς, κριθάς, etc., asynd., cf. ii. 4. 28.
2. ἐξῆν, *there was leave* for individuals. — ἐλάμβανον, *took for themselves.* — οἱ ἐξιόντες, v. l. omit οἱ : cf. McM.
3. κατῆγον, *put in,* or touched at the place. Cf. v. 1. 11.
4. πολίζει, mode? — ὅτι δέοι, 674 b. — ἐπεδείκνυεν...στρατιώταις, *showed them to the soldiers,* to avoid all suspicion of secret practice, and also, perhaps, hoping for an influence in favor of colonization. Some even translate, perhaps too strongly, *introduced* or *presented.* Cf. 1. 14.
5. οὐδέν, pos.? — οἰχόμενοι, by themselves. — ἄλλοι ἄλλῃ, v. l. omit ἄλλῃ : Born. conjectures ἄλλοσε. — ἀφαιρεθεῖεν, acc. to the rule adopted by the army, § 2, 8. — Δεξίππῳ, who had come with Cleander, see v. 1. 15; vi. 1. 32. — αὐτοῖς, σφίσιν, 537.
6. ἁρπάζειν, *to rob* him.
7. ἦν αὐτῷ...λοχίτης, *was a soldier of his company.* — ἀγόμενος, the man that was being carried off, etc. — ἀνακαλοῦντες, 530 a, cf. ἀνακαλοῦντες τὸν εὐεργέτην, τὸν ἄνδρα τὸν ἀγαθόν, *Cyr.* iii. 3. 4.
8. κατεκώλυον, *endeavored to stop them* (according to some, this). — οὐδὲν εἴη πρᾶγμα, *it was nothing* serious. — αἴτιον...ταῦτα γενέσθαι, the cause [that these things should be] *of this affair.* αἴτιος is often followed by τοῦ, 444 f.
10. εἰ...ἐκδώσει, cf. i. 3. 14 ; v. 6. 7.
11. διά (Lex.). — ἐξ οὗ, *on which account, wherefore.* — παρ' (Lex.) ὀλίγον ἐποιοῦντο, *they put Cleander beside a trifle,* by way of comparison : *they made small account of Cleander,* parvi faciebant. ποιεῖσθαι = æstimare, occurs in various forms : ἐν ἐλαφρῷ ποιεῖσθαι, περὶ πολλοῦ ποιεῖσθαι, δεινὰ ποιεῖσ., ἐν ἀπορρήτῳ ποι., vii. 6. 43. McM.
12. ἐμοὶ δέ, cf. iv. 6. 10 ; v. 5. 13. — ἡμῖν, connect with ἄπεισιν, 453 N ; i. 7. 20. — εἷς ἕκαστος, in appos. with subj. of εἰσι, 393 d, 501.
13. ἁρμοσταῖς, cf. v. 5. 19 N.
14. αἱ πόλεις ἡμῶν, ὅθεν ἐσμέν: Krüg. compares *ex tuis literis quas mihi misisti,* Cicero *Epist. ad Diver.* x. 13.
15. ἀκούω, tense? — οὐκ ἂν ἐποίησεν, 631 b. — ἐγὼ μὲν οὖν, repeated after the parenthesis. — αἰτίας, case 699 f. — ἐμαυτοῦ, case 699 a.
16. αἰτιᾶται, sc. Cleander ? — κρῖναι, voice ? cf. § 18. — εἰ...

οὐδ, cf. i. 7. 18 N; Küh. vii. 1. 29. — ἀντὶ δὲ τούτων, *on the contrary, in place of this.* — εἰρξόμεθα, *we shall shut ourselves out from,* or (as pass. excludemur) *we shall be excluded from,* 576 a.

17. θεούς, case 472 f. — ἦ μήν (Lex.). — ἀφειλόμην, 707 i; cf. v. 8. 10.

18. μὴ ἐκδῶτε, *v. l.* μὴ ἐκδότε. — τούτου ἕνεκα μήτε πολεμεῖτε, *on this account,* or, *so far as this is concerned, have no war.* — σώζοισθε ἀσφαλῶς, *may you be,* etc., 638, d, e. — ὑμῶν αὐτῶν, part. gen., *of your own number.*

19. ἔδωκεν s, *granted* [that he should go having selected] *him the privilege of selecting as attendants.* — ὁ ἀφαιρεθείς, order, cf. iv. 2. 18.

20. ἐκέλευσε, *v. l.* ἐκέλευε: cf. i. 7. 16 N. — σε, σὲ αὐτόν, emphat. repetition; *v. l.* σεαυτόν. — χρῆσθαι [sc. ἡμῖν or αὐτοῖς] ὅ τι ἂν βούλῃ, *to treat us as you may please;* cf. i. 3, 18 N, iii. 1. 40. — ἀξιοῦσι (numb.?) *deem it proper,* or *require.*

21. Δεξίππου, case 485 d, 661 b. Obs. the antithetic and sarcastic repetition here and in § 22.

22. ἐφ' ᾧτε, 557, 671 a; cf. iv. 2. 19.

23. Καί, τέ, καί, τέ, the office of each? — Τραπεζουντίους...πεντηκόντορον, case? — ἀπεστερήκαμεν: ἀποστερεῖν follows the syntax of ἀφαιρεῖσθαι (i. 3. 4); whereas στερεῖν more usually takes a *genitivus rei* (i. 4. 8). McM. — τὸ ἐπὶ τούτῳ, [as to that resting] *so far as rested on him.* — Ἥκουε... ὥσπερ ἡμεῖς, doubtless at Trapezus, as again at Cotyora, v. 6. 9. — Τοῦτον οὖν...ἀφειλόμην, sc. τὸν ἄνδρα, *from him, therefore, I rescued the man.* See § 21, where the genit. is used after ἀφελόμενος.

24. ἦγες, tense? — τῶν παρὰ σοῦ, const. præg., cf. i. 1. 5 N. — νόμιζε ...ἀποκτείνων (though infin. with νομίζω oftener), 657 f, 677 a. — ἄνδρα δειλόν...ἄνδρα ἀγαθόν, note antithesis.

25. ἐπαινοίη × ἐπαινοίη ἄν. — ἀξιοῦτε, *claim* for yourselves, 644 b.

26. τοῦτον, sc. Agasias.

28. τὸ μέρος, [the part given to him] *his part* or *share.* — τοῖς λῃσταῖς, § 5. — ῥήτραν, this term is applied to Lycurgus's unwritten laws; Plutarch, *Lyc.* 13. — τοιοῦτος, *such a person,* so concerned in the affair, yet claiming innocence. Cleander reserves his judgment, neither censuring nor acquitting.

29. τῶν ἀνδρῶν, τὼ ἄνδρε, § 30, etc., 494.

30. αὐτοῖς, numb. and gend.? — Δρακόντιον, why selected? — κατὰ πάντα τρόπον, cf. iv. 5. 16.

31. σοι ὑφεῖτο, ὅ τι ἐβούλου (conforming in time to ὑφεῖτο) ποιῆσαι, *submitted itself to you that you might do whatever you pleased.* — αἰτοῦνται καὶ δέονται, what is expressed by doubling the verb? — ἐμοχθησάτην: we have repeatedly remarked the eminent services of Agasias.

32. σου (also § 33), case, 434 a. — καὶ ὡς ἱκανοί s, *and, while submissive to their commander, how capable they are, with the favor of the gods, of meeting the enemy fearlessly.*

33. σου...παραγενόμενον, cf. i. 2. 1 N.

34. ναὶ τὼ Σιώ, i. e. by Castor and Pollux; *Hell.* iv. 4. 10. The Attic oath, νὴ τὼ θεώ, meant Demeter and Persephone. McM. — πολύ...ἀντίοι

...ἤ οὖς, [very different than] *quite the reverse of what.* — περὶ ὑμῶν ἐνίων, *concerning some of you.* Küh. regards ἐνίων as governing ὑμῶν, Krüg. as in appos. with it. Cf. v. 5. 11.

36. οὐκ ἐθέλει, *refuse.* — ἐξάγειν, like ἰέναι (ii. 2. 3 N.) [favorable] *for me to lead forth.* — ἐκεῖσε, i. e. to Byzantium.

37. διαθέμενοι, *having disposed of,* by sale, to traders touching at the port. — Βιθυνῶν (Lex.).

38. οὐδενί, *no booty.* — τὴν φιλίαν, sc. χώραν, where they would be on expense, and could not plunder. — ὑποστρέψαντας = *having turned sharp round,* they fell upon the Bithynians. — Χρυσόπολιν, Χαλκηδονίας (Lex.). Some editors use the form Καλχηδονία, Καλχηδών, wherever this word occurs. Cf. 167 b.

217

BOOK VII.

MOVEMENTS OF THE GREEKS IN THRACE. — MARCH TO PERGAMUS IN MYSIA.

CHAPTER I.

THE GREEKS INDUCED TO CROSS TO BYZANTIUM. — DISTURBANCES THERE. — XENOPHON'S COURSE.

1. "Ὅσα μὲν δή s, see p. 3, Notes, statement as to division into books, summaries, etc. — ἔπραξαν × ἐποίουν? (Lex. πράττω): the more definite term is here used with reference to the more recent events. — ἔξω τοῦ στόματος, i. e. ἔξω Βοσπόρου Θρακίου. Küh.

218

2. χώραν, v. l. ἀρχήν. — στρατεύηται, mode 653. — ὅσα δέοι, sc. ποιεῖν Φαρνάβαζον.

3. μετεπέμψατο...εἰς, 579, cf. i. 1. 2. — τῶν στρατιωτῶν, om. by some editors.

4. ὅτι ἀπαλλάξοιτο...ἀπό, *that he was about to take his leave of.* — συνδιαβάντα, *having crossed over with* (the army). — ἔπειτα οὕτως (so used separately after a participle, rarely both together); *then, in this condition of affairs,* i. e. having crossed with them into Europe.

219

5. Σεύθης, (Lex.) cf. 2. 32; v. 1. 15. — συμπροθυμεῖσθαι, iii. 1. 9. — καὶ ἔφη...ὅτι (rare after φημί, 659 h ; pos. 719 η, cf. § 11), *and promised him, if he would add his influence for this, that he should not repent of it.* — μεταμελήσει, v. l. μεταμελήσειν.

6. μηδέν...μήτε, on emphatic use of negatives, 713 b. — τελείτω, sc. Σεύθης. — προσφερέσθω ὡς ἄν...ἀσφαλές, *let him make such application as*

may seem to him safe, or (acc. to some) *sure of effect;* v. l. ὡς ἂν αὐτῷ δοκῇ, as *may seem to him best*.

7. ὡς ἀποπέμψων...ποιήσων, 598 b. — ἐπισιτίζεσθαι...πορείαν, *to procure provisions for the journey*.

8. ξένος, vi. 6. 35. — ἠσπάζετο, vale dicebat, *was bidding him farewell.* — μὴ ποιήσῃς, 628 c. — εἰ δὲ μή, 717 c ; iv. 3. 6 N. — οὐ ταχὺ ἐξέρπει, *is creeping forth* [not quickly] *so slowly.* Acc. to some, ἐξέρπει is taken from the mouth of Cleander in its more Doric sense, = ἐξέρχεται.

9. οἱ στρατιῶται αὐτοί, supply αἴτιοί εἰσιν.

10. πορευσόμενον, *as if about to march* with them. — ἐλθόντες...διαπραξόμεθα, (sc. the generals) *we will go and settle with Anaxibius*.

220

11. συνεσκευασμένους, v. l. συσκευασαμένους. — προσανειπεῖν, v. l. προσανεῖπεν. — ὅτι, pos. 719 η.

12. πρῶτον, v. l. πρῶτοι. — ἄρδην (Lex.) = παντελῶς. — Ἐτεόνικος (Lex.), Cf. Thuc. viii. 23. — ὡς, with fut. part. § 7 N. — μοχλόν, a strong bar placed across the double gate, and secured within a socket on each side.

13. τἆλλα τὰ ἐπιτήδεια = *other supplies.* Küh. omits τά.

14. Ἐπακούσαντες, *having overheard.* — ἢ καί, or [even] *perhaps.* — Ἱεροῦ, v. l. ἱεροῦ : the road into the Chersonese lay through this mountain: cf. 3. 3. A fortress Ἱερὸν ὄρος is mentioned by Demosthenes, *De Halon.* § 17 ; *De Falsa Leg.* § 156. — κύκλῳ, *round about*, or, *taking a sweep.* — διὰ μέσης, 508 a.

15. εἰσιόντες, as fut. part. See Lex. εἶμι.

16. ἔκοπτον, force of the impf.? 594. — εἰ...ἀνοίξουσιν, cf. i. 3. 14 N.

17. χηλήν (Lex.), *the breakwater* or *mole*, meaning here the projecting stone-work which protected the walls next the sea from the violence of the waves. See scholiast on Thuc. i. 63, quoted by Küh. — ὑπερβαίνουσιν,

221 rush over. — ἀναπεταννύουσι, v. l. ἀναπεταννύασι. — κλεῖθρα = μοχλόν, § 12. See Dictionary of Antiquities.

18. ἔθει καὶ συνεισπίπτει, see § 20, where, in the same way, the impf. and histor. pres. are joined together.

19. ἔνδον, *within*, i. e. their houses or abodes. — ἔξω ἔθεον, Küh. and others omit ἔθεον and supply as understood φεύγουσιν.

20. τὴν ἄκραν, i. e. τὴν ἀκρόπολιν, in next sentence. Krüg. compares *Hell.* vi. 1. 2, where the acropolis is mentioned, which in § 3 is called ἄκρα. — Χαλκηδόνος, cf. vi. 6. 38 N. — σχεῖν τοὺς ἄνδρας, *to sustain the expected onset of the soldiers.*

21. πολλοί, *in great numbers.* — Νῦν, cf. v. 6. 15 N. — ἔξεστιν, 459. — ἀνδρὶ γενέσθαι, virum te præstare, *to become a* (μέγαν, famous or eminent) *man*, 667 b. — ἔχεις, note repetition and asynd.

22. θέσθε τὰ ὅπλα s, *range yourselves under arms.* Xenophon's readiness and promptitude in so critical a case deserve to be noted.

222 **23.** εἰς ὀκτὼ ἐγένοντο, *fell in eight deep;* v. l. πεντήκοντα. — τὸ κέρας ἑκάτερον, 523 b.

24. οἷον, 556 a. — τὸ Θρᾴκιον, an open space within the walls, near the

gates, called *Thracian;* cf. *Hell.* i. 3. 20. McM. — ἔκειτο τὰ ὅπλα, iv. 2. 20 N; cf. τίθεσθαι τὰ ὅπλα, § 22. — συγκαλεῖ, *called round him.*
25. τιμωρησώμεθα, 579, 432 a. — οὐδέν (acc. of specification, 481), *in no respect.*
26. ἑωρακότας, sc. ἡμᾶς. — τὰ νῦν ἤδη γεγενημένα, cf. vi. 1. 32. Xenophon refers to the Peloponnesian war (B. c. 431-404), the result of which was that the Spartans gained the supremacy.
27. εἰσήλθομεν, *v. l.* ἤλθομεν. — τριακοσίων, *v. l.* τετρακοσίων. — ἐν τῇ πόλει, i. e. ἀκροπόλει, see Thuc. ii. 13. 24. — τῶν ἐνδήμων, *the home revenues.* — ὑπερορίας, sc. γῆς or χώρας. — τῶν νήσων: concerning the allies and tributaries of the Athenians in the great struggle with the Lacedæmonians, see Thuc. ii. 9. Also, for full and accurate information respecting the financial condition and management, the sources of revenue, etc., of Athens, the student must consult the work of Aug. Boeckh, "Staatshaushaltung der Athener," translated into English by Mr. A. Lamb (1857) under the title "The Public Economy of the Athenians."
28. ἄν, pos. 621 a. — ὅσοι, *v. l.* οἵ. — τοῦ ἄνω βασιλέως, i. e. the king of Persia : ἄνω, up the country, the interior region back from the sea-coast. — ὅστις, ii. 5. 12; 558. **223**
29. τοῖς ἡμετέροις [= ἡμῶν] αὐτῶν, *our own friends,* 498. — πάντες s, *all* (these friends and relatives) *are in those cities which,* etc. — δικαίως, sc. στρατεύσονται ἐφ' ἡμᾶς. — βάρβαρον, rather an exaggeration, since Trapezus, Sinope, and Heraclea are called Ἑλληνίδας πόλεις, v. 5. 14. McM. explains by saying, "they are styled *Barbarian* here, when compared with Byzantium, probably as being in Asia and under barbarian rule ; — the Persian king's authority over the *Asiatic* Greeks having been repeatedly acknowledged (during the Peloponn. War), as, for instance, in the treaties B. c. 411 (Thuc. viii. 58), and B. c. 387." — οὐδεμίαν, for μηδεμίαν. Küh. — καὶ ταῦτα, cf. i. 4. 12 N. — ἐξαλαπάξομεν, Homeric word for ἐκπορθήσομεν.
30. εὔχομαι, ἔμεγε, γενέσθαι, *I pray that I may be:* cf. iii. 1. 17 N. — ἐπιδεῖν, *look upon,* or, behold. — κατά, *down below,* or, *under.* — δικαίων τυγχάνειν, 427. — ἡμᾶς δεῖ...στέρεσθαι, *we ought not, wronged though we be, to deprive ourselves of the Grecian soil at least.*
31. εἰ δὲ μή, [but if not] *but if we obtain none,* 710, 717 c. — πειθόμενοι, sc. ὑμῖν.
32. οἱ μέν, asynd. Cf. i. 1. 9 N.
33. καθημένων, *seated,* i. e. in council, cf. vi. 2. 5 N. — Κοιρατάδης, see Lex. — οὐ φεύγων, *though not an exile.* — στρατηγιῶν, *an army-seeking fellow,* ambitious to be a general. — Δέλτα (Lex.). — μόλωσιν, poetic word, used only here by Xen. — σιτία, *v. l.* σῖτα. **224**
34. ἀκούουσι (asynd.)...τοῖς στρατιώταις, anacoluthon. Krüg. remarks, the writer began the clause as if ἔδοξε δέχεσθαι were about to follow. — τέλεσι, i. e. *the authorities* or *magistrates:* cf. ii. 6. 4. — ἀπαγγελεῖ, βουλεύσοιτο, for change of mood and tense, see ii. 1. 3 N.
36. ὅστις ἄν, *v. l.* ὃς ἄν. — πεπράσεται, 601 b; cf. i. 5. 16; ii. 4. 5.

37. εἰς, omitted by some before ἀνήρ. — ὡς ἐπί, cf. iv. 3. 11 N. — ἐθύετο, *was proceeding to take the auspices*, but was stopped before the act of immolation (ὡς θύων), § 40, where the narrative is resumed, §§ 38 and 39 being a parenthesis, stating what Xen. was doing meantime. McM.

38. ἐκέλευε (i. 6. 2 N) διαπρᾶξαι, v. l. ἐκέλευέν οἱ διαπρᾶξαι.

39. ἥκω, λέγειν, μέλλοις, obs. abrupt change of construction to oratio obliqua, and then to oratio directa. — ἔφη, sc. Cleander. — ἐκέλευεν (v. l. ἐκέλευσεν), sc. Anaxibius.

40. ἀσπασάμενος, cf. § 8 N. — οὐκ ἐκαλλιέρει, *had no favorable sacrifice*. — ἐστεφανωμένος, having on the garland or chaplet worn by one about to offer sacrifice. Cf. *Cyrop.* iii. 3. 34. — Κοιρατάδη, ἡγησόμενον, cf. i. 2. 1 N ; 667 e. — μή (Lex.), 686. — εἰ μὴ δώσει, for the more usual δώσοι: cf. i. 3. 14.

41. πολλῶν s, literally, *when there was wanting much to him, so that a day's food was not the lot of each of the soldiers,* i. e. his supply of provisions fell far short of one day's subsistence for each of, etc. — ἐνέδει, v. l. ἔδει. — ἀπειπών, *throwing up*, in disgust.

CHAPTER II.

OUTRAGEOUS CONDUCT OF ARISTARCHUS. — NEGOTIATIONS WITH SEUTHES, A THRACIAN PRINCE.

1. Φρυνίσκος, named as one of the generals, § 29. Cf. iii. 1. 47. — κατά, *over against, near*.

2. ἔπειθε, persuadere studebat, *was trying to persuade*. — ἔδωκε (as plupf.), *had given*. — ταὐτά, v. l. ταῦτα: cf. 6. 12.

3. ἀποδιδόμενοι, [giving for one's profit] *selling*. — κατὰ τοὺς χώρους, *through the districts* or *fields*. — κατεμιγνύοντο, v. l. κατεμίγνοντο.

4. διαφθειρόμενον (explanatory of ταῦτα), *was being dispersed* or *broken up*.

5. Κυζίκῳ (Lex.). — ὅσον οὔ, tantum non, prope, *all but*. — παρείη εἰς, cf. i. 2. 2 N.

6. εὕρῃ, v. l. εὕροι, or, εὕροιεν. — ἀναγκάζων s, *compelling* (the inhabitants) *to receive them into their houses*. — Ἀρίσταρχος...ἀπέδοτο, inexcusable cruelty on his part.

7. κατὰ τὰ συγκείμενα, *according to the agreement*, cf. 1. 2. He now calls on Pharnabazus to keep the agreement made between them. The satrap, however, thinking Anaxibius to be of no further value to him, treats his proposal with contempt, which stirs up Anaxibius to vindictive fury. — Ἀρίσταρχον, Ἀναξίβιον : Ἀναξιβίου, Ἀρίσταρχον, chiastic pos. — διεπράττετο τὰ αὐτά, *effected the same arrangement*.

8. Ξενοφῶντα, he seems to have been at the time with Anaxibius, 1. 39. — συνέχειν αὐτό, *to keep it together*. — προπέμψαι, *to send forward*, or, *escort.* — τοῖς ἵπποις, *with the horses* requisite or necessary for this purpose. — ἐπὶ τὸ στράτευμα, at or near Selybria, § 28. **227**

9. διαπλεύσας, *having sailed across* the Propontis.

10. ὑπισχνούμενος s, *promising to him that which he thought by mentioning* (it), *he would persuade him.*

11. ἀποσπάσας, sc. τοὺς ἑαυτοῦ, or, ἑαυτόν. — ἐν τῷ αὐτῷ (sc. τόπῳ), *on the same ground*, i. e. together.

12. ἔπραττε περί, *was bargaining* or *negotiating for.* — πεπεισμένος, *urged on.* — ἀπεῖπε μὴ διάγειν, [said that they should *not* transport] *forbade the shipmasters to transport*, 713 d.

13. ὅτι, cf. i. 6. 7 N. — καὶ ἐμέ, obs. change to oratio directa. — τοίνυν, cf. v. 1. 2 N. — τῇδε, *in this place*, in Perinthus as well as Byzantium, 6. 24.

14. ὄντων, sc. αὐτῶν. — πείσεται (Lex. πάσχω), euphemistic expression for *lose his life.* — τοὺς μέν = τούτους μέν. — προπέμπεται, force of mid.? cf. προπέμπει, § 19. — αὐτός, take with βούλοιτο. **228**

15. ἐθύετο, for force of mid. see Lex. θύω. — παρεῖεν, v. l. προεῖεν. — τοῦ κωλύσοντος, i. e. Aristarchus. — ἔνθα δή, v. l. ἔνθα δέ. — ἀνάγκη, sc. ἦν. — τῷ ἐκεῖ, i. e. Cyniscus, 1. 13.

16. ὁ μέν...εἶχεν, *he was occupied in these matters.* — ἐδόκει, sc. εἶναι.

17. αὐτῷ, v. l. αὐτῳ. — ἰέναι, cf. ii. 2. 3 N. — παρά...ἑκάστου, *from each.*

18. ἐρήμοις, i. e. *without sentinels* or *guards* stationed at them. — μετακεχωρηκέναι, *had changed his encampment* to some other place. — τῶν περί, 527 a. — τῷ Σεύθῃ, dat. as in 4. 19; cf. i. 7. 20; ii. 6. 8; iii. 4. 31. Its effect is to make Seuthes virtually the subject of the sentence: *that Seuthes had fires lit in front*, etc. See Arnold at Thucyd. iii. 97. McM. — μήτε ὁπόσοι μήτε ὅπου εἶεν, v. l. μηδ' ὅπου εἶεν : μήτε ὅπου εἰσί, μήτε ὅποι ἴοιεν. Kühl.

19. προπέμπει, cf. § 14 N. — ὁ ἀπὸ τοῦ στρατεύματος, i. e. ὁ ἐν τῷ στρατεύματι ὢν καὶ ἐκεῖθεν ἐλθών, Kühl.; qui praeest exercitui. **229** Born.

20. ἀναπηδήσαντες ἐδίωκον, *having leaped up* (i. e. mounted their horses, probably) *they galloped away.* — ὅσον, circiter, 507 f.

21. ἐγκεχαλ. ἐφυλάττετο, *he was keeping guard* (for himself) *with these ready bridled* for use. Born. reads, for ἐγκεχαλινωμένοις, ἐγκεχαλινωμένων, sc. αὐτῶν. Cf. i. 4. 12 N.

22. Τήρης (Lex.), cf. Thucyd. ii. 29; Hdt. iv. 80; vii. 137. — ὑπό, after ἀπολέσαι, denoting the agent. — ἀφαιρεθῆναι, 485 d. — μάλιστα νυκτός, *especially at night*, these, the Thyni, being most distinguished for carrying on successful warfare during the night.

24 Ἔπεμψας, cf. 1. 5. — ὑπισχνούμενος...ποιήσειν, after verbs of promising, etc., the infin. is oftener in the fut. acc. to the rule for indir. disc., *promising that you would do*, 659 g.

25. ἔφη, *assented*, or, *said yes.* — αὖθις, § 10. — τὰ χωρία, cf. 5. 8. — σέ...χρήσεσθαι (v. l. χρήσασθαι), *that I should experience you* (find **230** you) *as a friend.* — παρὰ σοῦ, cf. iii. 4. 9 N.

26. Ἴθι νῦν, v. l. νυν, enclit. Küh. — ἔφη, sc. Xenophon. — ἀφήγησαι τούτῳ, cf. 452 a.
27. οὐδέν, governed by τελεῖν. — αὐτός...ἀπιέναι, 667 f.
28. τί γάρ, quid igitur ? 708 b. — κατά, to or at, i. e. near to, in vicinity of. — διαβαίνειν, sc. χρῆναι, from οὐχ οἷόν τε preceding. Cf. Thucyd. i. 142.
29. ἔξω εἰσίν...ὁ πιστότατος, sing. nom. for plur. στρατιῶται or φίλοι.
30. πιστοτέραν...πρᾶξιν, the transaction or negotiation to be more binding. — κάλεσαι, call in these also. — τὰ ὅπλα, obj. of καταλιπεῖν.
31. οὐδενὶ ἄν...'Ἀθηναίων, he would distrust no Athenian. — συγγενεῖς. Krüg. rejects the claim of lineage or kinship, but Küh. holds that the traditions authorize the pretensions of Seuthes. — ὅ τι χρῆσθαι, Cf. i. 3. 18 N.
32. ἦν, for ἦσαν, agrees in numb. with ἀρχή the predicate. — τὰ πράγματα, 506, c. — ἐνόσησεν, this word, by an easy metaphor, is often applied to disorders in the state ; cf. Demosth. Phil. iii. 12, νοσοῦσι καὶ στασιάζουσι. — ἐκπεσών, expulsus, banished. — βασιλεῖ, i. e. of the Odrysæ.
33. ἐνδίφριος = ὁμοτράπεζος. — ἱκέτης δοῦναί μοι, as a suppliant (begging him) to give to me. — τοὺς ἐκβαλόντας...ποιοίην, I should inflict evil upon those who had expelled us (my family). — μὴ ἀποβλέπων, cf. v. 6. 27 N. — ὥσπερ κύων, these words are rejected by Küh. and others.
34. σὺν τοῖς θεοῖς, with the help of the gods.
36. κυζικηνόν, i. e. per month. — βούλωνται, 607 a ; 667.
37. ἀπό, Küh. reads ὑπό, cf. i. 2. 18 N. — ἀπιέναι...παρὰ σέ, to take refuge with you.
38. Σοί...θυγάτηρ, this passage is quoted as in favor of Xen.'s being older than is advocated in the present edition of the Anab. (see Introduction), cf. 6. 34 N. — Θρακίῳ νόμῳ, cf. Hdt. v. 6 ; Tacit. Germania, § 18. So too the ancient Greeks, Aristot. Polit. ii. 8. — Βισάνθην, cf. 5. 8.

CHAPTER III.

OPERATIONS OF THE GREEKS IN THE SERVICE OF SEUTHES.

1. δεξιάς, cf. ii. 4. 1 N. — ἕκαστοι, i. e. each deputation from the several divisions of the army, 2. 29 ; cf. iv. 5. 23 ; v. 5. 5.
2. ἔδοξε, force of aor.? — τὴν ὁδὸν ἐᾶσαι, to decline going.
3. οὗτος δὲ ὁ αὐτός, and this same person, 540. — 'Ιεροῦ ὄρους, cf. 1. 14. — ἢν κρατήσαντες τούτου, if having gained (i. e. crossed) this mountain. — πωλήσειν, i. e. Aristarchus, 2. 6. — ἐξαπατήσεσθαι, fut. mid. in pass. sense, with ὑμᾶς, cf. v. 5. 2 N. — περιόψεσθαι, i. e. Aristarchus, overlook or neglect you. Note the change of subj. with infin. in this section.
4. ἐκεῖνον, i. e. Seuthes. — εὖ ποιήσειν ὑμᾶς, he will do well for you. —

BOOK VII. CHAP. III.

τοῦτο, *about this,* i. e. whether to obey Aristarchus or to go to Seuthes. — ἐπανελθόντες, i. e. to the villages named in next section and 2. 1.

5. ἐῶσι, sc. the Lacedæmonians. — οἱ ἥττους, i. e. the Thracian villagers, weaker than ourselves. — ὅ τι τις ὑμῶν δεῖται, *what service each of these* (i. e. Aristarchus and Seuthes) *desires of you.*

6. 'Ἀνέτειναν, cf. iii. 2. 9 N. — τῷ ἡγουμένῳ, ii. 2. 4 N.

7. ἔπειθον, *tried to persuade;* force of imp.? 594. — αὐτῷ, i. e. Xenophon.

8. τῶν τοῦ Λακωνικοῦ = those with Aristarchus, the envoys of the Lacedæmonian. Krüg. regards τῶν as neuter, referring to things offered by the Lacedæmonian. — ἐξενίσθαι, *v. l.* ξενίζεσθαι.

9. εἶπεν, *v. l.* ἔφη. — 'Ἀλλά, 708 e. — ἀπεχούσας...ὅσον, *distant only so far as that.*

10. κυζικηνόν, 2. 36. — τὰ νομιζόμενα, *that which is customary,* i. e. double to the captains, and fourfold to the generals, 2. 36. — διατιθέμενος, *by the sale of.*

11. ἀποδιδράσκοντα, cf. i. 4. 8 N. — ἀνθίστηται, *v. l.* ἀνθιστῆται. — χειροῦσθαι, *to subdue* or *overcome.*

12. θαλάττης, i. e. the Propontis.

13. τῷ βουλομένῳ, leave was granted *to any one that wished to speak,* 678 a. — ἔλεγον...εἴη, *said to the same effect that the proposal of Seuthes was worth everything, for it was winter,* 643 c. — διαγενέσθαι, *to remain.* — ὠνουμένους ζῆν, *to live by purchasing* food. — εὕρημα, *a god-send,* an unlooked-for piece of good fortune, 633 d. Cf. ii. 3. 18.

14. ἐπιψηφιζέτω, *let him* (i. e. the proper officer) *put it to vote.* Krüg. and others read ἐπιψηφίζεσθε, *do you vote for these measures.* The mid. voice denotes "to *decree* by vote" (6. 14). Xenophon, in bidding them let the officer put the matter to the vote, instead of doing so himself (as at v. 1. 14), assumes the attitude of an indifferent party, lest hereafter (if matters went ill) he should be blamed for having influenced their choice. Cf. 6. 12, and foll. McM. — ἐπεψήφισε, *v. l.* ἐπεψήφισαν. — συστρατεύσοιντο, acc. to Rennell's calculation, it was now about the beginning of December, B. C. 400.

15. ἐσκήνησαν, cf. iv. 5. 15 N.

16. Μαρωνείτης, cf. Lex. — ἐνὶ ἑκάστῳ (τούτων) οὕστινας. — ἔχειν τι δοῦναι, cf. Thucyd. ii. 97. — πρῶτον μέν, correlative clause, Αἴθις δέ, § 18. — ἄγοντες αὐτῷ, 450 b, 540 f. — ἄνω, *up the country.*

17. διακείσεται = ἕξει τὰ πράγματα, melius vobis erit. Küh.

18. νομίζοιτο...δωρεῖσθαι, *it was usual...to make presents.* — καταγαγεῖν, Timasion was in exile at the time. — προύμνᾶτο, sued or *pleaded for.* — ἑκάστῳ, take with προσιών, as in § 16.

19. ἄλλοι, reference especially to Alcibiades (5. 8), *Hell.* ii. 1. 25; Corn. Nepos, *Alc.* vii. 4.

20. Εὔνους, see 444 d. — τούτῳ, *v. l.* τούτων. — οὐ...ἔχων...εἰ μή, *not having* (anything) *except.* — παῖδα, Wheeler renders here *son;* the ordinary meaning, *servant* or *attendant,* seems better. — ὅσον ἐφόδιον, *money just enough for the journey's expenses.*

NOTES.

21. τρίποδες, mensae tripedes (cf. Lex.). — ξυμῖται, v. l. ξυμῆτες.
22. τράπεζαι, Küh. says these are the same as the τρίποδες, § 21; Hutchinson and others understand the word to mean the dishes of food on the tables. — κατὰ τοὺς ξένους, i. e. *before the guests*. — ὅσον μόνον, *only enough*, 556 b.

236
23. φαγεῖν δεινός, *a terrible fellow at eating*. — τὸ μέν... χαίρειν, [bid farewell to] *let the distributing take care of itself*. — τριχοίνικον, a single choenix was the usual daily allowance.
24. περιέφερον, *they* (i. e. the attendants) *carried round*.
25. λέγοι, v. l. λέγει. — ἠπίστατο (ἐπίσταμαι).
26. προπίνω σοι, 460. — οὐ μή, 627, cf. ii. 2. 12 N.
28. ἵνα καὶ ἐγώ, [I say this to you] *in order that I also*. — τιμᾶν, sc. σέ.
29. ποιήσοι, v. l. ποιήσει. — ὀρέξαι, 450 b. — ὑποπεπωκὼς ἐτύγχανεν, *he happened to have drunk somewhat freely*, was pretty well warmed up with wine.

237
30. μᾶλλον ἔτι ἐμοῦ, *even more than I myself*.
31. προϊέμενοι, entrusting themselves, eager. — τὴν δὲ κτήσῃ, *and shall acquire territory in addition*. — ληΐζεσθαι, *to obtain by plundering*.
32. συγκατεσκεδάσατο...κέρας, *and then sprinkled what was left in the horn* on himself, or on his companions. Plato, *De Legg.* i. 9, says that the Thracians think this "an honorable and excellent custom": to us certainly it seems barbarous enough. — μαγάδι, 218 (Lex.).
33. ἀνέκραγε πολεμικόν, *he shouted the war-cry*, 478.
34. σύνθημα, cf. i. 8, 16 N. — ὅπως...εἴσεισι, 624 b: ὅπως with fut. indic. after a past tense is unusual. — οἵ τε γάρ...φίλοι, *for both those who are enemies to you are Thracians, and so also are those who are friends to us* Thracians.
35. αὐτούς, i. e. *by themselves*, 541 a.

238
36. ἀναμένετε, v. l. ἀναμενεῖτε, fut. for imperat. — ὁπόταν... ἥκω, *when it is the proper time, I will come*, 641 a.
37. εἰ...ἔχει, *whether the Greek custom is not preferable*, cf. iii. 2. 22 N. — βραδύτατον, cf. *Cyr.* v. 3. 37.
38. ἥκιστα...ἀλλήλους, *are least likely unconsciously to straggle away from one another*. — περιπίπτουσιν, *fall foul of*, cf. Thuc. ii. 65. — ἀγνοοῦντες, sc. ἀλλήλους.
39. τῷ νόμῳ, 524 a. — εἶπον, i. e. the Thracians. — Ἀθηναίαν, v. l. Ἀθηναῖοι, making it the subject of εἶπον. — συγγένειαν, 2. 31.
41. αὐτός...πορευόμενος, *that he himself when marching with even a few*.

239
— ὥσπερ δεῖ, *just as we require*.
42. ἀτριβῆ, *untrodden*.
43. καλῶς...ἔσται, 571 d. — τοὺς ἀνθρώπους...ἐπιπεσόντες, *we shall fall upon the men unperceived* by them. — τοῖς ἵπποις, *with the cavalry*.
45. οὐκ ἐμοῦ μόνον δέῃ, *you do not need me alone* or especially.
46. τριάκοντα, Schneider adduces this passage as evidence that Xenophon was a young man comparatively, about 30 years old. (See Introduction.) Some inferior MSS. have the reading πεντήκοντα.

BOOK VII. CHAP. IV.

47. Τάδε δή s, *this is just as you said* (§ 38), the fellows are caught; *but then I have lost my cavalry who are gone away without supports* (cf. iii. 4. 40). McM.

48. σὺν [τούτοις] οἷς ἔχω, 554 a N. — παρατεῖναι τὴν φάλαγγα, *to extend his line*. ἄλλα μύρια, on the use of ἄλλα, as here, see 567 e.

CHAPTER IV.

FURTHER OPERATIONS AGAINST THE ENEMIES OF SEUTHES.

1. ἄλλοις (sc. λογιζομένοις) οἷα πείσονται (πάσχω, Lex.), cf. i. 7. 4 N. — πείσονται, tense, 607 a, 645.
2. λείαν...διατίθεσθαι, cf. vi. 6. 37 N. — γένοιτο, *v. l.* γένηται. — ἄν, after ὅπως, with optat. denotes condition of attainment, cf. vi. 3. 18 N. — ἐκλιπόντες, sc. τὸ πεδίον.
3. ἀπεκαίοντο, cf. iv. 5. 3 N.
4. ἀλωπεκίδας, *fox-skin caps:* cf. Hdt. vii. 75; Ovid. *Trist.* iii. 10. 19. — ζειράς, long overcoats or wrappers, reaching to the feet, and buckled round the loins. Cf. Hdt. vii. 69. The Greek chlamys was a short cloak or mantle.
5. τῶν αἰχμαλώτων (part. gen.), *some of the captives*, 423. — ὅτι...ὅτι, 714; v. 6. 19. — ὑπό, with acc. *under, close under,* with the idea of motion.
6. συνεπισπέσθαι (Lex. συνεφέπομαι), *v. l.* συνέπεσθαι. — παρῆσαν, cf. i. 2. 2 N.
7. Ἐπισθένης (Lex.). — παιδεραστής, *a lover of boys*, a word mostly used in a vile sense.
8. Καὶ ὅς, 518 f. — δεῖται, *v. l.* δέεται. — συνελέξατο, aor. in plpf. sense. — τρόπον, *character*.
9. μέλλει χάριν εἰδέναι, *is likely to esteem it a favor*.
10. εἰ παίσειεν, *whether he should strike*, cf. i. 9. 19 N. — ἐκείνου, i. e. the boy. — Ὥρα, sc. ἐστί. — μοι διαμάχεσθαι, *to fight it out with me*.
11. ταῦτα μὲν εἴα, [allowed these things] *acquiesced in this*, and spared the boy's life. — μή, *v. l.* μηδ'. — ἐν τῇ...κώμῃ, *in the village highest up* (of all those) *under the mountain.* — καλουμένοις, cf. i. 2. 13 N.
12. ὥστε ἀπολέσθαι (671 a, b), *so as to be destroyed*, i. e. where they ran the risk of perishing.
13. πειθομένους, *so long as they were obedient.* — ἄρα, cf. iv. 2. 15 N.
14. εἰς, 704 a, cf. i. 2, 3; 7. 1. — περιεσταύρωντο, *were fenced about*.
15. ἔφασαν, i. e. the Thynian captives so said afterwards; or, it may be, they uttered these things as threats; see Küh. — ὡς, 680. — αὐτοῦ, *there*, where he was, within.
16. ἐφαίνετο, *was appearing.* — οἱ περί, 527. — ἔνδον, cf. 1. 19 N. — Μακίστιος (Lex.), a town not far from Scillus, Xenophon's resi-

dence for many years. For this reason probably he makes mention of Silanus by name. — ὀκτωκαίδεκα, some conjecture ὀκτὼ καὶ πεντήκοντα, on the ground that a youth of this age (about 18) could hardly blow a trumpet, as here stated. — ἐσπασμένοι τὰ ξίφη, *with drawn swords*, cf. i. 8. 29 N.

17. ὄπισθεν = ὥστε ὄπισθεν εἶναι, cf. v. 2. 16. — περιβαλλόμενοι, *throwing round* from front to back, to protect the rear; *slinging their bucklers* (τὰς πέλτας) *behind*. McM. — ἐνεχομένων, *being caught in* or *entangled*. — οἱ δὲ καί, cf. i. 10. 3 N.

18. παρ' οἰκίαν, [beside] *past a house*, 689 d. — ἠκόντιζον, *kept hurling javelins* out of the dark, etc. — εἰς τὸ φῶς ἐκ τοῦ σκότους, cf. v. 4. 31 N. — ἔτρωσαν (τιτρώσκω). — Εὐοδέα (Lex.).

19. τοῖς πρώτοις, *the first* that he met; others were on the way. — ἐπείπερ, *as soon as he perceived* how matters stood. — τὸ κέρας ἐφθέγγετο αὐτῷ, *his trumpet was kept sounding* or *blowing*. — ἐδεξιοῦτο, [gave the right hand] *congratulated*.

20. εἰ βούλεται, cf. i. 3. 14 N. — ἐᾶσαι, sc. στρατεύεσθαι.

21. τριπλασίαν, *three times as large* as before the arrival of the Greeks. — πράττοι, v. l. πράττει.

23. σπείσασθαι, Küh. reads σπείσεσθαι, and omits ἄν before ἔφη. — τιμωρήσασθαι, cf. 1. 25 N.

24. 'Ἀλλ' ἔγωγε (708 e), *well, I for my part*. — δίκην ἔχειν, *I have satisfaction, I am sufficiently avenged*. Cf. Hdt. i. 45. — συμβουλεύειν, note sudden change to indir. discourse. — ταύτῃ, sc. τῇ χώρᾳ.

CHAPTER V.

SEUTHES FAILS TO PAY THE GREEKS. — THE TROOPS BLAME XENOPHON. — EXPEDITION TO SALMYDESSUS.

1. Ὑπερβάλλουσι (histor. pres.), *they now crossed over*. Küh. following Krüg. by a change of punctuation, makes ὑπερβάλλουσι the dat. of the participle, depending on παρῆν, § 2. — Δέλτα (Lex.), cf. 1. 33. — Μαισάδου: ἦν οὐκέτι is not applicable to Mæsades, the father of Seuthes. He was dead (2. 32), and the Delta had never belonged to him, as appears from the context, but to the hereditary dominions of this family. The sense seems to be, " now this (Delta), though belonging to Teres, the Odrysian, an ancient prince of the family, had formed no part of the kingdom in the reign of Mæsades." The remark is made as showing that the Greeks had already accomplished Seuthes's object, the recovery of his father's territory. McM.

2. Ἡρακλείδης...παρῆν, cf. 4. 2 N. — διανεῖμαι, 454 e.

3. τοίνυν, cf. v. 1. 2 N. — καὶ αὖθις, *at another time* (on καί, see McM.). — τούτοις...δωροῦ, *bestow your gifts upon these, the generals* and captains, who have, etc.

4. οὐ πλεῖον ἐμπολῆσαι, *he had not sold any more* of the booty than would suffice for twenty days' pay : ἐμπολῆσαι, *v. l.* ἐμποδῆσαι, ἐμπωλῆσαι. **245**

5. ἀχθεσθείς, *being vexed* or *annoyed.* — καὶ προσδαν....καὶ ἀποδόμ., *either by borrowing...or selling.* — σαυτοῦ, *v. l.* ἑαυτοῦ, pron. of 3d pers. sometimes used for 1st or 2d.

6. ὅ τι ἐδύνατο, *in whatever way he could.* — διέβαλλε, *calumniated,* labored to bring into disgrace.

7. ἐνεκάλουν, *were finding fault with.* — ἤχθετο αὐτῷ, 661 b. — τὸν μισθόν, i. e. the full pay for the month.

8. τέως, *up to that time.* — ἀεὶ ἐμέμνητο, *he had been continually mentioning* or *saying.* — ὡς...παραδώσοι, *v. l.* παραδώσειν (659 e), cf. iii. 1. 9. — Βισάνθην (2. 38) s, see Lex. — ἐμέμνητο, 432 c. — καὶ...διεβεβλήκει, *had maliciously stated this also.*

9. ἔτι ἄνω, *further up the country.* — λέγειν τε s, *on the one hand bade them say that they could lead the army* [no less than] *quite as well as Xen.* (if he refused), *and on the other he promised,* etc. See McM. — σφεῖς, on this use of the pron. cf. 539 b. — ὑπισχνεῖτο, *v. l.* ὑπισχνεῖται. — ἔντος, om. by Küh. and others.

10. στρατευσαίμην ἄν, cf. v. 1. 4 N.

11. παρεκάλει, *v. l.* παρακαλεῖ. — πανουργίαν, *craftiness* or *knavery.* — ὅτι βούλοιτο, *in that he wished.*

12. ἐπεί...ἐπείσθησαν, 605 c. — Μελινοφ. (see Lex.). The coast in the vicinity of Salmydessus was noted for shipwrecks and the barbarous practice of plundering the wrecked vessels, and enslaving all who were caught in them. — ὀκέλλουσι καὶ ἐκπίπτουσι, *are grounded and cast on shore.*

13. ἕκαστοι λῄζονται, *each* (tribe) *plunders.* — τέως, *up to that time.* — ἔλεγον, ἁρπάζοντας, πολλούς, *v. l.* ἐλέγοντο, ἁρπάζοντες, πολλοί: subj. of ἔλεγον, the adherents of Seuthes, who made these statements about the people in the vicinity of Salmydessus.

14. βίβλοι γεγραμμέναι, *written books,* i. e. manuscripts. Some understand by βίβλοι here rolls of bark ; others say that the word is used for sails, ropes, coverlets, etc. Krüg. remarks that, "as so many books were written and read in Greece, it is not at all surprising that some of them should have been transported to the Greek colonies." — ταῦτα, *these regions,* as § 13, κατὰ ταῦτα (χωρία).

15. ἀεί, *successively, from time to time* (see Lex.); cf. iii. 2. 31 ; iv. 1. 7.

16. παγχαλέπως εἶχον, *were very hard in their feelings.* — οὐκέτι...διέκειτο, *was no longer on familiar terms* with Xen. — **247** ὁπότε...ἔλθοι (i. e. Xen.), 641 b. — ἀσχολίαι, *engagements,* or pressure of business. — ἐφαίνοντο, *were pretended.*

CHAPTER VI.

THE GREEKS INVITED TO MARCH AGAINST TISSAPHERNES. — XENOPHON'S DEFENCE OF HIMSELF AGAINST ACCUSATION.

1. Θίβρωνος, v. l. Θίμβρωνος. — δοκεῖ στρατεύεσθαι, *had resolved to take the field.* — Τισσαφέρνην. This wily satrap had returned to Asia Minor, invested with all Cyrus's former authority, and eager to obtain vengeance. The Ionian cities sought help from the Lacedæmonians against Tissaphernes; accordingly Thibron had been sent out with the title of harmost, and troops to the number of 4500. Cf. Xen. *Hell.* iii. 1. 3. — δαρεικός, cf. v. 6. 23 N.

2. ἐπί, *for*, i. e. for the purpose of taking away with them the army. — χαριεῖ (v. l. χαριῇ), *will confer a favor.* — ἀπαιτήσουσι, i. e. οἱ στρατιῶται.

3. παράγειν, *to bring in*, or *introduce* the Lacedæmonian envoys. — εἶπον ὅτι...ἥκουσιν: ἔλεγεν ὅτι...ἀποδίδωσι, 607; cf. i. 3. 14 N. — τε, connects ἀποδίδωσι with βούλεται. — ξενίᾳ, v. l. ξένια, cf. vi. 1. 3.

4. τίς ἀνήρ, *what sort of a man.* — χεῖρόν ἐστιν αὐτῷ, *it is the worse for him*, 453. — Καὶ οἵ, 518 f. — 'Ἀλλ', 708 e.

5. Ἆρ' οὖν...μή, *why, he will not oppose us*, (will he?) respecting the removal of the army? ἆρα μή indicates doubt and misgiving as to the reply. — τὸν μισθόν, *the pay*, cf. § 1. — προσχόντες (προσέχω) sc. τὸν νοῦν.

7. ὅτι, 644. — δοκεῖ, cf. § 1 N.

8. ἐν ἐπηκόῳ, see Lex., cf. ii. 5. 38. — ἑρμηνέα, see § 43, τὸν ἑαυτοῦ ἑρμηνέα.

9. 'Ἀλλ', 708 e. — καὶ πάλαι, jampridem, *long ago.* — οὐδὲν πεπαύμεθα, *we have had no rest.* Krüg. reads (after Stephens) πεπάμεθα (πάομαι), *we possess nothing.* — ὁ δέ...ἔχει, *he has our labors*, i. e. the fruit or results of our labors and privations. — ἰδίᾳ (Lex.). — ἡμᾶς...μισθόν, 480 c.

10. ὅ γε πρῶτος λέγων ἐγὼ μέν, *I, at least, who am the first one to speak out the truth in this matter.* — δίκην (Lex..διδόναι δίκην). — περιεῖλκε (see Lex.), *has dragged us around.* — τὸν μισθόν...ἔχειν, *I would, I think, deem that I had my pay.*

11. 'Ἀλλὰ πάντα s, *well, really* (after this), *a man may expect any kind of fate.* — ἐν ᾧ (with νῦν) s, *at a time when* [to myself at least I seem to be] *I am conscious*, etc. — παρεσχημένος, *of having shown.* — 'Ἀπετραπόμην, cf. 1. 4; 2. 8. — οὐ μά...οὗτοι, *no, by Zeus, not from learning*, etc. — ἀκούων...εἶναι, 657 k.

12. ὅθεν = ἐκεῖσε ὅθεν, cf. 2. 10, etc.; i. 3. 17 N.

13. δήπου, *of course*, perhaps a little ironical.

14. μέν, δέ, *on the one hand, on the other.* — πάντες...ταῦτα; *did you* (or did you not) *all say?* etc. Dind. and others omit the interrogation.

BOOK VII. CHAP. VI. 145

15. Ἐπεί, *since*. — εἰ ἐπαινῶ αὐτόν, *if I were to commend him* (649 c); i. e. supposing that *I do really* praise him, in *that* case, you may fairly accuse me, etc. McM. — διαφορώτατος, *most at variance*. — περὶ ὧν = περὶ τούτων ἅ, *concerning matters about which I am at variance with him*. **250**

16. ἔξεστι, *it is possible*. — ἔχοντα, sc. ἐμέ. — τεχνάζειν, *am trying to trick you out of it* (your money) by feigning enmity towards him. — εἴπερ ...Σεύθης, *if Seuthes paid me anything*, 454 e. — οὐχ οὕτως s, *he did not, assuredly, pay it with any idea that he should be both deprived of*, etc. — ἐπὶ τούτῳ, *with this purpose or intention*.

17. πράττητε, πράττειν, with 2 accus. *to exact from*, 480. — ἐὰν μὴ βεβαιῶ τὴν πρᾶξιν, *if I do not complete the business*.

18. Ἀλλά...ἔχειν, *but* [I am conscious of wanting much of having your money] *I am far enough from having any of your property*, cf. v. 4. 32 N. — ὀμνύω...θεούς, 472 f, cf. vi. 6. 17. — σύνοιδέ μοι, [knows with me] *knows as well as I*, whether, etc.

19. συνεπόμνυμι, *I swear further* or *in addition*. — μὴ τοίνυν μηδέ, *no, indeed, not even*, 713 b.

20. ὅσῳ μᾶλλον, τοσούτῳ μᾶλλον, *the more I, so much the more he*, etc. — συμφέροιμι, *I shared with*. — αὐτοῦ τὴν γνώμην, *his disposition*, ungrateful as it is.

21. Ναὶ μὰ Δία, 476 d. — ᾐσχυνόμην μέντοι, εἰ...ἐξηπατήθην, *I should be ashamed indeed, if I had been deceived;* ἄν omitted gives emphasis, cf. 632.

22. εἴ γε...φυλακή, *if indeed precaution is* (necessary) *towards friends*. — πᾶσαν, sc. φυλακήν. — ἠδικήσαμεν τοῦτον οὐδέν, 480 b. **251**

23. Kühner and others omit ἂν ταῦτα after ἐδύνατο. — ὡς = ὥστε. — ἅ.. εἶπον, *what I would never have spoken*. — τούτου, i. e. Seuthes. — ἐναντίον, *in the presence of*. Their lack of sense (ἀγνώμονες) and ingratitude (ἀχάριστοι) forced him to the humiliating acknowledgment of the distressed condition in which the Greeks were when they entered the service of Seuthes.

24. προσῇτε πόλιν; v. l. εἰ προσῇτε πόλιν, Ἀρίσταρ. — οὐκ εἴα, *forbid* or *prevent*. — ὑπαίθρια, *in the open air*. — μέσος χειμών, *midwinter*. — ὁρῶντες, ἔχοντες, *while you saw, while you had*. — ὅτων (253) gen. of price. — ὠνήσεσθε, Küh. and others make all these clauses interrogative, *did not Aristarchus? was it not midwinter?* etc., so also, § 25.

25. ἐπὶ Θρᾴκης, ad fines Thraciæ. — ἐφορμοῦσαι, *stationed outside*, blockading the coast. — εἶναι, sc. ἀνάγκη ἦν.

26. οὐδέν τι ἄφθονον, *in no great abundance* certainly. — ὅτῳ...οὐκ ἦν, *but we had no force whereby*, etc. — συνεστηκός, *in a body* or *organized*.

27. μηδ'...προσαιτήσας, *without having asked any pay whatever in addition*, 551 g. — ἂν ἐδόκουν, *should I seem?* — πρὸ ὑμῶν; *in your behalf?* 693.

28. Τούτων...κοινωνήσαντες, *for, surely, while you shared in these advantages*, in having the aid of these troops. — κατὰ σπουδήν, 696. Küh. and others read μᾶλλον repeated before μετέσχετε. **252**

29. κωλύοντες μηδαμῆ, 713 d. — κατ' ὀλίγους, *in small parties.*
30. μισθόν...τῆς ἀσφαλείας, cf. v. 6. 31 N. — τοῦτο...πάθημα, *is this the dreadful calamity* you are complaining of? — ζῶντα ἐμὲ ἐᾶν εἶναι; *to suffer me to live?* 679: v. l. ζῶντα ἐμὲ ἀνεῖναι (Krüg.), *to let me go alive?* cf. *Hell.* ii. 3. 51.
31. Οὐ, sc. ἀπέρχεσθε. — εἴ τι = ὅτι, 639 a; cf. i. 6. 1. — ταῦτα πράττοντες, *while faring thus.* — οὔτε...ἀπεβάλετε, *nor did you lose any alive,* i. e. by their being made captives.
32. Εἰ δέ τι...ὑμῖν, *if any honor had been gained by you,* 461; i. 8. 12. — πρὸς ἐκείνοις, *in addition to those things,* i. e. the reputation or glory acquired in Asia. — ὧν ἐμοὶ χαλεπαίνετε, *for which you are angry with me,* 456. — χάριν εἰδέναι, *be grateful* (Lex. χάρις).
33. πρὸς θεῶν, 697. — ἀπῆρα (ἀπαίρω), *I weighed anchor* or *set sail:* v. l. ἀπῇα (ἄπειμι). — ἄν με ἔπεμπον, (otherwise) *they would never have sent me,* impf. as of repeated acts, 2. 8, 1. 8; or of animus, "would not have been disposed to send." McM.
34. πρὸς Λακεδαιμονίους, join with διαβεβλημένος, *calumniated to,* i. e. *in the eyes of the Lacedæmonians.* — ὑφ' ὑμῶν, ὑπὲρ ὑμῶν, emphatic, indicating their ingratitude. — ἀποστροφήν, ii. 4. 22 N. — εἰ γένοιντο, i. e. *if I should have any.* These words bear on the question of Xenophon's age at the time, and clearly imply that he had neither wife nor children as yet. Subsequently he had two sons, Gryllus and Diodorus (by a wife named Philesia), the former of whom fell at Mantinea, B. C. 362: Plut. *Ages.* 20: cf. 2. 38 N.
35. ἐγὼ ἀπήχθημαί (ἀπεχθάνομαι) τε πλεῖστα, *I have incurred very great hatred.* — καὶ ταῦτα, 544 a. — κρείττοσιν, dat. of agent, after passive verb, 461. — πραγματευόμενος...ὑμῖν = καὶ οἷς πραγματ. in ordinary construction.
36. οὔτε ἀποδιδράσκοντα, *nor running away* stealthily. — κατακανόντες, Küh. reads κατακεκανότες, but it may be doubted whether there is any such perf. of καίνω to be found in use. See Veitch's "Greek Verbs." Cf. 679. — ἐν τῷ μέρει s, *in his* (proper) *share and beside* (beyond) *his share;* in his turn as well as out of his turn. — τρόπαια βαρβ., *trophies over the barbarians.* — πρὸς ὑμᾶς, contra vos, or apud vos, i. e. *against your caprices,* or *for you, for your sake.*
37. Καὶ γὰρ οὖν, cf. i. 9. 8 N. — Ὑμεῖς δέ...νῦν δὴ καιρὸς ὑμῖν δοκεῖ εἶναι; *You, then...does it now seem to you to be just the time?* anacoluthon, 402. — ὅτε, v. l. ὅτι. — πλεῖτε, *you are sailing,* i. e. you are at liberty to sail.
38. Οὐ μήν, sc. οὕτως ἐδόκει ὑμῖν. — ὦ...μνημονικώτατοι, *O ye, of all men* (I have ever known) *possessing most admirable memories!* ironical, of course. — οὗτοι, i. e. Charminus and Polynicus.
39. πρὸς ἡμῶν, *with us,* cf. § 4.
40. ἐπὶ τούτῳ, *next after him.* — τοῦτο, depends on στρατηγῆσαι as cognate acc. (ταύτην στρατηγίαν, i. 3. 15), *that you should first lead us as our generals for this,* viz. to exact, etc.

41. ταῦτα ἀποδόμενος s, *having sold these things, he has neither paid over the proceeds to Seuthes, nor to us,* 579. — ἐξόμεθα αὐτοῦ, *we shall keep hold of him,* 582.
42. μάλα, *v. l.* μᾶλλον, i. e. still more affrighted than at anything he had as yet heard. — ἢν σωφρονῶμεν, repeating the very words of Polycrates.
43. τὰ χωρία, cf. 5. 8. — ἐν ἀπορρήτῳ ποιησάμενος, *having communicated it as a secret;* cf. vi. 6. 11 ; Hdt. ix. 94. — Πολυνίκου, § 1. — ἔσται, sc. Xenophon. — ἀποθανοῖτο (*v. l.* ἀποθάνοι), change of mood. **255**
44. Ἐπέστελλον, i. e. by letters or messengers, or both. — ἐθύετο, *v. l.* ἔθυε, 455 g. — λῷον καὶ ἄμεινον, the usual form in consulting the gods, cf. vi. 2. 15 N. — ἐφ' οἷς = ἐπὶ τούτοις ἅ, *on the conditions Seuthes proposed.* — Ἀναιρεῖ, sc. Ζεύς, *Zeus replies:* the word is commonly used of responses by oracles, etc., cf. iii. 1. 6 ; vi. 1. 22.

CHAPTER VII.

EFFORTS TO INDUCE SEUTHES TO PAY WHAT IS DUE. — XENOPHON'S STRONG REMONSTRANCE SUCCESSFUL.

1. ἐσκήνησαν εἰς κώμας, const. præg., marched into the villages and took up their quarters there. — ὑπό, cf. i. 1. 6, where ἐκ is used, 586.
2. ἄνωθεν, *from the upper country.* — Καὶ ὅς, 518 f.
3. Προλέγομεν, *we warn you,* etc. — ὑπὲρ Σεύθου, *in behalf of Seuthes,* 693. — ὅδε ὁ ἀνήρ, Küh. reads ὅδε ἀνήρ. — Μηδόκου, king of the Odrysæ, cf. 3. 16. — εἰ δὲ μή, 710. — ἐπιτρέψομεν, sc. τὰς ἡμετέρας κώμας πορθεῖν. — ἀλεξησόμεθα, *v. l.* ἀλεξόμεθα.
4. Ἀλλὰ σοί...χαλεπόν, *well, even to give an answer to you, speaking in such terms, is disagreeable or annoying;* however, etc.
6. ὁπότε ἔλθοις, 641 b, iterative optat. Some read ἦλθες, but **256** cf. 1. 5 ; 2. 10. — ἐγκεχαλινωμένοις, cf. 2. 21.
7. δι' ἡμᾶς, 694. — σὺν θεοῖς, *with the help of the gods,* 533 c. — νῦν δή, *v. l.* νῦν δέ. — ἐξελαύνετε, *you are* (threatening us with) *driving us out,* somewhat sarcastic.
8. οὐχ ὅπως δῶρα δούς, *not only not bestowing any gifts:* on the use of phrases like οὐχ ὅπως, etc., see 717 g. Compare Lat. non dico. — ἀνθ' ὧν εὖ ἔπαθες, cf. i. 3. 4 N. — ἀλλ'...ἐπιτρέπεις, *but, as far as lies in your power, you do not allow us, just going away, even to encamp here* (note force of aor. ἐναυλισθῆναι).
9. ἀπὸ λῃστείας, [from] *by means of robbery,* 695. — ἔχοντα, sc. ἑώρα. — ἔφησθα, 2. 34.
10. τί καί, cf. 564 c. — ἔφη, Xenophon asked. — παρεδώκατε, 306 b. — οὐδὲν ἐμέ s, *in no wise calling me in* (to your counsels), cf. 6. 3. — θαυμα-

στόταтοι (ironical), *most wonderful men* that you are ! — ὅπως, 624, 701 c.
— χαρισαίμην, *I might gratify them*, and thereby secure their good-will.

11. κατὰ...καταδύομαι, *I am ready to sink under the earth*. — ὑπὸ τῆς αἰσχύνης, *with the shame* which I feel : see Küh. on the force of art. here.

257 — οὐδὲ γὰρ ἄν...ἐπαινοίη, εἰ ἐξελαύνοιμι τοὺς εὐεργέτας, *for Medocus, my king, would not approve of my conduct, if I should drive out our benefactors*, 631 d.

12. ἐλύπει, *distressed* or *vexed*. — ἡ χώρα πορθουμένη, *the devastation of the country*.

13. Καὶ ὅς, 518 f. — καλεῖ, 607 a, 645. — προερῶν (Lex. προερῶ), edicturus, *intending to warn* (them) as he had warned him, i. e. Xenophon. — ἀπιέναι, (viz.) *to depart*.

14. ἂν ἀπολαβεῖν, *you might recover*. — εἴποιτε, v. l. εἴπητε. — δεδέηται, v. l. δέδεκται, omitting ὅτι, and reading ὑμᾶς instead of ὑμῶν. — συναναπρᾶξαι, *to join in exacting*. — τούτων τυχόντες, *if they obtain* [these things] *this*, i. e. their pay. — φασι, i. e. the troops. — τότε, *then*, and only then.

15. δύνωνται, cf. i. 3. 14 N. — ἐπικαιρίους, cf. 1. 6. — λέγειν, sc. λέγε δή : εἰ δὲ μή, sc. ἔχεις : ἔχομεν, sc. λέγειν, 710, cf. 1. 31 N.

16. μάλα δὴ ὑφειμένως, *very submissively indeed*. — Σεύθης, sc. λέγει. — ἀξιοῦμεν...γεγενημένους, *we request that those who have become friends to us*, i. e. in the villages where the Greeks were now quartered, § 1. — ἤδη, *forthwith, then and there*.

17. καὶ νῦν, *even now*, after all that you have said. — ἐνθένδε, [from 258 hence] *from you*, to obtain, etc.

18. ἐπιτρέψαι s, *to leave it to these men* [whatever decision they should make] *to decide whether it is fitting that you should quit the country, or we?*

19. οὐκ ἔφη, sc. ἐπιτρέψαι ἄν. — οἴεσθαι, supply ἔφη. — πέμπειν, depends on ἐκέλευε.

21. ἠχθέσθης, cf. 5. 6, 7. — ἀπῄτουν, ἀποδοῦναι, ἀπολαβεῖν, Küh. calls attention to the force of ἀπό, in composition, viz. *back*, where something is due ; *to demand back, to give back, to take back*. — ὑπέσχον, aor. in plup. sense, *you had promised*.

22. μετὰ τοὺς θεούς, *next to the gods*. — εἰς τὸ φανερόν, *in a conspicuous position;* Xen. Cyr. viii. 7. 23 ; Agesilaus, 5. 6. — βασιλέα σε ἐποίησαν, 480 a. — λανθάνειν, supply ποιῶν, from ποιήσῃς following.

23. ἐδόκει, v. l. δοκεῖ. — εὖ ἀκούειν...ἀνθρώπων, [to hear agreeably, act. for pass. 575 a] *to be well spoken of by 6000 men*. — σαυτόν, λέγοις, change of construction from 3d to 2d person.

259 24. τῶν ἀπίστων, emph. pos. — πλανωμένους, *wandering about*, i. e. failing in accomplishing their object. — σωφρονίζειν (Lex.) *to bring to reason* or *obedience*. — τὸ ἤδη κολάζειν, v. l. τὰς ἤδη κολάσεις.

25. τί προτελέσας...ἔλαβες, *what it was that you paid us beforehand* (or *in advance*) *when you received us as allies*. — Οἶσθ', v. l. Οἶδ'.

26. Οὐκοῦν τοῦτο s, *is not, then, this, their confidence in you, that also which obtained your kingdom for you, bartered away by you for this sum of*

BOOK VII. CHAP. VII. 149

money? — χρημάτων, gen. of price. — πιπράσκεται; some omit the interrogation-mark.

27. πῶς μέγα ἡγοῦ, *how you considered it* (to be) *a great thing.* — ἅ... ἔχεις, *which you now hold by conquest,* 679 b. — εὔξω, v. l. ηὔξω, cf. 278 d. — χρημάτων, referring to the money due to the soldiers.

28. ὅσῳπερ, *inasmuch as,* in the same degree as. — ἀρχήν, [in the first place] *at all,* with negatives, 483. — πλουτῆσαι, φανῆναι, βασιλεῦσαι, incept. aor., *to become rich,* etc.; cf. πλουτεῖν, *to be rich,* etc.

29. ἐπίστασαι μέν, naturally there ought to follow, ἐπίστασαι δέ, ὅτι ἐπιχειροῖεν ἄν : a like construction is found in Sophocles, *Philoctetes,* 1056, πάρεστι μὲν Τεῦκρος...ἐγώ τε. — φιλίᾳ τῇ σῇ (object. use of pron.), *friendship for you;* cf. iv. 5. 13. — κατέχοι; some omit interrogation.

30. σωφρονεῖν τὰ πρὸς σέ, *would perform their duties towards you more discreetly.* — πρὸς σέ, 697. — ἄλλους...παραγενέσθαι, **260** supply εἰ νομίζοιεν, implied in εἰ ὁρῷεν, above. — τούτων ἀκούοντας, *hearing from these,* 432. — εἰ καταδοξάσειαν, *if they should form a bad opinion of you* (and judge) that *no others,* etc. — τούτους, the Greeks. — αὑτοῖς, i. e. the present subjects of Seuthes.

31. πλήθει...λειφθέντες, [left behind us] *inferior to us in numbers,* 406 b. — τοῦτο (for οὗτος) κίνδυνος, *is not this a danger?* is it not a matter of apprehension to you? — τούτων, i. e. the Greeks. — ὑπισχῶνται...συστρατεύεσθαι, cf. 659 g. — ἄν...ἀναπράξωσιν, *on condition that they should now* (at once) *exact what is due from you.* — συναινέσωσιν...ταῦτα; *may concede these things to them* (the soldiers)? Some place the interrogation after Λακεδαιμονίους; others omit it altogether.

32. γὲ μήν, *porro.* — ὑπό σοι, *under your power,* 691. — ἐπὶ σέ...σοι, 788 e.

33. προνοεῖσθαι...δεῖ, sc. σέ. — ἀπαθῆ κακῶν (object. gen.) μᾶλλον, *more free from suffering evils,* less exposed to harm. — ἐγκαλοῦσιν, *demand in payment.* This verb is used of a creditor summoning a debtor into court, in order to obtain judgment against him. See Küh., note.

34. τούτοις, v. l. τοῦτο. — ὀφείλοιτο, v. l. ὀφείλοιντο.

35. Ἀλλὰ γάρ Ἡρακλείδῃ, *But* (you may object to all this), **261** *for to Heracleides,* etc., cf. iii. 2. 25. — Ἦ μὴν πολύ s, *assuredly, it is a much smaller matter now for you to get and pay this money.*

36. ὁ ὁρίζων, *which determines.* — πρόσοδος, *revenue;* your present revenue or income will be (v. l. ἐστίν, is) greater than, etc.

37. ταῦτα...προενοούμην, *I have been considering these things* beforehand, as your friend, and in your interests. — ὧν...ἀγαθῶν, cf. 554 a. — διαφθαρείην, *be utterly ruined* in reputation.

38. οὔτ' ἄν...ἱκανὸς ἂν γενοίμην, cf. i. 3. 2 N.

39. σὺν θεοῖς, cf. iii. 1. 23 ; 2. 8, 11. — ἐπὶ τοῖς στρατιώταις, *for the soldiers,* i. e. for the sake of conciliating the troops and securing their services. — ᾔτησα, ἀπῄτησα, cf. v. 8. 4 N.

40. μηδὲ ἀποδιδόντος (sc. σοῦ) δέξασθαι ἄν, *I would not have received anything even if you had offered it.*—Αἰσχρόν, on omission of ἄν cf. 6. 21 N. — περιϊδεῖν, cf. 3. 3 N. — ἄλλως τε καί, 717 a.

41. λῆρος...πρὸς τό...τρόπου, *a trifle, in comparison with the holding on to the money by every means* in his power. — οὐδέν...κτῆμα, *no possession.* Cf. Xen. *Ages.* 3. 5.

42. πλουτεῖ...φίλων, *is rich in friends,* 414 a. — συνησθησομένους, *will share his joy* or *pleasure.*

43. Ἀλλὰ γάρ, *But* (I need not dwell upon this), *for.* — πάντως, *at any rate:* v. l. πάντας.

44. αὐτοί, *they themselves, on their part.* — ἐνεκάλουν...μοι, *brought against me the charge* (which I do not admit) *that I cared more,* 702 a.

45. τὰ δῶρα, obj. of ἔχειν. — ἐνιδόντας, *because they saw;* κατανοήσαντας, *because they observed.*

46. ἀποκεῖσθαι, v. l. ἀποδείκνυσθαι : see Küh. note. — ὅσα...ἐνεπίμπλασό, *you could not be satisfied with promising what great rewards should be mine.* — ὅσον...ἐδυνάμην, § 8 N. — νῦν...τολμᾷς, *have you the hardihood* (despite all that I have urged upon you) *to see with indifference that I am now thus dishonored among the soldiers?*

47. ὅτι...ἀποδοῦναι, depend on διδάξειν. — αὐτὸν γέ σε s, *that you yourself will not bear to see those reproaching you who freely laid out their services in your behalf, and trusted to your honor to compensate them.* The critics note that Xen. indulges in a little exaggeration here.

48. τῷ αἰτίῳ, 444 f. — οὔτε...πώποτε, *never at any time.*

49. ἀνομοίως ἔχοντα...ὅτε, *that I am differently esteemed in the army now, from what I was when,* etc.

50. ἄν τε μένῃς, *and if you will remain.* — τὰ χωρία, 2. 38 ; 5. 8.

51. ἔχειν οὕτως, 577 c. — Καὶ μήν, atqui, *and yet* in reality.

52. Ἀλλά = *well.* — ἐπαινῶ, *I thank you for,* a polite mode of declining a proffered kindness or favor. Cf. Lat. laudo, benigne. — νόμιζε, *be assured.*

53. Ἀργύριον...μικρόν τι, *I have no money* [other than] *except a little.* — τάλαντον = 300 darics, i. 7. 18 = about $1200. — ὁμήρους, cf. 4. 13, 20, 21. — προσλαβών, *taking in addition.*

54. ἐξικνῆται, *come up to* or *amount to* = ἐξαρκῇ. Cf. Hdt. ii. 135. — τίνος τάλαντον s, *whose talent shall I say that I have?* among which of the Greeks, when their number is so great, shall I divide this talent, which is so very small a sum? — Ἆρ᾽ οὐκ, ἐπειδή s, *is it not better, since danger also* (as you say, § 51) *threatens me, in going back at least* (to the army) *to guard against the stones?* cf. 6. 10. Born. and others give the sense of ἀπιόντα, *going back* to my own country and thus escape danger of losing my life. See Küh. note. — ἔμειναν, v. l. ἔμεινε.

55. ἐλάσοντας, 305 c. — ἔλεγον, *were saying* or were under the impression. — ἃ ὑπέσχετο, *what he had promised him,* 646 d.

56. δι᾽ ὑμᾶς, v. l. δι᾽ ἡμᾶς. — πολλὴν εἶχον αἰτίαν, *were much censured,* on the ground of having acted fraudulently.

57. οὐ προσῄει, *did not go near* Charminus and Polynicus, i. e. took no part in the proceeding. — οὐ γάρ...περὶ φυγῆς, *for not yet had a decree of banishment been passed against him at Athens.* See INTRODUCTION, p. ix. Cf. Thucyd. i. 119, 125. — ἀπαγάγοι, Küh. reads ἀπαγάγῃ.

CHAPTER VIII.

THE GREEKS CROSS TO LAMPSACUS. — ARRIVAL AT PERGAMUS. — XENOPHON ATTACKS ASIDATES, A PERSIAN, AND GAINS MUCH BOOTY. — ARMY HANDED OVER TO THIBRON.

1. **Λάμψακον**, see Lex. — ἀπαντᾷ τῷ Ξεν. 450 a. — τοῦ...γεγραφότος, *who wrote the* (work upon) *Dreams in the Lycæum :* McM. translates, "who painted the Dreams in the Lycæum" (a gymnasium at Athens, eastward of the city). The verb γράφω means either *to write* or *to paint*, but, if ἐνύπνια be the true reading, the former meaning seems most appropriate here : *v. l.* ἐνοίκια, and ἐνώπια. Küh. reads γεγραφηκότος for γεγραφότος, but that form is used only in later writers. — ἔχοι, *v. l.* ἔχει.
2. **ἦ μήν**, ii. 3. 26. — αὐτόν, Küh. reads αὐτόν. — ἐφόδιον, viaticum, *travelling expenses.*
3. **ἔθυε**, i. e. Xen. *was sacrificing.* — παρεστήσατο τὸν Εὐκ. = *got Euclides to stand by him,* cf. vi. 1. 22. — ἱερεῖα, *v. l.* ἱερά. Euclides conjectured Xenophon's present lack of means from the poor quality of the victims. — μέλλῃ, sc. χρήματα. — σὺ σαυτῷ, *you will be a hindrance to yourself,* i. e. you will allow your disinterestedness and neglect of your own interests to stand in the way, as heretofore.
4. **γάρ**, 708 c. — Μειλίχιος, *gracious* to those who propitiate him by offerings. Zeus was worshipped under this name at the Διάσια at Athens, when all the people offered sacrifices to this god. Cf. Thucyd. i. 126. — ὥσπερ οἴκοι εἰώθειν ἐγὼ ὑμῖν θύεσθαι, *as I was accustomed at home* (i. e. at Athens) *to offer sacrifice,* καὶ (= *namely, that is*) ὁλοκαυτεῖν, *to burn whole victims for you.* From this it may be inferred that Euclides and Xen. were on intimate terms at Athens. — ἐξ ὅτου, *since,* 557. — καθά, *v. l.* καὶ ἅ. — συνοίσειν s, *it would result to his advantage.*
5. **ὡλοκαύτει**, except in sacrifices offered to Zeus Meilichios it was not usual to burn the whole victim. — τῷ πατρίῳ (*v. l.* πατρῴῳ) νόμῳ, sc. τῷ ὁλοκαυτεῖν. — ἐκαλλιέρει (Lex. καλλιερέω).
6. **Εὐκλείδης**, another person of this name (not the same as in § 1), or perhaps the text is corrupt, as Küh. thinks (see Lex.). — ξενοῦνται, *are hospitably entertained* (in § 8 παρά goes with this verb). — ἵππον...δαρεικῶν, *the horse which he had sold in Lampsacus for fifty darics* (= about $200), 431 a. — τὴν τιμήν, *the price* paid for the horse.
7. **παρά**, *along,* cf. iv. 6. 4. — Λυδίας (partit. gen.)...πεδίον, sc. ἀφικνοῦνται, *they came to the plain of Thebe* (in, or belonging to) Lydia : *v. l.* Μυσίας.
8. **τῆς Μυσίας**, 522 h. — ξενοῦνται, cf. § 6 N. — Γογγύλου, cf. Thucyd. i. 128.
9. **αὐτόν** (after ἔφη), i. e. Xenophon. — καθηγησομένους, cf. 598 b.

266 **11.** τέ (after τούς) connects δειπνήσας and λαβών. — ὅπως εὖ ποιήσαι αὐτούς, *that he might do them a service,* viz. by giving them a share of the expected plunder. — βιασάμενοι, *having forced themselves into the company of Xen. and his chosen band.* — ἀπήλαυνον, *were for driving them off,* or *tried to drive them back,* in order that they might not be called upon to share the booty with these pertinacious volunteers, just as if, forsooth (δή), Xen. dryly remarks, the plunder was already in their hands.

12. τύρσιος (218. 2), depends on πέριξ. — χρήματα, *valuables,* i. e. here *cattle* and such like. — ἀπέδρα αὐτοὺς ἀμελοῦντας, ὡς, *escaped* (ran away from) *them, inasmuch as they neglected these in order that.*

14. ἐπί, with gen. i. 2. 15 N. — γηίνων, = ὀπτῶν, cf. ii. 4. 12 ; iii. 4. 7. — διωρώρυκτο, cf. 281 d. — διεφάνη, impers., *as soon as ever light shone through,* i. e. as soon as an opening was made. — βουπόρῳ ὀβελίσκῳ, *with an ox-spit,* cf. Hdt. ii. 135. — διαμπερές, cf. iv. 1. 18 N. — ἐκτοξεύοντες ἐποίουν, *by shooting arrows continually, they made* it unsafe any longer even to approach.

15. πυρσευόντων (Lex.). — Κομανίας, a castle or town not far from Pergamus. — ἄλλοι, cf. i. 5. 5 ; 7. 11 N. — ἄλλοι...ἄλλοι...ἱππεῖς, *cavalry, some from...others from.*

16. πῶς ἔσται, dir. for indir. disc. ὅπως ἔσοιτο, cf. i. 3. 14 N. — λαβόντες [sc. τοσούτους βοῦς] ὅσοι ἦσαν βόες, 551 c. — ποιησάμενοι, cf. i. 10. 9 N. — οὕτω, v. l. ἔτι. — μὴ φυγὴ εἴη ἡ ἄφοδος, *lest the departure should* (seem to) *be a flight,* 534. 3. — εἰ ἀπίοιεν, cf. iii. 4. 35 N. — νῦν δέ s, *but, as it was* (in fact), *they retreated as if intending to fight,* etc.

17. βίᾳ τῆς μητρός, *in spite of his mother,* who perhaps apprehended future retaliation on the part of the Persians. — Προκλῆς...ὁ ἀπό, cf. ii. 1. 3 N.

18. Οἱ περὶ Ξεν. 527 a. — κύκλῳ, *in the form of a circle.* — ὅπλα, i. e. shields. — πρὸ τῶν τοξευμάτων, *as a defence against the missiles.* The circular form would cause the missiles to strike the shield obliquely and glance off.

19. Ἀγασίας (Lex.). — πρόβατα...θύματα (507 f), *cattle enough for sacrifices,* but not enough for provisions or profit ; cf. § 21.

20. μακροτάτην, sc. ὁδόν. — Λυδίας, gen. depending on superl. 419 c. His plan was to throw Asidates off his guard by marching as far as possible on the road into Lydia, etc. — εἰς τὸ μή = ὥστε μή, *to the end that* (Asidates) *might not be in fear,* etc. Cf. Xen. *Mem.* iii. 6. 2.

21. ἐπ' αὐτόν, i. e. ἐπὶ τῷ ἰέναι ἐπ' αὐτόν, with a view to another expedition against him. — ὑπό...ἐχούσας, pertinentes, [having themselves under] *lying close under,* i. e. very near to and under the protection of, etc. Cf. Hdt. iv. 42.

22. συντυγχάνουσιν (hist. pres.), *fell in with.* — γυναῖκα, Küh. reads γυναῖκας. — ἀπέβη, [came off] *were fulfilled,* § 10.

23. οὐκ ᾐτιάσατο, *did not blame the god* any longer : the whole story is a curious mixture of piety and a free seizing upon other people's property !

BOOK VII. CHAP. VIII. 153

v. l. ἡσπάσατο, *hailed the god as his benefactor.* — συνέπραττον...ὥστε, [worked together...that] *joined together in bringing it about that*, etc. — ἐξαίρετα, *select* or *choice portions* of the *booty*: cf. Homer, *Il.* i. 334-367; Virg. *Æn.* viii. 552. **268**

24. Ἐκ τούτου, *v. l. ἐν τούτῳ*, i. e. in the spring of B. C. 399 (see "Record of Marches," etc. after the Appendix, p. 26).

25, 26. These sections are bracketed, as being of very doubtful authenticity. Krüg. regards them as a mere interpolation, and gives abundant and cogent reasons for his opinion. Dindorf, in his fourth edition (1867), and Schenkl (1869), print the paragraph in smaller type, as forming no part of the text of Xenophon. Cobet (1859) extrudes the sections entirely from his edition. Küh. brackets § 25, but gives § 26 as genuine.

26. Ἀριθμός, *the numbering* or *computation.* — καταβάσεως, i. e. to Cotyora, cf. v. 5. 4 ; ii. 2. 6 N. — διακόσιοι s, on the order of numerals in Greek, cf. 242 a. As to the numbers, however, as Küh. justly remarks, the MSS. vary to a large extent.

GEOGRAPHICAL NOTES.

[From MacMichael's "Anabasis."]

WALL OF MEDIA (i. 7. 15; ii. 4. 12). — PYLÆ (5. 5). — THE TRENCH (i. 7. 15). — CANALS (i. 7. 15; ii. 4. 13).

§ 1. Not the least remarkable of the discoveries which of late years have marked the progress of geographical inquiry in this most interesting region is the actual existence at the present time of an ancient wall stretching across Mesopotamia at the head of the Babylonian plain. Dr. Ross, who first examined it at its eastern terminus, in 1836, describes it, under the name *Khalú* (or *Sidd*) *Nimrúd* (Wall or Embankment of Nimrod), as a straight wall 25 *long paces thick*, and from 35 to 40 feet high, running S. S. W. ¼ W. as far as the eye could reach, to two mounds called *Ramelah* (Siffeirah, Ainsworth, pp. 81, 82), on the Phrat, some hours above Felujah. The eastern extremity was built of the *small pebbles of the country, cemented with lime of great tenacity*, but farther inland, his Bedwin guide told him, "*it was built of brick*, and in some places worn down level with the desert, — and was built by Nimrod to keep off the people of Nineveh, with whom he had an implacable feud" (*Journal of Royal Geogr. Society*, ix. pp. 446, 472; xi. p. 130). That it was constructed for purposes of defence, and not as a mere embankment[1] for purposes of irrigation, is indicated by its having on its northwestern face "*a glacis, and bastions at intervals of 55 paces, with a deep ditch 27 paces broad.*" It was further examined by

---

[1] Captain Jones, cited by Grote (*Greece*, ch. lxx.), represents it as "no wall at all, but a mere embankment, extending seven or eight miles from the Tigris, designed to arrest the winter torrents and drain off the rain-water of the desert into a large reservoir," etc. An embankment of the dimensions given above by Dr. Ross should hardly be required to arrest the winter torrents of a country remarkable for its drought (ἡ γῆ τῶν Ἀσσυρίων ὕεται ὀλίγῳ, Hdt. i. 193). Its true character as a line of defence is affirmed both by Layard, p. 579, and by General Chesney, i. pp. 29, 30, 118. The enormous breadth of the wall, "*25 long paces*," corresponds with that of the walls of Babylon (Hdt. i. 178). The preservation of the Sidd Nimrúd at its eastern extremity must be attributed to its material there (pebble, etc.) being useless for building purposes, so that it escaped the common fate of brickwork structures in having their materials used to build other cities. Rennell, *Geogr.*, i. pp. 496, 497.

Captain Lynch in 1844, and its eastern extremity determined to be in lat. 34° 3′ 30″, and long. 21′ 50″ W. of Baghdad. He galloped along it for more than an hour without finding any sign of its terminating. (*Journal of Royal Geogr. Society*, ix. pp. 472, 473.)

§ 2. The identity of this wall with Xenophon's *Wall of Media* was assumed by the explorers tacitly, but with every ground of probability. In the first place it is hard to imagine a "Wall of Media" in any other position than this, if its use was to protect from northern invasion the rich culture of Babylonia, with the entire canal area and system of irrigation, to which the plain owed its rare fertility. Hdt. i. 193. Then, too, of the great antiquity of Sídd Nimrúd there can be no question ; record of its origin there is none, except local tradition assigning it to Nimrod. On the other hand, the *continued existence* of a wall (corresponding to the *Median*) from Xenophon's age down to comparatively recent times is attested by a chain of scattered notices in later writers. Such a wall is mentioned by Eratosthenes (in the third century B. C., quoted by Strabo ii. 1 and xi. 14), as τὸ τῆς Σεμιράμιδος διατείχισμα, having its *eastern* terminus near *Opis*. Again, its *western* terminus was noticed in ruins by Ammianus Marcellinus (363 A. D.) at *Macepracta* on the Euphrates, near the head of a canal [*which he distinguishes from the Naha-Malcha* (Nahr Melik)], the *Saklawiyeh* apparently, a few miles north of which is the S. W. extremity of the *Sídd Nimrúd*. (See Ammian. Marcell. xxiv. 2.)

§ 3. Their identity is further attested by their occupying the same general position as a partition line between the rocky desert of Arabia and the fertile alluvial plain of Babylonia : "*the Sídd Nimrúd, for all practical purposes, distinguishes the Babylonian plain from the hilly and rocky country.*" (Ainsworth, p. 82, note 2.)

Layard (Nineveh and Babylon, p. 577) found the country N. of the Bridge of Herbah (N. E. of Babylonia). "a perfect maze of ancient canals now dry;... eight miles beyond the bridge *the embankments suddenly ceased; a high rampart of earth* (the Sídd Nimrúd) *then stretched as far as the eye could reach to the right and to the left;... to the north of it there are no canals nor watercourses except the Dijeil, which passes through the mound;* beyond the Median Wall we entered upon gravelly downs furrowed by deep ravines..." Now that a like position, between desert and cultivated plain, must be assigned to the *Median Wall*[2] is indicated by the name it bears ; for the *Medes* under Cyaxares had conquered all Assyria up to *Babylonia*,[3] a tract which Hdt. describes as one entire canal district

---

[2] "The wall of defence *against* the Medes," as "The *Picts*' Wall" means "*against the Picts.*"

[3] πλὴν τῆς Βαβυλωνίης μοίρης, Hdt. i. 806. This was after the overthrow of Nineveh by the Medes (B. C. 606 ?), and the extinction of the Assyrian monarchy, when Media and Babylonia became independent, and ultimately, if Herodotus' authority was good, antagonistic powers. He represents a jealous fear of *Median* encroachment prevailing at Babylon until both monarchies merged in the Medo-Persian (B. C. 538). The testimony, however, of Berosus (a Babylonian priest, who wrote a history of Babylonia, B. C. 260.

(ἡ Βαβυλωνίη χώρη πᾶσα κατατέτμηται ἐς διώρυχας, Hdt. i. 193), so that the "*Wall of Media*" as a barrier against Medish incursion would follow the northern outline of the old canal district; and that outline, as we have seen, is the line taken by the Sidd Nimrúd so far as it has been examined.

But, further, Xenophon represents the Desert of Arabia as terminating at a place called Pylæ (i. 5. 5). Now as the next marches given in his itinerary are said to be through Babylonia (7. 1), we conclude that *Pylæ* must have lain on the confines of Babylonia, and may be looked for at or near the western end of Sídd Nimrúd. This general conclusion is remarkably confirmed by comparing the distance of Sídd Nimrúd at its W. end, from Babylon with that of Pylæ from Babylon. General Chesney, in his great work on the Euphrates (vol. i. pp. 48 et seq.), gives us the distance by river from Thapsacus to Hillah (Babylon) as 613½ geographical miles, as obtained by the steamer in her course down the river. Now Xenophon gives the road distance from *Thapsacus* to *Babylon* as 210 parasangs, and of *Pylæ* from *Babylon* as 35 parasangs. If then 210 parasangs by road correspond to 613½ geographical miles by river, proportionally 35 parasangs by road will correspond to 102 geographical miles by river. We should look therefore for Pylæ at a point whose river-distance from Babylon is 102 geographical miles. Felujah is given as 91 geographical miles (Chesney), and 10 or 12 miles measured from Felujah up the river in Chesney's map brings us to the W. end of the Sídd Nimrúd, with which, therefore, Pylæ may be fairly identified. The result has all the more claim to our confidence that the route by land follows the course by river so closely as to make distance by one almost a measure of distance by the other; it is independent also of any arbitrary assumption respecting the value of a parasang.

§ 4. This coincidence, and the name itself of *Pylæ* (*gates* or *fortified pass*), suggest the conclusion that Pylæ was neither city (as Larcher surmised)

---

and whose authority is good) is that Media and Babylonia were friendly, and even allied powers, so long as the Median monarchy lasted (i. e. till B. C. 559), and that the real object of fear at Babylon was the *Medo-Persian* power founded by Cyrus, who, after conquering Lydia and all Asia Minor, finally turned his arms against Babylon and subdued it (B. C. 538). Probably this is the true account (see Rawlinson, vol. i. p. 428). If so, we must assign the construction of the wall to the interval between B. C. 559 and B. C. 538. It is probably a monument of the reign of Queen Nitocris (B. C. 558), whose great works are described by Hdt. as being purely defensive against Media (i. 185). He represents her as the mother of Labynetus, the last of the Babylonian kings; but her right place in history is not yet ascertained (see Rawlinson's *Herodotus*, vol. i. p. 427). At any rate, the vast dimensions of the wall (ii. 4. 12) point clearly to a period near to that at which Nebuchadnezzar could boast that he "*built this great Babylon*" (Daniel iv. 30), and among other structures a palace (the Kasr), whose vast ruins still exist, of which he declares, "*in fifteen days I completed and made it the high place of my kingdom*" (*Standard Inscription*, Rawlinson, ii. p. 487). The "Median Wall" came in later times to be called "the wall of Semiramis" (super § 2), the fashion in the East being to assign all great works of unknown origin to *Semiramis* (see Strabo, xvi.), as in our day to Nimrod.

nor mountain defile,[4] but the ancient pass into Babylonia through the wall[5] itself, at a time when it extended — as when entire it must have done — to the Euphrates. It certainly excites surprise that Xenophon makes no mention of their passing the wall at its west extremity, either at *Pylæ* or wherever else he passed it on the upward route. But it appears (Ainsw. p. 108) that all trace of the wall is lost between Siffeirah and the river (a distance apparently of some miles); and we may safely conclude that the wall at its western end was demolished when the Greeks passed it; for, assuredly, had it been entire, or capable of defence, the king would have defended it, if only to keep the enemy in check[6] till he could bring up his distant forces. In this view, therefore, there would be little trace of its existence presented to the Greeks beyond the name of "*The Gates*" still retained in the locality, and the ruins which Ammianus M. saw; but it was not the time to take note of ruins, or inquire about them; for when the Greeks were at Pylæ a battle seemed imminent. It was in the middle of the eleven days (i. 7. 18), when they had just come upon tracks of the enemy (6. 1), and were in almost hourly expectation of meeting him. It need excite no surprise, therefore, that at this juncture Xenophon remarked nothing of which he could afterwards give an account; and Pylæ is, in fact, the only place in the route that he is content to name and dismiss without comment or description of any kind; all we gather about it is, that it was at the end of the desert marches.

§ 5. If this assumption be admitted, that Xenophon was ignorant of the western terminus, and at the time he wrote (probably at Scillus) confused about the true direction of the wall, we have then some clew to explain his statement, ἀπέχει Βαβυλῶνος οὐ πολύ (ii. 4. 12). He knew that he had been within 36 miles of Babylon without falling in with the western end of the wall, and may have had a notion that it lay farther south than Cunaxa, which was 12 parasangs from Babylon. Himself laboring under some such misconception, it is not surprising that he should have both misled and perplexed his best geographical commentators, previous to the actual discovery of the wall. Rennell adopts his statement about the

---

[4] There is none such in this quarter (Renn. pp. 83, 84), who conjectures that the term "refers to the shutting up of the river itself between the mountains, which terminate at the same place on both sides of the river." See also pp. 300, 301.

[5] See the description of the Syro-Cilician gates (i. 4. 4); something similar at the eastern end of the Sidd Nimrúd seems to be described by Dr. Ross (*Journ. R. G. S.*, ix. p. 446).

[6] The barrier actually employed was the trench (i. 7. 14-16), commencing at the Median Wall (doubtless where its continuity began), and terminating at twenty feet from the Euphrates. This interval was left (according to Krüger) to prevent the water filling the trench. But why a dry trench should be *preferred*, and what would be the use of it, requiring to be defended for an extent of thirty-six miles, is not easy to conceive. It was probably filled with water from the canals, which are mentioned in connection with it; in which case, to have continued it on to the Euphrates would, in the low state of the river at that time (i. 4. 18), have only had the effect of emptying the water of the canals into the river (see *inf.* § 6); a narrow pass, therefore, was left to be defended.

proximity of the wall to Babylon, and represents it as crossing the isthmus, and touching the Tigris, between Baghdad and Ctesiphon ; but — as this is a distance of only 20 miles — he is obliged to give up Xenophon's other statement respecting the length of the wall, that "it was said to be 20 parasangs (about 50 geographical miles) long" (ii. 4. 12). Some difficulties there are which time and a better knowledge of the country may clear up; but others we must expect to meet with that are simply mistakes of the writer, inevitable under the circumstances; and few cases can be imagined more liable to mistake than this of the Greeks: they were moving about in the hands of those whose aim and main strategy was to mystify and mislead them; their own observation of the country must have been both limited and imperfect; and they could have little, if any, previous knowledge of it whereby to correct mistakes, whether of bad information, simple misunderstanding, hasty observation, lapse of memory, or whatever else goes to make up the sum of human error. Clearchus himself speaks as if he had no previous knowledge even of the Tigris (ii. 2. 3 ; 4. 6); and Xenias, who might have known something of Babylonia, had deserted (i. 1. 2 ; 4. 7). But further, there is always a doubt about interpreting such indefinite terms as *it is not far from Babylon;* for they are in their nature relative terms, and we do not know what Xenophon had in his mind when he used them. When Plutarch (*Artax.*, 7), speaking of Cyrus passing the trench, used the equivalent term τῆς Βαβυλῶνος οὐ μακρὰν γενόμενον, he could not mean less than 70 miles ; for he thought Cunaxa was 50 (*inf.* § 7), and the trench was more than 20 miles farther north ; and it is possible that Xenophon, writing in Greece, may, like Plutarch, be speaking[7] with reference to the whole length of the journey up, when he says of the wall, *it is no great distance from Babylon.* The use of the present tense (ἀπέχει) lends support to this view ; compare εἰσὶν αἱ διώρυχες (i. 7. 15) with αὗται (αἱ διώρυχες) ἦσαν... (ii. 4. 13), the present tense in each case intimating that the statement must be referred to the place where and the time when the narrative was written. I can only submit this, or the view given above, as possible solutions of an admitted difficulty.

THE CANALS AND TRENCH.

§ 6. Xenophon's account of the canals has been discredited on various grounds, physical and historical (see Rennell, p. 79 ; Ainsw. pp. 89, 90): 1st, because four canals, each of them 100 feet broad, and "extremely deep," must have entirely drained the river from which they were drawn, whether the Tigris, as Xenophon says, or (as some affirm he ought to have

---

[7] Exactly as Sir H. Rawlinson himself (who conceives the Median Wall to have been "the *enceinte* of Babylon," Hdt. i. p. 261, note 5) speaks of *Hit* and its bitumen pits as being "near to Babylon" (Hdt. i. p. 495). Hit was an "eight days' journey" from Babylon (Hdt. i. 179).

6   GEOGRAPHICAL NOTES.

said) the Euphrates, which is only 450 feet wide at Hillah (Rich.). 2dly, because it is the concurrent testimony of other ancient authors (Herodotus, i. 193; Ptolemy, v. 18. 8, 10; Arrian, vii. 7; Pliny, *N. H.*, vii. 26; Strabo, xvi. 1. 9), that the canals in the north of Babylonia flowed not from the Tigris into the Phrat, but from the Phrat into the Tigris; and that in fact the old canals still traceable in North Babylonia confirm their testimony, the Saklawiyeh (or Isa), Sersar, Nahr Melik, and Cuthiyeh being all derived from the Phrat. 3dly, that the slope of land north of Babylon favors the same conclusion, the bed of the Phrat being slightly (five feet) higher at Felujah than that of the Tigris at the opposite point. (Ainsworth's Researches in Assyria, etc., p. 145.)

In reply to these objections it may be urged in the outset that it is not easy to conceive how a careful intelligent observer, like Xenophon, could be mistaken on such matters of fact as the number and size of the canals. As to objection (1st), it has no force, except on supposition that a constant stream ran through all of them at all seasons. But there is no evidence[8] of this. The statements of Strabo and Arrian lead to the conclusion that they were open only during the season of flood, being afterwards converted by dams or flood-gates into *reservoirs* of water to be distributed over the plains during the dry season; when they became dry, or when the water in them fell below the level of the river, then the river would be drained to supply them.[9] They were filled during the season of flood, high embankments (constructed of old for this purpose, Herod. i. 184) lining the course of the river, and forcing its pent-up waters into the canals. On the flood receding, the communication with the rivers was cut off, and the canals left full of water to be applied (by hand-labor, Herod. i. 193) to the purposes of irrigation. For these a high level would be chosen, and embankments raised, so as to give the water elevation enough to be distributed at will by means of trenches and ducts all over the plain. "It is remarkable," says B. Fraser (*Mesopot.*, p. 31), "that all these canals, instead of having been sunk below the surface of the ground like those of the present day, were entirely constructed on the surface"; from these primary derivatives secondary irrigants were given off in all directions, having lofty "embankments from twenty to thirty feet in height"; these "lofty embankments stretching on every side in long lines till they are lost in the hazy distance, or magnified by the mirage into mountains, still defy the hand of

---

[8] Hdt., who visited this country fifty or sixty years before, speaks as if only one flowed into the Tigris : ἡ μεγίστη τῶν διωρύχων ἐστὶ νηυσιπέρητος, πρὸς ἥλιον τετραμμένη τὸν χειμερινόν, ἐσέχει δὲ . . . ἐς τὸν Τίγριν (i. 193).

[9] Strabo (xvi. 1) alludes distinctly to some such provision as this, and the effect upon the river when the canals are dried up in summer. Speaking, apparently, of the difficulty, from the nature of the soil, of damming up the mouths of the canals expeditiously or securely enough to prevent reflux, he says, καὶ γὰρ καὶ τάχους δεῖ πρὸς τὸ ταχέως *κλεισθῆναι* *τὰς διώρυχας, καὶ μὴ πᾶν ἐκπεσεῖν ἐξ αὐτῶν τὸ ὕδωρ. Ξηρανθεῖσαι γὰρ τοῦ θέρους ξηραίνουσι καὶ τὸν ποταμόν, κ. τ. λ. They served, he remarks, three distinct purposes : (1) they saved the crops from destruction by the floods; (2) from perishing by drought in summer ; and (3) they were serviceable for navigation.

APPENDIX. 7

time, and seem rather the work of nature than of man." (Layard, *Nin. and Bab.*, p. 479.) From these canals the trenches were filled (ii. 3. 10–13) in the dry season when the river was lower than had ever been known (i. 4. 18). Hence also we may explain why the trench (note 6) was conducted 12 leagues along the plain to the canals, instead of a few miles to the Phrat, doubtless because in its low state at that time, filling the trench from the river was impracticable.

2dly. As to the concurrent testimony of other authors that the canals of Northern Babylonia flowed from the Phrat into the Tigris, Herodotus is the only one whose testimony is really pertinent to this inquiry, he being the only one who saw and wrote of Babylonia under anything like the same conditions as Xenophon himself. Both wrote when the seat of government was on the Phrat at Babylon. The other historians speak of a wholly different state of things, when Seleucus, by building Seleucia on the Tigris, and making it his capital, had transferred the seat of government to the Tigris. From this era canals, one or more, from the Phrat to the Tigris, became a dynastic necessity, to place the new capital in communication with the Western Provinces and Europe.

It is these canals of communication, from their size and importance attracting the attention of later historians, that are alluded to by name from Polybius (B. C. 181) to Ammianus Marcellinus (A. D. 363). At the same time it is not denied that "canals of irrigation" also drawn from the Phrat did exist *in their day* in Northern Babylonia. The removal by Alexander the Great of the dikes on the Tigris (τοὺς καταρ῀)άκτας) (Arrian, *Anab.*, vii. 7. 7; Strabo, xvi. 1. 9), would necessarily break up the system of irrigation previously carried on from the Tigris (*Anab.*, ii. 4. 13) and transfer it mainly to the Phrat. These high dikes characterized the irrigation of the Tigris; from the height of its banks above its channel they would be far more of a necessity on the Tigris than on the Phrat, which, according to Arrian (vii. 7. 3), "*flows everywhere level with the land* (ῥεῖ ἰσοχειλὴς πανταχοῦ τῇ γῇ), *whereas the banks of the Tigris are high above its stream*" (μετεωροτέρα ἡ ταύτῃ γῇ τοῦ ὕδατος). Kinneir (*Journey*, p. 472) noticed this below Samarra, and remarked, "*consequently irrigation must always have been attended with difficulty.*" In fact, the dikes alone made it possible; remains of them are to be seen near Nineveh below Mösul and at the Band el Adhem; possibly also they may be found at the point where the waters of the Tigris are thrown into the two canals, — the Ishaki on the right, and the Burech on the left, — where the river forces its way through the Hamrin hills.

In Xenophon's day, the conditions of the case being reversed, that is to say, the seat of government being on the Phrat, and the dikes of the Tigris entire, the presumption is that the canal communication north of Babylon would be, as Xenophon says it was, from the Tigris to the Phrat. As regards Herodotus, his statements about the canals go a very little way to invalidate Xenophon's account, if indeed they do not confirm it; certainly, his remark that "the greatest of the canals" *goes into the Tigris* (note 8), implies that *some of the others did not*, that they either went into the Phrat (as the Shat el Hye does), or into the Persian Gulf, as the Nahr Sada did, or, as at present, that they were chiefly exhausted in the process of irrigation. Whether Herodotus knew anything at all about Northern Babylonia and the upper canal system (with which alone we are concerned) is more than questionable. That he did not come [10] to Babylon by the Phrat seems clear from his singular remark (i. 185), that "those who *go from our sea to Babylon when sailing down into the Phrat*[11] touch three times in three consecutive days at the same village (Ardericca)." His "Greatest Canal," the one which he describes circumstantially (*sup.* note 8), would be one which he saw — perhaps traversed himself — in the vicinity of Babylon, either the Nahr Nil or the Cuthiyeh (Cutha Canal); either would answer to his description ; but we have the testimony of Captain Bewsher that there are many ruins of the Babylonian era lining the banks of the Abu Dibbis and the Cuthiyeh,[12] so that we may assume the Cuthiyeh at any rate to have existed before Herodotus' day. Indeed, from the abundance of ruins on the Abu Dibbis and their rarity on the western branch (the present bed) of the Euphrates, Captain Bewsher surmises, with good reason, that the ancient bed of the river lay in the Abu Dibbis and its continuation the El Mutn ; and this conclusion I have adopted in the present edition, so far as to place Cunaxa on this, rather than on the western branch of the river.

SAKLAWIYEH. SERSAR. NAHR MELIK. CUTHIYEH.

It has been supposed, not unnaturally, that the four old canals in Northern Babylonia, still traceable and still partially in use, the Nahr Saklawiyeh, the Sersar, Nahr Melik, and Abu Dibbis or Cuthiyeh, are the identical four canals of Xenophon ; and this conclusion has influenced commentators[13] in placing Pylæ (which was 15 parasangs above the canals) considerably higher up the river than accords with Xenophon's distances, Rennell (p. 85) placing it 20 geographical miles below Hít, and Chesney 5 miles

---

[10] He would go either by the regular route, the royal road between Sardis, Nineveh, and Susa (which we know that he reached), or possibly by the caravan route over the Arabian desert from Egypt.

[11] καταπλέοντες ἐς τὸν Εὐφράτην. All this is a clear impossibility. Doubtless the whole account is given by Herodotus as a matter of hearsay, which he accepted simply as one wonder in a region of wonders, whatever the explanation of so strange a tale may be. There may have been three Arderiecas on the river a day's journey apart. There was certainly a second Ardericca near Susa, which Hdt. saw (vi. 119). Mr. Loftus' suggestion (*Travels*, p. 160) that the name is a corruption of *A'ra de Erek* ("Land of Erech") may give a clew to the right explanation. Erech — the modern Irka or Workha, in Chaldæa Proper — was one of Nimrod's four primeval cities (Gen. x. 10), and may be supposed to have planted colonies bearing its name.

[12] Notably *Tel Ibrahim*, "by far the largest mound in this part of Mesopotamia, 1,000 yards long and 60 high." (Bewsher, p. 178.)

[13] Ainsworth alone, in his later work, "Commentary" (p. 294), suggests that Xenophon's canals may really have been derived from the Tigris or from the marsh of Accad.

APPENDIX. 9

lower down, opposite Jarrah. But there is no trace of four in ancient history before the Christian era ; one, or perhaps two, having a continuous existence, though with some variety of name, figure in history subsequent to the Seleucian era. Almost conclusive evidence is supplied by the historians of Julian's campaign, in 363 A. D., that the four modern canals did not exist, as we have them, at that period. Julian, in order to get his fleet from the Phrat into the Tigris to co-operate with his army in the attack on Ctesiphon, had to open an old canal of Trajan's, from the Nahr Melik into the Tigris north of Ctesiphon. The account will be found in Gibbon (ch. xxiv.). It is plain that this operation could never have been necessary if Julian could have brought his fleet into the Tigris direct by either of the upper canals, the Saklawiyeh or the Sersar (Abu Ghurraib) Canal. The Sersar does not seem to have existed at all, and the Saklawiyeh did not debouch into the Tigris, being originally (as Amm. Marcell. describes it) a canal of irrigation merely, carried into *the interior* of Babylonia.

When we turn to Xenophon's narrative we find nothing whatever, beyond the number "four" common to both, to favor the idea that they were the same as the four we have been considering ; not only are the two systems represented as derived from different rivers, but their distance apart is itself an insuperable difficulty in the way of identifying the one with the other ; for on the supposition that they were the same, Xenophon's error in saying they were three miles apart is inexplicable ; if they were so, then they must have been distinctly in his mind as having occurred at intervals of an hour's ordinary journey, and as having all fallen within the compass of one day's march ; whereas the four existing ones cover ground that he took three or four days to traverse ; a discrepancy far too great to be attributable to ordinary errors of narration. Moreover, if we are to place any reliance on the distances given in Xenophon's itinerary, and modern investigation tends only to corroborate them, there was no canal in his day where the Saklawiyeh is now, nor any indication of a canal-system for twenty-five miles farther south. All that is stated in the Anabasis goes to show that the first four marches in Babylonia were through a district neither populous nor cultivated ; there is no mention of either cultivation or population, of cities or villages, either deserted or otherwise, between Pylæ and Cunaxa ; the canals themselves are not met with until the invaders had marched more than 30 geographical miles through Babylonia, at a point within 22 parasangs — 55 geographical miles — of Babylon. Even between the canals and Cunaxa there is still no mention of cultivation, nor yet on the retreat, though the second day's march, in company with Ariæus, would be into the interior of Babylonia, — not until the end of that day had brought the Greeks back again into the neighborhood of the canals where were trenches and date groves (ii. 3. 10) ; and we hear no more of canals or trenches till they passed within the Median Wall, where we find two canals of irrigation drawn from the Tigris (ii. 4. 13) serving the northeastern district of Babylonia.

The impression which the entire narrative leaves on the mind is, that the cultivation of Babylonia, north of Cunaxa, started from and was mainly confined to the northeastern quarter, being carried on by means of two canals drawn from the Tigris, of which the Ishaki[14] Canal probably was one, and the Dijeil[15] the other; that the cultivation, by means of irrigants, was carried as far westward as the slope of land allowed the water to go, and that the trench (i. 8. 15) was designed by Artaxerxes to cut off the invaders as long as possible from the cultivated lands on their left; in short, to starve the enemy that he was afraid to fight.

The third objection, that the slope of the land is against the notion of water getting into the Phrat from the Tigris, has no weight, if the water be drawn from the Tigris high enough up. This is the case with the Ishaki Canal, which we must conceive of therefore as a great trunk irrigant running down Northern Babylonia, distributing its waters right and left as far as the slope of the land would allow them to go, the trench marking the limit. In this view the four canals seen and described by Xenophon would only be the last of the series belonging to this system, the extent of which lying behind the trench would be unknown to him.

There is one natural feature of the Tigris that must always have given it an especial value, as compared with the Phrat, for purposes of irrigation; it is this, — that the Tigris is in flood[16] a month earlier than the Phrat, and yet seems to continue at flood three weeks longer. If the Tigris, compared with the Phrat, starts vegetation a month earlier, and supports it some weeks longer, there can be little doubt that the Tigris would be the chief agent employed in irrigating the Babylonian plain, before Alexander removed the dikes on which the irrigation depended.

Moreover, if the great Sada Canal existed then, as the Inscriptions lead us to believe it did, the Phrat would be largely drained to supply the canal before entering Babylonia. The Sada Canal must have been to the Phrat what the Nahr Wan was to the Tigris (see *infra*, § 10), the recipient of its overflow and the fertilizer of the deserts that skirt its western bank, — with this difference, however, that as the Nahr Wan, by intercepting the waters of such rivers as the Diyalah and the Adhem, must always have been a

---

[14] There is evidence that the Ishaki passes through the Median Wall, as the Dijeil is known to do (see Layard, *sup.* § 3).

[15] "Dijeil, 'the little Tigris,' is the diminutive of Dijla, anciently pronounced Diglah, Digl, Digr, or Tigr" (*Journ. of R. G. S.*, ix. pp. 472-474). It is the "Diglito" of Pliny (*N. H.*, vi. 27 [31]), who says of the Tigris, "Ipsi (nomen) quà tardior fluit Diglito." A derivative of the Tigris is evidently meant. The Tigris itself has its name from Tigra, old Persian for *arrow*, being so called from the rapidity of its stream (cf. Strabo, xi. 14. 8).

[16] The Tigris rises before the Phrat, being swelled by the snows lying on the *southern* slope of Mount Niphates, which melt sooner and run a shorter course than those on the northern slope, which flood the Phrat. Ainsworth (*Journ. R. G. S.*, xi. p. 72, note) states that the Tigris is in flood in April and May, the Zab in June and early in July. There being very little difference in respect of volume of water between the Tigris and Zab (the Zab, though narrower, being much deeper), it follows from Ainsworth's account that the later flood of the Zab must keep the Tigris high till the end of June. The Phrat is at its height from the end of May to the beginning of June.

APPENDIX. 11

goodly stream independently of the Tigris, Nahr Sada, on the contrary, must have been always dependent on the Phrat for its entire supply of water, there being no river in the Desert of Arabia to feed it, so that flowing as the Sada is known to have done for about 400 miles into the Persian Gulf, the drainage of the Phrat through this canal must have been so great and probably continuous, as to make it difficult to conceive of it as having any water to spare for the irrigation of Northern Babylonia, particularly if "the Great Canal" of Herodotus, drawn from the Phrat, be it the Nahr Cuthiyeh or the Shat el Nil, was a running stream, as Herodotus' account seems to imply.

There is, indeed, one incident in Xenophon's narrative which goes far to show that the waters of the Phrat were really thus employed in fertilizing the land on its right or southern bank at the date of the Anabasis. In the course of the desert marches before reaching Pylæ, the Greeks crossed the river to *Charmande*[17] for provisions, and found them in abundance. The geological character of the country being the same on both sides of the river, the fact that we find a desert tract on the one side, and a fertile district on the other, argues artificial irrigation present in the one case, and absent in the other.

THE TRENCH.

Xenophon states (i. 7. 15) that the Trench stretched up through the plain, a distance of *twelve parasangs* to the Wall of Media. When Xenophon gives figures or information from hearsay merely, he is so careful to tell us so (see ii. 2. 6, ii. 4. 12, and iv. 1. 3) by the use of ἐλέγετο or ἐλέγοντο, that where, as in this case, he makes an absolute statement, there is strong presumption that he writes from personal knowledge, that in fact the route lay along the western side of the Trench up to the Median Wall, the Satrap's object being to get the invaders away from the rich cultivation of Babylonia as quickly as possible.

The *direction* of the Trench, as indicated by παρετέτατο ἡ τάφρος ἄνω διὰ τοῦ πεδίου, is by no means clear; ἄνω meaning "up from the level of the river on to higher ground" (as at iv. 4. 3), would agree very well with διὰ τοῦ πεδίου ("across the plain"), but not so well with παρετέτατο, — for παρα- implies that when the Greeks came in sight of the Trench, it seemed to run nearly parallel to their line of march along the river. Now this would be the case if we suppose that the Trench started from the wall at no great distance from the western end, for then, if we take into account the length of the Trench (30 geographical miles), it would approach the

---

[17] *Charmande* (i. 5. 10) was near the close of the Desert : for we read of *herbage* burnt by the enemy (3. 1; compare 5. 5). — Ramâdi corresponds in position with *Charmande*, and seems to retain the name : for *Charmande* = *Harmande* (just as Χαῤῥὰν = *Harran*; Χεβρών = *Hebron*, etc.) : — and *Harmande* = *Ramande* by the same transposition of letters as take place in Gr. ἑρπ = Lat. *rep* = *creep;* and in ἁρπ-άζειν = *rap-ere*.

river at a small angle, and would be in sight running along the Greek left some time before it reached the narrow pass; in short, παρα- is in itself evidence that the Trench did not start far from the western end of the wall. ἄνω meaning "up," in a direction contrary to that of the stream, accords better with the Greek than ἄνω "up from the level of the river"; it was suggested to me by Mr. Long, and is, I believe, the true meaning, unless we suppose that a direction including both notions of "up" was in the writer's mind. ἄνω might also mean "up" towards Babylon (as in ἀν-ἤχθησαν, ii. 4. 1), and this appears to be the view on which Grote's Map is constructed (ch. lxx.); a map, it is said, "*accommodated to the narrative, and not depending on any positive evidence of remains now existing.*" Grote places Cunaxa north of the Median Wall, which he represents as starting from the Nahr Melik, and running northeast to a point north of Baghdad; its length is under 30 miles, and its shortest distance from Babylon 60 or 70. The canals are all south of the wall. The objections to this arrangement are: 1. It fails to account for the trenches full of water which the Greeks found north of Cunaxa before reaching the provision villages (C in Grote's Map), a defect inseparable from any arrangement that places Cunaxa north of the wall, and the canals south of it. 2. That Ammianus connects the wall at its western end, not with the *Nahr Melik*, but with another canal higher up the river (see § 2). 3. It does violence to the text in representing the three marches mentioned (ii. 4. 12) as reckoning from the station where the Greeks joined Ariæus, instead of that at which Tissaphernes took charge of them. By inadvertence apparently, the retreat in the map begins from A, the first station after passing the Trench, instead of B, the station before the battle, to which Ariæus had retreated. This correction being made, would (on the same east-by-south course) bring them nearly to the wall at the end of the first day of the retreat. Xenophon says they reached it on the fifth.

Captain Bewsher, it is true, describes a wall of bricks on the north side of *Nahr Melik*, called Hubl es Sukhr, which would correspond in position with Grote's wall. Its extent does not appear to have been ascertained, nor whether in this respect or in its construction it corresponds with Xenophon's wall, which was made "of bricks *laid in bitumen*"; but apart from the difficulty of reconciling such a position with the distance travelled between Cunaxa and the wall, it is perfectly clear that the Hubl es Sukhr cannot be the wall that Ammianus saw north of his upper canal, there being from his account a distance of at least 14 miles (xxiv. 3. 10) between that canal and the *Nahr Melik*. The wall in question has been long known to geographers. "Its remains, with the ruins of buildings," says Dr. Vincent (i. p. 536), "are seen by every traveller who comes by land from Hillah to Baghdad; they are noticed by Tavernier and Ives, and are represented in De Lisle's Map. What they are, whether the extension of old Baghdad, or of a wall built by Zobeida, wife of Haroun al Raschid, which extended across the desert to Mecca, is difficult to say (see Abd-ul-Khurren, p. 129)."

CUNAXA.

§ 7. The name given by Plutarch (*Artax.*, 8) to the battle-field. There was a village with a hill above it (i. 10. 11, n.), and Ainsworth is very probably correct in thinking that the Greeks received the name "from a Persian compound, of which *Kuh*, 'a hill,' formed the base, as in *Kuhistan*, 'the country of hills.'" Xenophon (ii. 2. 6) places Cunaxa at 360 stadia from Babylon; Plutarch, at 500 stadia. By the side of Xenophon's definite statement, Plutarch's looks like a round number. Captain Bewsher, however, following Grote (*Greece*, ch. lxix., note 2), adopts it, placing Cunaxa at *Kunecsha*, 50 miles by air-line from Babylon. No reasons are given for preferring Plutarch's authority to Xenophon's in such a matter, and I am unable to find any. Xenophon's intimate connection with Proxenus, one of the generals, would give him access to the best information on the point, and he would know how to use it. The distance, occurring among road distances, must be a road distance and no air-line. It would no doubt be given to Xenophon by the Persian authorities in the national standard, i. e. as 12 parasangs, which he would reduce (at the usual rate of 30 stadia to the parasang) to 360 stadia. Twelve parasangs give a road distance of about 30 geographical miles, or 27 by air-line, — little more than a two days' march, — from Babylon. With great significance, therefore, might the Greeks say, "*We have conquered the king's forces at his gates, and having laughed him to scorn, came away*" (ii. 4. 4).

For the (probable) position of Cunaxa on the Abu Dibbis branch, see *sup.* p. 8.

THE RETREAT.

§ 8. Ἐπεὶ ἡμέρα ἐγένετο, ἐπορεύοντο ἐν δεξιᾷ ἔχοντες τὸν ἥλιον (*Anab.* ii. 2. 13).

The direction in which the retreat commenced has been called in question: whether, in fact, the Greek means, "When it was day *they started, having the sun on their right*," i. e. in a northerly direction; or "*... they proceeded, keeping the sun on their right*," i. e. as Grote represents it (*Hist. Gr.* ch. lxx.) in an easterly direction, "as referring to the sun's diurnal path through the heavens"; and in his map, constructed on this view, the course laid down is south of east, in order that it may strike the wall of Media, which he conceives to have lain south of Cunaxa.

I do not know an instance of direction being either regulated or indicated by the sun's diurnal course; referred to his place of rising it is common enough. Thus, when Herodotus means to tell us that the Great Canal (see *sup.* note 8) runs south of east, he describes it as πρὸς ἥλιον τετραμμένη τὸν χειμερινόν. Grote cites indeed Herod. iv. 42; but surely the two cases are wholly distinct. Herodotus, speaking of the exploring party that circumnavigated Africa, and of their westward course along the south coast, says, ἔλεγον ἐμοὶ μὲν οὐ πιστὰ ὡς τὸν ἥλιον ἔσχον ἐς τὰ δεξιά. Herodotus is treating of a natural phenomenon, which he was told of, but could not credit, as at variance with all that he, in north latitude, had ever seen or heard of a westerly course. Whether a soldier was likely to use the expression to describe (by a curious curve) the direction of a day's march, is another and a very different question.

On the other hand, the remark, *They started, having the (rising) sun on their right*, falls from Xenophon easily and naturally enough, if we suppose him speaking of an incident which he had in his mind when he wrote, enabling him to fix the direction taken through a country in which he hardly knew the bearing of one point from another. This northerly direction is, in fact, confirmed by Diod. Sic. (xiv. 25, *ad fin.*), who tells us that the generals in council with Ariæus decided to start off *towards Paphlagonia; and for Paphlagonia they started*, indicating a more northerly aim than ἐπὶ Ἰωνίας did in Ariæus' message (*Anab.*, ii. 1. 3). The same expression "towards Paphlagonia" occurs again in Diodorus (xiv. 27) to describe the northerly route along the Tigris.[18]

We conclude, then, that they commenced the retreat (after joining Ariæus, ii. 2. 8) in a *northerly* direction, and continued it with Tissaphernes — who was journeying *homewards* (ὡς εἰς οἶκον ἀπιών, 4. 8) — far enough in this direction to pass out of Babylonia; for on the sixth day of the retreat "they passed within the Median Wall (παρῆλθον εἴσω[19] αὐτοῦ, 4. 12), — an expression which can only signify *an entry through it into Babylonia*. The line of route suggested by Ainsworth, viz. somewhere to the north[20] side of the wall, but not, I think, by *Pylæ*, which is not mentioned in the retreat, is apparently the only one consistent with the data, geographical and historical, of the problem. General Chesney considers that this movement to the northwest was made "in order to round the marshes and inundations of Akker Kuf." It may have been so, if the marsh (Khor) existed then. I am inclined, however, to think that the

---

[18] In fact, the direction that a Greek would understand by it would be almost due north; for not only did the Paphlagonia of the Anabasis extend considerably farther eastward (i. e. east of the Thermodon, v. 6. 6, 9) than in Herodotus' time, who places it west of the Halys, but the ancient geographers, from Herodotus to Strabo, labored under an error as to the relative positions of the Persian Gulf and the Euxine, which threw the Euxine too far to the east, in fact placed the *mouth of the river Phasis a little east of Babylon*, though it is really three degrees west. "This derangement," says Rennell, "was the probable cause of Xenophon's keeping too far to the *east* in his way through Armenia, *towards Trebizond*. He would adhere to the geographical system then in vogue through Greece (as given by Herodotus), *and expected to find Trebizond nearly in the same meridian with Babylon and Nineveh*, though it bore about north thirty degrees west from the latter." — Rennell, *Geogr.*, i. pp. 247 - 249.

[19] The adverb has here its common proleptic usage: *so as to get within it.* Cf. i. 6. 5; iv. 2. 12; v. 2. 16. Thus Xenophon and Plutarch mean the same thing, when (speaking of Cyrus passing the trench) Plutarch says, ταύτης Κῦρον ἐντὸς παρελθόντα περιεῖδε ὁ βασ.; and Xenophon, ἐγένοντο εἴσω τῆς τάφρου. See also Xen. *Hell.*, v. 4. 41, and *inf.* vii. 1. 18.

[20] This is implied in the remark that they accompanied Tissaphernes on the homeward route.

APPENDIX.   15

real object was to draw the Greeks out of the heart of Babylonia for the reason given below. It may well be, moreover, that the presence of an invading and victorious army would be a dangerous incentive to the slave population of Babylonia, alluded to probably in ἐργασομένων ἐνόντων (ii. 4. 22). Many were the captive nations beside Jews that had *wept beside the waters of Babylon*, their "lives made bitter" by forced labor in building the palaces and walled cities, and in digging those canals and trenches of Babylonia, among which they and their children would find at once a fast prison, a merciless taskmaster, and an early grave. The pride, rapacity, and cruelty of the Chaldæan towards the *many nations* that he had *spoiled* and *gathered to himself* are vividly portrayed in the prophecy of Habakkuk ii. 5–12. See also Psalm cxxxvii.; Josephus, *Antiq.*, x. 11; Eusebius, *Præpar. Evang.*, ix. 39. Under Persian rule the *Chaldæan* himself joined the list of subjugated races in Babylonia, the whole forming a population ripe enough for insurrection, as history shows. See Rawlinson on Hdt., iii. 150.

In taking the Greeks this circuit, we perceive Tissaphernes securing two objects distinctly alluded to in the course of the narrative: to withdraw them as much as possible from the heart of Babylonia, lest the value of the prize and ease of acquisition should tempt them either to immediate occupation of this inviting province, or to future invasion (see ii. 4. 22, and iii. 2. 26); and also to gain time, by circuitous marching or protracted negotiation, for bringing up his distant forces, and maturing plans for cutting off in the retreat the enemy that had beaten him in the field (ii. 4. 3 and 25).

Ariæus' plan, if he had any plan beyond that of providing for his own safety, was apparently to march along the Tigris, on a line where they could get provisions, till they should strike into one of the great western roads across Mesopotamia, either at Mösul, or higher up, near the Carduchi, where was a road "carrying to Lydia and Ionia" (*Anab.*, iii. 5. 15), by which in fact Tissaphernes returned to his satrapy, after he gave up pursuit of the Greeks (Diod. Sic., xiv. 27).

§ 9. SITTAKE (ii. 4. 13) was 15 stadia (about 1¾ geographical miles) west of the Tigris, 8 parasangs from the Wall of Media, and 70 parasangs from the ford over the Zab. Ainsworth places Sittake at Akbara, the summer residence of the Caliphs of Baghdad, and this is probably very near the true position. [This Sittake is not to be confounded with the "Sittake GRÆCORUM *Ab Ortu*" of Pliny (*N. H.*, vi. 27), which is placed by Ptolemy the geographer (vi. 1. 3 and 6) 2 degrees (about 80 geographical miles) east of Ctesiphon: *Sittake Græcorum* was doubtless one of that cordon of Greek "colonies built by Alexander's orders round Media to keep the neighboring barbarians in check" (Polybius x. 17. 3).]

§ 10. The river PHYSCUS (ii. 4. 25). After crossing the Tigris (Shat Eidha[21] at Sittake, the route *struck off from the river* (ii. 4. 25), and did

---

[21] Both Chesney and Ainsworth identify the Shat Eidha with the Tigris of Xenophon. See Commentary, p. 300.

not return to it for the next 10 marches, 6 of which lay through a desert tract, the desert of Media (ii. 4. 27, 28). How did these two large armies get their supply of water all this time? We have no difficulty in answering the question, if we suppose Xenophon's river Physcus to be represented by the Bureich and Resas Canal, and that the route lay along its course. This identification of Canal with River was originally suggested as possible by Sir H. Rawlinson, and though subsequently abandoned by him from a misconception apparently respecting the site of Sittake, appears to be the true solution of the question. Compare the case of the Daradax (i. 4. 10), and Masca (5. 4), and Pallacopas Canals called ποταμοί (note McMichael's *Anab.*, i. 4. 10).

§ 11. OPIS on the Physcus River (ii. 4. 25) was also on the Tigris (see Hdt. i. 189, and Strabo xvi. 1. 9, who perhaps — not by any means certainly — identified it with Seleucia; which is irreconcilable with its recorded distance from the river Zabatus). Opis was 10 marches, 50 parasangs, from the ford over the Zab. Reckoning this distance back from that ford (see § 12), we are brought near to *Eski* (old) *Baghdad* for the site of Opis. [The following adds confirmation to this view: Alexander we know from Arrian (*Anab.*, vii. 7. 6, 8) removed the dikes of the Tigris as far up as Opis. Now Dr. Ross (*Journal of Royal Geogr. Soc.*, xi. p. 127) gives an account [22] of the canal that leaves the Tigris at Kaim, which shows, I believe, certainly that a dike has been removed at this point; and if the age of this canal (which is said to be "of remote antiquity long before the Mohammedan era," Dr. Ross) goes back to Alexander's day, then Opis *cannot have been lower than Kaim*, and may have been higher.]

The reader will find the question touching the sites of Sittake and Opis discussed at length in the *Cambridge Journal of Philology*, vol. iv. no. 7, pp. 136 – 145.

§ 12. KÆNÆ (ii. 4. 28). There are no ruins on the right bank of the Tigris to represent Kænæ, except those at Kalah Sherkat, or (as Sir H. Rawlinson writes the name) *Kileh* Sherghat. If the latter be the right spelling, we may recognize Xenophon's *Kœnœ* phonetically [23] in *Kileh*, the nasal liquid *n* being often replaced by *l*, as it is in Bo*l*ogna = Bo*n*onia; *L*abynetus = *N*abonadius; and Ze*l*ebi = Ze*n*obia, etc. *Kileh Sherghat* was, under the name of Asshur, the original Assyrian capital from 1273 B. C. to about 930 B. C., before the seat of government was transferred to Nineveh by Asshur-idannipal, the warlike Sardanapalus of the Greeks. See Rawlin-

---

[22] "*It is difficult to imagine how the water ever entered this canal, its ancient bed being seen in section above fifteen feet above the surface of the Tigris, which now* (i. e. *in June*) *nearly at its highest level sweeps along the high perpendicular banks.*"

[23] I. e. if Xenophon received the name "Kineh" *orally* (as he probably did under the circumstances of the march, see ii. 4. 10) he would be likely enough to give it in the form of a Greek word resembling it; just as in the case of the next city Nimrûd, which he calls *Larissa*, a name familiar to the Greek ear, supposed by Layard to be a corruption of *Al Assur*, by Bochart, of *Al Resen*. Khi, found in the inscriptions as an epithet of Ashur, may have some connection with the name. Rawlinson, *Hdt.*, i. p. 483.

son, *Hdt.*, i. pp. 373 – 377. , *Cœnæ* was passed somewhere "in the course of the first march"[24] from the villages of Parysatis, i. e. on the fourth day before reaching the ford over the Zab. That ford was only two marches distant from the Tigris, at *Larissa;* and of these the first was but $2\frac{1}{2}$ miles (iii. 3. 11). Layard (pp. 60 and 226) identifies the ford with one 25 miles up the Zab, a little above the junction of the Gomar-sú (whose bed is the χαράδρα of iii. 4. 1). Reckoning back from this ford as a point pretty well ascertained (the first that is so in the route beyond the Tigris), we are brought opposite *Kileh Sherghat* in the course of the 4th march from the ford.

The fact of their leaving the Tigris and marching up the Zab before crossing it, though not expressly stated, is sufficiently indicated by the remark that "they *arrived at* the Tigris" near *Larissa* (iii. 4. 6) after two marches from the ford. Nor is this the only instance in the narrative of mention of a river being reserved for the point where it was crossed. The Phrat itself, for instance, is first mentioned at *Thapsacus*, though both Chesney and Ainsworth are convinced that the three previous marches must have been along its banks (Ainsworth, *Travels in the Track*, p. 66). The same remark may be applicable to the march along the Physcus before crossing it, and also to the marches between the rivers Phasis and Harpasus, some of which lay along the banks probably of both rivers up to the point where they were found to be fordable (see iv. 6. 4, 5; 7. 1 – 15).

ROUTE THROUGH ARMENIA.

The Greek route after crossing the Kentritis — admitted to be the river of Sert (the *Buhtan Chai*) — is a point on which the judgment of geographers is divided. The point really at issue is which of the head-waters of the Tigris represents the Tigris of Xenophon, of which he says (iv. 4. 3) that the Greeks "came beyond its sources" after a three days' march of 15 parasangs from the banks of the Kentritis.

We are to bear in mind that the Greeks were told on the frontiers of the Carduchi (iv. 1. 3) that "*in Armenia* they would either cross the head-waters (πηγὰς) of the Tigris, if they liked, or if they did not like, would go round them."

Now they entered Armenia after crossing the Kentritis; and if it can be shown, as I think it may, that the Greeks crossed this stream *before* its junction with the *Bitlis-su*, then I apprehend that the Bitlis-su (the Eastern Tigris) will aptly represent the Tigris of Xenophon and satisfy the conditions of the narrative better than any other stream; and the conclusion

---

[24] ἐν τῷ πρώτῳ σταθμῷ: cf. ἐν τούτοις τοῖς σταθμοῖς (i. 5. 5). Dindorf, however, has "ad castra prima," "*at the first station*," and so the English translators. But ἐν could not apply to a place beyond the river: they did not even cross over to it; so that in no way could it be conceived of as part of the encampment: they stopped only for provisions; the station was farther on.

will be that the Greek route followed the direct caravan-road between Sert and Bitlis, and that the plain of Mush where it is watered by the *Kara-su*[25] (Black water) represents the plain of the *Teleboas* (iv. 4. 7) "with its many villages on its banks" (iv. 4. 3). This view of the route is in the main that proposed by Major Rennell (*Retreat*, pp. 203 – 207).

The first question is where the Kentritis was forded. Layard's view (*Babylon and Nineveh*, pp. 49 and 63, 64) is, that the Greeks forded the *Buhtan Chai* (Kentritis) opposite Till or Tilleh, considerably *below* its junction with the *Bitlis-su*, at a point where he crossed it himself (with difficulty) at the end of September. But it is morally certain that the Eastern Tigris, the combined stream of the Bitlis-su and the Buhtan Chai, is not fordable *two months later*, the season at which the Greeks reached this quarter.

The state of this stream, as indeed of the entire river-system of the Niphates, varies regularly with the time of the year. The rivers rise in March and April with the melting of the mountain snows, are at their height by the end of May, and "commence gradually falling from the beginning of June to the end of July" (Kinneir, *Journey through Asia Minor, &c.*, p. 489). They are then at their lowest pitch, and continue so till the winter rains swell them in November and December. Kinneir on his way from *Sert* to *Redwan* crossed the *Bitlis-su* by bridge, at a point 12 miles from Sert, just above its junction with the Buhtan Chai, and found it even there "very rapid and *certainly not fordable anywhere near where I crossed it*" (p. 412). This was on the 12th of July, when the stream would be getting low; but further, he tells us (p. 488 n.), "I crossed the Euphrates and Tigris *in December* (1810), and they were at that time much fuller than when I crossed them afterwards in July." Now it was at the end of November, or early in December, at any rate *after the rains had set in* (see iv. 1. 15), that the Greeks forded the Kentritis. Indeed, Layard himself, speaking of a period a week or 10 days earlier, when the Greeks crossed the *Khabour*, supposes them to have taken "*the more difficult* road over the pass in order to cross the Khabour by a *bridge or ferry; it must be remembered that it was winter, and that the rivers were consequently swollen*" (p. 61, note).

We conclude then that the Greeks crossed the Kentritis before its junction with the Bitlis-su. They forded it, we are told, at a point where the

---

[25] Layard (*Babylon and Nineveh*, p. 64) says, "I am convinced that the *Teleboas* cannot be identified with the *Kara-su*, which would be at least forty or fifty parasangs (eight to ten days' march) from Tilleh"; no doubt from Tilleh (or Till), supposing the Greeks to have crossed here, which, however, is more than questionable. Layard seems to have adopted this view from the belief that the river (*Buhtan Chai*) narrowed between rocky banks is not fordable higher up (than Till), p. 63. But this is an error, as Ainsworth has shown; cf. *Commentary*, p. 316. Layard supposes that the Greeks, after fording the river at Till, and finding no road into Armenia through the Charzan mountains, followed the course of the *Bitlis-su*, which he identifies with the *Teleboas*, observing that Xenophon says "*they came to* (ἐπὶ), not that *they crossed* the Teleboas." But ἐπὶ is Xenophon's regular usage in speaking of rivers which certainly were crossed; cf. i. 4. 1 and 11.

APPENDIX. 19

Kurd mountains come down to within a mile of the river. The Greeks we presume came to the ford by a regular road, of which the made road (ὁδὸς ὥσπερ χειροποίητος), which they saw *leading over the hills beyond the river*, was a continuation (iv. 3. 5). Now Ainsworth, who visited this district in 1839-40, describes a ford (*Commentary*, p. 316) and "a road *carried up the face of a limestone rock partly by steps cut out of the rock, and partly by a causeway paved with large blocks of stone. This is the highway to Sert, and appears to be of remote antiquity.*" He adds that there may very well be other fords in this quarter. But assuming that the Greeks crossed here, the neighborhood of Sert agrees well with Xenophon's description of the first day's march beyond the Kentritis, "*it was all plain and smooth hills, not less than 5 parasangs*" (iv. 1. 2). Fraser (*Mesopotamia*, xii. p. 239) describes Sert as situated in "*a large undulating plain without a single tree, surrounded at a considerable distance by mountains.*" Nor is this the only coincidence in the case. The Greek march of 5 parasangs ended at a "large village where the Satrap had a palace, and *most of the houses had towers upon them.*" Now Kinneir (p. 403) describes Halisnu (a few miles north of Sert) as "a large village *unlike anything we had yet seen*, built of stone and mortar, and *each house is a castle, consisting of a square tower surrounded with a wall* to protect the inhabitants from cavalry or musket-shot." Whether Halisnu represents Xenophon's village or not, still, Kinneir's description shows this style of building to be peculiar to the district; at the same time it seems to be not uncommon within it, for Ainsworth informs me that the same kind of structure is to be seen at Sert.[23] We can hardly then be far from the Greek track at this point, whether we have hit upon the exact ford or not.

From this plain (of Sert) there are four[27] roads leading to the plain of Mush, which it remains to show corresponds in distance and in other particulars with the plain of the Teleboas. Of these roads, three go by Bitlis, this being, doubtless, with all its difficulties, the most practicable route; one of them taken by Colonel Sheil and Ainsworth, goes by Bakia; another diverging a little to the east of these, was travelled by Kinneir, who describes it in detail, almost mile by mile; the passage over the mountain south of the Bakia River, he says, "is one of the worst roads he ever saw."

---

[26] Sert will scarcely represent Xenophon's village, for it is hardly two miles from the river (Buhtan Chai), and Xenophon's remark that the Greeks were forced to make their long afternoon's march of five parasangs, because there were no villages *near the river*, owing to the wars with the Kurds, intimates more than two miles. As Xenophon's plain does not exclude "smooth hills" (iv. 1), he may be supposed to mean any place before reaching the mountains, which embosom the plain "at a considerable distance" from Sert (Fraser *sup.*) This undulating country, favorable for the growth of the vine, extends as far as Tasil, where are "extensive vineyards spread over the declivities of the neighboring hills" (Kinneir, p. 403).

[27] "From Sert to Bitlis there are three roads of 16, 18, 22 hours respectively. We travelled the road said to be 18 hours. Beside these there is a road of 38 hours to Mush direct, which does not pass through Bitlis. This must be the road which Kinneir supposed the Greeks to have taken." Col. Sheil, *Journ. of R. G. S.*, vol. viii. p. 77.

The third road *crosses the Bitlis-su* by one of the many bridges over this river, and strikes the road skirting the right bank of the Bitlis-su, by which Layard travelled from Bitlis to Tilleh, and where he saw the ancient causeway which, he thinks, "has probably been always the great thoroughfare between Western Armenia and the Assyrian plains." It is this last of the three roads that may very well have been meant by the captives when they told the Greeks "they might *cross* the head-waters of the Tigris if they liked."

Supposing *Halisnu* to represent the Satrap's palace, two marches of 10 parasangs along the first or second of these roads, the last march being by a rugged mountain pass, would bring them fairly over the river of Bakia (the *Bakia-su*), to near Eulak, 8 miles short of Bitlis. It is hereabouts that they are said to have "come beyond[28] the sources of the Tigris." Hence they made three days' march, 15 parasangs, to the river Teleboas (the Kara-su), a "*beautiful river, though not large*, having many villages about it."[29]

It is true that they would come upon the head-waters of the Kara-su in less than three marches, but it would be wholly out of character with Xenophon's brief lively narrative to take note of such an incident. Even in the case of large rivers, we have seen (see on the Zab, p. 17) that "three marches to a river" is Xenophon's ordinary form to express, not the point where the route first struck the river, but where it became a point of interest in the narrative, most commonly where it was crossed; and, in this case, also for its "beauty and many villages." In the present instance they would come upon the Teleboas (*Kara-su*) *within a few miles* of where they left the Bitlis River, the first two days' march lying over the eastern extremity of the great watershed between the Tigris and the Phrat, and the Teleboas would be the first tributary of the Phrat seen by them. It is possible that this narrow strip of land, within which they might observe their

---

[28] ὑπερῆλθον. The use of the aorist clearly, I think, implies *some definite point* at which Xenophon conceived that they "came beyond the sources." That point, to all intents and purposes, would be when they had crossed the last tributary stream, the *Bakia-su*.

[29] Kara-su is Turkish for "Black River." It may be a descriptive, but is certainly not a distinctive name; for there is at least one other Kara-su in this quarter. It is much to be regretted that such intruders should have been allowed to displace the old Armenian names. Possibly it is not too late to recover these latter, and to trace Xenophon's Teleboas in some local name containing the radical Telb. Teleboas is presumably, like Larissa and Kænæ (*sup.* n. 23), an adaptation of a Greek word to the local name sounding like it. Mr. Consul Brandt crossed the *Kara-su* at Irishdir, where he found it "knee-deep and fifteen yards wide" (*Journal*, p. 379). There is no part of Armenia that answers to Xenophon's description of the Teleboas and the plain in connection with it (iv. 7), as does this part of the plain of Mush watered by the *Kara-su*. Lord Pollington (p. 445) describes it as "*studded with villages*," "*excellent wine made in it.*" "It grows *grapes*, melons," etc. (Brandt). "Corn, *horses* of excellent breed, *cows and sheep, are numerous*" (Knight's Cyclopædia). Compare Xenophon's account (iv. 4. 9), "The Greeks found here all manner of good things, *live-stock, corn, old wine of good flavor, raisins*, and all sorts of pulse."

Tigris — the Bitlis-su — flowing one way, and the Teleboas flowing the other to join the Phrat, is the στενόν alluded to at iv. 1. 3.

This view of the six marches after crossing the Kentritis is, no doubt, like every other view that has been proposed, open to objections. In truth, the whole question resolves itself into a choice of difficulties. Layard and Ainsworth alike object to the badness of the road between Sert and Bitlis, carried as it is over steep and rugged mountains, and by a dangerous pass. This is no doubt true. Still the fact remains that, bad as the road may be, it is the regular caravan route between Sert and Bitlis travelled by Kinneir, Sheil, and Ainsworth, and therefore presumably not so bad as the other by the Kharzan mountains. Brandt, who travelled by the *Kolb-su* route, thought *that* "the worst he ever saw"; but bad as it was, the Kharzan route, he was told, was still worse. If it be said that there is nothing in the narrative here that indicates the difficulties of a mountain pass, the answer is that it is not Xenophon's way to give descriptions of country, except as illustrating the incidents of the march, and there is a dearth of incident in this part of the *Retreat*, which it is not difficult to account for. We should no doubt have learnt more about the country, had the Satrap thought fit to oppose the invaders at any of the passes along the route. But he had got to know his enemy too well for that. He had learnt on the banks of the Kentritis that he had no force wherewith to oppose an army that had fought its way through the mountain passes of Kurdistan; and to try conclusions with them hopelessly in the heart of his Satrapy, would, in case of defeat, only place his province at the mercy of a victorious and reckless soldiery. Behind him was the plain of Mush, with its many villages and fertile soil. These he might hope to save by coming to terms with the invaders; and this, as the narrative tells us, he was wise enough to do.

ON THE GEOGRAPHY OF XENOPHON'S ANABASIS.

"This remarkable work has been read, and its geographical details have been either taken for granted, or referred to proximate delineations of territory and places, which communicated to the mind anything but a sensible or positive satisfaction in tracing the progress of the armies. In many cases the reader was compelled, after much examination, to take for granted what the mind naturally required to be verified; and, in others, to forego all inquiry as entirely hopeless. A reader of modern military history would regard as very imperfect a work which would be found deficient in the necessary details of geography. In books of travel the defect would be felt still more. The Anabasis, independent of its merits arising from the grandeur of the subject, the high reputation of its author, and the military exploits which it records, contains a great variety of incident to recommend it; it combines with the character of a military history that of a book of travels likewise; and if military operations generally receive their character from the nature of the ground on which they are performed, how much more must they do so when combined with a lengthened journey through hostile countries, and amid inclement seasons! Nor can the mind be satisfied except when such details are accompanied by representations and descriptions, which at once serve to render manifest the several movements, and to develop the causes which led to them. — W. F. AINSWORTH, F. R. G. S., *author of* "*Travels in the Track of the Ten Thousand Greeks.*"

RECORD OF THE MARCHES, HALTS, ETC., DURING THE ANABASIS AND KATABASIS OF THE GREEKS.

I. THE EXPEDITION OF CYRUS.

'Ανάβασις. *Ephesus to Cunaxa.*

[February, B. C. 401, to September of the same year.]

	Days' March.	Para-sangs.	Days' Halt.
The march begun from the sea at Ephesus (ii. 2. 6), about first week in............*Feb.* B. C. 401. To Sardis. Cyrus musters his forces as for an expedition against the Pisidians. Of the Greek generals, Xenias, Proxenus, Sophænetus, Socrates, and Pasion are present with their forces. Xenophon, having sailed from Athens, overtakes Cyrus and Proxenus at Sardis as they are about to set forth.	...	18	...
To the Mæander (i. 2. 5).................*March* 6.	3	22	...
To Colossæ (i. 2. 6). Menon arrives	1	8	7
To Celænæ, to the palace of Cyrus (i. 2. 7). Clearchus arrives. Greeks reviewed and numbered ....*March* 20.	3	20	30
To Peltæ (i. 2. 10). Lycæan games...............	2	10	3
To Ceramorum Forum, Κεραμῶν 'Αγορά (i. 2. 10)	2	12	...
To Caystri Campus (i. 2. 11)...............*May* 1.	3	30	5
Soldiers demand pay, now due for more than three months. Epyaxa arrives with a large gift of money. Army paid for four months...............	...	...	...
To Thymbrium (i. 2. 13)	2	10	...
To Tyriæum (i. 2. 14). Army reviewed by request of Epyaxa	2	10	3
To Iconium (i. 2. 19)...............	3	20	3
Through Lycaonia (i. 2. 19). Menon sent to escort Epyaxa through the western pass of Mount Taurus............	5	30	...
To Dana	4	25	3
To the plain before the pass, Cilician gates (i. 2. 21).......	...	?	1
To Tarsus (i. 2. 23). Interview with Syennesis.....*June* 6. The soldiers refuse to proceed, but are induced through the crafty management of Clearchus (i. 3)	4	25	20
	...	...	...

24 RECORD OF THE MARCHES, HALTS, ETC.

To the Psarus (i. 4. 1)...	2	10	...
To the Pyramus..	1	5	...
To Issus. The fleet arrives, bringing Chirisophus and reinforcements...	2	15	3
To the Syro-Cilician gates, Pylæ Syriæ (i. 4. 4). Abrocomas retreats...	1	5	...
To Myriandrus (i. 4. 6). Xenias and Pasion desert, *July* 6.	1	5	7
To the Chalus (i. 4. 9)..	4	20	...
To the springs of the Dardes (i. 4. 10)........................	5	30	...
To Thapsacus on the Euphrates (i. 4. 11)............*July* 30.	3	15	5
Cyrus discloses the object of his expedition. Menon artfully induces his division to cross first........................	...	...	...
To the Araxes in Syria (i. 4. 19)	9	50	3
To Corsote (Arabia) on the Mascas (i. 5. 1-4). Animals found	5	35	3
To Pylæ (i. 5. 5). Hunger. Persian discipline......*Sept.* 1.	13	90	...
Charmande. Danger and rage of Clearches. Orontes attempts to desert, is tried and executed (i. 6)................	...	...	...
Through Babylonia (i. 7. 1). Review and preparation for battle..	3	12	...
March in battle array (i. 7. 14). Trench passed.............	1	3	...
March more negligently (i. 7. 19)................................	1	4?	...
To Cunaxa (i. 7. 20). Battle (i. 8). Success of the Greeks.	1	4	...
Death of Cyrus .... *Sept.* 7.	...	...	...
Panegyric on Cyrus (i. 9). Later movements of the day (i. 10). The surrender of the Greeks demanded and indignantly refused (ii. 1)...	...	...	...
	89	543	96

II. RETREAT OF THE TEN THOUSAND.

Κατάβασις. *Cunaxa to Cotyora.*

[Sept., B. C. 401, to May, B. C. 400.]

Night march to last station to join Ariæus (ii. 2. 8)..........	1	4	...
The Cyrean Greeks and barbarians swear mutual fidelity .... *Sept.* 10.	...	...	...
To Babylonian villages (ii. 2. 13). Truce with the king (ii. 3. 1, 9)..	1	...	...
To villages for obtaining supplies (ii. 3. 14). The dates now ripe and gathered or gathering. Treaty with the king through Tissaphernes.	1	?	3

RECORD OF THE MARCHES, HALTS, ETC.

Description			
Waiting for Tissaphernes. More than 20 days' halt..........	...	...	20
To the Wall of Media, with Tissaphernes and Ariæus (ii. 4. 12). Entrance within it and passage of two canals	3	?	...
To the Tigris near Sittace (ii. 4. 13). Stratagem to hasten the crossing of the Greeks .... *Oct.* 11.	2	8	...
To the Physcus at Opis (ii. 4. 25). The bastard brother of Artaxerxes meets the Greeks	4	20	...
Through a desert region with Tissaphernes. To the villages of Parysatis (ii. 4. 27).......................................	6	30	...
Through a desert region passing by Cænæ (ii. 4. 28)..........	4	20	3
To the Zapatas (ii. 5. 1)... *Oct.* 29.	...	...	...
Five generals treacherously seized (ii. 5). Their characters (ii. 6). General dejection (iii. 1. 2). Xenophon arouses and reinspirits the army. Other generals chosen (iii. 1. 47)	...	...	...
To villages (iii. 3. 11)	1	⅝	1
To the Tigris at Larissa, crossing a ravine, etc. (iii. 4. 6).	1	?	...
To Mespila (iii. 4. 10)	1	6	...
To villages (iii. 4. 13–18)	1	4	1
Through a plain, pursued by Tissaphernes (iii. 4. 18)	1	?	...
To villages around a palace (iii. 4. 24–31)	5	?	3
To a village in a plain...	1	?	...
Night march of 60 stadia (iii. 4. 37). Enemy dislodged from a height..	...	2	...
To villages (iii. 5. 1) beside the Tigris. Progress stopped by mountains (iii. 5. 7)	3	?	...
Towards Babylon (iii. 5. 13). Consultation and inquiry ...	1	?	...
Night march to the mountains (iv. 1. 5) .... *Nov.* 20.	...	...	...
To villages of the Carduchi (iv. 1. 10). Baggage lessened.	1	?	...
Mountain march, with fighting (iv. 1. 14).......................	1	?	...
March in heavy storm. Carduchi occupy the road. A party seize another path (iv. 2. 5)	1	?	...
Passage forced and villages reached (iv. 2. 22)	1	?	...
Marching without a guide. To the Centrites (iv. 3. 1) ...	3	?	1
Through Armenia to villages and satrap's palace (iv. 4. 2).	1	5	...
To the springs of the Tigris (iv. 4. 3)........................... .	2	10	...
To the Teleboas......:...	3	15	...
Through a plain followed by Tiribazus (iv. 4. 7).............	3	15	3
Much snow in night .... *Dec.* 6.	...	...	...
To camp of Tiribazus; but return to their own camp (iv. 4. 22).	1	?	...
To mountain pass (iv. 5. 1)...	1	?	...
To Euphrates (iv. 5. 2). Desert stages................ *Dec.* 13.	3	15	...
Through a plain, deep snow, severe wind (iv. 5. 3)	3	15	...

26 RECORD OF THE MARCHES, HALTS, ETC.

To a village, water-carriers, etc. (iv. 5. 9)	1	?	7
With a guide, through snow (iv. 6. 2)	3	?	...
To and along the Phasis (iv. 6. 4)	7	35	...
To a mountain pass defended by the Chalybes (iv. 6. 5, 27).	2	10	[15]
To village in a plain (iv. 6. 27)	1	...	...
Among the Taochi (iv. 7. 1). Capture of a stronghold stocked with cattle (iv. 7. 14)	5	30	...
Through the Chalybes, the bravest tribe found (iv. 7. 15).	7	50	...
To the river Harpasus .... *Feb.* 3, B. C. 400.	...	...	...
Through the Scythini, to provision villages (iv. 7. 18)	4	20	3
To the large city Gymnias; guide obtained for the mountain where the sea could be seen	4	20	...
To Mount Theches. The Euxine in sight (iv. 7. 21). Great joy, etc.	5	?	...
Through the Macrones, who aided their passage (iv. 8. 1).	3	10	...
To villages of the Colchi, forcing a passage (iv. 8. 9, 19).	1	?	4?
To Trapezus (Trebisond), to the sea (iv. 8. 22). Sacrifices and games (cf. Diod. Sic., xiv. 30)............*Feb.* 28.	2	7	30
Chirisophus sails to Byzantium for vessels (v. 1. 4). Treachery of Dexippus. Expedition against the Drilæ (v. 2. 1). The older men, women, children, sick, and the baggage sent by vessels to Cerasus. The rest march (v. 3. 1).....	...	...	...
To Cerasus (v. 3. 2). Review and numbering	3	?	10
Division of the consecrated tenth (v. 3. 4). Xenophon's disposition of his share.	1	?	?
To the Mosynœci (v. 4. 2). Treaty with a part of the tribe. Storming the chief fortress. Through Mosynœci to the Chalybes (v. 5. 1).	8	?	...
Through the Chalybes (v. 5. 1)	1	?	?
Through the Tibareni, as friends, to Cotyora (v. 5. 3), *May* 7.	2	?	45
Embassy from Sinope. Xenophon's plan of a settlement frustrated (v. 6. 15). Defends himself before the army (v. 7. 4). Rebukes disorder. Purification of the army. Trial of the generals (v. 7. 1). Halt of 45 days at Cotyora.	...	...	...
	118		92
			(107)

The army thence proceeded to Sinope and Heraclea, *July* 1. Advanced to Calpe and Chrysopolis (vi. 1. 6), *Aug.* 7. Sale of the spoils. Passed into Thrace, and occupied there for several months. Returned to Asia, and reached Lampsacus early in the following year. Joined Thibron (vii. 8. 24), *March* 5, B. C. 399.

INDEX

OF

CITATIONS FROM XENOPHON'S ANABASIS.

"Accomplished XENOPHON! thy truth hath shown
A brother's glory sacred as thy own.
O rich in all the blended gifts that grace
Minerva's darling sons of Attic race!
The Sage's olive, the Historian's palm,
The Victor's laurel, all thy name embalm!
Thy simple diction, free from glaring art,
With sweet allurement steals upon the heart;
Pure as the rill, that Nature's hand refines,
A cloudless mirror of thy soul it shines.
Thine was the praise, bright models to afford
To CÆSAR's rival pen, and rival sword:
Blest, had Ambition not destroyed his claim
To the mild lustre of thy purer fame!"

CITATIONS FROM THE ANABASIS.

[The following Index was prepared specially to accompany the Revised Edition of the Grammar (1871). The numbers inclosed in parentheses denote the sections of the Anabasis which are cited; those following them, the sections of the Grammar in which the citations are made.]

BOOK I.

CHAP. I. (1) 412, 445 a, 472, 494, 504, 568, 571, 700, 719, 720; (2) 393, 480, 505, 522, 561, 573, 579, 592, 658, 703, 719; (3) 444 b, 505, 518, 530 c, 530 e, 533, 577, 598, 643, 718 k, 718 n; (4) 393, 453, 511, 525, 691, 696; (5) 474, 501, 527, 577, 592, 641; (6) 406, 443, 483, 533, 553, 586, 680; (7) 419, 444 b, 472, 533, 595, 658, 674, 689, 718; (8) 432 b, 505, 524, 586, 661, 666, 696; (9) 460, 483, 509 c, 523 f, 524, 536, 576, 718, 677 f; (10) 445 a, 469, 533, 658, 703; (11) 393, 719.

CHAP. II. (1) 551, 571, 689, 711; (2) 456, 659, 666, 704; (3) 674, 711; (4) 450, 689, 711, 719; (5) 395, 533, 551, 688; (6) 482 a, 482 d, 522, 525, 605, 674, 689; (7) 393, 414, 459, 504, 522, 577, 641, 689, 719; (8) 395, 455, 537, 573, 719; (9) 475, 504, 531, 706; (10) 393, 478, 507 c, 522, 719; (11) 454 d, 479, 573, 696; (12) 218, 393, 506 b, 718, 719; (13) 450, 523 i; (14) 534, 576; (15) 240 f, 506 a, 506 c, 692; (17) 459, 507 d, 571, 641; (18) 704; (20) 482, 506 a, 522, 533, 540, 554, 699; (21) 435, 533, 657, 685, 699, 719; (22) 675, 689; (23) 395, 443, 481, 489, 508, 569; (24) 504, 605; (25) 508, 509 a, 523 f; (26) 408, 450, 583, 721; (27) 583.

CHAP. III. (1) 430, 588, 594, 662, 689; (2) 320 a, 482, 483, 607; (3) 393, 484, 537, 571, 628; (4) 485, 522, 633, 718; (5) 459, 523 c, 641, 713, 719; (6) 455, 480, 551, 621, 622, 680, 689, 714; (7) 540, 689; (8) 444 a, 450; (9) 419, 506 c, 678, 717, 719; (10) 598; (11) 432 d, 537, 598, 682; (12) 405, 572, 582, 641; (14) 480, 483, 549, 553, 579, 677, 679; (15) 553 a, 553 c, 554, 572, 624, 659; (16) 463, 644, 693; (17) 284 g, 467, 650, 677; (18) 466, 560; (20) 595, 659, 689; (21) 242 e, 416 b, 433 f, 459, 507 d, 522, 645, 689, 721.

CHAP. IV. (1) 533, 572, 689; (2) 242; (3) 689; (4) 445 b, 466, 500, 569; (5) 418, 436, 677; (6) 534; (7) 633; (8) 476 d, 496, 641, 671, 721; (9) 440, 480; (10) 581; (11) 467; (13) 405, 523 f, 563, 701;

(14) 455, 563; (15) 414, 454 d, 568; (16) 457, 536, 595, 685; (17) 408; (18) 650; (19) 414, 718, 719.

Chap. V. (1) 506 b; (2) 408, 523 i, 571, 641; (3) 788 f; (4) 440, 469, 586, 227; (5) 240 e, 419; (6) 446, 472 f, 497; (7) 423, 476 e, 559; (8) 418, 467, 542, 635, 694, 711; (9) 259, 468, 485, 507 d, 523 e, 695; (10) 394, 412, 414, 426, 466, 585, 719; (12) 405, 537, 540, 612; (13) 668 b; (14) 573, 643; (15) 419; (16) 401, 408, 484, 523 g, 601; (17) 691.

Chap. VI. (1) 419, 506 f, 639, 676, 719; (2) 405, 419, 452, 622, 719; (3) 553, 649; (4) 523 k, 538, 579, 719; (5) 394, 420; (6) 405, 524, 671, 719; (7) 549, 668; (8) 636, 685, 697; (9) 478, 524, 579, 599, 665, 697; (10) 426, 592, 674; (11) 567.

Chap. VII. (1) 444 a, 508; (2) 386 c; (3) 211, 280 b, 414, 431 b, 626, 636, 719; (4) 458, 528, 537, 698; (5) 317 c, 416 a, 686; (6) 557, 694, 720; (7) 538, 642, 686; (8) 419, 536; (9) 476 d, 538, 568, 708; (11) 509 e; (12) 408; (13) 678, 690, 693; (14) 395; (16) 495; (17) 569; (18) 433, 524; (19) 685; (20) 475.

Chap. VIII. (1) 467, 525, 550, 598, 711; (3) 530; (4) 489, 506 c; (5) 692; (6) 466, 523 b; (7) 573; (8) 416 a; (9) 522, 692, 722; (10) 680, 689, 689 k; (11) 467, 695, 718; (12) 452, 461, 540, 610; 690; (13) 485, 523 b; (14) 541; (15) 525, 671; (16) 432 a, 518, 530, 563; (17) 455, 568; (18) 344, 418, 467, 506 c; (20) 571; (21) 474; (23) 455, 609; (24) 541; (26) 530, 540, 603; (27) 402, 466, 580; (29) 579, 583.

Chap. IX. (1) 523 h, 586; (2) 481, 592; (5) 466, 694; (6) 453, 578; (7) 253, 315 c, 478, 579, 586, 692; (9) 482; (10) 315 c; (11) 480; (12) 690; (13) 420, 459, 571, 713; (14) 466, 550, 554; (15) 442; (16) 716; (19) 634; (21) 253, 624, 719; (22) 512; (23) 460, 538; (24) 467; (25) 433, 551; (26) 456; (28) 563; (29) 261 e, 456, 537, 544, 603, 689, 699; (30) 523 c, 534; (31) 693.

Chap. X. (1) 443 c, 497, 497 b, 527, 587; (4) 405, 499, 518; (5) 648; (6) 506 a, 577, 676; (9) 694; (10) 529 a, 529 b, 550, 598; (12) 443 c, 586, 716; (13) 567, 609; (14) 594, 689; (15) 476 e, 695; (16) 643; (17) 433; (18) 573.

BOOK II.

Chap. I. (1) 526, 666; (3) 227, 438, 645, 693; (4) 612, 615, 685; (5) 540, 611; (6) 482, 518; (7) 716, (10) 293 a, 484, 571, 595, 718; (11) 430; (12) 568; (13) 320 a, 451, 478, 677; (14) 454 d; (15) 393; (16) 497, 507 f; (19) 531, 676; (20) 708; (21) 680; (22) 502, 714; (23) 643.

Chap. II. (1) 432 f; (2) 537; (3) 675; (4) 506 e, 671; (5) 518; (6) 242; (10) 564, 577; (11) 433 e, 459, 523 a; (12) 445 a; (13) 533; (14) 690; (15) 569, 645, 709; (16) 533, 540, 547, 571; (17) 420, 671; (20) 394, 719; (21) 469, 523 b.

Chap. III. (1) 697, 705; (2) 641; (4) 643, 645, 689; (5) 571; (6) 491, 571, 645; (10) 679; (11) 282 c, 530,

THE ANABASIS.

634, 713; (13) 556; (14) 412; (15) 406, 481, 533; (17) 442, 695; (18) 450, 484, 633, 663; (19) 545; (20) 458; (21) 592, 595; (23) 472 f, 547, 636, 696; (24) 641; (25) 663; (26) 483, 571; (27) 506 b.

CHAP. IV. (1) 533; (3) 533, 649, 664; (4) 533, 547; (5) 671, 678; (6) 320 a, 458; (7) 505; (8) 523 c; (9) 450; (10) 695, 699; (12) 440, 533, 679; (13) 459; (14) 414, 445 c; (15) 548; (16) 497, 540; (19) 572, 642; (20) 642; (24) 533, 676, 679; (26) 567.

CHAP. V. (2) 598; (3) 225 d, 472 f; (4) 472 b, 657; (5) 485, 694; (7) 455, 641; (9) 502, 523 e; (10) 414;'(12) 558, 716; (14) 622; (15) 456, 547, 566, 636; (16) 624; (18) 421, 582; (19) 455; (20) 719; (21) 558; (22) 444 f; (23) 481; (32) 468, 548; (37) 528; (39) 484, 550; (41) 544; (42) 452.

CHAP. VI. (1) 481, 587; (2) 592; (6) 671; (8) 682; (9) 467, 559, 663, 667; (10) 477; (13) 466; (18) 507 a, 695; (19) 457; (20) 437 a, 446; (22) 451, 507 a, 663; (23) 253, 573, 699; (26) 698; (29) 481, 523 k; (30) 505, 690, 697.

BOOK III.

CHAP. I. (1) 690; (2) 526, 646; (3) 432 a, 501, 577, 690, 707; (4) 453; (6) 211, 477, 554; (7) 544, 550; (9) 659; (11) 416 a, 573; (12) 693; (13) 531, 713; (14) 680; (15) 563; (16) 419; (17) 562; (18) 664, 682, 687; (19) 413; (20) 459; (21) 538, 572; (23) 438 b, 489, 533; (24) 533, 628; (27) 478, 484, 514; (29) 313, 432 e, 450, 713; (31) 587; (32) 641; (35) 458, 633, 657; (36) 450; (37) 408; (38) 577, 621; (40) 433; (42) 711; (43) 460; (45) 560; (47) 662.

CHAP. II. (1) 577, 667; (2) 564, 703, 788 e; (4) 442, 484, 540, 550, 690, 708; (5) 442, 562, 685; (6) 638; (7) 425; (8) 612, 694; (10) 676; (11) 473, 661, 716; (12) 692; (13) 412, 530; (14) 409; (15) 661; (17) 425; (18) 534; (19) 467, 472 b, 663; (20) 472 f; (25) 657, 709; (28) 419, 553; (29) 460; (32) 709; (37) 418, 665; (38) 432 b, 594; (39) 432 e, 443, 657.

CHAP. III. (1) 675; (4) 645; (5) 679; (8) 682; (9) 556; (11) 433; (16) 414, 482, 514; (19) 530; (20) 394, 454, 587.

CHAP. IV. (1) 315 c, 567, 624; (2) 706; (5) 464; (6) 419; (7) 523 c, 529; (10) 533; (12) 575; (13) 692; (15) 632; (17) 453; (19) 572; (21) 240 f, 692; (23) 467, 593; (25) 609, 671, 695; (26) 595; (28) 540; (30) 467; (34) 460; (35) 464; (36) 571; (37) 469; (38) 609; (41) 541; (46) 506 b; (47) 691; (49) 689.

CHAP. V. (1) 527; 577; (2) 527; (3) 527; (5) 540; (7) 671; (8) 240 f; (9) 509 b; (10) 522; (11) 405, 713; (13) 643, 645, 657; (14) 474; (15) 460; (16) 421, 432 g, 689; (17) 553; (18) 320 a, 420, 474.

BOOK IV.

Chap. I. (3) 633; (5) 450, 533, 556; (6) 407; (9) 432 g; (10) 548; (11) 523 f; (13) 675; (14) 483, 518, 710; (20) 574, 592; (21) 483; (22) 491, 540; (23) 594; (27) 503, 659; (28) 431 b.

Chap. II. (2) 485; (3) 450, 674; (4) 703; (6) 524; (7) 523 f; (9) 419; (10) 523 f, 636; (11) 702; (12) 501; (13) 485; (15) 458; (16) 506 c, 689; (17) 506 a, 523 f, 689, 702; (19) 557; (20) 279 e; (23) 507 d; (28) 213 d.

Chap. III. (1) 523 a, 582; (2) 509 a, 550; (5) 722; (8) 234 f; 695; (9) 553; (10) 494; (11) 548; (13) 444 b, 455, 523 k; (28) 420, 689; (32) 571, 577.

Chap. IV. (2) 218, 489, 551; (4) 526; (7) 489; (13) 506 e; (14) 509 b, 529, 698; (15) 686; (17) 603; (18) 603, 679.

Chap. V. (4) 507 a; (5) 472 b; (7) 320 a, 474, 643; (10) 507 f; (11) 474, 476 e; (16) 509 a, 669; (17) 580, 582; (22) 423; (24) 482; (29) 474; (31) 375 a; (36) 469, 485.

Chap. VI. (2) 463, 705; (9) 526; (10) 708; (11) 510, 677; (12) 510, 689, 690; (13) 622; (14) 505; (21) 690; (22) 690; (24) 523 f; (25) 643; (26) 523 f.

Chap. VII. (1) 569; (3) 604, 612; (4) 527, 689; (5) 567; (6) 689; (7) 637; (8) 692; (9) 225 f; (10) 609; (11) 541; (12) 426; (16) 220 f, 556; (17) 554; (20) 444 d, 550, 701; (24) 401, 689; (25) 551, 569; (27) 533.

Chap. VIII. (1) 469; (2) 225 f; (4) 418, 699; (5) 592, 676; (6) 524; (8) 690; (10) 518; (11) 653; (13) 627; (14) 713; (18) 499; (20) 423; (22) 394, 689; (25) 550; (27) 479, 507 f.

BOOK V.

Chap. I. (1) 506 b; (2) 574; (8) 514, 551, 694; (9) 689; (13) 522; (15) 575.

Chap. II. (5) 509 e; (14) 559; (15) 567; (20) 582; (24) 548; (26) 573; (29) 522.

Chap. III. (1) 283; (2) 240. 3, 394, 509 a; (3) 575, 706; (11) 395, 699; (13) 437 a.

Chap. IV. (1) 689; (9) 556, 661; (10) 644; (11) 530, 695; (15) 407; (16) 557; (22) 507 d; (24) 592; (26) 225 f; (29) 523 i; (34) 560, 583, 635, 695.

Chap. V. (1) 432 g; (3) 394; (4) 242; (5) 242; (8) 612, 716; (11) 417; (12) 585; (15) 548; (20) 691; (21) 509 b; (22) 585; (25) 702.

Chap. VI. (1) 621; (7) 523 e; (9) 507 f; (12) 577; (16) 703; (17) 583; (20) 569; (21) 624; (27) 506 c; (29) 455; (30) 631; (32) 663; (37) 442, 644.

Chap. VII. (5) 533, 592; (7) 533; (8) 621; (9) 445 c; (10) 281, 453, 564; (12) 414, 706; (17) 418; (20) 699; (21) 677; (26) 317 b; (28) 480; (29) 612; (34) 694.

Chap. VIII. (3) 259, 432 a, 554, 675; (4) 282 c; (5) 662; (6) 476 d; (7) 536; (8) 560; (11) 548, 564; (12) 501, 515; (13) 676; (22) 259; (24) 523 a; (25) 432 c.

THE ANABASIS.

BOOK VI.

CHAP. I. (3) 695; (5) 567, 592, 609, 695; (6) 679; (8) 234 e, 481; (10) 477; (14) 482; (18) 506 b; (20) 483; (21) 454 c; (22) 452; (23) 509 b; (25) 643; (28) 677; (29) 633, 691; (30) 571; (31) 315 a, 504, 574, 658, 677, 707.

CHAP. II. (1) 218, 689; (2) 315 a; (8) 599; (10) 415, 706; (12) 464; (14) 538; (15) 261 a, 523 b; (18) 709.

CHAP. III. (1) 464, 528; (2) 240 f; (6) 477, 533; (11) 719; (14) 557; (15) 550; (16) 716; (19) 550; (25) 483.

CHAP. IV. (1) 462; (4) 529; (8) 605; (9) 240. 3, 460, 722; (11) 284 c; (13) 284 c, 523 h, 581; (14) 666; (18) 716; (19) 523 c, 686; (22) 680, 689; (23) 577; (24) 507 f.

CHAP. V. (5) 550; (6) 485; (10) 317 b, 432 h; (24) 523 b; (30) 705.

CHAP. VI. (1) 433; (4) 674; (5) 537; (7) 530; (11) 692; (13) 526; (15) 631, 699; (16) 451, 576; (17) 472 f, 707; (22) 557; (23) 691; (24) 657; (29) 494; (32) 434, 696; (33) 434; (34) 476 d; (38) 529.

BOOK VII.

CHAP. I. (6) 713; (8) 628, 717; (11) 719; (18) 506 b; (21) 459, 667; (22) 282 c; (23) 523 b; (25) 481; (27) 676; (29) 498; (30) 427, 482, 689; (33) 378 d; (34) 643; (36) 601, 719; (39) 659.

CHAP. II. (1) 689; (2) 716; (3) 315 a; (5) 450; (6) 553; (8) 553; (9) 509 c; (12) 713; (13) 469; (16) 433; (17) 433; (18) 225 f, 461; (20) 507 f; (24) 659; (25) 577; (26) 452; (29) 419; (32) 466, 506 c.

CHAP. III. (3) 540; (13) 643; (16) 450, 540; (20) 284 c, 444 d; (22) 556; (26) 460; (27) 460; (29) 450; (32) 218; (33) 478; (35) 541; (36) 641; (39) 524; (43) 571; (48) 554, 567.

CHAP. IV. (4) 689 f; (5) 423, 714; (16) 527; (18) 689; (19) 523 c.

CHAP. V. (2) 454; (5) 432 d; (7) 661; (8) 432 c; (9) 539.

CHAP. VI. (3) 607; (4) 453, 518; (9) 480; (11) 537, 577; (15) 649; (16) 454, 636; (19) 713; (21) 632; (22) 480; (23) 636; (24) 253; (27) 551, 693; (28) 696; (29) 466, 713; (30) 679; (32) 456, 461; (33) 697; (36) 550, 596; (37) 402; (38) 480, 659; (41) 579, 582; (44) 455.

CHAP. VII. (3) 693; (7) 533, 694; (8) 717; (9) 695; (10) 306; (11) 631; (15) 710; (22) 480; (23) 575; (27) 679; (28) 483; (29) 538; (30) 697; (31) 406, 659; (32) 691, 788 e; (33) 444 a; (41) 717; (42) 414; (44) 702; (53) 701; (55) 305 c, 646; (57) 225 i.

CHAP. VIII. (1) 450; (4) 557; (6) 431 a; (8) 522; (11) 507 d, 510; (12) 218; (14) 281; (16) 534, 551; (19) 507 f; (26) 242.

ON THE STUDY OF GREEK.

"THE REASONS why we spend so long a time in acquiring a mastery over the GREEK LANGUAGE are manifold. We do so partly because it is one of the most delicate and perfect instruments for the expression of thought which was ever elaborated by the mind of man, and because it is therefore admirably adapted, both by its points of resemblance to our own and other modern languages, and by its points of difference from them, to give us the IDEA, or fundamental conception, of all Grammar; i. e. of those laws which regulate the use of the forms by which we express our thoughts.

"Again, Greek is the key to one of the most astonishing and splendid regions of LITERATURE which are open for the intellect to explore, — a literature which enshrines works not only of imperishable interest, but also of imperishable importance, both directly and historically, for the development of human thought. It is the language in which the New Testament was first written; and into which the Old Testament was first translated. It was the language spoken by the greatest poets, the greatest orators, the greatest historians, the profoundest philosophers, the world has ever seen. It was the language of the most ancient, the most eloquent, and in some respects the most important of the Christian fathers. It contains the record of institutions and conceptions which lie at the base of modern civilization; and at the same time it contains the record, and presents the spectacle, of precisely those virtues in which modern civilization is most deficient.

"Nor is it an *end* only; it is also a *means*. Even for those who never succeed in reaping all the advantages which it places within their reach, it has been found to be, in various nations and ages during many hundred years, one of the very best instruments for the EXERCISE AND TRAINING OF THE MIND. It may have been studied irrationally, pedantically, and too exclusively; but though it is desirable that much should be superadded, yet with Latin it will probably ever continue to be — what the great German poet Goethe breathed a wish that it always should be — the BASIS OF ALL HIGHER CULTURE." — FARRAR'S *Greek Syntax*.

INFLECTION. — "GREEK presents the MOST PERFECT SPECIMEN of an *inflectional*, or *synthetic* language. A language which gets rid of inflections as far as possible, and substitutes separate words for each part of the conception, is called an *analytic* language; and next to the Chinese, which has never attained to synthesis at all, few languages are more analytic than the English. A synthetic language will express in *one* word what requires many words for its expression in an analytic language: e. g. πεφιλήσομαι, *I shall have been loved*, Ich werde geliebt worden sein : ᾤχετο, abierat, *il s'en était allé*.

"The advantage of a synthetic language lies in its compactness, precision, and beauty of form. * * *

"It is most important to observe that *no inflection is arbitrary*. Among all the richly multitudinous forms assumed by the Greek and Latin verbs, there is not one which does not follow some definite and ascertainable law. Parsing loses its difficulty and repulsiveness, when it is once understood that there is a definite recurrence of the same forms in the same meaning, and that the distorted shape assumed by some words is not due to arbitrary license, but to regular and well understood laws of phonetic corruption." — *Do.* (from § 7 - 14 of Pt. I.).

METHOD FOR LEARNING GREEK.

A. Let the student, with such aid as the teacher may supply or approve, so acquaint himself with a passage from a classic author that he can translate it into English, and also explain, illustrate, analyze, and parse it as fully as the teacher may wish, — learning such portions of the Grammar as are here needed. It is the order of nature, that the *language in its actual use* should be presented to the learner before its grammar, of which it is then the proper office to explain and generalize this use. If "THINGS BEFORE WORDS" is a sound maxim in education, "DISCOURSE BEFORE GRAMMAR" is no less so. Yet grammar, in its place, is not therefore any the less important. "Facts before philosophy"; but facts want their chief value, unless they lead to philosophy.

B. At the recitation, let *new sentences* based upon this passage (or upon previous attainment) be proposed to the student for immediate translation ; and let this lead at length to exercises in translating from some Greek book upon the first sight or hearing ("reading at sight," &c.).

C. For the next exercise, let the student make himself so familiar with the passage that, if the English is repeated to him, either word by word, clause by clause, or sentence by sentence, he can promptly return the corresponding Greek. Some change in the forms of the words or sentences will often render this exercise still more valuable ; and the words and constructions which are learned should be early made the basis for freer and more varied translation from English into Greek. The habit, which has so much prevailed, of translating in one direction only, renders those associations upon which the acquisition of a language depends *one-sided*, — both incomplete and insecure. *The nail is not clinched.*

D. Let a fourth exercise be a simple and easy form of GREEK DIALOGUE, consisting of questions and answers drawn from the passage. Freer exercises in Greek conversation or composition should follow as the student acquires strength for them. *To learn a language, we must use it.*

In what way these several exercises, all so important in the acquisition of a language, may be best carried forward together, the teacher will judge. In most cases, the same recitation may usefully combine the translation and analysis of the lesson of the day with retranslation into Greek from the previous lesson, and a brief dialogue upon the lesson still preceding, — thus maintaining, with the progress in advance, a double review, and fixing what is learned deeply in the mind, as a secure basis for rapid attainment. Other reviews at proper intervals will render the student's acquisitions still more firm, till they become an *inseparable part of himself.*

The translation into English or Greek, the analysis, &c., may be either brought to the instructor in writing ; or may be written before him on paper, slate, or blackboard ; or may be oral. Books should be open or closed, according to the nature of the exercise. The judicious teacher will give variety to the daily recitation, and as much active employment for each pupil as will consist with the needed instruction. Let the members of a class be accustomed to propose to each other the English to be retranslated into Greek (thus reviewing their previous translation into English) and new sentences for translation, to frame the Greek questions to be answered, and to correct each other's written or oral work. In his private study, let the learner do all he can to render the teacher's office needless ; and let him repeat *again and again* the Greek which he has learned, that the words may become directly associated with their ideas, without the intervention of another language ; and this often *aloud*, so that the voice and ear may coöperate with the eye in impressing the memory ; while *select portions* should be so learned as to be *repeated without book.*

This *fourfold method* evidently applies no less to other languages.

PRECEPTS OF EMINENT EUROPEAN SCHOLARS.

"If all the improvements in the mode of teaching languages which are already sanctioned by experience, were adopted in our classical schools, we should soon cease to hear of Latin and Greek as studies which must engross the school years, and render impossible any other acquirements; there would then be no need whatever for ejecting them from the school course, in order to have sufficient time for everything else that need be included therein." — JOHN STUART MILL.

"To learn languages is not a difficult task in itself; it is made so, only by the method in which they are studied. Adults are unwilling to imitate children in their mode of learning them. The latter, whose minds are unembarrassed and free from any violence, by constantly hearing others speak, soon attempt to express their own ideas in a similar way. In like manner, adults who learn languages from books, with a similar freedom of mind, should daily *read, repeat again and again* the reading, *hear* others read, *write* out what they read, and *peruse and reperuse* it, and assiduously persevere in this exercise of repeating, until what is read be deeply engraven upon the memory." — JAHN.

"What I choose is this: that every *day* the task of the preceding day should be reviewed; at the end of every *week*, the task of the week; at the end of every *month*, the studies of the month; in addition to which, this *whole course* should be gone over again during the vacations. I can truly say, that, if I have made any progress myself in Greek learning, I owe it to this practice of reviewing." — WYTTENBACH.

"The precepts either of general or particular grammar should be taught *as opportunity occurs*. So also the *principles*, as well as the application of them, must be inculcated: and at the same time, in connection with this, grammatical analyses should be made. Lectures wholly devoted to general or particular grammar can be given with profit, only after the student has attained considerable skill and ability in translating." — MICHAELIS.

"Every reflecting teacher must know, from his own experience, how much familiarity with *one particular* elementary book, which unites fulness with precision, contributes to lead in the safest and shortest way to that established knowledge, which it is the object of all instruction to convey. On the other hand, he will easily see how much loss of time, and embarrassment to the student, are occasioned by a change of his elementary books of instruction. For this reason, I must protest against the teacher's directing his pupil to the use of a skeleton-grammar, before he takes up this." — GESENIUS: *Preface to a Hebrew Grammar*.

"The best method of acquiring a foreign language, whether dead or living, will of course be that in which the greatest amount of HEARING, SPEAKING, READING, and WRITING can be compressed, in well graduated lessons, into a given amount of time. Some minds will profit more by one of these exercises, and others by another; but the greatest progress will unquestionably be made by him who avails himself of the resources of *all the four*. Writing must be conducted by a well-calculated application of the materials presented by reading; so that whatever is read to-day will certainly be required to-morrow, or next day, for the performance of the written exercise." — PROF. BLACKIE.

GREEK DIALOGUE. — "There is nothing to hinder the teacher and his pupils from talking together every day on the matter and in the words read; and I, by judiciously mingling repetitions of the old with the new lessons, a perfect command may thus be acquired over a whole book. The Greek language has been so taught for years in Dr. Hauschild's Gesammt-Gymnasium, Leipsic. The language must *live* for him who would appreciate its beauty: but it cannot live *for* him, unless it live *in* him, i. e. unless he use it for the expression of his own living thought. In this regard, SPEAKING is even a more important exercise than writing." — DR. CLYDE.

[These extracts have been taken with some abridgment, but with none changing the sense. Those from the distinguished philologians and teachers Gesenius, Jahn, Michaelis, und Wyttenbach, were translated by Prof. Moses Stuart and Hon. John Pickering.]

GREEK GENIUS AND CULTURE.

[Testimony of Oriental Scholars and of Statesmen.]

THE GREEK PROBLEM. "What the inhabitants of the small city of Athens achieved in philosophy, in poetry, in art, in science, in politics, is known to all of us; and our admiration for them increases tenfold if, by a study of other literatures, such as the literatures of India, Persia, and China, we are enabled to compare their achievements with those of other nations of antiquity. The rudiments of almost everything, with the exception of religion, we, the people of Europe, the heirs to a fortune accumulated during twenty or thirty centuries of intellectual toil, owe to the Greeks; and, strange as it may sound, but few, I think, would gainsay it, that to the present day the achievements of these our distant ancestors and earliest masters, the songs of Homer, the dialogues of Plato, the speeches of Demosthenes, and the statues of Phidias, stand, if not unrivalled, at least unsurpassed by anything that has been achieved by their descendants and pupils.

"*How* the Greeks came to be what they were, and *how*, alone of all other nations, they opened almost every mine of thought that has since been worked by mankind; *how* they invented and perfected almost every style of poetry and prose which has since been cultivated by the greatest minds of our race; *how* they laid the lasting foundation of the principal arts and sciences, and in some of them achieved triumphs never since equalled, is a PROBLEM which neither historian nor philosopher has as yet been able to solve. Like their own goddess Athene, the people of Athens seem to spring full-armed into the arena of history; and we look in vain to Egypt, Syria, or India for more than a few of the seeds that burst into such marvellous growth on the soil of Attica." — *Lectures on the Science of Language*, by MAX MÜLLER, Professor in the University of Oxford.

"GREECE [the real founder of Indo-European pre-eminence], enriching itself with elements drawn from the decaying institutions of older races, assimilated them, and made them lively and life-giving, with an *energy of genius* unrivalled elsewhere in the annals of the world. The wider the range of our historical study, the more are we penetrated with the transcendent ability of the Greek race." — *Language and the Study of Language*, by WM. D. WHITNEY, Professor of Sanskrit in Yale Coll.

"EUROPEAN civilization from the Middle Ages downwards is the compound of two great factors, the Christian religion for the spirit of man, the Greek (and in a secondary degree, the Roman) discipline for his mind and intellect." — WM. E. GLADSTONE, Prime Minister of England.

"IT is impossible to contemplate the annals of Greek literature and art, without being struck with them as by far *the most extraordinary and brilliant phenomenon* in the history of the human mind. The very language, even in its primitive simplicity as it came down from the rhapsodists who celebrated the exploits of Hercules and Theseus, was as great a wonder as any it records." — H. S. LEGARÉ, late Attorney Gen. of the United States.

"LET me repeat, that so far from dissuading from the study of Greek as a branch of general education, I do but echo the universal opinion of all persons competent to pronounce on the subject, in expressing my own conviction that the language and literature of ancient Greece constitute *the most efficient instrument of mental training* ever enjoyed by man; and that a familiarity with that wonderful speech, its poetry, its philosophy, its eloquence, and the history it embalms, is incomparably THE MOST VALUABLE OF INTELLECTUAL POSSESSIONS." — Hon. GEORGE P. MARSH: *Lectures on the English Language*.